Legal Aspects of International Terrorism

Edited by

Alona E. Evans
John F. Murphy

Published under the auspices of
The American Society of
International Law

Lexington Books
D.C. Heath and Company
Lexington, Massachusetts
Toronto

Library of Congress Cataloging in Publication Data

American Society of International Law.
  Legal aspects of international terrorism.

  Includes bibliographical references and index.
  1. Terrorism. I. Evans, Alona E. II. Murphy, John Francis, 1937-
III. Title.
  JX5420.A46   1978   341.77   78-404
  ISBN 0-669-02185-7

Contents

Preface

This book is the end product of a research project on "Legal Aspects of International Terrorism," undertaken by the American Society of International Law for the Department of State under Contract No. 1722-520057. By stressing "legal aspects," the society is not in any way suggesting that its project is of a highly technical nature of interest only to international lawyers. Rather, from the outset, the project envisaged the creation of an interdisciplinary working group to conduct the study under the guidance of Dr. John Lawrence Hargrove, the society's director of studies, and of the undersigned two codirectors, and emphasized the need to consider legal aspects as part of the economic, political, and social context in which international terrorism is taking place.

As is well known, there has been considerable debate over what definitional approaches to international terrorism are most appropriate. For its purposes, the project's working definition focuses on the threat or use of violence by private persons for political ends, where the conduct itself or its political objectives, or both, are international in scope. The working definition does not comprehend within its scope a variety of governmental acts, often classified as "state terrorism," such as illegal interception of international civil aircraft, suppression of political expression, violation of international humanitarian law by acts of genocide, or violation of the laws of war or the Geneva Conventions relating to prisoners of war or protection of civilians. This is not to say that state terrorism is irrelevant to the project. On the contrary, acts of state terrorism all too often create a political, economic, and social milieu that precipitates acts of individual terrorism. To the extent that state terrorism creates milieus conducive to particular manifestations of international terrorism, it might appropriately be taken into account as such a causal factor, although this sort of causal analysis is not the main burden of this project. International terrorism may also be engaged in by private individuals who are serving as government agents. Their status as government agents, however, in no way excludes them from the project's scope.

At the same time, the project is not limited to the forms of international terrorism that have already become a part of familiar experience. On the contrary, the project attempts to identify the most threatening current and foreseeable future manifestations of private acts of international terrorism. In the words of the society's proposal to the Department of State:

... [R]elatively recent or still emerging scientific and technological developments may present new opportunities for terrorism, which will be as threatening as those of the past and in some cases very much more so. This is true not only for new *techniques* of destruction which can be turned to terrorist purposes, such as nuclear explosive devices, or chemical or biological devices of mass destruction of human life (which may be found to be equally threatening, upon examination of the relative difficulties of control of access). It is true also of new *targets* of terrorist acts such as facilities and installations which may be especially attractive to terrorists because of high cost, physical vulnerability, special difficulties of control of access, or high potential for damage to health, property or environment in the event of destruction. Nuclear power plants, petroleum supertankers, fixed or floating installations for seabed mining or ocean thermal energy extraction, installations for seabed oil drilling or pumping, and submarine pipelines are examples which may exhibit some or all of these characteristics. Indeed, in some and perhaps all of these cases, calculation of the costs of rendering installations less vulnerable to terrorist acts, and the costs flowing from such acts should they occur, is a part of rational decision on the allocation of capital among competing technologies.

Over the summer of 1975 a working group for the project was established. (The members of the working group are listed on pp. 669-670.) The duties of members of the working group varied. Dr. Hargrove and the codirectors were responsible for managing the project. The codirectors also were responsible for editing the final report, and along with most other members of the working group, they had writing responsibilities. A few members had no writing responsibilities but served as consultants. In addition, the working group benefited from the services of several research assistants and an administrative assistant.

The working group functioned in the following manner. Individual writers of chapters of the report prepared drafts and sent them to the society for distribution to the other members. After the members had had an opportunity to read and evaluate the drafts, the working group met at the society's headquarters to discuss the drafts and to suggest revisions to the writers. After final revisions of each of the individual chapters were completed, the codirectors prepared a draft of each chapter, incorporating all the conclusions and recommendations of the individual writers. This chapter was then evaluated by a full meeting of the working group, in an attempt to reach a consensus as to the recommendations that were to be submitted to the Department of State in the project's final report. Between September 12, 1975, and February 26, 1977, the working group met on 10 different occasions.

Although they were not members of the working group, selected U.S. government officials were invited to attend the group's meetings in an advisory capacity. In no sense, however, were members of the working group U.S. government employees. Nor did the U.S. government exercise a veto power over the deliberations of the working group or over the ultimate publication of its conclusions and recommendations. At the same time, the working group benefited considerably, at various stages of the project, from the perceptive comments of government officials. Especially useful was a two-day conference at Coolfont, West Virginia, held March 26 through March 29, 1977, where officials from various government agencies commented on the draft conclusions and recommendations appended to the report.

A major and difficult task of the project was the collection of data on international terrorism. In large part the project relied on conventional sources, such as statutory material; decisions of U.S. and foreign judicial and administrative tribunals; congressional hearings, reports, and studies; reports of international organizations; interviews with public officials and representatives of business and industrial enterprises; as well as books and other secondary sources. In the early stages of the project an extensive bibliography on international terrorism was prepared and later supplemented by a research assistant. Individual members of the working group attended symposiums and conferences on international terrorism, where they often obtained papers and other information from participants. Efforts were made to keep in touch with other persons and institutions involved in research projects on international terrorism and to exchange data with them. Research assistants based in Washington, D.C., explored files in the Department of State and did research at the Library of Congress.

The project also, however, attempted to utilize more unconventional methods of data collection. Prior to establishing the working group—indeed prior to the awarding of the project to the society—the Department of State had circulated an airgram to all posts asking them to submit data on their host countries' law and practice on international terrorism. Specifically, the department asked each post to report on, and, if feasible, to supply texts of, statutes and regulations on terrorism with primary application within the host country; statutes and regulations implementing existing international conventions on terrorism; judicial or administrative decisions dealing with individual cases of terrorism; the host country's prosecution policy and practice; and official pronouncements on terrorism. As the replies from the field came in, they were summarized by research assistants and distributed through the society to members of the working group.

The data gleaned from these replies were of uneven quality, in large part depending on the degree of effort expended by, and the extent of expertise available to, the post. With respect to those replies that did not contain useful data, there were several responses. In some cases a supplementary airgram was sent to the post requesting additional information. In others the information received from the field was supplemented by research in State Department files or at the Library of Congress.

Because the department's airgram was drafted and sent out before the final parameters of the project were determined, some of the manifestations of international terrorism of concern to the project were not covered. This was especially true of such technical areas as ocean facilities. Unfortunately, subsequent attempts to obtain additional data from the field proved unavailing. Consequently, the chapter on "Ocean Vessels and Offshore Structures" contains no materials on the laws and practices of foreign countries.

In the same vein, after substantial consideration of available alternative sources of data, it was decided that two areas within the scope of the project—nuclear materials and facilities and practical problems of law enforcement—could best be explored by informal, off-the-record discussions with responsible officials in the field. The sensitivity of these subjects renders public sources of information at best uninformative and in some instances misleading. Accordingly, the writers of the chapters in these areas traveled extensively to conduct interviews with key officials, both in the United States and in Western Europe. Finally, the society maintained contact with officials of the Council of Europe in an effort to keep generally abreast of developments in Western Europe, particularly with regard to the drafting of the European Convention on the Suppression of Terrorism.

Members of the working group recognize that in spite of these efforts to improve the quantity and quality of data collected on national laws and practices concerning terrorism, their information in this area is of uneven reliability. In particular, with respect to national measures, there is often a discrepancy between the law on the books and the practice of states. The functioning of a national criminal justice system cannot be gleaned solely from the texts of its laws. Although discussions with foreign officials may serve to minimize this difficulty, they do not eliminate it, and the working group has borne this consideration in mind while formulating its conclusions and recommendations.

This report is divided into two parts. Part I includes chapters on those manifestations of international terrorism that, in the opinion of the working group, most require study. Each of these chapters has been organized, with slight deviations in some chapters, along the following lines. First, a thorough description of the problem is given, including, in technology-related areas, some forecasting of future trends. Second come a description and an assessment of existing national law and practice, both that of the United States and, to the extent feasible, that of other countries. Third, a description and an assessment of existing international law and practice are given. The fourth sections discuss the political, economic, and social milieus in which the manifestation of international terrorism is taking place. Fifth, and finally, conclusions and recommendations are given for changes in national and international law and policy. The recommendations in each chapter are those of the individual writer and do not necessarily reflect the views of the working group.

Part II, which focuses on international and transnational efforts to prevent and control international terrorism, contains chapters designed to cover and to tie together subjects common to the terrorist threats and use of force considered in Part I. As to these subjects, too, the chapters attempt to describe and assess the existing state of affairs with a view to making recommendations for possible improvements in national and international law and practice. Again, the conclusions and recommendations are those of the individual chapter writers.

The appendix contains the conclusions and recommendations of the study.

This appendix is divided into three parts. The first contains general recommendations, *i.e.*, those not necessarily limited to a subject covered by any single chapter and often advanced by more than one member of the working group. The second contains specific recommendations gleaned from and relating to the subject matter of the individual chapters. In the opinion of the codirectors, the recommendations contained in the first and second parts of this appendix had some measure of general support in the working group, although they were not necessarily supported by a majority of the members. It should be stressed, however, that no formal votes were taken on these recommendations. Recommendations included in the first or second parts of the appendix have had general support among most members of the working group. Recommendations receiving little or no support from the working group appear in the third part of the appendix with an indication as to the individual member of the working group who submitted them.

The crux of the report is this appendix on conclusions and recommendations, where we have attempted to keep in mind the need to provide the U.S. government with specific concrete suggestions, accompanied by supporting reasons, for actions it might take toward preventing and suppressing international terrorism.

To this end attention has been given to three broad categories of possible actions: unilateral, bilateral or regional, and multilateral or global. As to each proposal, the costs have been weighed against the benefits, and an attempt has been made to elaborate fully the reasons for concluding that the benefits outweigh the risks. If a recommendation suggests that the United States should take action in concert with other countries, these countries have been identified and reasons have been given why U.S. action with them would be especially helpful.

As a whole, this report contains a substantial number of recommendations on a great variety of subjects. We do not expect that all these recommendations will be accepted or will lead to changes in national or international law and practice. At a minimum, however, we hope that the report is a useful description and analysis of the legal aspects of international terrorism and that the recommendations contained therein will stimulate serious consideration of the issues they raise.

Alona E. Evans
John F. Murphy

Acknowledgments

Over the two years that this book has been in preparation, we have benefited from the assistance of, and thus are grateful to, a number of people. First and foremost, we owe a debt of gratitude to Dr. John Lawrence Hargrove, Director of Studies, American Society of International Law. Throughout the life of the project, Dr. Hargrove has lent invaluable assistance in drafting the original proposal to the Department of State; in planning and participating in meetings for the working group; in advising the codirectors and working group on the organization and editing of the report; and in contributing to the project in many other ways too numerous to mention. Dr. Hargrove has been ably assisted by Eva Sheldon, his administrative assistant, whose constant attention to the myriad details associated with the project greatly facilitated the successful completion of the report, and by Judith R. Hall, Administrative Director of the society, whose careful editing of the manuscript was invaluable in the publication process.

A special note of thanks and gratitude goes to Stephen R. Dorr. It is truly impossible to exaggerate the importance of Mr. Dorr's contribution to this project. In addition to his research on various facets of the project, Mr. Dorr prepared preliminary drafts of the appendix. He also did preliminary editing on the other chapters in the report. In all these and other tasks, Mr. Dorr's performance has been outstanding.

Christina Cerna, S. Jacob Scherr, and Linda Weinstein prepared summaries of the replies to the Department of State's airgram requesting information on host countries' law and practice regarding terrorism and engaged in other research tasks. Joseph R. Barnes prepared a substantial bibliography on international terrorism for the use of the working group and helped on the research for Chapter 5, "Protected Persons and Diplomatic Facilities" (in Volume II).

Thanks are due to the entire secretarial staff of the University of Kansas School of Law, who spent many hours typing materials for the project. In particular, Cleo Lown typed countless letters and placed numerous phone calls in connection with administrative details of the project.

We are thankful for the fine cooperation we have received from members of the working group who have striven to meet draconian deadlines and to produce high-quality work. It has been a pleasure working with them.

Last but not least, we acknowledge the financial and other support extended by the Department of State to this project. The assistance rendered by Ambassador L. Douglas Heck, Robert A. Fearey, Louis Fields, and Robert Myers, among others, has been invaluable.

Alona E. Evans
John F. Murphy

Introduction

As one can gather from a brief glance, this report on the legal aspects of international terrorism is voluminous. In an effort to make the report more useful to the reader, we have attempted to summarize the conclusions and recommendations of the report, as well as their underlying rationales, in an appendix. Admittedly, though, even these summaries are lengthy, perhaps unavoidably so, in light of the magnitude and complexity of the subject matter. At any rate, the purpose of this introduction is to give our individual, subjective views regarding the conclusions and recommendations that we regard as especially worthy of consideration and, perhaps, action. We hasten to add that we do so in our individual capacities only, and that other members of the working group may, and in some cases surely do, have different opinions.

In thus setting forth our views, we will proceed along the same line as does the appendix. That is, we will address ourselves first to general conclusions and recommendations that transcend or cut across the individual manifestations of international terrorism treated in the report. We will then examine the individual chapters of the report and attempt to glean from its mass of material conclusions and recommendations we regard as especially worthy of attention.

General Conclusions and Recommendations

Throughout the report, a basic issue raised is whether international terrorism should be combated through unilateral, bilateral or regional, or global means. Ideally, the approach should be multilateral and global, because by definition, international terrorism violates vital interests of the world community as a whole and the response thereto should be worldwide. Moreover, if ratified, a general international agreement that would define the offense of international terrorism, require states either to prosecute an accused or to extradite him to another jurisdiction for prosecution, make states that fail to comply liable for damages, and make states that condone or cooperate with international terrorists liable for payment of damages to the victims could be a major contribution toward the goal of preventing and punishing international terrorism.

However, the ideal does not necessarily comport with the real. Recent efforts to draft general treaty law on terrorism indicate that the utility of multilateral treaties is likely to be limited, and that the more like-minded (and thus narrower) the class of states participating in such exercises, the greater will be the likelihood of success either in the drafting effort itself or in the actual operation of the legal regime produced.

On the other hand, one should not give up hope that the political milieu may change so as to be more congenial to the conclusion of a general antiterrorist treaty. Especially shocking acts of international terrorism—such as the events at Dacca and Mogadishu and the brutal murder of Hanns-Martin Schleyer—as well as pressures such as those generated by the threatened international strike of airplane pilots, may result in an atmosphere where new initiatives in the United Nations General Assembly and in other appropriate international organizations may be feasible. The Department of State should closely monitor the current political climate and develop contingency plans in order to be able to take advantage of favorable developments.

As an alternative to general treaties, the United States should encourage regional efforts to develop conventions for the control of terrorism, such as the recently adopted Convention of the Council of Europe. The conclusion of new, or the revision of current, bilateral agreements also may be useful. The U.S./Cuba Memorandum of 1973 and the U.S./Canadian Extradition Agreement of 1971 may serve as models.

It should be remembered that in this field as in any other, international lawmaking is not limited to treaties. The process of customary international lawmaking may afford some possibilities for overcoming problems created by a lack of pre-existing political consensus on "gut" issues such as sanctuary or the obligation to extradite. Also, to this end quiet and patient negotiations are likely to be more fruitful than the polemical exchanges that all too often characterize meetings on terrorism in international forums.

The usefulness of unilateral or national efforts, taken either by the United States or by other countries, should not be underestimated. Definition of the offense and prescription of penalties for its commission through domestic legislation, development of security measures, such as screening devices at airports, and improvement of law enforcement techniques would appear especially helpful.

One area where legislation would *not* be useful is that of negotiations with terrorists. Here government officials and other persons involved in the negotiating process need to have maximum flexibility to adjust their strategies to rapidly changing circumstances. General policy guidelines and *ad hoc* decision-making, plus improved law enforcement techniques, should remain the principal methods for dealing with terrorists.

An area of special concern—although this project did not examine it in detail—is the possible relationship between media coverage and terrorist activities. In the view of the working group, guidelines (nonlegal standards, perhaps a code of ethics) should be formulated to govern the nature and extent of media coverage of terrorist activities. Questions that should be addressed would include the need for temporarily withholding publication of a kidnaping or extortion threat until the incident has been resolved; avoiding publication of tactical police information; the relationship between tone and emphasis in media coverage and the encouragement of terrorist activity; and the like.

Specific Conclusions and Recommendations

Terrorists' Threats and Societal Vulnerabilities

Aircraft and Aviation Facilities. Recent events have graphically demonstrated the overriding importance of rigorous national security measures to the protection of aircraft and aviation facilities against terrorist attacks. Highest priority should therefore be given to intensified FAA supervision of security measures in use in U.S. airports. The x-ray screening devices can become faulty very quickly, and the FAA's current quarterly inspections are not frequent enough to ensure continuous operating efficiency. Airport security programs also should be extended to cover General Aviation at the point where general aircraft meet with public air facilities.

In the same vein, the FAA should pursue with increased vigor its efforts to encourage the improvement of airport security at foreign airports. At many of these airports, security is at present lax or nonexistent, as recently evidenced by the apparent lack of effective controls at the Bombay, India, and Palma, Majorca, airports.

In spite of the failure of the 1973 initiative of the International Civil Aviation Organization, another effort should be made to conclude a multilateral convention that would be designed to enforce, by sanctions, the Tokyo, Hague, and Montreal conventions and any security convention that might be adopted. This convention would seek to strengthen the obligation to prosecute or extradite offenders of these conventions and to eliminate "hijack havens." The time for such action may be especially propitious in the wake of the shocking incidents at Dacca, Bangladesh, and Mogadishu, Somalia, and the threats by air pilots to strike if effective action is not forthcoming.

Nuclear Facilities and Materials. Perhaps the most striking conclusion drawn from this area is that international cooperation with respect to combating possible terrorist attacks or threats involving nuclear facilities and materials has been almost entirely lacking. Neither the Non-Proliferation Treaty, the IAEA statute, nor any other treaty covers the subject of physical protection of nuclear facilities and materials. There also is no systematic exchange among states of technical, administrative, or intelligence information concerning physical protection of nuclear facilities and materials or of information concerning terrorist threat potentials. Similarly, to our knowledge, no international organization or international coordinative mechanism has been designated or established to plan for or coordinate plans for the contingency of a theft of nuclear materials from one state to another. In the most extreme cases, where stolen nuclear materials were taken to a state that is unwilling or unable to cooperate in locating and recovering these materials, or where the location of stolen nuclear materials is not known, there is no mechanism through which states could plan or effect an efficient and timely coordinated search.

The primary recommendations in this area flow naturally from the above conclusions. The United States, in cooperation with other states, should seek to designate an international organization or to establish a formal mechanism to deal with physical protection matters. The United States should also aggressively seek the agreement of states on the principles and provisions of an international convention that would establish (1) the legal basis for national and international physical protection standards that uniformly cover nuclear facilities and nuclear materials at fixed facilities and in transit, including sanctions that may be imposed against states that fail to comply with such standards; (2) the rights and duties of states to cooperate with other states in the location and recovery of stolen nuclear materials; (3) the institutional mechanisms through which these rights and duties shall be exercised; (4) a crisis management center or mechanism that would operate in the event of a significant act of nuclear-related terrorism; and (5) the duty of states to prosecute or extradite individuals responsible for sabotage of nuclear facilities or theft of nuclear materials.

Pending the conclusion of such a convention, the United States should seek through discussions in appropriate forums the agreement of states on the foregoing principles. The United States and other nuclear supplier states should consider making such principles standard provisions of their bilateral agreements for cooperation on nuclear energy and of their trilateral safeguards agreements with nuclear-recipient states and the IAEA.

Ocean Vessels and Offshore Structures. Although terrorism on the oceans has to date not been a significant problem, the oceans contain many economic assets that are within the capabilities of terrorists to attack, and that, because of their economic or symbolic value, are potential targets. Allocation of jurisdictional competence over terrorist acts, at both the international and national levels, is a primary problem in this area. The present jurisdictional framework is an inadequate basis for allowing a state to protect assets beyond its territorial sea against terrorism. If an acceptable law-of-the-sea treaty is concluded, it may provide a basis under international law for national action.

On the national level, in the case of vessels, current U.S. legislation grants ample authority to enforcement agencies for preventive and enforcement activity. Clarifying legislative amendments are needed, however, with respect to offshore structures, preventive planning is inadequate, and ambiguities regarding allocation of jurisdiction among the several U.S. enforcement agencies should be resolved.

Accordingly, if an acceptable law-of-the-sea treaty should result from the current negotiations under United Nations auspices, the United States should ratify the treaty and enact legislation to extend federal criminal and civil law to all structures within the U.S. economic zone, under the jurisdictional provisions of the treaty. Failing conclusion or the coming into force of a law-of-the-sea treaty containing adequate economic zone articles, the U.S. government should consider extending the federal criminal and civil law so it applies to U.S. structures and objects off the U.S. coast that are not covered by the Outer Continental Shelf Lands Act (OCSLA) or the Deepwater Port Act. Upon completion of such an extension of U.S. jurisdiction, the Department of State should consider seeking to negotiate bilateral or multilateral treaties requiring either extradition or prosecution for those criminal acts committed on or against vessels or offshore structures.

With respect to the responsibilities of U.S. agencies, the Coast Guard, the Departments of Defense, State, and Justice, and other interested agencies should negotiate Memorandums of Understanding clarifying respective areas of jurisdiction. Upon such clarification, the U.S. Coast Guard should complete the development of (and make available to private parties as appropriate) a comprehensive set of contingency plans covering prevention of, reaction to, and follow-up after acts of ocean terrorism. In the same vein, offshore industries should be required to file their own contingency plans that would include data regarding pipeline cutoffs and other damage control procedures, responses to fire and pipeline rupture, and so on. Also, the U.S. government and private industries and institutions should cooperate in considering the possible vulnerability of offshore structures, deepwater ports, and vessels to terrorists, and the cost-effectiveness of design modifications to minimize such vulnerability.

Finally, it is important that a low public profile be maintained with respect to the problem of ocean terrorism. The possibility of publicity increasing the potential for attacks on ocean facilities would seem substantial.

New Weapons: The Threat to Communications Facilities and New Technological Systems. A primary conclusion in this area is that there are points of vulnerability in our complex technological infrastructure, as well as weapons that in the hands of a very few people can threaten to disrupt our society and afford opportunities for blackmail by fanatic groups or individuals. However, in terms of their ability to kill large numbers of people, terrorists have generally operated well below their technological ceiling. The apparent reasons for this are manifold. Technical difficulties, especially in the cases of chemical or biological weapons or fissionable nuclear material or other radioactive material, may be a restraint. Political or moral constraints also may be operative. Terrorists appear willing to kill a few persons to win publicity, to make a point, or to create fear; they have rarely been willing to kill many people to accomplish the same objectives, apparently because the public reaction against them would be instantaneous and would enable the government to crack down on them with public approval.

Thus terrorists have exploited the new vulnerabilities of advanced industrial societies in limited and special ways. A primary goal has been to force the government to take security measures that cause inconvenience. Terrorists have bombed transformers, but they have seldom tried to blow up power stations.

They have not interfered with water supplies. They have not forced evacuations by igniting fires in chemical manufacturing plants or by blowing up tanks of hazardous chemicals, although the recent publicity given to accidental chemical spills and fires may provide some inspiration in this direction. They have not attacked liquefied natural gas (LNG) facilities or tankers carrying LNG; this is, however, a comparatively new technology. Political extremists have on several recent occasions carried out acts of sabotage at nuclear facilities. The vulnerability that modern terrorists have regularly exploited is civil aviation, primarily because airliners are vulnerable and convenient containers of hostages or a guaranteed number of victims.

Terrorists may lose some of their unwillingness to kill large numbers of people if they can reach sanctuary and if governments are prevented from responding effectively out of respect for the sovereignty of other states and from political considerations. If a terrorist group does not depend on a local constituency for support and can rely on refuge elsewhere, it may be less concerned about alienating its target population. The apparent willingness of the Japanese Red Army terrorists to kill 156 persons aboard a hijacked airplane if their demands were not met lends support to this thesis.

The existing framework of liberty in the United States, and the explicit restrictions on the powers of government contained in the First, Fourth, Fifth, Sixth, Ninth, Tenth, and Fourteenth Amendments to the Constitution place significant limitations on the kinds of actions that may be taken for protection from exploitation by terrorists of societal vulnerabilities. Nonetheless, it may be possible to reduce the new risks by holding open nonviolent means to effective political action, and by some marginal tightening of legal restrictions on possessing substances with particular potential for politically disruptive effects and on the advocacy of certain kinds of acts.

Specifically, Congress should consider the possibility of amending the U.S. Criminal Code along the following lines:

1. Unauthorized possession of specified destructive substances for which there is no legitimate private use should be forbidden. Examples include all guided weapons systems—such as heat-seeking missiles and components specifically manufactured for use in them—nerve gases, nonbiodegradable herbicides, and biological substances potentially lethal to humans.

2. Unauthorized interstate trafficking in specified substances that may have legitimate private uses but that also have significant potential use as agents to disrupt essential services or amenities or threaten the life or health of people in any section of the country should be forbidden. These items might include explosives of any sort, explosive detonators, and incendiary substances.

3. Soliciting should be forbidden when that solicitation is likely to produce the unauthorized use of those substances or weapons on targets of high

sensitivity. Targets of high sensitivity would include such points of vulnerability as water supply systems, transportation systems, communications systems, energy systems, chemical and biological storage locations, and storage places for radioactive materials. It is recognized that, in the absence of an overt act to carry out a conspiracy, this extension of the criminal law might raise constitutional questions that should be exhaustively explored before this recommendation is implemented.

Several initiatives involving international cooperation might be usefully explored. In particular, international agreements that restrict the use of specified weapons (such as chemical and biological weapons) by states should be vigorously pursued and the widest possible ratification sought. It would help to diminish the likelihood that irresponsible groups might gain possession of some particularly dangerous substances if national stockpiles of these weapons were reduced or eliminated. Foreign countries should be encouraged, perhaps by offers of technical assistance, to enact national legislation to control the possession or use of dangerous substances or weapons by unauthorized individuals or groups within their jurisdiction. Other possibilities that should be explored with other countries are measures to limit or control the sale abroad of weapons, destructive devices and their components, and measures to identify certain substances or allow identification of their origin. Some limit on the dissemination of particularly dangerous or sensitive devices or components might be achieved by tagging them with radioactive nucleides or other substances.

Protected Persons and Diplomatic Facilities. The United Nations Convention on the Prevention and Punishment of Crimes Against Internationally Protected Persons, Including Diplomatic Agents, which the United States has ratified and is now in force, has the potential to become a major factor in the effort to combat one form of international terrorism. However, further steps should be taken to maximize the convention's potential. The United States should undertake a worldwide diplomatic effort to convince as many countries as possible to become parties to the convention. To this end, the United States should work closely with the U.N. secretary-general. Informal arrangements should be worked out between government officials and appropriate countries to encourage the utilization of the U.N. secretariat to exchange data and ideas concerning security measures for the prevention of attacks on diplomats and to urge other parties to the convention to report to the secretary-general on the steps they have taken to carry out their obligations under the convention.

As an alternative or supplement to the U.N. Convention, regional and bilateral international agreements should be concluded or more widely ratified. Regional agreements currently apposite include the OAS Convention to Prevent and Punish the Acts of Terrorism Taking the Form of Crimes Against Persons and Related Extortion That Are of International Significance, and the recently adopted European Convention on the Suppression of Terrorism. The United States has become a party to the OAS Convention, but the convention has not been widely ratified. The European convention is a major regional initiative toward the prevention and suppression of international terrorism. The Department of State should keep itself fully informed of the status of this convention and, when appropriate and feasible, consider using it as a model for future agreements or sign and ratify it if it is ever opened to non-European states and likely to become an effective "Atlantic" measure.

Bilateral agreements should be modeled, when feasible, after the U.S.-Canada Extradition Treaty of 1971, which expressly eliminates the political offense exception in the case of an attack on an internationally protected person. In cases where it is not feasible to eliminate the political offense exception entirely, the 1973 "Memorandum of Understanding" between the United States and Cuba concerning the hijacking of aircraft might be employed as a guide and drafted to apply to attacks on diplomats. The first treaty explicitly calls for extradition in cases that would include attacks on diplomats, and the memorandum incorporates the principle of *aut dedere, aut judicare* but goes beyond the U.N. convention by requiring that the accused person be submitted to trial for the "offense punishable by the most severe penalty" and that signatories prevent the use of their territory as a base for committing the illegal acts covered by the memorandum.

The Department of State should study the utility of the concept of strict state liability for injuries to diplomats, as both the OAS and U.N. conventions recognize that diplomats require special protection. Even if developing countries faced a special burden in this area, some form of financial assistance could be considered to ease that burden.

At the national level, high priority should be given to the research and development of technological devices designed to maximize the protection of diplomats and diplomatic facilities. Such efforts would appear especially desirable in light of recent attacks on diplomatic personnel and facilities in New York, Washington, and other major cities in the United States and abroad.

"Nonprotected" Persons or Things. The protection of "nonprotected" persons or things (*i.e.*, persons or things not enjoying special protection under international conventions such as those covering diplomats or aircraft and aircraft facilities) is one of the most difficult tasks facing the U.S. government in dealing with terrorism. In essence, the obligation of states to protect persons and things against international terrorism is part and parcel of their larger duty to respect human rights. This duty must include the rejection of general excuses for human rights violations that are couched in terms of "noninnocence," national liberation movement exceptions, aggression, worker struggles, and guerrilla warfare. The most effective response states can make to the "ideological war" terrorists are waging against society is actively to support, by word and deed, fundamental human rights and democratic values and the proposition that terrorism is impermissible as a strategy to coerce the attitudes and behavior of others.

Specifically, governments should not use the methods of terrorism to combat or sanction terrorism. Such methods lend credence to terrorist claims concerning the permissibility of using terror as a political weapon and undermine the credibility of governmental protestations. By way of affirmative action, the U.S. government should continue to publicly condemn serious violations of human rights (including use of torture and terrorism), whether engaged in by governments or by private parties, and fund and support, consistent with the federal nature of the U.S. system, programs directed at increasing an appreciation of human rights and strengthening institutions designed for the promotion of law and justice in respect of terrorist violence. Domestically, additional support of, and primary responsibility for, such programs should come from state boards of education, bar associations, and other governmental or private groups.

Personnel and Property of Transnational Enterprises. Terrorist attacks against the transnational business operation have increased substantially over the past few years. The threat of terrorism is forcing the transnational enterprise to rethink its traditional approach to security and to develop new modes of cooperative action with government authorities as well as within the private sector.

In general, the U.S. government should adopt policies that are designed to allow enterprises maximum flexibility in dealing with terrorism, encourage cooperative measures among enterprises to combat terrorism, and reinforce the general responsibility of states under international law to protect the personnel and property of all aliens against acts of terrorism. Specifically, the government should consider the following recommendations:

1. It should not foster a prohibition of ransom payments by business enterprises in their dealings with terrorists. Nor should it encourage efforts among states to establish such a prohibition.
2. It should take the position that hostage insurance is a private business matter to be regulated by supply and demand within the insurance industry. It should neither encourage the use of hostage insurance, for to do so could well increase the ransom expectations of terrorists, nor should it prohibit hostage insurance, because as recommended above, a prohibition of ransom payments should not be applied to the private sector.
3. It should not undertake a program to subsidize the security costs of private enterprise.
4. It should support and reinforce, where appropriate, the general responsibility of states under international law to protect the person and property of aliens within their jurisdiction against injury, including injury arising

from the acts and threats of terrorists. However, the United States should *not* attempt to establish a higher or special standard of protection with respect to acts and threats of terrorists directed against transnational business operations.

5. It should foster research on a wide variety of subjects dealing with the analysis of terrorist activities, their strategies, and lawful means of prevention in respect to transnational business operations. This research should be undertaken both within the government and within the private sector.

6. It should establish a data base through which the private sector is kept informed on a current basis, where appropriate, about the activities, movements, and organization of terrorist groups around the world. Such a resource base might be located within the Department of Commerce, but it should have access as needed to the information of the various intelligence agencies of the government.

7. It should foster the establishment of a resource center for the private sector, which would be owned and controlled by subscribing businesses. While the center would be located in the United States, it could furnish services worldwide to transnational business operations. Government funding might be necessary in the beginning phase.

Prevention and Control of Terrorism: International Responses

An International Control Scheme for the Prosecution of International Terrorism

International cooperation with respect to penal matters is minimal and should be increased. The already cumbersome process of extradition is seriously impeded by the "political-offense exception." Judicial assistance and other forms of cooperation in penal matters are varied and might be useful in this regard. However, they are seldom employed.

With respect to the problem of the political-offense exception, the feasibility of a multilateral treaty defining the "exception to the political-offense exception" in extradition should be considered. Such a treaty would list those internationally recognized crimes that are to be excluded from the political-offense exception in existing and future treaties, laws, and state practice.

There are other changes that the U.S. government should consider with a view to improvements in extradition law and practice. First, it should rely on multilateral treaties as an alternative to bilateral treaties as a basis for extradition. Second, it should enter into special agreements with states that deny extradition of their own nationals or deny extradition for offenses for which the death penalty could be imposed, in an effort to overcome these obstacles to extradition. These agreements should provide that: (1) the alleged offender shall be returned to the requesting state after trial in the United States, whether acquitted or convicted, and, if convicted, that the sentence be carried out in the requesting state; and (2) the alleged offender shall not be subject to the death penalty.

Apprehension and Prosecution of Offenders:
Some Current Problems

A key mandate of the antiterrorist treaties upon states parties is to extradite offenders or to submit them to prosecution. State practice indicates, however, that deportation is the more common method of rendition of offenders than extradition, but more information in this area is needed. Accordingly, a study of contemporary policy and practice of states with respect to the use of extradition, exclusion, and expulsion of international terrorists should be undertaken under private or international auspices. The study should determine the extent of use of each method as a means of international rendition of such offenders to states where they are wanted for prosecution, as well as reasons why extradition appears to be used less frequently than exclusion and expulsion as a means of international rendition.

Using information gained through such a study, the Department of State should seek to establish by multilateral convention a common standard regarding the use of exclusion and expulsion for purposes of international rendition with procedural safeguards for the interests of the offender as well as those of the states involved. Once such a common standard has been established, the words "lawful return" should be substituted for "extradition" in the treaty injunction "extradite or submit to prosecution."

Submission of an international terrorist to prosecution is the duty of the state to which he has been surrendered or of the state that, denying rendition, has retained custody of the offender. More information concerning the fulfillment or violation of this obligation by states is needed. Accordingly, a clearinghouse of information regarding instances of prosecution of international terrorists should be established with a view to determining the extent to which such prosecution takes place and the reasons for discrepancies in bringing offenders to trial and in sentencing. Similarly, there is a need for concerted development of a fund of information about policy and practice regarding the criminal justice systems of states. A greater knowledge of the practical operations of the criminal justice systems of various states, coupled with widespread development of judicial assistance procedures in criminal matters, would allay much of the reluctance of states to surrender international terrorists for prosecution or to undertake prosecution themselves. International cooperation looking to the establishment of an international minimum standard of criminal justice is needed before "extradite or submit to prosecution" becomes a widely meaningful formula for the legal control of international terrorism.

A suggested location for the clearinghouse of information proposed in the preceding paragraphs would be the Criminal Division of the Department of Justice.

The grant of political asylum to an offender is a distinctly separate matter from the obligation to submit an offender to prosecution; it must be considered subsequent to prosecution and on different terms. Therefore the formula "extradite or submit to prosecution" should be amended to recognize that prosecution is a separate act from granting political asylum to an offender after he has been prosecuted.

Last, but by no means least, the Departments of State and of Justice should emphasize the need for widespread development of various methods of judicial assistance and other forms of cooperation in penal matters through bilateral, and, where feasible, multilateral agreements as an inducement to lawful rendition and prosecution of international terrorists by states concerned about the quality of the criminal justice systems in other states.

Criminological Policy

It is important to realize that unlike the common criminal, a terrorist is an ideologically motivated offender—*i.e.*, a person who engages in acts of terror or violence not for personal gain but to accomplish a power outcome—and that general criminological policies and practices may therefore be ineffective when employed against terrorist violence. Such a person rejects in whole or in part the social and political system of the society of which he is a member and seeks to overthrow that system by violent means. When a specific target is chosen, the means used will depend on the anticipated psychological effects of the violent action. In this regard, the role of the media and its use by terrorists should be recognized as indispensable to the effective prevention and suppression of terrorism. Prosecution, followed by imprisonment, can be used to counter terrorism, but the most effective deterrent is preventive law enforcement.

Numerous agencies in the United States are interested in the enforcement of international criminal law; however, their interests and activities are overlapping and uncoordinated. Moreover, the United States is insufficiently involved, at the governmental level, in the international criminal law activities of private or public international organizations.

The U.S. government should take several actions, at both the international and national levels, with a view toward improving criminological policy in dealing with terrorists. At the international level, the U.S. government should encourage interested countries to harmonize their criminal laws and penalties for terrorist acts as a means of improving the effectiveness of apprehension and prosecution of such offenders. To that end, a U.S. study of comparative criminal law should be undertaken by a public agency or by private groups or institutions with public funding.

At the national level, the U.S. government should realize that it often cannot avoid, and in some cases might legitimately seek, a role in the development of broad public attitudes toward terrorism and public competence to cope with it. For example, it should avoid overemphasizing the significance of the dangers and threats of terrorism in order to help prevent creating a climate of fear and apprehension among the general population. To avoid attracting would-be martyrs, as well as for humanitarian considerations, it should oppose resorting to the death penalty for terrorists. LEAA, HEW, and other concerned federal agencies should place more emphasis on dispensing federal funds to appropriate state officials or private entities on the development of programs of education in law with respect to criminal justice, violence, human rights, peaceful resolution of international conflicts, and world public order. The U.S. government also should develop new training materials and help prepare qualified instructors to assist U.S. local law enforcement agencies in their efforts to implement new techniques of prevention and control of terrorist activities.

Practical Problems of Law Enforcement

In this crucially important area, the primary problem appears to be that law enforcement officials in the United States and in Western Europe are concerned about ambiguities in the scope of their authority to deal with international terrorism. Steps should accordingly be taken to close loopholes in the law enforcement response to terrorism.

Specifically, in the United States and in other countries, statutes and executive orders should be reviewed to ensure that they: (1) provide law enforcement and security officials with appropriate authority to discharge their responsibilities to combat terrorist activities; (2) do not impose unnecessary and undue restrictions on antiterrorist law enforcement activities; and (3) provide adequate guidelines for officials in discharging their responsibilities to combat terrorism.

In the United States, a review of Executive Order 11905 discloses a serious lack of definition of key terms. Both the 1975 Privacy Act and the Freedom of Information Act contain ambiguities of concern to law enforcement officials. The Presidential Memorandum establishing the Cabinet Committee to Combat Terrorism charges the Cabinet Committee with the responsibility to "coordinate, among the governmental agencies, ongoing activity for the prevention of terrorism. This will include such activities as the collection of intelligence worldwide. . . ." However, it is unclear precisely what this memorandum was intended to authorize. In the sensitive area of intelligence, such ambiguity is unwise.

If the recommendation to establish a central data base on terrorism, noted earlier, is adopted, care should be taken to ensure that the appropriate legal authority has been established for this action and realistic guidelines should be developed defining what information is to be collected, analyzed, and disseminated in order to ensure that this activity is kept within appropriate limits. These guidelines should be developed with guidance and support from the highest levels of the executive branch and in consultation with Congress. Consideration should also be given to establishing judicial or quasi-judicial review for certain threshold decisions, such as when to start and when to destroy a file on an individual.

State Self-Help and Problems of Public International Law

Measures of state self-help include, in descending order of intensity of coercion, the use of armed force, economic sanctions, international claims, diplomatic protests, and quiet expressions of concern through diplomatic channels. Such measures with respect to states that harbor, or at least do nothing to prevent and suppress the actions of, international terrorists should be employed cautiously. Moreover, when they are used, measures of state self-help should normally be of the variety that involve the least intensity of coercion. That is, quiet expressions of concern through the usual diplomatic channels to a state that is hindering efforts to combat international terrorism and demarches to induce that state to cooperate more fully with measures to control international terrorism will normally be more effective than dramatic confrontations subject to the full glare of publicity.

Most particularly, the Department of State should continue to stress the *sui generis* nature of the incident at Entebbe (which, unlike the 1977 Mogadishu raid, involved the use of armed force on the territory of a state without its consent) and should generally support the limitations international law places on the use of force by states against other states in the name of combating international terrorism. To this end, the State Department should stress the primary emphasis assigned by the United Nations Charter to avoiding the use of armed force and to settling disputes peacefully.

The State Department should not press for the adoption of multilateral or regional conventions enabling states parties to impose economic sanctions against a state that harbors international terrorists *unless* all further efforts at international cooperation fail. The United States should first make every effort to induce other states to become parties to and abide by applicable antiterrorist conventions and to take other steps toward the prevention and punishment of international terrorism. Only if all further efforts at international cooperation with recalcitrant states fail should the department renew and pursue proposals for the application of economic sanctions.

Further in this area of economic sanctions, the U.S. government (Congress and the executive) should carefully evaluate the utility of legislation compelling the president to impose economic sanctions against countries that grant safe haven to terrorists. Past experience indicates that legislation of this type (*i.e.*, the early version of the so-called Hickenlooper Amendment) tends to exacerbate already delicate U.S. foreign relations with the target state and fails to induce it to take action favorable to U.S. interests.

With respect to international claims, the Department of State should as a first step seek to ensure the inclusion of provisions applicable to states that aid international terrorists in the Document on State Responsibility that is to be ultimately adopted by the International Law Commission. These provisions should specify in precise terms the rights and responsibilities of states in this area. The department should further strongly encourage the ILC to complete its work on state responsibility on a high priority basis.

The State Department should protest vigorously against actions by states that hinder or interfere with the prevention or punishment of international terrorism. Moreover, where standing exists, such protests should be made even if no U.S. nationals are among the terrorists' victims.

Private Measures of Sanction

In the absence of effective responses by governments to individual acts of international terrorism, private measures of sanction have been proposed or employed to fill the vacuum. Prominent examples of such measures are the threatened international strike by airline pilots, the use of private police for security purposes or of private armies in retaliation for terrorist attacks, and economic boycotts of states perceived as aiding and abetting terrorist activities. Depending on the nature of the response, and the context in which it is made, individuals, groups, and private institutions can respond to terrorism creatively or destructively in terms of serving minimum world order and human dignity. Whether the cumulative effect of private choice will assist in preventing and controlling terrorism and in promoting minimum public order and human dignity may ultimately depend on popular awareness of and demands for a world of law, justice, and the values of a free society expressed in the human rights instruments of the twentieth century.

The U.S. government's ability to facilitate these broad conditions, while limited, is significant. Certainly the government can and should strive to enrich and improve access to the educational process, and more broadly employ an explicit ideological strategy aimed at widening understanding of the humane values that are most threatened by terrorism. On the international plane, this is one of the benefits of the newly invigorated human rights policy of the Carter administration.

By way of specific actions, the U.S. government should assure that the tactics, equipment, and training of private police are within relevant international and domestic legal standards. The government also should encourage the National Commission on Uniform Laws to consider, in the context of their present and future work, the amendment of federal and state law to assure civil and criminal immunity for persons acting reasonably to aid victims of terrorism, to compensate a victim if the victim is further injured by the person giving aid, and to compensate the individual for losses sustained while attempting to aid a law enforcement officer.

In concluding, we would like to reiterate that the conclusions and recommendations set forth above are only those that appear to us most worthy of attention and do not necessarily represent the views of the entire working group. Moreover, these conclusions and recommendations, as well as others, are developed more fully in the appendix and most fully in the individual chapters.

Alona E. Evans
John F. Murphy

Part I
Terrorists' Threats and Societal Vulnerabilities

1 Aircraft and Aviation Facilities

Alona E. Evans

Introduction

Hijacking, or the diversion of an aircraft from its scheduled destination by force or threat thereof, is a form of terrorist attack against international and domestic civil aviation. Having achieved spectacular success between 1968 and 1972, it continues to pose a threat, albeit a declining one. But aviation terrorism may also take the following forms: sabotage of aircraft on the ground or in the air; forced flights or the demand that terrorists be flown to an asylum state from the state in which they have committed an act of terrorism, a situation that may involve the extortion of ransom or release of "political" prisoners as well as the use of hostages; interception of aircraft by state authorities for reasons other than the protection of a state's jurisdiction over its airspace; and abduction of persons from aircraft that have landed routinely, by *force majeure* or by interception.[1] The reach of terrorism to civil aviation also comprehends what may be broadly described as "aviation facilities," including air terminals, cargo buildings, maintenance facilities, apron passenger vehicles, aprons, cargo areas, runways, taxiways, and off-airport processing facilities such as urban airline terminals and ticket agencies. Whatever the motive, an attack on aircraft and related facilities not only serves to "produce fear"—the distinguishing characteristic of terrorism[2]—but it is also peculiarly heinous because innocent persons dissociated entirely from the terrorist's personal or political ambiance are the victims. In addition, in an increasingly interdependent world, a major form of communication is subjected to disruption and often to destruction. Whatever the motive—escape from self, family, criminal process, or the furtherance of real or imaginary political objectives—interference with international and national civil aviation must be recognized as a crime and treated accordingly.

Aircraft hijacking, both international and domestic, has been brought under substantial control through proscriptive international and national legislation, rigorous national security measures, and the enforcement of same. The catalyst was the 1963 Convention on Offenses and Certain Other Acts Committed on Board Aircraft (Tokyo Convention), which entered into force December 4, 1969.[3] While it emphasized resuming unlawfully interrupted flights, this convention adumbrated the penal focus of the 1970 Convention for the Suppression of Unlawful Seizure of Aircraft (Hague Convention)[4] and of the 1971 Convention for the Suppression of Unlawful Acts against the Safety of Civil Aviation

This study was completed as of July 31, 1977. Certain additions incorporate recent events.

3

(Montreal Convention).[5] Subsequently, bilateral agreements—such as the 1973 Agreement on the Hijacking of Aircraft and Vessels and Other Offenses between the United States and Cuba,[6] looking to the control of hijacking, met real or anticipated regional manifestations of the problem. As early as 1961, the United States began to include hijacking as a distinct extraditable offense in its new or revised extradition treaties.[7] Federal legislation establishing the offense of "aircraft piracy" was adopted in the United States in 1961,[8] and it was followed by similar action in many other states. These treaties and statutes have been directed to deterrence through penal processes. The other side of the coin, deterrence through prevention, became the focus of attention in 1968. Security programs became progressively stricter until 1973, which saw the adoption of the stringent measures now in force in major air terminals in the United States and some other countries and apparently a concomitant of contemporary national and international air travel. In short, a variety of multilateral, bilateral, and unilateral approaches to the problem of controlling attacks on air transport have been undertaken gradually, at times fitfully, and then as international exasperation with an increasingly intolerable situation has grown, rigorously, and on occasion, ruthlessly.

This chapter will summarize the impact of terrorism on international and domestic civil aviation, the responses at the national and international levels to terrorist attacks on civil aviation, the economic and political milieus, and it will offer some suggestions looking to further development of controls over aviation terrorism.

The Problems of Terrorist Attacks on Civil Aviation and Aviation Facilities

Incidence of Attacks

Between January 1, 1960, and June 30, 1977, there were 487 hijackings of U.S. and foreign aircraft (see Table 1-1). Of these aircraft, 299 have been successfully hijacked to a destination, foreign or domestic, other than the scheduled destination; the remainder have been unsuccessful.[9] These figures include the seizure of aircraft in flight as well as attacks on aircraft "in service," *i.e.*, on the ground in preparation for or upon completion of flight.[10] From an average of five international or domestic hijackings per year between 1960 and 1967, the number increased to 35 in 1968 and spiraled to 89 in 1969. Between 1970 and 1973, there was an average of 72 hijackings per year. The average dropped to 24 per year between 1973 and 1976. There were 14 hijackings between January 1 and June 30, 1977.

Damage to or destruction of an aircraft, with or without injury or loss of life, may occur in the course of a hijacking scheme or as a deliberate act of

Table 1-1

Successful and Unsuccessful Hijackings of U.S. and Foreign Registration, 1960-1976

Year	United States	Foreign	Total
1960	0	9	9
1961	5	6	11
1962	2	2	4
1963	0	1	1
1964	1	1	2
1965	4	1	5
1966	0	4	4
1967	1	6	7
1968	21	14	35
1969	40	49	89
1970	29	59	88
1971	28	33	61
1972	32	33	65
1973	2	21	23
1974	7	20	27
1975	12	14	26
1976	4	18	22
1977 (Jan. 1-June 30)	1	13	14

sabotage.[11] The Federal Aviation Administration (FAA) reported 34 explosions on board aircraft in flight, which resulted in 949 deaths between January 1, 1960, and December 31, 1976.[12] These figures give no clue to the identity of the perpetrators of these acts of sabotage or their alleged motives. Occasionally, however, a terrorist group will associate itself with an act of sabotage; e.g., Cuban exile groups located in Miami and in Venezuela reportedly claimed responsibility for the destruction of the Cuban aircraft in October 1976.[13] It should be noted, however, that not all acts of in-flight sabotage result from terrorist plotting. Some have been perpetrated for felonious personal reasons, such as murder or suicide in order to collect insurance, and some have been perpetrated by mentally deranged persons.[14]

In the period covered by this study, there have been many acts of sabotage or attacks directed against aircraft on the ground at airports. Twenty-two of these attacks against aircraft have resulted in the deaths of 46 persons (30 in a Pan American World Airways aircraft at the Rome airport on December 17, 1973) as well as the destruction of 9 aircraft and substantial damage to 13 others. This type of offense is comprehended in the terms of the Montreal Convention if the aircraft was "in service," i.e., "from the beginning of the preflight preparation of the aircraft by ground personnel or by the crew for a specific flight until twenty-four hours after any landing" [art. 2(b)], provided that "(1) the place of takeoff or landing, actual or intended, of the aircraft is situated outside the territory of the state of registration of that aircraft; or (2) the offense is committed in the territory of a state other than the state of registration of the aircraft" [art. 4(2)].[15] The ground-to-aircraft-in-flight attack by missile or infrared homing device is another type of offense that has been attempted by terrorists at least twice recently, each time without serious consequence to the aircraft and passengers. It may possibly be reached by the Montreal Convention.[16]

In the same period numerous attacks have been made on various kinds of "aviation facilities," including a terminal building, transit lounge, apron, passenger gangway, baggage area, apron passenger vehicle, airline urban terminal, hangar, and control tower, as well as on aircraft not in service. In 1976 there were 23 such attacks, 11 of them directed against urban airline offices, 6 within air terminals, and 6 directed against aircraft not in service.[17] Twenty-seven of these types of attacks since 1968 have resulted in 57 deaths and injuries to some 375 persons.[18] The most serious single incident was an attack by members of the Japan Red Army in 1972 upon the baggage claim area of Lod Airport at Tel Aviv, in which 26 persons were killed and 80 injured.[19] As with hijacking, the attackers' identities and motives are not always clear. For example, the bombing of Los Angeles Airport on August 6, 1974, in which 3 persons were killed and 30 injured, appears to have been the work of a psychopath; on the other hand, the bombing at La Guardia Airport on December 29, 1975, which resulted in 11 deaths and injuries to 75 persons, apparently was perpetrated by persons unknown for reasons unknown.[20] The bombing of the offices of Mackey International Airlines in Fort Lauderdale, presumably by anti-Castro terrorists, appears to have achieved the terrorists' aim of forcing the carrier to cancel its proposed commercial flights to Cuba.[21]

Aviation facilities and aircraft that are not in service do not come within the purview of the Montreal Convention. This is one lacuna in the international legislation looking to control terrorist interference with civil aviation. Annex 17 to the 1944 Convention on International Civil Aviation (Chicago Convention)[22] as spelled out in implementing regulations (*see* pp. 10-19) makes airport security—*i.e.*, preventive measures—the responsibility of member states of the International Civil Aviation Organization (ICAO). But deterrence in the form of prosecution of offenders is provided for only within the framework of national law.

The phenomenon of the "forced flight" has become conspicuous in recent years. This form of interference with international civil aviation arises where a terrorist demands transportation out of a country and safe conduct to an asylum state with or without hostages and ransom. The forced flight may be part of the terrorists' basic plan, as in the incident of the December 22, 1975 kidnaping of

11 representatives of the Organization of Petroleum Exporting Countries who were attending a conference at Vienna.[23] Or, it may be the objective of the terrorist plan, as in the effort of three members of the Moro Liberation Front to reach Libya in an incident that began as a hijacking at Manila on April 7, 1976, and that was completed by international hedge-hopping on April 15.[24] The forced flight differs from the hijacking in that the state from which the flight began or the state of registration of the aircraft, if different, consents to the flight albeit under pressure of humanitarian, diplomatic, economic, or other considerations. Since 1969, there have been 35 forced flights, of which 31 have occurred in the past six years. More than half of these flights began as hijackings, and 22 involved the use of hostages before or during the course of the incident. In five instances, there has been an exchange of hostages in which a government official or airline representative has been substituted for the passengers or original crew as a guarantor of the terrorists' safety.[25] Hostages have usually survived their ordeal; however, there have been instances of flagrant murder of hostages by hijackers or in conjunction with a hijacking.[26]

The crude figures for incidents of hijacking, forced flights, aircraft sabotage, and attacks on aviation facilities indicate that all these offenses continue to thrive. It should be emphasized, however, that sabotage of aircraft and aviation facilities is the most serious of these offenses in terms of increasing incidence and destructiveness to persons and property.[27] Control involves national effort supported by cooperative and concerted action by concerned states. ICAO has established some relevant guidelines for security measures, which will be discussed later, but it has often assumed a passive stance in the matter, leaving the thrust of action to concerned states or to professional organizations *qua* interest groups, such as the International Federation of Air Line Pilots Associations (IFALPA).

Changing Character of Attacks on Civil Aviation

From 1960 through 1967, hijacking was committed primarily for private or personal reasons by persons seeking political asylum, escaping criminal process, evading family responsibilities, or suffering from psychological pressures. The private objective has continued to be one motive for hijacking.[28] But beginning in 1968, the public or political factor became pronounced, *i.e.*, hijacking to advance a political cause by providing financial support through the extortion of ransom for hostages or detained aircraft,[29] by rescuing compatriots of terrorist fronts, factions, or similar groups,[30] or simply by dramatizing an ideological position.[31] Extortions of money or the release of prisoners in conjunction with hijacking or forced flights began in 1969. There were 7 such demands in 1970, and 8 in 1971. The year 1972 saw 31 demands for ransom and 8 for prisoners. Since then, the number of extortionate demands has decreased from 9 in 1973 to 6 each in 1974, 1975, and 1976. There were 2 in the first six months of 1977. The factor of imitation that is evident in any examination of hijacking statistics was important in the burgeoning of ransom demands in 1972, especially in the United States, where in five instances hijackers also managed to parachute from the aircraft with their booty.[32]

Between 1960 and 1968, hijacking was accomplished mainly by the threat of force with little actual use of force beyond an occasional "roughing up" of a crew member or a passenger. Since 1968, however, violence has become a conspicuous feature of hijacking. Passengers, crew, ground personnel, police, and security guards have been killed or injured, and aircraft have been destroyed in a number of instances. Violence has emanated from both the hijackers and the persons trying to prevent or terminate hijackings. For example, six hijackers were killed and one wounded by security guards in an in-flight fracas on an Ethiopian aircraft on December 8, 1972.[33] In 1974, a man killed an airport policeman and the copilot of an aircraft, which was on the apron at Baltimore-Washington International Airport, in an attempted hijacking. He himself was killed by another policeman.[34] The use of force in an effort to frustrate a hijacking was dramatically demonstrated in the termination, on May 23, 1976, of a two-day "standoff" between Philippine troops and 6 hijackers at Zamboanga Airport in which 10 passengers and 3 hijackers were killed and the aircraft was destroyed.[35] This increasing resort to violence is not a hopeful portent where civil aviation is concerned. It suggests a kind of desperation on the parts of hijackers as well as government officials in which passengers and crew are the pawns. Moderation cannot be expected of the hijackers as long as the odds for the successful accomplishment of their objectives or for a safe conduct to a hijack haven are in their favor. Moderation on the part of government personnel responsible for aircraft and airport security is becoming less likely as government responses to terrorism move from acquiescence to obduracy.

Changing Responses to Attacks on Civil Aviation

"React, don't act" has been the approach to burgeoning aircraft hijacking and related offenses in the United States and abroad. It was evident in 1961 when Congress moved in three weeks to create the offense of "aircraft piracy," which it made punishable by a minimum of 20 years in prison and a maximum of the death penalty,[36] following the hijacking of three U.S. aircraft to Cuba and the frustration of another hijacking in dramatic circumstances. Hijacking was hardly a novelty in September 1961 when the statute was enacted: within the previous 17 months, there had been 17 successful or attempted hijackings, 7 of them to the United States.

Hijacking went into a decline for the next five years. In 1968 it began a rapid upswing, which lasted until 1973. The U.S. response was to try to control the menace by developing various kinds of security or policing measures. In 1968 it was announced that the FAA would develop a team of specially trained flight inspectors who would be assigned to flights on a random basis[37] and that searches of persons and baggage would be instituted.[38] The next development was the behavioral "profile," a set of distinguishing characteristics that would enable airport personnel to identify potential hijackers.[39] Since the inception of 100-percent screening, however, the use of the profile is no longer necessary.[40] In 1970, the "sky marshal" program was launched.[41] On January 5, 1973, the preboarding security program of full screening of boarding passengers and inspection of cabin luggage was instituted.[42] This program was expanded to a selective screening system for checked baggage, following the bomb explosion at La Guardia Airport on December 29, 1975.[43]

This evolutionary approach to the control of hijacking in the United States has had its counterparts to a greater or lesser extent in other countries, depending on how many attacks on airports or aircraft a particular state has experienced. The adoption of specific anti-hijacking legislation paralleled the increase in the number of hijackings beginning in 1968 and continuing into the 1970s, pursuant to the requirements of the Hague and Montreal conventions.[44] Other states have adopted airport security legislation gradually,[45] and they have been making only gradual efforts to apprehend and prosecute offenders.

The response to actual instances of hijacking took the form of a deprecatory attitude between 1960 and 1968, probably manifesting the theory that publicity only encourages this type of offense. As hijacking, together with related offenses, rapidly increased from 1968 on, a concessionary attitude was apparent in the reaction of victimized carriers and states. Extortion of money and prisoners was conceded, and hostages were allowed to accompany hijacked aircraft or forced flights. A trend toward obduracy on the part of carriers and states began to emerge in late 1975. For example, in August 1975 it was reported that Japan Air Lines would not cooperate in any more forced flights following a hijacking incident in that month. (Five Japan Red Army terrorists held 53 hostages at the U.S. Embassy at Kuala Lumpur and were then flown to Libya on a JAL aircraft accompanied by four hostages and by five compatriots who had been released from Japanese prisons.)[46] In September, Japan urged the United Nations Conference on Crime to focus on international cooperation looking to the control of terrorism.[47] Following the deaths of four persons during attacks on a train and on the Indonesian Consulate at Amsterdam by South Moluccan terrorists, the Dutch government announced the establishment of a special police force to deal with these offenses.[48] A few weeks earlier, the chief of the London Metropolitan Police warned: "To be perfectly blunt about it, what we are saying is that we are prepared to sacrifice the life of the hostages, if it comes to that. The only way to deal with these people [*i.e.*, terrorists] is to make no deals at all."[49] This draconic approach was also demonstrated in the Philippine government's standoff at Zamboanga in May 1976. A different manifestation of it appeared in the use of humanitarian intervention by Israel in Uganda, the Federal Republic of Germany in Somalia, and Egypt in Cyprus.[50] Even the Palestine Liberation Organization has been reported to oppose hijacking and to threaten the imposition of severe penalties on hijackers who might come within its jurisdiction.[51]

Existing National Measures for Controlling Attacks on Civil Aviation

Security Programs

In the United States, the FAA has general responsibility for maintaining and enforcing security measures affecting aircraft and air terminals.[52] It has "exclusive responsibility for the direction of any law enforcement activity affecting the safety of persons aboard aircraft in flight" involving aircraft piracy, interference with flight crew members, carrying weapons aboard aircraft, etc.,[53] but it may call on the Federal Bureau of Investigation (FBI) for assistance in deciding on appropriate law enforcement measures and in carrying them out.[54] When an attack is made on an aircraft on the ground with the doors open (a condition governed by the Montreal Convention), the FBI assumes the authority regarding appropriate law enforcement measures, including negotiation with hijackers, in consultation with the FAA, the pilot of the aircraft, and the carrier.[55]

As previously mentioned, the present full-screening program was instituted at the beginning of 1973. Following the unexplained explosion at La Guardia Airport on December 29, 1975, provision was made for screening checked baggage with the understanding that passengers might be "required to submit their baggage to inspection . . . [and] to provide positive identification."[56] The screening program is effective in 500 airports that handle scheduled flights.[57] The FAA regulations do not reach General Aviation aircraft, *i.e.*, private charters, air taxis, cargo carriers, or private aircraft. Each airport maintains its own police, who are trained at the Transportation Safety Institute in Oklahoma City. The FAA maintains a number of security inspectors who have been trained for duty as "sky marshals."[58] The cost to airlines of these security measures is met by a charge of 41 cents on each ticket sold by a U.S. carrier. Foreign carriers do not make this charge, as their rates are set abroad. They may also take the position that there are no security charges at foreign airports, although in fact these costs are simply subsumed in the costs of airport maintenance.[59] Foreign carriers operating in the United States are expected to meet U.S. security standards.[60] Airport operators will receive some funding for security equipment for terminals under the Airport and Airway Development Act Amendments of 1976 (P.L. 94-353).[61]

The success of the screening program has been evident. Between January 1 and June 30, 1976, for example, 191.1 million people were screened. More than 2800 weapons, explosives, and other incendiary devices were uncovered; those weapons included 1054 handguns.[62] In this same period, 422 persons were arrested as a result of the screening process.[63]

The constitutionality of the screening program has been challenged from time to time, but generally the courts have upheld it.[64] A court challenge to the safety of x-ray equipment used in the screening process was met by the FAA, which issued strict regulations regarding the safety standards for such equipment and requiring notification to passengers in the screening area about such equipment's effect on photographic film.[65]

Despite the effective screening program, hijacking and other attacks on civil aviation continue in the United States. For one thing, such a program is as effective as the personnel assigned to carry it out or as the detection devices in operation at a given time. In an attempted hijacking at Baltimore-Washington International Airport in 1974, the hijacker shot and killed an airport policeman who was monitoring the magnetometer and reached the aircraft by using the aisle reserved for debarkation.[66] In 1975, while a man who had tripped the magnetometer several times was boarding the aircraft, a handgun fell from his person. On search, he was also found to have a bladed knife.[67] As to the effectiveness of the electronic devices, the vice president of American Science and Engineering, Inc., a Massachusetts firm that makes x-ray screening systems, has observed that such machines can get out of order very quickly. Thus the FAA's quarterly inspections are not frequent enough to ensure continuous operating efficiency.[68] Certainly it does not take much experience in air travel in the United States to realize that there is a substantial difference in the sensitivity of screening devices in use by different carriers within the same airport or in different airports.

The security screening program operates in the boarding area of a terminal. It does not reach the boarding areas of General Aviation aircraft, which in some airports provide direct access to the apron where security-cleared aircraft and passengers are waiting. Nor are security screenings done in small airports that handle only General Aviation aircraft. Recognizing that "hijacking is the *number one* threat to GA security," and given the record of 23 successful and unsuccessful hijacking attacks on General Aviation aircraft between 1968 and 1975, some corporate aircraft operators, air taxi, and commuter carriers are voluntarily establishing security programs that are similar to those required of scheduled carriers.[69] For obvious reasons, "perimeter control" of the area surrounding a terminal requires a considerable staff if it is to be reasonably effective. It has been reported that O'Hare Airport has 32 police on each shift to patrol a 13-square-mile area.[70] Hijackings from O'Hare are not common, but other airports are less fortunate. For example, in 1972, a hijacker riding a bicycle, wearing a ski mask, and armed with a shotgun made his way onto the apron at the Reno airport through a hole in the fence.[71] A hijack attempt was made on a parked aircraft at Pensacola Airport in 1975 by a man who climbed over the fence.[72] In April 1976, a private aircraft was hijacked at Grand Island, Nebraska, by a man who reportedly drove through an open security gate onto the aircraft stand where the plane was being serviced.[73] The use of closed-circuit television, alarm systems, control of incoming freight by specially selected personnel, and isolated employee parking lots has been suggested as a means of protecting cargo from theft,[74] but these devices could also be used for perimeter control with regard to hijacking and related offenses. The main factor is cost; the question is whether the risk warrants the cost.

Information about airport security programs in other countries is not readily available. Where hijackings or attacks on aircraft on the ground or attacks on terminals and related facilities continue, it may be concluded that security is not effective. In some states, such as the United Kingdom, Canada, and the Philippines, security procedures are the responsibility of the carriers, and as in Japan, the country may not want to assume this responsibility. In other countries, the state assumes responsibility through its customs officers and police.[75] These variations make the adoption of international standards and the coordination of such standardized procedures more difficult. Experience, however, should have some effect on operating officials. Incidents in 1976, for example, indicate quite clearly that there are two significant areas of vulnerability at airports where security measures could be instituted or increased: transit areas where passengers leave one plane to embark on another, and baggage and customs areas where incoming baggage is received.[76]

Terrorist attacks usually produce increased attention to security. It has been reported that airport security at Rome was "modified" after the attack of December 17, 1973.[77] The presence of police and the use of "intensive aircraft boarding controls" have been reported at the Vienna airport.[78] Airport checks, metal detectors, airport guards, strict control of boarding areas, personal and luggage searches, and in-flight guards have been reported to be in use, singly or in combination, at airports in a number of states, including Cameroon, Fiji, Kenya, Norway, Oman, South Korea, and Sweden.[79] Some countries—e.g., Mexico—use security controls on international flights but not on domestic flights.[80] On the other hand, Oman is reported to have "particularly rigorous" security controls over flights from Muscat to Salalah.[81] While Israel has been one of the strictest supporters of security programs for both aircraft and airports, the need for security control over incoming luggage was evident in the recent explosion of two pieces of luggage at Tel Aviv Airport in the course of which 2 persons were killed and 10 were injured.[82] As an aftermath of the Entebbe incident of June 27, 1976, the Israeli government is said to be developing legislation that will require foreign air carriers to meet Israeli security standards.[83] Iceland, the transit point for considerable air traffic between the United States and Europe, is reported to maintain little security control, presumably for financial reasons.[84] Senegal has preboarding screening for weapons only on some international flights.[85] Malta's geographical situation relative to the Middle East and North Africa made it a transit point in the hijacking of a KLM B-747 from Beirut to Dubai on November 25, 1973, by adherents of the Palestine Liberation Organization; but that incident has not led to any special effort to install security controls at the Malta airport.[86]

The Greek experience with attacks on international and domestic civil aviation has included eight hijackings of Olympic Airlines aircraft, three attacks on aircraft on the apron at Athens Airport in which 2 persons were killed, and one attack on the transit area of the terminal in which 4 persons (3 Americans) were killed and 45 injured. The Athens airport has been the transit point or point of departure in six hijackings, the latest being the diversion of the Air France airbus to Entebbe, Uganda. While some security detection measures were in existence on August 5, 1973, when the attack was made on the transit area—because the victims were lined up for preboarding search[87]—and these measures were "improved" thereafter, it has been reported that laxity set in after the middle of 1974.[88] This report was confirmed respecting Air France during the June 1976 hijacking, as it is fairly clear that the hijackers embarked at Athens without a personal or hand baggage search.[89] It is understood that one U.S. carrier has now instituted its own preboarding search as a supplement to the regular airport search at Athens.

While Canada has not been one of the major victims of attacks on international or domestic civil aviation, between 1968 and 1974 it was involved in 13 hijackings, 7 having Canadian points of departure, 4 coming from the United States, and 1 attempt on an Air Canada aircraft in the Federal Republic of Germany.[90] On the basis of this experience, in 1974 Canada enacted a strict security program, including surveillance and search of persons, baggage, and cargo, and requiring Canadian registered carriers to report on the security measures that they had instituted.[91] Canada has just passed a law requiring foreign carriers to maintain security programs similar to those required of Canadian carriers.[92] Unlike the U.S. security regulations, the new Canadian regulations reach charter flights.

Under the terms of the Anti-Hijacking Act of 1974, which implements the Hague Convention, the president of the United States is authorized to suspend air service between the United States and any state that

is acting in a manner inconsistent with the Convention for the Suppression of Unlawful Seizure of Aircraft, or if he determines that a foreign nation permits the use of territory under its jurisdiction as a base of operations or training or as a sanctuary for, or in any way arms, aids, or abets, any terrorist organization which knowingly uses the illegal seizure of aircraft or the threat therof as an instrument of policy. . . .[93]

So far, these provisions have not been invoked. They are a last resort; more effective results can be obtained through negotiation and cooperative planning.

For example, the FAA has been working with foreign states to help develop effective security systems and to train their security personnel.[94] To ensure the maintenance of effective security by U.S. air carriers, the FAA makes periodic visits to foreign airports;[95] these carriers are obviously alert to the maintenance of effective security. Presumably, representations can be made informally or through the diplomatic channel, where there are marked lapses from a minimum-security standard ranging between the requirements of Annex 17 and the U.S. security program. As yet, no legislation implementing the Montreal Convention has been enacted in the United States.

It may be conjectured that the impetus for stringent minimum security standards at airports will come not just from Annex 17, but also from article 17 of the 1929 Convention for the Unification of Certain Rules Relating to Transportation by Air (Warsaw Convention) regarding carrier liability for accidents to passengers "in the course of any of the operations of embarking or disembarking."[96] In two recent cases arising from the attack on the Athens airport transit area on August 5, 1973, it was held that the "operations of embarking" comprehended injuries befalling passengers standing at a departure gate where the injuries resulted from a terrorist attack.[97] Rejecting the carrier's argument that its liability did not extend to injuries occurring within the terminal building, the Court of Appeals for the Second Circuit said in *Day* v. *Trans World Airlines, Inc.*:

We conclude, in sum that the protection of the passenger ranks high among the goals which the Warsaw signatories now look to the Convention to serve. We would add, however, that even if we restricted our interpretation to the intent and purposes of the Warsaw treaty as of 1929, we would reach the same result.

Since 1929, the risks of aviation have changed dramatically in ways unforeseeable by the Warsaw framers. Air travel hazards, once limited to aerial disasters, have unhappily come to include the sort of terrorism exemplified by the Athens attack. As that incident graphically demonstrates, these new perils often spill over into the airline terminal.

The Warsaw drafters wished to create a system of liability rule that would cover all the hazards of air travel. . . . The rigid location-based rule suggested by the appellant would ill serve that goal. . .

We believe, moreover, that the result we have reached furthers the intent of the Warsaw drafters in a broader sense. The Warsaw delegates knew that, in the years to come, civil aviation would change in ways that they could not foresee. They wished to design a system of air law that would be both durable and flexible enough to keep pace with these changes. Our holding today confirms the framers' belief that the ever-changing needs of the system of civil aviation can be served within the framework they created.[98]

As an aftermath of the Entebbe incident, actions for $145 million in damages have been brought in Chicago against Air France and Singapore Air Lines by 42 surviving passengers and the heirs of 3 deceased passengers, on the grounds that both airlines had negligently allowed armed hijackers to board their respective aircraft without security screening.[99]

In the last analysis, prevention has been the major control over hijacking and has provided the main deterrent to attacks on civil aviation. But a program of prevention faces two hazards. One is high cost, as was brought out by the delegate from Senegal to the ICAO Assembly in 1974; he questioned whether the United Nations Development Program could underwrite aviation security measures, as "not all States could afford to spend, as one had done, $28,000,000 for screening equipment." To this, the chair replied that the UNDP did not favor the supply of "operational equipment."[100] Another hazard is that success could be the downfall of the security focus, for as the incidence of attacks on aircraft and aviation facilities declines, the traveling public might begin to chafe at the severe scrutiny that it must undergo, or security controls in air terminals might be relaxed out of sheer ennui. The U.S. experience indicates, however, that eternal vigilance is the price of safe air transport.

Anti-Hijacking Legislation

Reference has been made to the evolution of U.S. legislation relative to the control of aircraft hijacking. In some countries—*e.g.*, Austria, Colombia, Italy, and Switzerland—acts that may be characterized as "terrorist," including hijacking and related attacks on civil aviation, are prosecuted under relevant provisions of the state's criminal laws or penal code.[101] There has been a trend, however, toward the adoption of specific antiterrorist legislation, as in the United Kingdom in 1974, where the problem has become significantly troublesome.[102] This legislation is not necessarily comprehensive enough to reach aircraft hijacking or other offenses against civil aviation. The Tokyo (art. 3), Hague (arts. 2, 4), and Montreal (arts. 3, 5, 10) conventions have placed an obligation on the parties to provide the necessary legislation to carry out their responsibilities thereunder. Of the 91 states surveyed here, 34 have specific anti-hijacking legislation. Seventy of these states are bound by one or more of the three conventions; of these, 33 have enacted legislation dealing with hijacking or, in a few instances, with sabotage.[103] Algeria, which is not party to any of the three conventions, also has amended its penal code to comprehend hijacking.[104] The effectiveness of this legislation lies in its deterrence value as demonstrated through the apprehension and prosecution of offenders.

Enforcement of Laws and Regulations

Between January 1, 1960, and June 30, 1977, there were 487 hijackings of aircraft, involving some 1009 hijackers. The decline in the incidence of hijacking since 1972 can be ascribed in large part to the preventive measures that have been in use in major U.S. and, to some extent, foreign airports. To a lesser extent, this decline may reflect the enforcement of anti-hijacking legislation or relevant laws. There is an explicit obligation on the states party to the Hague (art. 7) and Montreal (art. 7) conventions and implicit responsibility on those party to the Tokyo Convention (art. 15) to submit an accused to prosecution or to extradite him to another state where he will be prosecuted.

In the matter of obtaining custody of hijackers, the preferred method appears to be deportation, comprehending exclusion and expulsion, presumably because of the relative ease with which this process can be accomplished in most countries. Table 1-2 suggests the usefulness of this procedure.

The extradition process is more complex than deportation, involving as it does conventional and customary international law as well as considerations of international relations and national law and policy. The record suggests that extradition has been denied more often than it has been granted. In denying extradition, some states—such as Denmark, the Federal Republic of Germany, France, Italy, Spain, Sweden, Turkey, and Yugoslavia—have undertaken to prosecute offenders under their own laws, thereby meeting the requirements of the Hague and Montreal conventions. Of the 37 extradition requests for 87 persons listed in Table 1-3, 5 were granted, 19 were denied but have been followed by prosecution or prospective prosecution in the requested state, and 9 have been denied apparently without subsequent prosecution. Four requests are pending.

Where a state is willing to prosecute a hijacker found within its territory, surrender of the accused to the state in which the incident occurred or to the state of registration of the aircraft is not necessary. Moreover, the charge that the offended state might impose an unduly harsh penalty is avoided. Those interested in the regularization of international criminal proceedings, including acquisition of custody of fugitive offenders, will not welcome the trend toward "disguised extradition" in the form of exclusion and expulsion. On the other hand, the extradition process itself may be self-defeating in its effort to protect the interests of the states involved as well as those of the accused.[105]

It should be noted with regard to recovery of fugitives that the Convention on Status of Refugees may impose a limit on rendition.[106] This situation arose with regard to a Bulgarian request for extradition of a Bulgarian national from Greece on a hijacking charge. A Greek court granted the request; however, the representative of the High Commissioner for Refugees in the Middle East intervened in the proceeding on the grounds that the accused was a political offender. While the case was on appeal to the Supreme Court of Greece, the accused committed suicide.[107]

Acquisition of custody of offenders is one thing; prosecution is another. It is difficult to determine with any accuracy the total number of persons who have been apprehended in the period covered by the study or the disposition of their cases. The figures for the United States are reliable; those for other countries are variable. Nevertheless, the figures do suggest something of the current situation. Of the 257 persons involved in the hijacking of U.S.-registered

Table 1-2
International Rendition of Hijackers by Deportation

State	Instances
Albania	1
Algeria	7
Bahamas	1
Belgium	2
Bulgaria	1
Canada	2
Costa Rica	2
Cuba	41
to U.S. directly	8
to U.S. via Barbados	5
to U.S. via Bermuda	1
to U.S. via Canada	9
to U.S. via Czechoslovakia	1
to U.S. via Jamaica	4
to U.S. via Mexico	1
to Ecuador	10
to Mexico	2
Egypt	2
France	6
Lebanon	1
Libya	4
Malawi	2
Morocco	6
Netherlands Antilles	6
Saudi Arabia	3
Spain	3
Sweden	2
Trinidad and Tobago	6
Tunisia	4
Turkey	4
United Kingdom (Falkland Islands)	20
United States	1
Yugoslavia	4

aircraft since 1961, 158 have been apprehended. Of this number, 84 have been convicted in the United States, 3 acquitted, 29 did not stand trial or charges were dismissed because of mental condition, and 11 cases are pending.[108] Thirteen hijackers of U.S.-registered aircraft have been convicted in other countries on various charges; they are fugitives from the United States. Aircraft

Table 1-3
International Rendition of Hijackers by Extradition

Requesting State	Requested State	No. of Persons	Nationality	Result
Algeria	Yugoslavia	3	Algerian	Denied; prosecuted; suspended sentences; deported to Algeria
Argentina	Chile	6	Argentine	Denied
Argentina	Cuba	1	Argentine	Pending
Bulgaria	Greece	1	Bulgarian	Granted; while on appeal accused committed suicide
Bulgaria	Yugoslavia	1	Bulgarian	Pending
Canada	Cuba	1	American	Pending
Colombia	Paraguay	1	Colombian	Granted; on appeal
Cuba	Portugal	1	Cuban	Denied
Czechoslovakia	Federal Republic of Germany	2	Czech	Denied; prosecuted; sentenced 7 yrs.
Czechoslovakia	Federal Republic of Germany	10	Czech	Denied; prosecuted; sentenced 3 to 7 yrs.
Czechoslovakia	Federal Republic of Germany	1	Czech	Denied; prosecuted; sentenced 8 yrs.
Greece	France	2	Greek	Denied; prosecuted; sentenced 5 to 8 mos.
Greece	Sweden	1	Greek	Denied; prosecuted; sentenced 22 mos.
Greece	Sweden	1	Greek	Denied; prosecuted; sentenced 3½ yrs.
Hungary	Federal Republic of Germany	4	Hungarian	Denied; prosecuted; sentenced 2½ yrs.
Italy	Kuwait	5	Arab	Denied
Japan	Libya	4	Japanese	Denied
Mexico	Argentina	2	American, Guatemalan	Granted
Mexico	Cuba	5	Mexican	Denied
Mexico	Cuba	2	Mexican	Denied
Poland	Austria	1	Polish	Denied; prosecuted; sentenced 4 yrs.
Poland	Denmark	1	Polish	Denied; prosecuted; sentenced 6 yrs.
Poland	German Democratic Republic	1	Polish	Granted
Portugal	Spain	1	Portuguese	Denied
Romania	Federal Republic of Germany	4	Hungarian	Denied; prosecuted; sentenced 2½ yrs.
Soviet Union	Sweden	1	Soviet	Denied; prosecuted; sentenced 4 yrs.

Table 1-3 (cont.)

Requesting State	Requested State	No. of Persons	Nationality	Result
Soviet Union	Turkey	2	Soviet	Denied; prosecuted; released on amnesty
Sweden	Paraguay	3	Yugoslav	Pending
Sweden	Spain	3	Yugoslav	Denied; prosecuted; sentenced 12 yrs.; pardoned and deported
Switzerland	Belgium	1	Spanish	Granted
Turkey	Bulgaria	4	Turkish	Denied; prosecuted; sentenced 3 yrs.
United States	Argentina	2	American, Guatemalan	Denied; prosecuted; sentenced 3 to 5 yrs.
United States	Dominican Republic	1	Dominican	Denied; prosecution pending
United States	France	2	American	Denied; prosecuted; sentenced 3 to 3½ mos., fines
United States	France	4	American	Denied
United States	Italy	1	American	Denied; prosecuted; sentenced 3½ yrs.; amnesty
United States	Yugoslavia	1	American	Denied

piracy, interference with the flight crew, and kidnaping constitute two-thirds of the charges on which convictions have been obtained in the United States. The variety of charges listed in Table 1-4 suggests that plea bargaining is a factor in prosecution here as elsewhere in the criminal justice system.

Sentencing is as varied as the variety of charges listed in Table 1-4. As noted, aircraft piracy carries a minimum sentence of 20 years with a maximum sentence of death.[109] The death penalty has not been sought for this offense; however, life imprisonment has been imposed in 8 cases. Other sentences range from the minimum of 20 years, imposed in 12 cases, to 60 years. The average sentence is 22 years. Sentences on the charge of interference with a flight crew range from 2 years to 20, with 11 years as average. Kidnaping has been punished with sentences ranging from 6 years to 20, with an average of 12 years.

Information establishing a record of prosecutions or other dispositions of cases in countries other than the United States is difficult to acquire or to verify. Table 1-5 is hardly exhaustive, if one bears in mind that there have been 765 hijackers of foreign-registered aircraft in the period under study.

Existing International Measures for Controlling Attacks on Civil Aviation

Conventions and Bilateral Agreements

The Tokyo, Hague, and Montreal conventions constitute the basic international law relating to the facilitation of unlawfully interrupted flights, the offense of hijacking, and the offense of sabotage of aircraft, respectively. As of June 30, 1977, 87 states were bound by the Tokyo Convention, 80 by the Hague Convention, and 73 by the Montreal Convention. As of the same date, 140 states were bound by the Chicago Convention[110] and thus subscribe in theory, if not in fact, to its annex 17, which provides for standards of aviation security. The states bound by these conventions are listed in Appendix 1B. Another multilateral convention, but of a regional nature, has recently been adopted by members of the Council of Europe. It covers aircraft hijacking and sabotage, as well as attacks on internationally protected persons, kidnaping, the taking of hostages, and the use of bombs and other weapons and letter bombs designed to endanger lives.[111] On December 15, 1976, the U.N. General Assembly adopted a resolution establishing an Ad Hoc Committee on the Drafting of an International Convention against the Taking of Hostages.[112]

Bilateral agreements have the advantage of meeting a particularly difficult situation obtaining between two states, as in the relations between the United States and Cuba, in which hijacking was an exacerbating factor. By February 15, 1973, when the Agreement between the United States and Cuba on the Hijacking of Aircraft and Vessels and Other Offenses was signed, 87 U.S. aircraft had been diverted to Cuba.[113] The agreement, which covered vessels as well as aircraft, provided for the prosecution of an offender in the state in which he was found or the "return" of such offender to the other state, presumably for prosecution (Art. First). The use of the term "return" rather than "extradition" may have reflected the practical problem of resorting to extradition in the absence of diplomatic relations between the parties, but it also reflected Cuba's apparent preference for deportation as the convenient method of handling hijackers.[114] The defense of the political motive was made available to the hijacker under certain circumstances:

The party in whose territory the perpetrators of the acts described in Article FIRST arrive may take into consideration any extenuating or mitigating circumstances in those cases in which the persons responsible for the acts were being sought for strictly political reasons and were in real and imminent danger of death without a viable alternative for leaving the country, provided there was no financial extortion or physical injury to the members of the crew, passengers, or other persons in connection with the hijacking. [Art. Fourth][115]

An agreement with substantially the same terms as the U.S. agreement was concluded by Canada with Cuba on February 15, 1973.[116] Cuba has also made anti-hijacking agreements with Mexico (June 7, 1973), Venezuela (July 6, 1973),

Table 1-4
U.S. Charges and Convictions

Charge	Number of Convictions
Aiding and abetting aircraft piracy and conspiring to interfere with commerce by extortion [18 U.S.C. §§ 2, 1951; 49 U.S.C. § 1472(i)]	1
Aiding and assisting one sought for aircraft piracy [18 U.S.C. § 3; 49 U.S.C. § 1472(i)]	1
Aircraft piracy [49 U.S.C. § 1472(i)]	32
Aircraft piracy and interference with flight crew member [49 U.S.C. § 1472(i)(j)]	2
Aircraft piracy and kidnaping [49 U.S.C. § 1472(i); 18 U.S.C. § 1201]	6
Aircraft piracy and using firearm to commit felony [49 U.S.C. § 1472(i); 18 U.S.C. § 924]	1
Assault (state charge)	1
Assault with intent to commit murder (state charge)	1
Assaulting federal officer (18 U.S.C. § 111)	1
Assaulting federal officer and interstate transportation of stolen weapon (18 U.S.C. §§ 111, 922)	1
Attempted aircraft piracy [49 U.S.C. § 1472(i)]	1
Attempted kidnaping (state charge)	2
Bank robbery (18 U.S.C. § 2113)	2
Bank robbery and interference with flight crew member [18 U.S.C. § 2113; 49 U.S.C. § 1472(j)]	1
Carrying weapons aboard aircraft [49 U.S.C. § 1472(1)]	3
Conveying false information regarding attempt to commit aircraft piracy [49 U.S.C. § 1472(m)]	3
Conveying false information regarding destruction of aircraft (18 U.S.C. § 35)	1
Court martial (U.S.N.)	3
Custodial interference (state charge)	1
Endangering lives of crew members with dangerous weapons [49 U.S.C. § 1472(j)]	2
Escape from prison (18 U.S.C. § 751)	1
Interference with flight crew members [49 U.S.C. § 1472(j)]	12
Interruption of air commerce by threat of violence (18 U.S.C. § 1951)	2
Kidnaping (18 U.S.C. § 1201)	6
Kidnaping and aggravated assault (state charge)	1
Smuggling (18 U.S.C. § 545)	1

and Colombia (July 22, 1974), which are similar in text to the U.S. and Canadian agreements.[117] The Mexican agreement provided for consideration of the political defense but omitted the exception for acts of extortion or violence committed by a hijacker in the course of the offense (this exception is found in the American, Canadian, and Venezuelan agreements); the Venezuelan agree-

Table 1-5

Prosecutions for Aircraft Hijacking and Related Offenses in States Other than the United States

State	No. of Persons Charged per Incident	Nationality	Disposition of Case
Algeria	3	Algerian	Sentenced 6-12 yrs.
Argentina	20	Argentine	Sentenced 3-5 yrs.
Argentina	1	Argentine	Sentenced 6 yrs.
Argentina	2	American, Guatemalan	Sentenced 3 yrs., 5 yrs.
Australia	1	Australian	Sentenced 7 yrs.
Australia	1	Australian	Sentenced 5 yrs.
Australia	2	Australian	Sentenced 7 yrs., 15 yrs.
Austria	2	Polish	Sentenced 2 yrs., 27 mos.
Austria	1	Czech	Sentenced 1 yr.
Austria	6	Romanian	Sentenced 2-2½ yrs.
Austria	1	Polish	Sentenced 4 yrs.
Brazil	4	Brazilian	Sentenced 12-24 yrs., loss political rights 10 yrs.
Bulgaria	1	Turkish	Committed; deported later
Bulgaria	4	Turkish	Sentenced 3 yrs.
Bulgaria	4	Turkish	Sentenced 2-2½ yrs.
Canada	1	American	Sentenced 6 yrs.; deported later
Canada	3	Canadian	Juvenile detention
Canada	1	Canadian	Sentenced to life
Canada	1	Canadian	Sentenced 20 yrs.
Canada	1	Canadian	Committed
Canada	1	Canadian	Sentenced 7 yrs.
Cuba	5	Cuban	3 sentenced to death; 2 sentenced 30 yrs.
Cuba	3	American	Sentenced 15 yrs., 20 yrs., 20 yrs.
Cyprus	7	Palestinians	Sentenced 7 yrs.; pardoned
Czechoslovakia	5	Czech	Sentenced 18 mos.-9 yrs.
Denmark	1	Polish	Sentenced 6 yrs.
Denmark	1	Polish	Sentenced 3½ yrs.
Dominican Republic	1	Dominican	Sentenced 20 yrs.
Egypt	1	Greek	Sentenced 8 mos.
Egypt	2	Egyptian	Sentenced to life, 7 yrs.
Egypt	1	Egyptian	Sentenced 10 yrs.
Egypt	3	Egyptian	Sentenced to life
Federal Republic of Germany	8	Czech	3 sentenced 2½ yrs.; 5 sentenced 8 mos.-2 yrs. suspended

Table 1-5 (cont.)

State	No. of Persons Charged per Incident	Nationality	Disposition of Case
Federal Republic of Germany	1	German	Committed
Federal Republic of Germany	4	Hungarian	3 sentenced 2½ yrs.; 1 acquitted
Federal Republic of Germany	1	Italian	Sentenced 2½ yrs.
Federal Republic of Germany	2	Czech	Sentenced 7 yrs.
Federal Republic of Germany	9	Czech	Sentenced 3-7 yrs.
Federal Republic of Germany	1	Czech	Sentenced 8 yrs.
France	2	Greek	Sentenced 8 mos., 5 mos.
France	2	Polish	Sentenced 2 yrs.
France	1	French	Sentenced 8 mos.
France	1	French	Sentenced 5 yrs. suspended
France	2	American	Sentenced 3½ mos.; 3 mos., fines
Greece	2	Arab	Sentenced 17 yrs., 5 mos.; 14 yrs., 3 mos.
Greece	2	Arab	Sentenced 11 yrs., 18 yrs.
Greece	3	Arab	Sentenced 2 yrs.
Greece	1	Greek	Sentenced 8 yrs., 2 mos.
Greece	1	Greek	Sentenced 2 yrs.
Greece	13	Greek	1 sentenced 4½ yrs.; 4 sentenced 15-30 mos.; 7 suspended; 1 acquitted
Greece	2	Arab	Sentenced to death (commuted), 2 yrs. illegal possession of arms; 25 yrs. attempted murder; deported
Iran	2	Iraqi	Sentenced to death
Israel	2	Arab	Sentenced to life
Israel	1	Japanese	Sentenced to life
Israel	1	Libyan	Committed
Italy	1	American	Sentenced 3½ yrs., amnesty
Italy	1	American	Sentenced 27 mos.
Italy	3	Arab	Sentenced 5 yrs., 2 mos., fines; released on bond
Japan	5	Japanese	Prosecution deferred
Japan	1	Japanese	Sentenced 2½ yrs.
Japan	1	Japanese	Sentenced 20 yrs.
Japan	1	Japanese	Sentenced 7 yrs.

Table 1-5 (cont.)

State	No. of Persons Charged per Incident	Nationality	Disposition of Case
Japan	1	Japanese	Sentenced 10 yrs.
Japan	1	Japanese	Juvenile detention
Japan	1	Japanese	Juvenile detention
Japan	1	Japanese	Prosecution deferred
Jordan	1	Jordanian	Sentenced to death
Lebanon	1	French	Sentenced 9 mos.; released 2 wks.; deported
Lebanon	4	Arab	Sentenced to death; commuted to 5 yrs.
Malawi	2	South African, Lebanese	Sentenced 11 yrs.; deported after 30 mos.
Mexico	1	French	Sentenced 8 yrs., 9 mos.
Mexico	1	Mexican	Sentenced 25 yrs.
Mexico	2	American, Guatemalan	Sentenced 6 yrs., 10 mos.; 5 yrs.
Mozambique	2	Mozambique	Sentenced 14 yrs.
Netherlands	2	Arab	Sentenced 5 yrs.
Pakistan	3	Eritrean	Sentenced 1 yr.
Pakistan	1	Pakistani	Sentenced 3 yrs., fine
(Palestine (Liberation Organization)	5	Palestinians	Sentenced 10 to 15 yrs.
Philippines	1	Filipino	Sentenced to death
Philippines	3	Filipino	Sentenced to death
Philippines	2	Filipino	Sentenced to death
Poland	1	Polish	Sentenced 13 yrs.
Poland	3	Polish	Sentenced 2 yrs., 4 yrs., 12 yrs.
Soviet Union	2	Soviet	2 sentenced to death
Soviet Union	11	Soviet	2 sentenced to death, commuted to 15 yrs.; 9 sentenced 4-15 yrs.
Soviet Union	2	Soviet	Sentenced 10 yrs., 13 yrs.
Soviet Union	2	Soviet	Sentenced to death, commuted to 15 yrs.; 3 yrs.
Spain	3	Yugoslav	Sentenced 12 yrs., 1 day, fine; commuted; deported
Spain	1	Spanish	Sentenced 6 yrs., 1 day, fine
Sudan	7	Ethiopian	Sentenced 2 wks.
Sweden	1	Greek	Sentenced 22 mos.
Sweden	1	Colombian	Sentenced 1 yr., 8 mos.
Sweden	1	Greek	Sentenced 3½ yrs.
Sweden	1	American	Committed; deported

Table 1-5 (cont.)

State	No. of Persons Charged per Incident	Nationality	Disposition of Case
Sweden	1	Soviet	Sentenced 4 yrs.
Switzerland	3	Arab	Sentenced 12 yrs.
Turkey	2	Soviet	Proceedings ended by general amnesty
Uruguay	1	Argentine	Sentenced 1-2 yrs.
Venezuela	6	Venezuelan	Sentenced (penalty unknown)
Venezuela	5	Venezuelan	Sentenced 4 yrs., 7 mos.
Yemen (Sana)	1	Yemeni	Sentenced to death, commuted to life
Yugoslavia	3	Algerian	Sentences suspended; deported

ment specifically provided that neither party was under an obligation to return its own nationals to the other party.[118]

The Soviet Union has anti-hijacking agreements with Iran (August 7, 1973) and Finland (August 23, 1974); reportedly, it concluded one with Afghanistan in 1971.[119] The agreement with Iran, which was directed to the "hijacking/ theft of civilian aircraft" focused, as did the Tokyo Convention, on the facilitation of the interrupted flight (arts. 1, 2, 3, 4). With regard to the offender, the emphasis has been placed on the return of the person who has hijacked or stolen an aircraft to the state of registration [art. 2(4)]. No specific provision has been made for prosecution in the state of landing; however, this option may have been recognized in article 5, which provided that "[n]one of the provisions of this Agreement shall prejudice the right of the Contracting Parties to fully exercise their sovereignty and jurisdiction in accordance with their domestic laws and regulations."[120] The political defense has been ruled out by the provision that the return of the accused and his possessions to the state of registration, and the furnishing of information about the conduct of the hijacker during the commission of the offense, "shall apply irrespective of what aims and motives have guided those who have hijacked/stolen the aircraft."[121]

The Soviet agreement with Finland has also emphasized the return of the accused to the state of registration [art. 3(1)], subject, however, to procedural provisions that reflect procedures and caveats commonly found in the extradition process (arts. 4, 5, 6, 7). Nationals of the parties may not be returned, but they must be prosecuted by their own state [art. 3(2)]. Although the agreement has provided in terms for the return of an accused or the prosecution of an accused national "regardless of what have been the motives of those guilty of having hijacked the aircraft" [art. 3(3)] , consideration of the political motive is not barred, according to article 11: "The stipulations of this agreement do not affect the rights of the contracting parties or their points of view concerning the jurisdiction, the entering or the leaving of the country, the residence of foreigners, the right of asylum, the airway traffic or any matter concerning the legislation of above matters."[122] It has also been reported that there is an anti-hijacking agreement between Bulgaria and Yugoslavia.[123]

The usefulness of these agreements as a means of controlling aircraft hijacking is problematic, given the decline in hijacking since their conclusion, which must be ascribed in considerable measure to the preventive techniques of airport and aircraft security. Only one aircraft has been hijacked from the United States to Cuba since the 1973 agreement was concluded and that hijacker has not been returned.[124] The agreement does not reach offenses committed prior to February 15, 1973 (Art. First); however, 11 hijackers whose offenses were committed between 1961 and 1973 have returned to the United States from Cuba, directly or indirectly, since that date. The future of this particular bilateral relationship is uncertain, as the agreement was denounced by Cuba in October 1976, effective April 15, 1977, on the grounds of alleged U.S. complicity in the sabotage of a Cuban aircraft; however, a warming trend in relations between the two states has led Cuba to indicate that it would continue to enforce the agreement as a deterrent to hijacking.[125] The only hijacker of a Canadian aircraft to Cuba (actually a U.S. national) committed this offense before the agreement between the two countries was signed.[126] Cuba returned two hijackers to Mexico some years before these states concluded their anti-hijacking agreement in 1973. Information does not appear to be available about the return of hijackers from Cuba to Mexico since that time, nor is there information about the effectiveness of the agreement between Cuba and Venezuela. Similarly, there is no information as to whether any action has been taken under the agreement between the Soviet Union and Finland. The agreement between the Soviet Union and Iran, however, was invoked in October 1976 when Iran denied political asylum to the pilot of a mail plane and returned him to the Soviet Union.[127]

Of the 14 extradition treaties that the United States has concluded since 1961, all except 1 have made aircraft hijacking an extraditable offense.[128] Interestingly enough, the 1971 Extradition Treaty with Canada, which entered into force on March 22, 1976, specifically provides that the defense of the political offense is not available to a person accused of aircraft hijacking [art. 4(2) (ii)] .

Security Measures

ICAO, representing 140 states of diverse political and economic interests, is in a central position to provide leadership in preventing and controlling unlawful interference with civil aviation. It has been instrumental in developing the corpus of international law represented by the Tokyo, Hague, and Montreal conventions. ICAO's opposition to such interference has been expressed in a number of resolutions.[129] It has urged members to ratify the conventions and to adopt implementing legislation.[130] General standards and procedures for the protection of aircraft in flight and on the ground as well as related facilities have been recommended to members by ICAO and are set out in annex 9 and the more recent annex 17 to the Chicago Convention. These recommendations take the form of Recommended Practices and Standards, the latter of a quasi-mandatory nature. For example, effective December 30, 1976, the following recommended practices that were listed in Amendment No. 1 to annex 17 became standards: each contracting party must adopt a civil aviation security program; there should be a broadly representative security committee at each international aerodrome; and where an aircraft has been hijacked, states that are providing air traffic services thereto must keep other concerned states informed of its location.[131]

ICAO's security recommendations are spelled out in the *Security Manual for the Prevention of Unlawful Acts against Civil Aviation*, as amended, which has been prepared by a study group consisting of representatives of Brazil, France, Switzerland, the United Kingdom, and the United States, together with representatives of the Airport Associations Co-ordinating Council, the International Air Transport Association (IATA), and IFALPA. It is suggested that aviation security in each state be the responsibility of a National Civil Aviation Security Committee composed of representatives of government agencies concerned with aviation, law enforcement, immigration, customs, postal inspection, and foreign affairs as well as representatives of airlines, airport administrations, and where possible, aviation employees' organizations. The national committee should work through security committees at each airport, a provision that is now a standard for international airports.

The manual provides detailed suggestions for security measures and techniques, emphasizing *inter alia* the concept of the "sterile area" where passengers who have been through security clearance would be held prior to boarding. Procedures for dealing with actual hijackings, sabotage, and threats thereof are suggested. Interestingly enough, the Security Group does not urge uniformity among member states with respect to security procedures because of the diversity of international aviation operations. On the other hand, the group's statement that "in any pooling arrangements between operators, often of different nationalities, the adoption of uniform practices is an advantage" may be an intimation that uniformity is worth considering.[132] The study group does emphasize the importance of efficient exchange of information and cooperative endeavor among states, ICAO, the International Criminal Police Organization (Interpol), IATA, IFALPA, and the Universal Postal Union in dealing with threats and incidents. Pursuant to this concern for security, ICAO holds regional meetings from time to time for the exchange of information about security procedures.[133] This same concern for international cooperation in the control of terrorism was urged at a recent meeting of the ministers of interior and of justice of the European Economic Community countries.[134]

The provisions of the *Security Manual* are advisory; consequently, member states may act on all or any part of this advice. Overt refusal to comply with an ICAO standard could be effected by filing an exception thereto; laxity in acting is a different matter, however. There might be some psychological value, if nothing else, in having a multilateral convention establishing an international minimum standard of civil aviation security as a means of pointing up the importance of prevention as a control. Although security continues to be on the ICAO agenda, the focus of the organization is on the facilitation of air transport rather than on the urgency of expanding preventive measures.[135] It follows that the initiative for a security convention would have to come from concerned states. The cost factor has to be borne in mind, however, in advancing this proposal, so that a regional approach in the form of agreements among technologically advanced states, on the one hand, and among less technologically advanced states, on the other hand, might be the feasible line to consider.[136] IFALPA would probably prefer to focus the energies of interested states and aviation organizations upon the aim of widespread acceptance of the recommendations in annex 17 and the *Security Manual* as far as security measures are concerned, and to seek a new convention designed to enforce the Tokyo, Hague, and Montreal conventions.[137] In 1976, IATA embarked on an Intensified Aviation Security Program, which would expand the procedures recommended by ICAO; however, IATA would have some interest in a proposal for a security convention.[138]

Proposed Sanctions or Enforcement Convention

During the period covered by this study, certain countries have served often enough as destinations of hijacked aircraft or have been sufficiently involved in the protection of hijackers and other offenders against international civil aviation to be classified as "hijack havens" or sanctuaries. Cuba, Algeria, Libya, and Yemen (Aden) have been conspicuous examples.[139] The sanctions provision in the United States Anti-Hijacking Act of 1974 is directed against this type of activity. Domestic legislation is one way of reaching the problem, but it may not be the most effective way even for a state that engages in as much international air transport as the United States does. If the offending state does not maintain air transport relations with the United States, as is the case with Algeria, Libya, and Yemen (Aden), sanctions would have to be exerted through some other means. Effective sanctions require action by like-minded states, *i.e.*, they require a multilateral approach. But it is one thing to recognize the solution, and another to achieve it.

In 1970 the ICAO Legal Committee began to consider the project of international legislation designed to enforce the Tokyo, Hague, and Montreal conventions by penalizing states that refused to comply with their obligations thereunder.[140] The United States and Canada drafted a proposal in April 1971, for consideration by the ICAO Assembly at its meeting in June, but the assembly did not reach that item.[141] The burgeoning of hijacking in 1972, the massacre at the Lod airport in May, and IFALPA's boycott in June led to the creation of a Special Legal Subcommittee, which undertook with some sense of urgency the study of a feasible method of obtaining concerted action "within the framework of ICAO" against states that countenanced attacks on international civil aviation.[142] The charge to the subcommittee received further impetus from the massacre of the Olympic athletes at Munich, which occurred during its first meeting in September.[143] As a result of this meeting, the subcommittee drafted some articles that provided *inter alia* for (1) a commission of experts to hear complaints against states that had detained aircraft or had failed to prosecute or to extradite offenders, and for (2) suspension of an offending state's rights under the Chicago Convention and the 1944 International Air Services Transit Agreement[144] as well as bilateral air service agreements.[145] The frame of reference of any prospective sanctions convention was established at the January 1973 meeting of the Legal Subcommittee. Such a convention would have no binding effect on states that were not a party to it, allegations against such states would not be investigated without their consent, and sanctions would not be directed against such offending states.[146] There was evidence of considerable interest in formulating sanctions legislation as an amendment to the Chicago Convention, thus building on the sanctions provisions in this agreement.[147] Another approach, advanced by the Soviet Union, would amend the Hague and Montreal conventions by making extradition mandatory.[148]

These various points of view were discussed at the 20th Session (Extraordinary) of the ICAO Assembly and International Conference on Air Law at Rome between August 28 and September 21, 1973. The proponents of an independent convention—Denmark, Finland, Norway, and Sweden—offered a draft (called the Nordic proposal) that provided that a contracting state could request the ICAO Council, or a commission of experts appointed by it, to investigate the state's complaint that another party had illegally detained an aircraft or had failed to submit an offender to prosecution or to extradite him. If the council were satisfied about the merits of the complaint, it could recommend that the offending state "take appropriate measures to remedy the situation."[149] On the other hand, if the council failed to act or if the offending state failed to comply with the council's recommendation, any party to the convention could request the secretary general of ICAO to convene a conference to devise "appropriate measures to remedy the situation."[150]

The United Kingdom and Switzerland were among the proponents of amending the Chicago Convention. They offered proposals comprehending the offenses listed in the Hague and Montreal conventions and the commitment to facilitate the resumption of interrupted air service that appears in article 11 of the Tokyo Convention.[151] France suggested that the Hague Convention be incorporated into the Chicago Convention, thereby making it enforceable by the measures already available in the Chicago Convention.[152] The Soviet Union, opting for a more stringent Hague Convention, suggested that extradition to the state of registration of a hijacked aircraft be made mandatory unless the accused be a national of the state where he is found and that extradition should be based on treaty.[153]

Whatever the merits of the several proposals, they lost in a conference that was generally conceded to have been a fiasco. Not only did it suffer from organizational problems, but it was doomed at the outset by that insistence on the expatiation of the underlying causes of terrorism as against coming to grips with the overt manifestations of terrorism, which characterized the United Nations' approach to the subject in 1972-1973.[154] A dismal situation was rendered even more so by the Israeli interception of a Lebanese civil aircraft on August 10, 1973, barely a fortnight before the conference opened. The conference's significance was succinctly summarized by the chairman of the United States delegation, who observed that ". . . the international concern which brought about these meetings may ultimately have secondary consequences which are beneficial."[155] The International Federation of Air Traffic Controllers' Associations (IFATCA) made the point that the conference had had the result of focusing state attention for the first time on the necessity of joint action against states that were derelict in their responsibility to protect international civil aviation.[156]

The reaction of many ICAO member states to any approaches to a realistic solution to the enforcement problem reflected the same unwillingness to face the issue of terrorist attacks on civil aviation as one of criminal law, as has been exhibited in the United Nations since the introduction of the U.S. draft convention on terrorism in September 1972. The prospects for a sanctions convention appear to be dim as long as terrorism as an agenda item is given short shrift by the United Nations. Yet the move by Libya, Tanzania, and Benin (Dahomey) to withdraw their proposed resolution in the Security Council condemning Israel's "flagrant violation" of Uganda's sovereignty through the commando rescue at Entebbe Airport is a negative action that may have emanated in part from some grasp of the enormity of the hijackers' crime as compounded by the Uganda government's cooperation.[157] Admittedly, political reality indicated that the supporters of the hijacking would not be able to muster enough votes to pass the resolution; or if they did, it would have been vetoed by the United States, which took a strongly affirmative attitude toward the Israeli raid.[158] Yet the fact of backing down in the face of widespread denunciation of the hijacking and subsequent detention of passengers and crew as hostages may have brought into focus the basic issue that offenses against civil aviation must be subject to legal control whatever the motivation and whatever disposition is made of the offenders after prosecution. Similarly, the General Assembly's affirmative attitude in December 1976 toward the prospect of an agreement penalizing the taking of hostages may presage a new perception on the part of the United Nations of international independence in the control of crime. Nor can the influence of IFALPA and other aviation organizations be overlooked. In a recent letter to the president of ICAO, the president of IFALPA pointed out that "recent events justify all States being reminded of their obligations under the three Conventions, and that further consideration should be given to agreeing [on] a means of enforcement of the Conventions."[159] For its part, IATA would be prepared to give serious consideration to an initiative for an enforcement convention.[160] The Air Transport Association of America (ATA), while supporting international sanctions legislation whether by multilateral or bilateral agreement, has suggested that the impetus for consideration of the matter should come from Third World countries.[161]

Economic and Political Milieus

*Economic Considerations: The Cost
Factor in Hijacking*

The economic condition of international civil aviation is, in a nutshell, not good. According to ICAO, the growth rate of scheduled air traffic in 1975 was 2 percent as against 6 percent in 1974.[162] The total number of passengers carried in 1975 was 529 million for 676 million passenger-kilometers (420 billion passenger-miles), which consituted an increase of 3 percent over 1974. Air freight that showed a growth rate of 15 percent per year between 1965 and 1974 showed no growth in 1975.[163] Air mail traffic also showed no growth. But if 1975 was not good, 1976 was not much better. Increases in expenses because of increasing fuel prices and inflation led carriers to increase their fares and rates and to end up with a worldwide decline in net profits of 1.1 percent.[164] United States carriers experienced no change in net profits in 1972 and 1973, and they had only a 4.7 percent increase in traffic in these two years, whereas foreign carriers showed an increase in profits in both years, due in part to a growth in traffic of 14.7 percent.[165] That the situation in 1976 was not markedly improved was borne out, at least for Pan American World Airways, by a report that the carrier sustained a loss of $6 million in the second quarter of the year.[166]

An analysis of the Byzantine economics of the aviation industry is not the purpose of this study. Rather, the question is: What is the economic impact of terrorist attacks on civil aviation? Obviously, the high cost of insurance comes to mind. Hijacking is now accepted, at least in U.S. aviation law, as an "accident," comprehended by article 17 of the Warsaw Convention, an accident that may lead to personal injury suits involving claims for damages for both physical and mental injuries.[167] The extension of carrier liability into the transit area of a terminal opens the way for more actions of the type at issue in *Day* v. *Trans World Airlines, Inc.* and *Evangelinos* v. *Trans World Airlines, Inc.*[168]

Another source of loss to the carrier is damage to or destruction of an aircraft. The most notable recent case in this regard was *Pan American World Airways, Inc.* v. *The Aetna Casualty and Surety Co.,*[169] which involved a claim for $24,288,759 for the loss of a B-747 that was hijacked to Cairo on September 6, 1970, and destroyed by members of the Popular Front for the Liberation of Palestine. Holding that the all-risk insurers were liable for the plaintiff's entire loss, the District Court observed, and the Court of Appeals agreed, that a hijacking of an aircraft from Amsterdam, belonging to a carrier that served no routes to any belligerent state in the Middle East, could not be ascribed to the Arab-Israeli conflict, but was simply an act designed to disrupt international communications.

While ransom is not a concomitant of every hijacking, its cost must be added into any consideration of the economic impact of this offense. The government of the Federal Republic of Germany, a major stockholder in Lufthansa, paid $5 million to recover a B-747 and hostages from detention in Aden in February 1972.[170] The effect of a loss to ransom on the carrier's balance sheet is not known. But the effect of the loss to Southern Airways of $2 million in ransom, in November 1972, was certainly felt, according to the vice president of the carrier, who said that the ransom "if not returned, will exceed our profit for 1972, and this is the first time in 4 or 5 years that we have been in a profitable position."[171] Cuba returned the ransom on August 11, 1975.[172] Presumably, insurance coverage under a blanket crime policy would help in such a loss.[173]

Apart from these more spectacular financial effects of hijacking, consideration would have to be given to the effect in terms of cost accounting of delayed flights, extended flights involving added fuel costs, unusual wear and tear on equipment, additional landing fees and related expenses, and the loss arising from keeping an aircraft out of service for an extended time as, for example, in the Entebbe incident in which the aircraft was returned to the custody of Air France 26 days after the hijacking.[174]

In the United States, where the aviation security program is the carrier's responsibility, the cost may not be wholly met by the 41-cent charge on each passenger ticket. Delta Airlines reported spending $2,100,000 on security in the first three months of 1975. The ticket charge covered all but 6 percent of this cost.[175]

Economic Considerations: The Impact of Interest Groups

A number of interest groups are associated with the air transport industry. The carriers are represented by IATA and its national affiliates, such as the ATA.

Pilots are represented by IFALPA, which has national affiliates, such as the Air Line Pilots Association of America. Air traffic controllers are represented by the International Federation of Air Traffic Controllers Associations and its national affiliates (IFATCA). Airport operators are represented by the Airport Associations Co-ordinating Council. The growth of private ownership of aircraft is contributing to a growth in relevant organizations. The International Council of Aircraft Owner and Pilot Associations-Europe reported a membership of 188,000 in 1975.[176] Other organizations have a cognate interest in air transport, such as the International Transport Workers Federation (ITF), which includes members of civil aviation unions in 100 countries.[177] Organizations such as the American Society of Travel Agents or the American Jewish Congress may express themselves vigorously about particularly outrageous incidents of hijacking.[178] The main interest of all these groups is the facilitation of air transport for business reasons. "Facilitation," however, is subject to diverse interpretation when illegal interference with air transport enters the picture. The carriers are concerned about restoring interrupted service, while the pilots and air traffic controllers focus on the safety of passengers and crew.

IFALPA, with member associations in 65 states, sees itself as a "body of opinion" that is concerned with air safety and security and that "can afford to have a conscience" because it endeavors to influence ICAO and member states in educational terms rather than in political or economic terms.[179] This conscience is by no means passive. Control of hijacking and sabotage of aircraft became a central concern of the association in 1969. Since then, IFALPA and its affiliates have been committed to putting pressure on states to ratify and implement the Hague and Montreal conventions and to develop a convention designed to enforce these two and article 11 of the Tokyo Convention.[180] Member associations are urged to pressure states regarding these objectives when the states are negotiating new or renewing old bilateral air transport agreements.[181] Where a member association has been unable to approach its government on the matter or has been penalized for doing so, IFALPA may order a boycott of foreign and domestic air transport in the offending state.[182]

IFALPA's pressure tactics on states usually operate at the national level and through its representatives at ICAO meetings.[183] On June 19, 1972, however, in the face of a record of 38 international and domestic hijackings in the first five and one-half months of the year, IFALPA called a 24-hour boycott of worldwide civil air transport.[184] The aim was to draw attention to the increase in hijacking and the failure of states to take relevant action by becoming parties to the conventions, implementing them, and enforcing them. The boycott was a mixed success, substantially interfering with service in many European, Middle Eastern, African, and Latin American states and in Canada.[185] In the United States the effect was slight, as the Air Transport Association was successful in getting a temporary restraining order from the Court of Appeals for the District of Columbia, prohibiting the Air Line Pilots Association from cooperating in the boycott.[186] In the long run, IFALPA did not get its enforcement (sanctions) treaty from ICAO in 1973, but the number of parties to the Tokyo, Hague, and

Montreal conventions increased and the number of hijackings and related offenses began to decline. The boycott demonstrated a potential, if last resort, power of an important element in the air transport industry.[187]

IFALPA's action on June 19, 1972, was not a "strike" or "industrial" action; indeed, in some states that severely limit "industrial" actions, the boycott was treated as a stoppage "by mutual consent" between the association and the carriers.[188] This characterization of such a work stoppage was important with regard to collective bargaining agreements and other employee-employer relationships. The technique of the "wave of sickness" was demonstrated in June 1976 by members of the Canadian Air Traffic Control Association (CATCA) in a controversy over bilingualism in air traffic control operations.[189] Bilingualism has been a political as well as a socioeconomic issue of long standing in Canada. With respect to air traffic control, however, the issue of air safety became central in the face of prospective linguistic difficulties, especially in regard to aircraft operating under Instrument Flight Rules (IFR) and at airports serving national and international commercial carriers. As the president of CATCA summarized the issue:

It is obvious . . . that the loss of a common language in the air is a retrograde step. We do not agree with comparisons that are made with other countries which use more than one language in air traffic control. These countries have added English because it is the accepted common language of international aviation and are steadily expanding its use as advocated by the International Civil Aviation Organization which is the aviation arm of the United Nations. No country which has a bilingual ATC [air traffic control] system has the number or mix of aircraft experienced in Canada. The confusion engendered by the use of two languages is totally unacceptable where the protection of human life demands split second decisions and instructions.[190]

English was recognized as the official language for air traffic control in 1962, pursuant to the Aeronautics Act.[191] Following the adoption of the Official Languages Act in 1969, some pilots and controllers in Quebec began to use French, on the theory that the earlier act had been superseded in this regard. For the next six years, the issue was explored by the Ministry of Transport and various aviation organizations. In June 1974, the ministry authorized the use of French at five satellite airports in Quebec serving light aircraft under Visual Flight Rules (VFR). In April 1975 the ministry issued a report that recommended increased use of French for flights operating under VFR. From here on the situation became increasingly tense, especially after an air safety symposium conducted by IFALPA in Ottawa in March 1976 (in which the ministry refused to participate), which concluded that "a single language ATC [air traffic control] system is the safest method and that if a bilingual system was imposed for political reasons then any accidents would be the Minister's [of Transport] responsibility."[192] In May 1976, under threat of a strike, CATCA concluded a collective agreement with the ministry in which a public inquiry into the safety and cost factors of bilingualism was a central part. Learning thereafter that the ministry would be unwilling to reconsider its policy of developing bilingual air traffic control in the light of the results of such an inquiry and considering this position to be a "deliberate doublecross" in the light of the terms of the collective agreement, CATCA threatened a strike on June 20. On the government's motion, it was enjoined by an order forbidding CATCA from striking on any issue including language until the expiration of its contract on December 31, 1976.[193] The "wave of sickness" among controllers began on June 20. The Canadian Air Line Pilots Association found the situation too dangerous for air transport under IFR; thus for nine days, there was no IFR flying in Canada. Moreover, international flights from Ireland, the Netherlands, Mexico, Greece, Israel, Switzerland, Italy, Jamaica, Australia, the United States, Great Britain, and the Scandinavian countries were curtailed if not wholly stopped.[194] Ten U.S. carriers cancelled some 150 daily flights to Canada for safety reasons at the request of the Air Line Pilots Association of America.[195]

The terms under which the stoppage concluded indicated that the controllers had made their point. They compelled the creation of a Royal Commission of Inquiry (consisting of three judges from federal and provincial courts) to examine the safety features of bilingual air control communications, a free vote in the House of Commons when the commission's report (which would have to be unanimous) would come up for debate, and no expansion of existing bilingual air traffic control until the report had been approved.[196] In July 1976 the Ministry of Transport ordered English to be mandatory at all airports in Canada except for six satellite airports in Quebec, serving light aircraft under VFR. This order was upheld by the Federal Court of Canada in a decision on January 12, 1977, in an action brought by the Association des Gens de l'Air du Québec, a group of French-speaking pilots and controllers.[197] The commission's report is due in two years, so in the short term at least, CATCA's concern for monolingual air safety has prevailed. It should be added that IFATCA has taken the position that it is prepared to support member associations in any protest against state action that would endanger air navigation, a position that is directed against the closing of airports and denial of air traffic control instructions during a hijacking or the granting of a safe haven to a hijacker, but one that could presumably reach CATCA's concern about the linguistic issue.[198]

It is self-evident that control of aircraft hijacking, sabotage, and attacks on aviation facilities is fundamentally the responsibility of states and organizations of states, such as the United Nations or ICAO. IFALPA and other aviation organizations have demonstrated that they are prepared to cooperate with states and international organizations in developing and enforcing measures against these offenses. They are also prepared to use pressure when states and international organizations fail to act. The pressure group function is secondary to action by states, but it has a real and valid contribution to make in achieving the aim of security in international and national air transport.

Political Considerations

Politics is the persistent theme running through most instances of aircraft hijacking and related offenses against international civil aviation. Politics appears overtly in hijackings by seekers of political asylum; in hijackings, forced flights, and attacks on aviation facilities by persons seeking to dramatize their opposition to colonialism, particular regimes, or personally unpalatable ideologies; in extortion of ransom or the release of convicted criminals in furthering these acts; and in Cuba's denunciation of the Anti-Hijacking Agreement with the United States. Politics appears covertly in the denial of extradition of fugitive offenders *qua* political refugees on the ground that the territorial state has jurisdiction over their act;[199] in the persistent grant of asylum to perpetrators of attacks on civil aviation, whether terrorists, fugitives from justice, or psychopaths, as has been the case with Cuba *vis-à-vis* the United States, Venezuela, Colombia, and Mexico with which its relations have been broken or strained from time to time[200] or Libya *vis-à-vis* states whose policies do not coincide with current Libyan policy;[201] or in the aiding and abetting of a hijacking involving the threat of death to 103 hostages, as demonstrated by the government of Uganda in June 1976 for reasons, possibly of foreign policy, possibly of domestic policy, if not simply the personal whim of Ugandan President Idi Amin.[202]

Responses of states that have been victimized by terrorist attacks on civil aviation have also been affected by the political factor, although here the aim has been to reconcile politics with the humanitarian consideration of protecting hostages. The concessionary attitude taken between 1970 and 1975, when a number of convicted terrorists were released by various states—including the Federal Republic of Germany, Greece, Japan, Sweden, Switzerland, and the United Kingdom—contrasts with the vigorous intervention by Israel on behalf of the hostages held at Entebbe Airport.[203] This latter action raises the question whether humanitarian intervention is the latest alternative when states fail to fulfill their general obligation to control international criminal activity or to fulfill, as in the case of Uganda, their obligations under the Hague Convention.[204] Entebbe was followed by the West German commando attack in October 1977 on a hijacked Lufthansa aircraft at Mogadishu, Somalia, for the purpose of rescuing hostages, and the ill-fated effort by Egyptian commandos at Larnaca in February 1978 to rescue hostages held on board a Cyprus Airways aircraft that had been subjected to an abortive forced flight.[205] Humanitarian intervention is not only another phase of the hardening of government attitudes toward treating with terrorists, especially where the lives of hostages are at stake, but it also introduces a technique that can have a dangerous impact on the relations of the states involved.[206] The course of action now appears to be to negotiate with terrorists for as long as feasible, then to take vigorous measures, but not to concede to extortionate demands or threats against hostages. This procedure has at least two disadvantages: (1) it makes the hostages victims of both the hijackers and the negotiators, and (2) it works best in the limited ambiance of a national hijacking, *i.e.*, where the incident is confined to an airport within the state in which the incident began, so if necessary, local authorities can bring pressure to bear on their own responsibility.[207] Where a negotiation has to be carried out in a state other than the states of registration, of destination, or of takeoff of the hijacked aircraft or in a state whose relations with these states or with the states of nationality of the hostages is strained or broken[208]—*i.e.*, at long distance—force as the last resort is not likely to be a realistic choice for most countries; nor are the suggestions—advanced during the Entebbe incident—that a prisoner demanded by the hijackers should be killed for every hostage killed, or that all terrorists should be subject to the death penalty so that none would be available for purposes of extortion. Such draconic measures would only reduce civilized states to the level of the terrorists. Methods short of force—ranging from boycott of air transport with an offending state, suspension of trade or economic aid, to severance of diplomatic relations— are the most practicable techniques, certainly for large industrial states, which are the common victims of offenses against aviation.[209] These techniques can be usefully applied unilaterally, but they would have more impact if they had multilateral backing—*i.e.*, in a particular instance of hijacking, if the principal air transport states united against the offending state. The use of these measures is legitimate under the United Nations Charter and should not be relegated to wishful thinking in chancelleries.

There is always an offending state, one that does not respect its obligations relative to the protection of international civil aviation. It is interesting to note that among the states that have condoned or have temporized with aircraft hijackers or terrorists who have committed offenses against aviation facilities, Egypt, Iraq, Lebanon, Libya, and Tunisia are bound by one or more of the three relevant conventions.[210] These states, along with Algeria, Cuba, Kuwait, Syria, and Yemen (Aden), are also party to the Chicago Convention,[211] which provides the basis for the facilitation of international air transport. All of them, and most of the states that choose to follow their lead, have some international commitment to protect the integrity of international communications as represented by international civil aviation.

It is argued that "freedom fighters" or proponents of "wars of national liberation" are exempted from the onus of criminality, no matter how barbaric their acts. This is the political stumbling block that has led the United Nations to abdicate its responsibilities as a law-making and law-enforcing agency with respect to the control of international terrorism.[212] The question is whether criminal intent can be separated from political motive in regard to terrorist attacks on international civil aviation. The answer is affirmative, provided it is understood that the aim is the legal apprehension and prosecution of the offender for a recognized crime and that the ultimate disposition of the offender after conviction and serving of sentence is a separate matter that may involve a grant of political asylum or deportation to another state. If, in the support of the aim of prosecution, there is a general movement to develop international legislation on various forms of "judicial assistance," including exchange of information regarding criminal investigations, service of documents, interrogation of witnesses, transfer of criminal proceedings, enforcement of criminal judgments, and transfer to the home state and supervision of offenders convicted in another country, much of the latent fear that persons accused of terrorist acts would be subjected to political persecution could be overcome.[213] This approach does not derogate from the pursuance of political aspirations by persons who have real or fancied national or international grievances. It does force such persons, and those who would sympathize with them, to recognize that political aspirations are no justification for offenses against international civil aviation.

Conclusion

The thrust of international terrorism against international civil aviation reaches not only the hijacking of aircraft but also the sabotage of aircraft in flight and on the ground, forced flights, as well as attacks on "aviation facilities," including terminals, transit areas, baggage and customs areas, aprons, hangars, control towers, and urban air terminals. The recognition by states of their mutual responsibility for the protection of international civil aviation as evidenced by their commitment to the Tokyo, Hague, and Montreal conventions and, in particular, by their rigorous application and enforcement of preventive measures has markedly reduced terrorist attacks against international civil aviation. Despite these measures, there are a sufficient number of serious incidents, especially involving transit and incoming baggage areas in air terminals, aircraft not in service, and urban air terminals, that attention should be given to establishing international standards by convention that would be designed to protect these places. At the same time, the desirability of a convention for the enforcement of the Tokyo, Hague, and Montreal conventions should not be dismissed. If state authorities are not alert to the need for developing measures of control for the protection of international civil aviation, these matters will be brought to their attention through political and economic pressures of private organizations.

In handling terrorist incidents in the aviation field, prolonged negotiation rather than concession is becoming the preferred policy of authorities. When prolongation reaches an intolerable duration, however, the price of this policy in the form of the loss of hostages' lives may be too high. Nonetheless, negotiation is to be preferred to concession on the one hand and to humanitarian intervention in a foreign country on the other.

Concerted action by states to submit international terrorists to prosecution for their attacks on international civil aviation and the wide publicizing of the results provides the dimension of deterrence that is the concomitant of the preventive measures that are proving to be so effective.

International civil aviation will continue to present attractive targets for political dissidents, not to speak of psychopaths and the like. But prevention through security measures and deterrence through prosecution are proving to be the means of controlling this form of international crime.

Recommendations

Unilateral Action

1. The United States should amend 49 U.S.C. § 1472 so as to implement the Montreal Convention.
2. General Aviation operators should be encouraged to adapt aviation security controls to their facilities.
3. The FAA should be enabled by increased budget and staff to expand its supervision over the efficacy of security measures in use in U.S. airports.

Bilateral or Regional Action

1. Encouragement should be given to regional efforts to develop conventions for the control of terrorism such as the recent proposal of the European Economic Community states.
2. Major air transport states should consider developing a security convention establishing minimum security standards for international aviation facilities and making attacks on such facilities an international offense (*see* next section).
3. Major air transport states should consider developing an enforcement (sanctions) convention to carry out the commitments of the Tokyo, Hague, and Montreal conventions and any security convention (*see* below).

Multilateral or Global Action

1. A multilateral convention should be concluded, establishing minimum standards of security for aviation facilities as defined in this chapter and making attacks on such facilities an international offense.

2. A multilateral convention should be concluded that would be designed to enforce the Tokyo, Hague, and Montreal conventions and any security convention.

3. A conference should be held outside the auspices of the United Nations to consider a single convention on legal control of international terrorism:

a. defining the offense to include attacks on civil aircraft and aviation facilities, on internationally protected persons and places, etc.

b. emphasizing submission of offenders without exception to prosecution in regular courts

c. making any state that has failed to act to control international terrorism by adopting implementing legislation for relevant conventions, by extraditing or otherwise returning offenders for prosecution, or by submitting offenders to prosecution, liable for damages for death or bodily or mental injury of individuals or for loss or injury to real or personal property

d. making any state that condones or cooperates with international terrorists for whatever reason liable for payment of damages to victims and responsible for extraditing or otherwise returning such offenders for prosecution or submitting them to prosecution in its own courts.

Notes

1. *See* BULLETIN OF INTERNATIONAL COMMISSION OF JURISTS 28ff., no. 32 (Dec. 1967). Interception and abduction will not be treated in this chapter.

2. 2 L. JIMENEZ DE ASUA, TRATADO DE DERECHO PENAL 969 (1950).

3. 20 U.S.T. 2941; T.I.A.S. No. 6768; 704 U.N.T.S. 219.

4. 22 U.S.T. 1641; T.I.A.S. No. 7192.

5. 24 U.S.T. 564; T.I.A.S. No. 7570.

6. 24 U.S.T. 737; T.I.A.S. No. 7579.

7. Brazil, Jan. 13, 1961, 15 U.S.T. 2093; T.I.A.S. No. 5691; 532 U.N.T.S. 177. Sweden, Oct. 24, 1961, 14 U.S.T. 1845; T.I.A.S. No. 5496; 494 U.N.T.S. 141. For complete list, *see* note 128 *infra.*

8. 75 Stat. 466 (1961); 49 U.S.C. § 1472(i).

9. For the purposes of this study, the figures used are based on DOMESTIC AND FOREIGN AIRCRAFT HIJACKINGS, compiled by the FEDERAL AVIATION ADMINISTRATION, CIVIL AVIATION SECURITY SERVICE, and issued as of January 1, 1977. To these have been added certain incidents that seemed relevant together with a list of incidents covering the period January 1, 1977, through June 30, 1977. There are no uniform criteria for defining attacks on aircraft and related facilities for statistical purposes. The Hague Convention, for example, applies only where "the place of take-off or the place

of actual landing of the aircraft on board which the offence is committed is situated outside the territory of the State of registration of that aircraft; it shall be immaterial whether the aircraft is engaged in an international or domestic flight" [art. 3(3) *supra* note 4]. Any such incident would constitute an "international" hijacking. On the other hand, many hijackings involve "domestic" flights, *i.e.*, they take place entirely within the state of registration of the aircraft with or without the intent of diversion to a foreign destination. The seriousness of the offense warrants the inclusion of such incidents here. In addition to the illegal diversion of an aircraft from its scheduled flight plan, there is the classification of "attempt" where a would-be hijacker is foiled in his effort to interfere with the aircraft. The FAA list of DOMESTIC AND FOREIGN AIRCRAFT HIJACKINGS comprehends these three categories. The figures used in this study cover only civil aircraft or the occasional military aircraft used for civil transportation. This study does not cover theft of aircraft, such as the "small plane" used by a Czech aircraft mechanic to enable himself and his family to reach West Germany where they sought political asylum or a Soviet MIG-25, flown to northern Japan by its pilot. [Chicago Daily News, April 18, 1977, at 2, col. 3; Guardian (London), Sept. 7, 1976, at 1, col. 2.] To these have been added certain incidents that seemed relevant together with a list of incidents covering the period January 1, 1977, through June 30, 1977. *See* Appendix 1C.

10. Montreal Convention, art. 2(b), *supra* note 5.

11. *E.g.*, destruction of Air Vietnam B-727 by hijacker before landing with a loss of 70 lives, September 15, 1974. FEDERAL AVIATION ADMINISTRATION, CIVIL AVIATION SECURITY SERVICE, EXPLOSIONS ABOARD AIRCRAFT, at 10 (as of Jan. 1, 1977).

12. *Id.* Six aircraft were of U.S. registration; 28 were of foreign registration.

13. N.Y. Times, Oct. 24, 1976, § 4, at 3, col. 1.

14. One of the first instances of in-flight sabotage for the purpose of killing a passenger occurred in Quebec on September 9, 1949. The perpetrators were convicted of murder and executed. *Id.*, Sept. 24, 1949, at 1, col. 6; Mar. 15, 1950, at 3, col. 2; Jan. 9, 1953, at 2, col. 8. *See also* Graham v. Colorado, 302 P.2d 737 (S. Ct. Colo. 1956). On February 3, 1975, a deranged passenger attempted to set fire to a Pan American World Airways aircraft en route from Rangoon to Delhi. FAA, EXPLOSIONS ABOARD AIRCRAFT, *supra* note 11, at 10.

15. *Supra* note 5.

16. Three Arabs were prosecuted for an attempt to shoot down an El Al aircraft as it landed at Rome Airport on September 5, 1973. They were sentenced to five years and two months, fined $2500 each, and then released on bail of $32,500 each. N.Y. Times, Dec. 15, 1974, at 16, col. 2; Feb. 28, 1975, at 8, col. 4. *See* Summary of Responses to Department of State Circular Airgram Regarding Law & Practice on Terrorism, Italy, 3 (May 1976) [hereinafter cited

as Circular, name of country, page, and date of summary]. Two West German nationals and three Arabs accused of attempting to shoot down an El Al aircraft at Nairobi on January 25, 1976, were "brought" to Israel from Kenya and went on trial before a military tribunal on July 6, 1977. N.Y. Times, July 7, 1977, at 6, col. 1.

17. FEDERAL AVIATION ADMINISTRATION, CIVIL AVIATION SECURITY SERVICE, SIGNIFICANT WORLDWIDE CRIMINAL ACTS IN-VOLVING CIVIL AVIATION 1976 (1977) [hereinafter cited as FAA, CRIMI-NAL ACTS]. For example, an explosion in the boarding area at Istanbul Airport killed four persons and injured 16. N.Y. Times, Aug. 12, 1976, at 1, col. 1; Aug. 13, at 22, col. 1. Three persons were killed and some 100 were injured when a bomb exploded in a suitcase in the customs area of Baghdad Airport. *Id.*, Dec. 17, 1976, at 4, col. 4. *See also* attack on the office of South African Airways in New York on June 18, 1976. *Id.*, June 19, 1976, at 3, col. 5.

18. FAA, EXPLOSIONS ABOARD AIRCRAFT, *supra* note 11, Circular Belgium, 3 (Sept. 1975) *supra* note 16.

19. N.Y. Times, May 31, 1972, at 1, col. 8.

20. *Id.*, Jan. 18, 1975, at 32, col. 1; Dec. 30, 1975, at 1, col. 8; Aug. 8, 1976, at 27, col. 1.

21. *Id.*, May 26, 1977, at 18, col. 6.

22. 61 Stat. 1180; T.I.A.S. No. 1591; 15 U.N.T.S. 295.

23. N.Y. Times, Dec. 22, 1975, at 1, col. 8.

24. *Id.*, Apr. 17, 1976, at 5, col. 7. The longest hijacking in terms of distance arose out of a private domestic problem and involved the diversion of an Iberian Air Lines B-727 from Barcelona to Algiers, Abidjan, Seville, Turin, Zurich, Warsaw, and back to Zurich, a matter of some 10,000 miles. *Id.*, Mar. 15, 1977, at 11, col. 1; Mar. 17, at 2, col. 6.

25. Guarantors have included a representative of the International Red Cross in the Middle East, *id.*, July 23, 1970, at 1, col. 6; the Japanese Vice Minister of Transport, *id.*, Apr. 4, 1970, at 1, col. 4; two Japanese and two Malaysian government officials, Circular, Malaysia, 5-6 (Mar. 1976) *supra* note 16; a member of the Mexican Secretaría de Gobernación, N.Y. Times, May 21, 1973, at 11, col. 1; the Vice President of Philippine Air Lines, *id.*, Apr. 17, 1976, at 5, col. 7.

26. *E.g.*, German national aboard British VC-10 hijacked to Tunis. *Id.*, Nov. 22, 1974, at 6, col. 1; Nov. 24, 1974, at 1, col. 4; Nov. 25, 1974, at 1, col. 3; Dec. 8, 1974, at 9, col. 1. Passenger, having dual British and Israeli nationality, who had been removed to a hospital from an Air France Aérospatiale airbus hijacked to Entebbe, Uganda, was presumably killed by persons unknown in retaliation for the Israeli rescue of 103 passengers and crew held as hostages under threat of death. *Id.*, June 28, 1976, at 1, col. 2; July 11, 1976, at 1, col. 4; July 13, 1976, at 5, col. 1.

27. FAA, CIVIL AVIATION SECURITY SERVICE, FOURTH SEMI-

ANNUAL REPORT TO CONGRESS ON THE EFFECTIVENESS OF THE CIVIL AVIATION SECURITY PROGRAM, JANUARY 1-JUNE 30, 1976, 4-5, charts 1, 5 [hereinafter cited as FOURTH SEMI-ANNUAL REPORT].

28. *E.g.*, hijacking of private aircraft on April 19, 1976, by a man apparently suffering from personal and family difficulties, N.Y. Times, Apr. 20, 1976, at 60, col. 7; hijacking in Philippines on October 7, 1975, by a man seeking his kidnaped daughter, *id.*, Oct. 8, 1975, at 29, col. 3. A helicopter was hijacked to Southern Michigan Prison on June 6, 1975, where an inmate was removed, *id.*, June 7, 1975, at 1, col. 1. This same type of caper was carried out in Dublin on October 31, 1973, *id.*, Nov. 1, 1973, at 1, col. 1.

29. On February 22, 1972, five members of the Popular Front for the Liberation of Palestine hijacked a Lufthansa B-747 with 174 passengers and 14 crew to Aden. Crew and aircraft were released after the payment of $5 million ransom by the government of the Federal Republic of Germany, which is a major Lufthansa shareholder. *Id.*, Feb. 22, 1972, at 1, col. 2; Feb. 26, at 1, col. 8.

30. On September 15, 1972, three Croatians, members of Ustasha, hijacked an aircraft to Spain from Sweden, getting into the bargain the release of seven Croatian terrorists, two of whom had been convicted of the murder of the Yugoslav ambassador to Sweden, and $100,000. *Id.*, Sept. 16, 1972, at 1, col. 7.

31. *E.g.*, the hijacking to Paris of a TWA B-727 on September 10, 1976, for the purpose of dramatizing the Croatian cause. *Id.*, Sept. 22, 1976, at 22, col. 2.

32. The ransom-parachute syndrome began in the United States on November 24, 1971, with the hijacking of a Northwest Air Lines B-727 from Seattle by D.B. Cooper. *Id.*, Nov. 26, 1971, at 1, col. 4. This is the only extortionist-hijacker of a domestic flight in the United States who has not been apprehended.

33. *Id.*, Dec. 9, 1972, at 1, col. 7.

34. *Id.*, Feb. 23, 1974, at 1, col. 4.

35. *Id.*, May 22, 1976, at 2, col. 4; May 4, 1976, at 1, col. 1. *See also* obduracy as a policy and the use of force demonstrated by Dutch authorities in their effort to conclude the three-week "hijacking" of a train by South Moluccan terrorists and their detention of hostages in a school. In the course of recapturing the train, two hostages and six terrorists were killed. *Id.*, June 12, 1977, at 1, col. 1.

36. 75 Stat. 466 (1961); 49 U.S.C. § 1472(i).

37. HOUSE COMM. ON FOREIGN AFFAIRS, SUBCOMMITTEE ON INTER-AMERICAN AFFAIRS, 90TH CONG., 2d SESS., AIR PIRACY IN THE CARIBBEAN 5 (Comm. Print 1968).

38. Civil Aeronautics Board, Local and Joint Passenger Rules Tariff No. PR-5, CAB No. 117, at 9 (1968); *see* 49 U.S.C. § 1511.

39. The nature of the profile is confidential. Its use was discussed in United States v. Lopez, 328 F. Supp. 1077, 1086-87 (E.D.N.Y. 1971).

40. An analysis of 184 successful and unsuccessful hijackings of U.S.-regis-

tered aircraft between May 1, 1961, and December 31, 1976, shows that 109 offenders had the characteristics delineated in the profile, another 32 probably had them, and 34 did not meet the profile. It was not applicable in 76 instances (*e.g.*, charter flights are not subject to security controls). FAA, CIVIL AVIA-TION SECURITY SERVICE, CHRONOLOGY OF HIJACKINGS OF U.S. REGISTERED AIRCRAFT AND CURRENT LEGAL STATUS OF HI-JACKERS (as of Jan. 1, 1977).

41. N.Y. Times, Sept. 12, 1970, at 11, col. 5.

42. 37 Fed. Reg. 25934 (Dec. 16, 1972); 14 C.F.R. §§ 107.1, 107.4.

43. 14 C.F.R. § 121.538(b).

44. *E.g.*, Ley 17567, Jan. 4, 1968, amending art. 198(3), PENAL CODE (Argentina); art. 170, PENAL CODE FOR THE FEDERAL DISTRICT AND TERRITORIES *as amended* Dec. 19, 1968, DIARIO OFICIAL [D.O.], Dec. 24, 1968 (Mexico); Decree Law No. 1266, Sept. 16, 1969 (Cuba); Decree Law No. 975, Oct. 20, 1969, DIARIO OFICIAL [D.O.], Oct. 21, 1969 (Brazil); Loi No. 70-634, July 15, 1970, JOURNAL OFFICIEL DE LA REPUBLIQUE FRAN-CAISE [J.O.] 6657 (July 17, 1970) (France). *But see*, Crimes (Aircraft) No. 64 ACTS AUSTL. P., 266 (1963).

45. In 1974, the FAA reported that 18 major airports in Western Europe had lax standards of security. Montreal Star, Oct. 17, 1974, at A15, col. 1.

46. N.Y. Times, Aug. 19, 1975, at 4, col. 4; Aug. 5, at 1, col. 1; Aug. 7, at 1, col. 2.

47. Circular, Japan, 3 (Apr. 1976), *supra* note 16.

48. N.Y. Times, Jan. 17, 1976, at 8, col. 4.

49. *Id.*, Dec. 25, 1975, at 1, col. 5.

50. *See* note 26 *supra. See also* notes 205 and 206, *infra.*

51. N.Y. Times, Jan. 30, 1975, at 1, col. 1.

52. Pub. L. No. 93-366, § 316(e), 88 Stat. 409 (1974).

53. *Id.*, 49 U.S.C. §§ 1472(i)-(n). "Aircraft in flight" as defined in the Hague Convention, art. 3(1), *supra* note 4.

54. Memorandum of Understanding between the Federal Aviation Adminis-tration and the Federal Bureau of Investigation §II. A.1-5 (1975).

55. *Id.*, § B.1(c).

56. 14 C.F.R. § 121.538(b) as amended (1976). Explosives detection K9 teams operate in 24 large and medium hub airports widely located throughout the country. FOURTH SEMI-ANNUAL REPORT, chart 11, *supra* note 27, at 10-11.

57. The security system at LaGuardia Airport did not fail in the case of the hijacking of a TWA aircraft by five Croat terrorists in September 1976. They carried harmless components aboard and then assembled dummy bombs on board that were realistic enough to enable them to seize control of the aircraft. They left behind a genuine bomb, which exploded, while being defused, killing a police officer. *See* Aviation Security Bulletin (Nov.-Dec. 1976). The following

information regarding security procedures is based on an interview with V.L. Krohn, Chief, Operations Liaison Staff, Civil Aviation Security Service, FAA, on March 24, 1976.

58. The program of "sky marshals," which was instituted in 1970 consisted of 12 FAA "peace officers," volunteers from other federal agencies, 800 military police, and some 1500 to 1800 United States Customs security officers. It was phased out when the preboarding screening program was instituted in 1973.

59. At a meeting of the ICAO Technical Commission, the United Kingdom representative commented: "In the United Kingdom most airlines employed private security firms, while the Government provide advice and guidance and reimbursed the cost of the searching." Minutes of the Technical Commission, Twenty-first Session, Sept. 24/Oct. 15, 1974, at 62 (A21-Min. TE/1-13).

60. 14 C.F.R. § 129.25 as amended, effective Oct. 9, 1975.

61. FOURTH SEMI-ANNUAL REPORT, *supra* note 27, at 12.

62. *Id.*, 9-11, chart 9. Effective June 20, 1975, strict regulations were adopted regarding the carrying of firearms aboard aircraft by authorized persons. 40 Fed. Reg. 17551 (Apr. 21, 1975).

63. FOURTH SEMI-ANNUAL REPORT, *supra* note 27, at 10.

64. *See* United States v. Epperson, 454 F.2d 769 (4th Cir. 1972); United States v. Flum, 518 F.2d 39 (8th Cir. 1975).

65. FAA, News, Mar. 5, 1975.

66. N.Y. Times, Feb. 23, 1974, at 1, col. 4.

67. FAA, CIVIL AVIATION SECURITY SERVICE, SECOND SEMI-ANNUAL REPORT TO CONGRESS ON THE EFFECTIVENESS OF PASSENGER SCREENING PROCEDURES (Oct. 6, 1975) 8 [hereinafter cited as SECOND SEMI-ANNUAL REPORT].

68. Christian Science Monitor, Nov. 26, 1975, at 28, col. 1.

69. Jerome, *How to Combat Security Risks in General Aviation*, FLIGHT OPERATIONS 12, 14 (Dec. 1975); *Aviation Security–The Future Trends*, 2 TOP SECURITY 238 (1976). *See also* FOURTH SEMI-ANNUAL REPORT, *supra* note 27, at 14.

70. Chicago Tribune, Jan. 4, 1976, at 14, col. 4.

71. N.Y. Times, Aug. 19, 1972, at 1, col. 6; Aug. 20, at 24, col. 1.

72. SECOND SEMI-ANNUAL REPORT, *supra* note 67, at 3.

73. N.Y. Times, Apr. 20, 1976, at 60, col. 7.

74. Murphy, McCarthy, *Air Freight Security*, 31 ICAO BULL. 18, 20 (Jan. 1976).

75. ICAO, Technical Commission, Minutes of the Technical Commission, *supra* note 59 at 62, 65. Circular, Philippines, 2 (Dec. 1975); Circular, Sweden, 1 (Dec. 1975) *supra* note 16. In October 1975, Portugal established a National Commission on the Security of Civil Aviation, which was charged with formulating aviation and airport security standards to be carried out by local airport security committees. Decree Law No. 575/75, Oct. 6, 1975. Circular,

Portugal, 1 (Feb. 1976) *supra* note 16. This action conforms to Resolution A17-12, ICAO Assembly, Seventeenth Session (Extraordinary). (*See* pp. 26 ff.)

76. *See* FAA, CRIMINAL ACTS, *supra* note 17.

77. Circular, Italy, 3 (May 1976) *supra* note 16.

78. Circular, Austria, 5 (Sept. 1975) *supra* note 16.

79. Circulars, Cameroon, 4 (Jan. 1976); Fiji, 1 (Feb. 1976); Kenya, 2 (Jan. 1976); Norway, 4 (Dec. 1975); Oman, 1 (Mar. 1976); Republic of Korea, 2 (Sept. 1975); Sweden, 4 (Dec. 1975) *supra* note 16.

80. Circular, Mexico, 3 (Aug. 1975) *supra* note 16. The first hijacking within the United Kingdom was undertaken by a man who boarded with a pistol at Manchester for a flight to London. N.Y. Times, Jan. 8, 1975, at 7, col. 1.

81. Circular, Oman, 1 (Mar. 1976) *supra* note 16.

82. N.Y. Times, May 26, 1976, at 5, col. 1. The explosion of an unclaimed suitcase at New Delhi Airport caused little damage. Boston Globe, May 26, 1976, at 2, col. 2.

83. N.Y. Times, July 6, 1976, at 3, col. 3. French security controls are being increased. *Id.*, July 5, at 4, col. 5; Nov. 1, 1976, at 9, col. 1.

84. Circular, Iceland, 2 (Dec. 1975) *supra* note 16.

85. Circular, Senegal, 1 (Mar. 1976) *supra* note 16.

86. Circular, Malta, 2 (Mar. 1976) *supra* note 16; N.Y. Times, Nov. 26, 1973, at 1, col. 6; Nov. 27, at 1, col. 1.

87. *See* Day v. Trans World Airlines, Inc., 528 F.2d 31 (2d Cir. 1975), *cert. denied*, 425 U.S. 989 (1976).

88. Circular, Greece, 4 (Oct. 1975) *supra* note 16.

89. N.Y. Times, June 28, 1976, at 1, col. 2; July 5, at 4, col. 5; July 11, at 1, col. 4.

90. TRANSPORT CANADA, CIVIL AVIATION SECURITY, HIJACKING INCIDENTS INVOLVING CANADA (Mar. 1, 1976).

91. Civil Aviation Securities Measures Regulations, PC 1974-786, Apr. 2, 1974, SOR/DORS/74-226, Apr. 4, 1974, 108 Can. Gaz., Pt. II, No. 8, at 1301. Civil Aviation Security Measures Order, Apr. 21, 1974, SOR/DORS/74-227, Apr. 4, 1974, *id.* 1303.

92. Senate of Canada, Bill S-34, An Act to Amend the Aeronautics Act, May 19, 1976. This bill passed the House of Commons in June 1976.

93. Sec. 1114, Pub. L. No. 93-366, 88 Stat. 409 (1974).

94. Interview with V.L. Krohn, *supra* note 57. *See* FAA, News (Dec. 11, 1974). *See also* FOURTH SEMI-ANNUAL REPORT, chart 14, *supra* note 27 at 17-18.

95. Interview with V.L. Krohn, *supra* note 57.

96. 49 Stat. 3000; 137 L.N.T.S. 11.

97. Day v. Trans World Airlines, Inc., *supra* note 87. *See also* Evangelinos v. Trans World Airlines, Inc., 396 F. Supp. 95 (W.D. Pa. 1975), *rev'd* and

remanded, 550 F.2d 152 (3d Cir. 1977), in which the Court of Appeals concurred with the holding in *Day.*

98. Day v. Trans World Airlines, Inc., *supra* note 87 at 37-38.

99. Chicago Tribune, Mar. 25, 1977, at 8, col. 1; Chicago Daily News, Mar. 25, 1977, at 5, col. 1. Four of the hijackers reportedly boarded the Singapore Air Lines aircraft at Bahrain and transferred to the Air France airbus at Athens.

100. ICAO, Assembly, 21st Sess. Montreal, 24 Sept.-15 Oct. 1974. Minutes of the Plenary Meetings, at 743. Doc. 9119, A 21-Min. P/1-12.

101. Circulars, Austria, 1 (Sept. 1975); Colombia 1 (Oct. 1975); Italy, 1-2 (May 1976); Switzerland, 1 (Jan. 1976) *supra* note 16. *See also Attentats contre la navigation aérienne*, 52 REVUE DE DROIT PENAL ET DE CRIMINOLOGIE [RDPC], No. 3-4 (Dec. 1971-Jan. 1972) (Numéro Spécial).

102. Prevention of Terrorism (Temporary Provision) Act, 1974, c. 56, [1974] Law Rep. Stat. pt. 6 at 1823 (Oct. 1975). This act was superseded by the Prevention of Terrorism (Temporary Provisions) Act, 1976, c. 8, CURRENT LAW STATUTES pt. 1 (ann. 1976). *See also* Criminal Jurisdiction Act, 1975, c. 59, *id.*, pt. 7 (1975), extending the extraterritorial jurisdiction of Northern Ireland to terrorist acts committed in the Republic of Ireland.

103. *See* Appendix 1A.

104. Circular, Algeria, 1 (Sept. 1975), *supra* note 16.

105. *See* pp. 493-496.

106. 189 U.N.T.S. 150. The 1967 Protocol on the Status of Refugees to which the United States is party incorporates arts. 2-34 of the convention. 19 U.S.T. 6223; T.I.A.S. No. 6577; 606 U.N.T.S. 267.

107. Circular, Bulgaria, 1-2 (Jan. 1976) *supra* note 16.

108. *See* FAA, CIVIL AVIATION SECURITY SERVICE, LEGAL STATUS OF HIJACKERS SUMMARIZATION (AS OF JAN. 1, 1977), ADJUSTED TO JUNE 15, 1977. The 158 persons apprehended include 18 persons who have been killed in the course of being apprehended or who have committed suicide.

109. 49 U.S.C. § 1472(i) as amended. *See* 75 Stat. 466 (1961); 88 Stat. 409 (1974).

110. *See* notes 3, 4, 5, and 22 *supra.* For analyses of the Tokyo, Hague, and Montreal conventions, *see* Boyle & Pulsifer, *The Tokyo Convention on Offenses and Certain Other Acts Committed On Board Aircraft*, 30 J. AIR L. & COM. 305 (1964); Mankiewicz, *The Hague Convention*, 37 J. AIR L. & COM. 195 (1971); Thomas & Kirby, *The Convention for the Suppression of Unlawful Acts against the Safety of Civil Aviation*, 22 INT'L. & COMP. L. Q. 163 (1973). *See also* J.W.F. Sundberg, rapporteur, *Unlawful Seizure of Aircraft, General Report to Eleventh Congress*, ASSOCIATION INTERNATIONALE DE DROIT PENAL (1974) (Budapest).

111. Adopted Nov. 1, 1976. Council of Europe, Press Release, B(76)84, Nov. 11, 1976. For a discussion of this Convention, *see* pp. 497-499.

112. U.N.G.A., Provisional Verbatim Record (99th mtg.), 21, A/31/PV.99 (15 Dec. 1976).

113. *See* note 6 *supra.*

114. *See* Table 1-2.

115. *See* note 6 *supra.*

116. Canada, Treaty Series 1973, No. 11. Unlike the U.S. agreement, art. 2 of the Canadian agreement does not contain a clause penalizing the preparation of hostile expeditions directed from one state against the territory of the other.

117. Mexico: Granma Weekly Review, June 17, 1973; Venezuela: Department of State, Division of Language Services, LS No. 40288, T-125/R-XX (trans.); Colombia (summary): Department of State, FBIS, VI. 25 Jul. 74. F1. *See also* Circular, Colombia, 1 (Oct. 1975). This agreement is not in force.

118. Art. 4, Cuba-Mexico Anti-Hijacking Agreement; art. 7, Cuba-Venezuela Anti-Hijacking Agreement, *supra* note 117.

119. Iran: Department of State, Division of Language Services, LS No. 59449, AC/DZ (trans.); Finland: Department of State, Airgram, A-174, Oct. 9, 1974; Afghanistan: ICAO Legal Committee, 20th Sess. (Special), Jan. 9-30, 1973, 1 Minutes at 12 (1973).

120. USSR-Iran, Anti-Hijacking Agreement, *supra* note 119.

121. *Id.*, art. 2(7).

122. USSR-Finland, Anti-Hijacking Agreement, *supra* note 119.

123. N.Y. Times, June 24, 1977, at 3, col. 1.

124. General Aviation Aircraft, Dec. 14, 1974, *id.*, Dec. 16, 1974, at 5, col. 4.

125. *Id.*, Oct. 16, 1976, at 1, col. 5; Apr. 29, 1977, at 1, col. 6.

126. The hijacker has not been returned to Canada. Transport Canada, Civil Aviation Security, Hijacking Incidents Involving Canada, Mar. 1, 1976.

127. Chicago Tribune, Sept. 26, 1976; N.Y. Times, Oct. 24, 1976, at 7, col. 1. The United Nations High Commissioner for Refugees is reported to have chided Iran for not complying with the 1951 Convention on the Status of Refugees. *Id.*, Nov. 2, 1976, at 5, col. 1. Convention cited *supra* note 106.

128. Argentina, Jan. 21, 1972, 23 U.S.T. 3501; T.I.A.S. No. 7510. Australia, May 14, 1974, T.I.A.S. No. 8234. Brazil, Jan. 13, 1961, 15 U.S.T. 2093; T.I.A.S. No. 5691; 532 U.N.T.S. 177. Canada, Dec. 3, 1971, T.I.A.S. No. 8237. Denmark, June 22, 1972, 25 U.S.T. 1293; T.I.A.S. No. 7864. Finland, June 11, 1976, S. Exec. H, 95th Cong., 1st Sess. France, Supplementary Extradition Convention, Feb. 12, 1970, 22 U.S.T. 407; T.I.A.S. No. 7075. Italy, Jan. 18, 1973, T.I.A.S., No. 8052. New Zealand, Jan. 12, 1970, 22 U.S.T. 1; T.I.A.S. No. 7035. Paraguay, May 24, 1973, 25 U.S.T. 967; T.I.A.S. No. 7838. Spain, May 29, 1970, 22 U.S.T. 737; T.I.A.S. No. 7136. Sweden, Oct. 24, 1961, 14 U.S.T. 1845; T.I.A.S. No. 5496; 494 U.N.T.S. 141. Uruguay, Apr. 6, 1973, S. Exec. K, 93rd Cong., 1st Sess. (1973) ratified by United States. The Extradition Treaty with Israel of Dec. 10, 1962, does not include this offense. 14 U.S.T. 1707; T.I.A.S. No. 5476; 484 U.N.T.S. 283.

129. Resolutions A17-1, A20-2 (condemning all acts of unlawful interference with international civil aviation); A20-1 (condemning Israeli action in shooting down a Libyan civil aircraft on February 21, 1973, and intercepting a Lebanese civil aircraft on August 10, 1973). ICAO, ASSEMBLY RESOLUTIONS IN FORCE (as of 15 Oct. 1974) at 127, 128, 29. Doc. 9124 (1975).

130. *E.g.*, Resolution 21-9 (ratification of conventions), *id.*, 129.

131. Adopted by ICAO Council March 31, 1976. FOURTH SEMI-ANNUAL REPORT *supra* note 27 at 16. On the same day, the council changed two recommended practices in annex 9—regarding the carrying of unauthorized weapons aboard nonpassenger aircraft and control of explosives in baggage and cargo—into standards, effective December 15, 1976. *Id.*

132. ICAO, SECURITY MANUAL FOR THE PREVENTION OF UNLAWFUL ACTS AGAINST CIVIL AVIATION, foreword, ix, Doc. 8973 Restricted (1971) and Amendment No. 1 (Jan. 9, 1974).

133. Interview with V.L. Krohn, *supra* note 57.

134. N.Y. Times, June 30, 1976, at 10, col. 3.

135. ICAO, Report of the Technical Commission, Assembly, 21st Sess., Sept. 24-Oct. 15, 1974, Resolution A21-23 (1975); ICAO, Report of the Eighth Air Naviation Conference, Apr. 17-May 11, 1974, at 10. Doc. 9101, AN/CONF/8.

136. Letter of November 30, 1976, from Harry J. Murphy, Director of Security, Air Transport Association of America, Washington.

137. Interview with T.V. Middleton, Industrial Secretary, International Federation of Air Line Pilots Associations, London, September 6, 1976.

138. Letter of January 18, 1977, from G. Lauzon, Assistant Counsel, International Air Transport Association, Geneva.

139. *See* Appendix 1B.

140. Fitzgerald, *International Terrorism and Civil Aviation*, Canadian Council on International Law, PROCEEDINGS OF THE THIRD ANNUAL CONFERENCE 79, at 91 (1974).

141. *Id.*, at 93.

142. *Id.*, at 94-95.

143. *ICAO Special Subcommittee Meets at Washington*, 67 DEP'T. STATE BULL. 357 (1972).

144. 59 Stat. 1693; 84 U.N.T.S. 389.

145. 67 DEPT. STATE BULL. 357, 361-64. ICAO Special Subcommittee on the Council Resolution of 19 June 1972, Report, Sept. 15, 1972. LC/SC CR (1972).

146. ICAO, Secretariat Note, LC/Working Draft No. 833. Rev., 22/1/73 at 1-2.

147. *Supra* note 140, at 95-97.

148. *Id.*, at 98.

149. ICAO, Proposal by the Delegations of Denmark, Finland, Norway, and Sweden, LC/Working Draft No. 831. Rev. 24/1/73, at 3.

150. *Id.*

151. United Kingdom-Swiss Proposal, LC/Working Draft No. 829, 17/1/73.

152. French Proposal, LC/Working Draft No. 821, 17/1/73.

153. Soviet Proposal, LC/Working Draft No. 826, 9/1/73.

154. *See* U.N.G.A., Report of the Ad Hoc Committee on International Terrorism, 28 U.N. GAOR Supp. (No. 28) U.N. Doc. A/9028 (1973).

155. Report of the United States Delegation to the 20th Session (Extraordinary) of the Assembly of the International Civil Aviation Organization (ICAO) and International Conference on Air Law, Rome, Italy, Aug. 28-Sept. 21, 1973, at App. B (Jan. 22, 1974).

156. International Federation of Air Traffic Controllers Associations, Standing Committee VII, Working Paper No. 57, Hijacking and the Controller, 13 (Feb. 1976). Working paper provided by T.H. Harrison, Executive Secretary, IFATCA, Troon, Scotland.

157. N.Y. Times, July 15, 1976, at 1, col. 1.

158. *Id.*, July 13, 1976, at 1, col. 1.

159. Letter of October 25, 1976, IFALPA 77 a 133, Ref 2/5/2 JO'G/NMM.

160. Letter from G. Lauzon, *supra* note 138.

161. Letter from Harry J. Murphy, *supra* note 136.

162. Information compiled by ICAO, based on data from 131 states, excluding the Soviet Union before 1970 and the People's Republic of China. 31 ICAO BULL. 11 (Jan. 1976).

163. Air freight carried in 1975 amounted to 19 billion tonne-kilometers (13 billion ton-miles). *Id.*

164. ICAO, ANNUAL REPORT OF THE COUNCIL—1974, 16-18. Doc. 9127 (1975).

165. *Id.* The most recent year for comparative figures is 1973.

166. N.Y. Times, July 23, 1976, at D3, col. 4. French public and private airlines were severely affected by the 1973 oil crisis. Air France, a nationalized company, is still operating without a profit. French Embassy, Press and Information Division, FRANCE 4 (July/Aug. 1976). British Airways reported a profit in the first quarter of 1976, its first profit in two years. Guardian, Aug. 27, 1976, at 13, col. 1.

167. *See e.g.*, Husserl v. Swiss Air Transport Co., Ltd., 388 F. Supp. 1238 (S.D.N.Y. 1975).

168. 528 F.2d 31 (2d Cir. 1975), *cert. denied*; 425 U.S. 989 (1976); 396 F. Supp. 95 (W.D.Pa. 1975), *rev'd* and *remanded*, 550 F.2d 152 (3d Cir. 1977).

169. 368 F. Supp. 1098 (S.D.N.Y. 1973), *aff'd* 505 F.2d 989 (2d Cir. 1974). *See also* Sunny South Aircraft Service, Inc. v. American Fire & Casualty Co., 140 So.2d 78 (Dist. Ct. App. Fla., 3d Dist. (1962); *aff'd* 151 So.2d 276 (S.Ct. Fla. 1963).

170. N.Y. Times, Feb. 22, 1972, at 1, col. 2; Feb. 26, at 1, col. 8.

171. *Hearings on S. 39, Before the Subcomm. on Aviation of the Senate Comm. on Commerce*, 93rd Cong., 1st Sess., 29 (1973).

172. N.Y. Times, Aug. 12, 1975, at 3, col. 1.

173. Northwest Airlines recovered $180,000 of the $200,000 exacted as ransom by "D.B. Cooper" (identity never established), who parachuted from one of its aircraft over Oregon on November 24, 1971, and has not been heard of since. The Supreme Court of Minnesota ordered Globe Indemnity Company of New York to pay the carrier on the theory that the plane constituted "premises" of the carrier that were covered by a "blanket crime policy," which included a $20,000 deductible provision. Wall Street Journal, Jan. 27, 1975, at 12, col. 1.

174. There were eight bullet holes in the fuselage of the aircraft. France is reported to have been charged 500,000 francs for the hostages' food. Le Monde, July 24, 1976, at 3, col. 1.

175. Christian Science Monitor, Nov. 26, 1975, at 28, col. 4.

176. 30 ICAO BULL. 23 (Sept. 1975).

177. Speaking at the January 1973 special meeting of the ICAO Legal Committee on a prospective sanctions convention (*see* p. 28 ff. *supra*), the ITF observer warned that if ICAO did not make serious efforts to control hijacking, its affiliates "would take industrial action against States which demonstrably assisted hijackers and saboteurs or condoned the activity of such criminals by offering them sanctuary." 1 Minutes, *supra* note 119, at 25.

178. The American Society of Travel Agents, then representing 2400 travel agencies in the United States and Canada and 5000 associates abroad, was conspicuous in its denunciation of the hijacking of an El Al aircraft to Algeria on July 23, 1968, and the prolonged detention of some of its passengers and crew. N.Y. Times, Aug. 10, 1968, at 25, col. 7; July 27, at 1, col. 7. The American Jewish Congress, in an advertisement in the New York Times following the Entebbe incident, urged IATA and IFALPA to boycott countries that cooperated with hijackers, suspension of U.S. air service with such countries, and curtailment of U.S. aid to them. *Id.*, July 25, 1976, at 8, col. 1.

179. Interview with T.V. Middleton, *supra* note 137.

180. AIR LAW I(2) (1976) at 136; AIR LAW I(1) (Sept. 1975) at 52-53. Information from AIR LAW provided by A. van Wijk, Chairman, IFALPA Legal Study Group, Amsterdam.

181. AIR LAW I(1) (Sept. 1975) at 53.

182. *Id.*

183. *E.g.*, the IFALPA observer pointed out to the ICAO Legal Committee at its January 1973 meeting that IFALPA had gone on record at its Special Conference at Mexico City, in December 1972, to the effect that IFALPA was prepared to use both the "straight and secondary boycott" in cooperation with other transport associations against states that tolerated inadequate security programs or maintained havens for hijackers and the like. 1 Minutes , *supra* note 119, at 22.

184. IFALPA Press Release 2/5/2 CCJ/NMM, June 8, 1972. Joint statement by IFALPA and ITF, *id.*, June 19, 1972.

185. N.Y. Times, June 20, 1972, at 20, col. 2; June 21, at 20, col. 4.

186. *Id.*, June 19, 1972, at 1, col. 8.

187. *E.g.*, threatened boycott of Algerian air transport by the French National Union of Air Line Pilots over the hijacking of an El Al aircraft on July 23, 1968, and the prolonged detention of some of its passengers and crew. *Id.*, Aug. 15, 1968, at 1, col. 5; Sept. 1, at 1, col. 7. *See also supra* note 178.

188. Interview with T.V. Middleton, *supra* note 137.

189. Telephone interview with J.M. Livingston, President, Canadian Air Traffic Control Association, Inc., Oct. 12, 1976, Ottawa.

190. *Two Languages in Air Traffic Control, A Position of Protest*, 5 AIR SAFETY SYMPOSIUM, IFALPA, Ottawa, March 2-3, 1976. For ICAO, English is the recommended language "[p] ending the development and adoption of a more suitable form of speech for universal use in aeronautical radio telephone communications." Rec. 5.2.1.1.2, Recommendations on Aeronautical Telecommunications of the International Civil Aviation Organization (ICAO), annex 10, vol. 11, at 34 (July 12, 1974). The Canadian Air Line Pilots Association is also opposed to bilingualism under IFR or at busy airports. Canadian Air Line Pilots Association, THE CALPA POSITION ON THE USE OF TWO LANGUAGES IN AIR TRAFFIC CONTROL (Aug. 1976). A survey of languages used in air control operations in 19 non-English-speaking countries showed that English was either the primary language or was required for flying under IFR, in congested areas, or at international airports. The Financial Post, July 31, 1976, at 28, col. 1. Information provided by J.M. Livingston, *supra* note 189.

191. Background of the dispute is drawn from Canadian Air Traffic Control Association, Inc., A HISTORY OF EVENTS LEADING TO THE BILINGUAL AIR TRAFFIC CONTROL DISPUTE (Aug. 1976) [hereinafter cited as HISTORY].

192. *Id.*, at 3.

193. *Id.*, at 4. Telephone interview with J.M. Livingston, *supra* note 189.

194. HISTORY, *supra* note 191, at 5.

195. Boston Globe, June 26, 1976, at 4, col. 1.

196. Telephone interview with J.M. Livingston, *supra* note 189. Canadian Air Line Pilots Association, THE SETTLEMENT OF THE RECENT AIR TRANSPORTATION DISRUPTION IN CANADA (Aug. 1976).

197. Toronto Globe and Mail, July 24, 1976, at 1, col. 6; Jan. 13, 1977, at 1, col. 1.

198. Working Paper No. 57, *supra* note 156.

199. *E.g.*, the Federal Republic of Germany denied a request from Czechoslovakia in 1972 for the extradition of two hijackers, Czech nationals who had sought political asylum in West Germany, on the ground that German jurisdiction had been established under the 1929 Extradition Law. Potz, *Die strafrechtliche Ahndung von Flugzeugentführungen*, 24 ZEITSCHRIFT FUR DIE GESAMTE STRAFRECHTSWISSENSCHAFT 489, 493 (1974).

200. *E.g.*, there has been only one hijacking to Cuba from the United States since the 1973 agreement on the subject was concluded; the hijacker has not been returned. Another example was the detention of Venezuelan aircraft by Cuba for a week in retaliation for the seizure of the Cuban fishing vessel *Alecrin* in Venezuelan territorial waters two months earlier. N.Y. Times, Feb. 12, 1969, at 7, col. 1; Feb. 18, at 65, col. 5; Nov. 26, 1968, at 3, col. 1.

201. Asylum has been given to hijackers of aircraft of Ethiopian, Japanese, Jordanian, and West German registration.

202. *See* note 26 *supra.*

203. The Entebbe terrorists wanted the release of 53 prisoners held in Israel, Kenya, the Federal Republic of Germany, and Switzerland. The raid was costly in terms of lives: 4 hostages, 1 commando, 7 terrorists, and about 20 Ugandan soldiers were killed. *Id.*

204. 22 U.S.T. 1641; T.I.A.S. No. 7192. *See* Appendix 1B.

205. *See* N.Y. Times, Oct. 14, 1977, at 3, col. 1; Oct. 15, 1977, at 1, col. 4; Chicago Tribune, Feb. 20, 1978, at 1, col. 5; N.Y. Times, Feb. 21, 1978, at 1, col. 5.

206. *See* U.S. policy of refusing to negotiate with kidnapers of U.S. nationals abroad. *Id.*, Aug. 8, 1975, at 4, col. 5 *See also* pp. 9-10 *supra.* Somalia was apparently agreeable to the West German commando attack; however, there was some question about whether Cyprus had been consulted about the impending Egyptian attack, and, as a result, the Egyptian government withdrew its diplomatic mission in Nicosia and requested Cyprus to withdraw its diplomats from Cairo.

207. *See* shootout at Zamboanga, *supra* at 8.

208. It is reported that France, the state of registration of the aircraft, had to negotiate with Uganda through the Somalian Ambassador to Uganda. N.Y. Times, July 5, 1976, at 1, col. 2.

209. Various bills and resolutions have been introduced into Congress calling for the suspension of economic and military assistance to a state that aids or abets terrorists or for the conclusion of a sanctions convention. *See, e.g.*, S. 206, S. 77, H.R. Con. Res. 46, 95th Cong., 1st Sess. (1977).

210. *See* Appendix 1B.

211. *Id.*

212. *See* note 154 *supra.*

213. *See* pp. 501-503.

Appendix 1A: Legislation Relating to Control of Aircraft Hijacking

State	Law	Summary	Source
Algeria	Art. 417, Penal code, Dec. 14, 1973	Prison up to 5 yrs. for hijacking or injury to persons; death if any deaths occur	Circular, Algeria (Sept. 1975)
Argentina	Ley 17567, amending art. 198(3), Penal code, Jan. 4, 1968	Prison 3 to 15 yrs.	Penal code
Australia	Crimes (Aircraft) No. 64 (1963)	Up to 14 yrs. for destruction of aircraft; death if intent to kill; up to 14 yrs. for assaulting crew; up to 7 yrs. for endangering safety of aircraft; up to 7 yrs. for taking dangerous goods aboard	Acts of Parliament, 266 (1963)
Austria	Penal code	—	Circular, Austria (Sept. 1975)
Bahamas	Criminal law	—	Circular, Bahamas (Jan. 1976)
Barbados	Hijacking Act 1973-2, Feb. 22, 1973	Offenses punishable as with comparable criminal offenses	Circular, Barbados (Jan. 1976)
Belgium	Amendments to Extradition Law and Law on Regulation of Air Traffic, Aug. 6, 1973	Prison from 10 to 20 yrs. hard labor for acts involving destruction of aircraft or taking of hostages; life at hard labor if acts involve a death	Circular, Belgium (Sept. 1975)
	Law on Taking of Hostages, July 2, 1975	Life at hard labor; death if hostage seriously injured or killed; 10 to 20 yrs. if hostage voluntarily released without conditions	
Bolivia	Penal code	—	Circular, Bolivia (Feb. 1976)
Brazil	Decree Law 975, Oct. 20, 1969	Prison 8 to 20 yrs. for transporting terrorists or contraband by aircraft	*Diario Oficial*, Oct. 21, 1969

State	Law	Summary	Source
	Decree Law 5786, June 27, 1972	Prison 12 to 30 yrs. for illegal seizure of aircraft	Circular, Brazil, 2 (Jan. 1976)
Bulgaria	Penal code	—	Circular, Bulgaria (Jan. 1976)
Burma	Criminal law	—	Circular, Burma (Feb. 1976)
Cameroon	Penal code	—	Circular, Cameroon (Jan. 1976)
Canada	Criminal Law Amendment Act, 1972	Up to life for unlawful seizure of aircraft; up to life for endangering safety of aircraft; up to 14 yrs. for carrying offensive weapons aboard	21 Eliz. 2, 1972, c. 13
Chad	Criminal law	—	Circular, Chad (Feb. 1976)
Chile	Penal code	—	Circular, Chile (Oct. 1975)
Colombia	Penal code	—	Circular, Colombia (Oct. 1975)
Costa Rica	Penal code	—	Circular, Costa Rica (Oct. 1975)
Czechoslovakia	Law 45, April 25, 1973	Prison 8 to 15 yrs. and confiscation of property for use of force or threat thereof aboard aircraft; 12 to 15 yrs. if a death occurs in act; 3 to 10 yrs. for hijacking aircraft out of country; 10 to 15 yrs. if death occurs during act (confiscation of property with both offenses); conveying false information about hijacking punishable by prison up to 3 yrs., "corrective measures," or fine	Circular, Czechoslovakia, 1 (Jan. 1976)
Denmark	Art. 183(a), Penal code, amended Feb. 8, 1974	Up to 12 yrs. for illegal seizure of aircraft; 6 mos. to 12 yrs. for explosions causing injury to persons or property; up to 2 yrs. for threat of violence; up to 4 yrs. for arson	Circular, Denmark, 1-3 (Dec. 1975)

State	Law	Summary	Source
Dominican Republic	Penal code	–	Circular, Dominican Republic, 1 (Jan. 1976)
El Salvador	Art. 491, Penal code	Prison 3 to 15 yrs. for illegal interference with aircraft	Circular, El Salvador, 4 (Jan. 1976)
Ethiopia	Penal code	–	Circular, Ethiopia (Jan. 1976)
Fiji	Tokyo Convention Act 1967 (Overseas Territories) Order 1968, Legal Notice No. 37, 1969, extending United Kingdom Tokyo Convention Act 1967 to Fiji	–	Circular, Fiji (Feb. 1976)
France	Law No. 70-634, July 15, 1970	Prison 5 to 10 yrs. for hijacking; 10 to 20 yrs. if injuries occur during act; life if a death occurs during act; death if act constitutes "assassination," involved torture, or constituted an aggravation of another crime (Code Pénal, Arts. 302, 303, 304)	*Journal Officiel* 6657 (July 17, 1970); Circular, France (May 1976)
	Law No. 75-624, July 11, 1975	Prison 1 to 5 yrs. and/or fine for conveying false information about hijacking	
Gabon	Penal code	–	Circular, Gabon (Feb. 1976)
Gambia	Criminal law	–	Circular, Gambia (Feb. 1976)
Germany, Democratic Republic of	Law of July 12, 1973	Prison for 3 yrs. to life for hijacking; life if death involved in act or threat to number of people	N.Y. Times, July 13, 1973, at 62, col. 2
Germany, Federal Republic of	§ 316c, Penal code, Dec. 18, 1971	Prison 1 to 5 yrs. for unlawful seizure of aircraft; 10 yrs. to life if death occurs	*Bundesgesetzblatt* No. 128, Dec. 18, 1971, at 1977 Circular, Federal Republic of Germany, 1-3 (Sept. 1975)

State	Law	Summary	Source
	§ 239b, Penal code	Minimum of 3 yrs. prison for taking hostages	
Greece	Penal code	–	Circular, Greece (Oct. 1975)
Guatemala	Arts. 299, 300, Penal code	Prison 3 to 15 yrs. for unlawful seizure of aircraft or accomplice thereto	Circular, Guatemala, 1 (May 1976)
Guinea	Current policy	–	Circular, Guinea (Feb. 1976)
Guyana	Criminal law	–	Circular, Guyana (Jan. 1976)
Honduras	Penal code	–	Circular, Honduras (Jan. 1976)
Hungary	Decree-Law, Nov. 10, 1971	Amending penal code to include offense of aircraft hijacking	24 *Bull. Legal Developments* 253 (Dec. 18, 1971)
Iceland	Criminal law	–	Circular, Iceland (Dec. 1975)
India	Criminal law	–	Circular, India (Nov. 1975)
Indonesia	Criminal law	–	Circular, Indonesia (Nov. 1975)
Iran	Law, March 1971	Prison 3 to 15 yrs. for unlawful seizure of aircraft; life for threats with weapons; where death or injury, maximum punishment for similar offense under criminal law; 3 to 15 yrs. for sabotage of aircraft; death if death occurs in act; 1 to 3 yrs. for threats	Circular, Iran, 3 (Jan. 1976)
Israel	Air Navigation (Offenses and Jurisdiction) Act, 1971, No. 5731 (April 1971)	Maximum of life imprisonment for hijacking; mandatory life if a death occurs during act; 20 yrs. for endangering or threatening person or aircraft; mandatory life if death occurs during act; 15 yrs. for taking hostages; mandatory life if death occurs during act	Circular, Israel (May 1976)

State	Law	Summary	Source
Italy	Penal code	–	Circular, Italy (May 1976)
Japan	Anti-Hijacking Law, May 18, 1970	Prison 7 yrs. to life for hijacking; life at hard labor or death if death occurs during act; 1 to 10 yrs. at hard labor for attempted hijacking	RDPC, 397-98, *supra* note 101
Jordan	Military law	–	Circular, Jordan (Oct. 1975)
Kenya	Aircraft (Offenses) Act 1970	Maximum of life imprisonment for unlawful seizure of aircraft	Circular, Kenya (Jan. 1976)
Korea, Republic of	Criminal code	–	Circular, Korea (Sept. 1975)
Kuwait	Criminal law	–	Circular, Kuwait (Oct. 1975)
Laos	Criminal law	–	Circular, Laos (March 1976)
Lebanon	Penal code	–	Circular, Lebanon (Jan. 1976)
Lesotho	Colonial Civil Aviation Order 1970, as amended	Minimum of 15 yrs. for unlawful seizure of aircraft; minimum of 10 yrs. for assault or threat thereof aboard aircraft; minimum of 7 yrs. for endangering safety of aircraft	Circular, Lesotho (March 1976)
Liberia	Criminal law	–	Circular, Liberia (March 1976)
Libya	Current policy	–	Circular, Libya (March 1976)
Luxembourg	Penal code	–	Circular, Luxembourg (Jan. 1976)
Malagasy Republic	Penal code	–	Circular, Malagasy Republic (March 1976)
Malaysia	Criminal law	–	Circular, Malaysia (March 1976)
Malawi	Hijacking Act, Dec. 31, 1972	Up to life imprisonment for hijacking, sabotage, conveying false information, or other acts jeopardizing aircraft in flight	Circular, Malawi (Jan. 1976)

State	Law	Summary	Source
Malta	Criminal law	–	Circular (March 1976)
Mexico	Art. 170, Penal code, amended Dec. 19, 1968	Prison 5 to 20 yrs. for unlawful seizure of aircraft	*Diario Oficial* (Dec. 24, 1968); Circular, Mexico (Aug. 1975)
Nepal	Criminal law	–	Circular, Nepal (Feb. 1976)
Netherlands	Penal code, amended March 31, 1971	Hijacking made criminal offense	Circular, Netherlands (May 1976)
New Zealand	Aviation Crimes Act, Oct. 20, 1972	Up to life imprisonment for hijacking; up to 14 yrs. for assault or other acts directed against safety of aircraft; up to 5 yrs. for possession of firearms	Circular, Netherlands (Jan. 1976)
Nicaragua	Penal code	–	Circular, Nicaragua (Feb. 1976)
Niger	Penal code	–	Circular, Niger (March 1976)
Nigeria	Criminal law	–	Circular, Nigeria (March 1976)
Norway	Art. 151(a), Penal code	Prison 2 yrs. to life for unlawful seizure of aircraft	Circular, Norway (Dec. 1975)
	Royal Decree, Aug. 20, 1971	Prison up to 3 mos. or fine for unauthorized possession of weapons	
Oman	Current policy	–	Circular, Oman (March 1976)
Pakistan	Criminal law	–	Circular, Pakistan (Oct. 1975)
Panama	Penal code	–	Circular, Panama (Nov. 1975)
Paraguay	Penal code	–	Circular, Paraguay (April 1976)
Peru	Penal code	–	Circular, Peru (Jan. 1976)
Philippines	Anti-Hijacking Law (Republic Act 3625)	Prison 12 to 20 yrs. and fine for hijacking; 15 yrs. to death and fine for use of force or causing death or injury during act	Circular, Philippines (Dec. 1975)
Poland	Art. 136(1), Penal code, amendment effective Jan. 1, 1970	Minimum of 3 yrs. imprisonment for acts affecting security of	RDPC, 403; *supra* note 101

State	Law	Summary	Source
	Art. 148(1)	transportation by air and other means; 8 yrs. to death if death caused during act	
Portugal	Penal code	–	Circular, Portugal (Feb. 1976)
Rwanda	Penal code	–	Circular, Rwanda (March 1976)
Senegal	Penal code	–	Circular, Senegal (March 1976)
Singapore	Criminal law	–	Circular, Singapore (March 1976)
South Africa	Civil Aviation Offenses Act (No. 10), 1972	Prison 5 to 30 yrs. for unlawful seizure of aircraft	Circular, South Africa (Oct. 1975)
Soviet Union	Decree of Presidium, Jan. 3, 1973	Prison 3 to 10 yrs. for hijacking; up to 15 yrs. if threat of violence or accident results; 15 yrs. or death if death or serious injury results	25 *Current Digest of Soviet Press*, No. 1 at 7 (1973)
	Principles of Criminal Legislation of the USSR and the Union Republics, arts. 7(1), 23(1), 30, 44(1), 45(2), revised March 9, 1973	Revision of articles to comprehend aircraft hijacking	*Id.*, No. 18 at 19 (1973)
Spain	Penal and Procedural Law on Aerial Navigation	–	Circular, Spain (Oct. 1975)
Swaziland	Criminal law	–	Circular, Swaziland (March 1976)
Sweden	Law on Change of the Criminal Law, May 25, 1973, c.13, Item 5(a)	Prison up to 4 yrs. for hijacking; up to 4 yrs. for sabotage; up to 10 yrs. to life if life endangered during act	Circular, Sweden (Dec. 1975)
Switzerland	Penal code	–	Circular, Switzerland (Jan. 1976)
Syria	Current policy	–	Circular, Syria (Jan. 1976)
Tanzania	Current policy	–	Circular, Tanzania (March 1976)
Trinidad and Tobago	Current policy	–	Circular, Trinidad (March 1976)
Turkey	Penal code	–	Circular, Turkey (March 1976)

State	Law	Summary	Source
United Kingdom	Hijacking Act 1971	Up to life imprisonment for unlawful seizure of aircraft; acts constituting murder, attempted murder, manslaughter, culpable homicide, assault, or offenses under certain sections of the Offences Against the Person Act 1861 and the Explosive Substances Act 1883 shall constitute that offense if done in pursuance of a hijacking or attempt thereof	1971, c. 70; Circular, United Kingdom (Nov. 1975)
United States	Aircraft Piracy Act, 1961, amending Federal Aviation Act, 1958; Antihijacking Act of 1974	Prison for minimum of 20 yrs. for hijacking or attempt; life imprisonment or death if a death results from hijacking or attempt thereof; up to 20 yrs. and/or fine of $10,000 for interference with flight crew, up to life if dangerous weapon used in act; crimes defined in 18 U.S.C. §§ 113, 114, 661, 662, 1111, 1112, 1113, 2031, 2032, 2111 committed aboard aircraft are punishable as indicated in respective sections; prison up to 1 yr. and/or fine of $1000 for conveying false information about hijacking or attempt and up to 5 yrs. and/or fine of $5000 if done maliciously or in reckless disregard of safety of human life	75 Stat. 466 (1961) 49 U.S.C. § 1472(i)-(n); 88 Stat. 409 (1974)
Upper Volta	Penal code	–	Circular, Upper Volta (March 1976)
Uruguay	Penal code	–	Circular, Uruguay (Dec. 1975)
Venezuela	Penal code	–	Circular, Venezuela (Oct. 1975)
Yugoslavia	Penal code	–	RDPC, 463-64, *supra* note 101
Zaire	Penal code	–	Circular, Zaire (April 1976)

Appendix 1B:
States Parties to
Relevant Aviation
Conventions

	Chicago	Tokyo	Hague	Montreal
Afghanistan	x	x		
Algeria	x			
Angola	x			
Argentina	x	x	x	x
Australia	x	x	x	x
Austria	x	x	x	x
Bahamas	x	x	x	
Bahrain	x			
Bangladesh	x			
Barbados	x	x	x	x
Belgium	x	x	x	x
Benin (Dahomey)	x		x	
Bolivia	x			
Brazil	x	x	x	x
Bulgaria	x		x	x
Burma	x			
Burundi	x	x		
Byelorussian S.S.R.			x	x
Cambodia	x			
Cameroon	x			x
Canada	x	x	x	x
Cape Verde	x			
Central African Republic	x			
Chad	x	x	x	x
Chile	x	x	x	x
China, Republic of	x	x	x	x
Colombia	x	x	x	x
Congo (Brazzaville)	x			
Costa Rica	x	x	x	x
Cuba	x			
Cyprus	x	x	x	x
Czechoslovakia	x		x	x
Denmark	x	x	x	x
Dominican Republic	x	x		x

63

	Chicago	Tokyo	Hague	Montreal
Ecuador	x	x	x	x
Egypt	x	x	x	x
El Salvador	x		x	
Equatorial Guinea	x			
Ethiopia	x			
Fiji	x	x	x	x
Finland	x	x	x	x
France	x	x	x	x
Gabon	x	x	x	x
Gambia	x			
Germany, Democratic Republic of			x	x
Germany, Federal Republic of	x	x	x	
Ghana	x	x	x	x
Greece	x	x	x	x
Guatemala	x	x		
Guinea	x			
Guyana	x		x	x
Haiti	x			
Honduras	x			
Hungary	x	x	x	x
Iceland	x	x	x	x
India	x	x		
Indonesia	x	x	x	x
Iran	x	x	x	x
Iraq	x	x	x	x
Ireland	x	x	x	
Israel	x	x	x	x
Italy	x	x	x	x
Ivory Coast	x	x	x	x
Jamaica	x			
Japan	x	x	x	x
Jordan	x	x	x	x
Kenya	x	x	x	x
Korea, Republic of	x	x	x	x
Kuwait	x			
Laos	x	x		
Lebanon	x	x	x	
Lesotho	x	x		

	Chicago	Tokyo	Hague	Montreal
Liberia	x			
Libya	x	x		x
Luxembourg	x	x		
Madagascar	x	x		
Malawi	x	x	x	x
Malaysia	x			
Maldives	x			
Mali	x	x	x	x
Malta	x			
Mauritania	x			
Mauritius	x			
Mexico	x	x	x	x
Mongolia			x	x
Morocco	x	x	x	x
Mozambique	x			
Nauru	x			
Nepal	x			
Netherlands	x	x	x	x
New Zealand	x	x	x	x
Nicaragua	x	x	x	x
Niger	x	x	x	x
Nigeria	x	x	x	x
Norway	x	x	x	x
Oman	x	x		
Pakistan	x	x	x	x
Panama	x	x	x	x
Papua New Guinea	x	x	x	x
Paraguay	x	x	x	x
Peru	x			
Philippines	x	x	x	x
Poland	x	x	x	x
Portugal	x	x	x	x
Principe	x			
Qatar	x			
Romania	x	x	x	x
Rwanda	x	x		
Sao Tome	x			
Saudi Arabia	x	x	x	x
Senegal	x	x		
Seychelles	x			

	Chicago	Tokyo	Hague	Montreal
Sierra Leone	x	x	x	
Singapore	x	x		
Somalia	x			
South Africa	x	x	x	x
Soviet Union	x		x	x
Spain	x	x	x	x
Sri Lanka	x			
Sudan	x			
Surinam	x			
Swaziland	x			
Sweden	x	x	x	x
Switzerland	x	x	x	
Syrian Arab Republic	x			
Tanzania	x			
Thailand	x	x		
Togo	x	x		
Trinidad and Tobago	x	x	x	x
Tunisia	x	x		
Turkey	x	x	x	x
Uganda	x		x	
Ukrainian S.S.R.			x	x
United Arab Emirates	x			
United Kingdom	x	x	x	x
United States	x	x	x	x
Upper Volta	x	x		
Uruguay	x	x	x	x
Venezuela	x			
Vietnam, Republic of	x		x	
Yemen (Aden)	x			
Yemen (Sana)	x			
Yugoslavia	x	x	x	x
Zaire	x			
Zambia	x	x		

Source: Based on *Treaties in Force. A List of Treaties and Other International Agreements of the United States in Force on January 1, 1977* (Treaty Affairs Staff, Office of the Legal Adviser, Department of State, 1977), annotated through June 30, 1977. Treaties *supra* notes 22, 3, 4, and 5, respectively.

Appendix 1C: Domestic and Foreign Aircraft Hijackings, January 1, 1960- July 31, 1977

Year	Results	Date	Name	Airline
1960	1	4/12/60	Herrera, Gonzalo; Monnar, Francisco; Lopez, Angel E.; Enrique, Pedro	(F) Cubana
1960	1	7/5/60	Acosta, Miguel; Norbregas, Leslie	(F) Cubana
1960	1	7/17/60	Menendez, Jose P.	(F) Cubana
1960	1	7/18/60	Cardenas Adeas, Jose F.	(F) Private G/A (Cuban)
1960	2	7/19/60	Hildebrant, Alex	(F) Trans-Australia
1960	1	7/28/60	3 men, anonymous	(F) Cubana
1960	2	8/21/60	1 man, 1 woman, anonymous	(F) USSR
1960	1	10/29/60	9 men, anonymous	(F) Cubana
1960	2	12/8/60	Martinez Herandez, Diosdado; Moreno Bacallado, Enildo; Moreno Bacallado, Eloy; Villarreal Garcia, Cesar; Quian, Raul; Cabrera, Caridad	
1961	1	1/1/61	2 men, anonymous	(F) Cubana
1961	3	5/1/61	Ramirez Ortiz, Antulio	National
1961	1	7/3/61	11 men, 3 women, anonymous	(F) Cubana
1961	3	7/24/61	Oquendo, Wilfredo	Eastern
1961	6	7/31/61	Britt, Bruce	PAC
1961	4	8/3/61	Bearden, Leon F.; Bearden, Cody L. (J)	Continental

Type of Aircraft	Flight Plan	Disposition
Viscount	Domestic Cuba	Landed in Miami. Pilot and 2 crewmen were 3 of the hijackers.
	Madrid/Havana	Landed in Miami. Hijackers were the co-pilots.
Viscount	Havana/Miami	Landed in Jamaica. Pilot was the hijacker.
Single-engine	Havana/Vedado, Cuba	Landed in Fort Lauderdale.
Electra L-188	Sydney/Brisbane, Australia	Hijacker wanted Singapore. Overpowered by copilot and deadheading pilot. Sentenced to 7 yrs. imprisonment.
	Oriente Prov./Havana	Landed in Miami. Pilot hijacked plane with help of 2 passengers. Held security guard at gunpoint. 2 women and 2 children joined hijacker.
	Domestic USSR	Crew wounded but overpowered hijackers.
DC-3	Havana/Isle of Pines, Cuba	Landed in Key West. Security guard shot and killed. Pilot, copilot, and 1 passenger wounded. Copilot was one of the hijackers.
	Domestic Cuba	Pilot crash landed. 1 killed, 4 wounded. 4 hijackers condemned to death by firing squad; 1 sentenced to 30 yrs.
	Domestic Cuba	Landed in New York. Hijackers pointed pistol at pilot while in Havana terminal area; forced him to fly group of Batista supporters out of Cuba.
CV-440	Marathon/Key West	Arrested in Miami on 11/21/75. Sentenced to 20 yrs.
DC-3	Havana/Varadero, Cuba	Landed in Miami. Security guard shot and wounded.
L-188	Miami/Tampa	Fugitive.
DC-3	Chico/San Francisco	Shot and wounded ticket agent and pilot. Sentenced for attempted murder, three 1-to-14 yr. terms to run consecutively.
B-707	Los Angeles/Houston	20 yrs. and 5 yrs. concurrently. Cody Bearden sent to reform school (released 1965).

Year	Results	Date	Name	Airline
1961	3	8/9/61	Cadon, Albert	Pan American
1961	2	8/9/61	5 men, anonymous	(F) Aerovias (Cuban)
1961	2	9/10/61	Tumanyan, Serge; Sekoyan, Genrik; Movesesyan, Garegin	(F) Charter (G/A) USSR
1961	1	11/10/61	Inicio, Herminio de Palma, and 5 other men	(F) Transportes Aereos (Portuguese)
1961	1	11/27/61	5 men, anonymous	(F) Avensa (Venezuelan)
1962	3	1/6/62	Mims, R.	Charter
1962	2	3/17/62	1 man, anonymous	(F) French charter
1962	3	4/13/62	Healy, David; Oeth, Leonard	Charter (G/A)
1962	2	4/16/62	Da Silva, Edgar	(F) Royal Dutch Airlines
1963	1	11/28/63	Dilma, "Commander"; Dilma, Olga; Marin, Jose; Rojas, Alberto; Toledo, Patrick; Rojas, Armando	(F) Avensa (Venezuelan)
1964	3	2/18/64	Castillo Hernandez, Enrique; Lopez Rodriguez, Reinaldo	Charter (G/A)
1964	2	10/18/64	2 men, anonymous	(F) USSR
1965	2	6/15/65	1 man, 1 woman, anonymous	(F) USSR
1965	1	8/31/65	Fergerstom, Harry (J)	Hawaiian
1965	2	10/11/65	Heisler, Lawrence (S); Boyd, Richard (S)	Aloha
1965	4	10/26/65	Medina Perez, Luis	National

Type of Aircraft	Flight Plan	Disposition
DC-8	Mexico City/Guatemala City	Deported to Mexico; Prison (Mexico) 8 yrs., 9 mos.; released 1973. Fugitive from U.S. charges.
C 46	Havana/Isle of Pines, Cuba	Pilot and 2 others killed. 6 wounded. Co-pilot made crash landing.
YAK-12	Erwan/Yekhegnadzor, USSR	Pilot wounded by hijackers. One hijacker killed in crash near Yekhegnadzor, Armenia, USSR. 2 other hijackers sentenced to death.
L-1049	Casablanca/Lisbon	Circled Lisbon dropping leaflets. Landed Tangier, Morocco. Hijackers expelled to Senegal then went to Brazil and were granted asylum.
DC6B	Caracas/Maracaibo, Venezuela	Landed in Curacao; hijackers deported. Imprisoned for 4 yrs., 7 mos.
	Sioux City/Dallas	Sentenced to 15 yrs.; reduced to 5 yrs.
	Paris/St. Martin de L'Ardoise, France	Hijacker one of 32 prisoners aboard; shot and wounded by a guard.
Cessna 172	Miami (local)	Deported to U.S. 4/20/62. Sentenced to 20 yrs. and 1 yr. to run concurrently.
	Amsterdam/Lisbon	Hijacker wanted to go to East Berlin. Aircraft landed in Holland. Hijacker in custody.
Convair Twin Engine	Ciudad Bolivar/ Caracas, Venezuela	Landed in Trinidad; hijackers deported, tried, imprisoned.
Piper PA-23	Miami/Key West	Fugitives
AN-2	Shadur-Lungu/Izmail, USSR	Pilot and copilot wounded. Landed in Kishinev, USSR.
	Domestic USSR	Flight engineer shot and killed by hijackers. Other crew members overpowered hijackers.
DC-3	Honolulu/Kauai	Correction school. Paroled 11/3/67.
F-27	Molokai/Honolulu	Both sentenced to 4 yrs. imprisonment and dishonorable discharges from U.S. Navy; released September 1966.
L-188	Miami/Key West	Acquitted 6/24/66 on grounds of mental incompetence.

Year	Results	Date	Name	Airline
1965	4	11/17/65	Robinson, Thomas (J)	National
1966	4	3/27/66	Betancourt Cueto, Angel	(F) Cubana
1966	1	7/7/66	9 persons	(F) Cubana
1966	2	8/3/66	Shvachka, N.; Svistunov, V.; Maksimkin, B.	(F) USSR
1966	1	9/28/66	Varrier, Maria, and 19 others	(F) Argentine
1967	1	2/7/67	Hajjaj, Riyad Kamal	(F) Egyptian
1967	1	4/23/67	5 men	(F) Nigerian
1967	1	6/30/67	Bodenan, Francois	(F) Private (G/A) (United Kingdom)
1967	3	8/6/67	Buendia, Pedro; Rojas, Fermina; Lopez, Roberto; Alvarez, Julian; 1 other man	(F) Aerocondor (Colombian)
1967	3	9/9/67	Garcia, Ramino; Garcia, Fernando; Garcia, Joaquin	(F) Avianca (Colombian)
1967	3	11/20/67	Babler, Louis Gabor	Charter (G/A)
1968	2	2/9/68	Clark, William (S)	Pan American (military charter)
1968	3	2/17/68	Boynton, Thomas	Charter (G/A)
1968	3	2/21/68	Rhodes, Lawrence	Delta

Type of Aircraft	Flight Plan	Disposition
DC-8	New Orleans/Florida	Correctional school. Conviction set aside 9/24/69.
IL-18	Santiago/Havana	Pilot and guard killed after pilot landed in Cuba. Hijacker thought he was at Miami. Copilot wounded. Hijacker was flight engineer. Hijacker captured 4/11/66.
IL-18	Santiago/Havana	Landed in Jamaica; Pilot was one of the hijackers. Copilot wounded.
AN-2	Poti-Batumi, USSR	Landed in Batumi, USSR. 1 passenger wounded. Hijackers captured.
DC-4	Buenos Aires/Rio Gallegos, Argentina	Landed in Falkland Islands. Deported. 3 leaders sentenced to 5 yrs. Others sentenced to 3 yrs.
AN-24	Cairo-Hurghada, Egypt	Landed in Jordan. Escaped to Sweden, where he is serving long sentence for other crimes.
F-27	Benin City/Lagos, Nigeria	Landed in Enugu, Eastern Nigeria.
HS-125	Palma de Mallorca/Ibiza, Spain	Landed in Algeria; Moise Tshombe, former prime minister of Congo, aboard. Tshombe held by Algerians and died in captivity 6/29/69. Bodenan expelled 10/29/69.
DC-4	Barranquilla/San Andres Islands, Colombia	Landed in Cuba.
DC-3	Barranquilla/Magangue, Colombia	Landed in Cuba.
Piper Apache	Hollywood, Fla./Bimini	Fugitive
DC-6	DaNang, South Vietnam/Hong Kong	U.S. Marines courtmartial; sentenced to 1½ yrs. and bad conduct discharge additional sentence for crimes committed in prison. Convictions set aside 12/3/69. Medical discharge 9/2/70.
Piper Apache	Marathon/Miami	Returned via Canada 11/1/69. Sentenced 20 yrs. for kidnaping 5/12/70.
DC-8	Tampa/West Palm Beach	Surrendered in Spain, 2/10/70. Commited to mental institution. Hijacking charges dropped. Returned to jail for robbery trial (state charge) 7/8/71. Sentenced to 25 yrs. for robbery 7/17/72.

Year	Results	Date	Name	Airline
1968	3	3/5/68	Awadalla, Sami Salin Hussein; Villalobos-Rica, Aristides; Ortiz-Acosta, Jairo	(F) Avianca (Colombian)
1968	3	3/12/68	Armenteros, Jesus; Carrazana y Gonzales, Gilberto; Donato-Martin, Ramon	National
1968	3	3/16/68	2 men, 1 woman, 2 children, anonymous	(F) Private (G/A) (Mexican)
1968	3	3/21/68	3 men, anonymous	(F) Avensa (Venezuelan)
1968	3	6/19/68	Mendez-Vargas, Radhames	(F) Viasa (Venezuelan)
1968	3	6/29/68	1 man, anonymous	Southeast
1968	3	7/1/68	Velasquez Fonseca, Mario	Northwest
1968	2	7/4/68	Morris, John H. (P)	TWA
1968	3	7/12/68	Bendicks, Leonard S.	Private (G/A)
1968	4	7/12/68	Richards, Oran	Delta
1968	3	7/17/68	Hernandez Leyva, Rogelio	National
1968	1	7/23/68	3 male Arabs, anonymous	(F) El Al (Israeli)
1968	3	8/4/68	Jessie, Willis (S) and 3-year-old daughter	Charter (G/A)
1968	3	8/22/68	1 man, anonymous	Charter (G/A)
1968	4	9/11/68	Beasley, Charles L.	(F) Air Canada
1968	3	9/20/68	Suarez-Garcia, Jose	Eastern

Type of Aircraft	Flight Plan	Disposition
DC-4	Riohacha/Barran-quilla, Colombia	Landed in Cuba.
DC-8	Tampa/Miami	Fugitives
Twin Engine	Merida/Cozumel, Mexico	Landed in Cuba.
CV-440	Caracas/Maracaibo, Venezuela	Landed in Cuba.
DC-9	Santo Domingo, Dominican Republic/ Curacao, Netherlands Antilles	Sentenced to 20 yrs. by Dominican court, 8/13/70.
DC-3	Marathon/Key West	Fugitives
B-727	Chicago/Miami	Fugitives
B-727	Kansas City/Las Vegas	Sentenced to 5 additional yrs. 5/16/69 (escaped from prison).
Cessna C-210	Key West/Miami	Deported to U.S. Sentenced to 10 yrs. 3/4/71; 3 yrs. parole 6/27/72.
CV-880	Baltimore/Houston	Charges dismissed 9/3/69. Released from state mental hospital 1/10/70.
DC-8	Los Angeles/Miami	Fugitives
B-707	Rome/Tel Aviv	Pilot wounded. 1 hijacker took over controls and landed aircraft at Algiers, Algeria.
Cessna 182	Naples, Fl. (local)	Returned voluntarily via Mexico. Sentenced to 10 yrs. for kidnaping 6/26/69. Paroled 7/28/71.
Cessna 336	Nassau/Exuma, The Bahamas	Landed in Cuba.
Viscount 4-engine Turboprop	St. John/Toronto, Canada	Surrendered at Montreal. Asked for asylum. Sentenced to 6 yrs. in Montreal prison 12/10/68. Deported to U.S. 3/25/71. Sentenced to 10 yrs. and 5 yrs. concurrent for bank robbery and related offense on 8/19/68 in Texas.
B-720	San Juan/Miami	Fugitives

Year	Results	Date	Name	Airline
1968	3	9/22/68	Garcia, Ramon	(F) Avianca (Colombian)
1968	3	9/22/68	London, Carlos	(F) Avianca (Colombian)
1968	3	10/6/68	Vazquez, Judy, and 2 children	(F) Aeromaya (Mexican)
1968	3	10/23/68	Truitt, Alben W.B.	Charter (G/A)
1968	1	10/30/68	Garcia Zurita, Juan Francisco	(F) Seasa (Mexican)
1968	4	11/2/68	Pastorcich, Roger (J)	Eastern
1968	3	11/4/68	Johnson, Raymond	National
1968	1	11/6/68	Rabuya, M., and 3 other men	(F) Philippine
1968	1	11/8/68	Giovine, Umberto; Panichi, Maurizio	(F) Olympic (Greek)
1968	3	11/18/68	2 men, anonymous	(F) CMA (Mexican)
1968	3	11/23/68	Suarez Isarcia, Aramis; Mayor Velasques, Miguel; Arroyo Quintero, Alberto; Mendoza Viera, Irardo; Nunez de Mendoza, Teresa; Rodriguez Rodriguez, Moises	Eastern
1968	3	11/24/68	Rios Cruz, Jose R.; Pena Soltren, Luis A.; Castro Cruz, Miguel I.	Pan American
1968	3	11/30/68	Montesino Sanchez, Miguel	Eastern
1968	3	12/3/68	1 man, anonymous	National
1968	3	12/11/68	Patterson, James and Gwendolyn	TWA
1968	3	12/19/68	Washington, Thomas, and infant daughter	Eastern

Type of Aircraft	Flight Plan	Disposition
B-727	Barranquilla/ Cartagena, Colombia	Landed in Cuba.
DC-4	Barranquilla/Santa Marta, Colombia	Landed in Cuba.
HS-748	Cozumel/Merida, Mexico	Landed in Cuba.
Cessna 177	Key West (local)	Returned via Canada 2/69. Sentenced to two 20 yr. terms to run consecutively 8/13/69.
C-46	Tampico/Reynosa, Mexico	Landed in Brownsville, Texas. Deported to Mexico.
DC-9	Mobile/Chicago	Probation with psychiatric care 7/18/69; released 12/23/70.
B-727	New Orleans/Miami	Fugitive
Fokker Twin Engine	Abu/Manila, Philippines	Landed in Manila. 1 passenger killed, 1 wounded. All passengers robbed. Hijackers escaped. M. Rabuya reportedly received death sentence.
B-707	Paris/Athens	Hijackers passed out handbills and required aircraft to return to Paris. Sentenced to 8 and 6 mos. respectively.
DC-6	Merida/Mexico City	Landed in Cuba.
B-727	Chicago/Miami	Fugitives.
B-707	New York/San Juan	David Gonzalez and Alejandro Figuera acquitted of aiding and abetting air piracy. Rios Cruz apprehended in San Juan on 8/2/75 and sentenced to 15 yrs. 12/18/75. Castro Cruz apprehended on 2/3/76 in San Juan and was sentenced to 12 yrs. 5/4/76. Pena Soltren is fugitive.
B-720	Miami/Dallas	Fugitive.
B-727	Tampa/Miami	Fugitive.
B-727	Nashville/Miami	Fugitives.
DC-8	Philadelphia/Miami	Returned via Canada, Nov. 1969. Sentenced to 2 yrs. 3/24/70. Released 6/4/71.

Year	Results	Date	Name	Airline
1969	3	1/2/69	Austin, Tyrone and Linda, with infant daughter	Eastern
1969	1	1/2/69	Flamourides, George	(F) Olympic (Greek)
1969	3	1/7/69	1 man, anonymous	(F) Avianca (Colombian)
1969	3	1/9/69	Bohle, Ronald	Eastern
1969	3	1/11/69	Helmey, Robert	United
1969	3	1/11/69	Amaya Roseque, Jesus R.	(F) APSA (Peruvian)
1969	4	1/13/69	McPeek, Kenneth E.	Delta
1969	3	1/19/69	Navarro Payano, Aristofarez	Eastern
1969	3	1/19/69	Quevedo Mora, J.; Quevedo Mora, Angel; Quevedo Mora, Antonio; Quevedo Mora, C.; Centurion Onofre, J.A.; Pino, C.; Pino, L.; Viejo Romero, A.; Moreno Merino, V.; Moreno Merino, C.	(F) Ecuatoriana (Ecuadorian)
1969	3	1/24/69	1 man, anonymous	National
1969	3	1/28/69	Smith, Clinton; Booth, Byron	National
1969	3	1/28/69	Brooks, Larry; Mason, Noble; White, Everett	Eastern
1969	3	1/31/69	Sheffield, Allan C.	National
1969	3	2/3/69	Hernandez, Garcia, W.; Hernandez, Marina; Babin Estrada, J.	Eastern

Type of Aircraft	Flight Plan	Disposition
DC-8	New York/Miami	Tyrone Austin killed in bank robbery 4/22/71, New York City; Linda Austin is fugitive.
DC-6B	Crete/Athens	Landed in Cairo. Imprisoned in Egypt 8 mos. Sent to Sweden upon initiative of U.N. Refugee Commission. June 1970 sentenced to 1 yr., 10 mos. imprisonment in Sweden. Greek request for extradition denied Sept. 1970.
DC-4	Riohacha/Maicao, Colombia	Landed in Cuba.
B-727	Miami/Nassau	Returned via Canada 11/1/69. Sentenced to 20 yrs. 7/6/72.
B-727	Jacksonville/Miami	Returned via Canada, 5/5/69. Acquitted due to insanity 11/20/69.
CV-990	Panama City/Miami	Hijacker was returned to Mexico and sentenced to 25 yrs. on 5/6/73. He was released and flown to Cuba with 29 other prisoners released by Mexicans in effort to secure release of U.S. consul general who was kidnaped.
CV-880	Detroit/Miami	Sentenced to 15 yrs. 7/31/69.
DC-8	New York/Miami	Extradition requested 7/21/71. Will stand trial in Dominican Republic.
Electra L-88	Guayaquil/Quito, Ecuador	The two Moreno Merinos in custody. All convicted in Ecuadorian court.
B-727	Key West/Miami	Fugitive
DC-8	Los Angeles/Miami	Fugitives
DC-8	Atlanta/Miami	White arrested in Cleveland 4/30/75; sentenced to 10 yrs. 9/24/75. Brooks and Mason are fugitives.
DC-8	San Francisco/ Tampa	Expelled to Sweden by Yugoslavia 10/5/76; expelled to U.S. by Sweden, 10/7/76; arraigned on hijacking charges 10/8/76.
B-727	Newark/Miami	Fugitives.

Year	Results	Date	Name	Airline
1969	4	2/3/69	Peparo, Michael (J); Fitz-gerald, Tasmin (J)	National
1969	3	2/5/69	Domiguez Fuentes, L.	(F) SAM (Colombian)
1969	4	2/8/69	Romo, Victor	(F) Mexican
1969	3	2/10/69	Alvarez de Quesada, Pedro	Eastern
1969	1	2/11/69	Pinckney, J.	British W.I.
1969	3	2/11/69	3 men, anonymous	(F) Aeropostal (Venezuelan)
1969	3	2/25/69	Ervin, Lorenzo E., Jr.	Eastern
1969	3	3/5/69	Bryant, Anthony	National
1969	4	3/11/69	Caro Montoya, Juan	(F) SAM (Colombian)
1969	3	3/15/69	1 man, anonymous	(F) Aerocondor (Colombian)
1969	3	3/17/69	4 men, anonymous	(F) Faucett (Peruvian)
1969	3	3/17/69	Sandlin, Robert L.	Delta
1969	4	3/19/69	Dickey, Douglas A.	Delta
1969	3	3/25/69	Frese, Luis A.	Delta
1969	3	4/11/69	3 men, anonymous	(F) (Ecuadorian)
1969	3	4/13/69	Courouneaux Sanchez, H.; Vargas Aqueros, M.; Diaz Claro, J.; Ramirez Castenada, E.	Pan American
1969	3	4/14/69	3 men, anonymous	(F) SAM (Colombian)
1969	3	5/5/69	Charrette, J.P.; Allard, Alain	National
1969	3	5/20/69	Martinez Rusinke, Luis Eduardo; 2 other men	(F) Avianca (Colombian)

Type of Aircraft	Flight Plan	Disposition
B-727	New York/Miami	Correctional School 5/7/69. Paroled 12/7/70.
DC-4	Barranquilla/Medellin, Colombia	Sentenced in Sweden to 30 mos. 3/27/72.
DC-6	Mexico City/Villa Hermosa, Mexico	Hijacker overpowered by passengers.
DC-8	San Juan/Miami	Fugitive.
	Nassau/Miami	Acquitted, 11/4/69.
DC-9	Maracaibo/Caracas, Venezuela	Landed in Cuba.
DC-8	Atlanta/Miami	Surrendered at Prague Sept. 1969. Sentenced to life imprisonment 7/7/70.
B-727	New York/Miami	Fugitive.
DC-4	Medellin/Cartagena, Colombia	Landed Cartagena. Hijacker wounded and overpowered. Airline mechanic killed.
DC-6	Barranquilla/San Andres Islands, Colombia	Landed in Cuba.
B-727	Lima/Arequipa, Peru	Landed in Cuba.
DC-9	Atlanta/Augusta, Ga.	Returned via Canada 11/1/69. Committed to mental institution 2/1/72. Released on second 18-mo. furlough 12/5/73.
CV-880	Dallas/New Orleans	Charges dismissed on grounds of insanity. Committed to state mental institution 8/14/69.
DC-8	Dallas/San Diego	Died in Cuba in jail 10/20/75.
DC-6	Guayaquil/Quito, Ecuador	Hijackers accompanied by approximately 6 other men, 3 women, and 4 children.
B-727	San Juan/Miami	Fugitives.
DC-4	Medellin/Barranquilla, Colombia	Landed in Cuba.
B-727	New York/Miami	Fugitives.
B-737	Bogota/Pereira, Colombia	Landed in Cuba.

Year	Results	Date	Name	Airline
1969	3	5/26/69	Parra Zamora, Crecencio; Romero Cracial, Roberto; Bolivar Samon, Marino	Northeast
1969	4	5/30/69	Niemeyer, Terrance (P)	Texas International
1969	4	6/4/69	3 men, anonymous	(F) DTA (Angolan)
1969	3	6/17/69	Brent, William	TWA
1969	3	6/20/69	3 men, 1 woman, anonymous	(F) La Urraca (Colombian)
1969	3	6/22/69	Esquivel-Medrano, Agustin	Eastern
1969	3	6/25/69	Marquez, John	United
1969	3	6/28/69	Anthony, Raymond L., Sr.	Eastern
1969	3	7/3/69	13 people, anonymous	(F) Saeta (Ecuadorian)
1969	4	7/10/69	Herrera, Luis	(F) Avianca (Colombian)
1969	4	7/10/69	Olarte, David	(F) SAM (Colombian)
1969	3	7/26/69	Carrera Vasquez, David; Munos Ramos, Pilar	(F) Mexicana (Mexican)
1969	3	7/26/69	Crawford, J.C.	Continental
1969	4	7/29/69	1 man, anonymous	(F) Nicaraguan
1969	3	7/31/69	Perry, Lester E., Jr. (P)	TWA
1969	3	8/4/69	3 men, anonymous	(F) Avianca (Colombian)
1969	4	8/5/69	McCreery, John S.	Eastern
1969	1	8/11/69	7 students, anonymous	(F) Ethiopian

Type of Aircraft	Flight Plan	Disposition
B-727	Miami/New York	Fugitives.
CV-600	New Orleans/Alexandria, La.	Charges dismissed on grounds of insanity 4/15/71. Committed to state mental institution 1/29/71. Released on probation 10/10/73.
DC-3	Luanda, Angola/ Cabinda	Landed in Congo.
B-707	Oakland/New York	Fugitive.
DC-3	Villavicencio/ Monterrey, Colombia	Landed in Cuba.
DC-8	Newark/Miami	Fugitive.
DC-8	Los Angeles/New York	Fugitive.
B-727	Baltimore/Tampa	Returned via Canada 11/1/69. Sentenced to 15 yrs. 10/6/70.
DC-3	Tulcan/Quito, Ecuador	Landed in Cuba.
DC-4	Barranquilla/Santa Marta, Colombia	Hijacker overpowered by pilot returned to Barranquilla.
DC-4	Cali/Bogota, Colombia	Overpowered by stewardess and passengers. Landed in Bogota.
DC-6	Minatitlan/Villa Hermosa, Mexico	Extradition to Mexico denied by Cuba, 9/15/69.
DC-9	El Paso/Midland, Tex.	Returned via Canada 11/1/69. Sentenced to 50 yrs. 9/14/70.
	Managua/coast of Nicaragua	Subdued. Hijacker dressed as female.
B-727	Philadelphia/Los Angeles	Fugitive.
DC-4	Santa Marta/Riohacha, Colombia	Landed in Cuba.
DC-9	Philadelphia/Tampa	Charges dismissed 1/12/70. Committed to mental institution. Discharged 9/15/71.
DC-3	Bahr Dar/Addis Ababa, Ethiopia	Landed in Khartoum, Sudan; asked asylum.

Year	Results	Date	Name	Airline
1969	3	8/14/69	Torres-Diaz, Domingo; Mena Perez, Julio L.	Northeast
1969	1	8/16/69	Tsironis, Vassilies, with wife and 2 sons	(F) Olympic (Greek)
1969	1	8/18/69	El Moneiry, Mohamed Hashem; El Moneiry, Soliman Hashem, with wife and 3 children	(F) Misrair (Egyptian)
1969	3	8/23/69	2 men, anonymous	(F) Avianca (Colombian)
1969	3	8/29/69	Carballe Delgado, Jorge	National
1969	1	8/29/69	Khaled, Leila A.; Essawi, Salim K.	TWA
1969	3	9/6/69	4 men, anonymous	(F) Tame Commercial Airline, operated by Air Force (Ecuadorian)
1969	1	9/6/69	4 men, anonymous	(F) Tame Commercial Airline, operated by Air Force (Ecuadorian)
1969	3	9/7/69	Peterson-Coplin, Felix	Eastern
1969	4	9/10/69	Gonzalez-Medina, Jose	Eastern
1969	1	9/13/69	3 men, anonymous	(F) Ethiopian
1969	1	9/13/69	Huete, Carlos	(F) Sahsa (Honduran)
1969	1	9/16/69	Toker, Sadi	(F) Turkish
1969	3	9/24/69	Hernandez, Alfredo (S)	National
1969	3	10/8/69	4 men, anonymous	(F) Cruzeiro do Sol (Brazilian)
1969	3	10/8/69	Ugartteche, E.	(F) Aerolineas (Argentine)
1969	3	10/9/69	Rivera-Perez, F.	National

Type of Aircraft	Flight Plan	Disposition
B-727	Boston/Miami	Fugitives.
DC-3	Athens/Agrinion, Greece	Landed in Albania. Made way to Sweden, where sentenced on 7/7/71 to 3½ yrs. imprisonment.
Anatov	Cairo/Luxor, Egypt	Landed in El Wagab, Saudi Arabia; hijackers arrested and returned to Egypt aboard same plane. Soliman El Moneiry sentenced to life imprisonment, M. Hashem El Moneiry sentenced to 7 yrs. 12/21/70.
AV-748	Burcaramanga/Bogota, Colombia	Landed in Cuba.
B-727	Miami/New Orleans	Fugitive.
B-707	Rome/Athens	Landed in Damascus.
DC-3	Domestic Ecuador	Flew to Tumaco, Colombia; took off with 34 passengers and 7 crew in second plane; refueled in Panama; landed in Cuba.
DC-3	Domestic Ecuador	Copilot killed, radioman wounded when aircraft refueled in Tumaco; plane abandoned; continued journey in second plane (see previous entry).
DC-8	New York/San Juan	Fugitive.
DC-8	New York/San Juan	Charges dismissed 9/25/70; committed to mental institution 1/3/69. Released Dec. 1971.
DC-6	Addis Ababa/Djibouti, Fr. Somaliland	1 man shot, other 2 taken into official custody upon landing in Aden, South Yemen.
DC-3	La Cieba/Tegucigalpa, Honduras	Arrested when landed in El Salvador. Flight continued to original destination.
Viscount	Istanbul/Ankara, Turkey	Landed in Sofia; put in mental institution. Returned to Turkey 5/4/72.
B-727	Charleston/Miami	Fugitive.
Caravelle	Belem/Manaus, Brazil	Landed in Cuba.
B-707	Buenos Aires/Miami	Landed in Cuba.
DC-8	Los Angeles/Miami	Fugitive.

Year	Results	Date	Name	Airline
1969	1	10/19/69	Klemt, P.; Von Hof, H.U.	(F) LOT (Polish)
1969	3	10/21/69	Shorr, Henry (J)	Pan American
1969	3	10/28/69	2 men, anonymous	(F) Air Taxi (G/A)
1969	1	10/31/69	Minichiello, R. (S)	TWA
1969	3	11/4/69	Quezada Maldonado, Juan Jose; Lugo Valencia, Rena	(F) Lanica (Nicaraguan)
1969	3	11/4/69	5 men, 1 woman, anonymous	(F) Varig (Brazilian)
1969	2	11/6/69	2 men (convicts), anonymous	Australia East-West
1969	1	11/8/69	Posadas Malgarejo, Luis	(F) Austral (Argentine)
1969	2	11/10/69	Booth, David (J)	Delta
1969	4	11/12/69	Varas Flores, Pedro (J); Degach Vergue, Patricio F. (J)	(F) LAN (Chilean)
1969	3	11/12/69	1 man, anonymous	(F) Cruzeiro do Sol (Brazilian)
1969	3	11/13/69	6 men, anonymous	(F) Avianca (Colombian)
1969	3	11/18/69	1 man, anonymous	(F) (G/A) (Mexican)
1969	1	11/20/69	Szymankiewicz, W.; Zolotucho, R.	(F) Lot (Polish)
1969	3	11/29/69	1 man, anonymous	(F) Varig (Brazilian)
1969	3	12/2/69	Hamilton, Benny R.	TWA
1969	1	12/11/69	1 man, anonymous	(F) South Korean

Type of Aircraft	Flight Plan	Disposition
IL-18	Warsaw/East Berlin	Landed in West Berlin, French sector. Sentenced by French military tribunal to 2 yrs. 11/20/69.
B-720	Mexico City/Miami	Landed in Cuba; committed suicide in Cuba 9/28/70.
Beechcraft	Buenaventura/Bogota, Colombia	Landed in Cuba.
B-707	Los Angeles/San Francisco	Landed in Rome. Sentenced to 7½ yrs. 11/11/70; reduced to 3½ yrs. amnesty; released 5/1/71. Fugitive from U.S. charges.
BAC-111	Managua, Nicaragua/ San Salvador, El Salvador	Deplaned all but crew at Grand Cayman Island, Bahama Islands.
B-707	Buenos Aires/Santiago	1 man and his pregnant wife allowed to deplane during refueling at Santiago. Tried to overpower guards.
BAC-111	Cordoba/Buenos Aires	Talked into surrendering at refueling stop in Montevideo; sentenced 1-2 yrs.
DC-9	Cincinnati/Chicago	Used girl as hostage in boarding area; declared mentally incompetent 10/15/69. Juvenile detention. Released 4/6/71.
Caravelle	Santiago/Puerto Montt, Chile	Overpowered by crew. After changing to another plane at Antofagasta, Chile, and again taking off for Cuba, passengers released at Antofagasta.
YS-11	Manaus/Belem, Brazil	Landed in Cuba.
DC-4	Cucuta/Bogota, Colombia	Pregnant woman and 1 other person allowed to deplane during refueling at Barranquilla. Landed in Cuba.
	Merida/Cozumel, Mexico	Landed in Cuba.
AN-24	Wroclaw, Poland/ Bratislava, Czecho- slovakia	Landed in Austria. Sentenced to 27 mos. and 2 yrs., respectively, 3/12/70.
B-707	London/Rio de Janeiro	Landed in Cuba.
B-707	San Francisco/ Philadelphia	Fugitive.
YS-11	Kangnung/Seoul, South Korea	Landed in North Korea.

Year	Results	Date	Name	Airline
1969	2	12/12/69	2 men, anonymous	(F) Ethiopian
1969	3	12/19/69	Alarcon, Patricio	(F) LAN (Chilean)
1969	3	12/23/69	1 man, anonymous	(F) LACSA (Costa Rican)
1969	3	12/26/69	1 man, anonymous	United
1970	3	1/1/70	Allen Luz, Yanez; Sommers, Isolde; Magalhaes, Claudio C.; Silva, Luis A.	(F) Cruzeiro do Sol (Brazilian)
1970	2	1/6/70	Funjek, Anton	Delta
1970	2	1/7/70	Venturo Rodriguez, Mariano	(F) Iberia (Spanish)
1970	1	1/8/70	Belon, Christian R.	TWA
1970	4	1/9/70	Medrano Caballero, Jorge T.	(F) Rapsa (Panamanian)
1970	3	1/24/70	2 men, 2 women, anonymous	(F) ALM (Netherlands Antilles Airlines)
1970	4	2/6/70	Venezuela Bravo, Pedro L.; Vasquez, Omar M.	(F) LAN (Chilean)
1970	3	2/16/70	Lopez del Abad, Daniel	Eastern
1970	2	3/10/70	1 man, 1 woman (wife), anonymous	(F) Interflug (East German)
1970	3	3/11/70	Stubbs, Clemmie, and wife, 4 daughters	United
1970	3	3/11/70	4 men, anonymous	(F) Avianca (Colombian)
1970	3	3/12/70	De Souza, Romulo D.	(F) Varig (Brazilian)

Type of Aircraft	Flight Plan	Disposition
B-707	Madrid, Spain/Addis Ababa, Ethiopia	Hijackers slain by security guards aboard aircraft.
B-727	Santiago/Arica, Chile	Landed in Cuba.
C-46	Puerto Limon/San Jose, Costa Rico	Released 30 passengers at San Andreas.
B-727	New York/Chicago	Fugitive.
Caravelle	Montevideo, Uruguay/ Rio de Janeiro	Stopped in Peru and Panama. Landed at Havana 1/4/70, 46 hrs. after hijacking started.
DC-9	Orlando/Atlanta	Overpowered on ground, wanted Switzerland, pleaded guilty 7/7/70; sentenced to 25 yrs., 7/31/70.
Convair Twin Engine	Madrid/Zaragoza, Spain	Wanted Albania; surrendered in Zaragoza, Spain. Sentenced to 6 yrs., 1 day, $240 fine, 7/9/70.
B-707	Paris/Rome	Landed in Beirut; surrendered. Sentenced to 9 mos. 10/30/70; released 11/18/70; deported to France. Sentenced to 8 mos. 2/1/71; released 9/18/71. Fugitive from U.S. charges.
C-47	David City/Bocas del Toro, Panama	Shot and killed by militiaman when plane returned to refuel at David City.
Fokker F-27	Santo Domingo, Dominican Republic/ Curacao, Netherlands Antilles	Landed in Cuba.
Caravelle	Puerto Montt/Santiago, Chile	1 hijacker killed, 1 wounded; stewardess wounded by detectives disguised as crew. 2 detectives and uniformed policeman also wounded.
B-727	Newark/Miami	Fugitive.
	East Berlin/Leipzig	Couple reportedly committed suicide when attempt failed.
B-727	Cleveland/West Palm Beach	Shot and killed while attempting to escape from prison in Cuba 3/26/73. Family returned to U.S. 5/30/74.
B-727	Bogota/Barranquilla, Colombia	Landed in Cuba.
B-707	Santiago/London	Landed in Cuba.

Year	Results	Date	Name	Airline
1970	6	3/17/70	Divivo, John J.	Eastern
1970	3	3/24/70	Ortiz, Atilio; Herrera, Maria A.	(F) Aerolineas Argentinas
1970	3	3/25/70	Won, Tyrone; Lee, Edna	(F) Charter (G/A) (British Honduras)
1970	1	3/31/70	Tamiya, T.; Mariaki, W.; Shiro, A.; Yasumiro, S.; Takahiro, K.; Kimihiro, A.; Takeshi, O.; Yoshizo, T.; Kintaro, Y.	(F) Japan Airlines
1970	2	4/6/70	Little, L.L.	TWA
1970	2	4/16/70	1 man, anonymous	Czechslovak Airline
1970	2	4/18/70	Lindon, M.R.	LACSA
1970	3	4/22/70	Meeks, Ira D.; McKinney, Dianne V.	Charter (G/A)
1970	6	4/23/70	Wagstaff, Joseph	North Central
1970	3	4/25/70	1 man, anonymous	(F) Viacao Aerea do Sao Paulo (Brazilian)
1970	3	4/27/70	1 man, anonymous	Charter (G/A)
1970	3	5/1/70	Jacobs, A.; Wiggins, R.R.	(F) British West Indian Airways (Trinidad and Tobago)
1970	1	5/5/70	Verner, Pavel	(F) Executive Plane (G/A) (Czechoslovakian)
1970	3	5/12/70	De Los, Santos V.; Frias, Enrique; Nina, Miguel A.; Veloz, Arsenio; Taveras, F. Ventura; 2 other men	(F) Dutch Antillean Airlines (ALM)

Type of Aircraft	Flight Plan	Disposition
DC-9	Newark/Boston	Copilot killed; captain and hijacker wounded; landed safely in Boston. Committed suicide in prison 10/31/70.
COMET IV (British)	Cordoba/Tucuman, Argentina	After a 9-hr. repair stop in Lima, Peru, landed in Cuba 3/25/70.
Cessna 180	Domestic, British Honduras	Refueled in Mexico. Landed in Cuba. Won committed suicide.
B-727	Tokyo/Fukuoka, Japan	Armed with swords, youths wanted to go to North Korea; tricked into landing in South Korea. After 4½-day wait on ground, passengers exchanged for hostages and flight continued to North Korea, 4/3/70. Crew and hostages returned 4/4/70. Action pending against 5 other participants.
	San Francisco/ Pittsburgh	Charges dismissed. Committed to state mental institution.
	Prague/Karlovy	Overpowered by crew.
	Pto. Limon/San Jose	Surrendered to police.
Cessna 172	Gastonia, N.C. (local)	Hijacked taxi to airport; hired plane, refueled at Rock Hill, S.C., Jacksonville, Fla., and Ft. Lauderdale, Fla. McKinney arrested on 7/10/75, New York; Meeks arrested 7/21/76, New York; charges dismissed 12/6/76, Meeks incompetent to stand trial.
DC-9	Pellston, Mich./Sault St. Marie, Mich.	Hijacked bus to take him to airport; got on plane, where subdued after threatening crew. Committed to state mental institution.
B-737	Brasilia/Manaus, Brazil	Refueled at Guyana and deplaned 36 passengers; 1 male remained voluntarily and went to Cuba with crew and hijacker.
	West Palm Beach	Fugitive.
B-727	Jamaica/Senegal	Wanted to go to Algeria; diverted to Cuba.
	Pribram/Kosice, Czechoslovakia	Junior executive for Czech uranium plant knocked out his boss and stabbed pilot; wanted to go to West Germany for job but diverted to Linz, Austria. Sentenced to 1 yr. 9/2/70.
Fokker F-27	Santo Domingo, Dominican Republic/ Netherlands Antilles	Dutch Revolutionaries.

Year	Results	Date	Name	Airline
1970	2	5/14/70	Perrotis, Theodore N.	(F) Australian
1970	3	5/14/70	1 man, anonymous	(F) Viacao Aerea Do Sol Paulo (Brazilian)
1970	3	5/21/70	Silva Mahecha, D.; Silva Mahecha, A.; Silva Mahecha, M.; Patino Hormaza, J.	(F) Avianca (Colombian)
1970	3	5/24/70	Preskovski, V.L.P.; Mendez, Selva A.; Navarrete, F.; Pineda, L.E.P.	(F) Mexicana de Aviacion (Mexican)
1970	3	5/25/70	Quesada, Graciela, and son	Delta
1970	3	5/25/70	Molina, Nelson	American
1970	1	5/30/70	Stellini, Gianlucca	(F) Alitalia (Italian)
1970	3	5/31/70	Sanchez, Jose Armando; Bueno, Berta; and five children	(F) Avianca (Colombian)
1970	6	6/4/70	Barkley, Arthur G.	TWA
1970	1	6/5/70	Ivanicki, Zbiginew	(F) LOT (Polish)
1970	1	6/8/70	Cihakova, Stanislava; Cihak, Rudolf; Calasek, Jini; Porer, Jaroslav; Klementova, Vera; Galaskova, Eva; Cihakova, S.; Prochazkova, Marie; one child	(F) CSA (Czechoslovakia)
1970	2	6/9/70	Jasinski, Roman; Rybak, Andrzej	(F) LOT (Polish)
1970	2	6/15/70	Kuznetsov, E.; 10 others	Aeroflot

Type of Aircraft	Flight Plan	Disposition
	Sydney/Brisbane, Australia	Girl, 6, accidentally opened emergency exit door on plane as hijacker was threatening pilot with toy gun while plane on ground at Sydney Airport. Passengers escaped. Hijacker surrendered. Sentenced to 5 yrs. 10/30/70.
B-737	Brasilia/Manaus, Brazil	Refueled at Guyana and Curacao. Landed in Cuba.
DC-3	Yopal/Sogamozo en Boyaca, Colombia	Stopped in Barrancabermeja; refueled in Barranquilla. Landed in Cuba.
B-727	Merida/Mexico City, Mexico	Landed in Cuba.
CV-880	Chicago/Miami	Fugitive.
B-727	Chicago/New York	Refueled at JFK Airport in New York and deplaned passengers; fugitive.
DC-9	Genoa/Rome	Landed in Cairo.
AVRO-748	Bogota/Bucaramanga, Colombia	Landed in Cuba.
B-727	Phoenix/Washington, D.C.	Landed at Dulles, demanded $100,000 ransom; departed for upstate New York; returned for more ransom and was captured; armed with pistol, knife, and can of fluid; pilot and hijacker wounded. Acquitted on ground of temporary insanity 11/16/71.
AN-24 (Soviet)	Stettin/Gdansk, Poland	Landed in Copenhagen. Sentenced to 6 yrs. 10/5/70; on appeal, reduced to 3½ yrs. 1/4/71; restored to 6 yrs. by Supreme Court.
IL-14	Karlovy Vary/Prague, Czechoslovakia	Landed in Nuremberg, Germany; asked for political asylum. Tried in Munich. Convicted and sentenced to terms ranging from 2½ yrs. to 8 mos. 9/16/70.
	Katowice/Warsaw, Poland	Foiled by crew.
AN-2	Domestic	Wanted to go to Sweden; convicted of treason; 2 sentenced to death, commuted to 15 yrs.; 9 sentenced to 4-15 yrs.

Year	Results	Date	Name	Airline
1970	1	6/21/70	Mollahzadeh, Ali; Mollah-zadeh, Hassan; Hamidi Asl, Massoud	(F) Iranian National Airline
1970	1	6/22/70	Xhaferi, Haxhi	Pan American
1970	3	6/26/70	Cardenas, Jairo; Carrillo Del Castro, Mauricio E.	(F) Avianca (Colombian)
1970	3	7/1/70	Lopez, George E.	National
1970	4	7/1/70	Palha Freire, Eiraldo; Palha Freire, Fernando; Viera Souza, Colombo; 1 woman	(F) Cruzeiro do Sol (Brazilian)
1970	3	7/4/70	Afraytes, Carlos A.	(F) Cruzeiro do Sol (Brazilian)
1970	1	7/12/70	Al Harbi, Fahad Bakheet Salem	(F) Saudi Arabian
1970	2	7/22/70	Hardin, George (S)	(F) Air Vietnam (South Vietnamese)
1970	1	7/22/70	Abdel Megid, Farid; Abdel Megid Mona; Fakhi, Yusef; Abul Abd, Khaled; Abul Walid, Khaled; Seif Ed Din, Mansur	(F) Olympic (Greek)
1970	2	7/25/70	De Campos, L.; Da Silva, A.	(F) Etapa Air Taxi (G/A) (Portuguese)
1970	3	7/25/70	4 men, anonymous	(F) Aeronaves de Mexico
1970	4	7/28/70	Jurado Albornoz, Lorenzo E.	(F) Aerolineas Argentinas
1970	3	8/2/70	Rivera Rios, Rudolfo	Pan American
1970	2	8/3/70	Huber, Johann	Pan American

Type of Aircraft	Flight Plan	Disposition
B-727	Teheran/Abadan, Iran	Landed in Baghdad; received political asylum.
B-707	Beirut/Rome	Landed in Cairo. Arrested in Los Angeles 2/15/73. Sentenced to 15 yrs. 6/8/73.
B-727	Cucuta/Bogota, Colombia	Landed in Cuba.
DC-8	San Francisco/Miami	Hijacked by armed man after stop in New Orleans; 4 servicemen passengers roughed up at Jose Marti Airport, Havana. Fugitive.
Caravelle	Rio de Janeiro/Sao Paulo, Brazil	Captured by Brazilian authorities; hijackers hoped to exchange passengers for jailed terrorists. Sentenced 12-24 yrs. and loss of political rights for 10 yrs. 12/1/70.
	Belem/Macapa, Brazil	At Cayenne, French Guiana, allowed 40 to 56 passengers to leave plane. At Georgetown, Guyana, the remaining 16 were allowed to deplane.
B-707	Riyadh, Saudi Arabia/Beirut	Landed in Damascus, Syria.
DC-4	Pleiku/Saigon, South Vietnam	Held pilot at knifepoint for 2 hrs. before surrendering at Tan San Nhut Airport. Escaped 8/11/70; recaptured.
B-727	Beirut/Athens	Released passengers after Greek government promise to release 7 Arab terrorists; flew plane to Cairo.
	Porto Amelia, Mozambique/Island of Ibo	Attempted hijacking to Tanzania. Landed in Ibo. Hijackers captured 3/2/72; sentenced to 14 yrs.
DC-9	Acapulco/Mexico City	Made 30-min. refueling stop in Mexico City; no one deplaned.
B-737	Salta/Buenos Aires, Argentina	Hijacker pulled 2 pistols; plane refueled at Cordoba where 23 of 48 passengers deplaned. Refueled again at Mendozo. Andes snowstorm forced plane back to Cordoba, where hijacker surrendered to police. Sentenced to 6 yrs. 5/17/71.
B-747	New York/San Juan	Displayed "gun" and bottle of fluid; took hostage as he and stewardess remained outside cockpit door; fugitive.
B-727	Munich/West Berlin	Threatened crew with gun; wanted to go to Budapest. No charges. Committed to mental institution. Released 11/13/70.

Year	Results	Date	Name	Airline
1970	1	8/7/70	Frej, Waldemar	(F) Polish
1970	1	8/8/70	Rehak, Valdimir; Rehak, Jaromir; Rehak, Valdimar (son)	(F) Czechoslovakian
1970	3	8/19/70	Arrue-Martinez, Jose; Ramos-Cobas, Jesus; Torres-Llurdan, Brilan	Trans Caribbean
1970	4	8/19/70	Inagaki, Sachio	(F) All Nippon (Japanese)
1970	1	8/19/70	Krynski Krbvstov; 2 men and 2 women	(F) LOT (Polish)
1970	3	8/20/70	Graves, Gregory (S)	Delta
1970	3	8/24/70	Labadie, Robert (S)	TWA
1970	2	8/26/70	Olma, Rudolph; Olma, Leon; Kanikula, Maria	(F) LOT (Polish)
1970	1	8/31/70	Boultif, Rabah; Layachi, Allova; Tovanti, Muhamed	(F) Air Algeria
1970	1	9/6/70	2 men, anonymous	TWA
1970	1	9/6/70	2 men, anonymous	(F) Swissair
1970	1	9/6/70	Ali, Sa'id Ali; Ibrahim, Samir Abdel Majid; Khalil, Mazin Abu Mehanid	Pan American

Type of Aircraft	Flight Plan	Disposition
	Szcregin/Katowice, Poland	Hijacker with grenade denied entry into cockpit; landed in East Berlin; wanted to go to Hamburg. Extradited to Poland. Sentenced to 8 yrs. for aircraft hijacking, 5 yrs. for rape and blackmail 9/19/70.
IL-14	Prague/Bratislava, Czechoslovakia	Landed in Vienna, Austria; arrested on charge of misuse of arms.
DC-8	Newark/San Juan	Fugitives.
B-727	Nagoya/Sapporo, Japan	Ordered plane to land at Hamamatsu Kita Air Defense Base, demanded rifle ammunition in possible suicide plot. Overpowered by police. Sentenced to 7 yrs.
IL-14	Gdansk/Warsaw, Poland	One hijacker had hand grenade landed at Danish Island of Bornholm; asked for asylum. Sentenced to 3½ yrs.; charges dropped for other four.
DC-9	Atlanta/Savannah	Arrested in San Juan 6/1/75. Sentenced to 20 yrs. 10/25/75.
B-727	Las Vegas/Philadelphia	Deported to U.S. by Cuba 9/24/70. Unfit to stand trial 12/2/70; committed to state mental institution 2/28/72; released 10/30/73.
AN-24	Katowice/Warsaw, Poland	Threatened crew with bomb, which accidentally exploded, injuring hijacker and 10 passengers; wanted to go to Vienna; plane landed safely at Katowice. Sentenced to 25 yrs. 4/8/71; others sentenced to 2 and 4 yrs.
CV-640	Annaba/Algiers, Algeria	Wanted Albania; landing refused. Landed in Yugoslavia. Extradition denied. Given suspended sentences. Expelled to Algeria, sentenced to 6-12 yrs.
B-707	Frankfurt, Germany/ New York	Palestinian guerrillas hijacked plane after boarding at Frankfurt; taken to Dawsons Field, Jordan; plane blown up, 9/12/70. Fugitives.
DC-8	Zurich/New York	Palestinian guerrillas hijacked plane near Paris; taken to Dawson's Field; Jordan; plane blown up 9/12/70. Boarded at Zurich.
B-747	Amsterdam/New York	2 original hijackers joined by 7 others in Beirut during refueling; plane blown up in Cairo 9/7/70. Boarded at Amsterdam.

Year	Results	Date	Name	Airline
1970	2	9/6/70	Khaled, Leila; Arguello, Patrick	(F) El Al (Israeli)
1970	1	9/9/70	Haddad, M.J.; Ahmed, A.M.S.; Hassan, H.M.	(F) BOAC (United Kingdom)
1970	2	9/10/70	3 Arabs	(F) Egyptian
1970	2	9/10/70	McMahon, Thomas	(F) Aer Lingus (Irish)
1970	2	9/12/70	1 man, anonymous	(F) Egyptian
1970	1	9/14/70	Mamuzsits, Janos; Karaczony, Geza; Biro, Miklos; Biro, Piroschka; 2 children	(F) TAROM (Romanian)
1970	2	9/15/70	Irwin, Donald B.	TWA
1970	2	9/16/70	El Nasr, Sayed Seif	(F) Egyptian
1970	1	9/18/70	Keesee, Robert	(F) Bira Air Transport (G/A) (Thailand)
1970	3	9/19/70	Witt, Richard Duwayne	Allegheny
1970	4	9/22/70	Donovan, David Walter (P)	Eastern
1970	1	10/10/70	Bahrani, Hassan; Reza, Ali; Mahoudi, Mohammed	(F) Iran National Airlines
1970	1	10/15/70	Brazinskas, Pranas; Brazinskas, Algirdas (J)	(F) Aeroflot (USSR)

Type of Aircraft	Flight Plan	Disposition
B-707	Tel Aviv/New York	Armed El Al steward shot and killed male hijacker; female was overpowered by passengers. Plane landed in London. Khaled helped hijack TWA plane to Syria, 8/28/69. Boarded at Amsterdam. Released in deal for hostages on U.K. plane at Dawson's Field.
VC-10	Bombay/London	Palestinian guerrillas forced plane to refuel in Beirut before going to Dawson's Field; plane blown up 9/12/70. Boarded at Bahrain.
	Beirut/Cairo	Apprehended by security officers aboard aircraft shortly after hijacking attempt was initiated.
	Shannon/New York	Overpowered by crew.
	Tripoli, Libya/Cairo	Apprehended by security officers aboard aircraft while airborne shortly after hijacking attempt was initiated.
	Bucharest/Prague	Landed in Munich. P. Biro found innocent. Other 3 hijackers sentenced to 2½ yrs. 1/20/71. Extradition to Hungary/Romania denied.
B-707	Los Angeles/San Francisco	Wanted to go to North Korea. Sentenced to 12½ yrs. on state charge 11/23/71.
AN-24	Luxor/Cairo, Egypt	Disarmed by security officer aboard aircraft. Sentenced to 10 yrs.
Cessna 182	Domestic Northern Thailand	Landed in N. Vietnam. Released to U.S. authorities with a group of U.S. POWS 3/14/73.
B-727	Pittsburgh/Philadelphia	Fugitive.
DC-8	Boston/San Juan	Landed in San Juan. Federal charges dropped in favor of unrelated state robbery and murder charges. Sentenced to 6 yrs. for robbery and life for murder.
B-727	Tehran/Abadan, Iran	Diverted to Baghdad, Iraq; hijackers in custody. One steward wounded.
AN-24	Batumi/Sukhumi, USSR	Landed in Trebizond, Turkey; 2 pilots wounded, stewardess killed. Extradition denied. Released as political offenders 10/17/70; reversed by Supreme Court, 3/9/71; criminal proceedings terminated by general amnesty May 1974; asylum denied by U.S. 6/27/76; entered U.S. illegally Aug. 1976; deportation proceedings in progress as of July 31, 1977.

Year	Results	Date	Name	Airline
1970	3	10/21/70	5 men, 2 women, anonymous	(F) Lacsa (Costa Rican)
1970	1	10/27/70	Gilev, Nikolai F.; Pozdeyev, Vitali M.	(F) Air Taxi (G/A) Aeroflot (USSR)
1970	3	10/30/70	1 man, wife, and 5 children, anonymous	National
1970	3	11/1/70	Larrazolo, Felipe; 2 children	United
1970	1	11/9/70	3 men and 6 criminals, anonymous	(F) Air Taxi (G/A) (Iranian)
1970	2	11/9/70	Simokaitis, Vitavtas; Simokaitis, Grazina	(F) Aeroflot (USSR)
1970	1	11/10/70	1 man, anonymous	(F) Saudi Arabian Airlines
1970	3	11/13/70	1 man, anonymous	Eastern
1970	6	12/10/70	1 man, anonymous	Aero Taxi (G/A) (Czechoslovakian)
1970	4	12/19/70	Denis, Carlos	Continental
1970	2	12/21/70	Lopez Morales, V.	Prinair (G/A)
1971	3	1/3/71	Wilson, Arthur J.; Graves, Lolita K.; White, Carl and Norma; and 4 children	National
1971	3	1/22/71	Grant, G.J.	Northwest
1971	1	1/22/71	Sebhatu Selassie; Yohanneso, Michael	(F) Ethiopian Airlines
1971	2	1/23/71	Kim Sang-tae	(F) South Korean
1971	4	1/26/71	Jimenez Cano, Enrique	(F) Quisqueyana Airways (Dominican Republican)

Type of Aircraft	Flight Plan	Disposition
C-46	Limon/San Jose, Costa Rica	Transferred to second plane at San Andres. Landed in Cuba.
Morave IL-14	Kerchi/Sevastopol, USSR	Landed at Sinop, Turkey. Deported to USSR 12/20/71. Pozdeyev sentenced to 13 yrs.; Gilev sentenced to 10 yrs. 9/16/72.
DC-8	Miami/Tampa	Landed in Cuba. Fugitive.
B-727	San Diego/Los Angeles	Landed in Tijuana to refuel; proceeded to Cuba. Fugitive.
DC-3	Dubai, Trucial State/ Banda/Abbas, Iran	Refueled at Doha, Qatar; landed in Baghdad, Iraq.
	Vilna/Palanga, Lithuania	Averted. V. Simokaitis sentenced to death, commuted to 15 yrs. in labor camp. G. Simokaitis sentenced to 3 yrs. in a labor camp.
DC-3	Amman, Jordan/ Riyadh, Saudi Arabia	Landed in Damascus.
DC-9	Raleigh, N.C./Atlanta	Refueled at Jacksonville. Landed in Cuba. Fugitive.
Morave	Bratislava/Brno, Czechoslovakia	Hijacker overpowered by passengers while aircraft was in the air. Landed in Brno. One passenger wounded.
DC-9	Albuquerque/Tulsa	Sentenced to 5 yrs. 2/9/71.
Heron	San Juan/Ponce, Puerto Rico	Returned to San Juan where hijacker over- powered by crew. Charges dismissed. Com- mitted to mental institution. Released 11/29/73.
DC-8	Los Angeles/Tampa	C. White, N. White, and four children apprehended on 5/24/75 in San Juan. Charges against N. White dismissed. C. White sentenced to 20 yrs. Wilson and Graves arrested 11/18/75 in Chicago. Wilson and Graves sentenced to 20 and 5 yrs.
B-727	Milwaukee/Detroit	Fugitive.
DC-3	Bahar Dar/Gondar, Ethiopia	Landed in Benghazi, Libya.
F-27	Kangnung/Seoul, South Korea	Crash-landed Korean Coast where hijacker and copilot killed.
L-1049	Santo Domingo, Dominican Republic/ San Juan, Puerto Rico	Landed in Cabo Rojo, D.R., where hijacker was overpowered by the crew after Haiti refused landing.

Year	Results	Date	Name	Airline
1971	1	1/30/71	Qureshi, Ashraf; Hashim, Mohammad	(F) India Airlines
1971	3	2/4/71	Hines, Walter C.	Delta
1971	1	2/25/71	Paterson, Chapin (S)	Western
1971	2	3/8/71	Marston, Thomas K. (J)	National
1971	1	3/30/71	Lotibana, Daniel; Chua, Fructuoso; Mausisa, Edgardo; Baskinas, Domingo; Rosauro, Glen; Tigulo, Edgardo	(F) Philippines
1971	3	3/31/71	Ramirez, Diego	Eastern
1971	4	3/31/71	Matthews, John M. (J)	Delta
1971	3	4/5/71	Hernandez-Tranhs, Carlos L.	American Air Taxi (G/A)
1971	2	4/13/71	Howdle, Jeffrey (J); Lamirande, Leslie (J); Rusk, Gary (J)	(F) Transair Midwest (Canadian)
1971	2	4/21/71	Anile, Francisco	Eastern
1971	4	4/25/71	Rivadeneira	(F) Avianca (Colombian)
1971	4	4/29/71	Vega	(F) Avianca (Colombian)
1971	1	5/8/71	Moreno, Jose R.	(F) Avianca (Colombian)
1971	2	5/13/71	Yong Ki Chung	(F) All Nippon Airways (Japanese)
1971	2	5/17/71	Pennington	(F) Scandinavian Airlines System (Swedish)
1971	1	5/27/71	Miheller, Sandor; Moka, Adalbert; Papp, Janos; Papp, Joszef; Vamos, Robert; Veizer, Janos	(F) Tarom (Romanian)

Type of Aircraft	Flight Plan	Disposition
F-27	Srinagar/Jammu Kashmir, India	Landed in Lahore, Pakistan. Passengers and crew released 2/1/71. Aircraft destroyed by fire and explosion on 2/2/71 caused by hijackers. Both hijackers injured slightly.
DC-9	Chicago/Nashville	Apprehended on 9/27/75. Convicted on 4/23/76 on charges of air piracy.
B-737	San Francisco/Seattle	Landed in Vancouver, B.C. Deported to U.S. 3/8/71. Sentenced to 10 yrs. 6/11/71.
B-727	Mobile/New Orleans	Landed in Miami. Correctional custody, 3/10/71; indefinite term, Youth Corrections Act, 11/3/71
BAC-111	Manila/Davao City, Philippines	Refueled in Hong Kong where 20 of 44 passengers deplaned. Landed Canton, China. Aircraft, crew, and passengers returned to Miami. Hijackers remained in China.
DC-8	New York/San Juan	Deported to U.S. by Bermuda, 10/8/74.
DC-9	Birmingham, Ala./ Chicago	Sentenced to 3 yrs. probation.
Cessna 402	Key West/Miami	Fugitive.
Navajo	Dauphin/Winnipeg, Canada	Landed at Winnipeg. No charges, as 3 had already been committed to juvenile detention home.
DC-8	Newark/Miami	5 yrs. suspended sentence; 3 yrs. probation 2/15/72.
	Barranquilla/Medillin, Colombia	Hijacker overpowered by passengers and crew.
	Los Angeles/Bogota, Colombia	Landed in Panama. Hijacker arrested.
DC-4	Monteria/Cartegena, Colombia	Landed at Maracaibo, Venezuela. Hijacker detained.
YS-11	Tokyo/Sendai, Japan	Returned to Tokyo. Hijacker surrendered. Prosecution deferred.
DC-9	Malmo/Stockholm, Sweden	Averted on ground, Malmo. Convicted on charges of coercion and attempted gross blackmail 8/6/71. Deported to U.S. 10/14/71.
IL-14	Oradea/Bucharest, Romania	Landed in Vienna. Hijackers taken into custody. Sentenced to terms ranging from 24 to 30 mos. 12/71.

Year	Results	Date	Name	Airline
1971	2, 5	5/28/71	Bennet, James E.	Eastern
1971	3	5/29/71	Garcia Landaeta, Ivan G.	Pan American
1971	2	6/4/71	Riggs, Glen E.	United
1971	1	6/9/71	Rodrigues, Reis, J. (S); Rodrigues De Sousa, R.	(F) Air Taxi (G/A) (Angolan)
1971	2	6/11/71	White, Gregory L.	TWA
1971	2	6/18/71	White, Bobby	Piedmont
1971	4	6/21/71	Aanaya, J.	(F) Avianca (Colombian)
1971	2	6/29/71	1 woman, anonymous	(F) Finnair (Finnish)
1971	1	7/2/71	Jackson, Robert (S); Sanchez Archila, Ligia	Braniff
1971	6	7/11/71	Alvarez Lopez, Nelson; Lopez Rabi, Angel	(F) Cubana
1971	2	7/23/71	Obergfell, Richard	TWA
1971	3	7/24/71	Guerra-Valdez, Santiago M.	National
1971	2	8/16/71	Sarper, A.I.	United
1971	2	8/22/71	Farag, K.M.	(F) Egyptian
1971	2	9/3/71	Borges Guerra, Juan M.	Eastern
1971	1	9/8/71	Gabr, M.	(F) ALIA (Jordanian)

Type of Aircraft	Flight Plan	Disposition
B-727	Miami/New York	Landed in Nassau. Deported to U.S., 5/29/71. Acquitted 12/29/71. Committed to mental institution 12/30/71.
B-707	Buenos Aires/Miami	Hijacked on takeoff from Caracas. Fugitive.
B-737	Charleston, W. Va./ Newark, N.J.	Destination Israel. Landed at Dulles Airport to change aircraft. Taken into custody. Sentenced to two concurrent 20-yr. terms 1/7/72; affirmed 12/14/72.
	Luanda/Cabinda, Angola	Landed in Pointe Noire, Rep. of Congo.
B-727	Chicago/New York	North Vietnam destination. Killed passenger. Incompetent to stand trial. Committed to mental institution 10/7/71.
B-737	None	Attempted hijack ground Winston-Salem. Destination Cuba. Averted. Taken into custody. Sentenced to 5 yrs. 9/14/71.
DC-4	Monteria/Medellin, Colombia	Overpowered and disarmed by crew.
DC-9	Helsinki/Copenhagen	Overpowered by crew.
B-707	Mexico City/San Antonio	Wanted Algeria. Landed at Buenos Aires. Sentenced 5 and 3 yrs., respectively, 12/15/71. Extradition to U.S. denied. Extradition to Mexico 7/25/74. Sentenced to 6 yrs., 10 mos. and 5 yrs., respectively.
	Havana/Cienfuegos, Cuba	1 passenger killed; 3 injured by exploding hand grenade. Hijackers in custody.
B-727	New York/Chicago	Destination Italy. Shot and killed while attempting to change aircraft at New York.
DC-8	Miami/Jacksonville	Landed in Cuba. Hostess and passenger slightly wounded. Fugitive.
B-747	Los Angeles/Honolulu	Overcome by customs security officer.
IL-18	Cairo/Amman, Jordan	Destination Israel. Overpowered by sky marshals. Deported to Jordan.
DC-9	Chicago/Miami	Destination Cuba. Overpowered by deadhead crew and passengers. Hostess and 2 others slightly injured. Sentenced to 20 yrs. 3/16/72.
Caravelle	Beirut/Amman, Jordan	Landed in Benghazi, Libya. Hijacker taken into custody by Libyan police.

Year	Results	Date	Name	Airline
1971	2	9/16/71	Hassan, Hilal Abdel Kader	(F) ALIA (Jordanian)
1971	2	9/24/71	Pliskow, Barbara	American
1971	2	10/4/71	Giffe, George, Jr.; Wallace, Bobby W.	Charter (G/A)
1971	2	10/4/71	Awad, Wafa Abdel R.T.; Zaidan, Tewfik Hussein	(F) ALIA (Jordanian)
1971	1	10/8/71	Matazzi, C.	(F) Argentine
1971	3	10/9/71	Dixon, Richard	Eastern
1971	3	10/12/71	2 men, anonymous	(F) Avensa (Venezuelan)
1971	2	10/16/71	Yannopoulos, Constantine	(F) Olympic Airways (Greek)
1971	1	10/18/71	Thomas, Del L.	Wien Consolidated
1971	3	10/20/71	4 men, 2 women, anonymous	(F) Saeta (Ecuadorian)
1971	3	10/25/71	Lugo Casado, Angel	American
1971	2	10/26/71	Thalassinos	(F) Olympic (Greek)
1971	1	11/3/71	11 men, anonymous	Bolivian
1971	2, 5	11/12/71	Cini, P.J.	(F) Air Canada
1971	4	11/17/71	1 man, anonymous	(F) Arawak (Trinidad and Tobago)
1971	1, 5	11/24/71	1 man ("D.B. Cooper")	Northwest

Type of Aircraft	Flight Plan	Disposition
Caravelle	Beirut/Amman, Jordan	Destination Baghdad. Hijacker armed with hand grenade. Overpowered by sky marshals. Death sentence approved 10/7/71.
B-727	Detroit/New York	Plot to free two Black Panthers and transport them to Algeria. Captured by police. Sentenced to 2 yrs. probation 7/23/74.
Aero Commander Hawk 681	Nashville/Atlanta	Destination Bahamas. Giffe killed pilot, wife, and self when aircraft immobilized by FBI at Jacksonville. Wallace acquitted 6/21/72.
Caravelle	Beirut/Amman, Jordan	Wanted Iraq. Overpowered by security guards during flight.
B-707	Rio de Janeiro/ (destination unknown)	Landed in Mendoza; arrested.
B-727	Detroit/Miami	Returned to U.S. 1/8/76; arrested in Michigan 1/9/76; convicted 12/16/76.
Convair 580	Barcelona/Caracas	Landed in Cuba.
YS-11A	Kalamata/Athens, Greece	Wanted Beirut, claimed to have a bomb. Landed at Athens to refuel. Police boarded, arrested hijacker. Sentenced 1 to 8 yrs., 2 mos. 10/11/72.
B-737	Anchorage/Bethel, Alaska	Wanted Cuba. Landed in Vancouver, where hijacker surrendered. Deported to U.S. 10/19/71. Sentenced to 20 yrs. 5/12/72.
Viscount	Quito/Cuenca, Ecuador	Landed in Cuba.
B-747	New York/San Juan	Fugitive.
DC	Athens/Crete	Wanted Rome. Overpowered.
		11 Bolivian political prisoners hijacked aircraft to Puno, Peru.
DC-8	Calgary/Toronto, Canada	Wanted Ireland. Overpowered by crew. Attempted extortion. Sentenced to life imprisonment 4/12/72.
	Trinidad/Tobago	Wanted Cuba. Hijacker persuaded to surrender at Trinidad.
B-727	Portland/Seattle	Wanted Reno-Mexico. Hijacker parachuted with $200,000 extortion money en route to Reno. Fugitive.

Year	Results	Date	Name	Airline
1971	3	11/27/71	Finney, Michael; Goodwin, Ralph; Hill, Charlie	TWA
1971	2, 5	12/3/71	Kay, Jean	(F) Pakistani
1971	1	12/12/71	Mena Valladares, Leonel M.; Arana Irias, Raoul; Villanueva Valdes, Gustavo J.	(F) Lancia (Nicaraguan)
1971	4	12/16/71	Urdininea, Wilfredo	(F) Lloyd Air Boliviano
1971	6	12/22/71	Porcilio, Urbano M.	(F) Alas Del Caribe Air (Dominican Republican)
1971	2, 5	12/24/71	Holt, Everett	Northwest
1971	3	12/26/71	Critton, Patrick D.	(F) Air Canada
1971	6, 5	12/26/71	Coleman, Donald	American
1972	3	1/7/72	Sims, Allan G.; Robinson, Ida P.; 1 child	Pacific Southwest
1972	2, 5	1/12/72	Hurst, Billy E., Jr.	Braniff
1972	2, 5	1/20/72	La Point, Richard	Airwest
1972	2, 5	1/26/72	St. George, Merlyn	Mohawk
1972	4	1/26/72	McAlroy, Patrick	SFO Helicopter Co. (G/A)
1972	2, 5	1/29/72	Trapnell, Garrett	TWA

Type of Aircraft	Flight Plan	Disposition
B-727	Albuquerque/Chicago	Goodwin drowned in Cuba 3/4/73. Finney and Hill fugitives.
B-707	Paris/Karachi, Pakistan	Hijacker overpowered by police prior to takeoff. Sentenced to 3 yrs. (suspended) Oct. 1973.
Jet BAC-111	San Salvador/Managua, Nicaragua	1 hijacker killed during refueling at San Jose, Costa Rica. Two hijackers deported to Nicaragua. In custody, escaped during Nicaraguan earthquake, 12/23/72. Fugitives.
F-862	Sucre/La Paz, Bolivia	Hijacker killed pilot, wounded 2 other persons, and was killed by police.
Islander BN2A	Santiago/Santo Domingo, Dominican Republic	Landed in Dajabon, Dominican Republic. Hijacker then overpowered by pilot and passengers.
B-707	Minneapolis-St. Paul/ Chicago	Extorted $300,000. Crew and passengers deplaned. Hijacker surrendered. Committed to mental institution 6/21/72. Charges dismissed on 5/2/75 due to mental incompetence. Remanded to custody of state.
DC-9	Thunder Bay/Toronto, Canada	Landed in Cuba.
B-707	Chicago/San Francisco	Hijacker overpowered. Planned $200,000 extortion. Sentenced to two 10-yr. terms (concurrent) 7/28/73. Released on 5 yrs. probation 9/16/74.
B-727	San Francisco/Los Angeles	Wanted Africa. Landed in Cuba. Fugitives.
B-727	Houston/Dallas	Attempted $1 million extortion. Crew and passengers deplaned. Hijacker surrendered. Sentenced to 20 yrs. 2/2/73.
DC-9	Las Vegas/Reno	$50,000 extortion. Parachuted in vicinity of Denver. Captured. Sentenced to 40 yrs. 5/12/72.
FH-227	Albany/New York	$200,000 extortion. Killed by FBI.
Helicopter Jet	Berkeley/San Francisco	Surrendered prior to being provided an aircraft. Committed to mental institution by state 9/15/72.
B-707	Los Angeles/New York	Shot and captured by FBI. Attempted extortion of $300,000 and release of prisoners. Sentenced to life imprisonment and concurrent terms of 20 yrs. and 10 yrs. 7/20/73.

Year	Results	Date	Name	Airline
1972	2	2/19/72	Mustafi, Salah Mahdi	(F) Jordanian
1972	1, 5	2/22/72	Al Khatib, Yusef; Mohamed, Kasim Ben S.; Almaki, Abdel R.; Aljram, Sudan M.; 1 other man	(F) Lufthansa (West Germany)
1972	3	3/7/72	Brewton, James W.; Bennett, Joseph T.	Chalk's Flying Ser. (G/A)
1972	2	3/7/72	McKee, Edmond (J)	National
1972	1	3/11/72	Lazzeri, Attilia	(F) Alitalia (Italian)
1972	3	3/19/72	Jennings, John; Reed, Janyce	Tortugas Airways (G/A)
1972	3	3/21/72	Schwandner, Allan Charles; Pera, Steven	(F) Air Taxi (G/A) (Jamaican)
1972	2, 5	4/5/72	Harjanto, H.	(F) Merpati Nusuntara (Indonesian)
1972	2, 5	4/7/72	McCoy, Richard F.	United
1972	3	4/7/72	Lugo, Rodriguez, J.L.	Prinair
1972	4	4/8/72	Bustamente, J.; Vallejos, Juan A.	(F) Faucett (Peru)
1972	2, 5	4/9/72	Speck, Stanley H.	Pacific Southwest
1972	2	4/13/72	Chavez-Ortiz, Ricardo	Frontier
1972	6	4/16/72	Ojeda Perez, Uriel	Prinair (G/A)
1972	2	4/17/72	Smith, Kenneth	Alaska
1972	2	4/17/72	Greene, William H. III	Delta

Type of Aircraft	Flight Plan	Disposition
Caravelle	Cairo/Amman, Jordan	Ordered flight to Tripoli, Libya. Overpowered by Jordanian security guards.
B-747	New Delhi/Athens	Landed in Aden, South Yemen. $5 million ransom paid. Hijackers taken into custody by South Yemeni authorities; released 2/27/72.
Grumman 73	Miami/Bahamas	3 wounded. Brewton killed in Jamaica 12/15/75. Bennett is fugitive.
B-727	Tampa/Melbourne, Florida	Charges dismissed 7/25/73. Placed under state supervision. No charges brought by state.
Caravelle Twin Engine	Rome/Milan	Landed in Munich. Sentenced to 2½ yrs. 5/7/73.
Cessna 206	Key West/Tortugas Island	Landed in Cuba. Fugitives.
Cessna 182	Kingston, Jamaica (local)	Arrested in Cuba. Fugitives from U.S. charges.
Vicker Viscount	Surabaya/Jakarta, Indonesia	Extortion attempt−20 million rupiahs and a parachute. Landed in Jogjakarta. Hijacker killed by pilot.
B-727	Denver/Los Angeles	Extortion attempt $500,000. Arrested 4/10/72 following parachute jump near Provo, Utah. Sentenced to 45 yrs. 7/10/72. Escaped 8/10/74, killed in shoot-out while resisting capture 11/10/74.
	San Juan/ (destination unknown)	Abduction to Cuba, extorted $290,000. Fugitive.
B-727	Piura/Chiclayo, Peru	Overpowered and disarmed by crew.
B-727	Oakland/San Diego	Extortion attempt $500,000. Hijacker captured at San Diego. Committed to mental institution 12/19/72. Discharged 6/14/73.
B-737	Albuquerque/Phoenix	Sentenced to life imprisonment 7/24/72. Sentence reduced to 20 yrs. 11/29/72.
DH-114	Ponce/San Juan, P.R.	Captured at boarding ramp. Sentenced to 2 yrs. 8/18/72. Released 1/10/74.
B-727	Seattle/Annette Island, Alaska	Captured. Released from mental institution 7/10/73.
CV-880	West Palm Beach/ Chicago	Extortion attempt $500,000. Surrendered at Chicago. Sentenced to 20 yrs. 9/25/72.

Year	Results	Date	Name	Airline
1972	1	4/18/72	Dolezel, K.; Lerch, A.	(F) Czechoslovakian
1972	2	4/17/72	Maimone, M.V.	(F) Swissair
1972	1, 5	5/3/72	Aidan, Iashar M.; Akcha, Ainoulla A.; Shemshek, Seffer A.; Youlmaz, Mehmed H.	(F) Turkish
1972	1, 5	5/5/72	Hahneman, F.W.	Eastern
1972	3	5/5/72	Hansen, Michael	Western
1972	2, 5	5/8/72	Tannous, Rima I.; Halaseh, Therese I.; 2 males (Arab guerrillas)	(F) Sabena (Belgian)
1972	2, 5	5/23/72	Baguero Cornejo, J.V.	(F) Ecuadorian
1972	1, 5	5/24/72	Kamil, F.H.A.; Yaghi, A.J.	(F) South African
1972	2, 5	5/28/72	Savakis, E.	(F) Olympic (Greek)
1972	2, 5	5/30/72	Silva, G.D.J.	(F) Varig (Brazilian)
1972	1, 5	6/2/72	Holder, William; Kerkow, Katherine	Western

Type of Aircraft	Flight Plan	Disposition
L-140	Prague/Marienbad, Czechoslovakia	Landed in Nuremberg, Germany. Pilot wounded. Extradition denied 6/14/72. Sentenced to 7 yrs. 7/31/72. Political asylum denied April 1973.
DC-9	Geneva/Rome	Captured at Rome. Sentenced to 27 mos. 3/8/72. Released on provisional liberty on 3-million lire bond 3/14/73.
DC-9	Ankara/Istanbul, Turkey	Objective: Free 3 imprisoned members of Turkish Liberation Army. Surrendered at Sofia 5/4/72. Sentenced to 3 yrs. 11/3/72.
B-727	Allentown, Pa./ Washington, D.C.	$303,000 extortion. Parachute jump into Honduras 5/6/72. Surrendered in Honduras 6/2/72. Returned voluntarily. Sentenced to life imprisonment 9/29/72. Ransom recovered May 1973.
B-737	Salt Lake City/Los Angeles	Returned to New York from Cuba via Barbados 6/14/75. Sentenced to 10 yrs. 12/24/75.
B-707	Brussels/Tel Aviv	Objective to free imprisoned Palestinian guerrillas. 2 male hijackers killed and 2 females wounded by Israel authorities 5/9/72. 1 passenger killed. 2 females sentenced to life 8/14/72.
Electra Turbo-prop	Quito/Guayaquil, Ecuador	Hijacker killed at Quito. Had demanded $39,000 and 2 parachutes.
B-727	Salisbury, Rhodesia/ Johannesburg, South Africa	Aircraft flown to Blantyre, Malawi. All passengers and crew escaped 5/25/72. Police overpowered hijackers 5/26/72. Sentenced 9/18/72 to 11 yrs. Released by Malawi and deported to Zambia 5/21/74.
B-707	Iraklion, Crete/ Athens	Objective: Ticket to London for medical treatment and then to Athens for money. Police rushed aircraft and seized hijacker. Sentenced to 2 yrs. 2/10/73.
Electra L-188	Sao Paulo/Porto Alegre, Brazil	$250,000 plus 3 parachutes as extortion attempt. Troops rushed plane. Hijacker killed himself with pistol.
B-727	Los Angeles/Seattle	$500,000 extortion. Aircraft landed in San Francisco. Ransom delivered. Changed to B-720. Aircraft flew to Algiers with stop at New York. Hijackers under Algerian control. Ransom returned 6/28/72. Arrested in Paris 1/24/75. Extradition refused by French court 4/14/75. Convicted of using false passports 6/2/75. Sentenced to 3½ mos. and 1000-franc fine and 3 mos. and 800-franc fine, respectively; released immediately.

Year	Results	Date	Name	Airline
1972	2, 5	6/2/72	Heady, Robb D.	United
1972	1	6/8/72	7 men, 3 women, 1 child, anonymous	(F) Czechoslovakian
1972	2, 5	6/23/72	McNally, Martin J.; Petlikowsky, Walter J.	American
1972	2, 5	6/30/72	Carre, Daniel B.	Airwest
1972	2	7/2/72	Nguyen, Thai Binh	Pan American
1972	2	7/5/72	Smith, Charles E.	American
1972	2, 5	7/5/72	Alexiev, Dimitri; Azamanoff, Michael; Peichev, Lubomir	Pacific Southwest
1972	6, 5	7/6/72	Goodell, Francis M. (S)	Pacific Southwest
1972	6, 5	7/10/72	Bachalt, N.	(F) Lufthansa (West German)
1972	2, 5	7/12/72	Green, Michael; Tesfa, Lulseged	National
1972	2, 5	7/12/72	Fisher, Melvin M.	American
1972	2	7/12/72	1 man, anonymous	(F) UTA (French)

Type of Aircraft	Flight Plan	Disposition
B-727	Reno/San Francisco	$200,000 extortion attempt. Captured after parachute jump. Sentenced to 30 yrs. 8/25/72.
L-410	Marianske Lazne (Marienbad)/Prague	Wanted Nuremberg. Killed pilot, injured copilot. Landed small airfield inside West Germany. Extradition denied 6/16/72. Hijacker committed suicide in prison 1/13/73. Other 9 convicted 12/14/73; sentenced to terms ranging from 3-7 yrs.
B-727	St. Louis/Tulsa	$502,000 extortion. Parachuted in vicinity of Peru, Ind. Apprehended 6/28/72. Petlikowsky not on hijacked aircraft. Sentenced to 10 yrs. for aiding and assisting 5/18/73. McNally sentenced to life 12/14/72.
DC-9	Seattle/Portland	$50,000 extortion attempt. Apprehended at Portland. Committed to mental institution 7/5/72.
B-747	Honolulu/Saigon	Hijacker killed at Saigon by passenger.
B-707	None	Hijacker boarded parked empty aircraft at Buffalo, N.Y., demanded to be flown out of the area. Persuaded to surrender. Convicted in state court of custodial interference 6/7/73. Sentenced to 5 yrs. probation 7/18/73.
B-737	Sacramento/San Francisco	$800,000 extortion attempt. Hijackers killed by FBI. 1 passenger killed, 2 wounded. Peichev not on hijacked aircraft; sentenced to life plus 20 yrs. concurrent for aiding, abetting, and conspiring in the acts 12/21/72.
B-727	Oakland/Sacramento	$450,000 extortion attempt. Hijacker surrendered. Convicted of air piracy and use of firearm to commit a felony 1/17/73. Sentenced to 25 yrs. plus 5 yrs. 2/12/73.
B-737	Cologne/Munich	$400,000 extortion attempt. Apprehended aboard aircraft.
B-727	Philadelphia/New York	$600,000 extortion attempt. Surrendered. Green convicted 6/19/73; sentenced to 50 yrs. 3/18/74. Tesfa sentenced to 60 yrs. 12/2/74.
B-727	Oklahoma City/Dallas	$550,000 extortion attempt. Surrendered. Sentenced to life imprisonment 9/28/72.
	Abidjan, Ivory Coast/Paris	Aircraft diverted prior to landing at Abidjan, denying man opportunity to hijack it. Man shot and apprehended after he shot his wife.

Year	Results	Date	Name	Airline
1972	2	7/19/72	Suarez, B.	TAO
1972	1, 5	7/31/72	McNair, Melvin; McNair, Jean; Wright, George; Brown, George; Burgess, Joyce; 3 children	Delta
1972	1	8/15/72	Santucho, M.; 8 other men; 1 woman	(F) Austral (Argentine)
1972	2, 5	8/18/72	Sibley, Frank M.	United
1972	1	8/22/72	2 men, 1 woman, anonymous	(F) Al Yemda (South Yemeni)
1972	3	8/25/72	4 men, anonymous	(F) Opita Air Taxi (TAO) (Colombian)
1972	1, 5	9/15/72	Lisac, Nikila; Rebrina, Tomislav; Preskalo, Rudolf	(F) Scandinavian Airlines System (Swedish)
1972	2, 5	10/6/72	Boccaccio, Ivano	(F) Aerotransporti Italiani (Italian)
1972	2, 5	10/11/72	Schuetz, Friedhelm	(F) Lufthansa (West German)
1972	1, 5	10/22/72	Ataol, H.; Atakli, E.; 2 other men	(F) Turkish
1972	3	10/29/72	Tuller, Charles; Tuller, Bruce (S); Tuller, Jonathan; Graham, William (S)	Eastern

Type of Aircraft	Flight Plan	Disposition
VC	San Andres/Barran-quilla, Colombia	Killed pilot, wounded copilot; overcome by crew.
DC-8	Detroit/Miami	$1 million extortion. Refueled in Boston. Landed in Algiers 8/1/72. Ransom returned 8/23/72. Three children returned to U.S. 12/72. M. McNair, J. McNair, G. Brown, and J. Burgess arrested in Paris 5/28/76. U.S. extradition request denied Nov. 1976.
BAC-111	Trelew/Buenos Aires, Argentina	10 terrorists and convicts who escaped from a prison in S. Argentina hijacked a jetliner at Trelew, refueled at Puerto Montt, Chile, then flew to Santiago. Chile granted political asylum and allowed hijacker to fly to Cuba on a Cuban jetliner.
B-727	Reno/San Francisco	Sought $2 million. Shot and captured by FBI at Seattle. Convicted 10/18/72. Sentenced to 30 yrs. 2/28/73.
DC-6	Beirut/Cairo/Aden, South Yemen	Landed in Benghazi, Libya.
	Neiva/Bogota, Colombia	Refueled in Barrancabermeja, Colombia. Landed in Cuba.
	Goteborg/Stockholm, Sweden	Wanted $105,000 and release of 6 convicts. Landed at Madrid. Extradition to Sweden denied. 3 hijackers sentenced to 12 yrs. 12/4/72; pardoned 2/13/75. 6 went to Paraguay. Extradition requested by Sweden.
F-27	Ronchi Del Legionari/Bari, Italy	$344,000 extortion. Hijacker killed aboard aircraft during gun battle with police at Ronchi. 1 policeman wounded.
B-727	Lisbon/Frankfurt	Demanded several thousand marks and a car at Frankfurt. Claimed to have a bomb. Shot and captured while moving to car.
B-707	Istanbul/Ankara, Turkey	Landed in Sofia, Bulgaria. Threatened to blow up plane unless 13 prisoners freed and reforms by Turkish government. Pilot and 1 passenger wounded. Surrendered late on 10/23/72. Sentenced to 2-2½ yrs. 2/2/73.
B-727	Houston/Atlanta	Killed ticket agent; wounded ramp serviceman. Forced way aboard. Tullers apprehended in U.S. 7/7/75. Tullers convicted of aircraft piracy 6/24/76. Graham fugitive.

Year	Results	Date	Name	Airline
1972	1, 5	10/29/72	El Shahed, Samir Arif; Saleh, Mahmoud	(F) Lufthansa (West German)
1972	4, 5	11/6/72	Nakaoka, Tatsuji	(F) Japan Airlines
1972	1, 5	11/8/72	Segovia, German; Rodriguez Moya, Ricardo; 3 other men	(F) Mexicana De Aviacion
1972	3, 5	11/10/72	Jackson, Henry D.; Cale, Louis D.; Cale, Melvin C.	Southern
1972	2	11/15/72	Hrabinec, Miloslav	(F) Ansett Airlines (Australian)
1972	2, 5	11/24/72	Widera, Victor	(F) Air Canada
1972	2	12/72	Havelka, P.; Havelka, A.; Velek, A.; Drazny, V.; Rovicha, L.	Czech
1972	2	12/8/72	5 men, 2 women, anonymous	(F) Ethiopian Airlines, S.C.

Type of Aircraft	Flight Plan	Disposition
B-727	Beirut/Ankara, Turkey	Demanded release of 3 male Arabs, imprisoned for involvement in slaying of 11 Israelis at Munich Olympics. Landed in Zagreb, Yugoslavia. Prisoners boarded. Flew to Tripoli, Libya.
B-727	Tokyo/Fukuoka, Japan	Demanded $2 million and flight to Cuba or would blow up plane. Returned to Tokyo to get ransom and change to DC-8. Captured by police when entered DC-8. Sentenced to 20 yrs. 3/13/74.
B-727	Monterrey/Mexico City, Mexico	Demanded release of 6 terrorist colleagues being held in prison, 4 million pesos ($320,000), 2 machine guns with ammunition, and a doctor to accompany wounded prisoner. Returned to Monterrey. All demands met. Flew to Cuba. Extradition denied 11/30/72. Ransom and weapons reportedly returned 2/1/73.
DC-9	Birmingham/Montgomery, Ala.	Demanded $10 million, 10 parachutes, food, etc. Landed several places to refuel. Landed Havana 11/11/72. Again left Havana; flew to 2 U.S. airports. Refueled; returned to Havana. Passengers released. Copilot shot and wounded. Sentenced in Cuba; Jackson and L. Cale to 20 yrs., and M. Cale to 15 yrs. 9/27/73. Ransom returned 8/11/75.
F-27	Adelaide/Darwin, Australia	Demanded a light aircraft and a parachute at Alice Springs Airport. Shot by police when in light aircraft. Finally shot and killed himself. 1 policeman wounded.
DC-8	Frankfurt/Montreal	Hijacking initiated on the ground at Frankfurt. Demanded release of a Czech being held by West Germany for hijacking a plane from Prague to Nuremberg. Also demanded release of several other Czechs. Held stewardess hostage. Shot and killed aboard aircraft by police marksmen.
	Domestic	Sentences ranging from 18 mos. to 9 yrs. 1/19/73.
B-720	Addis Ababa/ Asmara, Ethiopia	When one of the hijackers announced the hijacking, security guards opened fire. 6 hijackers killed. Hijackers exploded 1 hand grenade, which tore hole in floor of plane, stopped 1 engine, and injured rudder. 7 passengers and 2 stewardesses wounded. Plane landed safely at Addis Ababa. 1 wounded female hijacker in custody.

65

Year	Results	Date	Name	Airline
1972	2	12/14/72	Stanford, Larry Maxwell	(F) Quebecair (Canadian)
1973	2	1/2/73	Wenige, Charles A.	Piedmont
1973	2, 5	1/4/73	Neilson, C.K.	(F) Pacific Western (Canadian)
1973	4	4/24/73	1 man, anonymous	(F) Aeroflot (USSR)
1973	3, 5	5/18/73	Botini Marin, Federico; 2 other men; 1 woman	(F) Avensa (Venezuelan)
1973	2	5/25/73	1 man, anonymous	(F) Aeroflot (USSR)
1973	1, 5	5/30/73	Lopez Dominguez; Francisco, Solano; Borjas Gonzales, Oscar Eusebio	(F) SAM (Colombian)
1973	1	6/10/73	Bhattari, Basanta; Subedi, Prasad; Dhungel, Nagendra P.	(F) Royal Nepal Airlines
1973	3, 5	7/4/73	Mazor, Basilio J.	(F) Aerolineas Argentinas

Type of Aircraft	Flight Plan	Disposition
BAC-111	Wabush/Montreal, Canada	Hijacker pointed rifle at stewardess. Required pilot to fly to Montreal then shuttle between Montreal and Ottawa. Passengers released. Hijacker surrendered after 10 hrs. Sentenced to 20 yrs. 4/20/73.
YS-11A	Washington, D.C. (DCA)/Baltimore	Hijacking initiated while on the ground at Baltimore. Hijacker surrendered after several hours' negotiations at Baltimore. Sentenced to 20 yrs. 2/16/73.
Convair	Vancouver/Penticton, Canada	$2 million extortion and passage to North Vietnam. Hijacking initiated on ground at Vancouver. Passengers released. Police boarded and arrested hijacker while still at Vancouver.
TU-104	Leningrad/Moscow	Copilot and hijacker killed when device held by hijacker exploded. Aircraft reportedly landed safely at Leningrad.
Convair-580	Valera/Barqui-simeto, Venezuela	Landed in Curacao, Panama, and Mexico. Threatened to blow up plane unless 79 Venezuelan prisoners flown to Cuba. Demand refused. Aircraft, passengers, and crew returned from Cuba 5/20/73.
TU-104	Moscow/Chita, USSR	Aircraft crashed in southern Siberia following gunfight. Number aboard unknown. No survivors.
Electra	Pereira/Medellin, Colombia	Threatened to blow up plane unless $200,000 ransom paid and 140 Colombian prisoners released. Landed several places in South America. Groups of passengers released or escaped at various stops. Hijackers received $50,000 but no prisoners released. Hijackers finally left aircraft 6/2/73 and escaped. Lopez Dominguez captured 6/8/73. Colombian extradition request granted 2/4/75; on appeal.
Twin Otter	Biratnagar/ Kathmandu, Nepal	Landed near Forbesganj, Bihar, India. Hijackers escaped into the jungle with 3 million Indian rupees (approximately $400,000), which were being transported by a Nepal state bank. Some arrests but not of those listed.
B-737	Buenos Aires/ Tucuman, Argentina	Demanded $200,000 in government grants to medical agencies. Government refused. Landed Mendoza, Argentina; Santiago, Chile; Lima, Peru; Panama City, Panama; finally Havana, Cuba. Passengers released at various stops. Extradition requested 7/6/73.

Year	Results	Date	Name	Airline
1973	2	7/11/73	Clark, Daniel (S)	Charter (G/A)
1973	1	7/20/73	Maruoka, Osamu; 4 other men; Thomas, Katie G.	(F) Japan Air Lines
1973	1	8/16/73	A-Touni, Mahmoud	(F) Middle East Airlines (Lebanese)
1973	1	8/25/73	Abu Bakr, Nasser Ahmed	(F) Yemen Air Lines
1973	2	10/2/73	Stremmer, Franz-Josef	(F) Royal Dutch Airlines
1973	2	10/10/73	Garcia Perez, Roberto	(F) Mexicana
1973	1	10/11/73	Riga, Roger; Naval, Armando; Montojo, Basilio	(F) Philippine Air Lines
1973	2	10/18/73	Cravenne, Daniele	(F) Air France
1973	3	10/20/73	Pagola Nicolini, Mario; Sierra Mata, Luis Arturo; Pedroso Silva, Mirtha Susana; Biere Diaz, Lidia Elena	(F) Aerolineas Argentinas
1973	1, 5	10/31/73	2 men, anonymous	Irish Helicopters, Ltd.

Type of Aircraft	Flight Plan	Disposition
Bell 47-G5 Helicopter	Gainesville, Tex./ Marietta, Okla.	Chartered helicopter. After flying over Marietta area, forced pilot at pistol point to fly to Wichita Falls, Tex. Captured in Dallas 7/13/73. Sentenced to 20 yrs. under Federal Youth Corrections Act 2/11/74.
B-747	Paris/Tokyo	Woman hijacker killed and purser wounded in accidental explosion of explosive carried by woman. Landed in Dubai, United Arab Emirates 7/20/73. Aircraft and all passengers and crew except dead woman and wounded purser held. Aircraft refueled and took off at about 7/23/73. Refueled at Damascus. Finally landed at Benghazi, Libya, where all passengers and crew were released and aircraft blown up. 4 male hijackers arrested by Libyan authorities. Hijackers released and flown to Damascus 8/13/74.
B-707	Benghazi, Libya/ Beirut	Landed in Tel Aviv. While hijacker's attention was diverted, Israeli security personnel boarded aircraft and captured him. Committed to mental institution 12/11/73.
DC-6	Taiz, North Yemen/ Asmara, Ethiopia	Landed in Kuwait after refueling at Djibouti. Hijacker surrendered after authorities guaranteed his safety in Kuwait.
DC-9	Dusseldorf, West Germany/Amsterdam	Hijacker disarmed while talking to pilot. Arrested when plane landed at Amsterdam.
B-727	Mexico City/ Monterrey, Mexico	Security officer dressed as a crewman boarded aircraft and captured hijacker before takeoff from Mexico City.
BAC-111	Davao/Bacolod, Philippines	Took airline president hostage in exchange for passengers. Landed in Hong Kong. Hijackers granted amnesty by Philippine government and surrendered.
B-727	Paris/Nice	Landed at Marseilles. 110 passengers and all but 2 crew members released. French police boarded disguised as stewards and shot, wounded, and captured hijacker, who died on way to hospital.
B-737	Buenos Aires/Salta, Argentina	Landed in Yacuiba, Bolivia. Released all but 5 persons and demanded smaller plane to go to Cuba. Bolivia officials refused. Released hostages and surrendered after promise of safe conduct to Cuba 10/22/73.
Alouette	Dublin/Stradbally, Ireland	Released 3 IRA members from prison. Landed at Baldoyle.

Year	Results	Date	Name	Airline
1973	4	10/31/73	Lorenzo, Jose Gabriel	(F) Avensa (Venezuelan)
1973	2, 5	11/2/73	4 persons	(F) Aeroflot (USSR)
1973	1, 5	11/25/73	Darwish, Fawzi; Al-Sanuri, Husayn Ahmad; Zhbgeen, Isnu	(F) Royal Dutch Airlines
1973	2, 5	12/1/73	Buholzer, Daniel	(F) Swissair
1973	1, 5	12/17/73	5 men, anonymous	(F) Lufthansa (West German)
1974	2	1/3/74	Sanchez, Rodobaldo S.	(F) Air Jamaica
1974	3	1/21/74	Tapia Carrion, J.	(F) Aeropesca (Colombian)
1974	1	1/25/74	4 men, anonymous	Irish Helicopters, Ltd.

Type of Aircraft	Flight Plan	Disposition
DC-9	Barquisimeto/Caracas, Venezuela	Threatened stewardess with pistol. When pilot told hijacker he was about to land at Caracas and had little fuel, hijacker shot and seriously wounded himself.
YAK-40	Bryansk/Moscow, USSR	Landed at Moscow. Demanded $1 million and flight to Sweden. After 5 hrs. of negotiations police stormed the aircraft, killed 2 hijackers and captured other 2; 2 persons wounded.
B-747	Beirut/New Delhi	Landed in Dubai after stops in 4 other countries. Demanded release of jailed Arabs in Cyprus and guarantees that Dutch would not assist Israel in war efforts or Soviet Jewish emigration to Israel. Released remaining 11 hostages and surrendered after promise of safe passage to undisclosed country 11/28/73.
DC-8	Zurich/Abidjan	Landed in Geneva. Demanded $50,000 for starvation-threatened Africa, ticket to New York, safe conduct. Released all but 4 crewmembers. Police boarded posing as newsmen requested by hijacker and quickly overpowered him.
B-737	Rome/Munich	Fired weapons in terminal of Rome Airport. Took 6 hostages. Threw incendiary grenades into a Pan Am B-707, 30 passengers killed. Then killed guard and boarded Lufthansa aircraft; only crew aboard. Landed in Athens threw off body of 1 hostage. Demanded release of 2 Arabs being held for 8/73 attack at Athens Airport. Greeks refused. Refueled at Damascus. Flew to Kuwait and surrendered after allegedly receiving safe conduct guarantee. Released as ransom in 11/22/74 hijacking of British Airways VC10. All taken into Tunisian custody 11/25/74.
DC-9	Kingston, Jamaica/ Detroit	Went through shop area, avoided terminal and boarded. When asked for his ticket, threatened to blow up aircraft unless flown to Miami. Claimed to have hand grenade wrapped in handkerchief. Overpowered by security guards before takeoff.
Vicker Viscount	Pasto/Popayan, Colombia	Refueled and 26 passengers released at Cali. 4 passengers released, 2 tires changed, and aircraft refueled at Barranquilla. Landed in Cuba.
	Dublin/Strabane, Ireland	Dropped bombs on Strabane.

Year	Results	Date	Name	Airline
1974	2	2/20/74	Nguyen, Cuu Viet	(F) Air Vietnam/ (South Vietnamese)
1974	6	2/22/74	Byck, Samuel J.	Delta
1974	1	3/3/74	Nuri, Adnan A.; Tanima, Sami H.	(F) British Airways
1974	2, 5	3/12/74	Owaki, Katsuhito (J)	(F) Japan Airlines
1974	2	3/20/74	Al-Azhar, Kasete; Kiflu, Niget	(F) East African Airways (Kenyan)
1974	6	3/30/74	Smith, Ernest J.	National
1974	2	4/9/74	Tobon, Elkin	(F) Cessnica (G/A) (Colombian)
1974	4, 5	5/10/74	Tabares, Carlos A.; Avila Campos Jorge E.; Rodriguez Hernandez, Pedro J.	(F) Avianca (Colombian)

Type of Aircraft	Flight Plan	Disposition
DC-4	DaLat/DaNang, South Vietnam	Landed in Hue, South Vietnam, after pilot convinced hijacker that fuel was needed, engines were malfunctioning, and they would land at Dung Ha (North Vietnamese-controlled area). Hijacker and 2 others killed when hijacker detonated explosives he had been carrying, after realizing they had landed at Hue.
DC-9	Baltimore/Atlanta	Hijacker shot and killed airport policeman. Then boarded aircraft and shot and killed copilot and wounded pilot. Airport policeman from outside aircraft shot through door's glass porthole and hit hijacker twice in the chest. Hijacker then shot and killed himself.
VC-10	Beirut/London	Landed in Amsterdam. Allowed passengers and crew to deplane. Threw inflammable liquids including plane's liquor supply around cabin and set plane on fire. Captured running from plane. Sentenced to 5 yrs. 6/6/74. Released as ransom in 11/22/74 hijacking of British Airways aircraft. All taken into Tunisian custody 11/25/74.
B-747	Tokyo/Naha, Okinawa	Landed at Naha. Demanded $55 million, 200 million yen, 15 parachutes, and mountain climbing gear. Captured by police. Sentenced to juvenile detention.
Fokker F-27	Nairobi/Malindi, Kenya	Landed in Entebbe, Uganda. Hijackers ordered plane to Libya but agreed to stop at Entebbe to refuel. After negotiating, hijackers surrendered to Ugandan authorities.
B-727	None	With 2 hostages and carrying shotgun, hijacker boarded parked out-of-service aircraft at Sarasota, Fla. and demanded to be flown out of the area. Fled after being disarmed by only other person aboard, a maintenance man. Hijacker captured about 4 hrs. later. Sentenced on state charges to 15 yrs. and 10 yrs. (concurrent) 9/16/74.
Beechcraft C-45	Medellin/Turbo, Colombia	Prior to takeoff at Medellin, 17-year-old hijacker pointed knife at pilot and demanded to be flown to Lima, Peru. Cargo handler grabbed hijacker from behind and overpowered him.
B-727	Pereira/Bogota, Colombia	Landed in Bogota, released 26 passengers, then flew to Cali Peria, and back to Bogota. Demanded 8 million pesos (approximately $317,300) and flight to Cuba. Officials refused to pay ransom. Police stormed plane and killed 1 hijacker and captured the other 2. 1 hijacker wounded in leg.

Year	Results	Date	Name	Airline
1974	2, 5	5/23/74	Kamaiko, David F.	Wall Street Helicopter, Inc. (G/A)
1974	2	6/26/74	Rowell, Edwin C.	(P) Air Charter Inc. (G/A)
1974	1	6/27/74	Kirkaldie, Douglas A.; Beck, William Henry C.; Naylor, Stanley D.	Big Horn Airways (G/A)
1974	2, 5	7/15/74	Iwakoshi, Akira	(F) Japan Air Lines
1974	5, 6	7/24/74	Martinez Rusinke, Luis Eduardo	(F) Avianca (Colombian)
1974	2, 5	9/4/74	Collins, Marshall III	Eastern

Type of Aircraft	Flight Plan	Disposition
Bell 206A Jet Ranger Helicopter	New York (local)	Took aircraft refueler hostage, boarded, and required pilot to fly to top of the Pan Am building, New York City. After landing, pilot ran from aircraft and was shot by hijacker. Hostage struggled with hijacker. Police rushed to helicopter and overpowered hijacker. Prosecution decision to be made after 1 yr. psychiatric treatment 12/30/74. Matter nolle prossed 1975.
Piper Comanche	Alexandria/Angola, La.	Prisoner under escort, produced gun while in flight; forced pilot to land at Hammond, La. Hijacker handcuffed deputy sheriff escort and pilot to tree and fled. Captured about 1 hr. later, approximately 1½ mi. from airport. Sentenced by state for aggravated kidnaping to 10 yrs. imprisonment to be served in addition to sentence of 34 yrs. for previous crimes 4/14/75.
Cessna 172	Ashland, Mont./ Sheridan, Wyo.	Hijackers had robbed bank. Used charter as escape vehicle. While in air, pilot agreed to change course to Yellowtail Dam, Mont. When he started to report change of flight plan, microphone was taken from him and guns were pointed at him. After landing at Yellowtail Dam, pilot was bound and left in plane. 2 captured 1 hr. later. Kirkaldie captured 7/6/74 in Janesville, Wis. Naylor and Beck sentenced to 20 yrs. for bank robbery 7/16/74 and 7/23/74, respectively. Reduced to 8 yrs. under Youth Corrections Act 10/21/74 and 10/22/74 respectively. Kirkaldie sentenced to 20 yrs. for bank robbery and interference with flight crewmember 11/11/74.
DC-8	Osaka/Tokyo, Japan	Landed at Tokyo. Hijacker demanded release of a leader of Japanese Red Army and plane to fly the 2 to North Korea. Authorities refused. Flew to Nagoya, Japan. Passengers escaped while hijacker in cockpit. Police boarded and captured hijacker. Sentenced to 10 yrs. 1/31/77.
B-727	Pereira/Medellin, Colombia	Landed in Cali. Demanded $2 million and freedom for several political prisoners. Passengers including hijacker's wife and baby escaped through emergency exit. Police boarded, shot, and fatally wounded hijacker. Hijacker participated in 5/20/69 Avianca hijacking.
DC-9	New York/Boston	Initiated hijacking after landing in Boston. All except pilot released. Hijacker kept arm around pilot's neck, cut him slightly with razor blade. Pressed nail into pilot's arm and hit him with emergency ax. Demanded $10,000 and flight out of area. After more than 3 hrs., hijacker persuaded to surrender. Escaped federal hospital twice 1975; in federal penitentiary.

Year	Results	Date	Name	Airline
1974	2	9/15/74	Tan, Le Duc	(F) Air Vietnam (South Vietnam)
1974	1	9/28/74	4 men, anonymous	(F) Dundalk Aero Club (G/A) (Ireland)
1974	2	10/7/74	1 man, anonymous	(F) Far Eastern Air Transport Corporation (Republic of China)
1974	1	11/6/74	Al Auran, Muhammad S.; Al Zaiban, Yassin; Hiyari, Salem	(F) Royal Jordanian Airlines Corp. (ALIA)
1974	1, 5	11/22/74	4 men, anonymous	(F) British Airways
1974	2	11/23/74	1 man, anonymous	(F) All Nippon Airways (Japanese)
1974	2	11/29/74	Djemal, Naim	(F) CP Air (Canadian)
1974	2	12/1/74	Aslam, Mohammad	(F) Swissair

Type of Aircraft	Flight Plan	Disposition
B-727	DaNang/Saigon, South Vietnam	Hijacker demanded to be flown to Hanoi, North Vietnam. Pilot started to land at Phan Rang, South Vietnam. Hijacker pulled pins on two hand grenades. Explosion caused plane to crash, killing all 70 aboard.
Rallye Club	None	Hijackers entered Aero Club office. 2 held persons in club at gunpoint while other 2 forced pilot to fly them to Jonesborough, N. Ireland, where homemade bomb was thrown from aircraft. Hijackers had 4 bombs and presumably intended to drop them on British targets in N. Ireland. First bomb struck a wing. Caused no damage but hijackers gave up further attempts to bomb. Aircraft landed in Ravensdale, Ireland. Hijackers fled.
Viscount 810	Tainan/Taipei, Taiwan	Hijacker armed with knife and 4 gasoline-filled bottles demanded to be flown to Mainland China. Captured by security guard and cabin attendant.
Caravelle 50	Amman/Aqaba, Jordan	Landed in Benghazi, Libya. When aircraft attempted to land in Beirut, officials closed airport. Passengers and crew released unharmed. Hijacker requested political asylum.
VC-10	Dubai, United Arab Emirates/Calcutta	At Dubai, forced way aboard firing automatic weapons. Wounded 2. Refueled at Tripoli, Libya. Finally landed at Tunis, Tunisia. Demanded release of 13 terrorist prisoners in Egypt and 2 hijacker prisoners in Netherlands. Shot and killed 1 male passenger. 5 prisoners from Egypt and 2 from Netherlands turned over to hijackers. All surrendered to Tunisian officials upon assurance of protection 11/25/74. Turned over to PLO 12/7/74. Reportedly sentenced to 10-15 yrs.
B-727	Tokyo/Sapporo, Japan	Brandished stick resembling dynamite. Overpowered by flight crewmember.
B-737	Winnipeg/Edmonton, Canada	Landed in Saskatoon, Saskatchewan. Held stewardess at knife point. Demanded to be flown to Cyprus. Agreed to landing at Saskatoon for fuel and surrendered to pilot. Sentenced to 7 yrs. for attempted hijacking 2/5/75.
DC-8	Bombay/Karachi, Pakistan	Pointed gun at crew. Demanded flight to Middle East. Landed at Karachi to refuel. Overpowered by crew. Sentenced to 3 yrs. and $200 fine for attempted hijacking 3/10/75.

Results	Date	Name	Airline
3	12/14/74	1 man, anonymous	Tampa Flying Service (G/A)
1974 2	12/25/74	Homolov, Joseph	(F) Air India
1975 2	1/3/75	Landers, Paul	National
1975 2, 5	1/7/75	Madjid, Saed	(F) British Airways
1975 2	1/13/75	Wright, Laughlin	Eastern
1975 2	2/22/75	Siqueira, Joel Jr.	(F) VASP (Brazilian)
1975 1	2/23/75	Al Awadi, Ali Ben Ali	(F) Yemen Airlines

Type of Aircraft	Flight Plan	Disposition
Piper Seneca	Tampa/Naples, Fla.	Chartered aircraft by phone before boarding. While in company operations facility, pointed handgun at pilot and demanded to be flown to Cuba. Fugitive.
B-747	Bombay/Rome	Hijacker entered cockpit brandishing small pocketknife. Claimed to have bombs aboard. Demanded gun and passage to place of his choice. Ordered pilot to go into sharp dive over Rome. Overpowered by flight crew.
B-727	None	Carrying rifle, hijacker climbed over fence at Pensacola, Fla., airport, boarded out-of-service aircraft and told 3 men who were cleaning the aircraft that he was going to hijack the plane. 2 of the men disarmed and overpowered him. Convicted of aircraft piracy 2/20/75. Committed suicide 2/23/75.
BAC-111	Manchester/London, England	Pointed pistol at stewardess, threatened to blow up plane with hand grenade. Landed in London; passengers deplaned. Hijacker demanded £100,000, parachute, and flight to Paris. Money and parachute delivered. Aircraft took off, pretended to go to Paris but landed at Stansted Airport, Essex, England. Hijacker captured while running from plane with hostage. Gun and hand grenade were not real.
B-727	Atlanta/Philadelphia	Pounded on cockpit door; demanded to be flown to San Juan, P.R. Agreed to land at Dulles Airport to refuel. On landing, hijacker locked himself in restroom. Passengers deplaned, then police boarded and apprehended hijacker, who was not armed. Committed to mental institution on 3/28/75.
B-737	Goiania/Brazilia, Brazil	Shortly after takeoff from Goiania, hijacker carried infant to cockpit. At door, put infant down and grabbed stewardess around neck and put gun to her head. Then took copilot's seat and pointed gun at pilot. During 8 hrs. of negotiations, hijacker demanded 10 million cruzeiros ($1.3 million), guns, parachutes, and release of 10 prisoners. 4 police slipped aboard when hijacker allowed women and children to deplane. Hijacker shot and captured; pilot wounded.
DC-3	Hodeida/Sana, Yemen	Armed with pistol, hijacker demanded flight to Abu Dhabi. Landed in Qizan, Saudi Arabia to refuel. Hijacker captured as soon as plane landed, sentenced to death 3/2/75. Commuted to life imprisonment 3/2/75.

Year	Results	Date	Name	Airline
1975	2, 5	2/25/75	Abarca, E.; Malay, C.	(F) Philippine Airlines
1975	1, 5	3/1/75	Naimi, Taha; Al-Qeitan, Faud; Hasan, Ahmad	(F) Iraqi Airways
1975	2	3/2/75	Grosser, Alexander P.	Air New England
1975	1	3/6/75	Gonzales, Ralph; Rodriguez, Edward E.	Sawyer Aviation (G/A)
1975	2	4/9/75	Oshima, Kazuo	(F) Japan Airlines
1975	4	4/25/75	Covey, Francis P.	United

Type of Aircraft	Flight Plan	Disposition
DC-3	Pagadian/Zamboanga, Philippines	Armed with hand grenades, hijacker took rifle from air marshal. Required return to Cebu City, Philippines, where 12 passengers were released; then flew to Manila. Demanded that Philippine president grant 1 of the hijackers a pardon on previous jail sentence. President agreed. After 10 hrs. negotiations, hijackers surrendered. Sentenced to death 12/17/76.
B-737	Mosul/Baghdad, Iraq	Landed in Tehran, Iran. Demanded $5 million and release of 85 Kurdish prisoners jailed in Iraq. Threatened to blow up plane and all aboard. During flight, security officer shot and seriously wounded Hasan and shot at others. Hijackers returned fire. 2 passengers killed, 7 passengers injured. After landing, passengers managed to deplane, and hijackers surrendered. Naimi and Al-Qeitan executed by firing squad 4/7/75. Hasan died from wounds received during hijacking.
Twin Otter	Hyannis/Nantucket, Mass.	Boarded aircraft preparing for aircraft positioning trip. Only pilot aboard. Claimed to have knife and demanded flight to New Haven, Conn. Pilot refused and radioed for help. Trucks blocked aircraft. Pilot deplaned. Police boarded and seized hijacker. Convicted 4/9/76 for carrying weapon aboard aircraft.
Cessna 310	Phoenix/Tucson	Hijackers chartered aircraft for flight to Tucson. Pointed gun at pilot and forced him to fly to private airstrip south of Nogales, Mexico. Hijackers turned plane and pilot over to group that met plane. Pilot escaped 3/7/75. Rodriguez captured in Las Vegas 3/31/75. Gonzales surrendered to federal agents 4/11/75. Both sentenced to 6 yrs. 7/17/75.
B-747	Sapporo/Tokyo, Japan	Pointed gun at steward and demanded 30 million yen (about $100,000). After landing at Tokyo, police boarded and overpowered hijacker. Sentenced to 2½ yrs.
B-727	Raleigh/Newark	Claimed to have gun and bomb. After landing at Atlanta, allowed all but 1 crew member to deplane. All passengers and crew got off. Law enforcement officers boarded and took hijacker into custody. He had no weapon or explosive. Sentenced to 5 yrs. 10/17/75.

Year	Results	Date	Name	Airline
1975	2	5/15/75	Crawford, Deborah Lynn	United
1975	1, 5	6/6/75	Colosky, Morris	Hi-Lift Helicopters Inc. (G/A)
1975	1	6/28/75	Gakof, Nodsio I.	(F) Bulgarian
1975	2	7/28/75	Oshima, H. (J)	(F) All Nippon (Japanese)
1975	2	8/16/75	McNair, Roper	(G/A)
1975	1	9/4/75	1 man, anonymous	Australian Air Force
1975	4	9/9/75	Laurent, P.; Laurent, C.; Charles, E.	(F) Haiti Air Inter
1975	2	9/15/75	Saloman, Fre	Continental

Type of Aircraft	Flight Plan	Disposition
B-737	Eugene/San Francisco	Approached stewardess saying that she did not want to go to San Francisco, that she had a knife and would use it if necessary. As plane came in for landing, hijacker placed under control until police arrived. Committed to state mental institution.
Bell 47-J2 Helicopter	Plymouth, Mich./ Lansing	After chartering flight, hijacker allegedly put knife to throat of pilot and demanded to be flown to Southern Michigan Prison. Aircraft landed and was joined by 1 waiting inmate. Flew to point 6 mi. north of prison, reportedly maced pilot in the face, then escaped in waiting vehicles. Convict apprehended 6/7/75. Colosky captured 6/17/75. Colosky sentenced to 20 yrs. for aircraft piracy 11/20/75.
Anatonov 24	Varna/Sofia	Armed with a revolver, hijacker forced plane to fly to Thessaloniki, Greece. Asked for political asylum; extradition to Bulgaria granted. Committed suicide while appeal pending 8/23/75.
Lockheed Tristar	Tokyo/Hokkaido, Japan	Youth broke into cockpit feigning to have knife. Allowed the plane to return to Tokyo, where all passengers and crew disembarked. Arrested by police; sentenced to juvenile detention.
Piper Cherokee	None	Approached plane as it was preparing for departure. Armed with gun, demanded to be flown to Jamaica, Puerto Rico, and Madrid. Pilot landed near Fayetteville, N.C. Hijacker took remaining hostage to airport; surrendered. Incompetent to stand trial. Committed to state mental institution 2/2/76.
	Baucau, Portugese Timor/Darwin, Australia	Timorese soldier forced plane on loan to Red Cross to fly 54 refugees to Darwin.
Dehavill and Twin Otter	Port Au Prince/ Cap Haitien	Hijackers entered cockpit, held knife to throat of pilot, and ordered flight to Cuba. Plane landed at Gonaives to refuel, where 2 passengers overpowered and subdued hijackers.
B-727	None	Hijacker, along with 2 hostages, entered parked aircraft, where he took 2 more hostages. 2 of the 4 subsequently escaped, 1 was shot by hijacker and seriously wounded. Hijacker stepped out of aircraft and pointed pistol at police officer. Fatally shot by police marksman.

Year	Results	Date	Name	Airline
1975	2	9/27/75	Marketos, S.	(F) Olympic (Greek)
1975	1	10/5/75	Several men, anonymous	(F) Aerolineas Argentinas
1975	2	10/7/75	Morales, Canislo	Philippine Air Lines
1975	1	10/7/75	Ralph, Ronald E.; Burke, David P.; Murphy, Jeffrey	Atlantic Aero (G/A)
1975	2	11/8/75	Johnson, Jack R.	Tri State Aero (G/A)
1975	1	11/24/75	Schmidt, Gary W.	California Air Charter (G/A)
1975	2	12/22/75	Rodelo, R.	SAM Airlines (Colombian) (G/A)
1976	2	1/5/76	Dono, Prudencio; Dono, Renato	Japan Airlines

Type of Aircraft	Flight Plan	Disposition
SC-7	Athens/Mikonos, Greece	Young man entered cockpit holding spray bottle claiming it contained nitric acid. Crew overpowered him and turned him over to authorities at Mikonos.
B-737	Buenos Aires/ Corrientes, Argentina	Aircraft hijacked by band of leftist guerrillas. Landed in small provincial capital of Formosa, where all passengers disembarked. Plane took off but ran short of fuel and landed at Rafaela, where guerrillas ran from aircraft and escaped.
BAC-111	Davao/Manila, Philippines	Hijacker armed with pistol and hand grenade demanded to be flown to Benghazi, Libya. Plane landed in Manila where hijacker allowed some passengers to disembark. Hijacker surrendered to authorities 9 hrs. after hijacking began.
Cessna 177	Greensboro, N.C./ Atlanta	Pointed gun at pilot and demanded to be flown to Florida. All 3 subsequently apprehended. Ralph and Burke sentenced to 20 yrs. 1/30/76. No proceedings against Murphy.
Cessna 150	Evansville, Ind./None	Young man chartered flight for "joy ride" around Evansville. Pointed gun at pilot and told him to dive aircraft into ground. As plane was in dive, pilot managed to push hijacker out of aircraft to his death.
Piper Navajo	Palomar, Calif./ Dallas	Man chartered aircraft reportedly to transport musical instruments to Dallas. Once in air, hijacker pulled gun and demanded to go to Mexico. Plane landed and became mired in mud. Several individuals approached aircraft and began to unload contents into waiting vehicles. Later they set aircraft on fire. Pilot was eventually released unharmed. Fugitive.
Beechcraft D-80	Barrancabermeja/ Medellin, Colombia	Man entered cockpit after takeoff. Permitted aircraft to land at Medellin. Upon landing, demanded $65,000 and safe conduct to unspecified location. Local authorities boarded aircraft, shot and wounded hijacker, and took him into custody.
DC-8	Bangkok/Tokyo	2 armed men seized aircraft as it was about to depart from Manila. Threatened a stewardess but eventually agreed to release all passengers in exchange for flight to Tokyo. Japan refused clearance for entry; hijackers surrendered to authorities.

Year	Results	Date	Name	Airline
1976	2	2/29/76	Cardona, José	Aces Airlines (G/A) (Colombian)
1976	1	4/5/76	Molina Avaral, C.	
1976	1, 5	4/7/76	3 men, anonymous	Philippine Airlines
1976	1	4/12/76	1 man, anonymous	
1976	2	4/18/76	Lentz, Roger	Heinzmann Engineering Co. (G/A)
1976	1	4/24/76	Hernandez, Alfonso	Avianca (Colombian)
1976	2	4/30/76	Ejder, Zeki	Turkish Airlines
1976	2	5/13/76	Solesby, Franklin M.	Royal American Flyers, Inc. (G/A)

Type of Aircraft	Flight Plan	Disposition
Saunders ST-27	Medellin/Apartado, Colombia	Armed hijacker demanded $300,000. Aircraft landed in Chigordo, where all passengers and a stewardess were forced to disembark. Plane then returned to Medellin, where hijacker entered into gun battle with police. Hijacker shot during battle and died later in hospital.
	Luanda/Lisbon	Cuban soldier granted asylum. Extradition to Cuba denied.
BAC-111; DC-8	Cagayan de Oro/ Mactan, Philippines	3 men hijacked aircraft and demanded $300,000 and release of numerous political prisoners. At Manila, exchanged all passengers for another set of hostages and $300,000 cash. During the next 6 days, hijackers flew to Kota Kinabalu, Kuala Lumpur, Bangkok, Karachi, and Benghazi. At Benghazi, released remaining hostages and asked for political asylum 4/15/76.
	Luanda/Lisbon	Cuban soldier; asked asylum.
Piper Navajo	Grand Island, Nebraska/None	Man armed with shotgun and pistol demanded to be taken to Mexico. Plane landed at Denver, departed Denver twice, but returned both times. Hijacker eventually deplaned small aircraft and boarded larger aircraft along with 2 hostages. Fatally shot by authorities as he walked down aisle of aircraft.
B-727	Pereira/Bogota, Colombia	Man armed with pistol hijacked aircraft as protest against "neglect of peasants." Surrendered to authorities at Bogota without incident.
DC-10	Paris/Istanbul	Man armed with knife threatened stewardess and attempted to force plane to land at Marseille or Lyon. Plane unable to land at either site and instead returned to Paris, where hijacker surrendered to authorities. Deported to Turkey on same plane.
Cessna 210	Denver/Houston	Man chartered small aircraft from Denver to Houston. After plane was in air, produced pistol and attempted to fire, but pistol failed to discharge. Struggle ensued between hijacker and one of 2 pilots aboard aircraft. Hijacker disarmed and subdued. Turned over to authorities at Lamar, Colo.

Year	Results	Date	Name	Airline
1976	2	5/21/76	6 men, anonymous	Philippine Airlines
1976	1	6/27/76	4 people, anonymous	Air France
1976	1	7/6/76	Hasdlumagid, Mustafa	Libyan Airlines
1976	2	8/23/76	Ali Ahmad, Osman; Muhammad Ahmad, Najib; Asmad Muhammad, Sulayman	Egyptair
1976	2	8/28/76	1 Vietnamese male, anonymous	Air France
1976	2	9/4/76	3 men, anonymous	KLM (Netherlands)

Type of Aircraft	Flight Plan	Disposition
BAC-111	Davao/Manila, Philippines	6 Moslem rebels hijacked aircraft and forced it to land at Zamboanga. Hijackers demanded $375,000 and aircraft to fly to Libya. After hours of negotiations, gun battle broke out between hijackers and security forces. Grenades set off aboard aircraft. 10 passengers killed, 22 injured. 3 terrorists killed, 3 injured. 3 surviving hijackers sentenced to death 11/4/76.
Airbus A-300	Tel Aviv/Athens/ Paris	Aircraft hijacked shortly after departure from Athens. Landed Benghazi, Libya, to take on fuel, then proceeded to Entebbe, Uganda. Hijackers and over 250 hostages left hijacked aircraft and entered airport building at Entebbe. Hijackers demanded release of 53 pro-Palestinian prisoners in numerous countries in exchange for hostages. During course of the negotiations, approximately 150 hostages released, leaving as hostage those with Israeli passports and Air France crew members. On 7/3/76 Israeli commandos launched rescue operation at Entebbe Airport. 3 hostages killed; all others rescued. All hijackers, some Ugandan troops, and 1 Israeli commando killed. Airbus returned by Uganda 7/22/76; France paid 500,000 francs for cost of hostages' food.
B-727	Tripoli/Benghazi, Libya	Man armed with two replica pistols and two knives hijacked aircraft and ordered it to Tunis. Aircraft denied landing; finally flew to Palma de Mallorca, where hijacker surrendered.
B-737	Cairo/Luxor, Egypt	Hijacking terminated in Luxor, where hijackers were overpowered by security forces. Supreme Egyptian Military Court sentenced hijackers to fines and prison for life 9/18/76.
Caravelle	Saigon/Bangkok	Aircraft commandeered as it was about to depart Saigon. Hijacker released passengers and crew. Authorities rushed aircraft. Hijacker then set off two grenades, killing himself and damaging aircraft.
DC-9	Nice/Amsterdam	Aircraft hijacked by 3 persons while en route from Spain to Amsterdam. Plane rerouted to Tunisia, Cyprus, and Israel, where it circled offshore. Plane returned to Cyprus; hijackers surrendered with safe conduct to Libya.

Year	Results	Date	Name	Airline
1976	6	9/10/76	6 men, anonymous	Indian Airlines
1976	1	9/10/76	Busic, Zvonko; Busic, Julienne; Matovic, Petar; Pesut, Frane; Vlasic, Mark	TWA-355
1976	2	9/15/76	Tanaka, Seiichi; Tanaka, Kimi	(F) (G/A) (Japanese)
1976	2	9/18/76	1 man, anonymous	(F) Aer Lingus (Irish)
1976	1	10/28/76	Becvar, Rudolf	(F) Czechoslovakian
1976	1	11/4/76	Karozinski, Andrzej J.	(F) LOT (Polish)
1976	6	12/21/76	Hinnant, Palmtree, Jr.	United
1977	2	2/13/77	1 man, anonymous	(F) Turkish Air Lines
1977	1, 5	3/14/77	Porcari, Luciano	(F) Iberia Air Lines

Type of Aircraft	Flight Plan	Disposition
B-737	New Delhi/Bombay	Hijacking occurred shortly after plane took off from New Delhi's International Airport. Destination unspecified. Forced to land in Lahore, Pakistan. Hostages released (77 passengers and crew). 6 men arrested. Pakistani government released 6 hijackers on grounds of insufficient evidence available for prosecution 1/5/77.
B-727	La Guardia Airport, New York/Chicago	4 men, 1 woman boarded at La Guardia. False bombs on 1 hijacker's person. No weapons, but claimed same. Demanded flight to major U.S. and foreign cities to drop Croatian Nationalist leaflets. Bomb left in N.Y., killing 1 policeman. Flight forced to Gander, Nfld., Iceland, and France. Hijacking terminated in France. Hijackers returned to N.Y. to face air piracy and murder charges. Busics sentenced to life 7/20/77; other 3 to be sentenced on federal charges (as of July 31, 1977).
	Domestic	Sightseeing trip; stabbed pilot and third passenger; assailants jumped overboard.
B-707	(Unknown)	Crew left plane on ground; hijacker surrendered.
IL-18	Prague/Bratislava, Czechoslovakia	Hijacker armed with submachine gun and pistol. Landed in Munich. Surrendered. Extradition denied. Sentenced to 8 yrs. 3/31/77.
TU-134	Copenhagen/Warsaw	Polish state airline hijacked to Vienna by male using dummy "bomb". Extradition denied. Sentenced to 4 yrs. 2/15/77.
DC-8	(Unknown)	United Air Lines employee boarded empty DC-8 while on ground at San Francisco Airport. Hijacker demanded to be provided crew to fly to somewhere on East Coast. Held 2 hostages. Hijacker surrendered. To be prosecuted on state charges.
DC-9	Istanbul/Izmir, Turkey	Wanted Yugoslavia. Wounded pilot and stewardess. Landed at Ismiz. Overcome by passenger.
B-727	Barcelona/Palma de Mallorca	Diverted aircraft to Algiers, Abidjan, Seville, Turin, Zurich, Warsaw, Zurich. Wanted to recover custody of children in Abidjan and Turin. Extorted 35 million Ivory Coast Francs ($140,000). Overcome by police on final landing at Zurich.

Year	Results	Date	Name	Airline
1977	2	3/17/77	1 man, anonymous	(F) All Nippon Airways (Japanese)
1977	2	3/17/77	Tanaka, Osamu	(F) All Nippon Airways (Japanese)
1977	1, 5	3/19/77	2 men, anonymous	(F) Turkish Air Lines
1977	2	4/25/77	1 man, anonymous	(F) LOT (Polish)
1977	2	4/26/77	2 men, anonymous	(F) Ethiopian Air Lines
1977	2	5/2/77	Ali Fargani, Abuaisha	(F) Iberian Airlines
1977	2	5/8/77	Trayer, Bruce	Northwest Orient
1977	1	5/26/77	Sosnovsky, Vasily	(F) Aeroflot
1977	1, 5	6/6/77	Nasser, M. Ali Abu Khaled	(F) Middle East Air Lines
1977	1	6/18/77	Dimitrov, Rumen Cancov	(F) Bulgarian Air Lines
1977	1	6/21/77	Tamayo, Carlos	(F) LAN (Chilean)
1977	1, 5	6/29/77	1 man, anonymous	(F) Gulf Air

Source: Federal Aviation Administration, Civil Aviation Security Service, edited and annotated by Alona E. Evans.

Note: Names of individuals listed as hijackers of non-U.S. aircraft have not been verified and may be aliases.

Legend:
1 Successful to other than Cuba
2 Unsuccessful to other than Cuba
3 Successful to Cuba
4 Unsuccessful to Cuba
5 Extortion or release of prisoners
6 Destination unknown—unsuccessful
F Foreign
J Juvenile
S Servicemen
P Prisoner under escort
G/A General aviation

Type of Aircraft	Flight Plan	Disposition
B-727	Tokyo/—	Wanted Sendai. Committed suicide on board aircraft.
B-727	Sapporo/Sendai, Japan	Overpowered by passengers.
B-727	Diyarbakir/Ankara, Turkey	Landed in Beirut. Wanted $300,000 in Turkish currency and fuel. Surrendered to police.
TU-134	Cracow/Nuremberg	Hijacker overcome by Polish security officers before takeoff.
—	—/Addis Ababa	Wanted Saudi Arabia. Killed by crew.
—	Madrid/Rome	Hijacker attempted to force aircraft to return to Madrid after landing at Rome. Overcome by pilot.
B-747	Tokyo/Honolulu	Wanted Moscow. Overcome by crew. Hijacker wounded. Aircraft returned to Tokyo.
—	Riga/—	Landed in Stockholm. Extradition denied. Sentenced to 4 yrs. 7/27/77.
B-707	(Unknown)	Landed in Kuwait. Wanted $1.5 million from Kuwait, Saudi Arabia, and Iraq. Overcome by army commandos.
—	(Unknown)	Landed in Belgrade. Extradition requested.
—	(Unknown)	Wanted Algeria. Landed in Mendoza, Argentina. Surrendered to police.
VC-10	London/Oman	Wanted $200,000. Denied landing at Dubai. Landed in Qatar. Surrendered.

Nuclear Facilities and Materials

Herbert H. Brown

Introduction

In the last 25 years, there has been dramatic worldwide commercial development of nuclear energy, which has manifested itself through the huge increase in commercial nuclear facilities and in the flow of nuclear materials among nations. This development in turn has begun to focus attention on the significant problem posed by terrorists or others intent on malevolent acts: the presence of nuclear facilities and materials offers these persons a potential means to carry out their unlawful purposes. This chapter briefly traces the development of commercial nuclear energy and then focuses on the significant problems of protecting nuclear facilities and materials posed by this development.

The Development of Commercial Nuclear Energy

The worldwide commercial development of nuclear energy received its biggest boost in December 1953, when President Eisenhower delivered his landmark "Atoms for Peace" address before the United Nations General Assembly. Thereafter, Atoms for Peace became the catalyst of intensive U.S. cooperation with foreign nations regarding the peaceful applications of atomic energy, and it created new channels of commerce between the U.S. nuclear industry and governmental and private customers abroad.

In the two decades subsequent to 1953, international nuclear commerce has expanded widely, and other industrialized countries have developed the capabilities to compete with the U.S. nuclear industry for sales of reactors, fuel, and related equipment and services. At present, this competition emanates from six countries—Canada, France, the Federal Republic of Germany (FRG), Sweden, the United Kingdom, and the Union of Soviet Socialist Republics. These competitors, together with the United States, interact with more than 100 nations, developed and developing, that administer national nuclear energy programs.

For nations without abundant long-term fossil fuel or hydro resources to generate electric power, nuclear energy has become an economic imperative that promises the only existing technology with which to achieve a relatively secure degree of national energy self-sufficiency in the next decade. Various countries— among them Italy, Spain, France, Iran, Japan, the Federal Republic of Germany, and Brazil—have already made major policy and financial commitments to nuclear power. The Arab oil embargo of 1973-1974 and its aftermath reinforced the practicality of these commitments by demonstrating to the world's oil-dependent nations the punishing consequences of an international economy built on a structure of quadrupled OPEC oil prices. It added emphasis to the growing realization that worldwide oil reserves are being rapidly depleted and that they might last for as little as another 35 to 40 years.

The Transfer of Nuclear Technology:
Dangers and Safeguards

Unlike international commerce in other energy technologies, the transfer of nuclear technology has always been known to possess an intrinsic danger: nuclear energy equipment, materials, and techniques can be applied under certain circumstances to military as well as to peaceful ends. Thus a nation with both the requisite technical capability and the political will could divert nuclear technology obtained for peaceful purposes in order to produce nuclear weapons. This has been a fundamental premise, if not fear, underlying international nuclear commerce from the outset, and it has been the object of extensive international "safeguards" that are intended to assure that peaceful nuclear commerce does not lead to the proliferation of nuclear weapons.

"Safeguards" and "nonproliferation" are legal and technical concepts that embrace a combination of treaty obligations, most notably under the Non-Proliferation Treaty,[1] and international verification procedures, principally under the International Atomic Energy Agency, designed to deter nations without nuclear weapons from acquiring them. A related legal and technical concept applied by national governments to their nuclear energy programs is "physical protection." This concept embraces the system of technical devices, control, surveillance, and response a government uses to preclude unauthorized access to nuclear materials and facilities within its jurisdiction. Specifically, physical protection seeks to prevent nuclear materials or facilities from becoming a means or an end of malevolent acts, such as the sabotage of a nuclear facility or the theft of nuclear materials. Thus although the concepts of safeguards, nonproliferation, and physical protection share the common objective of assuring that nuclear technology is used only for peaceful purposes, physical protection differs from safeguards and nonproliferation in the following important respect: safeguards and nonproliferation are international programs directed at national governments, whereas physical protection is a national program directed at individuals or groups at the subnational level.[2]

Given the existence worldwide of several hundred nuclear facilities and thousands of shipments of nuclear materials, there has been relatively little nuclear-related malevolence. No known act of malevolence related to nuclear energy has produced a radiological hazard to the public or has permitted an unauthorized individual or group to obtain special nuclear materials. Nevertheless, there have been many hoaxes, threats, and relatively minor acts of sabotage, more than 100 over the past eight years in the United States alone.[3] The increasing incidence of international terrorism has underscored the possibility that terrorists could attempt a significant nuclear-related act.

National governments have treated this possibility with seriousness and confidentiality, studying the vulnerabilities of their varying physical protection systems without disclosing any inherent weaknesses. Since 1975 there has been a substantial increase in both the national and international dialogue on physical protection among governments. Related to this development, the two international organizations with mandates concerning nuclear energy safeguards, the International Atomic Energy Agency (IAEA) and the European Atomic Energy Community (EURATOM) have cautiously begun to evaluate whether—and, if so how—they should participate in programs that might improve the physical protection of nuclear materials and facilities within their areas of competence. But the recent activities of national governments and international organizations have been inconclusive, thereby highlighting several basic unanswered questions: What, specifically, are the terrorist threats against which governments must establish physical protection systems? And what is the probability that terrorists will act on these threats?

Implicit in these questions is the widely held belief that any significant act of nuclear-related terrorism would be generally perceived as international in character, even if the physical impact of such an act were confined to a small area of a single country. In part, this is because there is a subtle interdependence among nuclear scientists and researchers, nuclear energy industries, and government regulators of nuclear energy in each country, with counterparts throughout the world. These individuals and organizations have historically built their promise of the future reliability and success of nuclear energy technology on a collective record of excellent performance. As a top European government official responsible for nuclear regulation tells his audiences, "[t]here is no such thing as someone else's nuclear accident."

Political Problems in the Development
of Nuclear Energy

Despite the technological success of nuclear energy over the past two decades, the nuclear industry continues to stand on a fragile political base, and its ultimate commercial success is by no means guaranteed. There continues to be strong minority opposition to nuclear power by political and public groups in several advanced countries—particularly in the United States, Japan, and the Federal Republic of Germany—and the same type of vigorous trial by public opinion that has historically faced the nuclear industry on safety issues is beginning to focus on the vulnerability of nuclear materials and facilities to potential acts of terrorism. Government promoters and regulators of nuclear power view this as a challenge, not unlike a challenge to the safety of a nuclear power plant, that requires a response sufficient to convince the public of the inaccuracy of the criticism or of the effectiveness of the remedial governmental action.

The result has been a recent acceleration of dialogue, study, research, and debate within and among nations and international organizations that are concerned with maintaining and further developing nuclear energy technology. These activities have centered largely on technical issues, for example, identifying the specific hardware and systems that are vulnerable to terrorist acts, establishing relevant research priorities for developing new physical protection equipment, and optimizing architectural and engineering designs to deter specific kinds of terrorist acts. These efforts have also, but to a much lesser extent, focused on determining whether there are or should be diplomatic, legal, and procedural means of assuring that all nuclear materials and facilities throughout the world are adequately protected by government-authorized persons, so that no nation will become an especially attractive target for nuclear thieves, saboteurs, or terrorists.

This chapter concerns one aspect of these governmental activities: the role that international law is exercising, and that it could exercise, through its norms, processes, and institutions, to deter and, if necessary, to respond to nuclear-related terrorism. The study embraces five sections: First, a description of the nuclear materials, facilities, and activities that are technically vulnerable to terrorist acts; second, a discussion of potential nuclear-related terrorist threats; third, an examination of existing national measures to prevent acts of nuclear-related terrorism; fourth, an examination of current international activities that concern the physical protection of nuclear facilities and materials; and finally, some conclusions and recommendations for improving the international regime to deal with the problems posed by potential nuclear-related terrorism.

Technical Vulnerabilities of Nuclear Materials and Facilities

The range of threats posed by nuclear-related terrorism embraces at one extreme the hoax—that is, a bluff by terrorists to use nuclear materials they do not actually have—and at the other extreme the detonation of a nuclear weapon. Between these extremes are numerous permutations, which pose serious potential risks to public health and safety, including sabotage of nuclear power plants, theft of a nuclear weapon or of special nuclear materials with which to fabricate such a weapon, and dispersal of radioactive materials.

Conceptually, the threats posed by terrorists to nuclear materials and facilities are: (1) acquiring special nuclear materials with which to fabricate a nuclear bomb or a radiological weapon; or (2) assaulting nuclear facilities, with the intent of sabotage. This section will discuss the points in a nation's nuclear energy program that are possible targets of such acts of terrorism.[4]

There currently are 175 nuclear power plants in operation in more than 30 nations, the largest number being in the United States, where there are 60. The Organization for Economic Cooperation and Development (OECD) has projected that within its 24 member states there will be greater than a fivefold increase in nuclear generating capacity during the 1975-1985 decade.[5] Increases are also projected for the Eastern Bloc nations.[6]

There are five types of nuclear reactors now being used to generate electric power: light water reactors (LWRs) of the type manufactured in the United States, the Federal Republic of Germany, France, the Soviet Union, and Sweden; heavy water reactors (HWRs) manufactured in Canada (a variation is currently under development in the United Kingdom and Japan); gas-cooled reactors (GCRs) developed in France and the United Kingdom (neither is now being manufactured); advanced gas-cooled reactors (AGRs) manufactured in the United Kingdom (two are currently in operation); high-temperature gas-cooled reactors (HTGRs) manufactured in the United States (only one commercial scale HTGR exists) and under development in the Federal Republic of Germany; and liquid metal fast breeder reactors (LMFBRs), of which there are demonstration-scale prototypes operating in the United Kingdom, France, and the Soviet Union.

Of the types of reactors now used throughout the world to generate electric power, LWRs represent the largest number; HWRs are next in number, followed by GCRs, and finally by AGRs. All these types are fission reactors that require a sustained chain reaction of "atom splitting" to produce heat, which in turn converts water into high-pressure steam to drive turbine generators that produce electric power. Both LWRs and AGRs are fueled by enriched uranium; HWRs and GCRs are fueled by natural uranium. The fission process in all these types causes the uranium fuel to be converted into several radioactive waste products and into new fissionable elements, most notably plutonium, an extraordinarily radiotoxic transuranic element that in sufficient quantities can be made into a nuclear weapon.

To support the operation of these types of nuclear power plants, there is a series of facilities, operations, and processes (some of which exist on a commerical scale while others are only now being planned by industry or government) that ranges from mining uranium ore to disposing of radioactive wastes. This series is technically called the "nuclear fuel cycle." For LWRs, the historically accepted concept of the total fuel cycle would include the following stages:

1. mining uranium ore
2. milling uranium ore to produce "yellowcake"

3. conversion of yellowcake to uranium hexafluoride
4. enrichment of uranium hexafluoride with 2 to 3 percent of the isotope U^{235}
5. transportation of enriched uranium from the enrichment plant to a fuel fabrication plant
6. fabrication of uranium fuel elements
7. transportation of the fuel elements from the fabrication plant to a nuclear power plant
8. irradiation of the fuel in the nuclear power reactor
9. storage of the "spent" fuel at the reactor site
10. transportation of the spent fuel to a reprocessing plant
11. reprocessing of the spent fuel to extract plutonium
12. transportation of radioactive reprocessing wastes to a storage facility
13. storage and ultimate disposal of the radioactive reprocessing wastes
14. transportation of the plutonium from the reprocessing plant to a fuel fabrication plant for "recycling" into mixed-oxide fuel elements (*i.e.*, fuel containing both uranium and plutonium)
15. transportation of mixed-oxide fuel elements to a nuclear power plant
16. irradiation of the mixed-oxide fuel in a nuclear power reactor

At present, there are no commercial scale reprocessing plants, mixed-oxide fuel fabrication plants, or permanent high-level waste disposal facilities operating anywhere in the world. Thus the actual nuclear fuel cycle for LWRs now ranges only from mining uranium ore to storing the spent fuel elements at the reactor site. Whether the reprocessing of spent fuel and the wide-scale use of mixed-oxide fuel will be permitted in the United States, thus "closing" the fuel cycle, is currently the subject of a major proceeding before the Nuclear Regulatory Commission (NRC).[7] A central focus of this proceeding is plutonium, and whether plutonium in wide use could be adequately protected by industry or government, or both, against theft or acts of terrorism.[8]

Of the total conceptual LWR fuel cycle, a recent study[9] performed by the MITRE Corporation for the NRC concludes that mining, milling, conversion of yellowcake, 2- to 3-percent uranium enrichment, and light water reactor fuel fabrication present no "practical" security concerns.[10] That is, sabotage of these facilities would not cause significant radioactivity to be released to the environment, and theft of these materials would not provide terrorists with plutonium that might be used to make a nuclear weapon.

However, the study further concludes that the following stages of the LWR fuel cycle are vulnerable to terrorist threats:[11]

1. *Nuclear power plants:* potential sabotage of the spent fuel storage pool
2. *Transportation of spent fuel:* potential sabotage of the shipping casks
3. *Fuel reprocessing plants:* potential sabotage or theft of plutonium

4. *Radioactive waste storage:* potential sabotage of storage containers
5. *Plutonium storage:* potential sabotage or theft
6. *Transportation of plutonium from reprocessing to nuclear power plants:* potential sabotage or theft of plutonium
7. *Mixed-oxide fuel fabrication plants:* potential sabotage or theft of plutonium
8. *Mixed-oxide fuel transportation from fabrication to nuclear power plants:* potential sabotage or theft of plutonium

The HWR fuel cycle has the same vulnerability to sabotage as does the LWR fuel cycle, but as its fuel is made of natural (*i.e.,* unenriched) uranium, its vulnerability to theft has no significant security consequences until after its spent fuel is reprocessed and plutonium is separated. At present, however, the Canadian government has no plans to reprocess the spent fuel of HWRs and plans only to store it as a waste product awaiting the development of permanent storage facilities. The GCR fuel cycle has vulnerabilities analogous to those of the HWR fuel cycle; and the AGR fuel cycle parallels that of the LWR.

On the other hand, the HTGR and LMFBR fuel cycles are more vulnerable to terrorist acts than are the LWR, HWR, GCR, and AGR fuel cycles. Each stage of the LMFBR cycle, beginning with fuel fabrication, includes the use of fuel elements containing about 20 percent plutonium and each stage of the HTGR fuel cycle, beginning with enrichment, includes the use of uranium that is highly enriched with either the isotope U^{235} or U^{233} materials suitable for producing a nuclear weapon if extracted and possessed in sufficient quantity.

A recent joint ERDA-NRC study of the 11 U.S. facilities licensed to possess strategic quantities of nuclear materials found that several such facilities were vulnerable to the terrorist threats postulated in the study.[12] The study recommended that both the ERDA and the NRC take actions to upgrade the current level of physical protection at these particular facilities and also to generally upgrade the level of physical protection at all such licensed facilities. Another study recently concluded by the NRC reached similar conclusions for nuclear power plants and resulted in new physical protection requirements[13] that substantially upgrade the NRC's previous physical protection standards. These actions well characterize a general current trend in all countries to identify and evaluate specific technical vulnerabilities of their nuclear fuel cycles and to impose new technical requirements on these facilities to upgrade physical protection measures.

The Threat to Nuclear Facilities and Materials

No one knows whether terrorists will adopt nuclear-related tactics. There is little empirical information, and expert opinions point in different directions. These differences are highlighted by recent testimony presented to a congressional committee investigating the adequacy of current physical protection measures.[14] J. Bowyer Bell of Columbia University stated:

There is about the entire subject of nuclear terrorism a dreadful lack of precision. There can be no absolute assurances. There may be those with the will, capacity, and the desire to steal plutonium or detonate a bomb in a powerplant to cause a meltdown. The chances are slim that there are many so inclined in the United States and slimmer that a foreign organization will be so attracted. But in nuclear matters a qualitative estimate that the threat is remote is cold comfort. Somewhat more reassuring is the obstacle facing any such terrorist venture; yet the terrorist may assume a vulnerability where little exists, may launch a failed operation so spectacular that a frightened public will perceive a present danger.[15]

In contrast, Brian Jenkins of the Rand Corporation testified:

We should not exaggerate the threat. The potential consequences of serious sabotage leading to a radioactive release, the fabrication of an illicit nuclear explosive device, or plutonium contamination are serious. But I have tried to point out why some of the more horrendous scenarios in which hundreds or thousands of lives might be imperiled appear less likely.

There are disincentives, even among those we call terrorists, to carry out these extreme acts. And they are not that easy to accomplish. Planting a bomb at a tourist attraction or seizing hostages in a consulate is a far easier task than destroying a nuclear reactor or making—not designing, but making—a nuclear bomb. We should not overestimate the capabilities of terrorists.

They tend to operate at a low level of efficiency.[16]

Most analyses of this subject have necessarily been somewhat conjectural, beginning with an assessment of the purely technical vulnerabilities of the nuclear fuel cycle and concluding with the admonition that nuclear-related terrorism is potentially so serious that it cannot be discounted. A recent ERDA report follows this pattern: "There is no way to predict from historical data the probability of such an event occurring, the form the threat would take, or the means that would be used by the adversary. The physical security aspects of the safeguards system must be based on an assumption that the possibility of a serious threat exists."[17]

This assumption, *i.e.*, "that the possibility of a serious threat exists," has had important implications for governments, because for all practical purposes it has required them to plan and respond as though the "possibility" were an actuality. Thus governments are performing independent assessments of particularly national and local terrorist motivations as part of their search for concrete evidence on which to structure a program of governmental deterrence. There are also governmental analyses underway to relate such terrorist motivations to the vulnerabilities of the type and design of the particular nuclear facilities within these nations and the technical, legal, and administrative constraints that would affect their program of governmental deterrence.

The point of reference for these analyses is the collation of past acts of nuclear-related malevolence. A recent study performed by the BDM Corporation that analyzed the terrorist threat to commercial nuclear facilities found that worldwide, between 1966 and 1975 there were 21 such nuclear-related incidents.[18] These incidents are shown in Table 2-1. The major conclusion concerning these incidents was that they tended to be more like common industrial problems causing a nuisance to industry, rather than broader security problems causing risks to the public.

Of the 21 incidents studied, the BDM study found that only four potentially endangered public health and safety: (1) the threatened crash of a hijacked commercial airliner into government-owned nuclear facilities at Oak Ridge, Tennessee, in 1972; (2) arson at the Indian Point no. 2 power plant in New York in 1974; (3) the seizure of the control room of a nuclear research reactor in Argentina in 1973; and (4) the dispersal of radioactive pharmaceuticals by a terrorist on two Austrian trains in 1974.[19]

Analyzing the characteristics of the 21 nuclear-related incidents, the BDM study found that 17 of them involved theft of material or harassment representing "low-casualty-potential," for example, theft of radium needles from a hospital and of mildly radioactive copper plates from a laboratory, and

Table 2-1
Nuclear-Related Incidents, 1966-1975

United States		Foreign	
Date	Incident	Date	Incident
Aug. 1966	Loss of radium shipment	Nov. 1966	Theft of fuel rods, U.K.
Oct. 1971	Intruder, Vt. Yankee PLT	July 1973	Argentine plant seized
Nov. 1971	Arson, Buchanan, N.Y., PLT	April 1974	Austrian 1131 dispersal
Nov. 1972	Threat of crash into ORNL	June 1974	Alleged theft, India
Feb. 1973	Topple site tower, Mass.	June 1975	Bombing of French plant
Aug. 1973	Theft of 1131 capsules	–	Attacks on EUCOM sites
June 1974	Theft of SR90 device	–	Plot to poison water
July 1974	Intruder in Nike site	–	Plot to purchase
Oct. 1974	Possible sabotage, Zion		
Oct. 1974	Theft of C060 plates		
Oct. 1974	Theft of BYU device		
Nov. 1974	Theft of radium needles		
Dec. 1974	Theft of CS-137 gauge		

Source: THE BDM CORPORATION, ANALYSIS OF THE TERRORIST THREAT TO THE COMMERCIAL NUCLEAR INDUSTRY, BDM/W-75-176-TR (Sept. 12, 1975), at 10.

discovery of intruders within nuclear facility sites.[20] Eleven of the incidents occurred at research and health facilities where the least dangerous radioactive materials were kept, and where there was no significant danger to the public health and safety. With respect to the perpetrators' motives in the 21 incidents, the BDM study found that eight were financial gain, one was extortion, one was disruption of a facility, three were protest, two were revenge, and one was "irrational."[21] The perpetrators tended to act alone or in small groups; 8 incidents involved a single person, 5 incidents involved 2 to 5 persons, 3 incidents involved 6 to 15 persons, and in 5 incidents the perpetrators were unknown. Of the 21 incidents, 5 were characterized as "terrorist" actions.

The BDM study also concluded that "the cooperation of an insider or actual attack by an insider himself was crucial for the covert theft of nuclear material. Without a 'fifth column' inside the facility, the chance of covert theft appears drastically reduced.'[22] This conclusion has important implications for governmental physical protection programs because it suggests that physical barriers and devices are not sufficient security measures. Rather, it would seem that in addition to such hardware, there must be adequate means of assuring that persons authorized to be within nuclear facilities do not themselves constitute security risks.

Finally, the BDM study concluded, "Significant and central to the problem of public safety is that no evidence suggests terrorist attempts to fabricate nuclear weapons. . . . The terrorist literature examined, with all its rhetoric about death and destruction, makes no mention of nuclear targets, and this can be taken to indicate their disinterest and/or fear."[23]

The BDM study identified "a series of [nuclear-related] malevolent actions that are plausible within the context of today's societal conditions or at some future time in a changed environment."[24] This series of actions, ranked from least to most severe in potential consequences to public health and safety, are hoaxes, threats, harassment to the exterior of a nuclear facility, interrupting operation of a facility, taking hostages at a facility, destroying a key component of a facility, releasing radioactive materials at a facility, stealing nuclear materials; dispersing radioactive materials in the public domain, and making a nuclear weapon. Based on this range of actions, the study states:

The most salient conclusion associated with the determination of the range of malevolent actions as it relates to societal consequences is the delineation of actions which cause the greatest public penalty. Those actions on the lower end of the malevolent actions scale do not pose a risk to the general public and include hoax, threat, harassment and disruption. These are essentially problems of the nuclear industry. However, beginning with the potentialities created by a hostage situation, the risk to the public is of such a dimension that the problem becomes one of safeguards. This lends increased importance to those actions on the upper end of the range of malevolent actions.[25]

Given this range of possible malevolent actions, and considering the obvious difficulties of sabotaging a protected nuclear facility or of stealing nuclear materials from such a facility and then designing and making a nuclear bomb, the BDM study identifies four principal "objectives" terrorists might have in taking nuclear-related actions:[26]

1. To gain a strong bargaining position with which the government is forced to deal.
2. To dramatize a political cause and capture wide publicity for it.
3. To paralyze society with an extremely dangerous threat to frighten the public and gain support through intimidation.
4. To destroy persons and property randomly and create civic and political anarchy.

Another objective could be to obtain nuclear materials for sale or transfer to a national government that desired to establish its own nuclear arsenal. An offer has reportedly been made by President Qaddafi of Libya to pay $1 million to anyone providing him with a nuclear bomb.

The key question of whether terrorists would be likely to pursue their objectives by attempting nuclear-related tactics remains open. If a terrorist group sought to obtain the release of a "political" prisoner from governmental authorities, or if it sought a large ransom for performing a specific act, the threat or commission of nuclear-related violence might provide a persuasive bargaining chip. Similarly, if terrorists sought to create civic chaos and political anarchy, a spurt of random terrorist acts using small amounts of nuclear materials coupled with the threat of more severe acts might also prove effective.

On the other hand, it has been argued that some kinds of nuclear-related terrorist acts would probably be ineffective because of the psychological impact that they would have on the public and on government officials. Experts on terrorist behavior often cite Lenin's maxim, "[T]he purpose of terrorism is to terrorize," that is, to cause fear, alarm, and shock rather than death and massive destruction. Such a concept puts limits on the probable instruments and scale of terrorist violence. It suggests that there is a threshold level beyond which the public and its leaders will not tolerate further actions. Thus relatively low-level violence of local concentration—such as the IRA's activities in Northern Ireland—might be acceptable for a long duration, but intense nuclear malevolence might cause major public reaction. Whereas governments might adopt stepped-up intelligence and enforcement measures to combat the former, nuclear violence might itself be counterproductive, not only by provoking extreme governmental countermeasures, but also by eroding whatever popular support the terrorists might have otherwise commanded.

Another theory of terrorist behavior, put forth by Brian Jenkins, suggests that major nuclear-related violence, such as detonating a nuclear weapon manufactured with stolen materials, is not in keeping with the character of past terrorist actions.[27] Although bombs have been a staple of terrorists, this theory argues that bombs have historically served symbolic purposes to gain publicity for the terrorists' cause or to provide means of extortion or retaliation. In essence, bombs have been deadly, but they have not been the instruments of either mass murder or long-term destruction as would be the case with a nuclear weapon.

A recent unclassified CIA research study further develops this theory:

That the threatened employment of such awesome ordnance would have profound political and psychological effects is undeniable. But it must be emphasized that there are major hazards that would be involved for the terrorists as well. The most important of these (and the one probably primarily responsible for the failure of terrorists to make more of an effort to exploit mass destruction technology in the past) is the high risk of adverse public reaction—particularly in the event that the group involved were to end up in a position where it felt compelled to make good its threat.

Although a few terrorist groups have, in fact, resorted to indiscriminate mass murder, such instances have been relatively rare, and in each case thus far the human toll has been negligible in comparison to the casualties that would result from the broadcast of only a few ounces or less of a highly toxic agent or the detonation of even a small nuclear device. Basically, terrorists are in business to influence people, not exterminate them. Moreover, those that aspire to some sort of political legitimacy—and this means most of them—are generally quite sensitive to the need to take some care to avoid alienating local and international opinion.

The fact remains, however, that weapons of mass destruction cannot help but hold considerable temptation for militants whose basic strategy of violence centers on wringing maximum political leverage from publicity and fear. Hence, it seems prudent to assume that sooner or later some group is bound to take the plunge.[28]

The CIA study's conclusion is shared by many government officials. Although these officials believe that it would be difficult and dangerous for terrorists to attempt to steal nuclear materials or to sabotage a nuclear facility, the mere possibility of such acts requires governments to take preventive measures. Indeed, to perfect a nuclear weapon from stolen nuclear materials would take a skilled and trained team of 10 to 24 experts one to two years.[29] But government officials cautiously concede that there are such experts and that one to two years may not be so long for a fanatic group.

A further consensus of government officials is that there is the likelihood of an increase in low-level nuclear-related violence that is an extension of the general contemporary trend in terrorist violence. Thus there may be an increase in hoaxes, minor acts of sabotage involving nuclear facilities (although not necessarily the nuclear materials within those facilities), and thefts and dispersals of nonexplosive radiopharmaceuticals or radiographic materials that pose a comparatively lower degree of danger to public health and safety. Such was the character of the bombings of a Swedish reactor site in 1977, the Fessenheim and Mt. D'Arée reactor sites in France during 1975, and the dispersal of radiopharmaceuticals on Austrian passenger trains in 1974. These kinds of acts follow the traditional pattern of terrorist tactics: they optimize local impact and maximize publicity.

Existing National Measures

In the United States and all other countries that administer nuclear energy programs, the government strictly controls access to nuclear materials and facilities. Unauthorized possession of such materials or unauthorized operation of such facilities is a criminal offense punishable by fine or imprisonment, or both.[30]

To assure that unauthorized persons do not gain access to nuclear facilities or materials, states have special rules and procedures relating to the physical protection of these facilities and materials. In the United States, the Federal Republic of Germany, Canada, Switzerland, Spain, Japan, and other countries that permit nuclear power plants to be owned and operated by private companies, and in the United Kingdom, France, and other countries in which electric power is generated by nationally owned, yet operationally independent companies, government regulatory bodies license these companies on condition that specific physical protection measures are implemented by the companies. In the Soviet Union and other countries in which electric power is planned, generated, and marketed by the central government, physical protection standards are mandated and implemented by the national government itself.

Despite these differences in administration, there are basic physical protection concepts and standards common to all national physical protection systems although it is commonly understood that the completeness and effectiveness of states' physical protection systems vary widely.

1. All states seek to establish physical protection measures adequate (a) to deter sabotage of nuclear facilities and theft of nuclear materials; (b) to detect whether nuclear materials have been stolen; (c) to minimize damage caused by sabotage of a nuclear facility; (d) to respond promptly to repel an attempted act of sabotage or an attempted theft of nuclear materials; (e) to recover nuclear materials if they are stolen.
2. All states protect fixed facilities by a combination of physical barriers, alarms and other detection devices, on-site guard forces, and off-site reaction forces. On-site guards may be private or government employees, depending on the state's constitutional system. Off-site reaction forces in all

states are government employees, in some instances civilian and in others military.

3. All states protect nuclear materials in transit by requiring: (a) secure containers and transport vehicles; (b) guards and escorts during transportation; (c) communications systems that assure continuing contact with the transportation vehicle; (d) reaction forces capable of responding to an attempted theft. In the United States, government-owned materials are transported in special government vehicles accompanied by government guards and linked to a central government command and communications network. Privately owned nuclear materials in the United States, on the other hand, are transported by commercial carriers employing private guards and are subject to governmental regulatory requirements.

4. All states protect nuclear facilities and materials according to the types of facilities and materials involved. The most stringent protection is afforded to plutonium and highly enriched uranium and to facilities containing these elements.

5. All states are now studying the adequacy and effectiveness of their physical protection requirements for nuclear facilities and materials. Most states, including the United States, are systematically upgrading these requirements. In part, the reason for such upgrading is that until recently little analytical study was performed to determine the objective threats against which to protect nuclear facilities and materials and to assess how likely such threats are to be successful under varying assumptions. Recently the United States and particularly the Federal Republic of Germany have been analyzing various terrorist "scenarios"—including armed attack—to determine objectively whether existing facilities are sufficiently protected.

The U.S. NRC's requirements for physical protection of nuclear facilities and materials,[31] which are among the most comprehensive national requirements, provide that "licensees shall protect facilities and transport vehicles against acts of industrial sabotage and special nuclear materials against 'theft' " by establishment and maintenance of a physical protection system of: "(1) Protective barriers and intrusion detection devices at fixed sites to provide early detection of an attack; (2) deterrence to attack by means of armed guards and escorts; and (3) liaison and communication with law enforcement authorities capable of rendering assistance to counter such attacks."[32]

For nuclear power plants, the NRC has recently promulgated substantially upgraded requirements to protect them against industrial sabotage. The "general performance requirements" for licensees of such plants necessitate establishment and maintenance of "an on-site physical protection system and security organization which will provide protection with high assurance against successful industrial sabotage"[33] by both of the following:

(1) A determined violent external assault, attack by stealth, or deceptive actions, of several persons with the following attributes, assistance and equipment: (i) Well-trained (including military training and skills) and dedicated individuals, (ii) Insite assistance which may include a knowledgeable individual who attempts to participate in both a passive role (e.g., provide information) and an active role (e.g., facilitate entrance and exit, disable alarms and communications, participate in violent attack), (iii) Suitable weapons, up to and including hand-held automatic weapons, equipped with silencers and having effective long range accuracy, (iv) Hand-carried equipment, including incapacitating agents and explosives for use as tools of entry or otherwise destroying the reactor integrity, and (2) An internal threat of an insider, including an employee (in any position).[34]

To satisfy these general performance requirements, a licensee's physical protection system must include at least the following elements:[35]

1. a physical security system including "properly trained and qualified" guards
2. physical barriers at stipulated areas of the site and the facility
3. controlled access to the facility
4. detection devices, such as alarms
5. a continuous communications system among guards, watchmen, and "armed response individuals"
6. systematic and regular testing of all physical protection barriers, detection devices, communications equipment, and other security-related hardware
7. response capabilities, including liaison with local law enforcement authorities; no less than 10 "guards, and armed, trained personnel immediately available at the facility" (unless fewer are authorized by the NRC); procedures to determine whether a threat exists and to assess the extent of it, as well as to prevent an act of industrial sabotage "by applying a sufficient degree of force to counter that degree of force directed against them, including the use of deadly force when there is a belief that it is necessary in self-defense or in the defense of others"[36]

For licensed nuclear facilities at which strategic quantities of special nuclear materials (SNM) are located,[37] the NRC has more stringent standards than for nuclear power plants. These standards contain the same basic elements as the regulations for nuclear power plants, but they are more precise. Unlike the NRC's performance standards for nuclear power plants, which do not specify specific "threat levels," the NRC's requirements for facilities possessing strategic quantities of SNM require the capability to protect "against hypothetical threats by at least three well-armed, highly motivated, well-trained attackers actively aided by a facility employee in any position, including that of a guard."

To satisfy this standard, the NRC has recently required facilities possessing strategic quantities of SNM to install the following: additional guards, greater capabilities for communicating outside the facility in an emergency, improved alarm systems, better search and surveillance procedures, formalized procedures for support from local law enforcement agencies, and strengthened controls over access to nuclear materials.[38] Similarly, as for the transportation of strategic quantities of SNM, the NRC has upgraded its standards by requiring an increase in the number and training of escort guards and the installation of back-up communications.[39]

For government-owned nuclear facilities possessing strategic quantities of SNM, such as the nation's three enrichment plants, and for government-owned and operated transportation vehicles, physical protection measures are mandated by ERDA and are not subject to NRC regulation. ERDA's physical protection standards tend to be more stringent than the NRC's; like the NRC's, in recent years they have been substantially upgraded. For example, the director of ERDA's Division of Safeguards and Security testified in 1976 before a congressional committee concerning transportation of nuclear material:

As a result of increased terrorism being experienced worldwide, ERDA in 1970 commenced development of an improved system. This improved system is designed to counter the threats of a terrorist group equipped with power tools and other special equipment from penetrating the shipments for a sufficient period of time to allow a reaction force to arrive on the scene.

Additionally, special communication equipment was developed to allow a continuous communication capability between escort vehicles and the transporter as well as the control point. The response time provided by the security of the trailer allows security forces provided by state and local law enforcement agencies, as well as the accompanying escorts, to arrive on the scene before access to the special nuclear material can be attained. After exhaustive testing this system was placed in operation for the various ERDA facilities and is performing satisfactorily. I would hasten to add that no terrorist attacks have occurred. The fact that such a system exists and is, in fact, being used is a strong deterrent against such attacks.[40]

Another ERDA witness testified before this congressional committee:

Our goal is to protect against an overt attack by a well-organized armed group with sufficient strength to overpower conventional security guards and security hardware. Such a group might be in collusion with a security system employee or employees. . . . Detection, assessment, communications, access denial, and response forces all serve to prevent loss of material control. If SNM is lost, then recovery capability enables timely recovery. Use denial techniques for despoiling the material make it difficult for a malefactor to use the material and increase the time available for recovery. All of these elements are being assembled in balanced protection systems of assured effectiveness. Appropriate publicity regarding the existence of such systems can result in psychological deterrence of malefactor actions. Thus, . . . there are five levels at which a malefactor action may be thwarted. Malefactors are forced to successfully complete an entire sequence of actions while the safeguards system to be effective needs only to interrupt one of the many steps in the sequence. This "protection-in-depth" approach, which underlies all safeguards development, means that single elements of an effective safeguards system need not be perfect. With regard to insiders who might attempt to circumvent the system, the protection-in-depth approach incorporates operational procedures and access-enabling interlocks which require a "sequence of independent actions" by several individuals to defeat the system. No one person can either defeat the system or be placed in a duress situation where he might be forced to contribute significantly to its defeat.

Protection of SNM from an incident during transport is generally considered more difficult than at any other time. An example of a current transportation safeguards system is the nationwide ERDA safe-secure transportation system, referred to earlier, for highway shipments of Government-owned SNM. This system incorporates special penetration-resistant and self-immobilizing vehicles, specially trained couriers in armored escort vehicles, a nationwide dedicated communications system for monitoring the status of all shipments, and prearranged response and recovery capabilities. The development of special vehicles which would greatly improve the security and safety of materials during surface transportation was begun over six years ago. The objective has been to prevent access to the cargo in order to allow law-enforcement response forces to arrive and assist in neutralizing an attack.[41]

The United States is the only country that treats physical protection of nuclear facilities and materials as an issue subject to discussion and debate in regulatory proceedings open to public participation. Other countries are willing to discuss openly concepts of a general character, but they consider their specific physical protection standards, techniques, and systems to be classified matters touching national security. As a result, it is not possible to compare the various countries' specific requirements.

Nevertheless, two significant changes in foreign physical protection systems, one in the United Kingdom and the other in France, have recently been made public. In the United Kingdom, the government, following extensive debates in Parliament, has authorized the use of firearms by civilian guards—the Atomic Energy Authority's Special Constables—at the four nuclear energy facilities where plutonium is present, and by escorts of plutonium shipments. This is the first time in British history that civilians have been permitted to hold firearms. The reason for this action, as stated by the Secretary of State for Energy, was "the growing threat of terrorism and the possibility that terrorists will turn their minds to dangerous nuclear materials."[42]

The French government has determined nuclear power plants to be "vital installations" and has placed such plants under a 1959 law that requires physical protection not only after they are in operation, but also during all phases of construction. Accordingly, Electricité de France, the nationally owned utility that is constructing the country's nuclear plants, is required to install physical barriers and to post guards from the moment construction begins at a nuclear power plant site. The extent of protection is required to increase as construction progresses and to reach its maximum when nuclear materials are brought into the site. These new requirements were promulgated shortly after the Fessenheim nuclear power plant, then under construction, was sabotaged by two bombs.

Even though states consider the physical protection of nuclear facilities and materials susceptible only to national programs, over the past three years they have begun to exchange ideas on the technical aspects of physical protection. These voluntary discussions have focused almost exclusively on hardware and have not led to any decisions that could compromise a state's interests in enforcing its domestic law or policing its own security.

Existing International Measures

Currently, there is no international legal regime for the physical protection of nuclear materials or facilities from terrorist or other malevolent acts. Rather, those physical protection systems in existence are imposed by each government and are applicable only to the limits of that government's jurisdiction. These physical protection systems are international only in the sense that they may be influenced through the exchange of technical information with other governments.

The reason for the national character of physical protection systems can be traced to the international legal principle of national sovereignty. Governments, to varying degrees, consider physical protection to be an intrinsically national responsibility tied to domestic police and security functions. Thus they claim not only the exclusive power to exercise such functions within their boundaries, but the inherent necessity to do so in the particular manner reflective of their respective constitutional and legal systems. Accordingly, while governments may agree on the need for, the objectives of, and even the essential elements of a physical protection system, they do not agree on any concept or activity that would permit a state or an international organization to impose or enforce physical protection standards against another state.

Notwithstanding the strongly national character of present physical protection systems, governments are beginning to change their perspectives of the dimensions and implications of the issue. While national sovereignty prevails as an inviolate principle, various states are in fact beginning quietly to pursue several lines of international cooperation on physical protection. This movement is slow and subtle, and although still of modest consequence, it may be laying the groundwork for more systematic and meaningful international cooperation. There are several reasons for this change:

1. Governments fear that nuclear material stolen from one country could be used by terrorists against the interests of another country.
2. Governments fear that without a more common understanding of the

problem and better knowledge of the most current techniques for physical protection, some states' systems may lag behind and become particularly attractive targets for terrorists.

3. Governments fear that the recent increase in public discussion of potential nuclear-related terrorism could feed this idea and actually encourage such terrorist attempts.

4. Governments fear that a serious breach of any state's physical protection system might permit a notorious incident that could bring into question the integrity of other states' systems, thus jeopardizing the public acceptance of these states' nuclear power programs.

The principal forum for international cooperation on nuclear energy has been the International Atomic Energy Agency, a U.N. agency whose secretariat has historically acted on a strong consensus of its board of governors. The IAEA was established in 1957 "to accelerate and enlarge the contribution of atomic energy to peace, health and prosperity throughout the world."[43] It was mandated to "ensure, so far as it is able, that assistance provided by it or at its request or under its supervision or control is not used in such a way as to further any military purpose."[44] The agency's functions are basically two-fold: to assist member states in the safe application of nuclear technology and "to ensure" that governments subject to its jurisdiction do not divert nuclear materials from peaceful to military ends, *i.e.*, the "safeguards" function.[45]

IAEA safeguards are intended to "prevent the diversion of nuclear material by the risk of early detection while minimizing interference with a nation's peaceful nuclear program."[46] In practice, the IAEA administers safeguards by an accounting system for nuclear materials, supplemented by the imposition of containment locks, seals, and other devices that preclude the removal of nuclear materials from critical points of the fuel cycle, and by surveillance devices that monitor movements of nuclear materials within a facility.

These safeguards apply to:[47]

1. projects of the agency and projects of member states where the states request the agency's assistance in providing nuclear materials or technical expertise
2. projects between member states, if so requested
3. projects of a single member state, if so requested
4. activities of states party to regional agreements calling for IAEA safeguards, of which the Treaty of Tlatelolco of 1970 is at present the only one[48] (the IAEA function is to verify compliance with the treaty)
5. activities of states party to the Non-Proliferation Treaty (NPT)

The IAEA administers safeguards in one of two ways: (1) pursuant to a bilateral agreement concluded between the agency and the requesting state or

(2) pursuant to a trilateral agreement among the IAEA, the nuclear supplier state, and the recipient state. If the recipient state is a party to the NPT or the Tlatelolco Treaty, the safeguards agreement covers all nuclear activities within the state. If the state is not such a party, the agreement applies only to the stipulated project or activities.

In contrast to its explicit treatment of safeguards issues, the IAEA statute is silent on the subject of physical protection. Reflecting this silence, its programs have scrupulously avoided this subject with only one notable exception: an agency-sponsored booklet entitled *Recommendations for the Physical Protection of Nuclear Material.*[49] These recommendations, published in 1975 and commonly called INFCIRC/225, update an earlier publication of physical protection recommendations prepared by a panel of experts convened by the director general of the IAEA in 1972. The objectives of the two publications were the same, but the three intervening years shaded their underlying emphasis. In April 1975, the *IAEA Bulletin* introduced the new recommendations with the following explanation:

It is widely recognized that since the previous meetings (1972) took place the need for the adequate physical protection of nuclear materials has increased considerably. Acts of terrorism have grown in frequency and severity. They are perpetrated by an ever-widening variety of groups with different motivations and a range of capability, training and equipment. Having concluded that more serious consideration than hereto must be given to the threat of dispersal of nuclear materials and non-nuclear radioactive materials against theft or sabotage the consultants have defined the elements that should constitute any state's system of physical protection; they have further classified nuclear materials and non-nuclear radioactive materials by their importance from the point of view of physical protection and, lastly, they have made recommendations regarding the level of physical protection needed for each of these classes of material.[50]

Significantly, INFCIRC/225, consistent with the present national character of physical protection systems, subordinates the IAEA's role on this subject to the principle of national sovereignty and concedes that the IAEA's function is only recommendatory and advisory. Thus INFCIRC/225 states that the IAEA's institutional "objectives" on physical protection are:[51]

1. To provide a set of recommendations on requirements for the physical protection of nuclear material in use, transit, and storage. The recommendations are provided for consideration by the competent authorities in the states. Such recommendations could provide guidance but could not be mandatory upon a state and would not infringe on the sovereign rights of states.
2. To be in a position to give advice to a state's authorities in respect of their physical protection systems at the request of the state. The intensity and the form of assistance required are, however, matters to be agreed on between the state and the agency.

For a state's physical protection system, INFCIRC/225 sets forth the following "objectives":[52]

1. To establish conditions that will minimize the possibilities for unauthorized removal of nuclear material or for sabotage.
2. To provide information and technical assistance in support of the state's rapid, comprehensive measures to locate and recover missing nuclear material.

INFCIRC/225 recommends that a state's physical protection system include the following "elements":[53]

1. promulgation of "regulations" to govern the physical protection of nuclear materials "whether in state or private possession." (there should be provision for regular review of the regulations)
2. "licensing" of nuclear activities "only when they comply with the physical protection regulations"
3. "categorization of nuclear material" to ensure "an appropriate relationship between the material concerned and the protective measures" required by the state, taking into account the potential hazard of the material
4. definition of "requirements for the physical protection of nuclear material in use, storage and transit," which definitions should consider "the category of nuclear material, its location (use, transit, storage) and the particular circumstances prevailing either in the state or along the transportation route"
5. establishment of a "system of information" that enables the state to be informed of any change at nuclear sites or transportation of nuclear material that may affect implementation of physical protection measures.

In support of these elements, INFCIRC/225 sets forth the following "Basis for Concern":

The possibility exists that the theft of plutonium, highly enriched uranium or uranium-233 could lead to the construction of a nuclear explosive device by a technically competent group. The theft of plutonium or other radioactive materials could also lead to the use of these materials as radiological contaminants. Finally, one or more individuals could carry out an act of *sabotage* against a facility involved in the nuclear fuel cycle or against a shipment of nuclear material in such a manner as to create a radiological hazard to the public. None of these possibilities can, however, be quantitatively assessed.[54]

Of particular importance is the third element listed, *i.e.*, the need to categorize nuclear material according to its "attractiveness . . . for unauthorized removal," and facilities according to their "attractiveness . . . for sabotage." The categorization adopted in INFCIRC/225 is set forth in Table 2-2.

Table 2-2
Categorization of Nuclear Material

Material	Form	Category I	II	III
1. Plutonium	Unirradiated			
	not easily dispersible	2 kg or more	Less than 2 kg but more than 500 g	500 g or less[c]
	easily dispersible	2 kg or more	Less than 2 kg but more than 10 g	10 g or less[c]
2. Uranium-235	Unirradiated, any chemical form			
	uranium enriched to 20% U^{235} or more	5 kg or more	Less than 5 kg but more than 1 kg	1 kg or less[c]
	uranium enriched to 10% U^{235} but less than 20%	—	10 kg or more	Less than 10 kg[c]
	uranium enriched above natural, but less than 10% U^{235}[a]	—	—	10 kg or more
3. Uranium-233	Unirradiated, any chemical form	2 kg or more	Less than 2 kg but more than 500 g	500 g or less[c]
4. Irradiated fuel		Reprocessing plant Storage facilities separated from reactor sites	Reactor site[b]	

Source: IAEA Doc. INFCIRC/225 (1975), at 6.

[a]Natural uranium, depleted uranium and thorium, and quantities of uranium enriched to less than 10 percent not falling in Category III should be protected in accordance with prudent management practice.

[b]Although the recommendations of the group of experts are for this level of protection, it would be open to states, upon evaluation of reactor characteristics, to assign a different degree of physical protection.

[c]Less than a radiologically significant quantity should be exempted.

To reflect this categorization, a state's physical protection measures "must be designed specifically for each facility after taking into account the geographical location and the state's assessment of the threat."[55] Thus the state's measures should provide "a designed mixture of hardware (security devices), procedures (including guard organization and duties) and facility design (including layout)."[56] Specific recommendations are made in INFCIRC/225 for each of its three categories of nuclear materials.

INFCIRC/225 also covers the protection of nuclear materials in transit and emphasizes that "the transport of nuclear material is probably the operation most vulnerable to an attempted act of unauthorized removal of nuclear material or sabotage. Therefore it is important that the protection provided [be] in depth. . . ."[57] INFCIRC/225 recommends specific requirements for each of its three categories of nuclear materials,[58] as well as for each "mode of transport": road, rail, sea, or air. As with materials in use or storage, physical protection measures for transit are recommended to be proportional to the seriousness of the risk.

In addition to the foregoing recommendations for hardware, procedures, and facility design, INFCIRC/225 provides that an objective of a state's physical protection system should be "to provide information and technical assistance in support of rapid and comprehensive measures by the state to locate and recover missing nuclear material."[59] Thus it recommends that "personnel trained in the facility should be prepared to meet all necessary demands of . . . recovery of nuclear material," and that "particular attention [be] given to the recovery system."[60] For example, with respect to transportation of nuclear materials, INFCIRC/225 provides:

Arrangements should be made to provide an adequately sized and trained team to deal with domestic emergencies. The emergency teams should reach the scene of an incident in transit either while the act of unauthorized removal of nuclear material or *sabotage* is in process so that they can prevent its successful completion, or immediately after its completion, when the possibility of recovery is most favourable. The emergency teams should be sited at strategic locations within the state.[61]

And for materials in use and storage, it provides:

Emergency plans of action should be prepared to counter effectively any possible threats, including attempted unauthorized removal of nuclear material or *sabotage*. Such plans should provide for the training of facility personnel in their actions in case of alarm or emergency. In addition, personnel trained in the facility should be prepared to meet all necessary demands of physical protection and recovery of nuclear material and should act in full co-ordination with external emergency teams and safety response teams, who should also be appropriately trained.[62]

Although INFCIRC/225 recognizes that "a state may delegate the administration of physical protection measures either to a national body, or to duly authorized persons,"[63] it emphasizes that "the responsibility for the establishment, implementation, and maintenance of a physical protection system within a state shall rest entirely with that state."[64] This concept of state responsibility, coupled with the principle of national sovereignty, has significant implications for the physical protection of nuclear materials in international transit because it has tended to preclude the development of an integrated mechanism for the protection of nuclear materials in international commerce. As a result, the physical protection measures for such a shipment often change at the border, and while one state may, for example, require the presence of armed escorts or other special security procedures, the other state may not. The overall pattern of physical protection requirements, therefore, is dominated by inconsistency; each state's physical protection system is keyed to that state's particular national law and policy, rather than to deliberate criteria that embrace the intrinsic protective requirements of the materials being shipped.

This situation regarding physical protection measures differs sharply from the IAEA's treatment of the safety aspects of the transportation of nuclear materials. Since 1959, pursuant to a formal directive of the Economic and Social Council of the United Nations, the IAEA has acted periodically in an official programmatic capacity to promulgate and update specific recommendations to serve as the basis of both national and international regulations for the safe transport of nuclear materials. At present, these recommendations underlie the regulations of nearly all the IAEA's member states and the codes of the principal commercial and international bodies concerned with the transport of goods by road, rail, air, and sea.[65]

The IAEA's different treatment of safety and physical protection measures stems from the commitment of the agency's member states to the rigid application of the principle of national sovereignty. Thus while safe transport requirements are designed to protect materials from unintentional damage or exposure under normal handling and shipping conditions, physical protection measures are designed to prevent deliberate damage or removal. In comparing the nature of these conditions and the different types of regulatory requirements they engender, therefore, the former can be viewed in the economic context of facilitating international commerce, while the latter invoke the security context of a state's domestic policy responsibilities.

Consistent with this interpretation, INFCIRC/225 addresses physical protection of materials in international transport with general language and provides that the responsibility for such physical protection measures should be the subject of agreement between the states concerned. While INFCIRC/225 does not recommend what the nature or content of such an agreement should be, it emphasizes the importance of "advance agreement."[66] Thus it states:

In the case of transit between two states sharing a common frontier, the state's responsibility for physical protection and the point at which physical protection responsibilities are transferred from one state to another should be the subject of an agreement between the states. However, with respect to the maintenance of communication regarding the continuing integrity of the shipment and with respect to the responsibility for carrying out physical protection measures and the recovery actions in the event that a shipment becomes lost, the agreement between the states should provide that this responsibility will rest with the shipping state up to the frontier and will then be transferred to the receiving state.

When international shipments transit the territory of states other than the sending state and the receiving state, the arrangements between the sending and receiving states should identify the other states involved in such transit with a view to securing in advance their co-operation and assistance for adequate physical protection measures for the recovery actions on the territory of such states in case of loss of an international shipment thereon.

. . . .

In addition to the international agreements mentioned above, in contracts or agreements between shippers and receivers involving international transit or material, the point at which responsibility for physical protection is transferred from the shipper to the receiver should be clearly stated.

When the contract or agreement involving international transit provides for delivery to a destination in the receiving state in the vehicle of the shipping state, this contract or agreement should provide that information be supplied in time to enable the receiver to make adequate physical protection arrangements.[67]

For the near term, INFCIRC/225 will probably be the IAEA's boldest endeavor on physical protection. It has generally been received positively by member states and affected commercial organizations—such as companies that insure nuclear materials in transport—as a sound conceptual basis upon which states can develop more precise national regulations and performance standards. In this regard, then, INFCIRC/225 can be viewed as a sound and positive step toward better physical protection of nuclear materials and facilities.

Nevertheless, among the most salient characteristics of INFCIRC/225 is its lack of specificity and mandate. This factor is significant when assessing the practical value of its recommendations as a means of preventing nuclear-related theft or terrorism because it may be possible for a state to believe that it has adopted all the recommendations of INFCIRC/225 and still find its physical protection system wanting for lack of attention to unique conditions within its jurisdiction.

Moreover, other than making general statements of the need for states to arrange for the recovery of stolen nuclear materials within their boundaries and to cooperate with other countries involved in a shipment of nuclear materials to define their respective jurisdiction in recovering stolen nuclear materials, INFCIRC/225 is silent on the issue of how states should plan and prepare for efforts to locate and recover stolen nuclear material. As it is possible that stolen nuclear materials could be taken to a country either unable or unwilling to assist in the search for and recovery of such materials, and as it is also possible that the location of such stolen materials within a region or a country might not be known, such contingency planning would seem to be extremely important. For example, how would states have reacted if the jetliner hijacked to Uganda in June 1976 had been carrying nuclear materials and President Idi Amin had permitted the terrorists to harbor the materials somewhere within the country? And what, if anything, could the United States have done if the nuclear materials were foreign-owned and in transit between foreign countries? These kinds of questions clearly demonstrate the need for stronger national cooperation on physical protection and on the mechanics of how states would cooperate to locate and recover stolen nuclear materials. The question now is what to do next.

Recent developments, both within and outside the IAEA community, point to four possible future actions toward this end:

1. an international convention on the physical protection of nuclear materials and facilities
2. the use of bilateral nuclear cooperation agreements to stipulate the nature of physical protection measures in the recipient country
3. the use of trilateral safeguards agreements, among the IAEA, the state supplying nuclear material, and the state receiving the materials, to provide some degree of IAEA involvement in the implementation of physical protection measures
4. agreement among the states supplying nuclear fuel and equipment to require recipient states to apply the physical protection recommendations of INFCIRC/225 as a condition of the transfer of nuclear technology

An International Convention

INFCIRC/225 recommends that "states should consider the possibility of establishing a convention whereby they could aid each other and in particular in the recovery of nuclear material in cases where such aid would be needed."[68] This convention presumably would cover physical protection measures for both national nuclear programs and international transportation. The U.S. government and other governments support such a convention, but its prospects in the near term appear dim. The reason for this gloomy appraisal is twofold: the obstacle imposed by the principle of national sovereignty, and the practical difficulty of quickly obtaining widespread national support for such a convention. Many states agree about the concept of international cooperation on physical protection, and some also agree that a convention is an effective long-range means to achieve it. Most states, however, seem to believe that the laborious process of drafting a convention on physical protection would itself frustrate hope for early success.

Indeed, these fears are perhaps justified, at least in part. It is likely that the preparation of a convention would take four to six years before the instrument could be opened for signature. Preparatory meetings, working groups, drafting committees, and a diplomatic conference could be required. Not only would the concept of physical protection provoke the kinds of national sovereignty arguments that have stalemated the Law of the Sea Conference and attendant proceedings, but it would also probably provoke complicated and emotional questions of what role the IAEA or other international bodies should play in helping to assure compliance with the convention. It can be assumed, based on the IAEA's difficulties over the past five years in gaining endorsement of physical protection recommendations by the agency's board of governors, that any effort to give the IAEA a function in verifying compliance with physical protection recommendations—for example, those of INFCIRC/225—would be resisted by several states, including some that are now suppliers of nuclear materials and equipment.

On the other hand, a convention dealing solely with the physical protection of nuclear materials in international transit would seem possible, principally because states might be willing to view this intrinsically transnational matter as being outside the narrow confines of their domestic police responsibilities and the principle of national sovereignty. Such a convention could stipulate the respective rights and duties of states under whose authority the materials are being transported, the supplier state, the recipient state, and, indeed, states through which or over which the materials are being transported.

The involvement of third-party states would be a particularly important matter because physical protection of materials transported through a state for the convenience or need of other states requires not only administrative coordination but also financial and personnel commitments to provide actual support. Moreover, to the extent that the supplier state wishes to maintain some degree of control over the protection of the materials while being transported through a foreign jurisdiction, the nature and extent of this police responsibility would have to be stipulated with the host state. Indeed, in the event of an accident—for example, the crash of an airplane or derailment of a train carrying nuclear materials—responsibilities for assuming protective custody over the materials would also have to be addressed.

An outstanding issue that must be considered is how to establish responsibilities among states for the location and recovery of stolen nuclear materials. At present, there is no international instrument that covers this subject, and an attempt to coordinate an effort to this end would present extraordinarily complex legal, technical, administrative, and diplomatic problems. While this matter would obviously raise the issue of national sovereignty and the extent to which intelligence and police cooperation could be effected among states, it is nevertheless so central to the integrity of a comprehensive physical protection system that it cannot appropriately be overlooked.

Bilateral Agreements

Transfer of nuclear materials, equipment, and technology from one state to another is based on specific bilateral agreements for cooperation on the peaceful application of nuclear energy. Such agreements cover the type of assistance to be provided, the terms and conditions of the assistance, and safeguard requirements as provided under the Non-Proliferation Treaty or the IAEA statute. The U.S. government's Agreements for Cooperation with states to which it provides assistance on peaceful applications of nuclear energy, for example, are executed by the executive branch and approved by Congress. Each Agreement for Cooperation provides for the application of IAEA safeguards. None, however, provides for physical protection of the equipment or materials transferred.

The absence of a provision on physical protection is based on the historical belief that physical protection was exclusively a matter of national jurisdiction and that the self-interest of the nation receiving the equipment or materials would be enough to assure adequate protection and security. However, recent U.S. negotiations with other states on new Agreements for Cooperation have departed from this precedent; they represent a new U.S. position on the relevance of physical protection to these agreements.

In particular, the recent U.S.-Egyptian Joint Statement on Proposed Cooperation in Fields Pertaining to the Peaceful Uses of Atomic Energy, which is an antecedent to an Agreement for Cooperation in the near future, provides: "[t]he government of Egypt guarantees to apply effective physical security measures to the facilities and nuclear material covered by the agreement."[69] It is still unclear what effect this statement of principle will have on the conditions inserted into the Agreement for Cooperation although the possibilities include: (1) stipulation by the United States of specific physical protection measures to be applied by Egypt; (2) stipulation by the United States of the recommendations in INFCIRC/225 with the further understanding that the United States and Egypt will agree on the specific measures to be applied by Egypt; or (3) the right of the United States to specify the particular physical protection measures to be applied by Egypt. A major issue raised by each of these alternatives is what means the United States could use to assure Egyptian compliance with the physical protection provision of the Agreement for Cooperation, and what remedies the United States would have in case of Egypt's noncompliance.

Trilateral Safeguards Agreements

The recent FRG-Brazil safeguards agreement with the IAEA—like all other trilateral agreements involving a supplier state, a recipient state, and the agency—provides for IAEA verification that Brazil has not diverted nuclear materials from the peaceful purpose intended by the transfer of nuclear technology.[70] Unlike all the trilateral agreements that predate it, however, the FRG-Brazil agreement provides: "Each contracting Government shall keep the Agency informed of the measures it will take for ensuring the physical protection of nuclear material, nuclear facilities and specified equipment."[71]

This unprecedented provision raises two fundamental questions: what role will the parties require, or, more likely, permit, the IAEA to play? And what effect, if any, will this provision have as a precedent on future trilateral safeguards agreements? As for the IAEA's role, the physical protection provision theoretically opens the possibility that the agency will do more than what a mere literal reading of the language suggests—that is, simply being kept "informed." Indeed, with such information on physical protection in its possession, the agency would have a factual basis for action (if it were to decide to act) such as assuring that the recommendations of INFCIRC/225 are followed, inspecting the actual physical protection measures applied by Brazil to the materials and facilities supplied by the Federal Republic of Germany and the materials in transit from Germany to Brazil, reporting to the IAEA board of governors on the adequacy of these measures, and even requesting modifications to these measures to suit particular national or local conditions in Brazil or along the route of transit.

Although these kinds of IAEA actions may be theoretically possible, it is virtually certain that the IAEA will not follow such a course in the near future. Member states have still not accepted the agency as an appropriate entity for requiring or ensuring the adequacy of national physical protection systems. The effect, therefore, of the innovative FRG-Brazil provision on physical protection will more probably be to inject a subtle, and perhaps even unintended, influence into the evolution of a longer-range role for the IAEA in matters of physical protection. Such an influence would most probably be realized in negotiations of the agency's secretariat with the parties to future trilateral safeguards agreements. In these negotiations, it would seem logical for the secretariat to use the physical protection provision of the FRG-Brazil safeguards agreement as a point of departure in discussing with states how physical protection and the recommendations of INFCIRC/225 will be treated.

In this regard, however, it is instructive to compare how the IAEA board of governors handled the France-Pakistan trilateral safeguards agreement[72] for the transfer of reprocessing technology with how it handled the FRG-Brazil safeguards agreement. Such comparison would seem to minimize the precedential importance of the provision of the FRG-Brazil safeguards agreement, the France-Pakistan agreement contains no provision on physical protection. Still, the board of governors approved it on the same day it approved the FRG-Brazil agreement, without objection even from Germany or Brazil, therefore suggesting that physical protection was not the IAEA's most important consideration in taking action on the two agreements.

This suggested interpretation of the board of governors' action finds support in the ongoing activities of the so-called London Suppliers Conference, a series of meetings held by the nuclear supplier states over the past two years to discuss certain common problems in the transfer of nuclear technology. Although the substance of the conference has been classified, it has been reported that physical protection has been a central subject of discussion and that the supplier states have agreed that their future transfer of nuclear technology will be conditioned on application of a physical protection system by the recipient states. Such an agreement at the London Suppliers Conference could explain why France did not include a physical protection provision in its trilateral safeguards agreement with Pakistan and why the IAEA board of governors approved the agreement without objection or reference to the contemporaneous FRG-Brazil agreement. As it can be presumed that France acted in compliance with agreements reached at the London Suppliers Conference, the inference is that even though a physical protection provision was absent from its agreement with Pakistan, France must have made a bilateral agreement with Pakistan to assure that Pakistan applies physical protection measures to the transferred technology.

It is too early to discern whether other suppliers will voluntarily choose to follow the FRG-Brazil precedent, or will instead, like France, treat physical protection as a purely bilateral subject in their agreements for peaceful nuclear cooperation. It can be assumed that the FRG-Brazil trilateral safeguards agreement will prompt other supplier states to consider whether the IAEA should have a more direct role in physical protection. The United States, for example, will face this issue in negotiating its safeguards agreement with Egypt.

The larger question is whether the United States would attempt, or even desire, to use such a trilateral safeguards agreement as a tactic to move the IAEA into a stronger role on physical protection. Indeed, it would be possible for this agreement not only to provide for Egypt and the United States to keep the IAEA "informed" of physical protection measures—as was done in the FRG-Brazil agreement—but also to provide that the IAEA will stipulate physical protection functions, for example, verifying Egypt's compliance with the recommendations of INFCIRC/225. This approach would dramatically raise the issue of the IAEA's role in physical protection before the agency's board of governors. And if the United States were to offer to finance the IAEA's verification services, this approach would force the resolution of this matter on the narrow issue of whether a broad interpretation of the IAEA statute authorizes such an IAEA function.

Given the pragmatism with which the board of governors functions, the various positions of member states would probably be couched in a mixture of legal and policy arguments. Surely, national sovereignty would be invoked to argue against such an IAEA role. But the agency's broad charter to provide technical assistance to member states on safety and safeguards might offset this argument if both parties to the trilateral safeguards agreement specifically requested the IAEA's assistance with physical protection and, indeed, if the United States provided the agency with the funds necessary to provide this assistance.

Although there is no evidence to suggest that such a scenario is being planned, recent developments at the IAEA indicate that member states are softening in their opposition to the possibility of some kind of IAEA role in physical protection. For example, a resolution of the IAEA General Conference in September 1975

[C]ommends the Director General for his timely action in dealing with the matter of physical protection . . . ; endorses the intention of the Director Genreral to assist member states at their request in the development and strengthening of their national systems for physical protection; and calls upon member states and the Director General to consider ways and means of facilitating international cooperation in dealing further with problems of physical protection. . . .[73]

This language reflects a greatly more sympathetic attitude of IAEA member states on the agency's role in physical protection than at any time in the past. It is concrete evidence that the member states are deeply concerned with the common threat of nuclear-related "theft, vandalism, terrorism, and hijacking," as specifically stated in the 1975 resolution.[74]

Conclusions

Nuclear facilities and materials provide targets that could serve terrorist objectives. Although it would be difficult for terrorists to sabotage nuclear facilities or to steal nuclear materials, a trained and skilled group could accomplish these ends. Such a group could be so motivated if it sought to sensationalize its cause, to attack a symbol of modern society, or to extort a major concession from the government. The likelihood of such acts is unclear, but the serious potential harm to public health and safety and to valuable economic resources, and the public fears that would be provoked by nuclear-related terrorism, require states to take effective measures to protect against such acts.

Neither the Non-Proliferation Treaty, the IAEA statute, nor any other treaty covers the subject of physical protection of nuclear facilities and materials. States have treated physical protection exclusively within the domain of their national sovereignty to exercise police power and domestic security responsibilities. There are no international agreements mandating the use of uniform physical protection practices among states and none to govern the security of nuclear materials in international transit. There is no systematic exchange among states of technical, administrative, or intelligence information concerning physical protection of nuclear facilities and materials or of information concerning terrorists' threat potentials.

No international organization or international coordinative mechanism has been designated or established to plan for or coordinate plans for the contingency of a theft of nuclear materials from one state to another. The efforts of states to commence a dialogue on physical protection matters through the London Suppliers Conference, the *ad hoc* IAEA panels, and bilateral information exchange meetings have been fragmented and piecemeal; they have not been guided by a common integrated purpose or a stipulated objective. These efforts are inadequate for effective contingency planning.

The responsibilities for action and response by states in the event of a theft of nuclear materials across international borders, and indeed, the kinds of administrative and logistic actions that would be necessary, are unclear and unarticulated for even the least complex situation, which would be where all states *are* cooperative. In the more complex situation, where stolen nuclear materials were taken to a state that is unwilling or unable to cooperate in locating and recovering these materials, the potential for confusion among states is great because no guidelines exist to channel an effective response. In the most extreme case, where the location of stolen nuclear materials is not known, there is no mechanism through which states could plan or effect an efficient and timely coordinated search. The international legal principles of national sovereignty and territorial integrity would complicate and perhaps frustrate emergency actions by one state or several states acting collectively to locate and recover stolen nuclear materials in another state.

Recommendations

1. The United States, in cooperation with other states, should seek to designate an international organization or to establish a formal mechanism to deal with physical protection matters. Among the possible options, the United States should consider proposing that this mechanism take the form of a standing committee—adjunct to the IAEA but not within the agency's secretariat—with continuing responsibility for the following:

a. To promote free and systematic exchanges of information concerning physical protection measures and terrorist threat analyses among IAEA member states.

b. To sustain a panel composed of technical experts from IAEA member states to monitor regularly, upgrade, and expand, as necessary, the IAEA's recommendations for physical protection.

c. To compile data and report regularly to the IAEA director general and board of governors on the extent of member state compliance with the IAEA's recommendations for physical protection.

d. To provide a central information and data bank on research and development activities of IAEA member states concerning physical protection systems and vulnerabilities and concerning terrorist threat analyses, and to disseminate regularly this information and data to member states.
e. To provide a forum in which the technical aspects of physical protection and the technical and logistic requirements to locate and recover stolen nuclear materials can be integrated with international legal principles governing the rights and duties of states and the imposition of sanctions where states fail to maintain effective physical protection measures.
f. To stimulate contingency planning among states, outside the forum of this committee and the IAEA, to locate and recover stolen nuclear materials.

2. The United States should aggressively seek the agreement of states on the principles and provisions of an international convention that would establish:

a. the legal basis for national and international physical protection standards that uniformly cover nuclear facilities and nuclear materials at fixed facilities and in transit, including sanctions that may be imposed against states that fail to comply with such standards
b. the rights and duties of states to cooperate with other states in the location and recovery of stolen nuclear materials
c. the institutional mechanisms through which these rights and duties shall be exercised
d. the establishment of a crisis management center or mechanism that would operate in the event of a significant act of nuclear-related terrorism
e. the duty of states to prosecute or extradite individuals responsible for sabotage of nuclear facilities or theft of nuclear materials

Pending the conclusion of such a convention, the United States, acting through the London Suppliers Conference and supplementary bilateral discussions, should seek the agreement of states on the foregoing principles. Among the alternatives for implementing these principles, the nuclear supplier states should consider making such principles standard provisions of their bilateral agreements for cooperation on nuclear energy.

3. The United States should include in its future nuclear energy Agreements for Cooperation, and should negotiate supplementary arrangements to existing U.S. Agreements for Cooperation to include, a provision requiring recipients of U.S.-supplied technology, equipment, and fuel (a) to comply with the IAEA's INFCIRC/225 recommendations for physical protection, and (b) to permit the United States, or the IAEA if such agency is so authorized by the United States, to verify compliance with such INFCIRC/225 recommendations.

4. The United States should include in its future trilateral safeguards agreements with nuclear-recipient states and the IAEA, and should negotiate

supplementary arrangements to such existing trilateral safeguards agreements to include, a provision that the IAEA shall be kept informed of the recipient states' application of the IAEA's INFCIRC/225 recommendations for physical protection; and that, further, if so authorized by the United States, the IAEA shall have the right to verify such compliance. The United States should agree to pay the cost of any such IAEA verification activities.

Notes

1. Treaty on the Non-Proliferation of Nuclear Weapons, July 1, 1968; entered into force on March 5, 1970 for the United States, Mar. 5, 1970, 21 U.S.T. 483; T.I.A.S. No. 6839; 729 U.N.T.S. 161.

2. In the United States, however, "safeguards" is a term commonly used to embrace both the international programs and the U.S.'s physical protection requirements for nuclear facilities and materials within the United States. Thus in the United States the terms "international safeguards" and "domestic safeguards" are often used to separate the concepts.

3. Threats of Violence and Acts of Violence to Licensed Nuclear Facilities, a list released by the Nuclear Regulatory Commission pursuant to a request under the Freedom of Information Act.

4. A third threat posed by terrorists, acquiring an existing nuclear bomb, will not be covered in this study. Because the security systems used by governments to protect their nuclear weapons from unauthorized access are highly classified, it is not possible in the present context to assess the vulnerability of these systems to acts of terrorism. Nevertheless, it is generally known that regulations of the Department of Defense prescribe specific conditions and procedures under which U.S. nuclear weapons must be stored and transported. It is also generally known that channels of communication for the exchange of classified information exist among both nuclear weapons states and non-nuclear weapons states. For the purposes of this study, it must be assumed that these channels are being used appropriately to maintain the security of nuclear weapons installations and transportation vehicles against potential acts of terrorism.

5. ORGANIZATION FOR ECONOMIC COOPERATION AND DEVELOPMENT AND INTERNATIONAL ATOMIC ENERGY AGENCY, URANIUM, RESOURCES, PRODUCTION, AND DEMAND, A JOINT REPORT (Dec. 1975).

6. C.M.E.A. COLLECTED REPORTS ON VARIOUS ACTIVITIES OF BODIES OF THE C.M.E.A. IN 1974 (Moscow, Mar. 1975).

7. NUCLEAR REGULATORY COMMISSION, IN THE MATTER OF GENERIC ENVIRONMENTAL IMPACT STATEMENT ON MIXED OXIDE FUELS, RM50-5 (1976).

8. On April 7, 1977, President Carter stated that the United States "will defer indefinitely the commercial reprocessing and recycling of the plutonium produced in U.S. nuclear power programs." The president took this action as one step in his effort "to find better answers to the problems and risks of nuclear proliferation. . . ." As an alternative to nationally owned and operated reprocessing plants, Carter proposed that various concerned nations "explore the establishment of an international nuclear fuel cycle evaluation program so that we can share with countries that have to reprocess nuclear fuel the responsibility for curtailing the ability for the development of explosives." Remarks of the President on Nuclear Power Policy, White House Press Release, April 7, 1977.

9. THE MITRE CORPORATION, THE THREAT TO LICENSED NUCLEAR FACILITIES, MTR-7022 (Sept. 1975).

10. *Id.* at 75.

11. *Id.*

12. ERDA-NRC, FINAL REPORT, JOINT ERDA-NRC TASK FORCE ON SAFEGUARDS (unclassified version), NUREG-0095/ERDA 77-34 (July 1976) [Hereinafter cited as JOINT ERDA-NRC REPORT].

13. Requirements for the Physical Protection of Nuclear Power Reactors, 10 C.F.R. § 73 (1977).

14. SUBCOMM. ON ENERGY AND THE ENVIRONMENT OF THE HOUSE COMM. ON INTERIOR AND INSULAR AFFAIRS, SAFEGUARDS IN THE DOMESTIC NUCLEAR INDUSTRY, 94TH CONG., 2D SESS., REPORT OF THE SUBCOMM. ON ENERGY AND THE ENVIRONMENT (Comm. Print No. 17, 1976).

15. *Id.* at 3.

16. *Id.* at 3-4. *See also* Jenkins & Rubin, *New Vulnerabilities and the Acquisition of New Weapons by Nongovernmental Groups*, ch. 4 in this book.

17. ENERGY RESEARCH AND DEVELOPMENT ADMINISTRATION, FINAL ENVIRONMENTAL IMPACT STATEMENT, U.S. NUCLEAR POWER EXPORT ACTIVITIES, ERDA-1542 (Apr. 1976), at 6-2.

18. THE BDM CORPORATION, ANALYSIS OF THE TERRORIST THREAT TO THE COMMERCIAL NUCLEAR INDUSTRY, BDM/W-75-176-TR (Sept. 12, 1975) at 10. [Hereinafter cited as BDM REPORT].

19. *Id.* at 12.

20. *Id.*

21. *Id.* at 16.

22. *Id.* at 17.

23. *Id.* at 19.

24. *Id.* at 23.

25. *Id.* at 26-27.

26. *Id.* at 31-48.

27. *Oversight Hearings on Nuclear Energy—Safeguards in the Domestic Nuclear Industry: Hearings Before the Subcomm. on Energy and the Environ-*

ment of the House Comm. on Interior and Insular Affairs, 94th Cong., 2d Sess. 38 (1976) (Statement of Brian Jenkins) [Hereinafter cited as *Oversight Hearings*].

28. U.S. CENTRAL INTELLIGENCE AGENCY, INTERNATIONAL AND TRANSNATIONAL TERRORISM: DIAGNOSIS AND PROGNOSIS, PR10030 (Apr. 30, 1976), at 31.

29. BDM REPORT, *supra* note 18, at 31.

30. For a summary of the provisions of nuclear legislation enacted by OECD-member states, *see* OECD/NEA, NUCLEAR LEGISLATION, ANALYTICAL STUDY (1972).

31. 10 C.F.R. pts. 50, 70, & 73.

32. 10 C.F.R. § 73.55.

33. *Id.*

34. 10 C.F.R. § 73.55(a)(1).

35. 10 C.F.R. § 73.55(b)-(h).

36. 10 C.F.R. § 73.55(h)(3)(v).

37. "Special Nuclear Materials" are commonly defined to be plutonium, uranium-233, or uranium enriched to 20 percent or more in the U^{235} isotope. *See e.g.*, JOINT ERDA-NRC REPORT, *supra* note 12, at i. Strategic quantities are commonly defined to be two kilograms of plutonium or five kilograms of uranium enriched to 20 percent or more in the U^{235} isotope. *Id.*

38. *Oversight Hearings, supra* note 27, at 140 (testimony of Kenneth B. Chapman, Director of the Office of Nuclear Materials Safety and Safeguards, Nuclear Regulatory Commission).

39. *Id.*

40. *Oversight Hearings, supra* note 27, at 514 (testimony of Harvey E. Lyon, Director of Safeguards and Security, Energy Research and Development Administration).

41. *Id.* at 518 (statement of Orval E. Jones, Director, Nuclear Security Systems, Sandia Laboratories, Albuquerque, New Mexico).

42. 906 PARL. DEB. H.C. (5th ser.) 701 (1976) (statement of Anthony Wedgwood Benn, Secretary of State for Energy).

43. Statute of the International Atomic Energy Agency, Oct. 26, 1956, art. II, 8 U.S.T. 1093; T.I.A.S. No. 3873; 276 U.N.T.S. 3.

44. *Id.*

45. *Id.*, art. 3.

46. IAEA Doc. INFCIRC/153 (1971).

47. *See* IAEA Statute, art. XII, *supra* note 43.

48. Treaty for the Prohibition of Nuclear Weapons in Latin America, Feb. 14, 1967, 22 U.S.T. 754; T.I.A.S. No. 7137; 634 U.N.T.S. 364.

49. IAEA Doc. INFCIRC/225 (1975).

50. IAEA BULL. 28 (Apr. 1975).

51. IAEA Doc. INFCIRC/225 § 2 (1975).

52. *Id.*

53. *Id.* § 3.

54. *Id.* § 4.1.1.

55. *Id.* § 5.1.1.

56. *Id.*

57. *Id.* § 6.1.1.

58. *Id.* § 6.

59. *Id.* § 2.1.

60. *Id.* § 5.2.19.

61. *Id.* § 6.2.9.1.

62. *Id.* § 5.2.19.

63. *Id.* § 3.2.1.3.

64. *Id.* § 3.2.1.1.

65. *See* Swindell, *The Safe Transport of Radioactive Materials*, 17 IAEA BULL. (Feb. 1975).

66. IAEA Doc. INFCIRC/225, §§ 6.2.11, 6.4.8, & 6.5.5 (1975).

67. *Id.*

68. *Id.* §§ 6.2.11.3, 6.4.8.3, & 6.5.5.3.

69. 73 DEP'T. STATE BULL. 732 (1975).

70. IAEA BOARD OF GOVERNORS Doc. GOV/1769, (Feb. 2, 1976).

71. *Id.*, art. 19.

72. IAEA BOARD OF GOVERNORS Doc. GOV/1775, (Feb. 16, 1976).

73. IAEA Doc. GC (XIX)/560, (Sept. 25, 1975).

75. *Id.* § (b).

Ocean Vessels and Offshore Structures

J.D. Nyhart and
J. Christian Kessler

Introduction

The nature and extent of human use of the oceans have changed dramatically since the end of World War II. There has been an equally dramatic increase in the use of international terrorism. A third development may ultimately be the most significant of all: the increasing tendency of states to consider international conventions and treaty-made law a useful tool in solving shared problems.[1] This chapter will examine the point at which these three trends come together: how international as well as domestic law can be used to ameliorate the problem of international terrorism against offshore structures, shipping, and other ocean activities.

The next section examines the political and economic milieu within which any solution to the problem of international terrorism will have to develop. The treaties and doctrines in international law that apply or might be brought to bear on the problem are then reviewed. Following this the various mechanisms provided in U.S. domestic laws will be examined. (Due to unfortunate constraints on time and resources, we were not able to analyze the municipal laws of other states that have substantial vessel and offshore structure activity along their coasts, as we had originally intended.) However, the first task is to establish the nature of the potential threat.

A definition of terrorism may be based on either behavior or intent. Some would define terrorism as any act done for a particular purpose, whether or not the act was violent or threatened violence (certain governments are wont to define terrorism this way). In this chapter, international terrorism will be defined as "the threat or use of violence by private persons for political ends where the conduct itself or its political objectives, or both, are international in scope."[2] This definition focuses on both behavior, "threat or use of violence," and intent, "for political ends." It does not consider any outcome of the act. Whether an act results in terrorizing the public or some group of public officials is a question of success, not of intent or behavior. We are concerned with preventing all such acts, whether successful or not.

Western, and especially U.S., jurisprudence does not make the distinction between violence as a political act and violence for some other reason. Yet violence, and often international violence, is committed in the name of national self-determination, which is a right established in international law.[3] Thus the most bitter of international political issues is brought directly into the problem of defining international terrorism for legal purposes.[4]

Although the practice of international terrorism has become all too familiar, acts against maritime objects are relatively rare and usually not well publicized. A brief examination of some of the more successful and well-publicized incidents will demonstrate the range of experience:

1. January 1961—A group of passengers took control of the Portuguese liner *Santa Maria*. In the fight one person was killed and another wounded. The captors declared themselves members of the Portuguese National Independence Movement and proclaimed their goal to be the overthrow of the Salazar dictatorship. After 11 days the ship sailed into Recife, Brazil, where the 560 passengers were freed and the 30 exiled rebels were granted asylum.[5]

2. June 11, 1971—A Liberian registry tanker under Israeli charter was attacked while passing through the Bab el-Mandeb. A launch came around Perim Island, fired three rounds from an antitank rocket-launcher, and then fled behind the island again. The ship suffered no fires or major damage.[6]

3. March 4, 1973—The Greek tour ship *Sanya*, carrying 250 U.S. tourists, was sunk by a limpet mine in Beirut, Lebanon. Haifa, Israel was the next port. The Black September Organization claimed credit.[7]

4. February 2, 1974—A Greek freighter was seized in Karachi, Pakistan, by the Moslem International Guerrillas, who threatened to blow up the ship unless the Greek government freed two Fedayeen then being held for an earlier terrorist attack on the Athens airport in 1973. The terrorists released their hostages and were flown out of Pakistan. Greece later expelled the two Fedayeen to Libya.[8]

5. August 25, 1975—A call to a newspaper in Great Yarmouth, Norfolk, England, claimed that there were bombs on three gas production platforms in the North Sea. Royal Navy divers searched the legs of the platforms but found no bombs.[9]

While these incidents give some indication of what might occur, there are too few known cases on which to base any meaningful generalizations. However, three variables are critical to describing the nature of terrorist attacks against economic targets such as maritime objects: motivations, capabilities, and tactics.

There are four basic motivations for a terrorist attack against an economic target such as a ship or an oil rig. First, terrorists often seek publicity for their cause and an opportunity to expound their beliefs. Second, they often attack to extort funds, gain freedom for comrades, or effect policy changes. Third, they usually seek to intimidate the members and supporters of the government they oppose. Finally, terrorists sometimes attack simply to oppose the specific economic activity that the target performs, *e.g.*, an attack on a production platform producing oil for a former colonial power.

In other forms of terrorism, U.S.-owned property, citizens, or diplomats have often been the targets of terrorist attack not because the terrorists' demands were directed against the United States, but because the United States is a symbol of strength and an important ally of the government that the terrorists oppose.[10] Not only does such an attack demonstrate the power of the terrorists, but it also forces the local government to take extreme actions to avoid further embarrassment over its inability to protect its friends within its own borders. As a large portion of the supertankers and mobile drilling rigs in the world are either owned by or under charter to U.S.-owned multinational corporations, the potential for attacks on these objects is considerable. In addition, terrorists may oppose the specific activities in which these rigs or tankers are engaged, or for whom they are engaged.

For a terrorist group to constitute a threat to society, it must also have the capabilities, personnel, equipment, and technical knowledge to plan and conduct successful attacks. Kidnapings and assassinations require no more than a person and a gun although more sophisticated capabilities may increase the chance of success. Hijacking aircraft was once equally simple, but it has become more complex with the installation of weapons detection equipment at airports. An attack on an offshore structure or ship will require more sophisticated capabilities, such as limpet mines and scuba divers or bazooka-type rocket-launchers and a fast boat. Given the unfortunate fact that these capabilities are obtainable, and that the appropriate detection equipment would be prohibitively expensive or does not exist, governments may have to rely on legal mechanisms to control terrorist activities at sea to an even greater extent than has been the case on land and in the air.

The tactics that terrorists choose will be influenced by both the motivations and the capabilities of the group. If the terrorists want publicity or ransom, and are fairly powerful, they may choose to capture and occupy an offshore structure or ship. A weak group, or a group motivated primarily by opposition to the activity involved or a desire to intimidate the government, would be more likely to destroy or heavily damage the target.

The rights and duties provided by international and municipal law constitute a fundamental aspect of any response to potential terrorism against ocean vessels and offshore structures. Law can provide a mechanism to make offshore structures and ships less vulnerable to attack, and the attackers more likely to be arrested and tried. In the case where terrorists capture and occupy a structure or ship, international law can also provide a mechanism for international cooperation to handle the attack while it is in progress.

Political and Economic Milieus

Any attempt to use international legal mechanisms to solve the problem of international terrorism must consider the context within which this attempt takes place. Many political and economic issues affect states' perceptions of individual incidents and the various legal mechanisms adopted to deal with terrorism. The political context within which any international attempt to respond to terrorism against ocean vessels or offshore structures will take place is the product of states' interests in three issue areas: the ownership and use of ocean resources; the legitimacy or illegitimacy of terrorism as a political tactic; and the status of international legal mechanisms to resolve shared problems. A state's position on these specific issues will to some extent be determined by specific attitudes and interests. However, positions will also be strongly influenced by interests at a second, more fundamental, level of international relations involving such basic concerns as security, development, and ideology. The current U.N. Law of the Sea Conference provides just one example of the degree to which states' parochial and item-specific interests are sometimes overridden by more general political and ideological interests.[11]

The International Context

International politics since the early sixties has been characterized by two cross-cutting cleavages.[12] Of these two, the East-West cleavage has not been of much recent direct influence in ocean-related issues except to make the position of the Soviet Union and East European states ambiguous on occasion. Many international issues are partially structured by an underlying cleavage between the "have" nations of the North and the "have-not" nations of the South. This cleavage often reflects both perceived state interests on the specific problems at issue and the broader communities of interest perceived on such fundamental issues as development and ideology. International agreements on rights to and allocation of ocean resources is one area where the North-South cleavage has been important;[13] the problem of international terrorism and the status of international law are others.

The developed states of Europe, North America, and Japan are the principal users of the oceans. These states have the deep-water navies, the large merchant fleets, the distant-water fishing fleets, and the capital and technology for offshore petroleum production. A substantial portion of this Northern maritime activity takes place off the shores of the less-developed countries (LDCs) of the South. (The following discussion concerns the context of general international solutions, not where acts of terrorism against ocean vessels or offshore structures may occur. Many acts of international terrorism occur in the developed nations of the North, and these nations have substantial maritime activity off their own coasts, as well as many indigenous terrorist groups.)

As most maritime activities are capital-intensive, the LDCs of the South are rarely able to compete with the developed states of the North, even directly off their own coasts. The LDCs often perceive this control of maritime activities by the developed states as neocolonialism. Thus the maritime activities of the developed states in the oceans of the Southern Hemisphere have sometimes become an important political issue. Examples of this tension can be seen in the attacks on Northern worldwide dominance of the liner trades,[14] the attempts to keep major-power navies out of the Indian Ocean,[15] and the debates at the U.N. Law of the Sea Conference on such issues as transit through straits or international control of manganese nodule mining.[16]

Other dimensions of international politics also are important to the international allocation of resources, such as the cleavage between the "geographically advantaged" and the "geographically disadvantaged" states.[17] Because these cleavages do not provide any intersection with comparable cleavages on the issues of international terrorism or international law, they would not have any significant impact on the problem of international terrorism against ocean vessels or offshore structures.

Another important aspect of the problem has to do with the purported ultimate objective of much international terrorism: national liberation. National liberation and the right of every people to national self-determination is one of the principal unifying ideological values among LDC governing elites. Thus terrorist groups that proclaim the liberation of some area or people as their goal enjoy substantial political legitimacy among the people and governments of the Third World. Many LDC governments have provided material and political support for these groups, and until recently most LDC governments have found it politically impossible to oppose these terrorist groups actively. This situation appears to be changing, as more and more LDC governments are refusing asylum to terrorists holding hostages and seeking escape.[18] Some LDC governments may be changing their practice of granting asylum and tolerating terrorist activities on their territory. But perceived legitimacy of these activities in the name of national liberation will remain a serious impediment to establishing international conventions requiring all states either to prosecute or to extradite terrorists.

Not only to the LDCs perceive the problem differently from the way developed states do, but they also have radically different perceptions of international law as a mechanism for resolving problems.[19] Many states, and not only LDCs, consider the process of making international law a political process. This view should come as no surprise, as this concept is the basis of parliamentary democracy. However, it has come as something of a shock that most LDCs also consider the subject matter political and believe that international law is just a formal cloak for the self-interest of the wealthy and powerful.[20]

This perception by LDCs of international law as an institutionalization of the interests of the rich and powerful states of Western Europe and North America has three important implications for the problem of terrorism.

First, in the first two Law of the Sea Conferences, as well as in many other forums, many LDCs have argued that elements of international law established before they became independent states are not binding law for them.[21] Thus traditional legal doctrines must be renegotiated and, unless specifically agreed to by the state in question, may still be rejected at a critical moment. Second, this problem is further complicated by many LDC governments' distrust of experts (most of whom have come from the developed states). This lack of faith in experts has often led the LDCs to prefer vague and general statements of international policy to the highly technical and specific obligations often preferred by Western democracies.[22] LDCs sometimes fear that the more specific language contains traps that they cannot perceive without experts, and therefore they want to maintain maximal flexibility.

Finally, the perception of international law as a cloak for self-interest and the mistrust of a technical approach have led the LDCs to reject legal doctrine *qua* doctrine.[23] Rather than accepting a particular legal doctrine as a general criterion for analyzing some class of conflicts, many LDCs believe that the value of a legal doctrine depends on the context and the nature of the problem. Any principle of international law that has been accepted for some other purpose is therefore not *a priori* transferable to the issue of international terrorism. The only firm basis for international law, in the perceptions of many LDCs, is the maintenance of flexibility to strive for a subjectively and contextually defined justice against the wealthy and powerful states of the North. As states have gained more experience in broad multinational negotiations, such as is provided in United Nations forums, this contrast in their perception of international law appears to have softened somewhat.

It is within this broad political context that the problem of international terrorism against ocean vessels or offshore structures must be considered. Reliance on ocean resources creates a web of dependencies and vulnerabilities among states. The allocation of ocean resources provides areas of contention that may serve as stimuli to international terrorism, and the utilization of these resources involves vessels and structures that are potential targets of such terrorism.

Ocean Uses and International Terrorism

These problems of allocating rights to ocean uses and resources stem from the fact that many resources of the oceans are now, or will soon become, scarce relative to the worldwide demand for them. In other instances, various uses of the oceans conflict with each other or with other activities or values. While it is the purpose of the current U.N. Law of the Sea Conference to resolve these problems or to develop the legal and institutional mechanisms by which they can be controlled, it is clear that even if a treaty is produced, many problems will remain unresolved, and some states will not accept the solutions established by the treaty. Problems of ocean use that are of particular relevance to the problem of international terrorism involve either the allocation of extractable economic resources (such as manganese nodules, petroleum, or fish) or the use of coastal areas for navigation or scientific research. Some potential future uses of ocean space for energy production must also be considered.

The problem of how to allocate exploitation rights to manganese nodules is "the most politically charged and intractable issue" at the Third U.N. Law of the Sea Conference (UNCLOS).[24] These nodules, which constitute a potentially rich source of manganese, copper, nickel, and cobalt, are found principally on the deep ocean floor of the Pacific, although substantial deposits also exist in the Atlantic and Indian oceans.[25] With some exceptions, these deposits lie beyond the continental shelf claims of any state, even under a 200-mile economic zone regime. Exploitation of this resource will involve very sophisticated technology and vast amounts of capital. It is the developed countries, principally the United States, that have both the capability to mine the nodules and the demand for the metals. But the LDCs consider manganese nodules to be part of the "common heritage of mankind," and insist that the profits, or much of the profit, from their exploitation should be divided among the LDCs.

The United States has rejected the proposals of the "Group of 77" (the developing country caucus in U.N. bodies, actually encompassing upwards of 100 countries) to establish an international body to exploit this resource, and bills introduced in Congress for the last several sessions threaten unilateral action unless the UNCLOS produces an agreement satisfactory to the United States. As the U.N. General Assembly passed a "Moratorium Resolution" in 1969 stating that all states "are bound to refrain from . . . exploitation of the resources . . . of the seabed . . . beyond the limits of national jurisdiction" (Res. 2574D),[26] many LDCs would consider any such unilateral action before a new Law of the Sea Treaty was completed to be an act of extremely bad faith. In such circumstances the sophisticated and expensive vessels used to mine nodules could become targets for terrorist attacks. While these vessels would be clear targets with strong and direct ties to a highly ideological issue, an attack on a large ship many hundreds of miles at sea is clearly beyond all but the very largest and most capable terrorist groups. Such an attack must be considered among the remotest of possibilities because of the extreme difficulty involved and because the concept of striking a highly vulnerable object to exercise leverage over some other less vulnerable group (such as deep-ocean miners) is one of the basic strategies of terrorism. (It should be re-emphasized that this chapter is considering only terrorist acts by private persons. Acts of state, whether disguised as terrorism or not, are a different problem from that considered here, and beyond most of the international legal mechanisms discussed below.)

Another important ocean resource is petroleum. As all economic deposits of oil are on the continental margin, the criterion by which this resource would be allocated was decided by the 1958 Convention on the Continental Shelf, which provides that all resources of the seabed and subsoil of the continental margin belong to the littoral state.[27] Numerous conflicts have developed concerning which state has jurisdiction over potentially oil-rich parts of the continental margin. In the North Sea such conflicts were resolved by adjudication and negotiation, but along the rim of Asia many such conflicts have developed which have either been resolved by force or not solved at all.[28] In other areas there are conflicts between the states' central government and regional separatists and in some cases (notably the oil off Scotland), the separatists claim that "their" oil is being stolen by the central government. These conflicts could be, and in the case of Scotland have been, exploited by terrorists.[29]

The offshore petroleum industry has created more desirable targets for terrorists than all other ocean activities combined. Oil and gas are currently produced off 34 states[30] with exploration off the shores of at least 17 more states.[31] The exploration for and exploitation of offshore petroleum involve many types of vessels and structures. Drilling ships and rigs, served by supply boats and tenders, drill to find the petroleum. Then production platforms, which are usually unmanned once drilling is completed, are built. The petroleum is usually taken ashore by pipelines, although tanks or barges to store the oil are sometimes built nearby. In the Java Sea, floating plants have been constructed that convert natural gas to fertilizer compounds even before it is taken ashore.[32] These facilities provide valuable, and in many cases quite vulnerable, targets for terrorists. Such attacks might be motivated by opposition to the government that licensed these facilities, to the government of their owners, or to the multinational corporation owners themselves. Attacks on offshore petroleum production or export facilities might also be motivated by opposition to the activity itself, although this motive would more probably be secondary. As noted previously, one threat against offshore production platforms has already been publicly recorded, and the possibility of future attacks cannot be discounted.

Petroleum transportation by sea provides other potential targets for terrorists. Although entirely a development of the last decade, today there are more than 500 supertankers over 175,000 deadweight tons (DWT) displacement.[33] Both the economic value of such a ship and the pollution resulting from its sinking make it a potentially dramatic, and thus highly attractive, target for terrorists. Liquid natural gas (LNG) tankers are a still more recent development that provide equally, if not more, attractive targets for terrorists desiring publicity. There are several instances of terrorist threats or actual attacks on petroleum tankers, although none has resulted in any significant damage. Along with offshore production facilities, petroleum tankers must be considered among the most likely maritime targets for terrorist attacks.

Over 40 states utilize special deep-water moorings to export or import crude oil on supertankers.[34] Most of these moorings are several miles or more offshore. The more complex, often known as "superports," involve several moorings combined with a fixed platform for the pumping station and control facilities. Like offshore production facilities, superports may provide tempting, if somewhat difficult, targets.

Although commercial shipping is ordinarily too prosaic to be of interest to terrorists, in some areas of the world transit rights or political control have become such volatile issues that this has not always been, and may not always be, the case. Many coastal LDCs have argued that the right of innocent passage through international straits (many of which would fall entirely within coastal states' territorial seas under a 12-mile rule) should be a much more limited right than has been the practice.[35] Any final treaty coming out of UNCLOS will be much less restrictive than the extreme demands made by some LDCs. Local dissident groups might choose to label their governments as "lackeys of imperialism" for not having pressed more extreme positions, and they might attempt to dramatize their words by attacking merchant shipping. This might especially be the case in some states that argued for the archipelagic doctrine, which would make all waters within an archipelago—in some cases including major international straits—internal waters of that state, thus severely restricting rights of transit. While merchant shipping would appear to be among the less probable targets for terrorists, most incidents of terrorism at sea have involved commercial vessels as targets.

The Panama Canal presents a similar situation with regard to the potential for terrorism. However, the legal regime in this case is ruled by the Hay-Bunau Varilla Treaty of 1903.[36] Because the Panama Canal is a unique case not subject to the same principles of international law as other transit issues, it will not be analyzed further.

Fishing would not appear to provide any issues of relevance or targets of interest to international terrorists. Although almost all ocean fishing takes place on the continental shelf, so that fishing vessels are relatively close to shore and thus vulnerable, individual vessels are not very valuable, nor is the industry ideologically controversial. Many conflicts of great bitterness have developed over fishing rights, however. Iceland and Great Britain are in the midst of their third "cod war." Ecuador continually arrests foreign, usually U.S., tuna boats that fish without proper licenses. Off the U.S. Atlantic and Pacific coasts, foreign fleets take heavy catches that have caused U.S. fishermen to complain for years. These complaints recently compelled the U.S. Congress to take unilateral action establishing a 200-mile limited zone in spite of administration opposition due to the on-going UNCLOS negotiations.[37] Many of these conflicts have been marked by some violence between the enforcement officials of the littoral state and the distant-water fishermen. Some of these conflicts also involve armed attacks by local fishing boats on the distant-water fishermen who have come to work the fishing grounds. In at least one case—the "prawn war" in the Gulf of Carpentaria on the north coast of Australia—these attacks have become regular occurrences.[38] While they are not international terrorism as ordinarily viewed, these acts clearly constitute a borderline case, similar to the hijacking of the *Santa Maria*, which may influence some states' preferences concerning the international legal mechanisms to be established.

Marine science has become a contentious issue, both at the 1958 Geneva law-of-the-sea (LOS) talks and during the current UNCLOS, because of the LDCs' concern for the economic and military significance of scientific informa-tion about the coastal zone and continental shelf areas.[39] While scientific vessels do not have the value, visibility, or direct relationship to some ideological issue to make them prominent targets for terrorists, scientific vessels, like merchant vessels, might provide local dissidents with a method of dramatizing accusations that the government is soft on imperialism and neocolonialism.

Many other uses of ocean space will develop in the remainder of this century, especially new methods of energy production. Floating nuclear power plants (FNPs) will probably appear first off the East Coast of the United States in the early 1980s.[40] Large plants that produce electricity by ocean thermal energy conversion (OTEC) may appear a little later.[41] Methods of producing power from tides, waves, sun, wind, and ocean currents are also being explored and may result in new classes of maritime objects.[42] While most of these proposals are not developed enough to evaluate as targets of terrorism, the potential for terrorist attacks on FNPs is clear: FNPs would represent a new step in the use of nuclear power, and they would be located within sight of shore (*i.e.*, they would be quite easy targets to locate and reach).

Ocean Terrorism in International Law

Prohibitions or denunciations of terrorism in international agreements and documents are many.[43] They presumably apply to acts on the oceans as on land. However, the continued persistence of terrorism indicates that inter-national law has yet to make a serious impact on the problem. A search for a more effective legal framework applicable to acts on the oceans begins with an examination beyond these general statements of the international law-of-the-sea framework.

The acts with which this chapter is concerned are likely to have several common elements, including:

1. the threat or use of violence
2. by private persons
3. for political ends and
4. with an international character.[44]

The first and last elements may offer the least ambiguity in the law of the sea. Threats or the use of violence[45] are on the surface comparatively readily identifiable. The "international character," however, requires more attention.

The International Element in Ocean Terrorism on the High Seas

Ocean terrorism on the high seas would appear to be "international in scope" by definition. The 1958 Convention on the High Seas[46] provides that "[t]he high seas being open to all nations, no State may validly purport to subject any part of them to its sovereignty."[47]

Thus it would seem that an act of terrorism on the high seas would be an international act although it would not necessarily fall into either of Bassiouni's two situations defining an "international element"—*i.e.*, when "the perpetrator and victim are citizens of different states" or when "the conduct is performed in whole or in part in more than one state."[48] While most likely the perpetrator and victim would in fact be of different states, the perpetrator's identity might be unknown, clouded, or open to question. In the case of structures and ships having complicated financing and ownership patterns, the victim's nationality may also be unclear. Alternatively, the presence of "an international element" that depends on the act's taking place in "more than one state" does not fit the case on the high seas. Thus it would seem best at the outset to recognize that the international character of a high seas act of terrorism is analogous to that of piracy.

It might be argued that a vessel's or structure's flying a flag, the law of the state of which is the applicable law on the vessel or structure, gives any act done to or on the vessel or structure a national rather than an international color. However, flying the flag of a nation does not create a state of sovereignty aboard the vessel but rather establishes a responsibility for jurisdiction over acts done by it and on board it, but not necessarily to it.[49] The international character of the high seas still would appear to provide an international element.

Piracy. One of two high seas crimes recognized by the Convention on the High Seas is piracy.[50] Article 15 defines piracy, and article 19 provides that on the high seas, or in any other place outside the jurisdiction of any state, every state may seize a pirate ship or aircraft or a ship taken by piracy. Acts of government vessels, including warships, under the control of a mutinous crew are assimilated to acts by a private ship (art. 17).

If terrorism could be subsumed under piracy, then its status as a recognized high seas illegal act would be established. However, the article 15 definition creates at least two stumbling blocks.[51]

First, it refers to illegal acts of violence committed for private ends. This chapter's definition of terrorism refers to acts by private persons for political ends. A political end is not inherently a public end. Private ends might also be political, but the use of the term "private ends" specifically suggests that such an interpretation was not intended. In terms of recent ocean terrorist activity, it is worth noting that in the *Santa Maria* case, characterization of the act as piracy was withheld because the group seizing the ship publicly identified themselves with a political movement whose coup was supposed to be happening at the same time in Portugal.[52]

Second, article 15's construction raises an interesting subordinate problem. Rubin points out that the inclusion of the word "illegal" to modify "acts" logically suggests the existence of acts that otherwise were legal and that are now rendered illegal when done under the conditions of the article.[53] At the municipal law level, this logic suggests that acts of rebels might be recognized as being governmental in nature. As Rubin points out, it is state practice to ignore, or at least not get in the way of, internal rebellions.[54] When rebels gain control they are recognized. The definition of piracy has been used against rebels by their being so labeled, but not in their support as the application of Rubin's analysis might make possible. The same analysis might be applied to terrorists in support of their activity.

Acts on High Seas over the Continental Shelf. The 1958 Convention on the Continental Shelf[55] preserves the international character of the high seas superjacent to areas of the seabed and subsoil that are being exploited by a coastal state while simultaneously giving the state the power to protect the structure, vessels, or other equipment involved in the exploitation. Article 2 provides that the coastal state has sovereign rights for the purposes of exploration and exploitation, while article 3 states that these rights do not affect the legal status of the superjacent waters.

Article 5(2)(3) provides for safety zones of 500 meters around installations and authorizes the coastal state to take measures necessary for the protection of the installations within the zones. Thus authority to maintain public order generally exists. Acts of terrorism involving structures and activities related to exploration and exploitation of the seabed and subsoil on the continental shelf would fall under the protective jurisdiction of the coastal state.

Ocean Terrorism Within the Territorial Seas and Contiguous Zone. Under existing international law, the coastal state would be free to deal with acts of violence defined here as terrorism as it chooses within its territorial sea. Article 1 of the 1958 Geneva Convention on the Territorial Sea and Contiguous Zone provides that the coastal state shall have sovereignty in its territorial sea,[56] subject to guaranteeing innocent passage to vessels[57] and to other rules of international law. Innocent passage is defined as "navigation through the territorial sea for the purpose either of traversing, . . . or of proceeding to internal waters, or of making for the high seas. . . ."[58] Acts of terrorism would not appear to constitute innocent passage.[59]

If an act of terrorism in the contiguous zone threatened to break a regulation that concerned customs, fiscal, immigration, or sanitary matters within its territory or territorial sea, the coastal state would have the authority to act to prevent such infringement.[60] The coastal state thus probably has authority to prevent (or punish) an act of violence against an offshore structure in the zone that is likely to result in the pollution of the territorial sea.

Several countries, including the United States, have established unilaterally special zones of jurisdiction beyond the territorial sea dealing with matters not covered by article 24. These special zones deal variously with security and defense,[61] fisheries,[62] broadcasting,[63] and environmental protection.[64] Thus the prospect of unilateral offshore jurisdiction authorized to deal with terrorism domestically should not be ruled out if such acts become a perceived, significant threat.

International authority derived from a new law-of-the-sea treaty must still be considered a viable alternative, in spite of the current pessimism surrounding the LOS negotiations.

The Prospective Impact on Terrorism of an International Law-of-the-Sea Treaty

While the Single Negotiation Texts of the Third United Nations Law of the Sea Conference make no explicit reference to terrorism, they do put forward several concepts which, if adopted in a final treaty, would substantially affect the coastal states' power to combat terrorism.[65] Committee II's text is particularly relevant.

The High Seas. Two general provisions could impose new duties on states that would affect their responses to acts or threats of terrorism. First, while the high seas are preserved as "open to all states" (art. 74) in which "no state may validly purport to subject any part . . . to its sovereignty" (art. 75), the use of the high seas "shall be reserved for peaceful purposes" (art. 74). Thus a new general prescription against violence is added, which might, if given credibility, bring international weight of law to bear on terrorism. This possibility is furthered by the reappearance of existing article 6, which provides that "[e]very State shall effectively exercise its jurisdiction and control in administrative, technical and social matters over ships flying its flag" (art. 80). Thus it may be that violence, including acts of terrorism *qua* national liberation activity, is banned on the high seas even though such acts may be acceptable to some nations when done on land.

A second new provision [art. 80(7)] requires states to hold an inquiry into "every marine casualty or incident of navigation on the high seas involving a ship flying its flag and causing loss of life or serious injury to nationals of another State or serious damage to shipping or installations of another State or to the marine environment." Presumably an inquiry into an act of terrorism would be required if it could be established that the attack involved a vessel flying a legally identifiable flag. Thus an international prescription to follow up and investigate, rather than ignore, terrorism on the high seas may emerge from a treaty.

The Economic Zone. Acts of terrorism are normally perpetrated against objects of economic or political value. Offshore, most of these objects will be within the 200-mile exclusive economic zone proposed in the negotiations. Under the SNT, within the zone's boundaries the coastal state would have:[66]

1. sovereign rights for the purpose of exploring and exploiting, conserving and managing the natural resources, whether renewable or nonrenewable, of the bed and subsoil and the superadjacent waters
2. exclusive rights and jurisdiction with regard to the establishment and use of artificial islands, installations, and structures
3. exclusive jurisdiction with regard to other activities for the economic exploitation and exploration of the zone, such as the production of energy from the water, currents and winds; and scientific research
4. jurisdiction with regard to the preservation of the marine environment, including pollution control and abatement
5. other rights and duties provided for in the present convention

The exclusive economic zone would be, of course, a new institution. The meanings of the working of its articles are not yet fully formed. As to coastal states' powers to deal with terrorism, much would probably turn on whether the wording of article 45(1) was read broadly or narrowly in at least two respects. First, would the granting of sovereignty in subsection (a) be applied generally to the subject matter—e.g., the natural resources of the bed, subsoil, and super-adjacent waters—or second, would sovereignty be confined to the action purposes identified—e.g., exploring, exploiting, conserving, and managing those resources? If the first interpretation were taken, then the right to protect associated structures and vessels against acts of terrorism might be derived from the general grant found in 45(1)(a). If the second interpretation were taken, then the question would arise whether "managing," or possibly "conserving," carried the right to protect the assets involved.

The presence of a separate 45(1)(b) raises additional questions, however. First, does the separate grant of exclusive rights and jurisdiction with regard to the establishment and use of artificial islands, installations, and structures mean that such objects associated with the purposes of 45(1)(a) are to be dealt with under (b) and not under (a)? If so, then the question discussed in the preceding paragraph becomes moot. But similar questions arise concerning (b). Do "exclusive rights and jurisdiction" include the general right to protect against terrorism? If not, do exclusive rights and jurisdiction with regard to their "use" contain that authority?

The issue is elaborated in article 48, which provides in part that the coastal state shall have exclusive rights to construct, authorize, and regulate the construction, operation, and use of these objects [art. 48(1)]. Their safety is directly addressed in article 48(4)(5), which provides for the creation of safety zones around them, up to a distance extending 500 meters from each point of their outer edge.[67] Within the safety zones, coastal states may take "appropriate measures to ensure the safety both of navigation and of the artificial islands, installations, and structures."

Within the safety zone, the coastal state's power to protect is clear, and that is the area of most concern. The question becomes less clear outside the safety zone. Under article 97, hot pursuit in cases of violations of the laws and regulations of the coastal state exists in the economic zone (and on the continental shelf), including the safety zones.[68] But authority to take anticipatory action would probably have to be derived from either the general language of article 45(1)(a) or (b), and/or from the words "managing" [art. 45(1)(b)], or "regulate" [art. 48(1)].

It would seem reasonable for the coastal state to have full panoply of power to act within the economic zone anticipatorily, at the time of a terrorist attack, and afterward, in view of the powers given it and reviewed above. That the proscription against violence on the high seas applies in the economic zone,[69] as does the responsibility for effective administration of vessels,[70] and inquiry into marine casualty incidents adds force to this conclusion.[71]

Similar analyses can be made to article 45(1)(c), granting exclusive jurisdiction with regard to other activities for the economic exploitation and exploration of the zone, such as the production of energy from the water,[72] currents, and winds; and scientific research. Further elaboration pertinent to terrorism is not apparent,[73] but the conclusions already drawn about the coastal state's power would seem applicable here.

Article 45(1)(d), providing jurisdiction with regard to preservation of the marine environment, likewise raises the question of whether power to combat terrorism is inherent. If the terrorist activities violate environmental laws, power to combat would seem to exist under an analysis similar to that provided earlier.

Territorial Seas under the SNT. Three changes or additions proposed in the SNT would significantly affect coastal states' authority and responsibility to combat terrorist activity.

First, the breadth of the territorial sea would be uniformly set at 12 miles.[74] For some nations, this determination would mean an extension of sovereignty seaward. Much terrorist activity would presumably take place close to shore, where ambiguities present in the economic zone are absent.

Second, there is a long list of activities that are considered to be prejudicial to the peace, good order, or security of the coastal state and therefore not within the meaning of innocent passage. These acts include:[75]

1. any threat or use of force against the territorial integrity or political independence of the coastal state or in any other manner in violation of the Charter of the United Nations
2. any exercise or practice with weapons of any kind
3. any act aimed at collecting information to the prejudice of the defense or security of the coastal state
4. any act of propaganda aimed at affecting the defense or security of the coastal state

5. the launching, landing, or taking on board of any aircraft
6. the launching, landing, or taking on board of any military device
7. the embarking or disembarking of any commodity, currency, or person contrary to the customs, fiscal, or sanitary regulations of the coastal state
8. any act of willful pollution, contrary to the provisions of the present convention
9. the carrying on of research or survey activities of any kind
10. any act aimed at interfering with any systems of communication of the coastal or any other state
11. any act aimed at interfering with any other facilities or installations of the coastal state
12. any other activity not having a direct bearing on passage

Most acts of terrorism would fall under one or another of these clauses (kidnaping persons not citizens of the coastal state is a conceivable exception). Article 18 provides that the coastal state may make laws and regulations relating to innocent passage through the territorial sea concerning a list of items, which includes "the protection of navigational aids and facilities and other facilities or installations,"[76] "the protection of cables and pipelines,"[77] "the prevention of infringement of the fisheries regulations of the coastal State, including, *inter alia*, those relating to fishing gear,"[78] "the preservation of the environment . . . ,"[79] and "the prevention of infringement of the customs, fiscal, immigration, quarantine or sanitary or phytosanitary regulations of the coastal State."[80]

Article 22 authorizes the coastal state to take "the necessary steps in its territorial sea to prevent passage which is not innocent." Article 23 establishes ships' liablity for damage for failure to comply with rules of navigation in the territorial sea, which might hold some significance if terrorists were apprehended.

Thus in the territorial sea, the coastal state is sovereign, subject to the major limitation of vessels' rights of innocent passage; noninnocent passage is defined to include most imagined acts of terrorism; coastal states may act to prevent noninnocent passage; and the state is empowered to make laws to regulate several aspects of innocent passage that might pertain to terrorism.

The specificity of the elaboration of the concept of innocent passage actually creates a substantial limitation on the total sovereignty of the coastal state. For this reason, it may be desirable not to consider the state's power to combat terrorism in its territorial sea in terms of noninnocent passage, but rather as a component of its routine sovereign power of self-preservation.

Significantly, however, there is apparent authority in the SNT's provisions on innocent passage to provide a substantial international basis for establishing the illegality of most acts covered by this chapter's definition of terrorism.

The Continental Shelf. Under the SNT, the coastal state would exercise sovereign rights over the continental shelf for purposes of exploration and exploitation of its natural resources (art. 63). Basically, the regulatory authority pertinent to protection against terrorism is the same as that in the economic zone, which is recognized in article 66.[81]

The International Element under the SNT

Earlier, it was argued that under the 1958 conventions, the international character imbued in the concept of the freedom of the seas, subject to the sovereignty of no nation, provided a sufficient basis for international legal concern over the subject of terrorism on the oceans. The Single Negotiating Texts go further. The high seas—and by incorporation, the waters of the exclusive economic zone—are reserved for peaceful purposes. Any violent act of a terrorist character in these ocean zones would violate that international norm. The international character has become clearer.

In the territorial seas, it is most likely that acts of violence contemplated in this study would fall among the noninnocent acts of passage. And here an international norm would be violated, providing an international element.

U.S. Legal Treatment of Ocean Terrorism

Jurisdiction

The current jurisdictional limits of U.S. authority are clearly set out in international and domestic law. Excellent statements of U.S. geographical jurisdiction abound, and the statutes need be only briefly summarized. At the edges, the jurisdiction is fuzzy, so those parts will be examined here. The prospective limits of jurisdiction are also defined to a reasonable extent, assuming that the apparent consensus in the United Nations Third Law of the Sea Conference regarding new limits holds.[82]

U.S. jurisdiction on the oceans may be delimited in a number of ways. Within its territorial sea, extending for 3 nautical miles from the baseline, the United States exercises sovereign power under the 1958 Convention on Territorial Sea and Contiguous Zone.[83] In its contiguous zone—which extends out to 12 nautical miles—the United States may exercise control necessary to prevent and to punish infringements of regulations pertaining to sanitary, fiscal, immigration, and customs matters.[84] On the high seas, which extend beyond the territorial sea, no nation may validly purport to exercise sovereignty,[85] with the exceptions to the concept that are made by the contiguous zone and by the outer continental shelf concept discussed below.

There is an additional jurisdictional basis for U.S. law enforcement and other regulatory activities under the 1958 Convention on the Continental Shelf[86] and the 1953 Outer Continental Shelf Lands Act.[87] The latter extends

U.S. laws and political jurisdiction to artificial islands and structures engaged in the exploitation and exploration of the resources of the seabed and subsoil on the continental shelf.[88] In the case of deep-water ports outside the territorial sea, similar provisions in the Deepwater Port Act of 1974[89] extend the reach of criminal and civil laws.

If a U.N. law-of-the-sea treaty is effected, there will probably be general agreement on the extension of the territorial seas to a distance of 12 nautical miles. In effect, the contiguous zone will disappear. And it is likely that the treaty will create a new jurisdictional concept, the economic zone, which would extend 200 miles outward from the baseline. This zone would provide for the extension of sovereign rights in many cases, and exclusive or nonexclusive jurisdiction in others.[90] The newly expanded territorial sea and the economic zone would encompass most of the activities that might be the objects of terrorist attack.

Vessels have the nationality of the nation whose flag they fly.[91] That nation, with a few exceptions, has exclusive jurisdiction on the high seas over vessels flying its flag.[92]

Pursuant to these jurisdictional bases, Title 18, Crimes and Criminal Procedures, of the United States Code extends part of U.S. criminal law to a "Special Maritime and Territorial Jurisdiction of the United States." This jurisdiction, defined in 18 U.S.C. § 7, includes:

the high seas, and any other waters within the Admiralty and Maritime jurisdiction of the United States and out of the jurisdiction of any particular state, and any vessel belonging in whole or in part to the United States, or any state, territory, district, or possession thereof, when such vessel is within the Admiralty and Maritime jurisdiction of the United States and outside the jurisdiction of any particular state.[93]

The offenses specifically listed in Title 18 as being within this special maritime and territorial jurisdiction cover a wide range of offenses of the sort likely to take place under terrorist attack.[94]

Thus while all the criminal code would be applicable in the case of the outer continental shelf and deep-water ports, only designated sections of the code apply in the special maritime and admiralty jurisdiction areas.

From this brief description, it can be seen that there is a jurisdictional gap in the present structure, which is of potentially critical significance. Offshore structures that are not vessels, that are outside the territorial sea, and that have nothing to do with the exploration and exploitation of the continental shelf's seabed or subsoil do not fall within the general jurisdictional ambit of the United States as now conceived. The exception is deep-water ports; the Deepwater Port Act of 1974 asserts the extension of U.S. law but carefully stops short of an assertion of jurisdiction.[95] Future structures for nuclear power plants, ocean thermal energy conversion operations, ocean airports, or similar purposes would require similar unilateral assertions of legal and political authority if located beyond the territorial sea. And they would present the issue of legitimacy of such assertions in light of the 1958 Convention on the High Seas. The ratification of an LOS treaty with an extended territorial sea and an economic zone would cure this jurisdictional gap.[96]

An additional issue arises as to what constitutes a vessel, given the existence of a wide range of floating industrial structures such as jackup rigs and submersible or semisubmersible platforms used either in drilling or in production. In the future, the variety of these floating platforms is likely to increase. Whether or not they are categorized as vessels may affect their jurisdictional status and the applicability of many statutes to activities on and around them.[97] In many instances, the term "vessel" has been given the broadest definition. In the Deepwater Port Act, for example, a "vessel" means "every description of watercraft or other artificial contrivance used as a means of transportation on or through the water."[98] However, the criminal code definition is one of the older forms that sheds little light on the types of structures considered to be vessels. 18 U.S.C. § 9 provides only that "the term 'vessel of the United States,' as used in this Title, means a vessel belonging in whole or in part to the United States, or any citizen thereof, or any corporation created by or under the laws of the United States, or any state, territory, district, or possession thereof." Thus the problem is not fully solved. It is minimized, however, due to the coverage of artificial islands and structures in the Outer Continental Shelf Act and the coverage of deep-water ports under the Deepwater Port Act, plus the widened acceptance of broader definitions of the word "vessel" in legislation as indicated below.

Finally, it should be noted that only in a limited number of cases does the United States assert jurisdiction over its nationals beyond its own territory or those jurisdictional areas listed above. These include the subpoena and return of witnesses required in criminal trials,[99] treason,[100] attempting to influence a foreign government in its relations with the United States,[101] the imposition of income tax,[102] and the hijacking of airplanes, since the adoption of the Antihijacking Act of 1974, which implements the Hague Convention by extending limited universal jurisdiction over hijackers of whatever nationality.[103] But there is no general assertion of control over criminal behavior of U.S. nationals globally.

Substantive Law

There is no statutory or regulatory offense in U.S. law dealing directly with terrorism *per se*, either generally or as specifically applied to the oceans.[104] However, there are at least five categories of law that bear on ocean terrorist activities and that could serve as a basis for preventive, corrective, and punitive action:[105]

1. the criminal code generally, and state criminal law
2. sections of the criminal code specially applicable to the maritime jurisdiction
3. laws not in the criminal code that nevertheless provide criminal or civil sanctions for activities related to those that terrorists might undertake
4. laws providing authority for regulatory provisions concerning terrorist activities
5. laws providing enforcement authority to federal instrumentalities

U.S. Criminal Law. As noted earlier, all U.S. statutes carrying criminal sanctions would be applicable on the waterfront, within the territorial sea, and under the coverage of the Deepwater Port and Outer Continental Shelf acts. In addition to the common felonious offenses, several laws might be pertinent, including those dealing with offenses such as civil disorders,[106] conspiracy to deprive civil rights,[107] theft from interstate commerce,[108] extortion,[109] kidnaping,[110] destruction of communication systems,[111] mutiny and mutiny-related activities,[112] interference with commerce by robbery or extortion,[113] stowaways,[114] and firing or tampering with vessels.[115]

In addition to federal law, state criminal law would be applicable unless pre-empted at waterfront facilities and within the territorial sea.[116] Beyond, both the Outer Continental Shelf Lands Act and the Deepwater Port Act provide that state law shall apply within their respective ambits if not in conflict with federal law.[117] But the issue of a state criminal law's assimilation into federal law under these provisions apparently has not been tested in the courts.

Criminal Provisions within the Special Maritime and Territorial Jurisdiction. There are several offenses explicitly within the special maritime jurisdiction discussed earlier that bear on terrorism. They cover acts that might comprise some or all of a terrorist incident on the oceans: homicide,[118] arson,[119] assault,[120] maiming,[121] false pretenses,[122] destruction or injury to property,[123] plunder of distressed vessel,[124] attack to plunder vessel,[125] robbery and burglary,[126] incitation of seamen to revolt or mutiny,[127] assault on or resistance to any person authorized to make searches and seizures,[128] destruction of vessel by nonowner,[129] and breaking and entering vessel.[130]

Laws Providing Authority for Regulatory Provisions Concerning Terrorist Activity. The criminal sanctions reviewed above would provide an enforcement basis of considerable scope in confronting terrorist activities on the ocean and related areas. In addition, however, a battery of laws exists that contains authority under which federal regulations could be issued to deal in more detail with terrorism. Although none of the major statutes regulating waterfront ports and harbor facilities, deep-water ports, and offshore structures prohibits or indirectly covers terrorist activity, they all contain adequate language on which to base regulations covering such incidents. Such language speaks mostly in terms of safety.

The basic statute providing for the security of U.S. ports is the Magnuson Act of 1950 (50 U.S.C. § 191). Passed as an emergency powers act, it remains the basis for the regulations relating to the safeguarding of vessels, harbors, ports, and waterfront facilities. The act provides that when the president finds that national security is endangered in any of several ways, including subversive activity or disturbances of U.S. international relations, rules and regulations may be issued to "safeguard against destruction, loss, or injury from sabotage or other subversive acts, accidents, or other causes . . . vessels, harbors, ports and waterfront facilities in the United States . . . and water . . . subject to the jurisdiction of the United States."[131]

According to 33 C.F.R. § 6.14-1, the commandment of the Coast Guard has the power to "prescribe such conditions and restrictions relating to the safety of waterfront facilities and vessels" in port as he finds to be necessary under existing circumstances. This delegation is amplified by 33 C.F.R. § 127, which provides for the establishment of security zones for the above purpose. Current regulations also provide that no person or vessel may enter a zone without permission; that all within shall obey the captain of the port, who may take possession of or remove anything from the zone; and that no one else may take anything in or out of the zone without his permission.[132] There are currently five such security zones identified in the regulations.[133]

The Ports and Waterways Safety Act of 1974 (33 U.S.C. § 1221 *et seq.*) provides ample alternative statutory mandate to provide protection against terrorism in ports. To "prevent damage to, or the destruction or loss of any vessel, bridge, or other structure on or in the navigable waters of the United States," the act provides the Coast Guard with a wide range of power, including the establishment of safety zones or other measures of limited or controlled access.[134] To date, no regulations have been promulgated under the above sections.

The Outer Continental Shelf Lands Act[135] provides in Section 1333(e)(1) that the Coast Guard has "authority to promulgate and enforce such reasonable regulations with respect to lights and other warning devices, safety equipment, and other *matters relating to the promotion of safety of life and property* on the islands and structures . . . or on the waters adjacent thereto . . . " [emphasis added]. The regulations thereunder (33 C.F.R. §§ 140-147) are concerned with safety provisions regarding construction, lifesaving appliances and equipment, and so on. Provision is made in 33 C.F.R. § 147 for the creation of safety zones around offshore structures, referred to above, in order "to promote the safety of life and property on the islands and structures, their appurtenances and attending vessels" and adjacent water.[136] Such regulations may serve to prevent or control activities or access by vessels or persons. It is the authors' understanding that safety zones have not been promulgated around offshore rigs.

Under the Deepwater Port Act of 1974, the secretary of transportation may similarly issue and enforce regulations with respect to the same subject matter, including "promotion of life and property in any deepwater port and the waters adjacent thereto."[137]

Other similar regulatory authorities apply offshore, including the U.S. Geological Survey's responsibility for approving fixed structures and artificial islands;[138] the Office of Pipeline Safety's responsibility for OCS pipelines;[139] and the Nuclear Regulatory Commission's responsibility for floating offshore nuclear power plants.[140]

The reasons for recording the above provisions in detail are twofold. First, present statutes and regulations pertaining to ocean activities do not anticipate and provide explicitly for the kind of terrorist activity under discussion. Second, there exist, however, ample statutory mandates to create and enforce such provisions under the major statutes that give the respective authorities wide scope in providing for safety of life and property. Thus certain activity could be made unlawful and subject to penalties, remedies, and other deterrents under law. Moreover, clear authority exists to provide the Coast Guard and others with enforcement responsibility to act should an incident occur (see below).

In addition, there are probably preventive actions concerning the design, construction, and use of facilities that would lessen the attractiveness of structures and vessels as terrorist targets. Current legislative concepts are sufficient, although perhaps clumsy. For example, it is doubtful that the simple creation of security zones under the Magnuson Act would be workable under the existing terms cited above. However, a modified concept of security zones might provide for standby security measures, for example, if a terrorist threat were anticipated or likely.

Similarly, the Coast Guard's system of inspection and approval over vessel design and construction would provide authority to mandate changes in design and construction not only of passenger and cargo vessels, but also of so-called industrial vessels, including mobile rigs such as jackups, semisubmersibles and submersible structures.

Executory Action

Emphasis on safety, life, and property is used to provide a very broad mandate for executory action by the Coast Guard in 14 U.S.C. § 88. That statute provides that to render aid to distressed persons, the Coast Guard may "perform any and all acts necessary to rescue and aid persons and protect and save property." Further, the Coast Guard may render aid to persons and save property at any time and in any place in which the "Coast Guard facilities and personnel are available and can be effectively utilized."

Enforcement

The Coast Guard is the primary law enforcement agency on the oceans. According to 14 U.S.C. § 2, "the Coast Guard shall enforce or assist in the enforcement of all applicable federal laws on or under the high seas and waters subject to the jurisdiction of the United States." The service has a broad statutory mandate with which to implement that charge in Title 14 U.S.C. § 89(2). That section provides that "The Coast Guard may make inquiries, examinations, inspections, searches, seizures and arrests on the high seas waters over which the United States has jurisdiction, for prevention, detection, and suppression of violations of the laws of the United States." The service may, when requested, use its personnel and facilities to assist any federal agency or state or other political subdivision in law enforcement.[141] When enforcing the law, the Coast Guard officers shall "be deemed to be acting as agents of the particular executive department or independent establishment charged with the administration of the particular law."[142]

The Coast Guard recognizes responsibility for enforcing 500 sections of the U.S. code.[143] In many sections, it is likely to be the primary or sole enforcement agency. In others, other agencies have enforcement responsibility, but it is held jointly with the Coast Guard in responsibility for enforcement on the high seas and navigable waters.[144]

Enforcement is both of a civil and criminal nature. When criminal prosecution is involved, it is up to the Justice Department to make the final decision about whether to go ahead with prosecution. In most cases the Coast Guard district commander decides whether to bring an incident to the attention of the district attorney. In serious cases involving homicide, casualties resulting in death, etc.–*i.e.*, the kind that are likely to be involved in some terrorist activity–the commandant makes the decision.[145]

The authority discussed above would offer a wide variety of courses of action for the Coast Guard in a terrorist event, depending on whether the object of attack was a vessel; was flying a U.S. or foreign flag; was in U.S. territory, U.S. internal waters, or in international waters; and had on board U.S. passengers whose safety was threatened. Depending on circumstances, the Coast Guard would have authority (1) to conduct surveillance; (2) upon request, to assist state or other federal law enforcement agencies in actions or in communications with respect to the attackers, depending on the nature of applicable consular treaties, general relations treaties, or other treaties with the vessel or structure's flag state; (3) to conduct a course of action under U.S. criminal laws; (4) in conformity with the above treaties, to board a ship to ascertain if any federal law has been violated; (5) to conduct hot pursuit of a foreign ship; or (6) to carry out other activities under direct presidential order.[146]

The law enforcement responsibility given the Coast Guard in the new

200-mile fisheries conservation zone apparently reaffirms that agency as the primary U.S. law enforcement agency on the oceans. It will probably set the pattern for the assignment of enforcement responsibility as other jurisdictional assertions are made out to the limits of extended jurisdiction. Two questions require review, however, in the terrorism context.

First, to what extent are activities countering terrorism likely to take on a coloration of defense or national security considerations rather than of law enforcement? If the former are likely to be prominent, then the role of the Navy may become pertinent. Any murkiness as to responsibility between the two services should be cleared.

Second, will the Coast Guard or the Navy be the primary protector of the physical security of the deep-ocean mining platforms in the middle of the Pacific? Again, a clear early determination of responsibility might help avoid confusion if terrorist attack, however unexpected, might be made against a nodule mining operation.

Status of Recent Antiterrorist Planning

Various branches and agencies of the federal government have expressed interest in the problem of terrorism against maritime objects. As early as 1973, the Coast Guard was examining the enforcement statutes reviewed above to determine its responsibility and ability to act. In late 1974, the U.S. Navy asked the Center for Naval Analyses to study the issue, and a task group of the Joint Chiefs of Staff examined its implications for the Department of Defense. The National Academy of Engineering held a conference at the Navy Post-Graduate School, Monterey, California, in fall 1975, which examined the problems of defending and protecting offshore assets as one of several important problems of ocean policy. A subcommittee of the House of Representatives Committee on Merchant Marine and Fisheries has held hearings on Coast Guard activities on this subject and on Coast Guard-Navy cooperation. A subcommittee of the National Advisory Committee on Oceans and Atmosphere (NACOA) is currently investigating which federal agencies have what responsibility for protecting against and responding to attacks on facilities and structures off the coasts of the United States.

Coast Guard planning for terrorist incidents has included a review of Coast Guard authority, not only under 14 U.S.C. § 89 but also under 14 U.S.C. § 2, and a review of the responsibilities of the district commander captain of the port in such instances. Planning efforts have called for the completion of appropriate memorandums of understanding with other federal agencies as to responsibility, the establishment and promulgation of training criteria as well as necessary communication links, the development and publication at the area commander and district commander level of antiterrorist contigency plans and guidance, and the focus of primary responsibility for security on the masters, owners, operators, and agents of vessels and facilities.

However, most of the contingency planning has been oriented toward a strike against a vessel, such as the passenger vessel, in the form of hijacking, bomb threat, etc. Terrorist attacks against waterfront facilities within territorial or internal waters also have been contemplated. The key point is that attacks on offshore structures beyond the territorial waters, not regular passenger or cargo vessels, have virtually been ignored, at least until very recently.[147] Thus as was the case with many of the criminal statutory provisions, attention focuses on vessels rather than on structures.

Conclusions

From the review of the incidence of, and pertinent law and administrative preparedness concerning, terrorism on ocean facilities, the following conclusions may be drawn:

1. The oceans contain many economic assets that are within the capabilities of terrorists to attack, and that are valuable (either economically or symbolically) and therefore potential targets.
2. International law assigns primary jurisdiction for an incident to some state (flag state for vessels under most circumstances; littoral state for existing continental shelf structures or structures within the territorial sea). At present the jurisdictional framework is an inadequate basis for allowing a state to protect its assets against terrorism beyond its territorial sea.
3. Resolution of this problem through established international legal forums, especially those dealing with law-of-the-sea matters, will become entangled in broader political issues. However, if an LOS treaty emerges that is acceptable to the United States, it is likely to provide an improved basis for national action.
4. In the case of vessels, there exists ample U.S. legislative mandate for preventive and enforcement activity for U.S. enforcement agencies. In the case of structures, additional clarifying legislative amendments would be useful.
5. Preventive planning to date is inadequate.

Recommendations

1. The United States should amend sections 18 U.S.C. § 1363 (destruction or injury to property), 18 U.S.C. § 6159 (attack to plunder vessel), 18 U.S.C. § 2273 (destruction of vessel by nonowner), and 18 U.S.C. § 2276 (breaking and entering a vessel), so that they apply to offshore structures.

2. The United States should amend 18 U.S.C. § 7 to bring within the special maritime jurisdiction of the criminal code all structures that are owned by U.S. citizens or corporations, and that are not covered by the OCSLA, the Deepwater Port Act, or the laws of another state governing its continental shelf under the jurisdictional basis provided by the 1958 Convention on the Continental Shelf or a superseding LOS treaty.

3. If an acceptable law-of-the-sea treaty should result from the current negotiations under U.N. auspices, the United States should ratify that treaty and enact legislation to extend federal criminal and civil law to all structures within the U.S. economic zone, under the jurisdictional provisions of the treaty.

4. Failing negotiation, ratification, or coming into force of a law-of-the-sea treaty containing economic zone articles, the United States should consider extending the federal criminal and civil law to apply to U.S. structures and objects offshore the U.S. coast that are not covered by the OCSLA or the Deepwater Port Act.

5. Upon completion of either the second, third, or fourth recommendation, the Department of State should consider seeking to negotiate bilateral and/or multilateral treaties requiring either extradition or prosecution for criminal acts committed on or against vessels and/or offshore structures.

U.S. Agencies' Responsibilities and Planning

1. The U.S. Coast Guard, and the Departments of Defense, State, and Justice, and other interested agencies should negotiate Memorandums of Understanding clarifying their respective areas of jurisdiction and responsibility for preventing, reacting to, and following up on, any ocean terrorist incidents. These memorandums should cover future deep-ocean mining activities.

2. Upon such clarification, the U.S. Coast Guard should complete development of (and make available to private parties as appropriate) a comprehensive set of contingency plans covering prevention of, reaction to, and follow-up after acts of ocean terrorism. Coast Guard planning would be based on authority provided in 14 U.S.C. § 2 and in the Commandant's Notice 3176 of February 13, 1975. The development of such contingency plans should involve other agencies as indicated by the Memorandums of Understanding referred to above. These contingency plans should be amended to include deep-ocean mining activities as soon as development or prototype activities are underway.

Contingency Planning: Industry

Offshore industries should be required to file their own contingency plans, which would include data regarding pipeline cutoffs and other damage-control procedures, responses to fire and pipeline rupture, etc. This action would bring these industries more closely into overall government contingency planning and improve security in an area not previously covered by Coast Guard contingency planning. Filing requirements should be consistent with the need to protect proprietary information.

Projecting U.S. Policy

A low public profile should be maintained with respect to the problem of ocean terrorism. This would help reduce the possibility that publicity will increase the potential for attacks on ocean facilities.

Design Improvements for Offshore
Structures and Vessels

The National Academy of Engineering Marine Board Panel, the National Advisory Committee on the Oceans and Atmosphere, or a similar body should consider the possible vulnerability of offshore structures, deep-water ports, and vessels to terrorist attack, and the cost-effectiveness of design modifications to minimize it. A study to determine the cost-effectiveness of various design changes should be made. The USCG and USGS could require the appropriate construction and design regulations over which they have responsibility to be changed to conform to new standards. Together, these actions would provide additional security in what is now a vulnerable area.

Notes

1. The creation of numerous U.N.-affiliated, specialized organizations, as well as many regional organizations and economic communities is testimony to states' interest in, if not always success at, using legal-organizational mechanisms to solve problems rather than each state going it alone or relying on *ad hoc* consultations. The increased number of treaties is also evidence of this fact. *See* RUDA, THE FINAL ACCEPTANCE OF INTERNATIONAL CONVENTIONS 6 (1976).

2. AMERICAN SOCIETY OF INTERNATIONAL LAW, LEGAL ASPECT OF INTERNATIONAL TERRORISM: PROJECT STATEMENT 3 (July 1975). Discussions of the problem of defining "terrorism" may be found in B.M. JENKINS, INTERNATIONAL TERRORISM: A NEW MODE OF CONFLICT (Jan. 1975); Hutchinson, *The Concept of Revolutionary Terrorism* 16 J. CONFLICT RESOLUTION 383 (1972); Hannay, *International Terrorism: The*

Need for a Fresh Perspective, 8 INT'L LAWYER 268 (1974); Baxter, *A Skeptical Look at the Concept of Terrorism*, 7 U. AKRON L. REV. 380 (1974); Bassiouni, ch. 8 of this book.

3. U.N. CHARTER, art. 1, § 2.

4. Hannay, *supra* note 2.

5. M. MCDOUGAL & W. BURKE, THE PUBLIC ORDER OF THE OCEANS, 821 (1962).

6. Bell, *Bab El-Mandab, Strategic Troublespot*, 16 ORBIS 975 (1973).

7. B.M. JENKINS & J. JOHNSON, INTERNATIONAL TERRORISM: A CHRONOLOGY, 1968-1974, 39 (March 1975) (RAND CORP.: R-1597-DOS/ARPA).

8. *Id.* at 53.

9. Washington Post, Aug. 26, 1975, at A14, col. 5.

10. JENKINS, JOHNSON, & RONFELDT, NUMBERED LIVES: SOME STATISTICAL OBSERVATIONS FROM 77 INTERNATIONAL HOSTAGE INCIDENTS, (Aug. 1975) (Unpublished study prepared for the Department of State by the Rand Corp.). *See also* D.L. MILBANK, INTERNATIONAL AND TRANSNATIONAL TERRORISM: DIAGNOSIS AND PROGNOSIS. (Apr. 1976). (Research Study, Central Intelligence Agency PR 76 10030).

11. Hansen, *The North-South Split and the Law of the Sea Debate*, in PERSPECTIVES ON OCEAN POLICY (1974) provides an excellent discussion of this issue. *See also* Nye, *Ocean Rule-Making from a World Politics Perspective*, *id.*

12. H. Alker & B. Russett, *World Politics in Assembly Policies*, in WORLD POLITICS IN THE GENERAL ASSEMBLY 218 (1965). *See also* Farer, *The United States and the Third World: A Basis for Accommodation*, 54 FOREIGN AFF. 79 (1975).

13. The limitations of this analysis are discussed in Hansen, *supra* note 11.

14. S. LAWRENCE, INTERNATIONAL SEA TRANSPORT (1972).

15. Misra, *International Politics in the Indian Ocean*, 18 ORBIS 1088 (1975).

16. SENATE COMM. ON FOREIGN RELATIONS, 94TH CONG., 1ST SESS., THE THIRD LAW OF THE SEA CONFERENCE CARACAS SESSION JUNE-AUGUST 1974 (Comm. Print 1975); R. OSGOOD, A. HOLLICK, G. PEARSON & J. ORR, TOWARD A NATIONAL OCEAN POLICY: 1976 AND BEYOND (1975).

17. Friedheim & Durch, *The International Seabed Resources Agency Negotiation and the New International Economic Order*, 31 INT'L ORGANIZATION 343 (1977).

18. MILBANK, *supra* note 10.

19. Friedheim, *The 'Satisfied' and 'Dissatisfied' States Negotiate International Law: A Case Study*, 18 WORLD POLITICS 20 (1965); *see also* Lissitzyn, *The Less Developed Nations*, 2 THE STRATEGY OF WORLD ORDER 243 (Falk & Mendlovitz, eds., 1966).

20. Friedheim, *supra* note 19, at 23-4.

21. *Id.* at 26.

22. *Id.* at 30.

23. *Id.* at 28.

24. OSGOOD, *supra* note 16, at 158.

25. Albers, *Seabed Mineral Resources: A Survey*, 29 SCI. PUB. AFF. 3 (1973).

26. Quoted in OSGOOD, *supra* note 16.

27. Convention on the Continental Shelf, Apr. 29, 1958, art. 2, 15 U.S.T. 471, T.I.A.S. No. 5578, 499 U.N.T.S. 311.

28. Choon-ho Park, Intervention Against Unilateral Exploitation of Seabed Resources: Possibilities in East Asia, paper read at the 17th Annual International Studies Association Convention, Toronto, Canada (Feb. 25-29, 1976).

29. *Buried Treasure*, THE ECONOMIST (London), Sept. 27, 1975, at 36.

30. INTERNATIONAL PETROLEUM ENCYCLOPEDIA, 290 ff. (1975).

31. *Rig Locations*, OFFSHORE 155 (Jan. 1976); Brown & Fabian, *Diplomats at Sea*, 52 FOREIGN AFF. 301 (1974). (Brown and Fabian claim that exploration is taking place off the shores of some 80 countries.)

32. OCEAN INDUSTRY 54 (Nov. 1975).

33. INTERNATIONAL PETROLEUM ENCYCLOPEDIA 422 (1975).

34. *Deepwater Port Facilities: Hearing on H.R. 7501 and Related Bills Before the Subcomm. on the Environment of the House Comm. on Interior and Insular Affairs*, 93d Cong., 2d Sess. 129-31 (1974).

35. OSGOOD, *supra* note 16, chs. 3 & 4 *passim.*

36. The Isthmian Canal Convention, Nov. 18, 1903, 33 Stat. 2234; T.S. 431; 10 Bevans 663.

37. Fishery Conservation and Management Act of 1976, Pub. L. No. 94-265, ap. 13, 1976.

38. *Prawn Harvest 'Explosion,'* Washington Post, Jan. 4, 1976, at A20, col. 1.

39. OSGOOD, *supra* note 16, ch. 8; *see also* Friedheim & Kadane, *Ocean Science in the UN Political Arena*, 3 J. MARITIME L. & COM. 473 (1972).

40. Friedlander, *Floating Reactor: 'Crisis' Solution?* IEEE SPECTRUM (Feb. 1973).

41. On the physical characteristics of OTECs, *see* Weeden, *Thermal Energy from the Oceans*, OCEAN INDUSTRY 219 (Sept. 1975); *see also* OCEAN THERMAL ENERGY CONVERSION: LEGAL, POLITICAL AND INSTITUTIONAL ASPECTS (G. Knight, J. Nyhart, and R. Stein, eds., 1977) [hereinafter cited as OTEC].

42. ENERGY FROM THE OCEANS: FACT OR FANTASY? (J. Kohl, ed., 1976). (Conference Proceedings, The Center for Marine and Coastal Studies, North Carolina State University, Raleigh, N.C., Jan. 27-28, 1976).

43. They include the U.N. Charter; the Universal Declaration of Human Rights; The International Covenant on Economic, Social and Cultural Rights;

the International Covenant on Civil and Political Rights; the Convention on the Prevention and Punishment of the Crime of Genocide; the International Convention on the Elimination of All Forms of Racial Discrimination; the European Convention for the Protection of Human Rights and Fundamental Freedoms; the American Convention on Human Rights; the Nuremberg Principles and the 1949 Geneva Conventions. M.C. BASSIOUNI, INTERNATIONAL TERRORISM AND POLITICAL CRIMES, xi (1975).

44. Bassiouni's comparable phrase is "international element," which is defined to exist when: "1) the perpetrator and victim are citizens of different states or 2) the conduct is performed in whole or in part in more than one state." *Id.* at xiv.

45. Bassiouni's comparable phrase is "individual or collective conduct employing strategies of terror violence." *Id.*

46. Convention on the High Seas. Apr. 28, 1958, 13 U.S.T. 2312; T.I.A.S. No. 5200; 450 U.N.T.S. 82.

47. *Id.* art 2.

48. BASSIOUNI, *supra* note 43, at xiv.

49. "[F]or purposes of the jurisdiction of the courts of the sovereignty whose flag it flies" a vessel may be "deemed to be a part of the territory of that sovereignty. . . ." United States v. Flores 289 U.S. 137 (1933). This characterization is limited. "[T]he statement sometimes made that a merchant ship is a part of the territory of the country whose flag she flies . . . is a figure of speech, a metaphor [citations omitted]. The jurisdiction which it is intended to describe arises out of the nationality of the ship . . . and partakes more of the characteristics of personal than territorial sovereignty." Cunard S.S. Co. v. Mellon, 262 U.S. 100, at 123 (1923). *See* authorities cited here for critiques of the vessel-equals-territory argument.

50. The other is slaving. Convention on the High Seas, *supra* note 46, art. 13.

51. "Piracy consists of any of the following acts: (1) Any illegal acts of violence, detention or any act of depredation, committed for private ends by the crew or the passengers of a private ship or a private aircraft, and directed: (a) On the high seas, against another ship or aircraft, or against persons or property on board such ship or aircraft; (b) Against a ship, aircraft, persons or property in a place outside the jurisdiction of any State; (2) Any act of voluntary participation in the operation of a ship or of an aircraft with knowledge of facts making it a pirate ship or aircraft; (3) Any act of inciting or of intentionally facilitating an act described in sub-paragraph 1 or sub-paragraph 2 of this article." Convention on the High Seas, *supra* note 46, art. 15.

52. MCDOUGAL & BURKE, *supra* note 5.

53. Rubin, *Is Piracy Illegal?* 70 AM. J. INT'L L. 92, 94 (1976).

54. *Id.*

55. *Supra* note 27.

56. Convention on the Territorial Sea and Contiguous Zone, Apr. 29, 1958, art. 1, 15 U.S.T. 1606, T.I.A.S. No. 5639, 516 U.N.T.S. 205.

57. *Id.*, art. 14.

58. *Id.*, art. 14 (2).

59. *Id.*, art. 14 (4).

60. *Id.*, art. 24.

61. G. KNIGHT, THE LAW OF THE SEA 102 (1975).

62. *Id.* at 697; Fishery Conservation and Management Act, *supra* note 37.

63. KNIGHT, *supra* note 61, at 120.

64. *Id.* at 124.

65. United Nations Third Conference on the Law of the Sea, Informal Single Negotiating Text, pts. I-III, U.N. Doc. A/Conf. 62/WP.8/Pts. I-III (May 1975), and letters to President from Co-chairmen of the Informal Working Group on Settlement of Disputes, S.D. Gp/2nd Session/No. 1/Rev. 5 (May 1975). Following the March 15-May 7, 1976 session of the conference, a Revised Single Negotiating Text was published: U.N. Doc. A/Conf. 62/WP.8/Rev.1/Parts I-IV (May 1976).

66. U.N. Doc. A/Conf. 62/WP.8 pts. I-III (May 1975), pt. II, art. 45 (1).

67. The distance of the safety zone may be altered by "generally accepted international standards or as recommended by the appropriate international organizations." *Id.*, art. 48(5).

68. *Id.*, art. 97.

69. *Id.*, art. 47(2).

70. *Id.*

71. *Id.*

72. *See* Proceedings, *supra* note 41.

73. *See* Revised Single Negotiating Text *supra* note 65, art. 49 for elaboration concerning research generally.

74. *Supra* note 66, art. 2.

75. *Id.*, art. 16(2).

76. *Id.*, art. 18(1)(b).

77. *Id.*, art. 18(1)(c).

78. *Id.*, art. 18(1)(e).

79. *Id.*, art. 18(1)(f).

80. *Id.*, art. 18(1)(h).

81. "The provisions of article 48 shall apply *mutatis mutandis* to artificial islands, installations and structures on the continental shelf." *Supra* note 66.

82. For a concise description, *see* Knight, *International Jurisdictional Issues Involving OTEC Installations*, in OTEC *supra* note 41.

83. Convention on the Territorial Sea and Contiguous Zone, *supra* note 56.

84. *Id.*, art. 24.

85. Convention on the High Seas, *supra* note 46.

86. *Supra* note 27.

87. 43 U.S.C. § 1331 *et seq.*

88. 43 U.S.C. § 1333 (a)(i).

89. 33 U.S.C. § § 1501 *et seq.*, 1518(a)(i).

90. *Supra* note 66, art. 45.

91. *Id.*, art. 5(1).

92. Convention on the High Seas, *supra* note 46, art. 6(1).

93. 18 U.S.C. 7.

94. This term, "Special Maritime and Territorial jurisdiction of the United States" as used in this title, was substituted for the words "the crimes and offenses defined in § § 451-468 of this Title" in an earlier version of the code. At one time, as early as the 1910 Criminal Code, all the penal provisions covering acts within the Admiralty and Maritime jurisdiction were collected. In 1948 these acts, then 18 U.S.C. ch. 11 (1940), were allocated throughout the chapters dealing with particular offenses and the qualifying language "within the Special Maritime and Territorial jurisdiction of the United States" was added. The legislative history makes clear that the "jurisdictional limitation will be preserved in all sections of said Chapter 11 describing an offense." Thus not all, but only a part, of the criminal code is applicable to offenses within the special maritime and territorial jurisdiction of the United States. (*See* Legislative History following 18 U.S.C. § 7.)

95. 43 U.S.C. *supra* note 88, § § 1502(a), 1503(a), 1518(a)(1), (b), (e).

96. A different gap exists in the regulatory jurisdiction of the Army Corps of Engineers in governing construction of obstructions to navigation. *See* J. KESSLER, LEGAL ISSUES IN PROTECTING OFFSHORE STRUCTURES 16-17 (1976) (Center for Naval Analyses Professional Paper No. 147).

97. Nyhart, *Problems of Legal Responsibility and Liability to Be Anticipated in OTEC Operations*, in OTEC *supra* note 41.

98. 43 U.S.C. *supra* note 88, § 1502 (19).

99. 28 U.S.C. 1783, Blackmer v. U.S., 284 U.S. 421 (1932).

100. 18 U.S.C. 2381.

101. 18 U.S.C. 953.

102. Internal Revenue Code § 1.

103. 88 Stat. 409.

104. For a discussion of the possibility of creating a criminal sanction, *see* Paust, *"Nonprotected" Persons or Things*, ch. 6 of this report, pp. 341-397.

105. In addition, there are laws not collected under the criminal code that create criminal or civil offenses and that might pertain to a terrorist incident. Three examples suffice. It is an offense to obstruct navigation without a permit from the Army Corps of Engineers, 33 U.S.C. § 403. The law applies on navigable waters and is extended for purposes of the Outer Continental Shelf Lands Act and to the Outer Continental Shelf Act, 43 U.S.C. § 1333(f). Thus if an attack on any object under the Outer Continental Shelf Lands Act resulted in an obstruction being created, an offense would have been committed.

The Federal Water Pollution Control Act makes unlawful the discharge of oil or hazardous substances not in accordance with the act. Section 402 (33 U.S.C. § 1341) sets a permit requirement for all ocean discharges into the territorial sea and, for the contiguous zone and ocean waters beyond, all discharges not from vessels or other floating craft. Section 311 (33 U.S.C. § 1321) makes it unlawful to spill oil and hazardous substances into or upon the navigable waters of the United States, adjoining shorelines, or into or upon the waters of the contiguous zone. A terrorist attack on an oil platform or tanker (under certain conditions) that resulted in a discharge or spill of oil would probably be an unlawful act under one or the other of these provisions.

It is provided in 46 U.S.C. § 1461(d) that no person may use a vessel in waters subject to U.S. jurisdiction in a negligent manner so as to endanger life, limb, or property of another. Though the intent here is to make small-boating safer, the section might be applied to some incidents involving terrorism.

106. 18 U.S.C. § 231(a).
107. 18 U.S.C. § 241.
108. 18 U.S.C. § 659.
109. 18 U.S.C. § 875.
110. 18 U.S.C. § 1201.
111. 18 U.S.C. § 1362.
112. 18 U.S.C. § 1657, 2192, 2193.
113. 18 U.S.C. § 1951.
114. 18 U.S.C. § 2199.
115. 18 U.S.C. § 2275.
116. 43 U.S.C. § 1312 sets the seaward boundaries of states at three geographical miles, excepting those whose boundaries at time of entry to the union extended beyond.
117. 43 U.S.C. § 1333(2), 33 U.S.C. 1518(b).
118. 18 U.S.C. § 1111(b).
119. 18 U.S.C. § 81.
120. 18 U.S.C. § 113.
121. 18 U.S.C. § 114.
122. 18 U.S.C. § 1025.
123. 18 U.S.C. § 1363.
124. 18 U.S.C. § 1658.
125. 18 U.S.C. § 1659.
126. 18 U.S.C. § 2111.
127. 18 U.S.C. § 2192.
128. 18 U.S.C. § 2231.
129. 18 U.S.C. § 2273.
130. 18 U.S.C. § 2276.
131. 50 U.S.C. § 191(b).
132. 33 C.F.R. § 127.15.

133. In Sandy Hook Bay, New London, Marcus Hook, Guam, and Port Valdez, Alaska.

134. 33 U.S.C. § 1221(3)(i), (8), (9).

135. *Supra* note 87.

136. *Id.* at § 1333(e)(1), art. 5 (2) (3).

137. 33 U.S.C. § 1501(10)(b).

138. Although the Outer Continental Shelf Lands Act nowhere extends a safety mandate to the United States Geodetic Survey, it is currently exerting responsibility for integral safety on structures under 30 C.F.R. § 250, anticipating that it will be asked to undertake further safety responsibilities.

139. Fed. Reg. 34,035 (1976) *amending* 49 C.F.R. § 195; 18 U.S.C. §§ 831-35.

140. Regulated under the Atomic Energy Act of 1954. *See* 10 C.F.R. § 50.

141. 14 U.S.C. § 141.

142. 14 U.S.C. § 89(b).

143. 33 C.F.R. § 1.07-23, app.

144. *Id.*

145. 33 C.F.R. § 1.07-15(b).

146. U.S. Coast Guard Commandant Notice 3176, Feb. 13, 1975, encl. (3).

147. It is the authors' understanding that a meeting between Coast Guard and owners and operators of offshore structures has taken place regarding this question of protection of their offshore assets. The indication of concern by the operators was low, with more concern being focused on attempts on the onshore control points rather than on the offshore platforms.

4

New Vulnerabilities and the Acquisition of New Weapons by Nongovernment Groups

Brian M. Jenkins and
Alfred P. Rubin

Introduction

Measured against the world volume of "traditional" violence, the amount of terrorist violence up until now has been trivial. Nevertheless, terrorists have been able to attract worldwide attention to themselves and to their goals, cause alarm, create incidents that governments have been compelled to deal with often before a world audience, and frequently win concessions. Terrorists have also forced governments to divert tremendous resources to security functions. Terrorists have achieved these results with tactics that, although shocking and alarming, have not killed hundreds or thousands. Thus far terrorists have not sought to acquire or threatened to use weapons of mass destruction. Neither have they attempted to sabotage vital systems nor attack vulnerable targets, the destruction of which would result in widespread public alarm and inconvenience. However, they could turn to such tactics and weapons in the future.

Power, defined in its most primitive sense as simply the capacity to disrupt or destroy, is descending to smaller and smaller groups, as such groups acquire weapons that enable them to cause mass casualties or to attack targets presently invulnerable to them. As new vulnerabilities are created by technological advance, it becomes conceivable that terrorist groups could threaten or cause widespread disruption, or even mass murder, and thereby begin to subvert political systems.

This chapter examines the following problems: (1) the new weapons, and some old ones, that may come into the hands of nongovernmental groups in coming years; (2) the new vulnerabilities that are being created as a by-product of technological advances and the social consequences of disruption, sabotage, or other exploitation of these vulnerabilities; and (3) possible legal and technological measures and instruments of control.

Weapons: Old and New

Terrorists bent upon mass murder can choose from a variety of means. ("Mass murder" is not a very precise term. For the purpose of this discussion, it is arbitrarily defined as something approaching a hundred or more potential deaths. Conceivably, thousands could be imperiled by some of the actions described, but those actions would be extremely difficult to carry out successfully.) The use of chemical or biological weapons is generally seen as the easiest and most available way to kill a large number of people. A crude nuclear explosive device, depending on its yield and where and when it was detonated, could cause casualties of greater magnitude. But the acquisition of the requisite material and fabrication of the device would require greater risks and technical skill on the part of perpetrators than would be involved in the case of either chemical or biological weapons. Dispersal of radioactive material rather than explosion of a nuclear device would involve fewer difficulties as to acquisition of the material, and the fabrication of a dispersal device is far easier than that of an explosive device, but the probable adverse effects of a dispersal of radioactive material are likely to be exceeded in magnitude by an effective dispersal of chemical toxins or biological agents.

When it comes to slaughter, terrorists actually have little need for such exotic or highly sophisticated weapons. They have already demonstrated their knowledge of explosives. Bombings are the principal form of terrorist activity. Detonated at places of assembly—railroad and subway stations, bus terminals, aircraft—conventional explosives can cause heavy casualties. But for all their bombings, terrorists thus far have rarely used explosives in ways calculated to kill great numbers of any civilian population. Nor have terrorists ordinarily used the primitive but potentially even more lethal weapon of fire against people. Moreover, some of the individual weapons now being developed for tomorrow's infantrymen—man-portable surface-to-air missiles, for example—seem potentially useful to terrorists and, used against certain categories of targets, are capable of causing heavy casualties.

Each of these possibilities—chemicals and biological weapons; nuclear explosive and dispersal devices; conventional explosives and incendiaries; man-portable, precision-guided munitions; and other advanced infantry weapons—will be considered with regard to their characteristics and present or future uses. First we shall discuss the nature of the weapons, recent developments that make the particular means of violence more accessible or more attractive to terrorists, some of the possible applications terrorists might consider and the possible effects, and some of the technical problems involved as well as the political and moral arguments that could be mustered within a political extremist organization for or against use of a particular weapon or means of violence. We shall then examine the historical record for any direct evidence of terrorists using or seeking to use the particular weapon under discussion and try to estimate the likelihood of future use.

Chemical and Biological Weapons

Terrorists or others entertaining schemes of mass murder using chemical or biological weapons will find plenty of inspiration in recent novels and screenplays, and in newspaper headlines describing such examples as the Central Intelligence Agency's reported use of shellfish toxin, Blackleaf-40 (a common insecticide), and other poisons in plots to assassinate foreign leaders; the mysterious "Legionnaire's Disease," which killed 29 conventioneers in Philadelphia and made 180 others ill, and which many suspected was an act of homicide, not an accident, until other cases were identified; and the recent revelations that the U.S. Army had actually used live bacteria on unsuspecting civilian populations in U.S. cities as part of its program of research on chemical and biological warfare.[1] Ironically, among those calling attention to the possibilities of chemical and biological weapons are some of the proponents of nuclear power. Responding to warnings by opponents of nuclear energy that the widespread availability of fissionable material will enable terrorists and criminals to hold cities for ransom, they have pointed out that chemical and biological weapons offer easier and more readily available methods of mass murder than nuclear material.

Moved in the direction of chemical or biological weapons, terrorists will have no difficulty in locating a number of books written for the layman on the concepts of chemical and biological weapons.[2] This literature provides a history of the development of chemical and biological weapons and of their use in warfare. It also identifies the chemical compounds and biological pathogens that have been examined as well as the technical problems of manufacture and delivery to the target, and it identifies sources of further information.

The reader is then directed to the technical literature, which is extensive. To go beyond the point of imagining scenarios, some technical knowledge and material are needed as well as some basic laboratory facilities. Unfortunately, the level of requisite technical knowledge is not extremely high; a college student in chemistry might be able to put together an extremely effective chemical weapon. The material is widely available; in fact, it can often be easily purchased. And only primitive facilities are required to carry out some threats.

Chemical warfare dates back to the use of chlorine and mustard gas in World War I. Despite the Geneva Protocol of 1925[3] which prohibited chemical warfare, research aimed at developing new and more toxic chemical weapons continued during the 1920s and 1930s when major scientific advances were being made in the fields of physics and chemistry. The search for more toxic insecticides led to the discovery of organophosphorous anti-cholinesterases, a class of chemicals that disrupt the nervous system. The discovery led to the development of chemical toxins commonly known as the "nerve gases." Although chemical weapons were not used by either side in World War II, research continued during and after the war. Nerve gases of even greater toxicity were produced. Binary systems of delivery were developed; these kept two nonlethal compounds separated until the moment of use, when they are combined into a deadly agent. Nonlethal incapacitants such as hallucinogens were developed and used in experiments.

Proponents of chemical warfare could never fully persuade the public that chemical weapons were a "legitimate" means of killing enemy soldiers. Public pressure against the use of chemicals has always been high. At the present time, very little military research is being conducted to find new chemical weapons; however, most advanced nations maintain limited chemical stockpiles as a deterrent to their use by any foe.

In the course of military research programs and research in related civilian areas, hundreds of poisons have been developed, examined, and described. Many of these are well-known toxins such as arsenic, strychnine, hydrogen cyanide, and Parathion. Many are commercially available as insecticides and rodenticides, or for industrial or pharmaceutical purposes. No technical sophistication at all is required to purchase and use these toxins.

Three categories of chemical toxins might be of potential interest to terrorists bent upon mass murder. These are the fluoroacetates, organophosphorous compounds, and botulinum toxin. Fluoroacetic acid and related compounds are found commercially as rodenticides. Sodium fluoroacetate, the commercial form, can easily be refined into more deadly compounds. In dust or liquid form, the poison can be absorbed by inhalation or ingestion, through the eyes, and through cuts and abrasions.

More lethal than the fluoroacetates are the organophosphorous compounds that are found in a number of commercial insecticides, *e.g.*, DFP (diisopropylphosphorofluoridate), Parathion, and TEPP (the most toxic of the commercially available insecticides). These are the bases of the nerve agents. They are anticholinesterases that kill by interrupting the signals sent through the junctions of the nervous system. They are highly lethal and work rapidly, killing within hours or minutes, depending on the dose. Organophosphorous compounds can be absorbed by ingestion or inhalation, or through cuts and abrasions. They do hydrolyze in water, however, making them unsuitable for most scenarios involving the contamination of water supplies.

Botulinum toxin is produced naturally by the bacterium *Clostridium botulinium*. Some, therefore, are inclined to consider it a biological weapon. However, botulism poisoning does not depend on absorbing the bacterium but rather only on the toxin it produces. Thus, strictly speaking, it is a chemical weapon, an extremely lethal neurotoxin. Theoretically, one ounce is enough to kill 60 million people. An ounce or two in a reservoir of 10 million gallons would, again in theory, kill anyone who drank a half-pint of water. Fortunately, there is a difference between theoretical and practical toxicity. It would be extremely difficult to disseminate the toxin evenly throughout the water supply; its presence would probably be detected, and boiling the water would suffice to make it harmless. Even at lower levels of heat, botulinum toxin rapidly loses its effect. It is commercially available through pharmaceutical sources.

Any of these three substances would be suitable for a scheme of mass murder, if not on the scale of a city, certainly against a more limited target—a hotel, an office building, or a convention center.

Biological warfare is the use of living organisms—bacteria, viruses, etc.—to cause disease or death in humans, animals, or plants. It evokes a medieval vision of pestilence and plague. The concept of biological warfare itself is not new. In ancient times, retreating armies threw the carcasses of dead animals into wells and rivers to contaminate the advancing army's water supply. Settlers are reported to have on occasion sold Indians blankets contaminated with smallpox. However, most of the scientific research in the area of biological warfare is of quite recent origin. It has paralleled developments in the fields of microbiology, pathology, and epidemiology: the identification and isolation of viruses, the development of continuous culture techniques that allow the mass production of microscopic organisms, and the discovery that live viruses can be grown in fertilized chicken eggs.

Research on the use of biological weapons began in the 1930s and accelerated during World War II. Extensive research continued into the 1950s and 1960s, when, it has recently been revealed, unannounced experiments with bacterial agents considered to be harmless were conducted in U.S. cities.[4] The primary advantage of biological weapons over chemical weapons is that given the biological agents' capacity to reproduce, much smaller quantities are required to infect a large population. On the other hand, biological weapons tend to be highly unpredictable. They can produce negligible results, or a worldwide epidemic that makes no distinction between friend and foe. Moreover, those most likely to be severely affected by disease are the elderly, the very young, and the infirm, those who by no means could be called combatants. Dissatisfaction with biological weapons on technical grounds, along with growing moral revulsion against their use, has led most nations to renounce biological warfare.[5] However, small research efforts, aimed at developing means of detecting and defending against biological warfare, continue.

A wide variety of pathogens have been examined for use in biological warfare. Some have been found to be unsuitable because they are difficult to cultivate; cannot be stored for any length of time; are susceptible to temperature changes; cannot survive in certain climates or atmospheric conditions; work too slowly; are too difficult to innoculate against, thereby increasing the risks to the manufacturer and user; are routinely innoculated against; are easily treated; or have other "defects" as weapons. The potentially more suitable ones include anthrax, bacillary dysentery, brucellosis, cholera, coccidioidomycosis, cryptococcosis, dengue fever, certain forms of encephalitis, encephalomyelitis, glanders, certain strains of influenza, meliodosis, plague, psitacosis, Q-fever, Rift Valley fever, Rocky Mountain spotted fever, salmonella, smallpox, tularemia, typhoid fever, typhus, and yellow fever. One group of scientists has identified eight of these as potentially attractive to terrorists because they are easy to acquire, cultivate, and disseminate: anthrax, brucellosis (undulant fever), coccidioidomycosis (San Joaquin Valley or desert fever), cryptococcosis, pneumonic plague, psittacosis (parrot fever), Rocky Mountain spotted fever, and tularemia.[6]

Anthrax, sometimes called "wool sorters' disease" because it often infects persons working with untreated wool, is one of the most lethal and hardy bacterial pathogens. It can infect by inhalation or ingestion, or it can be absorbed through cuts, although infection by inhalation is far more likely to be lethal. Its symptoms are vague, making diagnosis and treatment difficult. Untreated, it is invariably fatal, and its lethality is high even with treatment. Anthrax spores can survive in boiling water and have been known to survive in soil for decades after the original contamination. Pneumonic plague is spread by fleas from infected rodents to people. With timely treatment, the survival rate is good, but it is likely to be fatal if untreated. Unlike anthrax, pneumonic plague can spread from person to person, thus creating the possibility of an epidemic. Rocky Mountain spotted fever is normally spread by ticks, although, like anthrax and pneumonic plague, the pathogens could be dispersed by air. Without treatment, it is often fatal.

Terrorists seeking to use biological weapons would need some technical knowledge and skills, a quantity of the selected culture, a laboratory for production, and a mechanism for dispersal. None of these poses a major obstacle. As the diseases that could be used as weapons occur naturally, ample technical literature is available in the public domain on their identification, characteristics, cultivation, and pathology. The technical knowledge required would be that of an experimental microbiologist, probably at the level of at least a master's degree. Some knowledge of aerosol systems would also be required, although for a crude dispersal mechanism, this knowledge need not be advanced. Most cultures can easily be obtained by mail order from manufacturers who supply medical and research laboratories. Some organisms—including most of those suitable for biological warfare—are restricted, but this means only that the person ordering must be confirmed as a qualified investigator. The controls are not tight: the signature of a laboratory or department head is sufficient proof. It would be about as difficult as forging a prescription for an unqualified person to obtain these cultures. Samples could easily be stolen, unnoticed, from a laboratory or hospital. Cultivating the organism to produce larger quantities can be accomplished in a well-equipped basement laboratory. Depending on what organism the terrorists select and the sophistication of their skills and equipment, their own safety could be a problem. Fear of catching a dangerous disease probably dissuades many potential users from employing biological weapons. A trained person, however, would be aware of the necessary precautions.

As in the case of chemical weapons, the biggest problem faced by terrorists using biological weapons would be effective dispersal. Microorganisms can be spread in air, water, or food, or by vectors such as fleas, ticks, or infected rodents. Aerosol dispersal is probably the most effective means of dispersal for the microorganisms discussed here. (The technical problems of water dispersal are discussed later in this chapter.) Aerosol dispersal mechanisms may range from simple aerosol cans or air brushes to cloud generators. The smaller the target, the more likely terrorists are to succeed, especially if the target population resides or works within a sealed building with central air conditioning. Infecting a city seems less feasible, and a larger area even less so.

In the cases of both chemical and biological weapons, apart from some difficulties involved with large-scale dissemination, the primary constraints are not technical. Toxins can be obtained or manufactured, biological pathogens can be purchased or stolen and cultivated, home laboratories suffice, technical literature is widely available, and many persons possess the necessary skills. It would be far easier for terrorists or criminals to fabricate a chemical or biological weapon than to fabricate a nuclear device. In difficulty, the task probably ranks with the clandestine production of chemical narcotics or refinement of heroin.

Moral considerations and political utility provide the most important constraints. The fact that most nations have renounced chemical and biological warfare may suggest to any group considering their use that their action will provoke widespread revulsion. Of course, it can be argued that most terrorist acts provoke widespread revulsion anyway, so this cannot be considered a constraint. However, the historical record suggests that at least up to the present, terrorists have avoided indiscriminate attacks that could cause widespread casualties. Their attacks may be indiscriminate but limited. In only a few instances have they caused heavy casualties.

Neither is the political utility of widespread casualties fully demonstrated or necessarily apparent. As a threat, chemical and biological weapons believed to be in the hands of terrorists would have considerable value. The actual use of such weapons might be politically counterproductive. Except as an act of revenge or of extreme desperation where moral constraints and arguments based on political utility erode, it is hard to see how even terrorists could believe that mass casualties would serve their cause. Against a more limited target composed of some segment of the population or representative of the system despised by the terrorists—a church, a police station, a government office, the boardroom of a major corporation—one can more easily imagine the use of such weapons.

Moral and political considerations would, of course, not necessarily inhibit lunatics—for example, serial murderers such as Jack the Ripper, the Boston Strangler, the Zodiac Killer, or the Los Angeles Slasher—who may be attracted to the idea of murder on a grand scale, which is something quite different. Of those mentioned, all but the Zodiac Killer attacked only specific kinds of people; the Zodiac Killer apparently chose his victims at random. He was, in his words, gathering "slaves" for the afterworld.

Society cannot depend entirely on the good judgment of political extremists not to use chemical or biological weapons. However, physical protection against them is impossible or impractical. Marginal improvements could be made by increasing the obstacles to unauthorized users acquiring certain dangerous chemical compounds and cultures. The problem is that many chemical toxins and biological pathogens have legitimate benign uses as well. It may be possible, however, to identify specific chemical compounds that ought to be subject to licensing procedures with penalties for unauthorized possession. In general, controls on the provision of dangerous microorganisms should be increased.

Chemical toxins and biological weapons have occasionally appeared in the schemes of political extremists, criminals, and lunatics. An unconfirmed newspaper report claimed in 1970 that an undercover agent tipped off U.S. officials that members of the Weather Underground (at that time still called the Weathermen) were trying to steal germs from the bacteriological warfare center at Fort Detrick, Maryland, to contaminate a city water supply.[7] In 1972, two boys, one a biology student, were arrested for plotting to use typhoid bacteria to poison the water supply of the city of Chicago. They claimed to be organizers of RISE, a group dedicated to creating a new master race. The two had recruited six or seven members who were to be inoculated against the disease, but two of the recruits panicked and tipped off the police.[8] (The scheme would not have worked anyway, as routine treatment of the water with chlorine would have destroyed the bacteria.) In 1973, a biologist in Germany threatened to infect water supplies with bacilli of anthrax and botulinum unless he was paid $8.5 million.[9] According to another report, police searching one of the hideouts of the Symbionese Liberation Army in San Francisco found technical military manuals on germ warfare.[10] The same group's use of cyanide bullets would seem to indicate its fascination with exotic instruments of death. The so-called Alphabet Bomber of Los Angeles reportedly was in the process of making nerve gas when he was apprehended by police. Fifty-three canisters of mustard gas, which was used extensively in World War I, were stolen from an ammunition bunker in West Germany in 1975.[11] West German authorities received threats that unless the government granted immunity to all political prisoners, the gas would be used against the population of Stuttgart, where the leaders of the Baader-Meinhof gang were about to go on trial. It is not known whether this threat was authored by the same people who took the gas. Some but not all of the canisters were later found.

In a bizarre extortion scheme, executives in various cities of the United States were mailed "tick letters" in 1976. The envelope contained ticks that, according to the accompanying letter, were deliberately infected with a "dangerous disease."[12] Some of the ticks were smashed by postal cancelling machines; some died of natural causes awaiting delivery. There had been earlier reports of a "germ letter" written on paper impregnated with deadly bacteria that would infect the recipient. In February 1976, police in Vienna and Berlin arrested members of a gang involved in the manufacture of nerve gas. A quantity of the toxin was seized. According to various reports, the gang was attempting to sell the gas to bank robbers or terrorists.[13] The gang's motives were apparently purely economic. Later in 1976, U.S. postal authorities examined a suspicious small package. It was found to contain a small charge designed to explode a vial of nerve gas when the package was opened. According to press accounts, an Arab terrorist group was suspected.[14]

Except for the tick letters, which achieved no success, none of these extortion plots was ever carried out. No one is known to have died as a result of chemical or biological warfare by terrorists. Nevertheless, the incidents provide evidence that extremists and extortionists certainly have considered using chemical and biological weapons.

Nuclear Weapons

That terrorists might somehow acquire nuclear weapons either by stealing them, or by fabricating them using stolen nuclear material, has become a topic of increasing public attention and concern. Even a relatively crude improvised nuclear explosive device, if successfully detonated, would have the destructive force of several hundred tons of conventional high explosives. This would exceed by a thousand times the largest explosive devices ever used by terrorists. Certain highly toxic nuclear materials also could theoretically be used against a target population in the same way that terrorists might employ chemical or biological agents.

There has been considerable debate about the difficulty (or ease) with which terrorists might acquire nuclear material of weapons grade, design, and fabricate a nuclear explosive device, or acquire and effectively disperse radioactive material. The assumption merits discussion that terrorists would see utility in causing casualties of the magnitude that nuclear weapons would produce or would perceive some other peculiar advantage in going nuclear.

Nuclear material of weapons grade—highly enriched uranium and plutonium—has been available for several decades in weapons programs and in the fuels used for nuclear-powered naval vessels and some research reactors. Nuclear power reactors use uranium of a much lower level of enrichment than would be required for a nuclear explosive device. Plutonium is a by-product of nuclear fuel burning and, when separated from the other reactor waste products, could be recycled as fuel for reactors or used to make weapons. Because of the rapid expansion of a civilian nuclear power industry throughout the world, plutonium production is rapidly increasing. A standard reactor produces 200 kilograms of plutonium annually. The current annual production of plutonium is approximately 20,000 kilograms. By 1983 the estimated annual production of plutonium worldwide may increase to around 70,000 kilograms (plus or minus 20 percent owing to uncertainties), and by the end of the century annual production may reach 1 million kilograms.[15] Currently plutonium is not being commercially separated from the other products in spent fuel rods in the United States, where the economics and the dangers of recycling plutonium for reactor fuel are topics of considerable debate. Reprocessing is currently being done in the United Kingdom, France, Belgium, Japan, and on a small scale, India. By the early 1980s, Sweden, West Germany, Italy, Spain, Yugoslavia, Canada, Brazil, Argentina, and Taiwan may also have reprocessing capabilities. Only 6 kilograms of plutonium are required for a sophisticated nuclear explosive device. A crude device would require somewhat greater quantities of plutonium or enriched uranium, perhaps in the tens of kilograms.

Highly enriched uranium (uranium that contains a high concentration of the isotope U^{235}), which can also be made into explosive devices, will not be available in such large quantities, but anyone interested in fabricating an improvised nuclear explosive device may find it more usable, as the detonation of a U^{235} device requires a less complicated design than the detonation of one with plutonium.

Protecting vast amounts of nuclear material against diversion or overt thefts is and will continue to be an enormous task. Even keeping track of it is a major problem. No accounting system is perfect. In the United States, where accounting procedures are considered fairly strict, it has been estimated that approximately 150,000 pounds of nuclear material cannot be accounted for. This does not mean that it is known to have been removed. (Less than a gram is known to have been removed.) The rest may simply be lost somewhere in the pipes, filters, and machinery of the processing system, or it may have been discharged with other effluents. This, however, does not rule out the possibility that small amounts may have been pilfered. Of this 150,000 pounds, 6 to 7 percent or about 11,000 pounds (about 5000 kilograms) is weapons grade material.[16]

With increasing amounts of such material moving about (about 40 countries now have plutonium), the opportunities for successful clandestine diversion will be increased, or thieves may decide to seize a shipment or repository of nuclear material by force as an armed robbery. Although security measures are constantly being upgraded, the possibility that a determined group could acquire sufficient material for an explosive device must be conceded.

Assuming that terrorists could somehow obtain sufficient material for a nuclear explosive device, could they design one? In the beginning, the secrets of fission were closely guarded. However, much of the requisite technical knowledge has gradually come into the public domain, and a growing number of people have been instructed in the basic principles. A properly trained civilian without detailed knowledge of nuclear weapons design probably could design at least a crude nuclear explosive device.

There is, of course, a difference between designing a nuclear weapon and actually making a nuclear weapon. Here, there is some debate about feasibility. One former designer of nuclear weapons asserts that it could be done by one skilled person.[17] Others argue that it would require five or six persons skilled in different fields such as explosives and metallurgy.[18] The potential explosive yield of a bomb clandestinely built by a subnational group is estimated to be in the tenths of a kiloton; its detonation would be uncertain.

Thus to acquire the material and then design and fabricate a weapon, a group theoretically would have to include a skilled band of thieves willing to use force or inside accomplices to obtain the material, a designer educated in the principles of nuclear weapons, and one or a handful of skilled persons to actually fabricate the weapon. The operation would require considerable planning, perhaps several months of full-time effort to carry out, one or more secure hideouts, some special equipment, and the necessary logistics to support the entire operation. Obviously, it would entail serious risks.

These requirements would seem to place a nuclear operation well above the capacities of many of the smaller terrorist groups whose dedicated members seldom exceed a dozen part-time bombers and shooters. Theoretically, however, it would be within the human resources of several of the larger terrorist groups, particularly those with university students and urban workers as members.

Apart from the technical problems involved in the illicit fabrication of nuclear weapons, there are the political considerations. What advantage would a terrorist group with the necessary capabilities find in fabricating a nuclear weapon? And how might terrorists use it? The historical record suggests that there are upper limits on terrorist violence, self-imposed constraints that deter even those we call "terrorists" from carrying out certain actions. To detonate a nuclear weapon without warning in a heavily populated area and thereby cause thousands or even tens of thousands of casualties would gain the terrorists little more than infamy. To kill a lot of people is not an objective of terrorism. If it were, terrorists have ample non-nuclear means of doing so, although certainly none with the destructive potential or terrifying characteristics of a nuclear explosion.

The primary utility of a nuclear weapon would be as an instrument of coercion. With it, terrorists could create a mass hostage situation of unprecedented proportions. But it is not clear what enormous demand might be made that would be commensurate with a threat of this scale. Springing a handful of prisoners or collecting a few million dollars ransom do not warrant the investment and risks necessary to the fabrication of a nuclear weapon. At the other end of the spectrum, there are certain demands that it would be impossible to satisfy, whatever the threat. A government, for example, would not agree to liquidate itself. Demands made by terrorists with a nuclear weapon would also have to be of a finite nature, that is, the authors of the threat would have to demand an action or a decision that could not be reversed once the threat had been removed and that could be carried out fairly quickly. It would be difficult for terrorists to enforce a change in national policy unless they proposed to maintain the threat. A nuclear weapon probably cannot be used by a terrorist group to alter national policy permanently, overthrow a government, or to create a homeland for a particular ethnic group.

Conceivably, a nuclear weapon could be used to make demands that are spectacular and disruptive but that would not necessarily bring any measurable benefit beyond publicity to the group—such as a demand to release all convicted felons or to distribute baskets of food to the nation's poor on one day. That a group with the talents necessary to steal nuclear material and fabricate a nuclear weapon would find such payoffs worth their investment is difficult to conceive. It would seem that, technical considerations aside, nuclear weapons may be of limited utility to terrorists. Their enormous destructive power cannot easily be matched with negotiable benefits.

This does not overlook the fact that there are lunatics and crazy political fanatics who might find blowing up a city, or threatening to blow up a city, an attractive undertaking. Their reasons for doing so might, by any other view of the world than their own, be totally bizarre. But the requirements for fabricating a nuclear weapon are likely to exceed their capabilities, at least for now and the immediate future. Thus those most capable of mustering the resources to fabricate a nuclear device also are most likely to decide, for the reasons suggested above, not to do so, while those who may be disinclined to take such considerations into account at present lack the capabilities for fabrication. The long-range danger lies in the fact that the point at which the intentions and capabilities of these two intersect is not fixed. We have not yet reached the time when any bright lunatic can make an atomic bomb. As plutonium becomes more widely available and the opportunities for theft or diversion increase, and as the knowledge of how to use it in nuclear weapons becomes more widespread, a small group, without concern for a large constituency, unhindered by the requirements of political logic, pursuing some mad goal, might be able to require a nuclear capacity and be willing to use it.

A further danger arising from the increasing diffusion of nuclear material worldwide and the flaws in accounting for it would be the difficulty of assessing the credibility of a well-staged threat involving the use of nuclear material. We are entering an age of alarming hoaxes.

The deliberate dispersal of plutonium or of some other highly radioactive material is considered by some to be at least as likely as the fabrication of crude nuclear bombs, and strictly from the standpoint of feasibility, more likely. It requires no minimum strategic amount of plutonium as does a bomb. It makes no difference whether the plutonium is weapons grade or reactor grade, or whether it is in the metallic or oxide form. Dispersal that requires no knowledge of nuclear physics or of weapons design poses a few risks for the perpetrator. Only *some* plutonium (or other radionucleide) and a dispersal mechanism are needed. On the negative side, effective dispersal of plutonium over a large area is difficult, and the results are both unpredictable and delayed.

Plutonium, a carcinogen, is often billed as the most toxic substance known. One-millionth of a gram has been shown capable of causing cancer in animal tissue. Its effect on humans is debatable. Extrapolations from laboratory experiments using animals show that the internal deposition of the smallest particle of plutonium will inevitably lead to bone or liver cancer. Naturally, no human subjects have been deliberately contaminated in order to determine the effect on people, but there have been numerous accidental exposures to plutonium among workers in nuclear programs. A close watch has been kept on these persons over the years, and as of 1975 no deaths were attributable to the exposure. The only result up to 1975 is that one person accidentally injected with plutonium developed a benign growth on his arm.[19] Thus the experience of humans actually exposed to plutonium would seem to contradict the extrapolations from experiments with animals and suggest that the toxicity of plutonium may be lower than previously estimated. This experience, however, is far from conclusive, and many questions remain regarding the potential of plutonium for terrorist use.

The distinction between chemical toxins, which kill by causing a chemical change in the body, and radioactive toxins, which kill by radiation, is significant. Theoretically, small quantities of plutonium may be ingested and pass through the body without causing serious harm, as most of the plutonium will be eliminated before it can produce serious radiation effects; very little of it will be absorbed into the bloodstream. This eliminates effective dispersal in food or via the water supply. Dispersal by water also presents other problems: plutonium is not soluble in water, and it is extremely heavy. Even fine particles are likely to settle quite near the initial point of dispersal. (Additional technical problems of water contamination are discussed on pp. 241-244.)

Plutonium is most dangerous when inhaled. Fine particles may lodge in the lungs, ultimately producing lung cancer. Most dispersal scenarios assume air dispersal. However, open air dispersal also poses certain technical problems. Again, the heavy weight of plutonium will cause it to settle out of the atmosphere quite rapidly, reducing the size of the zone that can be contaminated. Unless the plutonium is extremely finely ground, only a fraction of the particles will be respirable, and of that only a fraction of the inhaled plutonium will be retained in the lungs. Finally, there is the dilution problem. The probability of an individual breathing in one or more particles is low. The effects of dispersal will depend on the amount of plutonium that is dispersed, on how finely it is ground, the height at which the material is released—most scenarios prefer the rooftops of tall buildings—the population density, and the atmospheric conditions. All these conditions make the results somewhat unpredictable. One scientist has estimated that the open-air dispersal of plutonium dust would cause one fatality for each 15 grams released without warning. This would amount to 400 deaths for 6 kilograms, about the minimum needed for a bomb.[20] The perpetrator could substantially increase the potential casualties by dispersing the material at a public gathering—a stadium for example—or into the ventilation system of a closed, climate-controlled building where the concentration would be higher and the plutonium would recirculate with the air, thereby subjecting the occupants to repeated exposures.

The victims of exposure to plutonium would not all die immediately. A few persons subjected to massive doses might die within a few days. Lung cancers, however, would not show up for 10 to 20 years after exposure. Given some movement of the exposed population subsequent to the exposure and the normal rates of lung cancer from other causes (smoking, air pollution, etc.), the overall statistical increase might be negligible. Thus the dispersal of plutonium would lack that immediate impact that terrorists normally seek—a handful of immediate deaths, not an unknown number of victims 10 or 20 years later. On the other hand, if the exposure were subsequently publicized, public fear is likely to attribute all subsequent cases of cancer to the dispersal, thereby increasing alarm and adding to the perceived magnitude of the damage.

Despite its obvious shortcomings as a means of mass murder, plutonium does have a potential attraction in a dispersal scheme, *i.e.*, its slow rate of radioactive decay. Plutonium has a half-life of 24,000 years. Property contaminated with plutonium would have to be decontaminated, an elaborate and costly process, before it could again be safely occupied, or it would have to be abandoned for thousands of years. That brings up the potential objectives of symbolic contamination or economic dislocation. Plutonium, or some other highly radioactive substance, could be used to contaminate property, and thereby prevent its use. This would be particularly attractive if the target had some symbolic value to society or to the perpetrator.

Spent nuclear fuel contains highly radioactive elements, in addition to plutonium, which could be employed as contaminants. This material would be most vulnerable to diversion during shipment from the reactor site to reprocessing or waste storage facilities. In the United States, spent fuel is shipped in large, sealed casks containing anywhere from a half ton to approximately three tons. Terrorists conceivably could hijack a truck carrying such casks, drive it rapidly to the selected target, and there breach the casks and disperse their contents with high explosives. This would be a high-risk operation that could be carried out clandestinely. Using a portable antitank weapon, someone also could attempt to breach one of the casks while in transit.

Scientists have also identified tritium, water in which the normal hydrogen element has been replaced with its radioactive isotope, as a material that could be used as a contaminant. Tritiated water looks and acts like ordinary water and can be absorbed into the body either through the skin or by ingestion. Tritium could not easily be used to contaminate a large water supply; again, the dilution would mitigate or eliminate the danger. However, it could be used to contaminate a smaller water system. Given that it *is* water reduces some of the technical problems.

There has been only one case of deliberate dispersal of a radioactive material. In 1974, an anonymous caller in Austria, calling himself a "justice guerrilla," warned that certain train coaches had been deliberately contaminated with radioactive material. Investigators found strong but not lethal traces of iodine-131, which is normally used for medical diagnosis. The "justice guerrilla" turned out to be an individual with a history of insanity, and he intended his actions to be a protest against the treatment of the mentally disturbed. In a separate case, Italian police reported uncovering a plot by right-wing terrorists to poison Italy's aqueducts with radioactive waste material. The allegations were never substantiated.

Threats of dispersal would be more credible than threats of setting off nuclear bombs simply because the author of threats would need much less material or technical expertise to carry out the threats. For this reason, extortion based on a dispersal threat would be effective—less likely to be called—than extortion based on a claim that the author possessed a nuclear bomb. As an instrument of mass murder, a nuclear bomb, if detonated successfully, appears more effective than dispersal. In both cases, nuclear bomb threats and nuclear dispersal threats, the threat mode would seem more likely to be performed by the political extremist than would actual use without warning or demand.

Explosives and Incendiaries

Advances have been made in explosives, detonators, and fusing devices. The chemicals for making explosives are more available now. Dynamite, gelignite, and military explosives can be purchased or easily stolen; enormous quantities are lost every year. The biggest advances have been made in fusing mechanisms. Terrorists are often ingenious in making bombs go off in new ways: day-date calendar watches; digital clocks that flip small panels; and small, powerful batteries can set off a time bomb weeks, even months, after it was planted. Small portable transmitters sold in hobby shops for radio-controlled model airplanes have been used in command-detonated mines. Mercury switches, the same ones that turn washing machines off when the lid is lifted, have been used as fuses. So have light meters, photoelectric switches, altimeters, and even test tubes filled with peas soaking in water (the peas swell and push a small plunger up to complete an electric circuit). Bomb squads must now be wary of not one but two or three fusing mechanisms.

The most significant development has been the spread of technical knowledge. Thousands of soldiers have been trained to use explosives. Some ex-demolition experts have become terrorist bombers. Leftist guerrillas and would-be guerrillas have received courses on improvised demolitions in the Soviet Union, North Korea, and Cuba. For those who lacked the opportunity to receive formal training, there are numerous books and pamphlets on how to improvise explosive devices. (Many of the publications available in the United States are once-classified military and Central Intelligence Agency technical manuals whose public release resulted from the new Freedom of Information Act.)[21] As a result, more and more people know, or can easily learn, how to make bombs at home. As the ingredients are available commercially and individually and have benign uses as well as potentially malevolent ones, control of materials seems impossible. The most critical component appears to be the detonator or blasting cap.

High explosives require detonators to set them off, and most improvised explosive devices with high explosives use commercial or military detonators, as it is difficult to fabricate detonators. Without detonators, only low-velocity explosives can be used, but bombs made with low-velocity explosives, in order to attain the same destructive power, must be much larger than those with high explosives, thereby making their concealment more difficult.

Detonators are made by only a few companies in the United States and by no company in Latin America. It is reported that almost all the Irish Republican Army's detonators come from a single plant in the Republic of Ireland. It would seem, then, that by controlling the distribution and sale of detonators more closely and by monitoring them by means of taggants, which will be discussed later, it would be possible to reduce the number of bombings. At the very least, it would limit the use of high explosives to experts capable of making their own detonators. Detonators can be fabricated by someone who has a thorough knowledge of how to make explosives, but the process is perilous, and homemade detonators are larger and less reliable than commercially made ones.

The use of incendiary weapons such as napalm in warfare has come under increasing international attack and may be proscribed by new international conventions. Operating against such constraints is the development of new incendiary weapons. Scientists have recently found a way to create controlled "fireballs" with temperatures equalled only by thermonuclear weapons. Probably this does not mean very much for terrorists, for incendiary weapons such as napalm are too bulky to use, and the production of thermal weapons is likely to remain a technically complicated task beyond the capabilities of most terrorist groups. For most terrorists, an incendiary weapon is a Molotov cocktail—a bottle of gasoline with a rag wick—or simply a match.

Terrorists have caused extensive property damage by using small incendiary devices. They have tended not to use fire against people. This is also true of the majority of terrorist bombings; they are intended to cause property damage, not casualties. The devices planted by the Armed Forces of National Liberation (FALN), a Puerto Rican separatist group, might be considered an exception to both observations, as their bombs characteristically include a small tank of propane gas. When this tank of propane is detonated by the accompanying dynamite, it has the effect of a powerful air-fueled explosion and is also an incendiary. These bombs have caused casualties, but as murder weapons, incendiaries are unreliable except when part of an explosive device. When terrorists want to kill someone, they appropriately resort to high explosives or guns.

The use of large incendiary devices to kill large numbers of people would bring up the same problem faced in the use of chemical, biological, or nuclear weapons: the creation of mass casualties or the use of indiscriminate weapons may be counterproductive to the achievement of the terrorists' goals. If indiscriminate mass murder is the terrorists' objective, sophisticated incendiaries are not required; simple arson in a high-rise building could be effective. In sum, at present, developments in incendiary weapons do not seem to have increased the terrorists' potential for violence significantly.

Man-Portable Precision-Guided Munitions

Tremendous developments have taken place in major weapons systems in the last 30 or so years. Nuclear weapons, jet-propelled aircraft, helicopters, intercontinental ballistic missiles, nuclear-propelled surface vessels and submarines, reconnaissance satellites, multiple independently targeted reentry vehicles, and cruise missiles have altered concepts of tactics, strategy, and indeed even concepts of international diplomacy. Meanwhile, the weapons of the individual soldier have changed far more gradually. The foot soldier of the late 1960s and early 1970s carried an automatic or semiautomatic rifle, improved to be sure but not markedly different from the semiautomatic rifle or submachine gun of World War II. He carried hand grenades, the range and accuracy of which still depended on his throwing skill, and possibly a pistol—an automatic of pre-World War I vintage or a revolver of even earlier design.

Now, however, we appear to be at a point of upswing in the development of individual weaponry. The technologies of space ventures and commercial electronics have been applied to the weapons of the infantryman. Propellants that are thermodynamically more efficient and small two-stage solid fuel propulsion systems have reduced the requirements for heavy gun barrels and increased the range of small projectiles. Improvements in metallurgy and plastics and glass fibers permit further reductions in the size and weight of firing tubes. New sighting and tracking devices and aerodynamic testing of projectile shapes have increased range and accuracy. Developments in explosive and shaped charges have added to destructive power. As a result, there are new classes of weapons that are smaller, lighter, more accurate at greater range, and more destructive than anything previously carried by an individual soldier. Some of these weapons are even disposable.

The most dramatic development in individual weaponry is man-portable precision-guided munitions (PGMs). PGMs are munitions whose course can be corrected in flight. Targeting accuracy approaches certainty. Man-portable PGMs are lightweight; they usually can be carried and operated by one man. They are easy to operate (an advantage to groups whose members may not be trained), and they are highly destructive. They have two primary purposes on the battlefield: the destruction of enemy tactical aircraft and the destruction of enemy tanks. A single missile suitable both against aircraft and tanks is now under development.

Examples of man-portable PGMs include the U.S.-made Redeye and Stinger and the Soviet-made Strela or SA-7. These are shoulder-fired, anti-aircraft missiles that have infrared, heat-seeking sensors in the projectile that guide it to the heat of an aircraft engine. Redeye and Stinger weigh about 30 pounds; the SA-7 weighs about 23 pounds. Their range is about two to three kilometers. The British Blowpipe portable anti-aircraft missile system requires the aimer to track the target. His commands are transmitted to the missile via radio. The Swedish RB-70 anti-aircraft missile flies to the target at supersonic speeds guided by a laser beam.

Antitank PGMs include the U.S. Dragon and TOW missiles, the French-German Hot and Milan weapons systems, and the Soviet Sagger missiles. They are all wire-guided, weigh between 23 and 30 pounds, and have effective ranges of one to three and one-half kilometers. The Dragon can penetrate up to two meters of concrete or more than a half meter of heavy armor.[22]

By the end of the 1970s, such weapons will be in the arsenals of the major military powers in the hundreds of thousands. First-generation PGMs such as Strela and Redeye will be available to 30 to 40 countries in the Third World.[23] It is not realistic to expect that all these countries will maintain strict security measures; some may find it in their interest to make these weapons available to nongovernmental groups. If we postulate a conservative worldwide loss rate, by theft or diversion, of 0.1 percent over the next five years, then man-portable PGMs will be "loose" in the hundreds by the beginning of the 1980s.

Military analysts are currently debating the ultimate effects that the deployment of large numbers of man-portable PGMs will have on the military battlefield of the future. What concerns us here is their employment off the battlefield by irregulars or civilians. In the hands of terrorists, man-portable PGMs are not likely to be used against tanks or tactical aircraft, but rather against more vulnerable civilian targets. The possession of man-portable surface-to-air missiles would enable terrorists to shoot down or threaten to shoot down civilian aircraft. Arab terrorists were captured near Rome's airport with Soviet-made SA-7s in their possession.[24] According to one report, they had acquired these from Libya, which had acquired them from Egypt, which in turn had acquired them from the Soviet Union. The government of Libya was aware of the intended target—an El Al airliner—when it provided the weapons to the group.

Man-portable antitank PGMs would make it possible for would-be assassins to destroy a moving car in a motorcade or a speaker's podium from a distance of several kilometers. They would also provide saboteurs with the means to attack hard targets such as oil tankers, fuel or chemical storage tanks, and nuclear reactor containment towers where close access may be denied.

Other Special Infantry Weapons

Although of less consequence than man-portable PGMs, there are other new infantry weapons of possible use to terrorists. New antitank and assault weapons have been developed, such as the Armbrust 300, a German-made short-range, disposable antitank weapon. The Armbrust is silent, has no muzzle flash, no smoke, and no infrared signature. It can be fired without detection. Unlike most rocket launchers, it has no back blast, which means that it can be fired from inside a small room or other confined space. It is an ideal weapon for urban guerrilla warfare, and it could be used as a weapon of assassination.

The new U.S.-made short-range, man-portable antitank weapons are not precision-guided and weigh only about 8 pounds, compared with the normal 18 to 45 pounds for other antitank weapons. They are easily concealed and could also be used to assassinate passengers even in vehicles that are armored for security.

New shoulder-fired, multipurpose assault weapons include multishot rocket launchers with warheads suitable both for anti-armor and antipersonnel missions. Silent grenade launchers, minigrenades, and weapons firing duplex or triplex cartridges that contain two or three bullets in tandem—thus making one shot actually a salvo of projectiles—would all increase the firepower of a small attacking group of the future.

The new multishot, shoulder-fired, squirtless flamethrower would seem to be potentially useful both for armed assaults and sabotage, particularly of facilities where flammable materials are present. Squirtless flamethrowers do not have the heavy tanks and fire streams of earlier flamethrowers. Rather, they are small and portable. One model is 35 inches long and weighs under 27 pounds, compared with the cumbersome old flamethrowers that weighed between 50 and 80 pounds. The new models fire a cartridge that ignites upon exposure to air or upon impact. They have multishot clips.

Where assault is to be avoided, there are new lightweight (25- to 30-pound) disposable mortars and portable multispigot launchers that fire a salvo of projectiles at a target of predetermined range. They can be fired remotely, or conceivably by a timing device. One thinks of the mortar attacks on Moslem neighborhoods in Algiers by members of the *Organization Armée Secrète* and the more recent attacks on an airport in Ulster by IRA members who used a homemade mortar.

In sum, we see weapons that are small and easily concealed, that can be fired without detection and in some cases remotely, or that would greatly increase the firepower of the individual and the small group. These weapons appear to be useful for assassination, armed assaults, and sabotage; many increase the chances of escape. What consequences will these developments have?

Thus far, for the most part terrorists have attacked easy, unprotected targets: airline terminals, embassies, office buildings. Attacks on innocent civilian bystanders is what, in part, makes them terrorists. As they are not interested in a fight, they have avoided assaults on facilities that might be guarded. Although this situation may not change, we must take into account, however, that in the future groups, well-armed possibly by some government or by means of theft, may be able to overwhelm civilian guard forces that are normally lightly armed. Police are already being outgunned by suspects they are trying to apprehend. One man with an M-16 rifle has the firepower equivalent to five men armed with police revolvers. In the past few years, police departments have been compelled to develop special weapons and tactics units in part to deal with heavily armed, barricaded suspects. The possession of advanced infantry weaponry by common criminals or by political extremists may increase their willingness to engage in shootouts. The current trend toward heavier, more advanced weaponry for police probably will continue. We may also see new demands to increase the armament of civilian guards at vulnerable facilities such as liquefied natural gas or nuclear facilities.

Preventing such weapons from falling into the hands of unauthorized users seems a rather remote possibility. As all are basic infantry weapons, they are likely to be manufactured and deployed in large quantities. Military organizations that see their great utility on the battlefield are not particularly interested in withholding such weapons from deployment or complicating their use and increasing their cost by putting coding devices or other hardware on them that would present greater obstacles to unauthorized users. They are intended for use by soldiers with minimal training in combat; their operation must be kept simple. Consequently, the acquisition of such weapons does not appear to be a major problem for criminals or political extremists; hence, control will be difficult. However, it may be possible to identify and provide extra security for new infantry weapons that might be particularly attractive off the battlefield to criminals and extremists. The U.S. armed forces have recognized this need and guard PGMs such as Redeye and Stinger more closely than other types of weapons.

New Vulnerabilities

Inherent in modern industrial society are new vulnerabilities that could be exploited by criminals or political extremists. In some cases a handful of determined, knowledgeable individuals could carry out operations that, if successful, might have far-reaching consequences. Two types of actions should be considered: (1) those that may cause disruption of vital systems leading to widespread inconvenience, possibly to some degree of public alarm, but that do not directly threaten life; and (2) actions that directly threaten or appear directly to threaten human life. Examples of the first type would be the interruption of telecommunications or the destruction of vital records stored in computers in order to disrupt a country's financial system. Either act would certainly create serious problems but would not directly imperil human life. Examples of the second type would be the sabotage of liquefied natural gas facilities or of tank cars carrying lethal chemicals—both could present a danger to public safety. The public might not be directly threatened by the seizure of hostages at a nuclear power reactor because the captors would still have to carry out some additional sets of actions to cause a core meltdown and produce a radioactive release. However, the mere holding by terrorists of any nuclear facility would appear directly threatening to public safety and undoubtedly would cause alarm.

A complete list of modern society's vulnerabilities would include water supply systems, transportation systems, energy systems, communications systems, computerized management and information systems, and certain critical industries. The vulnerabilities may lie in the complexity and interdependence of the systems themselves or in certain vulnerable portions of a given system. This chapter is primarily concerned with vulnerabilities that could pose a direct danger to public safety if they were exploited. Therefore we will set aside the disruption of communications systems and computerized information and management systems that could cause serious economic loss and widespread inconvenience but not directly threaten life. We will concentrate on vulnerabilities that, at least theoretically, can be exploited by small bands of profit-minded criminals or political extremists. Our primary concern, however, is not simple theft or extortion but the threats against society that can be created as a result. Of those that may pose a danger to public safety, there appear to be five theoretical areas of vulnerability that merit close examination: water supply systems, transportation systems (especially civil aviation), nuclear facilities and liquefied natural gas facilities—which are two increasingly important components of energy systems—and components of chemical industries that manufacture or utilize large quantities of highly dangerous chemicals. In each case, we shall attempt to describe the nature of the vulnerabilities, the ease or difficulty with which a small group could exploit them, the incentives and disincentives to such actions by criminals—or more importantly for this discussion, political extremists—and the potential dangers that such actions would pose to society. The chapter will also examine some recent incidents in each area in which criminals or political extremists have attacked the category of targets being discussed. Later, it will also examine some of the possible measures for protection and control and the consequences that these would have for municipal and international law.

Water Supply Systems

Water supply systems possess two potential vulnerabilities: the supply of water can be interrupted by some type of physical attack on the system itself, and the water can be contaminated. Both actions are difficult to accomplish on a grand scale. Water supply systems are made up of dams, aqueducts, reservoirs, pumping stations, and they are built of earth, concrete, and steel for the most part—in other words, they are targets that cannot easily be destroyed by small explosive charges. Indeed, experience from conventional military contests suggests that such targets are hard to destroy, even with large bombs. Small explosive charges at critical points could cause leakage and temporary shutdowns for repairs, but probably no critical water shortages. It would be possible to interrupt, temporarily at least, the flow of water to a particular neighborhood or building, but it is difficult to see what objective that would serve. A group determined to cut off a city's water supply would have to assemble and plant huge quantities of explosives, carry on a continuous campaign of sabotage aimed at disruption, or resort to schemes of contamination.

The popular scenario of someone spilling the contents of a vial into a city's reservoir and poisoning its citizens is somewhat exaggerated. Although many chemical and biological substances could be dispersed in water supply systems, the would-be killer would face several serious obstacles. First, he would have to find a chemical agent that is not decomposed in water. Organic compounds, for example, would quickly hydrolyze, thus losing their effectiveness. Second, the killer would have to overcome problems of dilution and dispersion. Hundreds of millions of gallons of water flow through a city's water supply system daily. Water from rivers and reservoirs is supplemented by water from local wells, further diluting contaminated water from any single source. Thus a small quantity of a chemical agent would not suffice. Tens of tons, possibly hundreds of tons, of the most toxic substances would be required to provide a lethal dose to a majority of the water's consumers. Only a small fraction of U.S. water is used for human consumption, about a quart or two out of an average per capita consumption of 200 gallons daily. The rest is used for agriculture and industrial purposes, to water lawns, flush toilets, wash clothes, and so on. Therefore the killer would have to find some means of effectively dispersing the substance evenly throughout the system.

Those who would seek to use hallucinogenic agents such as LSD would face the same problem of dilution and dispersion. Biological agents that multiply by themselves might assist the potential killer in overcoming the quantity problem. Typhoid fever, cholera, and various species of shigella that cause dysentery remain viable in water, but it is precisely such waterborne diseases that modern water supply systems are monitored and treated for. Routine methods of water purification—such as coagulation, flocculation, sedimentation, filtration, and chlorination—effectively destroy most harmful organisms. If the water supply is seriously contaminated, chemical antidotes can be added, or portions of the system can be flushed without interrupting the supply. A few people might get ill as a result of an attempt to poison a city's water supply, but mass casualties are not likely to result.

Smaller water supply systems, such as the pipes leading into a high-rise office building or a hotel, could be dangerously contaminated. Dilution would be considerably less, and the poison would be introduced into the system after the water had already been treated. This is perhaps the greatest vulnerability.

There are a few technical problems here as well, however. The water supply would have to be shut down at least briefly; otherwise the powerful force of water pressure would prevent access to the pipes. Once access is gained, the would-be killer would have to devise a means of dispersing his poison gradually and evenly or risk having the entire load flushed through a toilet somewhere. At a minimum, some plumbing skills would be required along with some specialized dispersing equipment although the obstacles are far fewer here than in the case of poisoning a city's water supply.

If not lethally contaminated, a large water supply system could theoretically be nonlethally contaminated in a way that could result in the disruption of the supply and costly clean-up procedures. One could, for example, dye the water or simply make it smell bad. The objective would not be to kill anyone but rather simply to create alarm and cause inconvenience and disruption so as to attract attention as part of some publicity or extortion scheme.

Water supply systems have been the target of political extremists and criminal extortionists on several occasions in recent history. In February 1976, local police and FBI agents discovered in the residence of seven suspected terrorists 150 pounds of explosives, reportedly along with a plan to disrupt a large city's water system. The complex plan was to be a coordinated effort with groups in California, Oregon, and Washington, and may have been directed against the city of Portland, Oregon.[25] The IRA has on occasion blown up water pumping stations.[26] However, most political extremists have not gone in for attacks on water systems. Such attacks more commonly have been motivated by disputes over water rights. One of the most famous episodes in the United States was the so-called Owens Valley Water War, which began when the Department of Water and Power of the City of Los Angeles began buying land in the Owens Valley of central California and draining the valley's water through a large aqueduct to Los Angeles. As a result of the lowering of the water table, the once lush farm and ranch land was gradually turned into a virtual desert. Acts of sabotage against the aqueduct were common, and on one occasion angry ranchers seized control of a pumping station, an act that resulted in a shootout with a sheriff's posse. All this took place back in the 1920s, but bombings of the aqueduct system have occurred as recently as 1976.

Welsh nationalists, protesting against their valleys being flooded to form reservoirs or their water being pumped to the cities of England, have planted bombs at aqueducts and pumping stations. Acts of sabotage directed against water supply systems also have been associated with labor strife.

There have been a few attempts to contaminate the water in major supply systems with chemical or biological agents. These are discussed on pp. 222-229 in this chapter. In November 1976, Philadelphia officials received a $1 million extortion demand together with a threat to contaminate the city's water supply with 1000 gallons of heating oil. Although such contamination would not have been lethal, it might have caused some vomiting, so the public was warned to test the water before drinking it. The biggest problem would have been a major clean-up operation. No contamination was ever detected. Several suspects were apprehended; their motives were not political.

In sum, water supply systems seem to be no more vulnerable to interruption or contamination than they were a half century ago. If anything, they are less vulnerable owing to modern water treatment systems. Land wars and labor disputes account for most incidents of sabotage. Contamination schemes appear to have been originated for the most part by lunatics or plain extortionists, not political extremists.

Civil Aviation

Transportation systems have always been attractive targets of armies and saboteurs. A small amount of destruction in the right place can have crippling effects on lines of communications, as lines are always difficult to protect. It is not for these reasons, however, that terrorists find certain targets in modern transportation systems attractive. As mentioned previously, terrorists for the most part have not carried out campaigns to create widespread destruction or disruption. Most terrorist violence, thus far, has been characterized by isolated but dramatic incidents. For terrorists, transportation systems are attractive because they contain concentrations of people in aircraft, in air terminals, and in railroad stations. One could find larger concentrations of people in crowded downtown streets and in football stadiums, but there are other features that make components of transportation systems more attractive. In transit, people are often in some type of vehicle that can be isolated, so the people can be held hostage easily. Passengers cannot easily jump off an aircraft, so to terrorists an airplane is a convenient and mobile container of hostages. They can order it to be flown to just about anywhere in the world, which is something they cannot do with a football stadium or a nuclear reactor. Trains on a fixed rail cannot be manipulated as can an aircraft, but they still are containers of human beings who can be isolated. A further attraction is that the people found in air terminals and aircraft are an aggregation of strangers who are not likely to notice or challenge the presence of others with whom they are traveling. Foreigners do not stand out as much; the terrorist blends in. (The same holds true for major hotels.) Except for security check points at predictable locations (and aircraft that regularly have armed undercover agents aboard), there are no policemen. Travelers aboard an aircraft are "between" law enforcement capabilities. Moreover, such places as air terminals—and to a lesser extent, land transportation terminals—are close to the terrorists' own lines of communications and routes of escape. Finally, national carriers are symbols of the nation itself. The nationality of the passengers is likely to reflect this. In other words, the intended victims will have the "right" nationality. Attacking El Al is like attacking Israel; attacking Swissair is like attacking Switzerland. In sum, it is not the transportation system itself that terrorists attack; it is the suitable and convenient collections of passengers.

Despite recent improvements in security, civil aviation—particularly national carriers—will continue to be a major vulnerability.[27] Although there has been a marked decline in aircraft hijackings since 1970, hijacking continues to be a serious threat to international civil aviation. Two spectacular incidents that occurred in 1976 are cases in point: the hijacking of the Air France airbus by Palestinian terrorists, and the hijacking of a TWA aircraft by Croatian extremists.[28] Well-informed and determined groups can still find airports where security measures are lax or ways to penetrate or obviate security systems. Governments appear to have become tougher in their handling of hijackers. A hijacking in 1976 or 1977 was more likely to end in assault by security forces than would have been the case several years ago. Governments are more likely to order their security forces to shoot at the tires of the aircraft or assault the aircraft even though such actions involve obvious risks for the passengers. In part, this reflects growing resistance to terrorist extortion. It also reflects greater confidence in recently formed antiterrorist commando units.

Acts of sabotage against passenger aircraft have increased in recent years. The usual method of attack has been to plant a bomb aboard an airliner and later claim credit for the explosion. Although these acts have been few in number, they are a disturbing trend because they indicate some groups' willingness to kill larger numbers of civilians. They represent the largest casualty scores made by terrorists, and they are on the edge of mass murder. Palestinian terrorists claimed responsibility for the explosion and crash of a Swissair aircraft in February 1970 in which 47 were killed. In January 1972, Croatian terrorists said they had put a bomb on a Stockholm-to-Belgrade aircraft that crashed, killing 26. Palestinian terrorists claimed "credit" for the on-board explosion that caused a TWA aircraft to crash into the Ionian Sea in September 1974, killing 88 persons.[29] In October 1976, anti-Castro extremists claimed "credit" for the crash of a Cubana airliner in the Caribbean, in which 78 persons were killed.[30] The four incidents add up to a total of 239 deaths, close to a fifth of all the persons killed in international incidents of terrorism between 1968 and 1976.

Another ominous development in the area of civil aviation is the growing availability of man-portable guided munitions.

Civil aviation is unique as an industry that has been identified by the international community as requiring special protection under international law.[31]

Nuclear Energy Systems

Much has been written lately about the attractiveness of nuclear facilities to criminals and terrorists. The rapid growth of a civilian nuclear industry, increasing traffic in plutonium, enriched uranium, and radioactive waste material, and the spread of nuclear technology all increase the opportunities for terrorists to engage in some type of "nuclear action." Growing public concern with the potential terrorist threat to nuclear programs virtually guarantees widespread publicity for any such act.[32]

The nuclear industry provides terrorists with a broad range of possible targets. The nuclear fuel cycle involves several kinds of facilities that serve to provide nuclear reactors with fuel and to dispose of their waste products. These facilities include conversion, enrichment, fuel fabrication, and fuel assembly plants where uranium ore is transformed into fuel for power reactors, the reactors themselves, reprocessing plants where residual uranium and plutonium are separated from the spent reactor fuel, as well as waste repositories, and the transportation links between the facilities. Other potential nuclear targets include those associated with the fabrication of nuclear weapons, those where fuel is made for nuclear-powered ships, as well as nuclear research facilities.

Terrorists could be attracted to nuclear facilities as a source of highly enriched uranium or plutonium that they could use in an explosive or dispersal device or offer to ransom back to its owners for cash or concessions. Terrorists could seek to disable or destroy nuclear facilities to cause economic damage to a corporation, power outages, or even widespread casualties and damage. Terrorists might try to seize control of nuclear facilities as they would hijack an airliner or seize an embassy for the purpose of making demands. Theft, sabotage, or seizure would attract more attention in a nuclear context than such acts normally attract in a non-nuclear context. Terrorists could find nuclear facilities attractive merely as a dramatic backdrop for some other action calculated to gain public attention.

This setting of potential high tragedy appears to be the biggest attraction and not the fact that the sabotage of a nuclear facility or fabrication of an illicit nuclear explosive or dispersal device would enable terrorists to cause mass casualties. Almost any terrorist action associated with the word "nuclear" would automatically generate fear in the public mind. Drawing attention to themselves and their causes and creating alarm—typical objectives of terrorists—may be achieved by taking relatively unsophisticated but highly visible actions. Any visible act of sabotage, not necessarily one that disables the facility or that is dangerous to the public, or even a temporary seizing and holding of a nuclear facility, would suffice to gain the perpetrators widespread attention and produce alarm.

Thus theft, sabotage, and seizure appear to be the three categories of actions that terrorists might wish to carry out. How vulnerable is the industry to these actions? A desire to steal nuclear material would lead the terrorists to seek out fuel fabrication facilities in the nuclear power industry, government weapons fabrication programs, or the transportation links in these areas. These are the places where they might acquire the necessary quantities for making a bomb or dispersal device. (Minute quantities of plutonium also may be found at research facilities.) Plutonium is not easily accessible once it has been combined with other material in reactor fuel rods, and the spent fuel rods that contain plutonium are too radioactively hot to handle without special protective equipment. Most experts agree that the biggest vulnerability would lie in shipping.

The incidents that have already occurred may offer some clues about what to expect from terrorists in the immediate future. In March 1973, members of the People's Revolutionary Army, a Trotskyist urban guerrilla group in Argentina, occupied a nuclear power plant under construction north of Buenos Aires. They overpowered the guards, painted slogans on the walls, raised their own flag over the facility, and stole weapons. But they made no demands for the release of their hostages and did not attempt to enter the reactor area or damage the facility.[33] In May 1975, two bombs exploded at a nuclear power plant under construction in eastern France.[34] The explosions started a fire, which caused considerable damage in a nonoperative area of the nuclear reactor complex. The reactor itself did not contain fissionable material at that time. The bombings were reportedly planted by the "Meinhof-Puig Antich Group," which was how a caller, who warned people to evacuate the site, identified himself. No one had previously heard of the group. It may be recalled, however, that Ulrike Meinhof was one of the leaders of an anarchist group in West Germany and that Puig Antich was an anarchist who was executed by the Spanish government. In August 1975, two explosions caused minor damage to another nuclear power plant in France. The bombs damaged an inlet for cooling water for the reactor and an air vent on the building housing the unit. The reactor itself was not damaged. No one claimed responsibility for the attack, but police suspected a Breton separatist group responsible for other acts of sabotage in the area. Recently, there have been several more bombing incidents at nuclear facilities in France and one at a reactor site in Sweden.[35]

Damage and bomb threats against nuclear facilities as well as against all industrial, commercial, and government buildings have become common. If these are indicators of the future, as the nuclear industry expands more bomb threats appear probable, as well as low-level acts of sabotage, and perhaps the seizure of hostages at a nuclear facility. The public alarm that these episodes are likely to create will probably exceed the actual danger to public safety. The major danger still comes from the possible acquisition of plutonium by political extremists or from the more remote possibility of serious sabotage of a nuclear facility leading to a radioactive release. To prevent such events, we will undoubtedly see increases in the size of guard forces and improvements in their armaments.

Liquefied Natural Gas

Liquefied natural gas (LNG) will play an increasingly important role in the supply of energy. Japan already is a major importer and Western Europe is increasing its imports. As geographically convenient sources of natural gas are exhausted, the United States will increase its imports of natural gas tenfold by 1985, according to current estimates. This gas will come from existing and new sources currently under development in Algeria, Libya, Abu Dhabi, Alaska, the Soviet Union, Indonesia, and Brunei.

Natural gas is moved cross country by extensive pipeline systems and overseas by ocean vessels. It is economic to transport natural gas by ship only when it has been liquefied by cooling and thereby reduced to 1/600th of its volume. This process requires facilities to liquefy the gas, special LNG ports for loading and unloading, regasification facilities, and specially constructed LNG tankers.

The transport of large quantities of LNG by ocean vessel poses some dangers. The principal danger is a large spill that may result from an accident, such as a ship collision, or conceivably from an act of sabotage. When natural gas is mixed with air and provided with a source of ignition, it explodes with enormous force. There have been some spectacular and costly accidents. The biggest one occurred October 20, 1944, when an LNG storage tank in Cleveland, Ohio, spilled 6200 cubic meters of gas. The resulting explosion and fires killed 128 persons, injured 300, and caused $6.8 million (at 1944 values) worth of property damage. A standard present-day LNG tanker carries 125,000 cubic meters of gas.

Scientists are not entirely certain what would happen in a major cargo spill. The cold liquid gas ($-160°C$) would immediately begin to vaporize, forming a large cloud of gas, which could dissipate harmlessly into the atmosphere if there were no source of ignition. If the spilling liquid gas were ignited close to the rupture, it could form a "pool fire" that would continue to burn as the liquid gas spilled out and vaporized. If a large vapor cloud were formed and then ignited, it could form a fireball, burning all around the edges, heating and vaporizing the colder gas, which would then fuel the fire. It has been estimated that a 25,000-cubic-meter spill (the contents of one tank aboard an LNG tanker) would produce a fireball of approximately one-half mile in diameter, which would burn for about 65 seconds. On the other hand, the gas could entirely vaporize and explode.

Because of the apparent dangers, most LNG facilities are or will be located in remote areas where a fire or explosion would not endanger a major population center. However, as urban centers expand and as new facilities are built, LNG facilities may be sited close enough to cities to cause some concern, and thus become a major issue of debate. The siting of proposed LNG facilities in southern California, for example, has aroused considerable local opposition. In the environmental impact report prepared for the project, it was estimated that as few as none or as many as 70,000 people could be imperiled by an offshore spill of a fully loaded LNG tanker, depending on such factors as the size of the release, whether or not it was immediately ignited, and atmospheric conditions.[36]

In the context of sabotage, it would appear that the greatest vulnerabilities in the transport system would be to the LNG tankers themselves, particularly when sailing through narrow straits or secured for unloading. The transfer lines, liquefaction, regasification, and storage facilities at the terminals would also be vulnerable.

Three possible motives might be served by attacks on LNG tankers or terminals. LNG may fit some scheme of threatened mass murder, particularly in view of the publicity about possible casualties from a major spill. Causing a major spill, however, may exceed the capabilities of the individuals or tiny groups who normally concoct such schemes. Drawing attention to the dangers of LNG, or preventing or delaying construction of LNG facilities, could provide a motive for low-level acts of sabotage but probably not mass murder. Interruption of supply and economic dislocation, traditional motives for sabotage, could apply in the case of LNG. The world's LNG will originate from a small number of liquefaction facilities and will be transported in a small fleet of specially constructed tankers that will offload at only a few points. No excess capacity is planned. Therefore disabling a tanker or single terminal would have serious economic consequences. Threats against LNG facilities, as opposed to direct attacks, may be associated with efforts to attract publicity, cause alarm, extort money, or gain other concessions.

Unpublicized bomb threats and low-level incidents of sabotage involving LNG probably have occurred as in other industries. There have been no publicized reports of terrorist attacks nor of special terrorist interest in LNG facilities. But although it is of unpredictable probability, sabotage is considered a real possibility. Perimeter fences, alarms, television scanners, guards, boat patrols, sonar systems, and other measures to prevent sabotage have been recommended.[37] The status of their implementation is unknown. Security at LNG facilities is probably lower than that at nuclear facilities, and it may possibly be lower than that at airline terminals.

The dangers inherent in the transport of LNG are well recognized, and measures to prevent catastrophic accidents are incorporated into the design, construction, and operating procedures of LNG facilities. International standards for LNG tankers and crews are being developed by the Intergovernmental Maritime Consultative Organization; however, these standards are not legally binding. LNG tankers entering U.S. waters must meet codes enforced by the U.S. Coast Guard. Local fire prevention codes also apply. The design features in the facilities and vessels provide a significant measure of protection against an act of major sabotage.[38]

The shipment of liquefied petroleum gas (LPG) shares some of the same problems involved in the transport of LNG. In a discussion of sabotage or terrorist attack, both types of gases may be considered on a common basis.

Hazardous Chemicals

Flowing through the arteries and veins of a modern industrial society is a lethal array of hazardous chemicals: flammable liquids, gases, and solids; corrosive liquids; highly toxic materials or poisons; oxidizing agents; poisonous gases; radioactive materials (already discussed); and unstable chemicals that may explode or burn spontaneously. Some of these chemicals are used only in small amounts, but because of their extreme toxicity, they may still pose serious dangers to society. Others are manufactured, transported, and stored in significant amounts. For example, hundreds of tons of chlorine are produced and transported daily.

Accidents involving hazardous chemicals are not uncommon. In July 1976, an explosion at a chemical factory in northern Italy released a cloud of trichlorophenol gas containing five pounds of dioxin into the atmosphere. Dioxin is a highly toxic chemical once used in the defoliants employed by the U.S. forces in Vietnam and known to cause liver and kidney damage and genetic alteration. Residents of the town of Seveso, Italy, were evacuated as hundreds of birds, chickens, rabbits, cats, and dogs died. Plants withered. Thirty persons were hospitalized with skin rashes, but no human deaths were reported. Italian soldiers enclosed a 172-acre area with barbed wire. Authorities forbade the eating of vegetables from the contaminated zone. Doctors advised women in the area against pregnancy for at least three months. To decontaminate the area, experts advised that the chemical plant be destroyed, that poisoned livestock and vegetation be buried in waterproof ditches and covered with concrete, and that one foot of topsoil be removed entirely.

Although few accidents are as serious as the incident at Seveso—which may lead to permanent contamination of the landscape—explosions, fires, spills, or major leaks of hazardous chemicals that require the evacuation of employees or nearby residents may occur at the rate of one per day. We have become accustomed to reading or hearing reports of evacuations of entire towns or portions of cities in the path of deadly fumes or in anticipation of imminent explosions.

A handbook prepared by E.I. du Pont de Nemours and Company lists 75 hazardous chemicals, all of them toxic, 30 of them explosive, and 34 whose vapors form explosive mixtures with air. Hazardous chemicals are generally categorized as flammable liquids, such as acetone, benzene, butyl and methyl alcohol, and ether; flammable solids, such as magnesium, phosphorous, potassium, and metallic sodium; corrosive liquids, such as various acids, alkaline, and caustic liquids that cause serious injury to living tissue, that may corrode containers of other hazardous chemicals, or that may cause fire when in contact with organic material or with certain chemicals; oxidizing materials, such as ammonium nitrate, ammonium perchlorate, potassium chlorate, or potassium permaganate that yield to oxygen readily to support combustion or that react readily to oxidize fuels or other combustible materials; highly toxic materials and poisonous gases, liquids, or solids, such as chlorine, fluoride, hydrogen cyanide, phosgene, carbolic acid, and nitrobenzene (many common insecticides and pesticides would be included in this category) that pose serious hazards to life; unstable, highly explosive chemicals, such as organic peroxides, nitro-methan, again ammonium nitrate (a common fertilizer), and picric acid.[39]

Dangers to public safety may result from the primary explosion, fire, the spread of explosive flammable or toxic fumes, or indirect contamination of water, soil, plant life, and livestock. The biggest dangers would seem to be explosion and direct contamination by toxic fumes.

Major accidents at manufacturing sites, which normally result in few fatalities (usually fewer than 10), almost always involve employees. The more dangerous the chemical, the more likely the manufacturing plant is to be located far from centers of population. Disasters involving widespread off-site casualties are more likely to occur at storage facilities—for example, those at ports where large quantities of materials may be stored for shipment by barge or ocean vessel—and during transportation, where the materials may be carried via rail, truck, or barge past cities. Highway accidents, train derailments, and collisions involving ships or barges probably are the most frequent causes of evacuations of nearby towns.

One expert has identified 13 hazardous chemicals as those most likely to cause a major disaster upon accidental release. The 13 were chosen because they are extremely toxic, caustic, flammable, or explosive *and* because they are produced in sufficient quantity so that a disaster is a significant possibility. The chemicals and annual production figures that met these criteria were:

1. acrylonitrate, a liquid that releases cyanide when burned (1 billion pounds)
2. anhydrous ammonia, a compressed gas whose caustic vapors can produce pulmonary edema (26 billion pounds)
3. ammonium nitrate, a common fertilizer used as a substitute for TNT during World War II and about 80 percent as effective (6 million tons)
4. chlorine gas, a deadly gas that was used against troops in World War I and that is used today in water purification and various chemical processes (19.5 billion pounds)
5. ethylene oxide, a highly explosive chemical found in liquid or gas form (3.6 billion pounds)
6. fluorine, a highly flammable and toxic gas (no estimate available)
7. gasoline (2.2 billion barrels)
8. hydrogen cyanide, a toxic gas or liquid that produces explosive fumes (650 billion pounds)
9. hydrofluoric acid, a toxic and corrosive chemical in liquid or gas form (317,000 tons)
10. liquefied natural gas, which has been discussed separately
11. parathion, a toxic liquid (no annual production estimate available)
12. tetraethyl lead, a toxic liquid whose vapors are explosive (350 million pounds)
13. vinyl chloride, a liquid or gas used in the plastics industry that is explosive

and flammable, and that upon combustion produces phosgene gas, another chemical agent used in World War I (4 billion pounds)[40]

Accidents involving chlorine and vinyl chloride are the most common causes of evacuations. Ammonium nitrate and natural gas are the most common sources of accidental explosions. Fluorine is the most toxic on the list.

The manufacture, storage, handling, and use of hazardous chemicals are controlled by local fire prevention codes. In the United States, Department of Transportation regulations also control transportation and storage. Permits are normally required to produce, store, ship, or use hazardous chemicals. The codes set requirements with respect to proximity to dwellings, places of assembly, public highways, and so on; and limitations on storable quantities, storage facilities, and containers.[41]

Outside of wartime, no disasters involving hazardous chemicals have been traced to deliberate sabotage, although in some cases charges of criminal negligence have been made. While it would not be technically difficult to blow up a pipeline, start a fire at a chemical plant, or breach a barge or a tank car filled with chlorine or some other explosive, flammable, or toxic gas, thereby forcing the evacuation of the nearby populace, it is not clear what objectives would be served. While such acts endanger the public, they would have many of the same shortcomings associated with the poisoning of water supplies, the dispersal of radioactive contaminants, or attacks on liquefied natural gas facilities. The effects would be unpredictable and indiscriminate, and, from a political standpoint, counterproductive.

One can more easily imagine attacks on chemical plants or chemicals in transport as a protest against the companies themselves because they manufacture explosives used in munitions or defoliants or herbicides used in war, or because they have polluted the environment. There also could be personal motives; individuals might carry out attacks in revenge for losses suffered as a result of a previous accident. Deaths, permanent disabilities, and birth defects that have resulted from some cases of pollution could provide ample motivation for attacks on culpable corporations.

It is also conceivable that terrorists or individuals could hijack a truck loaded with some hazardous chemical and disperse it by means of fire or explosives at some target of high symbolic value—*e.g.*, the headquarters of a despised corporation, the New York Stock Exchange, a government building, or a historic monument—thereby contaminating the facility, temporarily preventing its use, and causing disruption and economic damage. The use of hazardous chemicals to get attention and deface property would be an extreme form of graffiti, but it does have a mild precedent in the pouring of blood on the steps of the Pentagon, which was done to protest the continuation of U.S. involvement in the Vietnam War. But terrorist use of hazardous chemicals lies in the realm of grim speculation and reflects no discernible trend. Political extremists, perhaps for reasons already discussed, or perhaps because the idea never came to them, have not sought to exploit this vulnerability.

Current safety codes work to preclude any accident as well as any deliberate act of sabotage from endangering the public. Hazardous chemicals in transit through population centers present the most obvious vulnerability. To prevent disasters, current regulations require that some of the more dangerous materials be routed around cities rather than passing through them. Even when accidents have occurred, the population usually has had time to evacuate the endangered area; thus these accidents have rarely produced fatalities. There does not appear to be a need for changes in the criminal code nor for new international conventions to protect the hazardous chemicals industry.

Responses

Technology to Combat Terrorism

Not all technological developments favor terrorists. Advances are continually being made in alarms and anti-intrusion devices to improve security at facilities that must be protected. Metal detector portals have made it more difficult to smuggle arms aboard aircraft or into guarded buildings. X-ray equipment has facilitated the detection of guns and bombs at air terminals and in mailrooms. Explosive detection devices that sense vapors emitted by various explosives will increase the possibility that hidden bombs will be found. Improvements have been made in lightweight body armor. Equipment has been developed that enables bomb squads to examine and dismantle or detonate bombs remotely. The use of various chemical, metal, or radioisotope taggants to detect the presence of or to identify the origin of guns, explosives, or even certain chemical substances increases the possibilities of controlling dangerous weapons and raises the possibility of a useful international convention.

Considerable research has been devoted to the design and development of instrumentation that would detect the presence of explosives through their natural properties, either by the vapors they emit or by their physical properties. Vapor-emission techniques work well only for nitroglycerin-based explosives. Neutron activation and x-ray techniques offer some promise for other categories of explosives. However, no single technology has yet been identified that will detect all explosives. This has led to the idea of inserting into explosive materials or detonators at the point of manufacture some substance that would facilitate detection and identification.[42]

Tagging for purposes of identification is somewhat easier than tagging for purposes of detection, and it involves different techniques. The objective in tagging for identification is to ascertain that an explosion was caused by explosives, to identify the explosive used and its origin, and to be able to trace the chain of distribution from point of manufacture to point of acquisition for illegal use. All this information is vitally important in criminal investigations and court proceedings.

Tagging for identification can be accomplished by including minute amounts of tiny particles in explosives at the point of manufacture. The particles—polyethylene-coated, laminated plastic particles or polyethylene-coated phosphor particles—are color coded. Combinations of color in a single particle allow for the creation of thousands of codes. Investigators retrieve the particles, which survive the explosion. Microscopic examination then allows positive identification of the type of explosive, the manufacturer, the plant where the explosive was produced, the date of production, and the package size. Careful bookkeeping by manufacturer and distributor will then allow a rapid trace to the point of acquisition for illegal use.

Tagging for detection is technically more difficult. Various kinds of taggants have been examined, including chemical compounds that emit easily identifiable vapors such as sulphur hexafluoride; other highly fluorinated compounds, and deuterated ammonium salts; heavy metals such as depleted uranium, bismuth, and thorium; radar harmonic tags that have identifiable radar signatures; and radioisotopes that emit alpha and beta particles and gamma radiation. The basic principle is simple. The taggants will give off an easily identifiable vapor, emit radiation, or have a characteristic herald that detection devices can be tuned for. When the device recognizes the odor, signal, or emission, it sets off an alarm.

Detection devices could be implanted at airports just as metal detectors and baggage x-ray machines are now used; at luggage storerooms; at post office mailrooms; at the entrances to sensitive facilities, such as government buildings; and at other potential targets. Depending on the sensitivity of such devices, those that detect minute vapor emissions could be placed at points in the ventilation systems of large buildings.

Legislation would be needed to require explosives manufacturers to use both identification and detection tags, and manufacturers and distributors to keep the careful records needed to implement a tagging program effectively. A central data bank would keep track of the codes and rapidly trace identification tags. Ideally, international agreement could be obtained to ensure that all manufacturers of explosives use identification and detection tags. International cooperation also would be needed to keep track of the identification codes. Because there are numerous manufacturers of explosives throughout the world and because the quantities produced are quite large, blasting caps, which are made by relatively few manufacturers, may offer greater opportunities for the use of detector tags.

The concept of tagging can also be applied to certain categories of weapons that might be used by terrorists. In weapons systems, it would make sense to place the tag within the component most critical to the weapon's operation and for which a substitute cannot easily be fabricated.

The obstacles to tagging are not technological ones; rather, they relate to legislation and international cooperation. A list of items or materials that are to be tagged would have to be agreed on, basic codes would have to be established, manufacturers would have to be required by law to tag their products according to the designated code, and detection devices would have to be deployed.

Legal Controls

As noted earlier, new weapons have enhanced the military power of nongovernmental political groups, and new vulnerabilities now exist that the traditional techniques of governments can no longer effectively protect against the threats posed by nongovernmental political groups. It remains to be seen whether the traditional and constitutional limits on the powers of government in the United States will block the development of adequate control techniques.[43]

Accepting the spread of technology as unavoidable—or avoidable only at a cost in the openness of U.S. society that citizens must be unwilling to pay—what is the maximum regulation of the spread of militarily useful devices that can be achieved within existing legal and political realities?

Making the possession of potential weapons or conspiracy to use them (or even perhaps conspiracy to possess them) areas for international cooperation would necessarily fix a very early moment when rule-enforcers would be conceded the authority to act against individuals or groups. But even if fixing law enforcement authority at such an early moment were desirable and feasible within every municipal criminal law system, it is not necessarily true that international cooperation in the enforcement of criminal law is desirable at such an early stage. Would it be consistent with the Constitution and traditions of the United States to make mere possession of firearms a crime under Federal law? And is international consensus possible regarding what precise implements should be banned as "weapons" or "vital parts of weapons"? Assuming that these rather technical problems can be overcome, there would remain the major policy question of whether it is really in the interest of the United States to elevate "order" to such a high priority in the scale of values of the international society that international cooperation for control of weapons be required in circumstances that until now have been regarded as involving areas of individual freedom. In other words, would it be consistent with the U.S. Constitution and traditions to make a distinction, now unclear, between free speech and "conspiracy" that would be clear enough to permit engaging international responsibility? This last policy question is reflected in the balance achieved in various municipal legal systems between the police authority and the safeguards against what the judiciary have labeled "abuses of that authority." It underlies, for example, the prohibitions against unreasonable search without a warrant embodied in the Fourth Amendment to the Constitution. The question, then, is whether the threat to the international legal order is great enough to justify a reconsideration of that balance even though the threat to the governmental orders of individual states is not sufficient to overcome their individual traditions that safeguard privacy and free expression.

It is beyond the scope of this study to resolve these serious questions. A complete analysis of U.S. constitutional and common law traditions relating to the proper extent of governmental power at the expense of relevant individual and group freedoms—including, for example, the right of the people peaceably to assemble as envisaged in the First Amendment to the Constitution[43]—would be a book in itself. Yet these questions cannot be fully answered without such an analysis. Indeed, it is possible that such an analysis would show these questions to be beyond the power of legal resolution, that any "resolution" would interfere with the political dynamics that lie at the base of the U.S. legal order. But it is possible to consider the degree to which at least some traditional U.S. legal concepts can be used to help identify the earliest possible moment at which law enforcement officials might be authorized to enter into arrangements envisaging international cooperation to suppress international terrorism.

The fact that some incidents of international terrorism might bring some actions of the executive branch of the U.S. government into the general foreign relations area does diminish traditional and constitutional restraints on executive power. Such restraints have been more or less explicitly affirmed by the U.S. Supreme Court,[44] although there was earlier inconsistent comment that seems, on cursory review, phrased far more broadly than the principles necessarily involved in the earlier cases before the Court.[45] Certainly, the Supreme Court has been particularly concerned with extradition by executive fiat, insisting that either a treaty with senatorial advice and consent or appropriate legislation exist as a basis of executive branch action when it comes to surrendering fugitives to foreign authorities.[46] Thus to the extent that international cooperation in the suppression of terrorism might take the form of easier rendition by U.S. officials to foreign officials, constitutional problems and problems of legal tradition are raised. There are also questions of reverse sensitivity concerning the procedures by which foreign states render fugitives to U.S. officials.[47] The Supreme Court has not ignored the problem, and an analysis of its effect on international cooperation to suppress international terrorism is best left to Chapter 9, which focuses on extradition.

Thus ruling out executive branch actions that do not have clear common law, treaty, or legislative foundations, and considering that treaties, acts of Congress, as well as executive branch action purportedly based on inherent power, would have to conform to the requirements of constitutional law and practice, it seems appropriate to examine the limits that the U.S. legal tradition places on the criminal consequences of behavior. The object is to discover the earliest moment consistent with the Constitution and binding tradition at which the acts of unprivileged persons can be interdicted; to limit the threat of international terrorism, in view of new weapons and vulnerabilities, to a time before the unprivileged persons have a reasonable chance of achieving their goals.

Theoretical Considerations. The powers of government in the United States, when applied to suppressing the behavior of nongovernmental groups or individuals, take the form of prescriptions that derive their force from the Constitution or the common law and take the form of legislation and executive branch action, including executive branch action to conclude international agreements either in coordination with the Senate or, in some cases, by the executive authorities alone. In either case the common law relating to *habeas corpus* proceedings ensures that the judicial branch has the opportunity to measure against fundamental rules aimed at preserving our ordered liberties the impact of such prescriptions as result in the bodily restraint of any individual. Even if judicial review were not a concern, since it is an object of governmental control in the United States to preserve the fundamental liberties of Americans, controls that disregard the constraints inherent in the U.S. constitutional and common law tradition must be rejected.

For purposes of this discussion, the phrase "international terrorism" will be used to denote the behavior of a nongovernmental political group that accepts the use of new weapons or action against new vulnerabilities. The phrase "nongovernmental political group" will be replaced by the phrase "unprivileged persons" to emphasize that, for purposes of this discussion, once a group becomes a serious pretender to governmental power, even if not recognized as such by any state, the legal restraints on constitutional government change in both municipal law and international law. It is not this chapter's function to analyze the powers of the U.S. government under martial law nor the implications in international law of the existence of an "armed conflict not of an international character." It is, of course, recognized that there may be borderline situations, as there always are when legal terms of art are used. But the starting point for present purposes is the determination that the basic constitutional and traditional limitations of the powers of government are to be observed and that the nongovernmental political groups involved are not in a position effectively to claim any "privilege" in international law to limit governmental response to their threatened depredations.

It is possible that unprivileged persons might engage in acts inconsistent with the U.S. national interest to which the United States does not attach legal consequences in its municipal criminal law (including when applicable the criminal laws of the 50 states). But as a threshold of concern for purposes of this study, U.S. criminal laws must be regarded as setting the minimum of concern. Since the defense of the U.S. constitutional order and the international legal order is presumed to be the object of the attempt to control international terrorism, and since the feasibility of international cooperation in the control of international terrorism must be examined—and that cooperation is unlikely in the case of acts not sufficiently reprehended by the United States to be punishable under criminal laws in the United States—an investigation of behavior not forbidden by U.S. criminal laws seems futile. Furthermore, as will be seen, it would be disquieting or worse for the United States to consider as the object of suppression through international cooperation acts permitted under the Constitution and other U.S. laws.

Not all acts violating the criminal laws of the United States or even disrupting the U.S. legal order threaten the stability of the constitutional order of the international legal order. Thus, ordinary crimes, such as murder, robbery, and kidnaping, as defined by the United States or any state within the United States, are not necessarily within the purview of this chapter, whether or not subject to extradition, simply because "ordinary" crimes and "ordinary" cooperation among states in the international community in suppressing crime do not raise extraordinary problems. Similarly, "political" crimes, or "ordinary" crimes with self-proclaimed political motives, normally threaten the constitutional order of only the state within whose territorial or maritime jurisdiction (including vessels and aircraft) the proscribed act occurs. There is no reason to request international cooperation in the suppression of such "political" activities, for such a request must raise questions of status under the provisions of international agreements relating to armed conflicts, *i.e.*, questions of privilege. There is no reason to expect such cooperation even if requested. A decision to aid a second state in suppressing its own political opposition—even if that political opposition is also to some degree responsible for the commission of crimes as defined in the municipal laws of all states—is a political decision with regard to which no state is likely to agree to international commitments short of a treaty of alliance or some major reordering of the international legal order, as the Holy Alliance did 160 years ago in its effort to support legitimacy in Europe.

There are "extraordinary" municipal law crimes whose suppression already involves cooperation among states in the international community, for example, aircraft hijacking, the protection of diplomats and other internationally protected persons, and other offenses of significance to international stability. The key to the distinction between "ordinary" and "extraordinary" in this sense seems to lie in the fundamental assumptions of the international legal order. Meaningful cooperation can only be expected and is desirable only in those cases where ideological considerations seem subordinated to other interests, and those cases involve only situations in which the threat posed is a threat of instability that cannot be confined to the borders of ideological antagonists. Thus while it is presumed futile to seek the cooperation of self-proclaimed socialist states in suppressing self-proclaimed revolutionaries in Western Europe, and equally futile to expect the United States to cooperate in suppressing threats perceived by several states in Eastern Europe by the continued outspoken opposition to their current governments of various exile groups in Western Europe or the United States, there are some threats to international stability where international cooperation may be feasible, such as unprivileged persons' use of new weapons and the catastrophes that might result from attacks on newly vulnerable targets.

Possible Courses of Action and Limitations Thereon

Conspiracy and Solicitation. The United States Code attaches criminal conse-quences to "conspiracy" in 22 different sections.[48] In addition, in other sections not using the word "conspiracy," the idea is expressed that a mere agreement to commit a prohibited act can be a crime in itself.[49] There are provisions of the code outside of the formal codification of the penal law in Title 18 that attach criminal consequences to "conspiracies."[50] And, of course, the United States Code as a whole does not fully express all the penal laws in the United States; each U.S. state and territory has its own penal code, and in many cases local law rather than federal law may be the essential proscription.[51]

"Solicitation" traditionally seems to have merited criminal consequences only in the most extraordinary circumstances. In Title 18 of the U.S. Code, the only provisions making mere solicitation a crime are § 1954 (influencing the operations of an employee benefit plan), §§ 663 and 917 (falsely soliciting contributions to the United States or the Red Cross), § 2192 (soliciting mutiny), and § 2198 (soliciting the seduction of a female passenger on board a U.S. flag vessel). Of these provisions, the only ones not involving patent corruption in the act of solicitation itself are the two relating to the special vulnerability of the master and passengers in a vessel. To the extent that the concept might be applied to inhibit international terrorism, legislation fixing criminal responsibility for whoever "knowingly or willfully advocates, abets, advises, or teaches the duty, necessity, desirability, or propriety of overthrowing or destroying the government of the United States . . . "[52] already seems to go as far as the Constitution permits. But advocacy cannot be the grounds for criminal consequences unless the mere advocacy creates a "clear and present danger" of bringing about the illegal object of the advocacy.[53] Indeed, even the advocacy of the use of force under that standard has been held beyond the reach of a state legislature under First Amendment standards as applied through the operation of the Fourteenth Amendment to the Constitution, unless the advocacy is directed to inciting or producing "imminent lawless action and is likely to incite or produce such action."[54] Under these interpretations, it seems difficult to advance the moment of criminality: to "advocate a conspiracy" is hardly likely to be regarded by the Supreme Court as a fit object of criminal sanction unless the advocacy amounts to a solicitation and the conspiracy itself is regarded as lawless action.

tion or confederacy between two or more persons formed for the purpose of committing, by their joint efforts, some unlawful or criminal act, or some action which is innocent in itself, but becomes unlawful when done by the concerted action of the conspirators, or for the purpose of using criminal or unlawful means to the commission of an act not in itself unlawful."[55] In some cases the mere act of conspiring has been held to warrant criminal punishment.[56] On the other hand, the general "conspiracy" provision of 18 U.S.C. provides "If two or more persons conspire either to commit any offense against the United States, or to defraud the United States . . . and one or more of such persons do any act to effect the object of the conspiracy, each shall be fined . . . or imprisoned . . . or both."[57] Obviously, an overt act is required to complete the offense. Similarly, 18 U.S.C. § 2385, which makes criminal the advocacy of overthrowing or destroying the U.S. government, also requires an overt act to complete the offense.[58] Thus in federal law, a "conspiracy" to "advocate" an illegal action would be criminal only if there were an overt act to carry out the conspiracy,[59] while advocating a conspiracy would be illegal only if there were a "clear and present danger" of imminent action. And since an overt action to effect the object of the conspiracy is necessary before the "conspiracy" can be said to have been consummated under this legislation, there is some doubt that mere advocacy of a conspiracy could be given criminal consequences under existing U.S. constitutional doctrine.

Soliciting a conspiracy might more easily be made criminal. For example, under antitrust legislation, the risk that trade be restrained as the result of agreement among ostensible competitors, or, under civil rights legislation, that civil rights be abridged by concerted threats, are precisely the risks the legislation seeks to guard against. Thus there is clear logic to giving the "conspiracy" criminal consequences at the moment the combination is formed; the formation of the combination is itself in both cases the overt act toward achieving the reprehended result. In the case of threats to overthrow the U.S. government, in the early 1950s Congress and the Supreme Court clearly evaluated the danger to the U.S. constitutional order to be both "clear" and "present." Even so, neither mere advocacy amounting to solicitation without a "clear and present danger" of action, nor a conspiracy without overt action, was regarded as enough to warrant criminal consequences in the light of the U.S. Constitution and traditions. Indeed, the wisdom of the framers of the Constitution and its amendments is even clearer in retrospect, as the restrictive interpretation of the powers of the federal and state governments under the First and Fourteenth Amendments did not in fact increase any perceptible threat to basic U.S. institutions; the dangers in retrospect appear to have been overrated.

The question then becomes whether international terrorism involves a "clear and present danger" in the sense of the Supreme Court's interpretation of the First Amendment, which is sufficient to justify attaching criminal consequences to mere advocacy or solicitation, and whether international terrorism of which concerted action is a part is inherently a threat to legally protectable values.

The answer to the first part of the question must be that in the light of the increased vulnerabilities of both national and international society to catastrophic disruption, and in the light of the ready availability of new weapons to precipitate such a catastrophic disruption, solicitation in some cases certainly creates the clear and present danger necessary to satisfy constitutional doctrine. In the light of the most recent cases and the evolution of attitudes in the United States since the excesses of the anti-Communist enthusiasms of the early 1950s—now being revealed as part of the general exposure of executive branch presumption and legislative branch dereliction building up to the Watergate scandals—it is doubtful that general condemnations of soliciting international terrorism would conform to constitutional imperatives. But solicitation coupled with the possession of the means to create a serious disruption of a vital system or for the perpetrator to escape personally from the catastrophe he might cause would seem to meet U.S. constitutional requirements.

Much detail would have to be worked out before a satisfactory statute or an international commitment could be drafted. For example, if the solicitor himself has to create the catastrophe, his soliciting the unnecessary support of a second person might decrease, rather than increase, the risk to society. The solicitation to be proscribed would have to be solicitation that increases the "clear and present danger." Furthermore, since in some situations the mere availability of a telephone or common wirecutter might be sufficient "means" to provoke a widespread communications breakdown, the prescription must be drafted to distinguish solicitation that has some rational relationship with action from solicitation that merely reflects adolescent depression. If the word "advocacy" is used instead of the narrower but constitutionally sounder word "solicitation," restrictions on the interpretation of the word "advocacy" in the context of the laws forbidding advocating the overthrow of the U.S. government would have to be sharpened and included in the new prescriptions. The catastrophe against which the prescriptions guard must be defined as clearly as possible; it would seem excessive and would raise serious constitutional problems if free speech aimed at diminishing the power of a foreign government or group of governments were made punishable by U.S. law. However deplorable a catastrophe abroad may be, unless the acts leading to it were either a crime where done and subject to an extradition arrangement or a catastrophe affecting interests in the United States that are the subject of legal protection,[60] the legality within the existing Westphalian system, and the prudence as a matter of policy, of excessive U.S. sensitivity are questionable.

In sum, new legislation or international commitments along the lines of 18 U.S.C. § 2385 (quoted above) would seem to be feasible and desirable to enable prosecution or extradition for prosecution in another state of any person who knowingly or willfully solicits the doing in any place of acts that would disrupt essential services or amenities or threaten the life or health of people in any section of the country,[61] when the effect of such solicitation is substantially to increase the likelihood that the acts will in fact be done. The job of drafting a text for presentation to the Congress or to foreign governments is extremely complex and is best undertaken only after it has been decided in principle to seek legislation or international agreement along the lines suggested.

If legislation to forbid soliciting international terrorism is passed, the general "conspiracy" provision of the United States code (18 U.S.C. § 371) will apply to it. But as noted previously, that definition of "conspiracy" relies also on the doing of an overt act to effect the object of the conspiracy. It is possible that there are some acts that would be so catastrophic, and so simple to perform if more than one person were involved, that to await the overt act is to permit the catastrophe itself. With regard to those acts, new legislation or international agreement along the lines of the antitrust and civil rights legislation might be appropriate to give criminal consequences to the mere existence of the illegal agreement, *i.e.*, to the conspiracy itself. Again, there would seem to be great complexity in drafting such new legislation or international agreement. The principal problem would appear to be to define the object of the conspiracy in such a way as to exclude from the definition the questionable agreements that the U.S. legal tradition has held insufficient in themselves to carry criminal consequences: those for which some overt act to effect the object of the conspiracy would still be appropriate. The interest to be protected by observing the traditional limits on the law relating to "conspiracy," aside from the interest in allowing a prospective criminal some *locus poenitentiae*, some chance to repent of his prospective wickedness, includes the consideration of the substantial risk that excessive enthusiasm in seeking to detect a "crime" for which no overt act is necessary would lead to action on the part of law enforcement officials that would threaten values of U.S. society other than the value of security against some disruptions.

Attempt. The concepts of advocacy, solicitation, and conspiracy all involve a second person: one with whom the solicitor or conspirator (or coconspirator) is communicating. But the legal order is sufficiently vulnerable to individual attack that it seems necessary to consider the earliest moment at which criminality can attach to an individual acting entirely alone.

The farthest movement toward suppressing political action by a single actor in the United States at this time is probably the 1968 statute making it a crime to attempt to "obstruct, impede, or interfere with any fireman or law enforcement officer lawfully engaged in the lawful performance of his official duties" in connection with "a civil disorder."[62] But the problem is not to define the ultimate crime, but to determine the earliest moment consistent with U.S. constitutional and legal traditions from which criminal consequences can flow. It is certainly possible to assert that an "attempt" to perform an illegal act can be considered to create a crime by itself. But the concept of attempt is directly linked to the definition of a crime; common law defines an attempt as not only a step toward a punishable offense, but also one that comes dangerously near to success.[63] Thus to establish an unsuccessful attempt as the threshold of criminality involves accepting the very risk sought to be avoided. It is thus necessary to look farther to find an early moment of criminality that would be relevant to the risks of catastrophe involved when focusing on international terrorism.

Preparation. The state before an "attempt" is "preparation." But under current concepts of criminal law, preparation to commit an offense is not itself an offense. It is, of course, possible to propose legislation or an international agreement that would transform mere "preparation" to commit an offense into an offense itself, by analogy to "attempts." But the very precision by which "attempt" is defined so as to exclude acts that move toward the commission of a crime but that fall short of a high likelihood of success reflects the tradition that preserves the maximum freedom for individuals to act without criminal consequences and restricts the vigilance of law enforcement officials to cases where the degree of threat posed to the good order of society is sufficient to justify the inevitable disruption of society that law enforcement action itself involves.

Another possibility is to propose legislation or international agreement attaching legal consequences to mere preparation *plus* the formed intention to commit the proscribed acts. But evidence of the additional factor of "intention" would seem to be derivable only from two sources: (1) "solicitation," which has already been recommended as an object for legislation and which can be supported without the additional factor of "preparation"; and (2) "possession" of the tools of crime. Because "solicitation" has been discussed already, there is no need to discuss it again; it involves a second person, and as an additional factor to "preparation," it seems to delay rather than advance the moment at which criminality can properly attach. Thus this approach to "preparation" seems futile.

Possession. It would seem to be consistent with U.S. legal tradition to attach criminal consequences to "possession" and if not "preparation" to achieve possession, at least "attempts" to achieve possession, of the tools of crime. Federal legislation already forbids the possession of some exotic items, for example, various categories of materials involved in nuclear weaponry[64] and various controlled substances such as heroin.[65] Enforcement authority with regard to the narcotics laws is given to the secretary of the treasury. This is evidence of a substantial constitutional problem relating to the power of the U.S. federal government to govern sedentary activity (such as mere possession) occurring entirely within the borders of a single state of the United States. Although it is possible to argue, as Representative Jonathan Bingham has done,[66] that Congress's commerce power[67] is a sufficient basis for federal legislation regarding the possession of any commodity that Congress construes to pose a threat or burden on interstate commerce, there is substantial opposition to that argument,[68] and the law cannot be said to be definitively settled. Indeed, as Representative Bingham points out in his short and clear comment on the subject, the drug laws were originally based squarely on the taxing power, and the rationale for federal action was shifted to the Commerce Clause only with the enactment of the Comprehensive Drug Abuse Prevention and Control Act of 1970.[69] Whether that rationale will suffice for all purposes has not yet been tested in the courts. The Gun Control Act of 1968,[70] which is probably the clearest precedent for any "possession" law that might be applied to the tools of international terrorism, is based on the Commerce Clause. But it is significant that this act does not purport to criminalize the mere possession of forbidden firearms or destructive devices. What is made illegal is the trade in forbidden items without a license issued by the secretary of the treasury, and the qualification that the forbidden acts bear some relationship to a movement in interstate or foreign commerce is repeated in every operative provision.

It is possible that this extremely awkward phraseology and indirection in regulating the possession of firearms and destructive devices reflect political bargaining more than constitutional inhibitions on Congress. But it is undeniable that the forum for the political compromises is constitutional language, and the apparent strength of feeling on the part of some congressmen that the legislative power of the federal government is limited in ways that mere citation to the Commerce Clause cannot overcome, despite the broad reading that might be given to some Supreme Court cases.[71] On the other hand, the most recent pronouncements of the Supreme Court in this area seem to have allowed for broad federal powers to define criminal behavior based on the congressional authority over interstate and foreign commerce, reaching even intrastate loan shark operations forbidden by the Consumer Credit Protection Act of 1968.[72]

When the actions to be prohibited can be related to "international terrorism" in some rational way, Congress's power to regulate "foreign commerce" would seem to be an adequate basis for legislation. The problem would thus seem to reduce itself to a single issue: to identify items the possession of which bears a close enough relationship to international terrorism to be considered criminal. From the special point of view of this chapter, the problem seems to disappear when phrased in this way. There does not appear to be any threat to the international legal order that would not also be a threat to interstate commerce in the United States; to the maintenance of U.S. legal rules in ships, aboard aircraft, or among overseas officials of the United States; or to the fulfillment of U.S. commitments under general international law already in force. Thus the issue appears to be less a battle between state and federal purview than of substantive restrictions on federal authority contained in the first 10 amendments to the U.S. Constitution. It is a problem for the framers of municipal law, not distinguishable from other problems of defining the municipal order; it does not seem to be a problem best analyzed by the Department of State or by the American Society of International Law.

Of course, possession of weapons or components of devices that, when used, may have an impact on the international legal order may itself be denominated the overt act necessary to complete a "conspiracy" in the restrictive sense embodied in the general "conspiracy" provision of the United States Criminal Code, although giving "possession" that legal effect might require legislation. Similarly, possessing the tools of a criminal might be evidence important to the question of whether the constitutional requirement of "clear and present danger" is met before mere advocacy or solicitation can carry criminal consequences, and a statute creating a presumption to that effect might be appropriate.

Abuse of Right. A final possibility must be considered. Do the obligations of the United States at general international law, such as the obligation not to permit U.S. territory to be used, even by private individuals, in such a way as to endanger the legally protected interests of other states,[73] include an obligation to seek out and apprehend any individual or group before it has the chance to attempt action that would injure another state? If so, then whatever action is necessary to discharge that obligation is legally required by international law, and constitutional inhibitions would be no basis for evading that obligation.[74] But whatever the constitutional responsibilities of officials of the executive branch of the federal government for representing the United States in international affairs, and indeed whatever the responsibilities of the United States under international law and the implied authority of the federal government as a whole to meet those responsibilities under the Constitution,[75] the Constitution, not international law, would be the only source of authority for U.S. officials. The supremacy of the Constitution as a matter of U.S. municipal law, and the limitation on U.S. officials that they can exercise only the powers conferred on them by municipal law in the United States, are deep traditions not to be overcome in practice whatever the apparent persuasiveness of counterarguments.[76] Therefore it would be futile here to analyze further the possible international obligations of the United States that might seem to require the governmental law-making organs or law enforcement agents to exceed their constitutional authority as limited by the first 10 amendments to the Constitution.

It would appear that U.S. obligations under international law to forbid the use of its territory as a base for unauthorized actions against foreign public authorities abroad would be substantially discharged by the vigorous enforcement of existing provisions of the U.S. Criminal Code, which already forbid (1) conspiracy to injure the property of a foreign government when an act to effect the object of the conspiracy is performed within the jurisdiction of the United States (18 U.S.C. § 956); (2) providing or preparing a means for any military enterprise against foreign territory (18 U.S.C. § 960); (3) fitting out or arming a vessel for use by any foreign people to commit hostile acts against people with whom the United States is at peace (18 U.S.C. § 962); (4) acting as an agent of a foreign government in the United States without first notifying the secretary of state (18 U.S.C. § 951); or (5) exporting arms, ammunition, or implements of war from the United States without a license (22 U.S.C. § 1934). It would seem that to the extent these and related provisions of law are enforced, U.S. practice confirms the force of the international legal obligations suggested here and indicates how they are being discharged consistently with the division of municipal law powers contained in the Constitution.

Constitutional Amendment. On the other hand, it remains conceivable that some aspects of U.S. obligations under international law are not covered by current municipal law, such as the possible duty to control terrorist acts of U.S. nationals abroad or to refuse haven to accused foreign terrorists who have not committed criminal acts within the jurisdiction of the United States and who, because of the political coloring of their acts, might be considered not subject to extradition under existing extradition treaties of the United States. It is possible, therefore, that constitutional and traditional limitations on the powers of government in the United States not only place the United States in a position in which its international obligations might be violated, but also might lead to a situation of helplessness before serious threats to the fundamental legal order of both international society and the United States itself. If it is true that those limitations now have that effect, then serious consideration must be given to the adoption of a constitutional amendment designed to endow the federal government (although not necessarily the executive branch acting alone) with the powers necessary to cope with the problem. But it would properly be for those arguing the existence of that threat to show its dimensions, the capacity of law under any formulation to deal with it, and to show that law conforming to the existing Constitution and legal tradition of the United States is incapable of dealing with it. It does not flow logically from the mere existence of new weapons and new vulnerabilities that to the extent the newly perceived threat exceeds the capacity of the U.S. legal order to deal with it, modifications of that legal order would either be capable of significantly diminishing the threat or that any degree of diminution would be worth the price in the traditional values that would have to be sacrificed on the altar of security. Indeed, a more logical, although equally unpersuasive, argument might be made that the best safeguard against international terrorism would be complete openness to all the weapons of terror so that no group could gain a rational advantage over any other group by having recourse to tactics of terror. Now if terrorism is to be impermissible as a safety valve for overheated members of society to find release (a safety valve that cannot be used without scalding innocent bystanders is surely more a weapon for instability than against it), it may be hoped that other paths for release are available. Thus it would seem that legal mechanisms to be effective against international terrorism must permit open, even influential, ways of expressing unhappiness without recourse to terrorist weapons or tactics. It is in this sense that any proposals to forbid "conspiracy" or "solicitation" must be measured, and proposals to limit possession of components of terror devices must be designed to avoid the possible confusion between devices that spread physical disruption (which must be controlled) and devices that spread mere propaganda or strengthen the credibility of obnoxious political opinion.

Conclusions

There are points of vulnerability in the complex technological infrastructure, and weapons that in the hands of a very few people can threaten to disrupt society in ways serious enough that blackmail by some fanatic groups or individuals is feasible.

Among the weapons that may afford terrorists an increasing capacity for violence and murder, explosives have been and are likely to remain for some time the most reliable and popular instrument of terrorist violence. Terrorists have used bombs to cause property damage and occasionally to cause limited casualties. With a few recent exceptions in which bombs were planted aboard aircraft, terrorists have not used conventional explosives to kill large numbers of people. Terrorists have rarely used fire as a weapon against people, although they have used incendiary devices, such as bombs, to cause property damage.

Terrorists have also used whatever portable and concealable weapons they have been able to obtain. This suggests that as some of the more advanced and exotic infantry weapons become more widely available, terrorists will acquire and use them.

Terrorists have not been associated with any plots involving the use of chemical or biological weapons with a few exceptions, for example, the stolen canisters of mustard gas and "tick letters." Political considerations or moral constraints may be operative here. Plots to poison large numbers of people are more often the product of lunatics than of political extremists.

The historical record provides no evidence that any terrorist group has ever made an attempt to acquire fissionable nuclear material or other radioactive material for use in an explosive or dispersal device. Again, apart from technical difficulties, terrorists may be guided more by political and moral constraints than is normally believed.

In terms of their ability to kill large numbers of people, terrorists have generally operated well below their technology ceiling, perhaps simply because thus far it has been unnecessary for them to escalate their violence beyond what we have seen. They are willing to kill a few to win publicity, to make a point, to create fear; they are rarely willing to kill many to accomplish the same objectives.

Terrorists have exploited the new vulnerabilities of advanced industrial societies in limited and special ways. Ironically, although they are willing to kill "handfuls" of people to gain attention and cause alarm, they apparently are unwilling to anger a large number of people by some act of sabotage that could cause widespread inconvenience. Terrorists would rather force the government to take security measures that inconvenience the public; compelling the British government to surround the Belfast shopping area with a security fence and search shoppers going in and out is an example. Terrorists have bombed transformers, but they have seldom tried to blow up power stations. They have not interfered with water supplies. They have not forced evacuations by igniting fires in chemical manufacturing plants or by blowing up tanks of hazardous chemicals, although the recent publicity given to accidental chemical spills and fires may provide some inspiration in this direction. They have not attacked liquefied natural gas facilities or tankers carrying LNG. On several recent occasions, however, political extremists have carried out acts of sabotage at nuclear facilities. The intent in these cases appears to have been publicity and disruption, not widespread casualties.

Terrorists seem careful not to kill a great many people or to make a lot of people angry at them so that the government, with public approval, would be encouraged to crack down on them. This constraint will erode in the case of terrorists operating internationally if the terrorists can reach sanctuary and if governments are prevented from responding effectively by respect for the sovereignty of other states and by political considerations. If a group does not depend on a local constituency for supply and can rely on refuge elsewhere, it may be less concerned about alienating its target population.

The vulnerability that modern terrorists have regularly exploited is civil aviation, primarily because aircraft are vulnerable and convenient containers of hostages or a guaranteed number of victims. It is impossible to protect ourselves fully within the existing framework of liberty in the United States, and the explicit restrictions on the powers of government contained in the First, Fourth, Fifth, Sixth, Ninth, Tenth, and Fourteenth Amendments to the Constitution. Nonetheless, it is possible to reduce the new risks by holding open nonviolent means to effective political action and by some marginal tightening of legal restrictions on possessing substances with particular potential for politically disruptive effects. It would also seem possible to reduce the likelihood of such blackmail in some cases by criminalizing the advocating, soliciting, advising, or teaching the doing of acts that would disrupt essential services or amenities or threaten the life or health of people in any section of the country, when the effect of that advocacy, solicitation, advice, or teaching would substantially increase the likelihood that the acts would in fact be done or when the advocacy, and so on, are coupled with the possession of the means to perform such acts and the items possessed are possessed in order to perform forbidden acts.

Because the limits on governmental action in this area are fixed by the Constitution, no action should be taken without full consultation with the officials of the executive branch of government responsible for assuring compliance with constitutional imperatives, particularly the attorney general. It must be borne in mind that the form of treaty or international agreement cannot, under current approaches taken by the Supreme Court, overcome limitations on the powers of the federal government contained in the Constitution. Even if they could, the political ramifications of attempting to evade constitutional limits on congressional powers by concluding treaty commitments that envisage changes in the criminal laws of the United States are too great to permit recourse to such approaches in this area.

Despite the faint reassurance that may be drawn from the fact that terrorists thus far have not used exotic weapons of mass destruction or conventional weapons to cause mass casualties, and that they have not, with the exception of civil aviation, struck at the technological vulnerabilities of modern society, we cannot depend on the permanence of political or moral constraints on the activities of political extremists. Therefore we ought to consider instruments and measures of control, both technological and legal instruments (domestic and international), to prevent certain kinds of threats, to establish responsibility for certain kinds of acts, and thereby possibly to deter national governments from lending their support to certain types of crimes.

Recommendations

Unilateral Action

1. Unauthorized possession of specified destructive substances for which there is no legitimate private use should be forbidden. Precedent exists for such legislation in the Atomic Energy Act of 1954, as amended. Items that could be specified might include all guided weapons systems—such as heat-seeking missiles, and components specifically manufactured for use in them—nerve gases, non-biodegradable herbicides, and biological substances potentially lethal to humans. Of course, governmental and other socially useful production or use of any of these items could be licensed.

2. Unauthorized interstate trafficking in specified substances that may have legitimate private uses but that also have significant potential uses as means for the disruption of essential services or amenities or that threaten the life or health of people in any section of the country should be forbidden. Precedent exists for such legislation in the Gun Control Act of 1968. Items that could be specified might include explosives of any sort, explosive detonators, and incendiary substances. Sales could be licensed on condition that the seller maintain reliable records of the purchaser's identity.

3. Soliciting the unauthorized use of specified substances or weapons in the possession of the solicitor or the person being solicited should be forbidden when that solicitation is likely to produce the unauthorized use of those

substances or weapons on targets of high sensitivity. The specified substances and weapons should be those forbidden to interstate traffic but possibly legally possessed. Targets of high sensitivity would include such points of vulnerability as water supply systems, transportation systems, communications systems, energy systems, chemical and biological storage locations, and storage places for radioactive materials. In the absence of an overt act to carry out a conspiracy, even this limited extension of the criminal law might raise constitutional questions. Therefore this recommendation is made as a suggestion for further study, not for immediate implementation.

International Cooperation: Bilateral, Regional, and Multilateral or Global

1. International agreements that restrict the use of specified weapons by states should be vigorously pursued and the widest possible ratification sought. It would help to diminish the likelihood that irresponsible groups might gain possession of some particularly dangerous substances if national stockpiles were reduced or eliminated. The negotiation and conclusion of other agreements such as the Convention on the Prohibition of the Development, Production and Stockpiling of Bacteriological (Biological) and Toxic Weapons and on Their Destruction (April 10, 1972) would help toward that end.

2. International agreements by which states would undertake to control the possession or use of dangerous substances or weapons by unauthorized individuals or groups within their jurisdiction should be encouraged among states whose national legislation would be made more effective by such agreements. While it is not likely that the United States could join in such international agreements without significant questions being raised about the scope of the federal government's treaty-making power, other states might find it easier to implement treaty obligations than to enact municipal legislation in this area without such international commitments.

3. Foreign states should be encouraged to enact national legislation to control the possession or use of dangerous substances or weapons by unauthorized individuals or groups within their jurisdiction. The United States could offer technical assistance to help foreign countries identify substances with potentially destructive uses and areas in their industrial infrastructure that would be less vulnerable to disruption if subject to special protection by legislation.

4. Measures to limit or control the sale abroad of weapons, destructive devices, and their components should be explored. National regulations exist in the United States and its allied members of the Coordinating Committee to control the import and export of militarily useful commodities and technical data. It might be possible to gain wider international agreement under which states would find it easier to coordinate measures to limit private exports and imports of interest to terrorists.

5. Measures to identify certain substances or allow identification of their origin should be explored with other nations. Even in the absence of agreement on export and import controls, some limit on the dissemination of particularly dangerous or sensitive devices or components might be achieved by tagging them with radioactive nucleides or other substances.

6. Special classes of weapons, destructive devices, and components should be identified, perhaps by an international body, so that they could be subjected to special security standards and controls to which all nations would be encouraged to subscribe. Such weapons might include man-portable, conceal-able, easy-to-operate, mass-produced, highly destructive precision weapons, and substances that are likely to do great harm off the battlefield against civilian targets. Even in the absence of agreement on export and import controls, some limit on the dissemination of particularly dangerous or sensitive devices or components might be achieved by tagging them with radioactive nucleides or other substances. (The concern is not simply terrorist groups but political extremists, lunatics, and criminal entities, national or international).

7. Nations that fail to meet international standards of security for aliens in their territory, or fail to meet their obligations under general international law to prevent their territory from being used as a base for armed bands attacking the territory of other states, bear international responsibility for their defaults to the extent that those defaults contribute to injury done to other states. The United States should state a position at every appropriate opportunity, asserting such responsibility against haven states. The general international law in this area is evidenced by consistent state practice, including the assertions of the Ugandan representative in the U.N. Security Council immediately after the Entebbe incident, and is partially codified in UNGA Res. 2625 (xxv), adopted by consensus October 24, 1970, and UNGA Res. 3314 (xxlx), adopted by consensus December 14, 1974.

Notes

1. *See* N.Y. Times, Aug. 8, 1976, at 33, col. 1; Aug. 31, 1976, at 11, col. 1.

2. *See* S.M. HERSH, CHEMICAL AND BIOLOGICAL WARFARE (1968); R. CLARKE, THE SILENT WEAPONS (1968).

3. Protocol for the Prohibition of the Use in War of Asphyxiating, Poisonous or Other Gases, and Bacteriological Methods of Warfare, June 17, 1925, T.I.A.S. No. 8061, 94 L.N.T.S. 65.

4. N.Y. Times, Dec. 23, 1976, at 12, col. 1.

5. *See* Convention on the Prohibition of the Development, Production and Stockpiling of Bacteriological (Biological) and Toxin Weapons and on their Destruction, Apr. 10, 1972, 26 U.S.T. 583, T.I.A.S. No. 8062.

6. ADVANCED CONCEPT RESEARCH (ADCON CORPORATION),

SUPERVIOLENCE: THE CIVIL THREAT OF MASS DESTRUCTION WEAPONS, 858-59 (Sept. 1972). This is the most comprehensive unclassified discussion of the possible use by terrorists of weapons of mass destruction and includes chapters on chemical, biological, and nuclear weapons.

7. Griffith, *Biological Warfare and the Urban Battleground*, ENFORCEMENT J. 14 (1975), citing a Jack Anderson column of Nov. 20, 1970.

8. N.Y. Times, Jan. 19, 1972, at 18, col. 1. The two accused fled the country and subsequently hijacked an aircraft from Jamaica to Cuba. Chicago Today, July 6, 1972, at 12, col. 1.

9. N.Y. Times, Nov. 24, 1973, at 24, col. 4.

10. Lowell Ponte, KABC radio broadcast, Los Angeles, Oct. 23, 1975.

11. *Terrorist Use of Gas Feared*, Washington Post, May 13, 1975, at A17, col. 1.

12. N.Y. Times, June 17, 1976, at 24, col. 3.

13. *Terrorist Gangs Reaching for Nerve Gas, Gruesome New Weapons*, Boston Globe, Nov. 7, 1976, at 1, col. 1.

14. *Id.*

15. According to calculations of Dr. Kenneth Solomon, Rand nuclear engineer.

16. U.S. General Accounting Office, Summary of GAO Report Evaluating ERDA's Safeguards Systems, 122 CONG. REC. H7,838 (daily ed. July 27, 1976) (Staff Summary of GAO Report entitled Shortcomings in the Systems Used to Control and Protect Highly Dangerous Nuclear Materials—Energy Research and Development Admin.).

17. M. WILLRICH & U. TAYLOR, NUCLEAR THEFT: RISKS AND SAFEGUARDS (1974).

18. Letter from J. Carson Mark, quoted in SCHMIDT & BODANSKY, THE FIGHT OVER NUCLEAR POWER 104 (1976).

19. R.K. MULLEN, THE INTERNATIONAL CLANDESTINE NUCLEAR THREAT 18 (1975) (Technical Research Unit, Research Division, International Association of Chiefs of Police, Gaithersburg, Md.

20. B.L. COHEN, THE HAZARDS IN PLUTONIUM DISPERSAL (1975).

21. Freedom of Information Act of 1974, Pub. L. No. 93-502, 88 Stat. 1561 [codified at 5 U.S.C. § 552 (1974)].

22. For a description and discussion of new man-portable PGMs, *see* J. DIGBY, PRECISION-GUIDED WEAPONS, Adelphi Paper No. 118 (1975).

23. This estimate is based on the author's calculation that the nations that possessed advanced precision munitions, although not necessarily man-portable weapons, in 1974 would have man-portable precision-guided munitions by 1980.

24. *See* Summary of Responses to Department of State Circular Airgram Regarding Law and Practice on Terrorism, Italy, 3 (May 1976) [hereinafter cited as Circular, name of country, page, and date of summary].

25. Washington Post, Feb. 22, 1976, at A2, col. 1.

26. N.Y. Times, Jan. 24, 1975, at 2, col. 8.

27. *See* Evans, *Aircraft and Aviation Facilities*, ch. 1, of this report.

28. *See* N.Y. Times, June 28, 1976, at 1, col. 2; Sept. 22, 1976, at 22, col. 2.

29. *See* FEDERAL AVIATION ADMINISTRATION, CIVIL AVIATION SECURITY SERVICE, EXPLOSIONS ABOARD AIRCRAFT 10 (Jan. 1, 1977).

30. *See* N.Y. Times, Oct. 7, 1976, at 1, col. 5; Oct. 24, 1976, § 4, at 3, col. 1.

31. *See* Convention on Offenses and Certain Other Acts Committed on Board Aircraft, Sept. 14, 1963, 20 U.S.T. 2941, T.I.A.S. No. 6768, 704 U.N.T.S. 219; Convention for the Suppression of Unlawful Seizure of Aircraft, Dec. 16, 1970, 22 U.S.T. 1641, T.I.A.S. No. 7192; Convention for the Suppression of Unlawful Acts Against the Safety of Civil Aviation, Sept. 23, 1971, 24 U.S.T. 564, T.I.A.S. No. 7570.

32. For a discussion of the prospects of nuclear terrorism, *see* B. JENKINS, WILL TERRORISTS GO NUCLEAR? (1975) (California Seminar on Arms Control and Foreign Policy, Santa Monica, Calif.).

33. N.Y. Times, Mar. 9, 1973, at 12, col. 3.

34. N.Y. Times, May 4, 1975, at 7, col. 1.

35. N.Y. Times, Apr. 17, 1976, at 5, col. 8; Apr. 19, 1976, at 8, col. 5.

36. DRAFT ENVIRONMENTAL IMPACT REPORT FOR THE PROPOSED OXNARD LNG FACILITIES, app. B (1976) (Socio-Economic Systems, Inc., Los Angeles).

37. Williams, *Details on the Hazards of Liquified Natural Gas in Marine Transportation*, 29 PROCEEDINGS OF THE MARINE SAFETY COUNCIL (U.S. Coast Guard) (1972). *See also* J. MURRAY, D. JAQUETTE, & W. KING, HAZARDS ASSOCIATED WITH THE IMPORTATION OF LIQUEFIED NATURAL GAS, The Rand Corporation, (1976); A. VAN HORN & R. WILSON, LIQUEFIED NATURAL GAS: SAFETY ISSUES, PUBLIC CONCERNS, AND DECISION MAKING (1976).

38. *See* Nyhart & Kessler, *Ocean Vessels and Offshore Structures*, ch. 3 of this report.

39. The description of hazardous chemicals is based on a table found in A CONDENSED LABORATORY HANDBOOK 20-27 (1971) (E.I. du Pont de Nemours and Company) and FIRE PREVENTION CODE 192-202 (1976) (American Insurance Association, Engineering and Safety Service). The code that is recommended by the American Insurance Association has been adopted by 4000 U.S. cities.

40. Solomon, *Meteorological Aspects of Chemical Spill Study*, HAZARD PREVENTION 6-11 (May-June 1975). *See also* K. SOLOMON, M. RUBIN, & D. OKRENT, ON RISKS FROM THE STORAGE OF HAZARDOUS CHEMICALS (1976).

41. FIRE PREVENTION CODE 1976, *supra* note 39.

42. For a discussion of measures to defeat terrorist bombers, *see* Styles, *Defeating the Terrorist Bomber*, INT'L DEFENSE REV. 121 (Jan. 1977).

43. U.S. CONST. S. Doc. No. 92-82, 92d Cong., 2d Sess. 1030-34 (1973).

44. Reid v. Covert, 354 U.S. 1 (1957).

45. *See* analysis in U.S. CONST., *supra* note 43.

46. Valentine v. United States *ex rel.* Neidecker 299 U.S. 5, 8 (1936). For the historical basis for the U.S. commitment to extradition by treaty or statute, bearing in mind U.S. CONST. art. VI, para. 2, *see inter alia* 1 MOORE, A TREATISE ON EXTRADITION AND INTERSTATE RENDITION 21, 23 (1891); 1 Op. Att'y Gen. 506 (1821); United States v. Robins, 27 F. Cas. 825 (No. 16,175) (D.S.C. 1799); *In re* Metzger, 17 F. Cas. 232 (No. 9511) (S.D.N.Y. 1847).

47. *See* separate concurring opinion by Judge Oakes in U.S. v. Lira, 515 F.2d 68, 72-73 (2d Cir. 1975), *cert. denied* 423 U.S. 847 (1975). For the extensive use of exclusion and expulsion as measures of international rendition of fugitive offenders, *see* Evans, *Apprehension and Prosecution of Offenders: Some Current Problems*, ch. 9 of this report.

48. 18 U.S.C. §§ 241, 286, 371, 372, 757, 793, 794, 956, 1201, 1403, 1751, 1792, 1951, 2192, 2271, 2274, 2384, 2385, 2516, 3286, 3287, and 3291.

49. *E.g.*, 18 U.S.C. § 1954: "Whoever [within a defined class] . . . agrees to receive or solicit any fee . . . shall be fined . . . or imprisoned. . . ." It is not possible without inordinate effort to find all the provisions of the code attaching criminal consequences to mere agreement or solicitation of agreement.

50. *E.g.*, 15 U.S.C. § 1: "Every . . . conspiracy, in restraint of trade or commerce . . . with foreign nations, is declared to be illegal: . . . punished by fine . . . or by imprisonment . . . or by both. . . ."

51. *E.g.*, Wildenhus' Case, 120 U.S. 1 (1887) (denying a Belgian application to release three accused men from the custody of the keeper of the common jail of Hudson County, New Jersey, where they were held for violation of New Jersey law).

52. 18 U.S.C. § 2385.

53. Dennis v. United States, 341 U.S. 494 (1951); Scales v. United States, 367 U.S. 203 (1958). The "clear and present danger" exception to the First Amendment, which limits Congress's power to limit free speech, was first stated by Justice Holmes in Schenck v. United States, 249 U.S. 47, 52 (1919).

54. Brandenburg v. Ohio, 395 U.S. 444, 447 (1969).

55. BLACK'S LAW DICTIONARY 382 (4th ed. 1951).

56. *E.g.*, the antitrust laws of the United States. *See* 15 U.S.C.A. § 1, annotation 437, citing Nash v. United States, 229 U.S. 373 (1913); United States v. Trenton Potteries Co., 273 U.S. 392 (1926); United States v. Socony-Vacuum Oil Co., 310 U.S. 150 (1940); and many others. *See also* 18 U.S.C. § 241, Williams v. United States, 179 F.2d 644 (5th Cir. 1950), *aff'd* 341 U.S. 70 (1951); United States v. Morado 454 F.2d 167 (5th Cir. 1972), *cert. denied*, 406 U.S. 917 (1972).

57. 18 U.S.C. § 371.

58. *See* Yates v. United States, 354 U.S. 298 (1957); United States v. Silverman, 132 F. Supp. 820 (D. Conn. 1955).

59. Dennis v. United States, 341 U.S. 494 (1951).

60. This can create serious problems. There is not universal approval in the international community of the extraterritorial reach of such protective legislation as the U.S. antitrust laws. *See* R.Y. Jennings, *Extra-territorial Jurisdiction and the United States Antitrust Laws*, 33 BRIT. Y.B. INT'L L. 146 (1957).

61. This last phrase, taken from § 7 of the Clayton Act, 15 U.S.C. § 18, has been upheld as meaningful in the context of U.S. antitrust law. *Cf.* United States v. Von's Grocery, Inc., 384 U.S. 270 (1966). It is not suggested as the best for legislation in the area of international terrorism.

62. 18 U.S.C. § 231(a)(3). The wording of this provision of the Omnibus Crime Act of 1968 (Pub. L. No. 90-284, 90th Cong., 2d Sess.), and indeed many other provisions of the act relating to civil disorders, renders its actual meaning almost undecipherable.

63. BLACK'S LAW DICTIONARY 162 *supra* note 60, citing State v. Ainsworth, 146 Kan. 665, 72 P.2d 962.

64. "Special nuclear material," 42 U.S.C. § 2073; "source material," 42 U.S.C. § 2092; and "byproduct material," 42 U.S.C. § 2111.

65. *See* 21 U.S.C. § § 812, Schedule I(b)(10), 844, 846.

66. *Firearms Legislation: Hearings on H.R. 11193 Before the Subcommittee on Crime of the House Committee on the Judiciary*, 94th Cong., 1st Sess. 443-44 (1975) [hereinafter cited as Firearms Legislation Hearings].

67. U.S. CONST. art. I, § 8, cl.3.

68. *E.g., Firearms Legislation Hearings, supra* note 66, at 120-23 (statement of Senator James A. McClure, citing arguments raised by representatives of the National Rifle Association in opposition to proposed federal gun control legislation).

69. 21 U.S.C. § 801 ff.

70. 18 U.S.C. § 921 ff.

71. *See* Wickard v. Filburn, 317 U.S. 111 (1942).

72. Perez v. United States, 402 U.S. 146 (1971). *See* the dissent by Justice Stewart at 157. *See also* 18 U.S.C. § 960.

73. This is the rule of international law usually referred to in its Latin version, *sic utere tuo ut alienum non laedas.* The leading cases include The Corfu Channel Case (1949), I.C.J. Rep. 4; Trail Smelter Case (United States v. Canada) (1938, 1941), 3 R. Int'l Arb. Awards 1905, 1911 (U.N. 1949).

74. *See* M. WHITEMAN, DIGEST OF INTERNATIONAL LAW 1 103-16 (1963).

75. The extent of all those responsibilities and the implied authority to meet them under the Constitution is the subject of considerable debate. *See* L. HENKIN, FOREIGN AFFAIRS AND THE CONSTITUTION (1972) *passim.*

76. The counterarguments are not very persuasive anyhow in the light of

the clear subordination of executive authority to the Constitution most dramatically affirmed in United States v. Nixon, 418 U.S. 683 (1974), and the long-standing interpretation of the U.S. Constitution placing treaty obligations of the United States on the same level as statute law, not as law superior to inconsistent statute. *Cf.* Reid v. Covert, 354 U.S. 1 (1957); Head Money Cases, 112 U.S. 580 (1884).

5

Protected Persons and Diplomatic Facilities

John F. Murphy

Introduction

Diplomatic privileges and immunities are a subject of vast dimensions about which a number of lengthy and learned treatises have been written.[1] No attempt will be made here to duplicate or even approximate these efforts. Rather, the focus will be on a particular facet of a diplomat's privileges and immunities, namely, the inviolability of his person and of his residence and property against "serious" attacks involving the threat or use of force. Accordingly, there will be no discussion of such subjects as the immunity of a diplomat from judicial process in or taxation by the receiving country.

This chapter will first set forth a brief background to and an overview of threats and the use of force against diplomats. The background material will include a discussion of the primary theoretical bases of inviolability as found in such instruments as the Vienna Convention on Diplomatic Relations.

An analysis of national law and practice regarding the protection of diplomats will follow. Selected examples of foreign legislation and security measures will be examined, insofar as data collected to date permit. This first section will also examine some case histories of attacks on diplomats and governmental responses thereto, drawing on data provided by several recent studies. A discussion of U.S. law and practice will focus solely on U.S. legislation as it existed prior to 1976. An examination of the 1976 amendments to U.S. legislation on the protection of diplomats will be deferred until the section of the chapter dealing with the OAS Convention to Prevent and Punish the Acts of Terrorism Taking the Forms of Crimes Against Persons and Related Extortion That Are of International Significance, and the U.N. Convention on the Prevention and Punishment of Crimes Against Internationally Protected Persons, Including Diplomatic Agents.

Next, the chapter will attempt to describe and assess existing international legal measures, *i.e.*, measures other than the OAS and U.N. conventions will be assessed critically with a view to ascertaining the extent to which these conventions remedy deficiencies in traditional law and practice and highlighting additional problems not adequately dealt with by the conventions.

Then the current milieu in which efforts toward the protection of diplomats are being undertaken will be analyzed. This section will include an exploration of the utility of the use of force against diplomats as a revolutionary tactic; the political, economic, and social barriers to ratification of the OAS and U.N.

conventions or the adoption of other measures toward the prevention and punishment of the use of force against diplomats; and countervailing considerations favoring ratification of the conventions and the adoption of other measures.

Finally, the conclusions and recommendations of the chapter will focus on three broad categories of actions the Department of State might take or support toward the prevention and suppression of attacks on diplomats: unilateral, bilateral and regional; and multilateral or global. These conclusions and recommendations will relate to possible changes in both the texts of written law and governmental practice and policy. In the event of a recommendation relating to action other than unilateral, the chapter will identify the countries with which the United States might wish to act in concert.

The Threat and Use of Force against Diplomats: Background and Overview

The inviolability of a diplomat's person, his property, and diplomatic facilities is one of the most ancient and widely accepted principles of international law.[2] There has been less agreement on the theoretical basis of the inviolability principle, and at least a dozen theories have been advanced to justify the extension of special protection of diplomats.[3] Most jurists, however, have focused their attention on three traditional theories: the theory of personal representation, the theory of extraterritoriality, and the theory of functional necessity.

According to the theory of personal representation, the diplomat is the personification of his ruler or of a sovereign state, and an attack on a diplomat is tantamount to an attack on his ruler or the sovereignty of his state.[4] With the decline of the monarchy and the rise of the modern nation-state system with its concomitant concept that ultimate sovereignty resides in the people, this theory has lost support among jurists. However, the International Law Commission (ILC) has recognized that the theory still enjoys a measure of acceptance, at least when coupled with the theory of functional necessity.[5]

The theory of extraterritoriality emerged with the rise of the nation-state system and the practice of countries maintaining permanent missions in foreign states.[6] It was based on two separate but closely related legal fictions: the concept of residence and the concept of territory. Under the concept of residence, the diplomat is not subject to local law because he does not reside in the host country; according to the concept of territory, diplomatic premises are considered to be the same as foreign territory. Although the theory of extraterritoriality traditionally had considerable support, modern jurists have largely abandoned it.[7]

The most widely accepted theory today is the theory of functional necessity.[8] Based on the premise that the interdependence of states requires freedom of movement and freedom of communication for the diplomat in order that states may carry on international intercourse, the theory of functional necessity is especially useful to explain the extension of privileges and immunities to international organizations and their personnel, since such organizations are without territory or representational status.

Whatever its theoretical basis, the principle of diplomatic inviolability has now been codified in a number of international conventions. Excluding for present purposes the OAS and U.N. conventions on the protection of diplomats, these include the Vienna Convention on Diplomatic Relations;[9] the Vienna Convention on Consular Relations;[10] the Convention on the Privileges and Immunities of the United Nations;[11] the Convention on Special Missions;[12] and the Vienna Convention on the Representation of States in Their Relations with International Organizations of a Universal Character.[13] The prototype provisions on diplomatic inviolability are articles 22 and 29 of the Vienna Convention on Diplomatic Relations. With respect to diplomatic premises, article 22 provides in pertinent part:

(1) The premises of the mission shall be inviolable. The agents of the receiving state may not enter them, except with the consent of the head of the mission.
(2) The receiving state is under a special duty to take all appropriate steps to protect the premises of the mission against any intrusion or damage and to prevent any disturbance of the peace of the mission or impairment of its dignity.

Similarly, as to a diplomat's person, article 29 provides that "[t]he person of a diplomatic agent shall be inviolable. He shall not be liable to any form of arrest or detention. The receiving state shall treat him with due respect and shall take all appropriate steps to prevent any attack on his person, freedom or dignity."

The scope of the receiving state's obligation to protect the person of a diplomatic agent is further indicated by the commentary on article 27 of the International Law Commission's final draft on diplomatic intercourse and immunities, which formed the basis for article 29 of the Vienna Convention:

This article confirms the principle of the personal inviolability of the diplomatic agent. From the receiving State's point of view, this inviolability implies, as in the case of the mission's premises, the obligation to respect, and to ensure respect for, the person of the diplomatic agent. The receiving state must take all reasonable steps to that end, possibly including the provision of a special guard where circumstances so required. Being inviolable, the diplomatic agent is exempt from measures that would amount to direct coercion. This principle does not exclude in respect of the diplomatic agent either measures of self-defence or, in exceptional circumstances, measures to prevent him from committing crimes or offenses.[14]

As to the obligation of the receiving state to protect diplomatic premises, the commentary on article 20 of the ILC's draft, which became article 22 of the Vienna Convention, specifies that the receiving state "is under a special duty to take all appropriate steps to protect the premises from any invasion or damage, and to prevent any disturbance of the peace of the mission or impairment of its dignity.... The receiving state must, in order to fulfill this obligation, take special measures—over and above those it takes to discharge its general duty of ensuring order."[15]

The principle of diplomatic inviolability has recently been sorely tested. Even the most casual observer of the world scene is aware that attacks on diplomats and diplomatic premises have greatly increased in number and in the level of violence employed. The *Revue Général de Droit International Public* publishes in each of its four yearly issues a "Chronique des Faits Internationaux." This chronicle of diplomatic happenings has of late become a catalogue of violence against diplomatic representation. For example, a quick survey of incidents reported in the "Chronicle" for the years 1973 to 1974 reveals at least 34 incidents of violent attacks on diplomats or diplomatic personnel. This trend continued into 1975, with 8 such incidents reported as of August 4, 1975. Moreover, as will be seen later in this chapter, the last months of 1975 in particular saw some especially spectacular attacks against diplomatic personnel and diplomatic premises.

United States diplomats have not been immune from such attacks. To give just some recent examples, in April 1974, USIA officer Alfred Laun was wounded while being kidnaped in Cordoba, Argentina. He was released the same day, apparently because of the seriousness of his wounds. In August 1974, U.S. Ambassador Roger Davies was assassinated in Nicosia, Cyprus. In February 1975, U.S. Consular Agent John Egan was kidnaped and later found murdered after the demands of his kidnapers were not met. In August 1975, in Malaysia, a group of five gunmen of the Japanese Red Army Organization occupied the American Consulate and the neighboring Swedish Embassy in Kuala Lumpur, taking 52 persons hostage, including the U.S. consul and the Swedish chargé d'affaires. The terrorists demanded the release of seven Red Army members held in Japanese prisons. The Japanese government acceded to these demands, and the hostages were released as the five gunmen, the released prisoners, and four new hostages (including two Japanese officials) were flown to Tripoli, Libya, where the terrorists were granted sanctuary in exchange for the safety of their hostages. Finally, in December 1975, CIA agent Richard Welch was shot and killed outside his home in Athens, Greece.

A primary, but by no means the sole, reason for the large number of violent attacks against diplomats is that the threat and use of force against diplomats has become an integral part of the revolutionary strategy of the urban terrorist.[16] According to this strategy, the diplomat may be either a primary or an instrumental target, *i.e.*, he may be attacked for "crimes" he allegedly committed personally, or he may be viewed merely as the instrument his attackers use to induce certain behavior, especially concessions, from target governments. An example of the diplomat as primary target might be Welch's murder in Athens, which, although the motives of the killers have not been definitely ascertained, has the hallmarks of an execution for "crimes" committed by Welch as an agent of the CIA, the agency most associated with U.S. "imperialism."[17]

The majority of attacks on diplomats involve situations where the diplomat is the instrumental target. That is, the terrorists may have nothing personal against the diplomat they attack but have as their primary target the government of the receiving state, the government of the country the diplomat represents, or the government of some third party state. According to newspaper reports, the killings in October 1975, within two days of each other, of the Turkish ambassadors to Austria and France by "The Secret Armenian Army for the Liberation of Armenia" were committed to publicize Turkey's World War I killing of hundreds of thousands of Armenians, and to gain support for the cause to "liberate" Armenians from Turkish rule.[18]

Most attacks on diplomats as instrumental targets have involved kidnapings. A recent study by the Rand Corporation indicates that of 77 international hostage incidents that took place between August 1968 and June 1975, 52 involved diplomats, honorary consuls, or other government representatives serving abroad.[19] Again, U.S. officials and citizens have been popular targets. According to the Rand Corporation, they were the hostages or the targets of kidnaping attempts in 38 percent of the episodes during the period under study.[20] Interestingly, the Rand Corporation reports that in only three cases was the United States explicitly the target of the kidnapers' demands, and suggests that "kidnappers often chose their hostages for the value they possessed as representatives of governments which were considered important or believed to be influential, and not because their government was necessarily the enemy or the principal target of the kidnappers."[21] In any event, these kidnapings have been undertaken for purposes of inducing payment of ransom or release of political prisoners and gaining publicity for the terrorists' cause, or in an effort to discredit the receiving government in the eyes of the local population and to weaken its communications with the world community.

The Rand Corporation has categorized these kidnapings as two basic types: the traditional situation and the barricade-and-hostage situation.[22] The traditional kidnaping involves seizing the victim and transporting him to an underground hideout. The whereabouts of the victim is known only to the kidnapers, and they also control communications with the family, corporation, or government upon whom demands are being made. In the barricade-and-hostage situation, kidnapers seize one or more hostages but either make no attempt to reach a hideout or are prevented from doing so. Barricaded in a public place—often in an embassy—the kidnapers are in effect hostages themselves. In the ensuing negotiations, the kidnapers include their own release as part of the bargain.

As will be shown in later sections of this chapter, these attacks on and kidnapings of diplomats have precipitated a variety of governmental responses at both the national and international levels. These responses indicate that the overwhelming majority of countries—regardless of ideology—have concluded that the protection of diplomats and diplomatic premises is in their vital interest. However, disagreement remains as to what measures are required and what policies will best serve to protect this interest.

Existing National Measures: Description and Assessment

National Legislation on the Protection of Diplomats

Foreign Legislation on the Protection of Diplomats. Data compiled up to the time of this writing indicate that many, perhaps most, countries provide expressly in their penal codes that attacks or attempted attacks against diplomats will be subject to severe criminal penalties.[23] The data also indicate that countries whose penal codes do not expressly criminalize attacks on diplomats or diplomatic premises nonetheless have jurisdiction under general provisions of their penal codes relating to such crimes as homicide, assault, kidnaping, and breaking and entering to prosecute offenders for serious violations of diplomatic inviolability.[24]

The Penal Code of the Republic of Uruguay, authorized December 4, 1933 (Law No. 155) and entered into force August 1, 1934 (Law 9.414 of June 29, 1934), in book II, title I, chapter II, § 138 provides:

Whoever on the territory of the State, by direct acts, attempts against the life, physical integrity, liberty or honor of the Chief of a foreign state, or of its diplomatic representatives, shall be punished, in case of an attempt on the life with four to ten years in a penitentiary, and in the other cases with two to six years.

If the acts result in death, the penalty shall be fifteen to thirty years in a penitentiary.[25]

A more recent example of penal provisions specifically referring to crimes against diplomats is the Penal Code of the People's Republic of Poland, which entered into force January 1, 1970. In the Special Part, chapter 36, § 283, it provides:

§ 1. Whoever on the territory of the Polish People's Republic, commits an active assault upon a person holding a leading position of a foreign state, upon the head of the diplomatic representation of a foreign state, who is accredited to the Polish People's Republic, or upon a person enjoying similar protection by virtue of law, treaty or generally accepted international custom, shall be subject to the penalty of deprivation of liberty for from one to 10 years.

§ 2. Whoever on the territory of the Polish People's Republic, commits an active assault upon a person belonging to the diplomatic personnel of a representation of a foreign state or upon a consul of a foreign state in connection with the exercise by him of official functions, shall be subject to the penalty of deprivation of liberty for from 6 months to 5 years.

§ 3. Whoever on the territory of the Polish People's Republic, insults a person mentioned in § 1 or 2, shall be subject to the penalty of deprivation of liberty for up to 3 years.[26]

By their terms, these provisions are limited in application to attacks on diplomats that occur within the territory of the receiving country. This appears, moreover, to be the general pattern, although jurisdictional scope may be extended in some cases to include attacks that take place on a plane or ship of the receiving country.[27]

There are exceptions, of course. Some countries may exercise criminal jurisdiction over attacks against diplomats occurring outside territorial limits on the basis of the nationality principle of international criminal jurisdiction. That is, a state may exercise jurisdiction over an attack on a diplomat abroad if the attack is committed by one of its nationals or, in some cases, by an alien domiciled in the state and if other requisites to jurisdiction are present. An example is article 7 of the Danish Penal Code of 24 June 1939, which provides:

Danish criminal jurisdiction shall henceforward extend to the following offenses committed outside the territory of the Danish State by a person having Danish nationality or domiciled within that territory:

(1) An offense committed outside the internationally recognized territory of a state and of a kind punishable by a severer penalty than detention;
(2) An offense committed within such territory and punishable also under the law which is in force there.[28]

The legislation of some countries may go beyond the nationality principle and authorize the exercise of criminal jurisdiction on the basis of the passive personality principle. Under the passive personality principle, which is not generally recognized and which is arguably inconsistent with international law,[29] criminal jurisdiction may be based on the nationality or national character of the person injured by the offense. The Penal Code of Mexico, adopted January 2, 1931, in title II, chapter II, § 148, provides:

Imprisonment of three days to two years and a fine of one hundred to two thousand pesos shall be imposed for:

(1) The violation of any diplomatic immunity, real or personal, of a foreign sovereign, or of a representative of another nation, whether residing in the Republic or passing through it.[30]

While section 148 appears to apply only to attacks on foreign diplomats that occur in Mexico, the general scope of Mexican criminal jurisdiction is wide. The articles of the penal code apply to Mexican embassies and consulates abroad and to foreign embassies and consulates located in Mexico. Moreover, crimes committed in foreign territory by a Mexican against a Mexican or against foreigners, or by a foreigner against a Mexican, are punished in the republic in accordance with federal laws, if the following requisites concur:

1. the accused is found in the republic
2. the accused has not been definitely judged in the country where he allegedly committed the crime
3. the act committed is a crime under both the law of the place where committed and the law of Mexico[31]

Although there seems to be no apposite case, the law and practice of some countries might be interpreted so as to authorize the exercise of criminal jurisdiction over an attack on a diplomat abroad on the basis of the protective or universality principles of international criminal jurisdiction. For example, article 8 of the Danish Penal Code of 24 June 1939 provides in pertinent part:

(1) Danish criminal jurisdiction shall also comprehend an offense committed outside the Danish State irrespective of the domicile of the offender:
  (i) If the offense is prejudicial to the independence, security, constitution or public authorities of the Danish State, or constitutes a breach of official duties or interests protected by law in the Danish State by reason of their special relationship thereto.[32]

Arguably, an attack on a Danish diplomat abroad, or perhaps even on a foreign diplomat accredited to Denmark, could be regarded as "prejudicial to the independence, security, constitution or public authorities of the Danish State" in that it would interfere with the important Danish interest in diplomatic intercourse with the rest of the world. On the other hand, it must be noted that the protective principle of international criminal jurisdiction has generally been narrowly interpreted so as to apply only to a few offenses in time of war directly affecting state security[33] or to offenses involving government administrative functions such as the counterfeiting of currency and false statements made to diplomatic officials at their foreign posts.[34]

One of the most expansive—perhaps the most expansive—exercises of extraterritorial criminal jurisdiction is to be found in the terms and recent application of a 1972 amendment to the Israeli Penal Law (Offenses Committed Abroad). The amendment provides in pertinent part:

The courts in Israel are competent to try under Israeli law a person who has committed abroad an act which would be an offense if it had been committed in Israel and which harmed or was intended to harm the State of Israel, its security, property or economy or its transport or communications link with other countries.[35]

Under this legislation, an Israeli military court in 1973 convicted Faik Bulut, a 23-year-old Turkish citizen, of the offense of belonging to Al-Fatah in Lebanon and Syria, and sentenced him to seven years in prison.[36] Bulut had been captured in February 1972 during an Israeli raid 100 miles into Lebanon. In response to contentions by defense counsel that the statute and its application violated international law, the court cited the protective principle in upholding the validity of the statute and ruled that Bulut's involuntary abduction from Lebanon without extradition did not preclude jurisdiction.[37] Although the court expressly avoided relying on the universality principle, the prosecution and defense counsel argued as if it were a primary basis of jurisdiction.[38]

The principle of universality—the right to assume jurisdiction, despite nationality or place of crime, merely on the basis of custody—is recognized as applying only to crimes that affect the international community and are against international law. Although universal jurisdiction has generally been recognized as applicable to various international crimes in addition to piracy,[39] these do not include membership in a terrorist organization, or even most terrorist acts themselves.[40] Arguably, however, it would be permissible under international law for a state to assume jurisdiction over attacks on diplomats on the basis of the universality principle in light of the principle of diplomatic inviolability established by the Vienna Convention on Diplomatic Relations and other international conventions.

Be that as it may, it is beyond the scope of this chapter to discuss the validity of the Israeli statute under international law. It suffices for present purposes to note that the statute's scope appears sufficiently expansive to cover an attack abroad on an Israeli diplomat or a diplomat accredited to Israel. If this interpretation is correct, the Israeli statute represents a deviation from the general pattern of national legislation whereby states exercise jurisdiction over attacks on diplomats only when they take place within their territory.

U.S. Legislation on the Protection of Diplomats. In 1972, the United States substantially expanded the scope of its federal legislation on the protection of diplomats and diplomatic premises.[41] The primary purpose of these amendments was to afford the U.S. jurisdiction, concurrent with that of the states, to proceed against those who violate diplomatic inviolability. Under the law as it existed prior to the amendments, in most cases of attacks on diplomats, the federal government could do little more than to encourage local enforcement of the law.

The 1972 amendments extend federal criminal jurisdiction to cover a variety of attacks on diplomatic personnel and diplomatic premises. For example, under section 1116 of Title 18 of the United States Code, criminal penalties of up to life imprisonment are provided for anyone who kills a "foreign official," a term that covers high-ranking officials of foreign governments and international organizations, as well as members of their families who accompany them,[42] or an "official guest." Section 1116 defines an official guest as a "citizen or national of a foreign country present in the United States as an official guest of the government of the United States pursuant to designation as such by the Secretary of State."[43] Thus foreign citizens who might come to the United States as members of an Olympic contingent could be designated "official guests" by the secretary of state and thereby become entitled to special protection under federal law. Not surprisingly, a primary motivating factor behind the introduction of this provision was the 1972 murder of the Israeli Olympic competitors at Munich.[44]

Another especially noteworthy provision of the 1972 amendments is revised section 1201 of Title 18, which expands federal jurisdiction over kidnaping. Under revised Section 1201, federal jurisdiction is provided when: (1) the victim is transported in interstate or foreign commerce (as under the law as it existed prior to 1972); (2) the kidnaping occurs within the special maritime and territorial jurisdiction of the United States; or (3) in the special aircraft jurisdiction of the United States; or (4) the victim is a "foreign official" or an "official guest" as defined in Section 1116 of Title 18.

The 1972 amendments entitle a foreign official, a member of his family, or an official guest to wide-ranging protection. As the Senate report pointed out at the time the 1972 amendments were under consideration, with the amendments, federal legislation on the protection of diplomats would:

(1) Make murder or manslaughter of a foreign official, a member of his family, or an official guest, or conspiracy to murder such an individual, a Federal offense punishable as a felony.
(2) Make the kidnapping of a foreign official, a member of his family, or an official guest a Federal felony if committed anywhere in the United States.
(3) Make the assaulting, striking, wounding, imprisoning or offering of violence to a foreign official or an official guest a Federal offense punishable as a felony.
(4) Make the intimidation, coercion, threatening, harassment or willful obstruction of a foreign official or an official guest a Federal offense punishable as a misdemeanor.
(5) Prohibit certain demonstrations within one hundred feet of foreign government buildings for the purpose of intemidating [sic], coercing, threatening or harassing any foreign official or official guest, or willfully obstructing such individual, and make this punishable as a misdemeanor.
(6) Make the willful injury, damaging or destruction, or attempted injury, damaging or destruction, of real or personal property within the United States belonging to or used or occupied by a foreign government, foreign official, international organization, or official guest, a Federal offense punishable by a felony.
(7) Make several changes in the Federal kidnapping law as it will apply generally. In this regard, the law is amended to make the thrust of the offense the kidnapping itself rather than the interstate transporting of the

kidnapped person. This effort to clearly differentiate the question of what is criminal from the question of what criminal behavior falls within Federal jurisdiction not only makes the sanction more rational but also has the practical effect of assuring that a kidnapping which occurs in a hijacking situation is an extraditable offense from a country which does not recognize an offense keyed to interstate transportation.[45]

The drafters of the 1972 amendments clearly intended that these provisions should supplement and not pre-empt state law and practice on murder, kidnaping, and assault. Primary responsibility to investigate, prosecute, and punish these common law crimes remains with the states.[46] In this connection, the law of the District of Columbia prohibits certain demonstrations within 500 feet of any "building or premises within the District of Columbia used or occupied by any foreign government or its representative or representatives of an embassy, legation, consulate, or for other official purposes," unless granted a permit by the superintendent of police of the District.[47]

The 1972 revisions of federal kidnaping law got their first test in 1974 and 1975 in *United States* v. *Lechoco.*[48] In that case, Lechoco, an immigrant Philippine lawyer armed with a pistol concealed in a briefcase, went to the Philippine Chancery on November 18, 1974, to keep an appointment he had previously made with the Philippine ambassador. After entering the ambassador's office, Lechoco took the ambassador hostage at gunpoint; threatened the ambassador's secretary at gunpoint; shot and wounded a Philippine economic attache; and fired at a D.C. metropolitan police officer. Lechoco initially demanded publicity for his acts and later also demanded the safe conduct of his son from the Philippines to Washington.

Lechoco held the Philippine ambassador hostage for over 10 hours. He finally surrendered to metropolitan police and FBI agents after an agreement was reached with Philippine President Ferdinand Marcos to place Lechoco's son on the first available flight from Manila.

On June 19, 1975, Lechoco was convicted by a jury in the District Court for the District of Columbia of kidnaping of and assault on a foreign official. In the sentencing proceedings before the district judge, Lechoco's attorney, pleading for a light sentence, contended that this case should not be considered one of "political terrorism" because Lechoco's motivation in kidnaping the ambassador was to unite his family, and that the separation of Lechoco and his family had already imposed sufficient punishment on him. In response, the government argued that Lechoco's actions were no different from those of numerous others who had hijacked planes or kidnaped diplomatic personnel. According to the government, Lechoco's intent to commit a terrorist act was shown by his bringing a gun and other terrorist equipment with him to the appointment with the ambassador. The government further pointed out that this was the first prosecution under the 1972 revisions to the federal kidnaping law and that the diplomatic community was vitally concerned that a severe penalty be imposed in order to deter future kidnapings of and other attacks on diplomatic personnel.

The court imposed a 10-year sentence on Lechoco under the federal kidnaping count, as well as shorter sentences under other counts, all of which were to run concurrently. In so ruling, the court stated that the violent circumstances of the case "cannot be overshadowed by the natural sympathy which we have to extend to this defendant."[49] It noted further that "Congress considered this crime to be so abhorrent that it provided probation and split sentence alternatives were not available to the Court, thus mandating that the Court impose a jail sentence. Under the terms of the statute itself, it must be for a term of years."[50]

The court also rejected Lechoco's motion that he be released on bond pending appeal. Taking note of the Bail Reform Act's standard of danger to the community or to other person or persons, the court was of the opinion that if Lechoco were released, the Philippine ambassador or his representative might be in danger, and that they should not be subjected to a "lingering fear" of attack from Lechoco. In support of this conclusion, the court stated that it was not convinced that Lechoco's sole motive in attacking the ambassador had been a concern for his son. According to the court, the record indicated that Lechoco was also motivated by a "long-standing hostility toward the Marcos regime in the Philippines. . . ."[51]

In sum, then, the District Court followed a hard-line approach in the *Lechoco* case, imposing a severe sentence and rejecting Lechoco's plea that he be released on bond pending appeal. It is noteworthy that the question of Lechoco's motivation was not raised until the sentencing stage. The only defense raised during the trial was insanity. Hence the defense did not contend that Lechoco's motivation in kidnaping the ambassador could excuse his actions, but only that it might serve as a mitigating factor in the sentencing process.

With respect to sentencing; the court implied that Lechoco's motivation might be taken into account as a possible mitigating circumstance but found that he had failed to prove that his sole or even his primary motive in the kidnaping was to have his son reunited with him. The court also interpreted the federal statute in such a way as to limit its discretion in imposing a lenient sentence. Finally, the court stressed the interest of the Philippine ambassador and embassy, as well as that of the diplomatic community, in freedom from the threat or use of violence, as support for its conclusion that Lechoco should remain in jail pending appeal.

The primary deficiency in U.S. legislation on the protection of diplomats prior to the 1976 amendments was that its jurisdictional scope was too limited to deal effectively with international and transnational attacks on diplomats, a deficiency also present, as noted previously, in the national legislation of most other countries. That is, jurisdiction is usually based on the territorial principle, and unless the attack on the diplomat takes place within the territory of the receiving country, or perhaps on a place or ship of that country, national criminal laws regarding the protection of diplomats are simply inapplicable by their terms. Moreover, the country where the offender is found may be unwilling or unable to extradite the offender to the country where the crime was committed or to the country whose diplomat was attacked because of the lack of an extradition treaty—where such a treaty is required under national law—or an exception to national extradition law such as the political offense doctrine. As will be seen later in this chapter, a primary purpose of recent international measures in this area has been to induce states to revise national law to remedy these deficiencies in jurisdiction and in extradition law and practice, and the United States has now ratified these measures and revised its national legislation accordingly.

National Security Measures for the Protection of Diplomats

As important, or perhaps more important, than domestic legislation designed to punish the perpetrators of violent attacks on diplomats are security and other measures adopted to prevent such attacks. In this area it is extremely difficult to secure hard data because of classification problems. This is especially true with respect to security measures adopted by countries other than the United States.

. Nonetheless, even conventional sources of information indicate that more and more emphasis is being put on protective measures as terrorist attacks increase in frequency and intensity.[52] Many of these measures are designed to prevent terrorist violence in general and not attacks against diplomats in particular. For example, there has been a general tightening of visa, immigration, and customs procedures in an effort to detect known or suspected terrorists before they enter the country. Similarly, domestic intelligence operations geared to the gathering of data regarding terrorist acts have been expanded, as have international interchanges of such data and of police techniques and technology among law enforcement officials. Postal services have been alerted to be on the lookout and have been supplied sophisticated technological devices for the detection of letter bombs, which have been circulating internationally by the hundreds.[53]

Other measures have been undertaken specifically for the protection for diplomats. The Australian government has recently held two exercises in Canberra involving the hypothetical seizure of a diplomat by a terrorist group, and extensive protection is provided to embassies that might be subjected to terrorist attack. The Australian government maintains close consultation with the United States and other governments in an effort to keep up-to-date lists of potential terrorists on file. Partly as a result of these efforts, two suspected Japanese terrorists were arrested and deported upon arrival in Australia during the Japanese prime minister's visit in October 1974.[54]

A variety of security controls for the protection of diplomats have been introduced unilaterally by national governments. In some cases diplomats have permanent bodyguards riding with them in their limousines or following them in trailing vehicles. Embassy and consulate staffs have been reduced in size to lessen the potential number of targets. In other cases, unnecessary travel has been eliminated and essential trips have been shrouded in secrecy. To keep potential terrorists off balance, work hours have been switched and staggered on a daily basis.

Similarly, embassy limousines, equipped with oversize rearview mirrors for travel in convoys, have been employed to pick up entire staffs from their homes, deliver them to the mission, and return them home after work. This technique has run into difficulty in congested urban areas, where convoy groupings can easily become separated. Efforts have also been made to reduce diplomatic visibility, such as the removal of diplomatic license plates from cars and the use of smaller and less ostentatious vehicles. Some diplomatic personnel carry arms, although others regard this as dangerous and provocative to terrorists. Security measures for U.S. diplomats have reportedly been carried to such an extreme in places like Nicosia, Beirut, and Buenos Aires that U.S. embassies there resemble fortresses.[55]

The U.S. government has also become increasingly concerned with the security of foreign missions located in Washington and New York. According to the Department of State, from January to October 1971, 79 major documented incidents against foreign diplomatic, consular, and semiofficial officers and personnel occurred in the United States.[56] These incidents were a prime motivating factor in the State Department's support of the 1972 legislation and the establishment of a 700-man Executive Protective Service set up to increase security for diplomats in the Washington area.

During the early 1970s the security of foreign missions to the United Nations and that of their personnel became an issue in the wake of numerous attacks on mission premises (especially those of the USSR and Eastern European countries) and on individual diplomats. In response to charges from some member states that security measures at the missions were inadequate, the United States described in detail steps taken under federal and state law by federal and New York City authorities to provide security for the missions.[57] At the conclusion of discussions on the subject, the United Nations secretariat summarized proposals for improved security that various member states had submitted. These included, *inter alia:*

1. extending the federal ban on picketing and demonstrating before foreign missions from a distance of 100 to 500 feet in order to bring it into accord with the situation in the District of Columbia
2. 24-hour police protection, employing special guards, if necessary, or, at a minimum, the use of additional guards who would participate in frequent but irregularly timed patrols

3. the introduction of electronic surveillance systems such as security alarm systems
4. the creation of special security zones with notices stating that the premises are the object of special police protection
5. more intensive education of the public regarding the principle of diplomatic inviolability[58]

Partly in response to these suggestions, the Secret Service has reportedly created 23 additional fixed posts at U.N. missions in New York,[59] and Congress has enacted legislation[60] that extends the protection of the Executive Protection Service to foreign diplomatic missions located in metropolitan areas other than the District of Columbia where there are 20 or more such missions headed by full-time career officers, and that increases the maximum number of EPS officers from 850 to 1200. The secretary of the treasury may utilize, on a reimbursable basis and with their consent, the services, personnel, equipment, and facilities of state and local governments. No more than $3.5 million is authorized to be appropriated for purposes of reimbursement for any fiscal year, and is to remain available as provided in appropriation acts.

Most recently, the Soviet Union has complained to the Committee on Relations with the United States as Host Country about a series of demonstrations at the Soviet mission to the United Nations by people carrying placards saying "Russian Blood in the Streets of New York" and "Seize Soviet Diplomats as Hostages" and about several violent attacks against Soviet diplomatic facilities, responsibility for which has been claimed by an underground group called the Jewish Armed Resistance.[61] In response to these attacks, U.S. embassy officials and their families in the Soviet Union have also come under harassment.[62]

In committee debate, the Soviet delegate charged that the harassment of Russian officials in New York was increasing because U.S. authorities had not taken effective countermeasures and, in spite of advanced criminal detection methods, had failed to find the guilty persons. William M. Scranton, the U.S. ambassador to the United Nations, responded by reporting that additional police security measures had been arranged for Soviet facilities and that intensive investigations were being conducted by the New York police and federal authorities. He also reported that the 1972 amendments to the federal law concerning the protection of diplomats were being reexamined to determine whether the display of placards with inflammatory calls for violence would constitute an offense under that law.[63]

The problem of what constitutes "adequate" security measures for the protection of diplomats and diplomatic premises is not easily resolved because the cost of providing enough protection to prevent the determined terrorist from carrying out an attack may be enormously high. Not only may the cost be high in terms of time and financial resources, but also overly stringent security measures may prevent the diplomat from performing his functions. The diplomat cannot fulfill his duties of representing his country and keeping abreast of current developments in the receiving country if he spends all his time in a fortress-like embassy or residence.

Previous studies have indicated that to a certain extent, the diplomat views himself as assuming the risks inherent in his profession. Moreover, at least as of 1960 and 1961, a survey of retired U.S. Foreign Service officers indicated that a majority of those surveyed believed that the protection they had received in the posts where they had served had been at least adequate,[64] although the comments were more favorable with respect to posts in the industrialized countries than they were in regard to service in the developing or Communist countries. Were a similar survey taken today, there might be more negative comments on the adequacy of protection in the developing countries. On the other hand, the protection of diplomats in the Communist countries appears to have improved considerably.

The delicate balance to be struck, it would seem, is between maximizing protection of the diplomat and of diplomatic premises while minimizing interference with diplomatic functions. The balance will be more heavily weighted toward one side or the other depending on circumstances in each individual country, *e.g.*, the presence or absence of terrorist activity, the extent to which diplomats are likely targets for terrorist attack, and the effectiveness of the receiving country's antiterrorist campaign.

Governmental Responses to the Kidnaping of Diplomats

Governmental responses to the kidnaping of diplomats have varied considerably and have depended in part on whether the kidnaping was traditional or the barricade-and-hostage type. In the traditional kidnaping case, some governments have viewed the welfare of the kidnaped diplomat as overridingly important and have readily granted all the terrorists have demanded. With one possible exception, this has resulted in the release of the diplomat unharmed.[65]

Other governments, including that of the United States, have adopted a hard-line approach, refusing to accede to any terrorist demands. The primary rationale advanced to justify the great risk to the kidnaped diplomat of the no-concessions policy is that it has a deterrent effect as to future kidnapings. As will be seen later, this thesis is subject to serious question in light of the findings of the Rand Corporation and other recent studies.

Still other governments have adopted a position somewhere in the middle of the spectrum, granting some but not all of the terrorists' demands. For example, the government may initially refuse to agree to demands for the release of a large number of political prisoners or the payment of a large ransom, yet subsequently agree to more "reasonable" terms involving a smaller ransom and fewer prisoners.[66] Or the government may refuse to release political prisoners or pay ransom but agree to the publication of the kidnapers' political manifesto.[67] In most of these cases the diplomat has been released unharmed.

Somewhat different considerations arise in kidnapings of the barricade-and-hostage type. As pointed out by the Rand Corporation, a barricade-and-hostage kidnaping usually affords the kidnapers an opportunity to obtain a larger number of hostages than is possible if the kidnaping is of the traditional type, and it may require relatively few persons to carry out.[68] On the other hand, a barricade-and-hostage kidnaping involves the considerable disadvantage to the terrorists of increasing the government's bargaining power and maximizing its options. Since the terrorists are themselves hostages, the government is in a good position to minimize their rewards because it is in a position to maximize the risks to the kidnapers if they attempt to harm their hostages. This advantage is not present in the traditional kidnaping case, where the hideout has not been discovered.

To illustrate this contrast between traditional and barricade-and-hostage kidnapings, it may be instructive to examine in some detail the 1970 kidnapings in Canada by members of "Le Front de Libération du Québec" (FLQ) of James Cross and Pierre Laporte.[69] On October 5, 1970, the FLQ, a terrorist group that had concluded that its goal of independence for Quebec would be achieved only by a revolutionary overthrow of the established order, kidnaped James Cross, a senior British consular officer, by abducting him at gunpoint from his residence in Montreal. In a note found at the University of Quebec, the kidnapers demanded that the government release 23 political prisoners, provide them with a plane for flight to Cuba or Algeria, pay $500,000 in ransom, and publish the FLQ political manifesto in all Quebec newspapers. The note stated that the deadline for a favorable response from the Canadian government was 48 hours, and a subsequent communication from the terrorists stated that if their demands were not met within the time limit, they would not be responsible for the consequences.

Reportedly, the Canadian government was initially uncertain about how to respond to the kidnapers' demands. By October 7, however, an official position had been reached. Foreign Secretary Sharp announced that the government considered the kidnapers' demands for ransom totally unacceptable and would not meet them. At the same time he indicated that the government was willing to publicize the FLQ's political manifesto and to engage in negotiations with the kidnapers about the terms for Cross's release. For their part, the kidnapers extended their deadline several different times.

For the first five days after the Cross kidnaping, then, the Canadian government and the kidnapers maintained effective communication. On October 10, however, the situation became considerably more complicated. At that time, the provincial Quebec government announced that it would give the Cross kidnapers safe conduct out of the country in return for Cross's release, but that it would not release the 23 political prisoners demanded. Fifteen minutes after this announcement, in order to increase leverage on the government, Quebec's Labor Minister, Pierre Laporte, was abducted from his home. Apparently this kidnaping was effected by another group, or "cell," of the FLQ, and there are indications that Cross's kidnapers were completely surprised to learn of the Laporte kidnaping.[70] Be that as it may, following Laporte's abduction, the FLQ reiterated its ransom demands and set new deadlines on both Cross's and Laporte's lives if the stipulated demands were not met.

On October 11, Quebec's Premier Bourassa rejected the demands but broadcast an appeal to the kidnapers to provide proof that both Cross and Laporte were still alive and to open negotiations with the government. In response, both cells of the FLQ suspended the deadlines on the lives of the hostages and proposed that the FLQ and the government agree on an intermediary to carry on negotiations between them. On October 13 talks began in Montreal between a representative of the FLQ and a representative of the Quebec government.

These negotiations led to a Quebec government offer (on behalf of itself and the federal government) to exchange five prisoners for the two kidnaped men. An October 16 deadline set by the Quebec government passed without an official response from the FLQ, although in the negotiations their representative had instantly rejected the offer as a mockery. The Quebec government regarded the representative's reaction as made in his personal rather than his official capacity.

An hour after the Quebec government's deadline passed, Prime Minister Pierre Trudeau invoked the Canadian War Measures Act with a Proclamation that Canada was threatened with insurrection by the FLQ's activities.[71] Under the act, the government had the extraordinary power, without consulting Parliament, to enact its own laws regarding arrest, deportation, censorship, or any other measure it might decide was necessary for the security, defense, peace, order, and welfare of Canada. In supplementary regulations adopted by the cabinet providing additional emergency powers to deal with the insurrectionists, the FLQ was declared to be an unlawful organization. After the invocation of the act, various reports estimated that between 150 to 300 arrests were made in over 150 raids.[72]

On the night of October 17, Pierre Laporte's body was found in the trunk of a taxicab in downtown Montreal. While denouncing the killing of Laporte as a "cruel and senseless" act, Prime Minister Trudeau refused to change his position on the release of the 23 political prisoners. Rather, the government reiterated its offer to provide the terrorists with free passage to Cuba if they would free Cross unharmed. On October 19, the Canadian House of Commons lent its support to the hard-line position by endorsing the government's proclamation of emergency powers under the War Measures Act.

Large numbers of arrests and investigations continued to be made, and finally on December 2 the police succeeded in locating the hideout house in North Montreal where the kidnapers were holding Cross, and surrounded it with armed force. Thus trapped, the kidnapers offered to negotiate. Government officials then entered the house and arranged for the release of Cross in exchange for the safe conduct of the kidnapers out of Montreal to Cuba. Cross was released in good mental and physical condition, and his kidnapers and members of their families were flown to Cuba.

As the preceding discussion indicates, both the Cross and Laporte kidnapings were initially traditional, but successful investigative work on the part of the Canadian police turned the Cross kidnaping into a barricade-and-hostage situation, and was in all probability primarily responsible for the different outcome in the two cases. It is important to note that, although from the outset the Canadian and Quebec governments adopted a hard-line negotiating stance, they did not adamantly insist on "no negotiations"[73] or no concessions. Rather, while refusing to pay ransom, at one stage or the other in the negotiations, the government agreed to publish the FLQ's political manifesto, to allow the kidnapers safe conduct out of Canada, and even to release a small number (five) of political prisoners. Also, and perhaps most important, the government made every effort to enter into and maintain negotiations with the kidnapers. Although the point is certainly debatable and the data are ambiguous, it is arguable that the invocation of emergency measures under the War Measures Act rather than any governmental refusal to grant demands, was a major contributing factor to the kidnapers' decision to murder Pierre Laporte.

On the other hand, the invocation of the act, and measures taken thereunder, may have been in part responsible for the police's success in finding the hideout of the kidnapers who were holding James Cross. In any event, the government's actions once the hideout was found and surrounded are noteworthy. The Canadian government did not direct the police to storm the hideout—an action that, as the Rand Corporation has pointed out—has usually resulted in the death of hostages.[74] Instead, government officials entered into negotiations with the kidnapers and secured Cross's release in exchange for their safe passage out of the country.

More recent barricade-and-hostage kidnapings suggest that the Canadian government may have been overly generous in granting Cross's kidnapers safe passage. For example, in December 1975, terrorists seized the Indonesia consulate in the Netherlands in an effort to win support for their fight to gain independence for the South Moluccan Islands in the Indonesian archipelago. During the terrorist takeover, one man died while trying to escape, and a group of Indonesian school children were released shortly after the terrorists gained control of the consulate. Thereafter the Dutch police kept the gunmen and the remaining hostages cooped up in the consulate while refusing to accede to the terrorists' demands and maintaining steady psychological pressure on them in order to induce them to surrender. After 15 days, this strategy succeeded, and the terrorists gave themselves up to Dutch authorities without harming the hostages.[75]

Other barricade-and-hostage incidents, however, indicate that the strategy employed by Dutch officials with respect to the South Moluccan terrorists may not necessarily be successful in all situations. For example, on March 1, 1973, eight members of Black September occupied the Saudi Arabian embassy in Khartoum, Sudan, and seized several hostages, including the U.S. ambassador, the U.S. deputy chief of mission, the Belgian and Jordanian chargés d'affaires, and the Saudi Arabian ambassador. The terrorists demanded the release of 60 Palestinian guerrillas being held in Jordan, all Arab women detained in Israel, Sirhan Sirhan (the killer of Robert Kennedy), and imprisoned members of the Baader-Meinhof gang in the Federal Republic of Germany. After all the target governments refused to accede to their demands, the terrorists executed the two U.S. diplomats and the Belgian chargé on the night of March 3. Although a Sudanese court sentenced the eight terrorists to life imprisonment, Sudanese President Nimeiri commuted their sentences to seven years and ordered that they be turned over to the PLO in Cairo.[76] This suggests that, even in a barricade-and-hostage situation, kidnapers may be willing to murder their hostages if they perceive that the authorities to whom they surrender are unlikely to impose severe penalties for these crimes.

The December 1975 occupation of the OPEC headquarters in Vienna by Palestinians is another example of a barricade-and-hostage situation where a no-concessions policy might not succeed in ensuring the safety of the hostages. In Vienna the stated motives of the terrorists were to bring renewed attention to the Palestinians' plight and to break the alliance between "American imperialism" and reactionary forces in the Arab countries. They demanded a plane to fly them and 30 hostages to Algeria, and then to other capitals in the Arab world in order to publicize their political views. Austrian Chancellor Bruno Kreisky quickly acceded to these demands, and some have sharply criticized him for doing so.[77] It must be remembered, however, that the terrorists, who had already killed 2 persons in occupying the OPEC headquarters, were holding 80 hostages, 11 of whom were senior oil ministers. If harm had come to these high officials because of refusal to provide a plane, the political repercussions could have been enormous. The application of a no-concessions policy in this situation might reasonably be seen as involving disproportionately high risks in light of the relatively modest demands made by the terrorists.

Based on its study of 77 international hostage incidents, the Rand Corporation has concluded that tough anticoncessionary policies have had little if any deterrent effect as to future kidnapings, and that tough antiterrorist campaigns by governments in such countries as Brazil, Uruguay, Guatemala, and Turkey have been "the more decisive factor in deterring or preventing future incidents."[78] These antiterrorist campaigns may themselves raise serious questions, since in some cases they have reportedly involved egregious violations of human rights, including torture. In Uruguay the antiterrorist campaign succeeded in destroying not only the Tupamaro movement but also Uruguayan democracy.[79]

A case study of United States policy and practice in international hostage incidents undertaken by the Carnegie Endowment for International Peace is similarly reaching the conclusion that the U.S. no-concessions policy does not deter kidnapers. The study reportedly bases this conclusion in large part on the finding that a primary motive of kidnapers in international hostage incidents is to gain publicity for their cause, a goal that does not usually depend on the United States granting concessions.[80]

Similarly, a study of hostage situations currently being conducted by Ernest Evans at the Massachusetts Institute of Technology questions the deterrence value of the no-concessions policy on the ground, *inter alia*, that the goal of securing ransoms and releasing prisoners is only one of several in hostage cases sought by terrorists, and is not necessarily the most important. The other primary goals of such terrorists, Evans contends, are unaffected by a no-negotiations, no-concessions policy, and include: (1) harassment and intimidation of authorities; (2) the provoking of repression; (3) aggravation of state-to-state relations; and (4) publicity. Evans recommends that the United States publicly disavow its policy of no negotiations, no concessions in favor of a policy of negotiating with terrorists and of making certain "cosmetic concessions" to them, such as promising a fair trial and humane treatment, or "tactical" concessions required by the bargaining situation, *e.g.*, allowing food and water to be brought to the hostages and their captors.[81]

On the other hand, the Department of State reportedly has classified information in its files based on contacts with terrorists or potential terrorists that indicates terrorists are aware of the U.S. policy and are deterred by it from kidnaping U.S. diplomats and private citizens. In any event, arguments other than its purported deterrent effect may be advanced in support of a no-concessions policy. The payment of ransom, the release of political prisoners, the publication of political manifestoes, and the provision of safe passage out of the country for kidnapers may substantially strengthen terrorist movements, and governments may be expected to resist terrorist demands for such actions. The crucial question to ask in cases of diplomatic kidnaping may be whether minimizing or denying demanded benefits to the terrorist is—in terms of a cost/benefit calculation—worth the substantial risk to the life of the diplomat involved in adherence to such a policy.

The proper strategy and tactics for governments to employ in response to kidnapings and other attacks on diplomats are key elements in any policy designed to enhance diplomatic protection, and a later section of this chapter will return to them. For present purposes, it is submitted that the case histories considered previously suggest that no set of strategies or tactics should be set in cement. On the contrary, governments should strive to maintain constant communication with terrorists, be flexible in their responses, and ready to adapt their policies to rapidly changing circumstances. The factual circumstances in individual instances of attacks against diplomats involve so many variables that no one set of strategies and tactics would appear suitable for application to all cases.

Existing International Measures:
Description and Assessment

Traditional International Legal Measures
(pre-OAS and U.N. Conventions)

Although, as has been shown above, the principle of diplomatic inviolability has long been established in both customary and conventional international law, experience in the twentieth century with incidents involving attacks on diplomats and diplomatic premises clearly demonstrates the deficiencies of traditional international legal measures as a system for the protection of diplomats.[82] First, under traditional law and practice, the range of persons entitled to special protection is unclear. While it has been widely accepted by states that heads of state or government, and permanent diplomatic personnel and consular officials, are within the scope of the receiving state's duty of special protection, no such consensus exists with respect to officials of international organizations or *ad hoc* (itinerant) diplomats. With respect to these persons, such obligations of protection as do exist are set forth in treaty provisions that state practice has not yet expanded into customary international law.[83]

Second, traditional international law has been ambiguous about the nature of measures that should be taken to ensure diplomatic inviolability. As has been noted earlier, article 29 of the Vienna Convention on Diplomatic Relations requires receiving states to "take all appropriate steps" to prevent any attack on diplomats but does not further specify what steps might be "appropriate." Rather, this decision has been largely left to the receiving state's discretion, although in the event of internal disturbances, strained relations between the sending and receiving states, or threat of an attack against diplomats, a duty on the part of the receiving state arises to increase security measures for diplomats and diplomatic premises. If a successful attack on a diplomat nonetheless occurs thereafter, the sufficiency of these measures may become the subject of dispute between the receiving and sending states.[84]

As to sanctions against persons who attack diplomats and diplomatic premises, the receiving state is under an obligation to use due diligence to apprehend the offender and to set in motion the administrative and judicial machinery that normally deals with the prosecution and punishment of offenders. More debatable, however, is the proposition that the receiving state is also under an international obligation to try the offender and punish him. Although there is support for this thesis—especially in the form of arbitral decisions[85]—the latitude that states give to their prosecuting authorities to decide whether to bring an accused to trial and to their judiciaries and executives to determine whether to convict and punish belies it. Moreover, as will be shown later, the negotiating histories of the OAS and U.N. conventions on the protection of diplomats indicate quite clearly that the scope of the duty of states' parties with respect to an offender they may apprehend is (in the event they do not extradite him to some other country) solely to submit the accused to the appropriate authorities for purposes of prosecution. The conventions impose no limitations whatsoever on prosecutorial discretion as to whether to bring the accused to trial.

Traditional international legal measures have been particularly inadequate in cases where the attack against the diplomat is committed in one state, and the actor flees to another state seeking safe haven. Here the effort to suppress and punish acts of international terrorism has run into problems arising from the complex matrix of asylum, extradition, and the political offense. Although Grotius was of the opinion that natural law required states either to punish fugitive offenders found within their territories or to surrender them to the other state,[86] no such legal obligation has developed. On the contrary, extradition is the prerogative of the requested state, and, in the absence of a bilateral treaty between the requesting and the requested state, there is no international legal duty to extradite. Even where there is an applicable extradition treaty, the scope of the duty to extradite may be narrow. First, extradition may be requested only for offenses listed in the treaty. Second, and most important, even as to these offenses, the political offense exception may determine whether the alleged offender will be returned to the requesting state or granted asylum by the requested state. In all cases the decision whether to grant extradition rests with the executive of the requested state. A discussion of the various approaches that states have taken to the political offense exception to extradition is beyond the scope of this chapter. It suffices for present purposes to note that attacks on diplomats may be classified by some of them as a political offense.[87]

Finally, traditional international legal measures have lacked established procedures for international cooperation in preventing and punishing violations of diplomatic inviolability. As will be discussed later, many of the recent efforts with respect to the protection of diplomats have been undertaken with a view to remedying this deficiency.

The OAS Convention

By way of brief background, it should be noted that during the 1960s, Latin America suffered from a rash of acts of terrorism arising from revolutionary activities.[88] In response to these acts, the General Assembly of the Organization of American States, on June 30, 1970, resolved, *inter alia:*

1. To condemn strongly, as crimes against humanity, acts of terrorism and especially the kidnaping of persons and extortion in connection with that crime.
2. Also to condemn such acts, when perpetrated against representatives of foreign states, as violations not only of human rights but also of the norms that govern international relations.
3. To declare that these acts constitute serious common crimes. . . .
4. To recommend to the member states that have not yet done so that they adopt such measures as they may deem suitable . . . to prevent and when appropriate to punish crimes of this kind. . . .
5. To request the governments of the member states to facilitate . . . the exchange of information that will help in the prevention and punishment of crimes of this kind.[89]

The resolution further directed the Inter-American Juridical Committee to prepare an opinion and a draft convention on procedures and measures necessary to fulfill the purposes of the resolution in cases where the proscribed acts might have international repercussions. This led in turn to a Draft Convention on Terrorism and Kidnapping of Persons for the Purposes of Extortion prepared by the committee and sent to the OAS General Assembly, January 8, 1971.

A conference of foreign ministers on the draft convention produced a wide range of views on how to approach the problem of international terrorism in the hemisphere. Six governments favored a wide-ranging convention that would seek to deal generally with problems of international terrorism,[90] and walked out in protest when the conference instead adopted a convention on the specific issue of the kidnaping of diplomats, namely, the Convention to Prevent and Punish the Acts of Terrorism Taking the Forms of Crimes Against Persons and Related Extortion That Are of International Significance.[91] On the other hand, 3 governments either abstained or voted against the convention because they believed that certain of its provisions infringed excessively on state sovereignty.[92] Of the 22 governments attending the conference, only 13 voted for and signed the pact.[93] At this writing, only 6 states, including the United States, have become parties.[94]

In view of this lack of support, it is immediately apparent that the convention has not been an effective international legal instrument for the protection of diplomats. At the same time, the strengths and weaknesses of the convention are worth a brief examination, if only because the convention was the first international legal instrument to deal directly with the protection of diplomats, and because it served as a primary model for the United Nations Convention.

With respect to the range of persons covered by its provisions, the OAS Convention does little to clarify ambiguities in traditional law and practice.

Article 1 obligates states' parties to cooperate "to prevent and punish acts of terrorism, especially kidnaping, murder and other assaults against the life or physical integrity of those persons to whom the state has the duty according to international law to give special protection, as well as extortion in connection with those crimes." By this reference to other sources of international law, the convention leaves unsettled the issue whether it encompasses such persons as visiting ministers, legislators, governors of states or provinces, officials of a foreign government or an international public organization acting in their official capacities, and family members residing with or accompanying any of these persons. Negotiating history indicates that the convention was not intended to deal with crimes against a class this large,[95] and in any event, extending special protection to a class of this size would be a practical impossibility for most countries. Precisely how far the convention's scope of protection does extend is a matter of conjecture.

The convention is also ambiguous concerning the persons to be deterred from or punished for attacks on diplomats. By its terms, the convention appears to cover only principals involved in the crimes covered by the convention, and not persons who are co-conspirators and accessories not directly involved in the proscribed acts.[96] On the other hand, some commentators have suggested that an injured government might read the convention broadly to include all members of a political group to which the perpetrators and their assistants belong, thus violating fundamental human rights.[97]

The convention's key provisions are those that focus on extradition or punishment through national legislation of alleged offenders. First, the convention classifies the proscribed acts as "common crimes of international significance, regardless of motive."[98] On its face, the purpose of this classification seems to be to exclude violent attacks against diplomats from the political offense exception in extradition law and practice. According to the Inter-American Juridical Committee, "the political and ideological pretexts utilized as justification for these crimes in no way mitigate their cruelty and irrationality or the ignoble nature of the means employed, and in no way remove their character as acts in violation of essential human rights."[99]

Other provisions of the convention, however, cast doubt on the conclusion that the "political offense" exception to extradition is unavailable to states parties. Specifically, article 3 provides that "it is the exclusive responsibility of the state under whose jurisdiction or protection such persons are located to determine the nature of the acts and decide whether the standards of this convention are applicable." Although some have interpreted this provision as authorizing a state party only to determine whether the proscribed acts actually occurred, and not to classify the acts in terms of the political offense/common crime distinction,[100] article 3 must be read in the light of article 6 of the convention. Article 6 provides, in categorical terms, that none of the convention's provisions "shall be interpreted so as to impair the right of asylum." The elimination of attacks on diplomats from the political offense category would perforce affect extradition practice and the right of asylum as they currently exist in much of Latin America. At a minimum, this apparent conflict of provisions creates a major ambiguity as to the continued viability of the political offense doctrine under the convention.

Under article 5, if extradition is denied "because the person sought is a national of the requested state, or because of some other legal or constitutional impediment, that state is obliged to submit the case to its competent authorities for prosecution, as if the act had been committed in its territory." States parties are also obliged, under article 8(d), to "endeavor to have the criminal acts contemplated in this convention included in their penal laws, if not already so included." At first blush, these provisions might appear to assure severe punishment for persons who attack diplomats. In fact, however, if it decides not to extradite, a state party is entirely free to decline to prosecute an alleged offender without violating the convention. The obligation on the party is only to submit the accused to the appropriate authorities for purposes of prosecution. Once the case is in the hands of government attorneys, they retain complete discretion as to whether to bring the case to trial. While their decisions may be based on such traditional grounds as insufficiency of evidence or unavailability of witnesses, they may also turn on considerations of political expediency clothed in legal terms.[101]

Besides the ambiguity of its provisions, a major deficiency of the convention is that it fails to come to grips with some key problems concerning the protection of diplomats, *e.g.*, conduct, if any, on the part of a diplomat that might cause him to lose his right to special protection by the receiving state. One possible manifestation of this problem was explicitly suggested by Ambassador Caicedo Castilla, a member of the Juridical Committee.

[C]ertain matters must be stated with the frankness due the truth. One of these is the fact that there are foreign officers who belong to what are called, with notable discretion, "intelligence services" (as if the other employees were not equally intelligent), or, to put it bluntly, international espionage. Would it be correct, or desirable, or popular to extend to such officers the guarantees reserved for ambassadors? I do not hesitate to say that it would not.[102]

Similarly, the convention contains only the most general of provisions concerning security measures for the protection of diplomats.[103] These provisions encourage states parties to cooperate with respect to such measures, but they do not set forth any guidelines for such cooperation or the parameters of an ultimate agreement among states parties on security measures.

Finally, the convention contains no provisions regarding the policy that states parties should adopt with respect to demands terrorists may make as conditions for the safe release of kidnaped diplomats. For its part, the Juridical Committee at least recognized the existence of the problem and recommended the following tentative procedure for dealing with one facet of it:

Each contracting state may, in serious and exceptional circumstances, decide whether or not it would be correct to authorize departure from its territory by, or to deport, as the case may be, any person who is detained or in prison. . . . The interested contracting states may reach an agreement, in cases of the specific type referred to in the preceding paragraph, regarding the legal status of the persons involved.[104]

The negotiating history of the convention contains no indication why this provision was not incorporated into the convention, or why alternative approaches to the problem it addresses were not considered.

On the positive side, the convention does establish a system which states that become parties in good faith can employ to assist them in their endeavors to prevent and punish attacks against diplomats. By defining serious attacks against diplomats as common crimes of international significance subject to principles of universal jurisdiction, the convention enables a state to exercise criminal jurisdiction over such attacks regardless of whether they occurred in its territory or in the territory of another state that is party to the convention. Through these provisions, the convention attempts to fill "jurisdictional lacunae" regarding attacks on diplomats present in traditional international law and practice. Also, for all their inadequacies, the provisions of the convention that call for cooperation among states at least set up a framework within which these states may engage in further efforts toward the protection of diplomats, a contribution not to be dismissed lightly.

The convention is further commendable for its attention to the rights of the accused. Article 4 provides that "[a]ny person deprived of his freedom through the application of this convention shall enjoy the legal guarantees of due process." Similarly, article 8(c) obliges states parties "[t]o guarantee to every person deprived of his freedom through the application of this convention every right to defend himself."

In sum, the convention has some potential to make a contribution toward the protection of diplomats in the hemisphere through its establishment of a system of universal criminal jurisdiction over attacks on diplomats, and of a system of *aut dedere, aut judicare*, and through its provisions for cooperation among states parties. Moreover, its safeguards for the rights of the accused help to place efforts to protect diplomats in proper perspective and to enhance support for fundamental human rights. However, because the convention contains so many ambiguities and fails to deal with crucial problems, its effectiveness in practice is problematical. For sure, as long as only six countries in the hemisphere are parties, the convention will remain largely irrelevant to efforts to protect diplomats against terrorist attack. In all events, as a regional and not a global international legal measure,[105] the OAS Convention may at a maximum be regarded as only a "first step"[106] toward the prevention and suppression of worldwide attacks on diplomats and diplomatic premises.

The U.N. Convention

The adoption by the United Nations General Assembly (on December 14, 1973) of the Convention on the Prevention and Punishment of Crimes Against Internationally Protected Persons, Including Diplomatic Agents,[107] was in effect the first successful outcome of intensive U.S. efforts to induce the United Nations to take action against international terrorism. Largely at the urging of the United States, and in response to the attack on Israeli athletes at the Munich Olympics the previous summer, in September 1972 Secretary-General Waldheim had requested the General Assembly to consider "measures to prevent terrorism and other forms of violence which endanger or take innocent human lives or jeopardize fundamental freedoms."[108] As a focal point of discussion, the United States introduced a Draft Convention for the Prevention and Punishment of Certain Acts of International Terrorism.[109] After heated debate on this item by member states, on December 18, 1972, the General Assembly established an Ad Hoc Committee on Terrorism, composed of 35 members, which met from July 16 through August 10, 1973. For a variety of reasons beyond the scope of this chapter,[110] the committee was unable to reach any agreement on recommendations to submit to the next General Assembly, and the U.S. Draft Convention was shelved.

United Nations work on the protection of diplomats preceded Secretary-General Waldheim's initiative on international terrorism and then proceeded simultaneously with the assembly's consideration of the U.S. Draft Convention. In 1971, in response to a large number of terrorist attacks on diplomats, the International Law Commission proposed to prepare a set of draft articles on the protection of diplomats. The General Assembly promptly accepted the proposal and requested that member states submit comments on the subject to assist the ILC in its preparation of the draft articles. After 27 members had submitted their comments,[111] and drawing on several proposed draft conventions,[112] in 1972 the ILC adopted a set of draft articles and transmitted them to the twenty-seventh session of the General Assembly.[113] The General Assembly in turn again requested member states to submit comments—this time on the completed draft articles.[114] Finally, in the twenty-eighth session of the General Assembly, the Sixth Committee completed work on the convention, which the General Assembly then adopted by consensus.

In the initial deliberations of the ILC, some participants had expressed a preference for a wide-ranging convention that would attempt to protect mankind generally from terrorist attacks. However, the majority of member states was of the opinion that in view of the traditionally protected status of diplomats under international law, a convention focusing on the diplomatic victim was urgently needed and that the "elaboration of a legal instrument with the limited coverage of the present draft is an essential step in the process of formulation of legal rules to effectuate international cooperation in the prevention, suppression, and punishment of terrorism."[115]

Detailed discussions of the negotiating history and of the terms of the convention may be found in several other forums.[116] For present purposes, this chapter will focus only on the convention's key provisions, in an attempt to evaluate the convention's strengths and weaknesses as an international legal instrument designed to prevent, suppress, and punish attacks on diplomats. To this end, negotiating history will be drawn upon when, as, and if it appears appropriate.

With respect to the range of persons covered by its provisions, the convention introduces a new concept into international jurisprudence: the "internationally protected person." Under article 1(1), the internationally protected person is defined as:

(a) a Head of State, including any member of a collegial body performing the functions of a Head of State under the constitution of the state concerned, a Head of Government or a Minister for Foreign Affairs, whenever any such person is in a foreign State as well as members of his family who accompany him;

(b) any representative or official of a state or any official or other agent of an international organization of an intergovernmental character who, at the time when and in the place where a crime against him, his official premises, his private accommodation or his means of transport is committed, is entitled pursuant to international law to special protection from any attack on his person, freedom or dignity, as well as members of his family forming part of his household.

The terms of article 1(1) indicate that there are two kinds of internationally protected persons. That is, a person within article 1(1)(a) is entitled to special protection whenever he is in a foreign state, for whatever reason. The scope of article 1(1)(b), on the other hand, extends only to a person entitled to special protection "at the time when and in the place where" the crime is committed. In the General Assembly, the United Kingdom representative stated his delegation's understanding of article 1(1)(b) as follows:

[A]s regards article 1(1)(b) and as the language of the provision itself makes clear, we understand that the persons who, in the circumstances specified in that subparagraph, are within the ambit of that subparagraph are those who fall within any of the following categories of persons, that is to say: persons who are entitled to the benefit of article 29 of the Vienna Convention on Diplomatic Relations, article 40 of the Vienna Convention on Consular Relations or article 29 of the New York Convention on Special Missions; persons who are high officials or agents of international organizations and who, under the relevant international agreements are, as such, entitled to the like benefit; and persons who, under customary international law or by virtue of some other specific international agreement, are entitled to special protection from any attack on their person, freedom or dignity. The subparagraph, of course, also covers members of the families of such persons, forming part of their households.[117]

In the same vein, the report of the Sixth Committee interprets the term internationally protected person "as applying to nationals of third states appointed by sending states to international organizations if such representatives or officials are accepted by the international organizations in question, provided that they are not nationals of the host states where such international organizations have their headquarters."[118]

As to the crimes covered by the convention and the persons to be deterred from or punished for attacks on diplomats, article 2 provides:

1. The intentional commission of:
    (a) a murder, kidnapping or other attack upon the person or liberty of an internationally protected person;
    (b) a violent attack upon the official premises, the private accommodation or the means of transport of an internationally protected person likely to endanger his person or liberty;
    (c) a threat to commit any such attack;
    (d) an attempt to commit any such attack; and
    (e) an act constituting participation as an accomplice in any such attack shall be made by each State Party a crime under its internal law.
2. Each State Party shall make these crimes punishable by appropriate penalties which take into account their grave nature.
3. Paragraphs 1 and 2 of this article in no way derogate from the obligations of States Parties under international law to take all appropriate measures to prevent other attacks on the person, freedom or dignity of an internationally protected person.

The intent of the drafters was for the convention to cover only crimes of a "serious" nature, such as murder and kidnaping, and the text of the Sixth Committee's drafting committee had referred specifically to "murder, kidnapping or other serious attack."[119] The word "serious" was ultimately dropped in the Sixth Committee on the grounds that it might restrict the convention's scope by introducing an element of uncertainty. The basic concept of restricting the scope of the convention to serious crimes was retained.[120]

The term "intentional" in article 2 has a twofold meaning. First, the act must be committed intentionally and not merely negligently; second, the offender must know that the victim is an "internationally protected person," i.e., he must be aware of his victim's status.[121]

Following the model of the OAS Convention, the ILC's draft contained the words "regardless of motive" after "intentional commission."[122] Some commentators have suggested that the Sixth Committee's deletion of these words is a serious omission because it undermines the ILC's position that terrorist attacks on diplomats were under no circumstances to be construed as "political crimes."[123] Others have contended that the words were dropped because it was felt that they were political rather than legal and might create confusion in a domestic tribunal. In the view of these commentators, the deletion does not affect the basic meaning of the paragraph.[124] At a minimum, however, the deletion of the words "regardless of motive" would seem to raise a question about the extent to which the political offense doctrine may be applied by states parties to attacks against diplomats, especially when one considers that the convention incorporates a limited right to asylum.

Article 2(1) avoids an ambiguity present in the OAS Convention by clearly including within its coverage not only actual attacks on diplomats but also threats or attempts to commit, and participation as an accomplice in such attacks. The coverage of article 2(1) will vary somewhat depending on the domestic laws of states parties to the convention because the precise definition of the offenses may differ under individual systems of law.

The requirement under article 2(1) that the acts covered by the convention "shall be made by each State Party a crime under its internal law" should not require much modification in the substantive criminal law of most states parties. As has been mentioned previously, under the domestic law of most countries, the crimes set forth in article 2 are already "punishable by appropriate penalties which take into account their grave nature."

Article 3 of the convention, in specifying the circumstances in which a state party is obliged to establish its jurisdiction over the crimes set forth in article 2, sets up a system of primary and secondary jurisdiction. That is, under paragraph 1 of article 3:

1. Each state party shall take such measures as may be necessary to establish its jurisdiction over the crimes set forth in article 2 in the following cases:
   (a) when the crime is committed in the territory of that state or on board a ship or aircraft registered in that state;
   (b) when the alleged offender is a national of that state;
   (c) when the crime is committed against an internationally protected person as defined in article 1 who enjoys his status as such by virtue of functions which he exercises on behalf of that state.

Article 3(1)(a) is based on the territorial principle of jurisdiction, which is a widely accepted norm of customary international law requiring no comment.[125] The nationality principle, upon which article 3(1)(b) is based, is also widely accepted as a permissible basis for the exercise of international criminal jurisdiction, although fewer states have actually incorporated it into their substantive criminal law and procedure.[126] On the other hand, article 3(1)(c) appears to follow the controversial "passive personality" principle and probably represents an extension of the jurisdiction a state may exercise under customary international law.[127]

Article 3(2) of the convention establishes a system of secondary jurisdiction. It requires each state party to provide for criminal jurisdiction "in cases where the alleged offender is present in its territory and it does not extradite him pursuant to article 8 to any of the states mentioned in paragraph 1 of this article." In such cases, jurisdiction would be based on the universality principle. The ILC had proposed in its draft that the acts specified as crimes "shall be made by each States Party a crime under its internal law, whether the commission of the crime occurs within or outside of its territory," and that "each State Party shall take such measures as may be necessary to establish its jurisdiction over these crimes."[128] Many countries, however, were unwilling to accept such an extension of the universality principle as the basis for primary jurisdiction.[129] Rather, they were of the opinion that primary jurisdiction should be exercised in accordance with more traditional principles by the state where the offense was committed, the state of which the alleged offender was a national, or the state of which the injured diplomat was a national—the states with primary interest in the incident—and that the state where the alleged offender was found should normally extradite him to one of the states primarily concerned. At the same time, these countries realized that the country where the alleged offender was found would have authority to refuse extradition. In such a case, these countries concluded, the state where the offender was found should be required to take jurisdiction itself over him, and such jurisdiction would have to be exercised in accordance with the universality principle. In short, the provision in article 3(2) for a secondary jurisdiction was necessary to carry out a system of *aut dedere, aut judicare*. Article 3 will, of course, require substantial modifications in the domestic law of most states parties.

The key provision in the convention is article 7, which states: "The state party in whose territory the alleged offender is present shall, if it does not extradite him, submit, without exception whatsoever and without undue delay, the case to its competent authorities for the purpose of prosecution, through proceedings in accordance with the law of that state." Unfortunately, the drafting history of this provision clearly reveals that it fails to eliminate a crucial weakness in traditional international law and practice, and in the OAS Convention, *i.e.*, the absence of any limitations on absolute prosecutorial discretion. Comparable provisions in the Hague and Montreal conventions on civil aviation,[131] which were among the models for the U.N. Convention,[132] contain a second sentence: "Those authorities shall take their decision in the same manner as in the case of any ordinary offence of a serious nature under the law of that state." In the Sixth Committee, the representative of Sweden proposed the inclusion of such a sentence.[133] However, the proposal was referred to a drafting committee and never again saw the light of day. Hence under article 7, the obligation on a state party is solely to submit the accused to its prosecuting authorities. In the words of the ILC's commentary to its draft articles: "It will be up to those authorities to decide whether to prosecute or not, subject to the normal requirements of treaty law that the decision be taken in good faith in the light of all the circumstances involved. The obligation of the state party in such case will be fulfilled . . . even if the decision . . . is not to commence criminal proceedings."[134]

It is submitted that the "normal requirement of treaty law that the decision be taken in good faith" is slim assurance indeed that states parties will process through normal channels persons accused of attacking diplomats, in the same manner as they would any person accused of murder, kidnaping, or other serious attack. Specifically, there is nothing whatsoever in the terms of the convention that precludes prosecuting authorities from deciding not to prosecute an alleged offender because of sympathy with his motives. Whether such a decision could be regarded as one taken in "bad faith" under the convention is problematical at best.

On the more positive side, the convention does take a major step toward limiting the possible application of the doctrine of asylum to attacks on diplomats. Article 12 provides: "The provisions of this Convention shall not affect the application of the Treaties on Asylum, in force at the date of the adoption of this Convention, as between the states which are parties to those treaties; but a state party to this Convention may not invoke those Treaties with respect to another state party to this Convention which is not a party to those Treaties." The latitude that article 12 gives to the continued application of treaties on asylum among states parties to the convention is carefully circumscribed. It refers only to treaties on asylum in force at the date of the adoption of the convention, *i.e.*, on December 24, 1973. Moreover, the article in no way affects the position of states parties that are not also parties to the treaties on asylum. As the U.S. representative explained to the Sixth Committee:

The article states that this Convention shall not affect the application of treaties on asylum in force as between parties to those treaties *inter se*. That is to say, even if the alleged offender is present on the territory of one party to such a treaty and the state on the territory of which the crime has taken place is also a party to such a treaty, if the internationally protected person attacked exercised his functions on behalf of a state not party to such a treaty or the alleged offender was a national of a state nor party to such a treaty, the state where the alleged offender is present may not invoke that treaty with respect to the non-party state. Thus, the non-party state can hold the state where the alleged offender is present to its obligations under article 7 and may, if it wishes, request extradition under article 8.[135]

The convention contains a number of provisions requiring states parties to engage in cooperative efforts toward the prevention, suppression, and punishment of attacks against diplomats. With respect to prevention, states parties are required to cooperate in order to prevent preparations in their territories for attacks on diplomats within or outside their territories, and to exchange information and to coordinate the taking of administrative measures against such attacks.[136] If an attack against a diplomat takes place, and an alleged offender has fled the country where the attack took place, states parties are to cooperate in the exchange of information concerning the circumstances of the crime and the alleged offender's identity and whereabouts.[137] The state party where the alleged offender is found is obliged to take measures to ensure his presence for purpose of extradition or prosecution and to inform interested states and international organizations of the measures taken.[138] Finally, states parties are to cooperate in assisting criminal proceedings brought for attacks on diplomats, including supplying all evidence at their disposal that is relevant to the proceedings.[139]

With respect to the rights of alleged offenders, article 6(2)(a)(b) states that an accused has the right "to communicate without delay with the nearest appropriate representative of the state of which he is a national or which is otherwise entitled to protect his rights or, if he is a stateless person, which he requests and which is willing to protect his rights; and ... to be visited by a representative of that state." Under article 9, an accused is guaranteed "fair treatment" at all stages of criminal proceedings against him. According to the ILC's report, the term "fair treatment" was "intended to incorporate all the guarantees generally recognized to a detained or accused person."[140] As an example of such guarantees, the report referred to article 14 of the International Covenant on Civil and Political Rights."[141] On the other hand, some commentators have suggested that the concept is imprecise and that "[w]hat is fair treatment in one state party may not be fair treatment in another."[142]

The dispute settlement provisions of the convention are striking. Article 13(1) provides:

1. Any dispute between two or more states parties concerning the interpretation or application of this Convention which is not settled by negotiation shall, at the request of one of them, be submitted to arbitration. If within six months from the date of the request for arbitration the parties are unable to agree on the organization of the arbitration, any one of those parties may refer the dispute to the International Court of Justice by request in conformity with the statute of the Court.

These provisions set up a meaningful system of dispute settlement in that only one of the parties to a dispute need request that it be submitted to arbitration, or, if the parties are unable to agree on the organization of the arbitral tribunal, to judicial settlement, in order to activate dispute settlement procedures. However, under paragraph 2 of article 13, any state party may file a reservation declining to be bound by this system of dispute settlement, and several ratifying states have already done so.[143]

Also, in the area of implementation, a significant omission is the paucity of provisions requiring states parties to report to the Secretary-General on steps they have taken to carry out their obligations under the convention. Under article 6(1), a state party in whose territory an alleged offender is present is required to provide information about the steps it has taken so as to ensure his presence for the purpose of extradition or prosecution to specified states or international organizations, either directly or indirectly through the secretary-general.[144] There is, however, no provision in the convention requiring states parties to report on changes they have made in domestic law and policy or on steps they have taken in cooperation with other states parties under the convention toward the prevention and punishment of attacks against diplomats. This omission is unfortunate. An annual reporting system by states parties on steps they have taken to implement the convention could establish a useful data base on which all countries might draw to assist them in their efforts to protect diplomats.

The resolution[145] by which the General Assembly adopted the convention introduces a substantial ambiguity into the situation. Operative paragraph 4 of that resolution provides that the General Assembly:

Recognizes also that the provisions of the annexed Convention could not in any way prejudice the exercise of the legitimate right to self-determination and independence, in accordance with the purposes and principles of the Charter of the United Nations and the Declaration on Friendly Relations and Cooperation among States in accordance with the Charter of the United Nations by peoples struggling against colonialism, alien domination, foreign occupation, racial discrimination and *apartheid*.

Operative paragraph 6 of the resolution provides that the resolution, "whose provisions are related to the annexed Convention, shall always be published together with it."

Operative paragraph 4 itself represents a compromise. In the Sixth Committee, a large group of African and Middle Eastern delegations had proposed the addition of the following draft article to the Convention: "No provision of the present articles shall be applicable to peoples struggling against colonialism, alien domination, foreign occupation, racial discrimination and *apartheid* in the exercise of their legitimate rights to self-determination and independence."[146]

It appears clear that the insertion of such an article in the convention would have created a double standard and rendered the convention inapplicable to an attack on a diplomat by a member of a national liberation movement. The effect of the compromise language employed in paragraph 4 of the resolution is at best unclear.

On the one hand, the resolution is not part of the convention, even if it is by its terms related to it and to be published with it. Also, the language of paragraph 4 seems merely to state the "self-evident fact" that the convention cannot in any way prejudice the right to self-determination, and not to affect the legal obligations set out in the convention itself.[147]

On the other hand, in the General Assembly some countries argued that the effect of paragraph 4 was the same when included in the accompanying resolution as it would be were it included in the convention.[148] As to the proper interpretation to be given to the language of paragraph 4, the minority view was expressed most strongly by the delegate from Algeria:

Our complete support for this principle has as its corollary an unconditional support for the national liberation movements, excluding any interference in their internal affairs, including the manner in which they wage their battles. In other words, my delegation cannot accept that the provisions for the protection of diplomats or internationally protected persons may be used to hamper the struggle of peoples for their liberation or the restitution of their rights, the affirmation of their national identity or the preservation of their dignity.[149]

The crucial issue regarding paragraph 4 of the resolution does not seem to be its legal effect, if any, on the obligations of states parties under the convention. Rather, it seems to be the effect the paragraph may have on the willingness of states to ratify the convention and to ensure that the convention realizes its full potential as a measure toward the protection of diplomats. At least one Western European country deeply concerned about the protection of diplomats is reportedly undecided whether to ratify the convention because of uncertainty concerning the effect of the resolution.[150] Moreover, the substantial support received by the draft article exempting wars of national liberation from the provisions of the convention may indicate that the Algerian interpretation of operative paragraph 4—regardless of its validity as a legal proposition—enjoys more support than that formally expressed during the debates in the General Assembly. If this is the case, the chances that the convention might become an effective measure for the protection of diplomats would appear slim. At this writing, only 25 states, including the United States, have become parties to the convention.[151]

If the convention is to play any role in the effort to protect diplomats, it is indispenable that it be ratified on a worldwide basis. Good faith adherence to the convention by a large number of states with a view to preventing, suppressing, and punishing attacks on diplomats while safeguarding the rights of the accused would go a long way toward resolving issues raised by the convention's terms (discussed above). However, as in the case of the OAS Convention, it must be realized that the convention fails to deal with some key problems regarding the protection of diplomats.

With respect to the crucially important area of *prevention* of attacks on diplomats, article 4 of the convention is, in effect, an agreement among states parties to agree at some future time on standards for the security of diplomats and on specific security measures. It is not at all clear, moreover, that such an agreement on standards for security measures should or could take the form of a formal international agreement. The need for flexibility and secrecy regarding protective measures for diplomats might dictate the use of more informal working arrangements among personnel primarily responsible for security.

In this same vein, the convention does not consider the issue of possible state liability for injury to diplomats. We have seen previously that insofar as one can ascertain principles of state liability in this area, they seem to be based on a concept of "fault" on the part of the receiving state. If so, is it necessary to develop minimum standards of security for diplomats, which could serve as the basis of a finding of liability on the part of a receiving state? Could principles of no-fault or strict liability be applied to the receiving state's protection of diplomats? What principles of liability, if any, might apply to third states that grant asylum to persons who attack diplomats, and how might they be enforced? These and related questions await definitive answers.

Assuming, as will surely be the case, that not all members of the world community will adhere to the convention, states parties may be faced with the very difficult problem of third-party frustration of the convention's purposes. This in turn raises the question of possible sanctions against states that grant safe haven to persons who attack diplomats. The ICAO's failure in the summer of 1973 to adopt measures of sanction against states that provide sanctuary to hijackers of airplanes is not a helpful precedent in this regard. If the likelihood of multilateral agreement on such sanctions is thus not great, should states turn to unilateral or perhaps regional measures of sanction? In this connection, the United States Anti-Hijacking Act of 1974 authorizes the president to adopt such sanctions in the hijacking area,[152] and an amendment to the International Security Assistance and Arms Control Act of 1976-1977 would terminate military and economic assistance to any country granting sanctuary from prosecution to international terrorists unless the president determines that national security considerations justify the continuance of such aid, in which case he must file a report with Congress stating the reasons for his decision.[153]

Finally, as has been noted above, there is the question of appropriate strategy and tactics for negotiating with kidnapers of diplomats. There is substantial disagreement within the United States and among countries as to what tactics should be adopted with respect to kidnapers of diplomats. Assuming agreement on strategy and tactics, should these be set forth in an international agreement?[154] Or is this an area more suitable for informal working procedures? Again, these and related questions await definitive answers.

Amendments to U.S. Legislation Implementing
the OAS and U.N. Conventions

At the same time that he ratified the OAS and U.N. conventions, the president signed into law the 1976 amendments to U.S. legislation on the protection of diplomats.[155] Although the Senate had previously given its advice and consent to ratification of both Conventions, as a policy matter, ratification had been delayed until Congress adopted legislation implementing the conventions.

In principal part, these amendments revise title 18 of the United States Code so as to:[156] (1) introduce the concept of the "internationally protected person" into federal criminal law; (2) allow the United States to exercise jurisdiction over a person who engages or attempts to engage in a serious attack (*i.e.*, murder, kidnaping, or assault) on an internationally protected person, regardless of the place where the offense was committed or the nationality of the victim or of the alleged offender, if the latter is present within the United States; (3) prohibit threats to kill, kidnap, or assault internationally protected persons as well as extortion related to such threats; and (4) classify as federal crimes attempts and violent attacks on the premises, private accommodation, or means of transport of an internationally protected person, foreign official, or official guest, which are likely to endanger his person or his liberty.[157]

In addition, section 970 of Title 18 was amended by inserting a new subsection (b), paragraph (1) of which penalizes those who "willfully with intent to intimidate, coerce, threaten, or harass" thrust an object or themselves into premises occupied by foreign officials or official guests and for whatever reason no damage to property occurs. Paragraph (2) of this new subsection (b) prohibits the refusal to vacate premises occupied by a foreign official or official guest if a lawful demand is made on the intruder. Examples given of conduct that might be subject to these provisions were the throwing of smoke bombs onto diplomatic premises or chaining oneself to immovable objects within diplomatic premises. In the report of the House Committee on the Judiciary,[158] four members of the committee criticized these provisions as expanding the "definition of criminal activity to cover innocent or constitutionally protected actions that in no way interfere with the personal liberty, safety or official business of foreign emissaries."[159]

The four dissenting members took especial exception to revised section 112(b) of Title 18, which reads as follows:

(b) Whoever willfully —
  (1) intimidates, coerces, threatens, or harasses a foreign official or an official guest or obstructs a foreign official in the performance of his duties;
  (2) attempts to intimidate, coerce, threaten, or harass a foreign official or an official guest or obstruct a foreign official in the performance of his duties; or
  (3) within the United States but outside the District of Columbia and within one hundred feet of any building or premises in whole or in part owned, used, or occupied for official business or for diplomatic, consular, or residential purposes by—
    (A) a foreign government, including such use as a mission to an international organization;
    (B) an international organization;
    (C) a foreign official; or
    (D) an official guest;
    congregates with two or more other persons with intent to violate any other provision of this section; shall be fined not more than $500 or imprisoned not more than six months, or both.

In the dissenters' view, this subsection would punish peaceable assembly, in that mere intent to violate provisions of the legislation, not action, is sufficient to give rise to criminal liability.[160] They also contended that it punishes innocent conduct by making it a crime to "obstruct a foreign official in the performance of his duties."[161] Finally, the dissenters claimed that by penalizing "harassment" of foreign officials without defining the term, the subsection might subject "Americans to arrest for such constitutionally protected acts as heckling or booing a foreign representative who makes a public speech."[162]

By way of response to such criticisms, the executive branch pointed to subsection (d) of section 112, which provides that nothing in the section "shall be construed or applied so as to abridge the exercise of rights guaranteed under the first amendment to the Constitution of the United States."[163] With respect to subsection (b)(3), they contended that, like a conspiracy, the

... numbers in a "congregation" enhance the risk of harm and, given the requisite unlawful intent, intervention by the government is warranted even though action has not progressed to the attempt stage. In practice, we envision a police warning to persons within one hundred feet of the protected premises who become unduly rowdy that their actions evince an unlawful intention and that they are subject to arrest if they do not remove themselves beyond a hundred feet from the premises. Once beyond the hundred feet, such persons may gather and act as they please, at least until their conduct rises to the level of an attempt prohibited by the section.[164]

Parenthetically, it may be noted that the amendments, in various sections, permit an exception to the prohibition in 18 U.S.C. § 1385 against the use of the armed forces of the United States as a *posse comitatus* to enforce the laws. For example, revised 18 U.S.C. § 1116(d) expressly provides: "In the course of enforcement of this section [regarding murder or manslaughter of foreign officials, official guests, or internationally protected persons] and any other sections prohibiting a conspiracy or attempt to violate this section, the Attorney General may request assistance from any Federal, State, or local agency; including the Army, Navy, and Air Force, any statute, rule, or regulation to the contrary notwithstanding." This authorization may be of considerable usefulness in the event of an attack on a diplomat in a rural area where local law enforcement officers may not be properly trained to deal with such cases.

Political, Economic, and Social Milieus

From the terrorist perspective, the available evidence indicates that the threat and use of force against diplomats and diplomatic facilities has been a very successful tactic indeed in the context of revolutionary struggle. With regard to the key area of kidnaping of diplomats, the conclusions of the Rand Corporation's study of 77 international hostage episodes are especially apposite:

Rough estimates as to the payoffs and risks involved in kidnapping indicate that the terrorist tactic of seizing hostages for bargaining or publicity purposes is far from being irrational, mindless, ineffective, or necessarily perilous. There is almost an 80 percent chance that *all* members of the kidnapping team will escape death or capture, whether or not they successfully seize hostages. Once they make explicit ransom demands, there is a close to even chance that all or some of those demands will be granted—and virtually a 100 percent probability of achieving worldwide, or at least national publicity.[165]

Moreover, it should be recognized that the use of terrorist tactics against diplomats may result in substantial benefits to the cause of the individual terrorists. At least in part the increased willingness of the world community to recognize the need for Palestinian participation in a Middle East settlement is a result of the attention focused on the Palestinian cause by the acts of terrorists. In Latin America, terrorist kidnapings have gained substantial funds by way of ransom payments for revolutionary groups, and have created economic and political instability for the receiving country's government.[166]

A primary reason for the poor performance of the world community with respect to international controls of terrorism has been the lack of consensus among countries as to fundamental values and goals. Many member states of the world community believe actions that the United States and other developed countries would classify as terrorist—including attacks on diplomats—are legitimate uses of force in response to state terrorism. According to this view, for example, Israel is engaging in state terrorism by forcefully occupying Arab and Palestinian territory, thus denying these peoples their right to self-determination. The military might of Israel, the argument continues, has rendered the conventional use of force by the Arabs and the Palestinians largely ineffective. Accordingly, it is necessary to turn in desperation to such unconventional uses of force as attacks on Israeli civilians, hijacking of airplanes, and the kidnaping of diplomats in order to weaken the morale of the Israeli people and the Israeli economy by a war of attrition. It has also been argued that the Palestinians have been driven to such measures by the world community's failure to recognize their right to self-determination and that these actions force the world community to focus on wrongs done to the Palestinian people.

Similar arguments can and have been advanced in support of the kidnaping of or attacks against diplomats or foreign businessmen in Latin America. From this perspective these actions are not illegitimate attacks on innocent representatives of third party states. Rather, such diplomats and foreign businessmen represent a foreign country whose aid is helping to perpetuate the power of a repressive government, which in turn is frustrating the exercise of the right to self-determination by engaging in state terrorism.

One may emphatically reject the validity of such reasoning—as well as the values it reflects—and still recognize that it enjoys a considerable measure of support in the world community. It contributed substantially to the U.N.'s rejection of the United States Draft Convention, and it helped block all efforts at the ICAO Rome Conference in the summer of 1973 toward the adoption of sanctions against states serving as sanctuaries for airplane hijackers.

In light of these circumstances, the adoption without objection by the General Assembly of the U.N. Convention seems an anomaly. What accounts for the seemingly widespread acceptance of this convention by an assembly that otherwise failed to reach any agreement on measures to combat terrorism? Surely the reasons are manifold and complex. But perhaps part of the answer lies in an examination of the subject matter and the terms of the convention itself. First, the convention contains no reference to terrorism. Rather, it refers to *crimes* against diplomats and other internationally protected persons. Second, in limiting its protection to a single class of victims, the convention focuses on functions of prime concern to all member states regardless of ideology. In the language of the convention, "crimes against diplomatic agents and other internationally protected persons jeopardizing the safety of those persons create a serious threat to the maintenance of normal international relations which are necessary for cooperation among states."[167] Omission of the term "terrorism" from the convention's text may have served to obviate much of the heated debates and emotional exchanges that invariably accompany discussion of this subject. Similarly, limitation of the convention's coverage to diplomats as victims especially worthy of protection due to their functions avoids, or at least minimizes,[168] fruitless debates on the degree of innocence, or lack thereof, of particular victims of terrorist attacks. In other words, the convention seeks to resolve the definitional problems of terrorism by avoiding them.

On the other hand, although the convention was adopted by consensus, to date relatively few states have become parties to it. It is one thing to support the protection of diplomats in principle by not opposing a convention on the subject in the General Assembly; few, if any, states would wish to take a public position in opposition to such an action. It is quite another thing to become party to an international legal instrument that obligates states to adopt measures, at both the national and international levels, designed to prevent and punish attacks on diplomats. Many states may resist taking the latter step because of their sympathy with terrorist causes.

Admittedly, little progress can be expected unless and until there is a change in the attitudes of these states. But these states may view international legal controls of attacks on diplomats more favorably as their diplomats become the victims of terrorist attacks. In this connection, it will be interesting to see whether the terrorist attack in Vienna involving the Arab oil ministers induces the Arab states to ratify the convention. Reportedly, the Arab states are delaying further steps toward becoming parties to the convention until agreement is reached among them on what the Arab position toward ratification should be.[169] Pressure on the Arab states to ratify the convention may come from their allies in OPEC. According to newspaper reports,[170] the governments of Venezuela and Colombia have proposed that a special session of the United Nations General Assembly be held to reconsider the need for a convention on international terrorism.

Also, crucially important international conferences currently being held or soon to be held on such matters as energy, raw materials, trade, food, population, the environment, the laws of war, and transnational corporations may highlight the need for effective measures to prevent and punish attacks on diplomats. The chances of a successful conclusion to such conferences would appear slim if they are conducted in an atmosphere where the possibility of terrorist attack against the participants is great.

Conclusions and Recommendations

The primary purpose of this section—a difficult one to fulfill—is to recommend what action or actions the Department of State might take toward the prevention and punishment of attacks on diplomats and diplomatic premises. These actions, of course, might take a variety of forms. In some instances the State Department might merely be urged to make an internal decision to change its policy as, for example, in the case of strategies to be employed in the event of a diplomatic kidnaping. In others, the department might be asked to propose, in conjunction with other appropriate agencies such as the Department of Justice, certain changes in federal legislation concerning the protection of diplomats. Or it might be suggested that the department seek to work closely with law enforcement and security personnel in the United States to ensure that these officials are doing everything possible to protect diplomats accredited to the United States, or to international organizations located in the United States, while minimizing interference with diplomatic functions and offense to diplomatic personnel. In any event, these actions would be of a unilateral nature. That is, they would be taken unilaterally by the United States and not in cooperation with other countries.

Cooperation with other countries would be carried out primarily, although not exclusively, by the Department of State through informal working arrangements between government officials or through the conclusion of treaties and other forms of international agreements. These arrangements and agreements might be bilateral with one other country or regional with several countries. "Regional" arrangements or agreements are not necessarily limited to countries located in geographical proximity. For example, the United States might enter into an agreement with member states of the Council of Europe, and this would qualify as a "regional" arrangement.

Finally, the State Department might take multilateral, or global, action. In particular, actions of a global nature would include those that might be taken in the United Nations.

Unilateral Actions

Amendments to U.S. Legislation. By and large, with the adoption of the 1976 amendments, federal legislation should allow the United States to discharge its international obligations under the OAS and U.N. conventions fully, and it should constitute an effective national measure toward the protection of diplomats. One possible revision in legislation that might be considered would be to amend section 112(b)(3) of Title 18 to extend the ban on demonstrations before diplomatic premises from 100 feet to 500 feet in order to bring federal law into accord with the law of the District of Columbia. The D.C. law seems to have worked well in practice, and the extra 400 feet of protective zone might assist law enforcement officers in performing their obligation to protect diplomatic premises while allowing people an opportunity to protest and otherwise express their views.

On the other hand, the Department of Justice reportedly is opposed to an extension of the protective zone to 500 feet outside the District of Columbia, on the grounds that congested conditions in other cities such as New York render a zone of this breadth unfeasible. This writer is not familiar enough with technical details of the problem to evaluate the Justice Department's position, but would suggest that at a minimum the matter should be kept under review in order to ascertain whether these technical difficulties are truly insurmountable.

At this time no legislation should be enacted that would compel the president to impose economic sanctions against countries that grant safe haven to terrorists who attack diplomats. As noted previously, Congress has passed legislation that would require the president to terminate military and economic assistance to a country that grants sanctuary to an international terrorist unless the president finds that national security considerations require continuance of such aid. An earlier version of this provision had given Congress the authority to override by concurrent resolution the president's decision to continue assistance. This was dropped in the final version.

At least in the context of the first Hickenlooper Amendment, U.S. experience with unilateral sanctions has not been happy.[171] Such sanctions have tended to exacerbate already delicate relations between the United States and other countries, and they have failed to induce the target state to take action favorable to U.S. interests. In hearings on the Anti-Hijacking Act of 1974, the Department of State was of the view that "the specific provision for primary boycott would be helpful if used in the context of international joint action," but such "power would be used sparingly, in urgent circumstances, where it would have clear effectiveness. In the usual case it would be joint measures which would have impact."[172] Even as to joint measures, the "President would exercise caution in utilizing this new authority—taking into account all the U.S. interests that may be involved."[173] In light of the U.N. experience with economic sanctions against Rhodesia, one might go further and question as well the utility of joint economic measures. At any rate, it is submitted that economic sanctions against states harboring terrorists should be taken only by the majority of the world community, and then only in a situation where all other means have been exhausted. The world community is already too involved in confrontational politics.

U.S. Security Measures for the Protection of Diplomats. As indicated previously, the United States appears to have given considerable attention in recent years to security measures, both for the protection of foreign diplomats in the United States and for the protection of U.S. diplomats abroad. Although there have been attacks on diplomats and diplomatic premises in the United States, the government has not yet had to face the kidnaping of a foreign diplomat. However, with the United Nations in New York, and the large number of "internationally protected persons" participating in U.N. proceedings, there is an acute danger that high-ranking officials of foreign governments or of the United Nations might be kidnaped and held for ransom.

The kidnaping of a diplomat puts special pressures on the governments of the sending and receiving states, and every reasonable effort should be taken to prevent such an occurrence. It is especially important that if in spite of security measures, a diplomat is kidnaped in the traditional manner, his whereabouts be discovered in order to minimize the kidnapers' bargaining power. To this end, it would be helpful if diplomats could be supplied with effective transmitting devices that could be concealed on their persons and utilized in tracing their location during a kidnaping. Unfortunately, the technical state of the art would appear to be not very advanced at this juncture. The most advanced device currently available is the size of a pen and has a maximum range of only three to four blocks. Other limitations on these devices are that they are incapable of functioning inside buildings with steel structures; they can become incapacitated by electrical interference; and they have often failed to function in actual kidnaping situations. In addition, diplomats are reluctant to use these devices, because of the substantial danger that they will be discovered by kidnapers. In such a case the kidnapers may become angry and injure the diplomat.

There is some question whether a transmitting device on the person of a diplomat could ever be effective even if technological developments were to permit its concealment from the naked eye. The argument is that as a practical matter, the very success of such devices in leading law enforcement officials to the hideout of the kidnapers would cause future kidnapers automatically to assume that diplomats were carrying transmitting devices and force the diplomat, by torture if necessary, to reveal the device's whereabouts in order to destroy it.

An alternative approach is to place a transmitter in the automobile in which the diplomat is traveling. However, in the usual kidnaping situation, the diplomat is transferred from his automobile to that of the kidnapers, which, of course renders the transmitter in his vehicle useless.

It is recommended that highest priority be given to research and development of technology designed to maximize the security of diplomats. However, unless and until more technologically sophisticated transmitting devices are developed, and authorities are otherwise satisfied with their usefulness as security measures, they should not be used because of the danger involved to the diplomat.

U.S. Responses to the Kidnaping of Diplomats. When discussing strategy and tactics the United States might employ in the event of the kidnaping of a diplomat, one must distinguish between kidnapings of foreign diplomats within the United States and kidnapings of U.S. diplomats abroad. In the latter situation, the receiving country has the primary responsibility to protect the U.S. diplomat, and the U.S. government does not act on its own or make contact with the kidnapers unless the receiving country has given its consent or has indicated to the U.S. embassy its unwillingness or inability to fulfill its responsibilities. The receiving country normally makes the ultimate decision on policy, although the U.S. embassy will advise the receiving country of its responsibility to obtain the release of the diplomat, inform it of U.S. policy in such situations, and offer the receiving country its cooperation. If the kidnaping is of a foreign diplomat in the United States, the roles are reversed, and the U.S. government is responsible for policy decisions.

One must also distinguish, as indicated earlier in this paper, between the traditional and the barricade-and-hostage types of kidnapings. In the barricade-and-hostage situation, the government's bargaining power is at a maximum, and the no-negotiations, no-concessions policy is likely to be at its most effective. Even in the barricade-and-hostage situation, however, several caveats should be noted. First a no-negotiations policy should never mean no discussions with the kidnapers. On the contrary, recent experience—such as the South Moluccan incident—indicates the crucial importance of constantly communicating with the kidnapers and maintaining steady psychological pressure on them to induce them to surrender. Psychologists believe that the longer the kidnapers are confined with their victims, the less likely they are to kill them, if for no other reason than that the kidnapers and their victims come to know and sometimes even to like each other.

Second, although the no-concessions policy often has maximum utility in the barricade-and-hostage situation, even here there may be exceptions. Assume, for example, that kidnapers succeed in taking over the British mission to the United Nations and hold the British, French, and German prime ministers hostage. Assume further that after discussions with the kidnapers, and a study of their past records, it appears that there is a great risk that they will kill their hostages unless they are granted certain concessions. In such a situation, it is submitted, it would be unwise, if not irresponsible, to adhere adamantly to a no-concessions policy. At a minimum, the international repercussions of doing so would be enormous. This is not to say that even in this situation, the U.S. government should immediately grant all the kidnapers' demands. Rather, the government should negotiate with the kidnapers and attempt to work out the best deal it possibly can, *i.e.*, a deal that involves granting a bare minimum of concessions. Publishing the terrorists' manifesto and granting them safe passage out of the country in particular might qualify as negotiable demands.

Different considerations arise in the traditional kidnaping situation. Here the government's bargaining leverage is weak, and the kidnapers' leverage is at its maximum strength. The kidnapers are in a position where they may kill the diplomat if their demands are refused with minimal risk that such killing will result in their punishment. The record indicates, moreover, that adamant refusal to grant any concessions has usually resulted in the diplomat's death.

In the traditional kidnaping situation, it would appear especially important to begin and maintain communications with the kidnapers. As noted previously, this may improve chances that the kidnapers, as they get to know the kidnaped diplomat, will refrain from killing him. Also, as time goes on, the chances that law enforcement authorities will locate the kidnapers' hiding place improve considerably.

Whether these discussions should include negotiations on the kidnapers' demands might depend on the facts of the particular situation. If the demands are modest—e.g., publication of a political manifesto, safe passage out of the country—a good argument can be made that they should be granted to save the life of the diplomat. On the other hand, if the demands include the payment of ransom or the release of political prisoners, they should not be granted unless the kidnaped diplomat is regarded as so important as to require taking extraordinary measures. It may be unpleasant to contemplate that the life of one official may be worth more to the U.S. government than that of another, but there is no denying that such may be the case.

With regard to recommendations for possible changes in policy, a distinction should be made between *stated* policy and the policy applied in the context of an actual diplomatic kidnaping. As to stated policy, the State Department should continue to announce that it will grant no concessions to terrorists. In effect, this statement will constitute the department's initial bargaining position if the kidnaping of a diplomat occurs. However, the department should quietly discontinue its reference to "no negotiations." The "no negotiations" phrase is a recent addition to U.S. policy statements, and government officials have not always consistently coupled it with "no concessions." As mentioned earlier, the phrase "no negotiations" is inherently ambiguous and imprecise. If it is interpreted to mean "no discussions" with terrorists, it is inappropriate and indeed dangerous to the kidnaped diplomat. If it means that the State Department will not negotiate with terrorists on concessions, it is redundant. At any rate, if the government engages in discussions with kidnapers, it is thereby negotiating with them, if only in an effort to convince them that they should release the kidnaped diplomat.

As to the appropriate policy to be followed in a diplomatic kidnaping, the Department of State should take a low-key public position and *not* reiterate its no-concessions policy in its reaction to the incident. Rather, the department should announce to the public simply that it has the matter under advisement or, if pressed, that its "policy regarding such matters is well known." What should be avoided are categorical statements of no negotiations or no concessions that might create a danger that the kidnapers will kill their victim or that, at a minimum, might restrict the government's flexibility in responding to the crisis.

The no-concessions policy—or any other policy, for that matter—should not be applied in a rigid, inflexible manner, but should rather be adaptable to individual circumstances. Some of the variables, among others, that the State Department should consider before it determines what action it should take might include the nature of the concessions demanded; the likelihood that the kidnapers will kill their victim if their demands are refused; the possibility of extending the discussions (negotiations) with the kidnapers and thereby enhancing the chances of finding their hideout; and the likely repercussions—both domestic and international—if the kidnaped diplomat is killed.

It is submitted further that the State Department's primary goal in kidnaping cases should be the safe return of the diplomat. If the facts indicate that the diplomat will be killed unless concessions are granted, they should be granted, unless, to be blunt, the "price is too high," or unless all available evidence supports the proposition that refusal to grant the concessions will deter future kidnapings and thereby greatly enhance the protection of all diplomats.

Department officials claim that they have "repeated, convincing evidence that our government's no negotiations, no concessions policies are widely known by terrorist groups abroad, that they are believed, and that they are having important deterrent effect."[174] However, several recent studies, at a minimum, question the deterrent effect of this policy. The data presently available are insufficient to judge the effectiveness of the policy, but the State Department should carefully evaluate the findings and conclusions of these studies to determine whether its original premises regarding the deterrent effects of the present policy are correct. As suggested earlier, there are reasons other than deterrence for adhering to a hard-line approach. But at a minimum, the deterrent effect or lack thereof of any particular policy is one important factor to be considered in those difficult moments when one is deciding how to react to a diplomatic kidnaping. The final judgment on the deterrent effect of present policy should be made only after a full consideration of all available data.

Bilateral and Regional Actions

Bilateral actions by the United States may prove especially effective as measures toward the protection of diplomats. The models for such action might be the recently ratified extradition treaty between the United States and Canada[175] and the 1973 "Memorandum of Understanding" between the United States and Cuba concerning the hijacking of aircraft and vessels.[176]

Article 4(2)(i) of the U.S.-Canadian extradition treaty provides that "[a] kidnaping, murder or other assault against the life or physical integrity of a person to whom a Contracting Party has the duty according to international law to give special protection, or any attempt to commit such an offense with respect to any such person" is not to be considered a political offense for purposes of the treaty. By this provision, the two governments have agreed to refuse political asylum to fugitives wanted in either country for an attempted or actual attack on a diplomat and to extradite such fugitives back to the requesting country unless some exception other than the political offense exception to extradition under the treaty should be applicable.

Under article 1 of the treaty, each party agrees to extradite to the other party persons found in its territory who have been charged with, or convicted of, offenses specified in the treaty and "committed within the territory of the other; or outside thereof under the conditions specified in Article 3(3) of this Treaty." Article 3(3) of the treaty states:

When the offense for which extradition has been requested has been committed outside the territory of the requesting state, the executive or other appropriate authority of the requested state shall have the power to grant the extradition if the laws of the requested state provide for jurisdiction over such an offense committed in similar circumstances.

Since both the United States and Canada now have legislation establishing extraterritorial jurisdiction over attacks on diplomats, requests for extradition of persons charged with such an offense should be granted in most instances.

The Department of State may find it possible to revise other extradition treaties along the lines of the U.S.-Canadian model and should seek to do so as a matter of priority. In some instances, however, especially with respect to countries with a strong tradition of granting political asylum, the United States may find the other party to the extradition treaty unwilling to agree to a categorical exclusion of attacks on diplomats from the political offense category. If so, the United States should turn to the U.S.-Cuba Anti-Hijacking Memorandum as the model, even though the memorandum was terminated on April 15, 1977, pursuant to Cuba's denunciation.[177]

The language of the U.S.-Cuba Memorandum is instructive. The first article provides that any person who hijacks an aircraft or vessel registered under the laws of one party and brings it to the territory of the other party shall either be returned to the party of registry of the aircraft or vessel or "be brought before the courts of the party whose territory he reached for trial in conformity with its laws for the offense punishable by the most severe penalty according to the circumstances and the seriousness of the acts to which this Article refers." In other words, the memorandum incorporates the *aut dedere, aut judicare* principle.[178] It does so, however, in a more meaningful way than does article 7 of the U.N. Convention. Unlike article 7, the memorandum requires that the accused person actually be submitted to trial for the "offense punishable by the most severe penalty" and not just "for the purpose of prosecution."

The second article of the memorandum is also noteworthy. It requires each party to try "with a view to severe punishment" any person who, "within its territory, hereafter conspires to promote, or promotes, or prepares, or directs, or forms part of an expedition which from its territory or any other place carries out acts of violence or depredation against aircraft or vessels of any kind or registration coming from or going to the territory of the other party or . . . carries out such acts or other similar unlawful acts in the territory of the other party." By this article, each party expressly recognizes an affirmative obligation to prevent the use of its territory as a base for committing the illegal acts covered by the memorandum.

The Department of State should seek agreement on a bilateral basis on the insertion of provisions along the lines of the first and second articles in the U.S.-Cuba Memorandum—modified to apply to attacks on diplomats rather than to aircraft or vessel hijacking—either in extradition treaties or in separate agreements or "understandings." In quiet negotiations, not subject to the glare of publicity accompanying U.N. deliberations, the United States might reach agreements for the protection of diplomats with countries that will never—or at least not until some time in the distant future—become parties to the U.N. Convention.

With regard to regional action, on November 10, 1976, the Council of Europe adopted the European Convention on the Suppression of Terrorism.[179] Under article 1 of the convention, a variety of terrorist actions are excluded from being considered as political offenses, including "a serious offense involving an attack against the life, physical security or liberty of internationally protected persons, including diplomatic agents." Article 7 sets forth the principle of *aut dedere, aut judicare* in language along the lines of that of article 7 of the U.N. Convention. However, article 7 of the European Convention adds the important sentence found in the Hague and Montreal conventions: "Those authorities shall take their decision in the same manner as in the case of any offense of a serious nature under the law of that State."

At the same time, in article 5, the convention evinces concern for the rights of the accused:

Nothing in this Convention shall be interpreted as imposing an obligation to extradite if the requested State has substantial grounds for believing that the request for extradition for an offence mentioned in Article 1 or 2 has been made for the purpose of prosecuting or punishing a person on account of his race, religion, nationality or political opinion, or that that person's position may be prejudiced for any of these reasons.

On the basis of similar grounds, under article 8(a) of the convention, one state may refuse to render another mutual assistance in criminal matters.

Under article 13 of the convention, a state may make a reservation to extradition for article 1 offenses that it may consider to be political. However, if a state does so, it must:

take into due consideration, when evaluating the character of the offence, any particularly serious aspects of the offence, including:

a. that it created a collective danger to life, physical integrity or liberty of persons; or
b. that it affected persons foreign to the motives behind it; or
c. that cruel or vicious means have been used in the commission of the offence.

Also, even if a reserving state should refuse to extradite an accused on the political offense ground, it presumably would remain under an obligation pursuant to article 7 of the convention, to submit him to the appropriate authorities for prosecution.

In its present form, the convention is open to signature only by member states of the Council of Europe. Reportedly, a majority of the committee that drafted the convention was at one time in favor of the convention being open to nonmember states as well. It is thus possible, although admittedly unlikely, that the convention might be revised at some future date to allow nonmember state participation. In any event, the Department of State should keep itself fully informed of developments concerning this convention and be prepared to give comments on its provisions if, in light of all the circumstances, this would seem appropriate. If the convention were to be opened to nonmember states, the department should consider whether the United States's signature and ratification would contribute to the convention's becoming an effective "Atlantic" measure for the protection of diplomats. At a minimum, the convention may serve as a model for future bilateral or regional agreements or eventually for U.N. action.[180]

Multilateral or Global Actions

Now that the United States has ratified the U.N. Convention, the Department of State should undertake a worldwide diplomatic effort to convince as many countries as possible to become parties. As the convention has come into force, the department also should work with the other parties and with the secretary-general, with a view to enhancing prospects that the convention will fully realize its potential as a measure for the protection of diplomats.

Specifically, the department should urge the other parties to report to the secretary-general on the steps they have taken to carry out their obligations under the convention, including the adoption of national legislation and other measures. The secretary-general should be requested to make the data submitted to him available to states parties to the convention and to other interested states.

The State Department should also utilize the secretary-general and the U.N. secretariat to exchange data and ideas among states parties to the convention and other interested countries concerning security measures for the prevention of attacks on diplomats and strategies and tactics for dealing with the kidnapers of diplomats. These areas do not lend themselves well to the conclusion of formal international agreements. However, it might be feasible and desirable to work out informal arrangements between government officials in appropriate countries.

At this time it is recommended that the State Department make no efforts to reach agreement with other parties to the convention on a system of sanctions against states that grant safe haven to terrorists who attack diplomats. Future developments may force a re-evaluation of this conclusion, or at the very least suggest that states parties might wish to make a joint protest to the offending country. For the present, however, it would appear preferable to wait and see whether the spirit that resulted in the convention's being adopted by consensus in the General Assembly will obviate the consideration of the drastic step of sanctions.

Finally, there is the question of state liability for injury to diplomats. Although it is generally accepted that a receiving state owes an especially high duty of care with respect to the protection of diplomats, and there is some support for the proposition that a standard of strict liability governs in situations involving successful attacks on diplomats,[181] on balance, the "fault" standard of state liability appears to apply in the event of injuries to diplomats as it does in the case of injuries to other aliens.

The International Law Commission is currently considering the subject of state responsibility. Article 11 of a draft prepared by Roberto Ago, special rapporteur on the subject, would provide for state responsibility for acts of individuals injuring aliens where the state "ought to have acted to prevent or punish the conduct of the individual or group of individuals and failed to do so."[182] This provision would thus maintain the "fault" standard of state liability for injuries to aliens.

It is recommended that the State Department consider whether a strict liability standard may not be more appropriate for determining a receiving state's liability for an injury or damages within its territory to a diplomat or diplomatic premises. It is beyond this chapter's scope to go into a detailed discussion of the merits of such a proposition. However, it is submitted that the concept of strict liability for injuries to diplomats is worthy of further study for the following primary reasons.

1. By the OAS and U.N. conventions, as well as by earlier conventions, the diplomat has been recognized to require special protection beyond that accorded to the ordinary alien.

2. While strict state liability for injuries to aliens by private individuals might constitute an unacceptable burden on states—in view of the immense amount of business and travel in today's world community—the same considerations may not apply to diplomats. Admittedly, the situation of the developing countries would constitute a special problem. But their problems with a strict

liability standard might be resolved or at least mitigated if the standard were coupled with technical assistance to developing countries in regard to security measures for the protection of diplomats. Another possible method of meeting the developing countries' needs might be to set up an international system of liability insurance, with special benefits for the less-developed countries.

3. At least some of the policy reasons that have supported the extension of strict liability standards in domestic tort law may be present in the case of an injury to a diplomat. For example, the diplomat carries on a function of substantial benefit to the receiving country. In spite of all reasonable precautions being taken by the receiving country, an injury to a diplomat by a private person may nonetheless occur. The question then arises about who or what should bear the burden of these injuries: the diplomat, the sending state, or the receiving state. A good argument can be made that it should be the receiving state. Holding the receiving state liable on a strict liability basis might encourage receiving states to maximize efforts to provide for the security of diplomats. The receiving state should be able, perhaps in some cases with the assistance of developed countries, to make provision through insurance or bonds for compensation to the sending state if injury in fact occurs to its diplomat. Through a system of international liability insurance, it would be possible for the receiving state to spread the risk of an injury to a diplomat within its territory among the members of the world community.

On the other hand, cogent arguments can be made against establishing a strict liability standard for the receiving state. For example, if a receiving state were to be held liable for an injury to a diplomat within its territory regardless of fault, it could be argued that this would prompt terrorists to attack diplomats in an effort to bankrupt the receiving state's government. Although a system of international liability insurance might minimize the potential economic burden on developing countries, the argument continues, it would also defeat the deterrence goal of the strict liability standard. With such insurance available, many countries might relax their security standards or be more willing to grant kidnapers' demands for ransom, thereby encouraging terrorists to engage in diplomatic kidnapings.

It should be emphasized that this is *not* a proposal that strict state liability for injuries to diplomats be established. Rather, the proposal is that the concept be studied with care. If, after such study, strict state liability for injuries to diplomats appears feasible, the department might consider introducing a proposal to that effect in the deliberations of the International Law Commission.

Notes

1. *See, e.g.*, C. WILSON, DIPLOMATIC PRIVILEGES AND IMMUNITIES (1967); E. PLISCHKE, CONDUCT OF AMERICAN DIPLOMACY (1967); E. SATOW, GUIDE TO DIPLOMATIC PRACTICE (1958).

2. C. WILSON, *supra* note 1, at 1.

3. *Id.*

4. *Id.* at 1-2.

5. *Id.* at 5.

6. *Id.*

7. *Id.* at 16.

8. *Id.* at 17-25.

9. 23 U.S.T. 3227, T.I.A.S. No. 7502, 50 U.N.T.S. 95 (1965).

10. 21 U.S.T. 77, T.I.A.S. No. 6820, 596 U.N.T.S. 261 (1973).

11. 1 U.N.T.S. 16 (1949).

12. 21 U.N. GAOR Supp. (No. 30) 1, U.N. Doc. A/7630 (1969).

13. U.N. Doc. A/CONF. 67/16 (1975); 69 AM. J. INT'L L. 730 (1975). For a critical commentary on this convention, *see* Fennessy, *The 1975 Vienna Convention on the Representation of States in Their Relations with International Organizations of a Universal Character*, 70 AM. J. INT'L L. 62 (1976).

14. 2 ILC YEARBOOK 97 (1958).

15. *Id.* at 95.

16. *See* C.E. BAUMANN, THE DIPLOMATIC KIDNAPPINGS 4-31 (1973).

17. Shortly before being shot, Welch had been identified as chief of the Athens CIA station by an Athens newspaper and an anti-CIA U.S. publication, *Counterspy.*

18. N.Y. Times, Oct. 25, 1975, at 1, col. 5.

19. Jenkins, Johnson, & Ronfeldt, Numbered Lives: Some Statistical Observations from 77 International Hostage Episodes (Aug. 1975). (Unpublished Rand Corporation study prepared for the Department of State.)

20. *Id.* at 6.

21. *Id.* at 8.

22. *Id.* at 9.

23. For an earlier conclusion to the same effect, *see* C. WILSON, *supra* note 1, at 47.

24. C.E. BAUMANN, *supra* note 16, at 49.

25. The text of the Uruguayan law was very kindly provided by William S. Kenney, President, American Section, International Association of Penal Law.

26. 19 THE AMERICAN SERIES OF FOREIGN PENAL CODES, THE PENAL CODE OF THE POLISH PEOPLE'S REPUBLIC 111-12 (1973).

27. *See, e.g.*, INDIA PEN. CODE § 4.

28. The text of article 7 of the Danish Penal Law may be found in Summary of Responses to Department of State Circular Airgram Regarding Law and Practice on Terrorism, Denmark, 1 (Dec. 1975) [hereinafter cited as Circular, name of country, page, and date of summary].

29. Harvard Research in International Law, *Introductory Comment, Jurisdiction with Respect to Crime*, 29 AM. J. INT'L L. 435, 445 (Supp. 1935). *See also* Letter from Mr. Bayard, Secretary of State, to Mr. Connery, Chargé to Mexico, FOREIGN REL. U.S. 751 (1888); 2 J. MOORE, INTERNATIONAL LAW 232-40 (1906).

30. The text of the Mexican law was very kindly provided by William S. Kenney, President, American Section, International Association of Penal Law.

31. Circular, Mexico, 2 (Aug. 7, 1975), *supra* note 28.

32. Circular, Denmark, 1 (Apr. 1976), *supra* note 28.

33. For example, the French Code of Criminal Procedure provides: "Every foreigner who outside the territory of the Republic renders himself guilty, either as perpetrator or as accomplice, of a felony or misdemeanor against the security of the state ... may be prosecuted and tried according to the provisions of French law if he is arrested in France or if the Government obtains his extradition." C. PR. PEN. art. 694 (13 ed. Petits Codes Dalloz 1971), cited in Sahovic & Bishop, *The Authority of the State: Its Range with Respect to Persons and Places*, in MANUAL OF PUBLIC INTERNATIONAL LAW 363 (M. Sorensen ed. 1968).

34. RESTATEMENT (SECOND) OF FOREIGN RELATIONS LAW, § 33 (1965).

35. *See* note, *Extraterritorial Jurisdiction and Jurisdiction Following Forcible Abduction: A New Israel Precedent in International Law*, 72 MICH. L. REV. 1087, 1088 (1974).

36. *Id.*

37. *Id.* at 1092.

38. *Id.*

39. Examples would include war crimes, slave trading, and traffic in women and children. Also, airplane hijacking and airplane sabotage have been made subject to a limited form of universal jurisdiction by the Hague and Montreal conventions. *Id.* at 1097-98.

40. *Id.* at 1099.

41. Pub. L. No. 92-539. These amendments have been codified in various sections of Title 18. *See especially* § §, 112, 113, 970, 1116, 1201, 1202.

42. Under § 1116, subpara. (c)(3), " 'family' includes (a) a spouse, parent, brother or sister, child, or person to whom the foreign official stands in loco parentis, or (b) any other person living in his household and related to the foreign official by blood or marriage."

43. Subsection (c)(4).

44. *See* 3 U.S. CODE CONG. AND ADMIN. NEWS, at 4318, 92d Cong., 2nd Sess. (1972) (Statement of Senator McClellan).

45. *Id.* at 4317-18.

46. *Id.* at 4317.

47. 22 D.C. Code § 1115 (Supp. 1975).

48. The facts of the *Lechoco* case, as set forth in the following text, are taken from the transcript of sentencing proceedings, which took place on August 22, 1975, before the District Court for the District of Columbia, the Honorable Howard F. Corcoran presiding (hereinafter cited as "Proceedings"), and from Judge Corcoran's Findings of Fact and Conclusions of Law, dated August 25,

1975. These documents were supplied the writer by Louis G. Fields, Assistant Legal Adviser for Special Functional Problems, Department of State. Neither of them has been published in the law reports. Upon appeal, in United States v. Lechoco, 542 F.2d 84 (D.C. Cir. 1976), the Circuit Court of Appeals for the District of Columbia Circuit reversed and remanded the case to the District Court on the ground that it was reversible error for the lower court to exclude proffered testimony relating to defendant's truthfulness during the cross-examination of psychiatrists who testified in support of the defendant's insanity defense and that the issue was crucial to defendant's guilt or innocence. However, the Circuit Court did not question any of the other findings of fact or conclusions of law made by Judge Corcoran.

49. Proceedings, *supra* note 48, at 10.

50. *Id.*

51. *Id.* at 19.

52. The conventional sources on which the writer has primarily relied include: Fearey, *International Terrorism*, 74 DEP'T STATE BULL. 394 (Mar. 29, 1976); Baumann, *The Diplomatic Kidnappings: An Overview*, INTERNATIONAL TERRORISM 30 (1974); J.B. BELL, TRANSNATIONAL TERROR 79-89 (1975).

53. Effective security measures in this area need not take sophisticated technological form. In Great Britain, letter bomb incidents fell off sharply after authorities made mailbox slots smaller and thus less able to accommodate bombs. Wall St. J., Jan. 4, 1977, at 1, col. 1.

54. Circular, Australia, 1, (Aug. 7, 1975), *supra* note 28.

55. Remarks made by Robert A. Fearey, Special Assistant to the Secretary of State and Coordinator for Combatting Terrorism, during an informal briefing session at the Department of State, January 14, 1975. Reportedly, the Department of State has spent $15 million to $19 million per year since 1974 on added protection for its overseas diplomats. Wall St. J., Jan. 4, 1977, at 1, col. 1.

56. *Senate Report No. 92-1105 on P.L. 92-539*, U.S. CODE CONG. AND ADMIN. NEWS at 4317, 92d Cong., 2nd Sess. (1972).

57. U.N. Doc. A/AC.154/36 (1974).

58. Secretariat Note on Security of Missions and Safety of Their Personnel, U.N. Doc. A/AC.154/23 (1974).

59. J.B. BELL, *supra* note 52, at 84.

60. Pub. L. No. 94-196, 3 U.S.C.A. § § 202, 209 (Supp. 1976).

61. N.Y. Times, April 7, 1976, at 7, col. 7.

62. *Id.*

63. *Id.*

64. C. WILSON, *supra* note 1, at 49.

65. *See* Baumann, *supra* note 52, at 37; Jenkins, Johnson, & Ronfeldt, *supra* note 19, at 28. On March 22, 1974, U.S. Vice-Consul John Patterson was

kidnaped in the Northern Mexican city of Hermosillo. A few hours later a note in his handwriting demanding a ransom of $500,000 reached the U.S. consulate in Hermosillo. Although Mrs. Patterson put an advertisement in the local newspaper offering to pay the money, the diplomat was later found murdered. On March 7, 1975, in the Federal District Court for the Southern District of San Diego, one Bobby Joe Keesen pleaded guilty to a charge of conspiracy to kidnap a diplomat. On April 28, 1975, he was sentenced to 20 years in prison. Interestingly, the court relied on United States v. Erdos, 474 F.2d 157 (4th Cir. 1973) (District Court had jurisdiction under the special maritime territorial jurisdiction of the U.S., 18 U.S.C. § 7, to try a U.S. citizen for a crime committed within a U.S. embassy located in a foreign country) in upholding its jurisdiction over Keesen, stressing in addition Mr. Patterson's status as the security officer of the U.S. consulate (*see* 18 U.S.C. § 7). The decision in the case, Criminal No. 74-1736, had not been published at the time of writing.

66. For example, on January 22, 1973, terrorists kidnaped the U.S. ambassador to Haiti and held him hostage along with the U.S. consul general. The kidnapers originally demanded the release of 30 prisoners and a ransom of $1 million. However, in subsequent negotiations they agreed to accept the release of 12 prisoners and $70,000. The kidnapers released their hostages after 18 hours and flew with the released prisoners to Mexico. Jenkins, Johnson, & Ronfeldt, *supra* note 19, at 40.

67. This was, for example, the initial reaction of the Canadian government to the demands made by the kidnapers of James Cross, a senior British consular officer. C.E. BAUMANN, *supra* note 16, at 113.

68. Jenkins, Johnson, & Ronfeldt, *supra* note 19, at 10-12.

69. The description of the Cross and Laporte kidnapings that follows in the text is taken largely from C.E. BAUMANN, *supra* note 16, at 111-28.

70. *Id.* at 114, n. 10.

71. *Id.* at 116.

72. *Id.* at 117.

73. Apparently, current U.S. "no-negotiations" policy does not necessarily preclude discussions with kidnapers, but such discussions "are strictly confined to such matters as the well-being of the hostage and to humanitarian and other factors arguing for his unconditional release." Fearey, *supra* note 52, at 398.

74. Jenkins, Johnson, & Ronfeldt, *supra* note 19, at v, 24.

75. N.Y. Times, Dec. 20, 1975, at 3, col. 4.

76. L. BLOOMFIELD & G. FITZGERALD, CRIMES AGAINST INTER-NATIONALLY PROTECTED PERSONS: PREVENTION AND PUNISHMENT 18-22 (1975).

77. N.Y. Times, Dec. 22, 1975, at 1, col. 8.

78. Jenkins, Johnson, & Ronfeldt, *supra* note 19, at 35.

79. THE MITRE CORPORATION, THE THREAT TO LICENSED NU-CLEAR FACILITIES 23 (Sept. 1975) (MTR-7022).

80. Unpublished study made available to the author, courtesy of the Carnegie Endowment for International Peace.

81. Ernest Evans, personal communication to the author.

82. Rozakis, *Terrorism and the Internationally Protected Person in the Light of the ILC's Draft Articles*, 23 INT'L & COMP. L.Q. 32,33 (1974).

83. *Id.* at 41.

84. *See generally*, C.E. BAUMANN, *supra* note 16, at 43-53.

85. *See, e.g.*, the Glenn Case, 3 MOORE, HISTORY AND DIGEST OF THE INTERNATIONAL ARBITRATIONS TO WHICH THE UNITED STATES HAS BEEN A PARTY 3138 (1898); the Cotesworth and Powell Case, *id.* at 2082; the Janes Case, 4 U.N.R.I.A.A.86. Even these cases are not entirely apposite to the question whether the receiving country is under an international duty to try and punish an accused person it has in custody, because they involved factual situations where the host country either failed to take any action whatsoever to apprehend or punish the culprits, or intervened in the judicial process by declaring an amnesty. The relevance, if any, of these cases lies in the expansive language of their opinions stating, for example, that "[t]he culprit is liable for having killed or murdered an American national, the Government [Mexico] is liable for not having measured up to its duty of diligently prosecuting and properly punishing the offender. . . ." The Janes Case, at 86. The writer is unaware of any case expressly stating that a country is under an obligation to place limits on prosecutorial discretion regarding the bringing to trial of offenders who attack aliens. Parenthetically, it should be noted that not all countries grant their prosecutors unlimited discretion. *See* Langbein, *Controlling Prosecutorial Discretion in Germany*, 41 U. CHI. L. REV. 439 (1974).

86. GROTIUS, DEJURE BELLO AC PACIS, bk. ii, ch. XXI, § IV, at 527 (Carnegie Endowment ed.).

87. For general discussions of the political offense doctrine and extradition, *see* M.C. BASSIOUNI, INTERNATIONAL EXTRADITION AND WORLD PUBLIC ORDER 370-487 (1974); 6 M. WHITEMAN, DIGEST OF INTERNATIONAL LAW 799-859 (1968); and Evans, *Reflections upon the Political Offender in International Practice*, 57 AM. J. INT'L L. 1 (1963).

88. *See* Comment, *The Inter-American Convention on the Kidnapping of Diplomats*, 10 COLUM. J. TRANS. L. 392, 393 (1971).

89. OAS Res. AG/Res. 4 (I-E/70) (1970).

90. Comment, *supra* note 88, at 394.

91. *Done* Feb. 2, 1971, T.I.A.S. No. 8413, Serie Sobre Tratados [S.S.T.] No. 37, OAS/Off. Doc. OAS/Ser. A.17 [hereinafter cited as OAS Convention].

92. Comment, *supra* note 88, at 394.

93. *Id.*

94. The parties to the OAS Convention, and the dates of their ratification, are Costa Rica, October 16, 1973; Dominican Republic, May 25, 1976; Mexico, March 17, 1975; Nicaragua, March 8, 1973; Venezuela, November 7, 1973; United States, October 20, 1976.

95. Comment, *supra* note 88, at 397.

96. The convention contains no mention of persons who take part in the conception, preparation, or execution of crimes against diplomats and under article 3, limits measures applicable under the convention to "persons . . . charged or convicted for any of the crimes referred to in Article 2. . . ." By contrast, the draft convention of the Inter-American Juridical Committee had expressly covered coconspirators and accessories not directly involved in the proscribed acts. Article 5, Inter-American Juridical Committee, Draft Convention on Terrorism and Kidnapping of Persons for Extortion, OAS Off. Records/ Ser. G., CP/Doc. 54/70 Rev. 1, at 17-22 (1970) [hereinafter cited as Committee Draft Convention].

97. Comment, *supra* note 88, at 400-01.

98. OAS Convention, *supra* note 91, at art. 2.

99. *See* the opinion of the Inter-American Juridical Committee accompanying the Committee Draft Convention, *supra* note 96, at 10 [hereinafter cited as Committee Opinion].

100. *Id.* at 42.

101. Comment, *supra* note 88, at 406.

102. Quoted in *id.* at 397.

103. Article 1 of the OAS Convention provides that the states parties "undertake to cooperate among themselves by taking all the measures that they may consider effective, under their own laws, and especially those established in this convention, to prevent and punish acts of terrorism, especially kidnapping, murder, and other assaults against the life or physical integrity of those persons to whom the state has the duty according to international law to give special protection, as well as extortion in connection with those crimes." Under article 8(a) and (b), the parties agree "[t]o take all measures within their power, and in conformity with their own laws, to prevent and impede the preparation in their respective territories of the crimes mentioned in Article 2 that are to be carried out in the territory of another contracting state" and "[t]o exchange information and consider effective administrative measures for the purpose of protecting the persons to whom Article 2 of this convention refers."

104. Committee Draft Convention, art. 9, *supra* note 96.

105. To be sure, the OAS Convention could become a global international legal measure. Article 9 provides that the convention "shall remain open for signature by the member states of the Organization of American States, as well as by any other state that is a member of the United Nations or any of its specialized agencies, or any state that is a party to the Statute of the International Court of Justice, or any other state that may be invited by the General Assembly of the Organization of American States to sign it."

106. *See* the Department of State's Statement on the approval by the OAS General Assembly of the OAS Convention, 64 DEP'T STATE BULL. 231 (1971).

107. U.N. Convention on the Prevention and Punishment of Crimes Against Internationally Protected Persons, Including Diplomatic Agents, Dec. 14, 1973, *see* G.A. Res. 3166, 28 U.N. GAOR Supp. (No. 30), U.N. Doc. A/9030 (1973) [hereinafter cited as U.N. Convention].

108. U.N. Doc. A/8791 (1972).

109. U.N. Doc. A/C.6/L. 850 (1972).

110. For a consideration of some of these reasons, *see e.g.*, Murphy, *International Legal Controls of International Terrorism: Performance and Prospects*, 63 ILL. BAR. J. 444 (1975); Franck & Lockwood, *Preliminary Thoughts Toward an International Convention on Terrorism*, 68 AM. J. INT'l L. 69 (1974).

111. These countries included: Brazil, Colombia, Iran, Israel, Jamaica, Kuwait, Niger, Great Britain, Norway, Sweden, the United States, Australia, Canada, Czechoslovakia, Denmark, Japan, Netherlands, Ukrainian SSR, France, Madagascar, Yugoslovia, Ecuador, the Soviet Union, Belgium, Argentina, Cuba, and Rwanda. *See* U.N. Doc. A/CN. 4/253 (1972); U.N. Doc. A/CN.4/253/Add. 1 (1972); U.N. Doc. A/CN.4/253/Add. 2 (1972); U.N. Doc. A/CN.4/253/Add. 3 (1972); U.N. Doc. A/CN.4/253/Add. 4 (1972).

112. These draft conventions included a working paper submitted in 1971 by Uruguay; a draft convention submitted by Richard D. Kearney, chairman of the International Law Commission; and the so-called Rome draft transmitted by Denmark. Other documents that served as primary source material for the U.N. Convention were the Vienna Convention on Diplomatic Relations; the Vienna Convention on Consular Relations; the Convention on Special Missions; the Hague Convention for the Suppression of Unlawful Seizure of Aircraft; the Montreal Convention for the Suppression of Unlawful Acts Against the Safety of Civil Aviation; the OAS Convention; and the International Law Commission's Draft Articles on Representation of states in their relations with international organizations. L. BLOOMFIELD & G. FITZGERALD, *supra* note 76, at 53.

113. U.N. Doc. A/8892, at 4 (1972) [hereinafter cited as the Commission's Draft Articles]. For the text of and commentary on the draft articles, *see* Report of the International Law Commission on the Work of Its Twenty-fourth Session (May 2-July 7, 1972), U.N. Doc. A/8710 (July 22, 1972). The text and commentary are reproduced in 11 INT'L LEGAL MATERIALS 977 (1972).

114. G.A. Res. 2926, 27 U.N. GAOR Supp. (No. 30) 113, U.N. Doc. A/8730 (1973). By letters dated January 31, 1973, the secretary-general, pursuant to the above resolution, requested comments on the draft articles from interested states, specialized agencies, and intergovernmental organizations. U.N. Doc. A/9127, at 4 (1973). For a compilation of the comments and observations of member states on the draft articles, *see* U.N. Doc. A/9127 (1973); U.N. Doc. A/9127/Add. 1 (1973).

115. Int'l L. Comm'n, Report, 27 U.N. GAOR Supp. (No. 10) 90, U.N. Doc. A/8710/Rev. 1 (1972).

116. In particular, *see* L. BLOOMFIELD & G. FITZGERALD, *supra* note 76, at 24. *See also* Wood, *The Convention on the Prevention and Punishment of Crimes Against Internationally Protected Persons, Including Diplomatic Agents*, 23 INT'L & COMP. L.Q. 791 (1974); Rozakis, *supra* note 82; and Note, *Convention on the Prevention and Punishment of Crimes Against Diplomatic Agents and Other Internationally Protected Persons: An Analysis*, 14 VA. J. INT'L L. 705 (1974).

117. U.N. Doc. A/PV.2202, at 112 (1973).

118. U.N. Doc. A/9407, at 11 (1973).

119. U.N. Doc. A/C.6/SR. 1434, at 12 (1973).

120. In the words of the U.S. representative to the General Assembly:

The Legal Committee decided to cover serious crimes, as was the initial intention of the International Law Commission. Subparagraph 1(a) has been clarified so that instead of referring to "violent attack" it refers to "murder," "kidnapping" or "other attack." Obviously, the words "other attack" mean attacks of a similar serious nature to those expressly mentioned—murder and kidnapping. Covering threats, attempts and accessoryship is appropriate, because of the initial seriousness of the acts covered under subparagraph (a) and (b) of paragraph 1. [U.N. Doc. A/PV.2202, at 134 (1973).]

121. The International Law Commission commented on this point as follows:

The word "intentional," which is similar to the requirement found in article 1 of the Montreal Convention, has been used both to make clear that the offender must be aware of the status as an internationally protected person enjoyed by the victim as well as to eliminate any doubt regarding exclusion from the application of the article of certain criminal acts which might otherwise be asserted to fall within the scope of subparagraphs (a) or (b), such as the serious injury of an internationally protected person in an automobile accident as a consequence of the negligence of the other party. [11 INT'L LEGAL MATERIALS 984-85 (1972).]

122. The Commission Draft Articles, art. 2(1), *supra* note 113.

123. Note, *supra* note 116, at 714.

124. Wood, *supra* note 116, at 804.

125. For a recent discussion of theories of international criminal jurisdiction, *see* Bassiouni, *Theories of Jurisdiction and Their Application in Extradition Law and Practice*, 5 CALIF. WEST. INT'L L.J. 1 (1974). *See also* Harvard Research in International Law, *supra* note 29.

126. Wood, *supra* note 116, at 808.

127. *Id.*

128. The Commission's Draft Articles, art. 2(1)(2), *supra* note 113.

129. Note, *supra* note 116, at 715.

130. *Id.*

131. Article 7 of the Hague Convention and article 7 of the Montreal Convention, which contain identical language.

132. *See* note 112, *supra*.

133. L. BLOOMFIELD & G. FITZGERALD, *supra* note 76, at 103.

134. 11 INT'L LEGAL MATERIALS 990 (1972).

135. U.N. Doc. A/PV.2202, at 135-36 (1973).

136. U.N. Convention, art. 4, *supra* note 105.

137. *Id.*, art. 5.

138. *Id.*, art. 6.

139. *Id.*, art. 10.

140. 11 INT'l LEGAL MATERIALS 994 (1972).

141. *Id.*

142. *See, e.g.*, Note, *supra* note 116, at 721.

143. These include: Finland; Tunisia; the German Democratic Republic; Poland; the Soviet Union; Byelorussian SSR; Ukranian SSR; Bulgaria; Mongolia; Ecuador; Czechoslovakia; Hungary; Romania; and Ghana. Department of State, Treaty Record.

144. Under Article 6(1) of the U.N. Convention, the states or international organizations to be notified include: (a) the state where the crime was committed; (b) the state or states of which the alleged offender is a national or, if he is a stateless person, in whose territory he permanently resides; (c) the state or states of which the internationally protected person is a national or on whose behalf he was exercising his functions; (d) all other States concerned; and (e) the international organization of which the internationally protected person concerned is an official or an agent.

145. U.N. Doc. A/9407, at 63, 64 (1973).

146. *Id.* at 50.

147. *See* Wood, *supra* note 116, at 787-98.

148. Note, *supra* note 116, at 727.

149. U.N. Doc. A/PV.2202, at 26 (1973).

150. Circular, Belgium, 2 (Sept. 1975), *supra* note 28.

151. Based on a list supplied the writer by the Office of the Legal Adviser, Department of State.

152. Pub. L. No. 93-366; 49 U.S.C.A. § 1514 (Supp. 1976).

153. Pub. L. No. 94-329 § 620A, 22 U.S.C.A. § 2371 (Supp. 1976).

154. Professor Thomas M. Franck has proposed a "Draft Convention of the Duty of States Not to Encourage International Terrorism by Complying with Terrorist Demands," which, as the title implies, would require states parties to take a very hard-line position in negotiating with terrorists. It would, in article 4, prohibit absolutely the accession to demands of terrorists that involve: (a) release of prisoners held in accordance with process of law; (b) making available weapons, ammunition, implements of violence, financial help, or means of

transportation; (c) granting safe passage out of the country; or (d) granting refueling rights to an aircraft unlawfully seized. Remarks by T. Franck in CANADIAN COUNCIL ON INTERNATIONAL LAW, PROCEEDINGS OF THIRD ANNUAL CONFERENCE 180-81 (1974).

155. *See Statement by President Ford*, 75 DEP'T STATE BULL. 554 (Nov. 1, 1976).

156. For a summary of the 1976 amendments, *see Internationally Protected Persons Bills Unsworn Declarations Bills: Hearing on H.R. 12942, H.R. 13709, H.R. 11106, and H.R. 11217 Before the Subcomm. on Criminal Justice of the House Comm. on the Judiciary*, 94th Cong., 2d Sess. 14 (1976) (statement of Jay C. Waldman) [hereinafter cited as *Internationally Protected Persons*].

157. As to attacks on the official premises, private accommodation, or means of transport of an internationally protected person, *see* 18 U.S.C. § 112 (a).

158. HOUSE COMM. ON THE JUDICIARY, IMPLEMENTING INTERNATIONAL CONVENTIONS AGAINST TERRORISM, H.R. REP. NO. 94-1614, 94th Cong., 2d Sess. 1, *reprinted in Internationally Protected Persons, supra* note 156, at 71.

159. *Id.* at 85.

160. *Id.* at 84.

161. *Id.*

162. *Id.* at 85.

163. Statement of Jay C. Waldman, *supra* note 156, at 16.

164. *Id.* at 16-17.

165. Jenkins, Johnson, & Ronfeldt, *supra* note 19, at v.

166. *See* Murphy, *supra* note 110, at 449.

167. U.N. Convention *supra* note 107, preamble, para. 2.

168. The question of the innocence, or lack thereof, of diplomats has arisen. *See* note 102 *supra* and accompanying text.

169. Circular, Jordan, 1 (Oct. 10, 1975), *supra* note 28.

170. N.Y. Times, Dec. 28, 1976, § 4, at 2, col. 1.

171. *See* Lillich, *Requiem for Hickenlooper*, 69 AM. J. INT'L. L. 97 (1975).

172. *Anti-Hijacking Act of 1973, Hearings on H.R. 3858 Before the Subcomm. on Transportation and Aeronautics of the House Comm. on Interstate and Foreign Commerce*, 93d Cong., 1st Sess., pt. 1, at 406, 407 (statement of Mark Feldman, Acting Deputy Legal Adviser, Department of State).

173. *Id.*

174. Fearey, *supra* note 52, at 398-99.

175. The report of ratification of the treaty may be found in N.Y. Times, March 25, 1976, at 10, col. 7. The text of the treaty may most conveniently be found in 65 DEP'T STATE BULL. 741, 744-46 (1971) and in 11 INT'L LEGAL MATERIALS 22 (1972).

176. Cuba-United States Memorandum of Understanding on the Hijacking of Aircraft and Vessels, 68 DEP'T STATE BULL. 260 (1973); 12 INT'L LEGAL MATERIALS 370 (1973).

177. *See* Washington Post, Oct. 19, 1976 (editorial), at A18, col. 1.

178. In 1975, Cuba reportedly returned three U.S. citizens who allegedly had hijacked planes to Cuba to the United States by way of transfer to FBI agents in Barbados, in order that they might be subject to prosecution here. Washington Post, June 3, 1975, at 11, col. 1.

179. The text of the Convention may most conveniently be found at 15 INT'L LEGAL MATERIALS 1272 (Nov. 1976).

180. *See* a suggestion to this effect in the report prepared for the Department of State by the Procedural Aspects of International Law Institute, SANCTUARY AND SAFE-HAVEN FOR TERRORISTS: THE RELEVANCY OF INTERNATIONAL LAW 37 (Dec. 1976).

181. *See* the arbitral decisions and other sources cited and analyzed in Lillich & Paxman, *State Responsibility for Injuries to Aliens Occasioned by Terrorist Activities*, 26 AM. U.L. REV. 217, 232-35, 249-51 (1977).

182. [1972] 2 Y.B. INT'L L. COMM'N 126, U.N. Doc. A/CN.4/Ser.A/ 1972/Add. 1 (1974).

"Nonprotected" Persons or Things

Jordan J. Paust

Introduction

The Problem: Protection

This chapter directs prior analysis by this writer to a more detailed consideration of the protection of "nonprotected" persons or things from impermissible terroristic violence.[1] By "nonprotected" persons or things, the author refers to those without some *special* status or protection under international law. All persons are protected by international human rights law and also, in time of armed conflict, by the law of war;[2] but here the term is used in contrast to "internationally protected persons," *i.e.*, diplomats and other specially protected persons.[3]

The fundamental problem is that even though legal rules protect ordinary citizens from terrorist attacks or the effects of such attacks, formal rules of international and domestic law are themselves inadequate.[4] The norms exist; the problem is that these norms must become more effective and restraints must be placed on the targeting of, or the spillover injuries that affect, the general populace.

Another problem arises from the fact that terrorism against nonprotected persons and things is being reported with increasing frequency in the media. Attacks are directed at children; shoppers; hotel, restaurant, and bar patrons; workers; postal facilities; trains; civil aircraft; athletes; historic sites; leftists; party and union offices; businessmen; mayors; policemen; and others throughout the world.[5] However, the distinction in status often drawn between combatants and noncombatants in "law-of-war" contexts, is seldom underlined in certain cases of terrorism. When reference is made to the permissibility of targeting under the laws of war, many people may fail to differentiate between "official" targets, such as governmental officials and policemen, and nonofficial targets.[6] Indeed, an alarming laxity of any distinction and a blurring of even feigned categories is on the increase as self-justifying claims to use terrorism against more of the ordinary citizenry gain acceptance among those who would resort to violence for personal or political advancement or change.

A recent study by T.R. Gurr of targeting by terrorists for the 1961 to 1970 period concludes that persons "who are the most likely targets of terrorist action are leading politicians and officials, with the military and police coming in second."[7] Most of these persons would not be specially protected under international law and many would be proper military targets in time of war. This points to a possible trend during the 1960s in which more "combatant"-oriented non-specially-protected persons were targeted. But Gurr's study also discloses that "noncombatants" (excluding military and police) suffered injuries in some 54 percent of all cases.[8] He adds: "Security forces and the terrorists suffered casualties in only a small fraction of cases—14 percent in each instance."[9] Thus, Gurr concludes, the one lesson to be drawn "is that political terrorism has been a relatively low-risk tactic for those who use it. Rioting and guerrilla warfare—two alternative forms of violent political action—can be shown to cause disproportionately large numbers of casualties among rioters and guerrillas by comparison with either the security forces or, usually, noncombatants."[10] Another lesson evident in these statistics is that when terrorism is used against non-specially-protected persons, injury and suffering are shifted somewhat from terrorist precipitators and combatant targets to the general populace. This trend in casualties indicates the general problem—that even though terrorists may have valid ideological or political grievances against combatant targets in nonwar contexts, the noncombatant elements of the populace are the ones who bear the brunt of the injuries and suffering. Another aspect of the problem involves the fact that some elite and counterelite groups strongly argue against the need for legal or humanistic distinctions to be drawn between targets in certain contexts.

Possible Solutions

The effective implementation of laws designed to protect nonprotected persons rests, in part, on a re-emphasis by concerned governments of human rights and the impermissibility of general excuses for violence and illegality. This is of critical import because it is far more difficult, if not generally impossible, for the police or the military to protect the general citizenry effectively than to protect government officials or even specific private industries or persons.[11] An ideologically based strategy may provide the *best* overall protection; further, it can be utilized where military, economic, and diplomatic strategies are generally insufficient.[12] Counterterror and counterassassination by the FBI[13] or the CIA will only be counterproductive in the long run as distinctions in targeting become blurred and a spiraling illegality of death squad warfare results.[14]

The use of current rhetoric, such as "just" and "unjust" struggle, "self-determination" struggles, "worker" struggles, "guerrilla" tactics, "innocent" and "noninnocent" persons, "oppressors," and the like must be addressed.[15] If law prohibits the justification of terroristic violence by such rhetoric, then one way to protect nonprotected people more effectively is to devise ideologic and diplomatic strategies that utilize education, public opinion, advice, communication, promotion, and prescription to counter simplistic justifications based on dichotomous distinctions between the "just" and the "unjust," the "oppressors" and the "oppressed," and so forth. Similarly, other broad excuses for murder and human suffering must be opposed. However, the rationale of terrorism rests on more than ideological rhetoric. Therefore to be realistic and effective, responses to terrorism must not ignore other conditions (predispositional and physical) that spawn the use of terrorism by private or public persons, groups, and institutions because these conditions can also be addressed and reoriented to prevent terrorism or to defeat its efficacy as a strategy to control patterns of thought and behavior.

To facilitate approaches to solution, this inquiry will adopt several jurisprudential insights and guidelines set forth by Myres McDougal and Harold Lasswell in a general theory about law, including the use of various sociological tools. By using these guidelines, new insights into present legal deficiencies may assure a more realistic, policy-serving effort to provide recommended alternatives.[16]

Targeting: The Question of "Innocence"

Words that have appeared in recent debates and studies on the general question of international terrorism such as "innocent" or "indiscriminate" seem to evince a groping for a legal distinction between direct attacks on noncombatants, attacks on combatants, and indiscriminate uses of armed violence. The use of the word "innocent" in reference to targeting or protection has permeated recent governmental statements on the general question of international terrorism. It is not clear, however, if these states actually intended to hinge the question of permissibility on such a nebulous concept, or if they even considered the policy ramifications of the implied opposite of "innocent"—namely, "guilty"—with its potential for divergent moral, political, and ideological applications as well as the summary decisional procedures it could engender. Most likely, the word "innocent" has merely been repeated from the use made in the Secretary-General's Report on Terrorism.[17] This practice could have dangerous implications, for the word "innocent" is fraught with human rights problems connected with the prohibition, under the law of war, of summary executions, and related prohibitions under general human rights law of the denial of a fair trial.[18]

Compared with the word "innocent," the use of the word "indiscriminate" is less extensive, and no clear consensus as to its criterial values has been reached.[19] Nevertheless, this word has been used in the law-of-war context to distinguish between discriminate attacks on combatants and indiscriminate attacks on the general population, or between permissible and impermissible targets. By considering words found primarily in the normative content of the law of war—words such as "object of attack," "incidental," and "indiscriminate"—we obtain some identifiable goal values and criteria for arriving at a rational and comprehensive decision in cases involving terror outcomes and effects resulting from attacks on impermissible targets. These goal values are further clarified by the use of the general law-of-war principles of proportionality, humane treatment, and the avoidance of unnecessary suffering, including the requirements of protection and respect for persons protected by Geneva law. Further, they provide a useful consensus for future decisions about impermissible forms of terrorism.

When making formal speeches, phrases such as states and persons "not directly involved" in the conflict, persons "unconnected with—or not responsible for—the basic cause of the grievance," and "third states" are also used.[20] However, the use of such phrases in commenting on international terrorism is strikingly imprecise and unhelpful. Most of the comments are short and vague, perhaps intentionally so. Considerations of human rights law and other legal norms are often absent from these statements.

It is important to note that a great deal of the philosophic and ideological literature seeking to justify acts of terrorism against nonprotected persons contains exculpatory references to concepts of "innocence" and "noninnocence" or to related distinctions between the "oppressed" and the "oppressors."[21] Much of this literature states the truism that none of us are purely "innocent." But it takes a giant ideological leap to conclude that, after all, no one should stand in the way of "the revolution" or of the state, *all* people are expendable, and the terrorist murder of noninnocents is a good thing.[22] Thus "defined," the incidents at My Lai, Athens, Lod Airport, Dacca, Jerusalem, Belfast, Ghinda (Ethiopia), Kuala Lumper (Malaysia), Tanzania's animal research center, Djibouti (East Africa), Holland, and elsewhere are supposed to be justifiable, but they are not. The simple blurring of "innocence" and "oppression" not only weakens the inhibiting impact guilt may have on a terrorist contemplating bombing a marketplace, or killing Olympic athletes, nurses, or children and babies, but it also undermines the humanistic distinctions that are fundamental to law and society.[23]

The danger posed by referring to "innocence" as justifying terror is that ideological literature often takes giant leaps through shadings of "guilt" or "innocence" and leaves potential terrorists with all the justifications they require. When Mao Tse-tung stated that "politics is war without bloodshed while war is politics with bloodshed,"[24] and others add that "an honest man today must consider the liberal as the true enemy of mankind,"[25] then leftist terrorists know full well, as do their rightist death squad counterparts in Argentina and elsewhere, that it is perfectly proper to kill and terrorize. As Kwame Nkrumah adds: "all propaganda media must convey the following ideas, encouragement and information . . . the struggle to the death against . . . all reactionaries."[26] Hence "liberals" and "reactionaries" are proper targets, and the list expands.

Some legal scholars even favor the expansion of "legitimacy" for the targeting of civilian participants (administrative or political) in an armed conflict setting.[27] This view, however, could lead to the destruction of the distinction between combatants and civilian nonbelligerents. Farer has argued that in "many civil wars, the whole issue is which administrative structure, including the police and army, shall govern. . . . People who occupy administrative positions assume a common risk in time of civil war whether they wear a three-piece suit or a uniform."[28] Farer has also argued that the law should be changed to allow the assassination of civilians who are "active participants in the struggle for power" as opposed to the assassination of the "more or less passive bulk of the citizenry." He adds:

Why should the guerrilla be castigated for failing to distinguish between the commander of a district paramilitary force and the civilian official from whom he receives his orders? Why should the Minister of the Interior ensconced in his office be legally immune . . . ? Nor can such a distinction be considered necessary in response to the dictates of humanity for who could be less innocent.[29]

One might wonder if the category of the noninnocent would include three-piece-suit-wearing capitalist businessmen, party and union officials and officers, bar patrons, shoppers, and children.[30] How and where would the line be drawn? The phrase "active participants in the struggle for power" would allow a broad interpretation of the "legitimacy" of terror and death inflicted on almost anyone and thus would tend to escalate terror and death. To avoid this, numerous legal norms require that a distinction be made between persons engaged in hostilities as armed combatants and those not so engaged.

Falk has stated that "the insurgent faction in an underdeveloped country has, at the beginning of its struggle for power, no alternative other than terror to mobilize an effective operation."[31] He has added that "[a]n important element of differentiation is that insurgent terror tends to be discriminating in its application and to involve relatively small numbers of victims."[32] Beyond the factual problems inherent in such statements, it is important to realize that the number of victims does not lessen the illegality of the act, nor the dangers inherent in legalizing violence directed toward persons who do not engage in an armed conflict as armed combatants. Law and human dignity rest instead on a common need to minimize and control violence and to extend human rights protection. In nonwar situations as well as in war situations, every effort should be made to limit permissible targeting.

National Measures: Defining a Crime of Terrorism

Multilateral efforts to create a general convention on international terrorism have bogged down in unnecessary political rhetoric[33] and have been generally unhelpful in expanding consensus against numerous types of terrorist targeting. Nevertheless, a multilateral convention is still possible. Bilateral efforts may also be useful as a short-term approach. Efforts within the United States to supplement existing criminal laws seem more likely to stimulate greater protection at home than abroad, where similar foreign effort has not occurred at the national level. However, U.S. legislation might stimulate foreign, bilateral, and even multilateral effort.

The Problems

One of the problems of implementing criminal sanctions concerns acts of terrorism that produce a terror outcome by threats of violence, without actual physical injury to any human or nonhuman target. Criminal lawyers might view this problem through legalistic lenses framed by concepts of attempt, assault, and conditional assault, and the penalties, if any, might be conditioned upon such a focus. Standard criminal law treatises advise that "threatening words alone, without any overt act to carry out the threat" will not create the crime of assault.[34] Take, for example, a situation where a terrorist group phones a person to inform him that his family will be bombed if he does not support the terrorist objectives. Many criminologists may find that there has been no crime of assault because there is no overt act to carry out the threat. Intimidation may create criminal responsibility in some states if a felony is involved, which is highly likely in the case of threats of violence, but state and federal law can be supplemented to include a specific offense of terrorism to meet this and other problems (e.g., degrees of penalty and gravity of demonstrated concern). The following discussion shows how this might be possible.

Legislative efforts to create a crime of terrorism, at the international or state level, should include a definition that realistically mirrors the terror process. An effort to punish terroristic conduct by using an overly broad definitional or jurisdictional focus (viz., as simply murder, attempted murder, threats, or assault) is unwise and unworkable in the long run. At the national level, an attempt to prosecute as "terrorism" many types of conduct that produce no actual terror outcome would seem politically and functionally unwise and constitutionally unsound. A generally accepted definition of terrorism requires an element of "terror" and a coercive purpose.[35]

Due process requires some minimal connection between criminal distinction and reality. Furthermore, any legislative draft should mirror expectation and fact. The alternative is to regulate activity without attaching the term "terrorism" to the legislative provision. But any definition of terrorism should mirror expectation about "terrorism," or else constitutional restraints on the criminal sanction may be compounded by popular expectations. As social scientists are becoming increasingly aware, the effective *implementation* of law requires some deference to common expectation in the community.[36] Overly broad definitions or criminal enactments against conduct that cannot be properly viewed as "terrorism" could reduce respect for authority and undermine attempts at prohibiting such conduct. This would be contrary to the goal of preventing and deterring terrorism. Legislative or executive pronouncements, for example, that characterize conduct or attitudes that "damage the interests of a state" as impermissible forms of "terrorism" are unrealistic and may also isolate the "state" from new attitudes, beliefs, or change by any means.

International and domestic political effects may also thwart the overall goals by overly broad prescriptions against terrorism. Attempts by certain state elites to control nearly all counter attitudes and behavior in the name of antiterrorism may be a greater threat to law, authority, and human rights than most forms of terrorism. This type of legislative or executive control can lead opposition groups to feel less restrained in using *any* means appropriate to serve *their* ends. Furthermore, overly broad state attempts at control can condition attitudes in at least two negative ways: (1) toward an undermining of governmental authority due to the belief that the government has gone too far, and (2) toward an acceptance of terrorism by recognizing that power seems to take precedence over "law." Again, state responses are ideologically and politically significant.

Domestic Example: Texas Statute, 1973

For a specific example, we turn to actions recently taken by the state of Texas. In 1973, the Texas legislature enacted a statute, making "terroristic threat" an offense, in order to punish those who threaten to commit "any offense involving violence to any person or property with intent to:

(1) cause a reaction of any type to this threat by an official or volunteer agency organized to deal with emergencies;
(2) place any person in fear of imminent serious bodily injury; or
(3) prevent or interrupt the occupation or use of a building; room; place of assembly; place to which the public has access; place of employment or occupation; aircraft; automobile, or other form of conveyance; or other public place.[37]

It seems curious, however, that such offenses are punishable merely as a misdemeanor,[38] and that terror outcome is not required for "terroristic threat."[39] Only subsection 2 requires some production of a "fear outcome"; the other subsections merely require a "reaction" by an official or volunteer agency, or evidence of the prevention of the enjoyment of public facilities. Perhaps this definition is "fair" with regard to the penalty imposed (*i.e.*, a misdemeanor), but since the possibilities of violative conduct are so broad and could be nearly innocuous in some cases (such as a phone threat to punch the mayor of Houston in the nose), the legislation is far too vague for useful guidance in defining terrorism or devising effective criminal sanctions. If terrorism is to be defined adequately as a separate offense, there must be some awareness of the need for a "terror outcome"—an outcome that is the primary factor separating terrorism from "normal" acts of murder, assault, and so forth. Definitions that merely delineate "acts of violence," the "threat or use of violence," "repressive acts," and similar categorizations[40] are incomplete. By ignoring the critical need to focus on the terror process that involves the use of "intense fear" or "anxiety" to coerce a primary target into particular behavior or attitudinal patterns, such approaches will be unhelpful in guiding efforts to design realistic and effective responses to terrorism. One solution, with a chance for international adoption, would make a terroristic threat combined with a terror outcome punishable as a felony. Furthermore, a provision could be created as a standard for uniform state and federal law. In Appendix 6B, such a proposal is detailed.

Examples of Foreign Legislation

A brief comparison of foreign legislation in this area may also highlight certain points made above. In the vast majority of the cases examined, foreign law does not seek to create a new, separate crime of terrorism. In other cases, foreign governments have simply expanded censorship and detention powers under an antiterror/antisubversion label without defining a new crime of terrorism. Most governments utilize martial law powers, expand military jurisdiction, create new security courts or procedures, or operate by police or military decree on an *ad hoc* basis to counter terrorism. Also, several states have adopted sweeping measures for detention, search, media control, and other powers in the name of antiterrorism without defining terrorism or with a definition so broad as to include almost any antigovernment utterance or conduct.[41] These approaches are usually overly broad, may prove harmful in the long run, and would be unconstitutional if adopted in the United States.

Whenever an attempt is made to define terrorism under foreign law, the definitional approach is too broad for U.S. purposes (*i.e.*, they overregulate and/or proscribe in an unconstitutionally vague or overly broad manner). The Czechoslovakian Penal Code takes the simple approach by proscribing the "terrorizing" of another person.[42] Although presumably more specific than most (since a "terrorizing" outcome or effect would seem to be required), this approach does not seem to be conditioned by any requirements of "intentional" activity or violent acts (*i.e.*, unintentional conduct and conduct or threats of conduct of a nonviolent nature may also be prohibited, especially in view of Communist theories of "objective" crime, which do not adhere to Western *mens rea* requirements). What seems to be a Czech requirement of terror outcome or effect is mirrored in nearly all other foreign definitional attempts, with the exception of the Soviet Union. However, the need for a "terror" outcome or effect has been diluted. What is required for "terrorism" in these countries is some threat or state of "alarm, fear or terror."[43] These provisions seem to go too far and may well be constitutionally suspect if adopted in the United States. The Soviet penal provision is even broader in this regard; it does not require any fear, alarm, or terror outcome.[44]

Most of these definitions are also more restrictive than the proposal in Appendix 6B with regard to the types of conduct utilized to produce the proscribed public or private alarm.[45] In this sense, they seem needlessly restrictive in focus. A requirement of a threat or use of violence would seem sufficient to cover all delimiting factors, with one possible exception. For example, typical lists of the means utilized to produce public alarm include the use of weapons, explosives, incendiary materials, poisonous gases, toxins, infectuous microbe agents, and other devices capable of harming the public.[46] All these seem to be covered by the "threat or use of violence" factor in Appendix 6B, and the broader phrase seems preferable so as not to exclude any particular mode not enumerated in a list. What might cause difficulty, however, is the question whether a "threat or use of violence" includes the use of poison and microbes. It would seem that it could be so interpreted;[47] to be safe, the phrase "or threat or use of poisons or microbes" could be added.

With regard to the "threat" versus "attempt" problem considered above, each foreign definition includes prohibitions against threats or is sufficiently broad to include any "act" (i.e., threat, attempt, and so forth) that produces prohibited outcomes. The only exception here is the Soviet Union, whose penal code requires a "killing" or "grave bodily injury," thus presumably excluding attempts or threats to do so.[48] The approach used in Appendix 6B proscribes both the threat and use of violence.

It should also be noted that only three of the states considered limit their definitions by some reference to the terrorists' political objectives, although many states without a definition seem aware of the need to differentiate between political terrorism and, say, mafia terrorism. Nicaragua and Mexico require a purpose: to disturb the public order, to cause unrest in the land (Nicaragua), to attempt to damage the authority of the state (Mexico).[49] The Soviet Union requires a "purpose of subverting or weakening the Soviet regime."[50] Again, it seems very useful to distinguish between political and nonpolitical motivation, but the specific "political" effects detailed by Mexico, Nicaragua, and the Soviet Union would not need to be copied or listed in any U.S. legislation. Finally, it is simply noted that the most comprehensive definition is found in the Mexico Penal Code; it contains most of the elements of a definitional focus that are useful,[51] but it is still too broad in its prohibition of acts that produce "alarm" and "fear."

International Perspective

General legal policies and divergent justifications for the use of terrorism are considered here with reference to norms applicable both in time of war and in times of relative peace. Although this study does not relate directly to contexts of armed conflict, it seems useful to consider general legal policies applicable to both contexts for two reasons: (1) the two sets of relevant legal policies are usefully considered in relation to each other, as they often supplement our understanding of policy-serving approaches to similar problems; and (2) justifications are often couched in arguments that warfare conditions, and even the laws of war (such as prisoner-of-war protections for terrorists), exist in what are, more objectively, nonwar contexts.

The Use of Violent Strategies: General Limitations

Initially, one can observe that whether or not an armed conflict or armed "struggle" exists, not all strategies for violent coercion are permissible[52] and that the "justness" of one's political cause does not necessarily "justify the means" utilized.[53] Indeed, the U.N. secretary-general has put it more directly in his report on international terrorism:

At all times in history, mankind has recognized the unavoidable necessity of repressing some forms of violence, which otherwise would threaten the very existence of society as well as that of man himself. There are some means of using force, as in every form of human conflict, which must not be used, even when the use of force is legally and morally justified, and regardless of the status of the perpetrator.[54]

Another relevant trend in expectation has excluded the offense of terrorism from "political" crimes in conection with norms of extradition;[55] and relevant human rights instruments allow no exception to human rights protections on the basis of a postulated political purpose in cases of conduct that would amount to acts or threats of terrorism.[56] The recognition of legal restraints on violent coercion and the unacceptability of "just" excuses *per se* is a key to the efficacy of norms proscribing terrorism. Without a shared acceptance of these two basic premises, law can have little effect on the participants in the power process, and they will increasingly defer to raw, violent power as the "just" measure of social change.[57]

Numerous examples of claims to utilize any means of violence, to expand permissible target groups, or to excuse human rights deprivations on the basis of a "holy" or "just" macropolitical purpose appear in recent writings. Furthermore, misconceptions of legal norms and goal values (policies) are far too frequent in legal literature.[58] Moreover, much of the philosophical literature of certain revolutionaries contains the argument that violence permeates all societies and institutions; man is exploited, tyrranized, alienated; violence is a cleansing force and frees the alienated; and violence is "necessary" in politics or for the dominance of one's own political predilection.[59] A typical statement is that of Marcuse: that violence used to uphold domination is bad but that violence practiced by the "oppressed" against the "oppressor" is good.[60] The average terrorist would probably be convinced by that statement. However, problems arise once one begins to map out the types of participants, perspectives, arenas of interaction, resource values, strategies employed, outcomes, and effects in connection with the "violence" in society and the strategies of "resistance" by the "oppressed." As a result, one finds insufficient guidance in the words "oppressed" and "oppressors," as with the errant meaning of the word "just." The "oppressed" who use coercive violence are going to become the "oppressors" of someone else or some other thought, so the "guidance" results in circular confusion and leaves mankind in a spiral pursuit of self-destructive terror and counterterror.[61] To add that terrorism is "necessary" so that the "will of the people" can be expressed is similarly unattractive. Intentionally created terror necessarily suppresses the free expression of all viewpoints and the free participation of all persons in the political process.[62] States should, therefore, seek international recognition of legal restraints through the development of conventional international law.

A precise, realistic definition devised at the international level is necessary for common opposition to impermissible terrorism. As already pointed out here, the word "terrorism" is often used as an epithet to describe the despised conduct of an enemy; it is used in many disparate ways; and what seems to have inhibited effective international cooperation in 1972 was an unnecessary confusion about what some states sought to proscribe and, more important, what was not sought to be proscribed.[63] An overly broad approach that does not mirror the realities of terroristic process or common expectation will fail to aid in promoting the consensus needed for a cooperative global sanction effort. By agreeing about what "terrorism" actually is, we may indeed leave certain forms of political coercion unregulated, but we can form a consensual basis for action that should reinforce authority and restrain those who seek to rule or disrupt by raw power and terror.

In this regard, it seems worth emphasizing that the 1937 League of Nations Convention attempted to deal with the process of terrorism. Its work, however, was incomplete and its focus misdirected.[64] Moreover, that convention failed to consider the problem addressed in this work: the protection of "unprotected" persons or things. The 1972 U.S. Draft Convention did attempt to regulate the use of terroristic strategy against certain "unprotected" persons, although it did not address the use of nonhuman instrumental targets to produce intense fear or anxiety in human primary targets.[65] The problem with the U.S. draft was that it potentially prohibited more than just the conduct or the effect of terrorism. The broader potentialities of the U.S. draft probably contributed to the suspicion on the part of several states that the United States was attempting to regulate, beyond a shared consensus, what ought to be regulated. Further, the use of the qualifying word "unlawfully" with regard to "kills, causes serious bodily harm or kidnaps another" is not a useful way to guide future decisions or to obtain the consensus needed for convention ratification.[66] It merely begs the question, offering no criteria for choice in its application.

Laws of Armed Conflict

Those willing to explore the relevant juristic effort of mankind will find that recent trends in prescription and authoritative pronouncement that are themselves additional forms of legal response to terrorism have been sufficiently clear in recognizing that there are limits to permissible death, suffering, and competitive destruction, no matter what the cause or type of participants. A basic human expectation incorporated into the customary law of war has been that even in times of armed conflict, people expect that each party to the conflict will conduct its operations in conformity with the laws and customs of war. Also, it has been generally expected that these norms "do not allow to belligerents an unlimited power as to the choice of means of injuring the enemy"[67] and that respect for the law is not merely owed to the enemy but to all mankind. Furthermore, there is respected authority for the position that the customary law of war and practice has prohibited terrorism as an intentional strategy.[68] There were at least two commissions established early in the twentieth century for the purpose of articulating the established norms of the law of war, and they identified a widespread denunciation of terrorism as well as murder, massacres, torture, and collective penalties.[69] A third group charged with the investigation of the German control of Belgium in World War I concluded that a deliberate "system of general terrorization" of the population to gain quick control of the region was contrary to the rules of civilized warfare, and that German claims of military necessity and reprisal action were unfounded.[70] The pre-World War I German staff and jurists had openly favored terrorization of civilians in war zones to hasten victory or in occupied territory to ensure control of the population,[71] but these views and implementary actions during the war were widely denounced as unlawful strategies.[72]

Since World War II, distinguished authorities have recaptured the need for a peremptory norm that prohibits the intentional terrorization of the civilian population as such or the intentional use of a strategy that produces terror that is not "incidental to lawful" combat operations.[73] Underlying these viewpoints are policy considerations involving: (1) the need for limiting the types of permissible participants and strategies in the process of armed violence; and (2) a shared awareness of the need to prohibit the deliberate terrorization of populations, both to preserve any "vestige of the claim that war can be regulated at all" and to save from extinction the "human rights" limitations on the exercise of armed coercion within the social process.[74]

As if to reaffirm these trends in expectation, the 1949 Geneva Conventions contained a specific peremptory prohibition of "all measures" of "terrorism,"[75] and numerous humane treatment provisions prohibited these and related acts of violence in all circumstances. Specific prohibitions include: violence to life and person, cruel treatment, torture, the taking of hostages, summary executions and other forms of murder or punishment without judicial safeguards, outrages upon personal dignity, and humiliating and degrading treatment.[76] A nonabsolute ban on all forms of "physical or moral coercion" against protected persons is also contained in the conventions, and Pictet states that the prohibition is very broad although the drafters "had mainly in mind coercion aimed at obtaining information, work or support for an ideological or political idea."[77] Coercion of a violent or violence-threatening nature to induce behavioral or attitudinal outcomes in the primary target (either the captured person or some "home" audience) in connection with an effort to gain "support for an ideological or political idea" is, however, just the sort of thing envisioned in the definitional framework provided above. The acts mentioned above, which the Geneva Conventions prohibit, are the means or strategies often employed by terrorists. Thus prohibiting torture and inhumane treatment, for example, can help limit the possible methods terrorists might seek to employ in carrying out their activities.

Recent efforts to supplement the Geneva Convention norms through two new protocols to the convention have also contained specific reiterations of the prohibition of terrorism as well as the prohibition of any other form of armed violence directed at the civilian population as such.[78] Included in a 1972 draft of the International Committee of the Red Cross were "terrorization attacks" and "acts of terrorism, as well as reprisals against persons." An early 1973 draft included changes such as: "acts and measures that spread terror," "attacks that spread terror among the civilian population and are launched without distinction against civilians and military objectives"[79] and "violent acts of terrorism perpetrated without distinction against civilians who do not take a direct part in hostilities."[80] If properly framed, the new prohibitions of terrorism in the Geneva protocols will be important because they might help to implement customary and current expectations that attacks on the civilian population as such should be prohibited, whereas the present conventions primarily protect persons already in control of the military force or in occupied territory and the wounded, infirm, women, children, or "other persons" who are "exposed to grave danger."[81]

Related claims to the right to control the population of an occupied territory in times of war through a process involving the taking of hostages and their execution in response to local population resistance have been authoritatively denied after both world wars. After the Second World War, it was further declared that the executions of hostages without strict compliance with reprisal principles and certain minimum judicial safeguards "are merely terror murders" and are impermissible regardless of a "reprisal" or other objective.[82] Now the Geneva Conventions also prohibit the taking of hostages in any type of armed conflict and for any purpose.[83] To serve a similar policy, they also prohibit collective penalties and reprisals against protected persons, no matter what the postulated need of those engaged in the armed struggle.[84]

General Human Rights Law

Today, it also seems reasonable to conclude that all forms of violent terrorism against noncombatants and captured persons and governmental or private terrorization of others in order to prevent their free participation in the governmental process would violate human rights as documented in numerous international instruments. The 1948 Universal Declaration of Human Rights stated that "[e]veryone has the right to life, liberty and security of person" and that "[n]o one shall be subjected to torture or to cruel, inhuman and degrading treatment or punishment."[85] This is the same language as that contained in the 1949 Geneva Conventions, and it would seem to document a similar expectation that all forms of terrorism through acts of violence or threats thereof to persons are prohibited.[86] Similar language also appears in the 1966 Covenant on Civil and Political Rights[87] and two regional human rights conventions.[88] In addition to these trends in the documentation of human rights, other authoritative pronouncements have declared that acts of terrorism constitute serious violations of the fundamental rights, freedoms, and dignity of man.[89] The U.N. secretary-general has added that "terrorism threatens, endangers or destroys the lives and fundamental freedoms of the innocent,"[90] and a recent resolution of the U.N. General Assembly stated that that body was at least "deeply perturbed" over acts of international terrorism that take a toll of innocent human lives or jeopardize fundamental freedoms and human rights.[91] In 1969, the Red Cross Istanbul Declaration also provided that "it is a human right to be free from all fears, acts of violence and brutality, threats and anxieties likely to injure man in his person, his honour and his dignity."[92] Necessarily included in such a ban would be acts of violent terrorism.

Not only do expectations about human rights seem to favor the prohibition of almost all forms of violent terrorism *per se*, but terrorism utilized as a strategy to coerce others from free and full participation in the governmental process would undoubtedly offend norms designed to assure a full sharing of power in the political process for all participants in the social process and the full sharing of enlightenment or the free exchange of ideas.[93] These fundamental human goals are supplemented by specific human rights references to equality, the impermissible distinction of persons on the basis of conflicting political or other opinion,[94] and the shared principle of self-determination. Indeed, terrorism, as a strategy to coerce others through violence, offends both collective and individual freedom and dignity.[95] Such coercive interference with the political process is an attempt to deny the full sharing of power by all participants in a given social process, or the denial of "self-determination."[96] Moreover, when such attempts at elitist control of the political process are made by parties or states outside a particular social process (especially outside a state boundary), such "exported" terrorism for that purpose would offend norms governing intervention. More specifically, a widely recognized customary prescription declares: "Every state has the duty to refrain from organizing, instigating, assisting or participating in acts of civil strife or terrorist acts in another state or acquiescing in organized activities within its territory directed toward the commission of such acts. . . ."[97] A similar prescription prohibits related attempts to "organize, assist, foment, finance, incite or tolerate subversive, terrorist or other armed activities";[98] and the U.N. secretariat has stated that a punishable act should include the incitement, encouragement, or toleration of activities designed to spread terror among the population of another state.[99] The above prescriptions are also supported by a long history of expectation usually categorized in terms of aggression or intervention.[100]

In view of the numerous documented expectations prohibiting acts of violence relevant to terrorism, one might conclude that any new convention on terrorism would only reaffirm these trends and would be most significant for its procedural mechanisms for implementation.[101] Already supplementing the law of armed conflict and human rights, of course, are the more specific air hijacking and sabotage conventions[102] and the regional OAS Convention on Terrorism.[103] But one might ask, if there are numerous norms prohibiting terrorism in armed conflicts, as well as in certain other contexts, then why are there still problems ahead for the complete, rational, and policy-serving regulation of terrorism? First, some states have recently articulated claims for particular exceptions to the seemingly complete ban on terrorism; and second, there are hidden gaps within the present coverage of this matter by the law of war. Moreover, some overriding cases of "necessity" may balance against a normal prohibition of terrorism if the community has not already placed an absolute ban on that particular activity.

Claimed Exceptions

National Liberation Movements. Claims, which may conflict with the Geneva Civilian Convention, are being made by some states that community efforts to regulate terrorism should not apply in the context of a national liberation movement where a people are legitimately seeking self-determination.[104] It is difficult to judge, however, how many states made this claim in connection with the general debate on international terrorism. Some 14 states seem to take a similar stance openly, but many of these merely claim that a ban on international terrorism "should not affect" the inalienable right to self-determination and independence of all peoples or "the legitimacy of their struggle" (or words of similar effect).[105] Such a claim seems merely to affirm that an otherwise legitimate use of force or overall struggle for self-determination should not itself be considered as impermissible *per se*.[106] It would seem, however, that even these states do not claim that during such self-determination struggle *any* means of force, including terrorism, directed against civilians protected under the Geneva Civilian Convention is to be permissible in that context. Each claim as to the permissibility of terrorism would have to be analyzed by the world community in terms of the actual context with a comprehensive reference to participants, perspectives, basic values or resources, situations of interaction, strategies utilized, actual outcomes, and long-term effects, as well as the goal values involved, impacts on goal value realization, and so forth.[107] A few states seem to have specifically claimed that *any* means utilized in such a self-determinative process should be legal, but their uncompromising and extreme viewpoints seem to have convinced no one else thus far.[108]

Defense against Aggression. Another related and recently advanced claim[109] is that any means utilized to confront an "aggressor" should be permissible and thereby excluded from a ban on terroristic acts of international significance.[110] This claim flies in the face of the well-documented international consensus, inherited and present, that no exception to the coverage of the law of war and human rights should be made on the basis of the "aggressor" status or "unjust" quality of the actions of one or more of the parties to a particular armed conflict. Underlying this consensus is the recognition that it is often difficult to determine which party is an aggressor and that without an authoritative determination on such a matter, each party to the conflict might refuse to apply the law of war to the other parties to the conflict in the context of conflicting assertions and escalating inhumanity. Moreover, the law of human rights in times of armed conflict, which is designed to assure protection to all noncombatants regardless of race, color, religion, faith, sex, birth, wealth, political opinion, or similar criteria, is based on an obligation owed to all mankind, not only to the participants actually involved in the fray.[111] Further, the goal values covered in that law are deemed too important to give way to such a claim, and most norms are of a peremptory nature allowing for no derogation on the basis of state status, political or ideological pretext, military necessity, or state or group interest unless specifically so permitted for a particular prescription. Whatever the fate of such a claim in the debate on international terrorism in general, under the law of war it is doomed to failure since it conflicts with the widely shared expectations of the world community and the important goal values underlying all human rights.

Worker Struggles. A third related claim would exclude worker struggles from the regulation of terrorism.[112] Presumably, lack of support for this view beyond the Soviet frontiers will lead to its demise in the general debate. Although a little more specific than references to "oppressors" and "oppressed," this worker struggle exception suffers from a similar criterial ambiguity. This claim has never been specifically raised in a law-of-war context, and there does not seem to have ever been demonstrated any shared policy reason why "workers" should be allowed to terrorize everyone else.

Guerrilla Warfare. A fourth related claim that has not appeared in recent general debates on international terrorism, but that has arisen in the context of efforts to revitalize certain provisions of the law of war, is that any means employed by insurgent guerrillas, including the terrorization of noncombatants, should be permissible.[113] Some have even advocated that in a guerrilla warfare context all participants should be allowed to escape the regulation of the law.[114] Both these claims are minority viewpoints and both run counter to customary law and Geneva law, which recognize no sweeping exceptions for guerrillas or guerrilla warfare.[115] Indeed, the law of war was developed with both a guerrilla warfare and an insurgent/belligerent power struggle background; adherence to its norms and goal values by the world community will more greatly assure the fulfillment of human rights, the lessening of indiscriminate suffering, the protection of noncombatants, restraint on armed violence, the abnegation of raw power as the measure and force of social change, freedom from inhumane or degrading treatment, and the serving of all other policies intertwined with human dignity and minimum world public order.[116]

It seems that none of these four types of claimed exception will find community approval. They all seek to exclude a whole context of violent interaction from legal regulation rather than to advocate a particular policy that will balance decision-making in the regulation of all contexts though showing deference to certain policies in cases where conflicting policies present themselves with an otherwise relatively equal weight. If the community chooses to give a strong policy weight in favor of self-determination, for example, then that preference should be balanced in terms of context, conflicts with other goal values, and the decisional question familiar to law-of-war specialists categorized in terms of "military necessity," "proportionality," and "unnecessary suffering." Where, however, higher preference has been demonstrated for certain human rights goal values such as the peremptory Geneva law protections, these preferences should continue to be balanced against claimed "self-determination" exceptions to any ban on terrorism. Thus the world community should identify all goal values at stake in a given context of armed violence and also rank the goal values for decisional consideration in terms of peremptory goals, higher order goals, lower order goals, and so on (and make these choices known). This type of approach might well lead to a conclusion that a specific form of self-determination process is permissible in general even though its outcome is somewhat of a terroristic nature. But it might also lead to a conclusion that within such a self-determinative process, a particular attack on a civilian population is impermissible in view of the peremptory goal values that regulate the means of carrying on any armed conflict. Another conclusion that seems possible is that within that general process, conflict, or struggle, a terroristic attack on "counter" participants of a military character, in a specific subcontext, can be permissible.

Military and Police Targets

A slightly different problem is posed by the targeting of military or police personnel in time of nonwar. These types of targets are not given special protection under international law and are considered by many to be armed "combatants." Moreover, Gurr's study of trends in targeting during the 1960s indicates that military or police are the second most frequent "principal" or instrumental human targets.[117] Adding certain revolutionary perspectives and behavior patterns together, one could aver that a general "legal" expectation among terrorist revolutionaries is that military and police targeting is permissible. Such a conclusion, however, raises several legal problems. First, there is insufficient data concerning actual revolutionary perspectives. Second, Gurr's study indicates that domestic public, foreign political, and private political targeting is over four times more frequent.[118] This suggests that *noncombatant* political targeting is the main focus of terrorist groups, not the targeting of police and military personnel. Two conclusions could follow: (1) that revolutionaries view both types as proper targets; or (2) that there is little attention paid to claims of legal permissibility since what might be a more convincing claim to target "combatant" elements of the state is not in fact mirrored in practice.

A third problem posed, however, involves the near futility of drawing realistic conclusions from present data. Gurr's study of the 1960s discloses that revolutionary terrorism was quite rare and that precipitators "were more often motivated by hostility toward *particular* policies and political figures than by revolutionary aspirations."[119] This shows that terrorism is indeed typically "political," but that the use of terrorism as part of a revolutionary campaign is not frequently the case. From general data, then, it is difficult to address one of the gray areas of possible permissibility—the targeting of armed combatant state elements in a revolutionary context. It is most difficult also to address any claim by revolutionary groups that permissible targeting under the laws of war (*e.g.,* the use of terroristic strategy in time of war to attack a military headquarters with a rocket barrage)[120] should also be permissible in an insurgency context or in a nonarmed conflict setting. At a minimum, however, the targeting of military and police personnel in a nonwar context raises several concerns.

First, it follows from the preceding analysis that an attack on such targets in general by a revolutionary group in a nonwar context with a claim that such elements keep the state elites in power and are, therefore, not innocent is the sort of sociological truth that is nevertheless far too simplistic to support claims to permissibility under law. General human rights law does not permit the summary execution of such targets, which an assassination of a police officer on the streets entails. For similar reasons, the state cannot engage in assassination of "known" radicals or criminals of a leftist or rightist persuasion. Indeed, assassination is illegal even in time of war.[121]

Second, to argue that police officers may be hit at random, which seems the more frequent practice,[122] is far too close to the claims of collective guilt denounced by the Nuremberg courts as violating civilized decency and international law. Equally unimpressive is the argument that when the population is being oppressed in a vicious manner with the aid of the police, police officers can be utilized at random as instrumental targets to terrorize other policemen or the political oppressors. What appears far more humane in such a case is to engage in tyrannicide, nor terrorism. Indeed, this precision in targeting, the murder of the tyrant, is *not* a form of terrorism *per se*. Contrary to several trends in prescription that would label an assassination of a head of state as an act of terrorism, the elimination of a head of state might well involve no terror objective and no terror outcome. The same might be true of the elimination of a particular police official or the death of several military persons during a fire-fight with a revolutionary cell or an attempt by foreigners to free their countrymen from the inhumanities of a Mexican jail.[123] Not only are such forms of violence *not* terrorism, but they raise more difficult questions of permissibility under claims relating to self-help and self-defense. These are gray-area concerns, but they are not addressed further in this inquiry.

We should note, however, that this form of precision targeting without terror objectives is far different from the bomb in the marketplace or the random assassination strategies considered earlier. These latter practices raise serious human rights questions, and a proper approach to inquiry must address all the relevant legal policies at stake in a given situation as well as all the actual features of context that appear important for a more realistic and policy-serving decision.[124] At a minimum, however, we must condemn the use of nonjudicial murder except in cases of extreme necessity. Current trends reflect little awareness of even this minimal requirement; for although Gurr's study is not presently usable for tight inquiry into claims to utilize nonjudicial murder in "self-defense" or in contexts of extreme value deprivation with few, if any, alternatives to such a form of self-help sanction, he does indicate a possible concern: "Probably most striking is the fact that political terrorism was relatively less common in poorer, authoritarian, Third-World states than in the prosperous democracies of Europe and Latin America."[125] From this, one is led to believe that terrorism is most often *not* a necessary response to oppression, but a useful form of political rebellion. As Gurr adds, "Their [*i.e.*, the terrorists'] public motives were not notably different from those of groups using other unconventional methods of political action."[126]

Conclusions and Recommendations

In this section, several problem areas that are deemed most useful for implementary attention are highlighted. It is important to keep in mind, however, that numerous and varied approaches to the protection of the mass of persons and things in global society that are not given special status are possible, and many general and special measures of protection are actually utilized to secure well-being, power, wealth, enlightenment, and other patterns of value growth, enjoyment, and distribution. Nearly any effort to ensure respect for and implementation of general human rights and fundamental freedoms will have implementary consequences with regard to the threat or use of terroristic strategy by others, as will nearly any thwarting of such human right and freedom goals. Further, within such an effort, the implementation of well-being goals through general criminal and tort law sanctions will have an important overall effect. Here, attention is directed to specific responses involving an aggressive, concurrent effort by state, federal, and international governmental entities to secure rights and freedoms through joint and separate implementary action.[127]

Ideological Strategies

Educational Devices. In addition to ideological responses to the claims considered earlier, the consideration of possible educational efforts by private individuals, groups, and institutions[128] provides another focus for state response. State and federal governmental entities within the United States can play a far more creative and effective role in the education of all persons in U.S. society concerning human, constitutional, and civil guarantees and the problems posed to a free society from illegal and inhumane strategies and conditions. As outlined in Chapter 13, "Private Measures of Sanction," more creative and effective coordination with the media and other enlightenment groups and institutions can lead to greater protection from terrorism for the "nonprotected" persons and things within U.S. society or in global society. Indeed, the need for promoting legal obligations to respect and ensure respect for human rights has been widely discussed in the literature.[129] Such an effort would fit nicely with the Carter administration's efforts to implement human rights at the international level.

Specific possible approaches are numerous. The federal government could encourage greater use of high school government and civics classes, senior problems classes, history classes, and other classes for investigation, analysis, and discussion of general human rights norms and implementary approaches. Related educational programs and concerns can be developed for other levels, including more general but important cooperative and individual-oriented learning in elementary and preschool process.

Educational efforts such as these can be supplemented by government-sponsored "implementation advisory teams" to engage in service to educational groups and institutions as well as law enforcement agencies, local governmental bodies, media groups, civic organizations, religious groups and institutions, penal institutions, health groups and institutions, and others. Government-sponsored fellowships for further study and the development of related efforts in the private sector can be initiated or redirected. Publications of a short, general nature and also of a more detailed, scholarly format can be stimulated, published, and distributed, as well as other forms of communication (*e.g.*, films, slides, and so forth); and there could be more encouragement of seminars, conferences, and other enlightenment forums.[130] A useful step toward human rights implementation is the appointment by the Department of State of a coordinator of human rights activities.[131] A knowledgeable, energetic, and effective person in this position could work within the State Department framework, along with the assistant legal adviser for human rights in the Office of the Legal Adviser, to plan, initiate, and coordinate an interagency, intergovernmental, and community-wide approach to implementation.

Ideological Warfare. A useful long-term response to terrorism against nonprotected persons or things might be termed "ideological warfare." If law and authority are necessarily antagonistic to the use of terrorism and other forms of intensely coercive change or control, then waging an ideological war against intensely coercive strategies to control people and ideas could add significantly to the implementation of law by conditioning predispositional patterns for preventive, deterrent, and related sanction effects. The educational approaches just mentioned are merely certain forms of ideological strategy within which this attempt can take place. It is most important that governments seeking a proper response to terrorism via this ideological warfare must not appear hypocritical by engaging in illegal activities. To engage in counterterrorism, for example, would seem in the long run only to lend credence to terrorist claims concerning the permissibility (legal, moral, or otherwise) of the use of terror as a political weapon. If patient firmness has a useful effect in meeting terror-hostage situations, it seems that a patient firmness demonstrated by a lawful sanction response in general will also be useful. A lawful response pattern could condition the use of terrorism as a strategy by increasing political and ideological risks and making the strategy far less attractive.

Sanctions based on ideological strategies and educational efforts that have been recommended as possible solutions for the problem of terrorism should also be attempted at regional or international levels though bilateral or multilateral agreements or working arrangements. The 1949 Geneva Convention provisions on training and general education concerning human rights in time of armed conflict can serve as patterns for bilateral and multilateral agreements on a general human rights education and implementation program. As any agreements would help to further implement articles 1(3), 55(c), and 56 of the United Nations Charter, efforts might usefully begin with the airing of general approaches in the appropriate U.N. entities (*e.g.*, ECOSOC, UNESCO, and the Human Rights Commission).[132] The question of implementation may be dealt with by an attempt to secure general approval for cooperative educational and advisory approaches to human rights implementation as a general means of combating terrorism. There should be no opposition to such a resolution, since it would be agreed that cooperative approaches are useful and that the use of general human rights as an educative vehicle should not lead to overt disapproval. Not even the Soviets would dare to vote against human rights.

The U.S. government must become more actively involved in the implementation of human rights. The approach taken by former Secretary of State Henry Kissinger at the OAS meeting in Santiago, Chile, is encouraging,[133] and the Carter administration's efforts to demonstrate a consistent commitment to human rights should prove highly useful in the long run. At the OAS meeting, Kissinger announced his concern about violations of human rights in Chile and Cuba, declared that human rights violations in Chile have "impaired our relationship with Chile and will continue to do so," and noted that if human rights are not preserved and defended in this hemisphere, "then they are in jeopardy everywhere."[134] The Carter administration has been no less active in its open opposition to violations of human rights law. Serious violations of human rights wherever and whenever they occur should be openly and consistently condemned, especially the use of torture and terrorism by governments. Tougher sanction approaches should be taken against governments that refuse to implement basic human rights. The sanctions contemplated against Chile[135] are certainly more useful than a mere statement, such as former Secretary of Commerce Elliot Richardson's statement to the regime in South Korea, that the United States continues to be "concerned."[136]

If we are really concerned about stopping private terrorism, then some attention has to be paid to the threats posed by governmental deprivations of basic human rights. We are beginning to realize with regard to South Korea, Chile, Angola, Rhodesia, and South Africa that human rights are also relevant, if not at times key factors, to stability and power patterns. As Kissinger stated at the 1976 OAS meeting, nearly mirroring a Jeffersonian approach to international relations, "A government that tramples on the rights of its citizens denies the purpose of its existence."[137] One might add that such a government may also deny regional or international peace and may pose significant threats to national security interests of other governments if private forms of terror and counterterror are exported to other countries.

Ideological responses can take myriad forms, but it is useful to follow up on an approach attempted by Senator Jacob Javits with bills to cut off communications and transportation with the so-called safe haven states for terrorists. Besides military, economic, and related sanctions against governments that fail to comply with international legal norms of state responsibility that require a state to refrain from financing, promoting, assisting, tolerating, or acquiescing in exported or transnational terrorism, the United States can continue to speak out against such state involvement and can become more active in education, media, and other ideological forums in opposing governmental failure to promote basic human rights.

Economic Strategies

As in the case of private economic sanctions,[138] international, national, state, and local governmental entities can and should respond in an effective manner so as to eliminate or at least minimize the relative deprivation and social tension that can spawn acts of terrorism and other destructive forms of violence. The control of economic patterns to prevent or counter terrorist threats is similarly possible, and governments should seek to supplement the strategies described on pp. 577-587 of Chapter 13. At present, it appears that economic decision-making at the federal level lacks coordinated consideration of overall prevention of social violence goals.

In addition to problems of overall economic response, there is the problem of what action governments should take in response to private sources of financing of international terrorism.[139] Should they, for example, employ embargoes, boycotts, or other economic tactics against those who support international terrorism? Should they seek to control or confiscate sources of terrorist wealth within their jurisdiction?[140] Or should they take steps to limit the ready market availability of weapon systems most useful for terroristic outcome and effect?[141] Can the government control wealth patterns designed to promote illegality? What criteria can one identify for permissible governmental intervention? Must there always be compliance with necessity and proportionality standards, especially when funds are destined for use abroad?[142] These and related problems are beyond the scope of this study. However, they should be explored on a priority basis by appropriate government agencies and by private scholars.

Diplomatic Strategies

The consideration of diplomatic strategies for the protection of nonprotected persons and things involves inquiry into strategies concerning negotiations with terrorists and strategies concerning the improvement of international protection. With regard to negotiations with terrorists, it is thought best to leave such efforts unrestrained by a mantle of new laws. Whether there should be an effort made to prohibit or allow governmental or private negotiation seems best met by general policy and effective *ad hoc* decision. In this regard, it is assumed that federal, state, and local law enforcement entities and special skill groups will continue to refine and improve various response techniques.[143]

An alternative approach to the protection of nonprotected persons and things would be the creation by an international agreement of additional categories of specially protected persons or things as a supplement to general human rights law and other legal norms. Difficult questions with respect to the tradeoffs involved would have to be answered. For example, are medical personnel, food production and distribution patterns, and energy production and distribution patterns as vital to international society as diplomats and civil aviation? Out of the very transnational complexities and involvements that can stimulate the use of terrorist strategy, can there occur new cooperative responses to terrorism and other problems of social violence and global concern? There appears to be a new opportunity for a more detailed consensus concerning the rights of children and the need for more meaningful international protection for children; the special status of food and energy production and distribution group and institutional patterns; and the importance of special protections for aliens (tourists, businesspersons, and so forth).

Agreements for the special protection of children and medical personnel might be administered by such United Nations entities as UNICEF and the World Health Organization and by the International Committee of the Red Cross. The problem of special protection for interdependent and global food and energy patterns, however, presents greater difficulties. Although interdependence amid resource scarcity presents new opportunities, there are complex matters that might inhibit any new agreement. First, certain Third World perspectives challenge international competence to create legal prescriptions relating to the production and distribution of earth resource patterns.[144] Second, some states claim the right under the law of war to target energy production and distribution groups and institutions. Can the world community refrain from targeting such energy complexes in time of war? If not, how can consensus for immunity from terrorist destruction proceed at the international level? Is it best to leave regulation at the nation-state level, where attacks by private groups on such complexes are illegal? Does this present an inhibiting inconsistency that will fail to convince terrorists and that will limit the likelihood of achieving more effective restraints on terrorist targeting even though restraints in the targeting of children and medical personnel could be more likely?

In certain cases the consensus against targeting children, medical personnel and facilities, large food storage facilities—such as the grain storage facilities in many port areas—and other persons or things will not restrain those who seek the effect of terror for the sake of terror. Terror can sometimes be more effective if targeting seems irrational or insane to the average observer. Nonetheless, a consensus among governments and peoples to reaffirm lines drawn under human rights law, coupled with a general effort to create special protections for children, medical personnel and facilities, and food and energy complexes,[145] could be useful to inhibit further injury or destruction of such persons or things. What might follow later would be an effort to gain special protection by international agreement for shopping areas, hotels, restaurants, entertainment centers, sporting facilities and events, museums, educational and cultural institutions, and so forth. The categories for which effective consensus is least likely would relate to political leaders and policemen, since they are viewed by many as too involved with power and military patterns to be given the special protection that children and diplomats could enjoy.

Gurr's study of trends in targeting seems to support these conclusions. It shows that property targets are by far the most numerous, some 67 percent of targets in general, and some 86 percent of those in Europe.[146] Domestic political figures and military or police were the most prevalent among human targets, some 31 percent overall.[147] His study indicates that "private" human targets constituted only 24 percent, and some of these were "private political groups."[148] From these percentage figures, it appears that the best prospects for a consensus would be with regard to a condemnation of "private" human targets in general, leading to more specific guarantees for children, medical personnel and facilities, and other private persons and institutions.

Other diplomatic strategies might involve the creation of international instruments stimulating greater use of education and general ideological responses as outlined earlier, and should include the recognition of the permissibility, where necessary and proportionate, of economic and military sanctions designed to punish terrorists and to thwart the "safe haven" policies of certain states that fail to adhere to the prosecute-or-extradite principle. Diplomatic strategies may also be devised to assist in the protection of transnational business persons and property. In the next chapter, Clarence Mann underscores the utility of placing the wife and children of a businessman held hostage on television and radio in an effort to make the terrorist realize that the businessman is not an abstract, ideologically justified target but a human being. Such an approach is not only sound diplomatic strategy but also useful as part of an ideological counter to efforts by terrorist propagandizers or others to dehumanize targets and to blur the distinctions found in human rights law. In this regard, particular attention should be paid to working more effectively with the media concerning the reporting of incidents, communication with terrorists, and the media code of ethics, as Chapter 13 suggests.

International Legal Strategies

Finally, it should be stressed that the United States should attempt to engage in efforts leading to a new international convention that prohibits terroristic targeting of certain persons. In this regard, ideological strategies should be utilized to coincide with a general attempt to implement human rights in order to gain acceptance of more specific prohibitions. Those who aver that it is impossible to reach an international consensus on prohibitions of terrorism, that we must continue to refrain from mentioning the word "terrorism" and seek prohibitions of "hijacking," attacks on diplomats, and so forth, are wrong.

All states and all ideologies should be open to the acceptance of an international prohibition of the terroristic targeting of children.[149] The question was raised several times at a recent meeting of scholars on international terrorism in New York, and no one opposed the suggestion to begin an effort to proscribe certain forms of terrorism with a consensus on the impermissibility, under any circumstances, of the terroristic targeting of children. Indeed, Ambassador Fereydoun Hoveyda of Iran thought the suggestion well worth attempting. He also thought that efforts could be directed at a general convention to prohibit the taking of any hostages and to prohibit terrorist attacks on international postal facilities or the terroristic use of the mails. Many could agree to refrain from using letter bombs, even in a war of national liberation, but all should agree on a proscription of terroristic attacks on children.

Already, the U.N. General Assembly has unanimously declared that children have a special status and are entitled to *special protection.*[150] The Declaration of the Rights of the Child, in principle 2, declares that the child "shall enjoy special protection." Principle 8 of the declaration adds: "The child shall in all circumstances be among the first to receive protection and relief." Supplementing such a priority and "special protection" status is the affirmative requirement of protection against "all forms" of "cruelty" recognized in principle 9. With such a consensus already recognized by the General Assembly, it would seem worthwhile to press for a multilateral agreement that children have special status and cannot, under any circumstances, be the object of a terroristic attack. Such an agreement may provide the first realistic building block for the construction of greater multilateral treaty protection of the nonprotected people of this world, although one could argue that children are, by the declaration, already specially protected (*e.g.*, within the meaning of the 1971 OAS Convention).

In another publication, this writer surveyed several response strategies available to a state, especially the exchange of data for prevention and prosecution, trends concerning investigation and prosecution, related aspects of extradition and immunity, trends concerning more general approaches to prevention, restraints on exported terrorism, state self-help strategies, and relevant sanctions by international organizations.[151] The analysis is not reproduced here, but it is worth repeating its conclusion that any new international instrument designed to aid in the prevention of impermissible terrorism directed at nonprotected people should at a minimum include:

1. articles on the advantages of data collection and sharing with pragmatic coordination through U.N. entities
2. warning requirements
3. articles on cooperative investigatory procedures[152]
4. requirements for search and arrest and prosecution where extradition is not utilized
5. procedures for the cooperative application of the law through more transnationally oriented prosecution tribunals for states that are agreeable to the arrangement
6. a specific denial of POW status or "political" offense impediments to a uniform prosecution effort

Similarly, political asylum should not be granted to international terrorists, since the offense is against humankind and not merely against a particular state or geopolitical system.[153] In supplementation of these cooperative efforts and prosecutorial requirements, the policy of requiring an exchange of all implementary legislation should be followed. Implementary regulations and outlines or the content of programs for instruction should be exchanged for comparative analysis and a further coordination of implementary functioning. A recent development in this regard is encouraging. During an international law conference held under U.N. auspices, the United States and the Soviet Union agreed to cooperate in an attempt to end terrorism, although it may take a year until a "commission of inquiry" can be functional. Some believe that a world criminal court may be forthcoming from such an effort within five years.[154] Any improvement in this direction would be helpful.

Notes

1. Paust, *Terrorism and the International Law of War*, 64 MIL. L. REV. 1 (1974), *reprinted in* 14 REV. DE DROIT PENAL MILT. ET DE DROIT DE LA GUERRE 13 (1975).

2. *See id; see also* pp. 349-358 *supra.*

3. *See also* Murphy, *Protected Persons and Diplomatic Facilities*, ch. 5 of this report. Murphy, *The Role of International Law in the Prevention of Terrorist Kidnapping of Diplomatic Personnel*, in INTERNATIONAL TERRORISM AND POLITICAL CRIMES (M.C. Bassiouni ed. 1975). It should also be noted that a distinction between private and public targets does not reflect the split in concern, as many public targets, such as local politicians and police, are not "private," nor are they specially protected under international law. A distinction between "specially protected" and "protected" seems more realistic.

4. *See, e.g.*, Lasswell & McDougal, *Criteria For A Theory About Law*, 44

S. CAL. L. REV. 362 (1971); Paust, *An International Structure for Implementation of the 1949 Geneva Conventions: Needs and Function Analysis*, 1 YALE STUDIES IN WORLD PUB. ORDER 148 (1974). For the writer's definitional approach, *see supra* note 1 at 1-5, and Paust, *Private Measures of Sanction*, ch. 13 of this report. Here we are concerned with effort by precipitators who seek to utilize the strategy of terrorism against "nonprotected" persons or things as instrumental targets or to coerce "nonprotected" persons as primary targets.

    5. *See* Appendix 6A.

    6. *See* T. FARER, THE LAWS OF WAR 25 YEARS AFTER NUREM-BERG 42-43 (1971); C.E.I.P., REPORT OF THE CONFERENCE ON CONTEMPORARY PROBLEMS OF THE LAW OF ARMED CONFLICTS 78-79 (1971) (statement of T. Farer); Falk, *Six Legal Dimensions of the United States Involvement in the Vietnam War*, 2 THE VIETNAM WAR AND INT'L LAW 216, 240 (1969); G. SOREL, REFLECTIONS ON VIOLENCE 132 (1950).

    7. Gurr, *Characteristics of Contemporary Terrorism*, THE POLITICS OF TERRORISM: A READER IN THEORY AND PRACTICE (M. Stohl ed. forthcoming). His study shows that domestic political figures and military or police personnel were principal targets in some 31 percent of the overall cases, with "random victims" constituting only 8 percent from 1961-1970. *See id.*

    8. *See id.*

    9. *Id.*

    10. *Id.*

    11. "Nonprotected" targets are numerous, soft, and often "spectacular." *See* Crozier, Houston Post, Jan. 18, 1976, at 5, col. 1; N.Y. Times, Sept. 3, 1975, at 16, col. 1.

    12. Here are employed the four general categories of strategy utilized by McDougal and Feliciano in their study of coercion and public order. *See* M. McDOUGAL & F. FELICIANO, LAW AND MINIMUM WORLD PUBLIC ORDER (1961).

    13. *See* allegations contained in A.C.L.U. report, N.Y. Times, June 27, 1975, at 4, col. 4; L.A. Times, Jan. 26, 1976, at 1, col. 6. A recent revelation of FBI terrorism conducted against domestic radicals is contained in news accounts of kidnapings and threats in the New York area. *See* N.Y. Times, June 25, 1976, at 1, col. 3.

    14. *See also* N.Y. Times, June 25, 1976, at 6, col. 4; N.Y. Times, June 28, 1976, at 12, col. 3; Houston Post, Feb. 11, 1976, at 4, col. 3 (Argentina); also *see* Appendix 6A. Such "warfare" would only leave markets, restaurants, streets, and homes as the battlefield of political-ideological controversy and the stage for spiraling nondistinction in targeting.

    15. *See also* Evans, *Aircraft and Aviation Facilities*, ch. 1 of this report, at 37-38; Murphy, *Protected Persons and Diplomatic Facilities*, ch. 5 of this report, at 315; Mann, *Personnel and Property of Transnational Business Operations*, ch. 7 of this report, at 444.

16. *See, e.g.*, note 73 *infra* and note 12 *supra*; Lasswell & McDougal, *supra* note 4; McDougal, Lasswell, & Reisman, *Theories About International Law: Prologue to a Configurative Jurisprudence*, 8 VA. J. INT'L L. 188 (1968).

17. The use of the word "innocent" appears in some 39 of the 55 replies made to the secretary-general by August 1973 or contained in the G.A. *Ad Hoc* Committee Report on International Terrorism, Observations of States Submitted in Accordance with General Assembly Resolution 3034 (XXVII), U.N. Doc. A/AC. 160/1 & Adds. 1-5 (1973) [hereinafter cited as U.N. Doc. A/AC. 160/1 & Adds. 1-5].

18. For relevant legal norms *see, e.g.*, Convention Relative to the Protection of Civilian Persons in Time of War, dated at Geneva, Aug. 12, 1949, arts. 3, 5, 22, 33, 71, 147 6 U.S.T. 3516, T.I.A.S. No. 3365, 75 U.N.T.S. 287 [hereinafter cited as G.C.]; Convention Relative to the Treatment of Prisoners of War, dated at Geneva, Aug. 12, 1949, arts. 13, 82-108, 130 [hereinafter cited as G.P.W.]; U.S. DEP'T OF ARMY, FIELD MANUAL NO. 27-10, THE LAW OF LAND WARFARE (1956) [hereinafter cited as FM 27-10]; United States v. List, 11 TRIALS OF WAR CRIMINALS BEFORE THE NUREMBERG MILITARY TRIBUNALS 1253, 1270 (1950) [hereinafter cited as T.W.C.]. *See also* Paust, *My Lai and Vietnam: Norms, Myths and Leader Responsibility*, 57 MIL. L. REV. 99, 138-39 (1972), on the potential for human disaster and massacres inherent in the use of such an ambiguous criterial referent as "innocent."

19. The use of the word "indiscriminate" appears in some 7 of the 55 replies made to the secretary-general. *See* U.N. Doc. A/A.C. 160/1 & Adds. 1-5, *supra* note 17. Included here are replies from the Federal Republic of Germany, France, Israel, Italy, Norway, Romania, and South Africa.

20. *See id.* Included are replies from Austria (particularly countries that have nothing to do with the conflict), Barbados (third states), Belgium (third states having no connection with the state of war), Canada, Czechoslovakia ("unconcerned" persons *re*: political or other motives), Federal Republic of Germany ("not involved" in the conflicts), Iran (persons "unconnected with—or not responsible for—the basic cause of the grievance"), Ireland, Italy (particularly persons with "no link" and arenas "beyond areas of tension"), Netherlands (concentrate on those "not parties" to a conflict), Norway (concentrate on acts against a third state), Yugoslavia (acts "outside the areas of belligerence").

21. *See* notes 59 & 60 *infra*.

22. *See* note 14 *supra* and note 60 *infra*. *See also* Friedlander, *Sowing the Wind: Rebellion and Terror-Violence in Theory and Practice*, 6 DEN. J. INT'L L. & POL'Y 83 (1976).

23. *See, e.g.*, U.N.: Report of the Secretary General, Measures to Prevent International Terrorism Which Endangers or Takes Innocent Human Lives or Jeopardizes Fundamental Freedoms, And Study of the Underlying Causes of Those Forms of Terrorism and Acts of Violence Which Lie in Misery, Frustration, Grievance and Despair and Which Cause Some People to Sacrifice Human

Lives, Including Their Own, in an Attempt to Effect Radical Changes, 27 U.N. GAOR, C.6 Annexes (Agenda Item 92) 41 U.N. Doc. A/C.6/418, Annex 1 (1972) [hereinafter cited as U.N. Doc. A/C.6/418].

24. ON PROTRACTED WAR 58 (1967); G. SOREL, *supra* note 6, at 132. *See also* VON CLAUSEWITZ, ON WAR (Jolles trans. 1943).

25. Gerassi, *Violence, Revolution and Structural Change in Latin America*, LATIN AMERICA: THE DYNAMICS OF SOCIAL CHANGE 116 (1972). *See also* G. SOREL, *supra* note 6.

26. HANDBOOK OF REVOLUTIONARY WARFARE 100 (1972).

27. *See* T. FARER, *supra* note 6.

28. *Id.* at 42-43. This, of course, begs a fundamental question.

29. *Id.* at 43.

30. *See* Appendix 6A.

31. Falk, *supra* note 6. T. TAYLOR, NUREMBERG AND VIETNAM: AN AMERICAN TRAGEDY 137 (1970), classified this as a "military necessity" argument in his view, but terrorism and killing in violation of positive rules of international law are never allowed even if viewed as necessary by guerrillas or professors. *See* United States v. List, *supra* note 18; *see also* R. FALK, A STUDY OF FUTURE WORLDS 340-41 (1975).

32. Falk, *supra* note 6. *See also* G. SOREL, *supra* note 6. For a related conclusionary "questioning" of the utility of law in the context of guerrilla warfare and a conclusionary attempt to justify unilateral decisions by the parties to armed conflict as the binding decisions of legality on all others in the community (not to mention all other signatories of the Geneva Conventions), *see* A. Rubin, *The Status of Rebels Under the Geneva Conventions of 1949*, 21 INT'L & COMP. L.O. 481-82 (1972); *also see id.* at 477-79 concerning treaty interpretation. Gurr's initial conclusion that "political terrorism appears to be a tactic of political activists who lack the broad class support needed for large-scale revolutionary activity" supports the conclusion that terrorists usually *lack* political support, and that terrorism in such cases thus inhibits a full and free self-determination process. *See* Gurr, *supra* note 7. Gurr would agree with Falk that terrorism tends to involve relatively small numbers of victims, but both seem to ignore the effects of terror on the broader audiences of primary targets or spill-over victims. Moreover, Gurr's findings indicate that actual injury and suffering among "targets" is rather indiscriminate, with noncombatants injured more often. *See* Gurr, *supra* note 7, at 18-19.

33. *See* Paust, *supra* note 1, at 1-3; Paust, *A Survey of Possible Legal Responses to International Terrorism: Prevention, Punishment and Cooperative Action*, 5 GA. J. INT'L & COMP. L. 431-33 (1975).

34. *See, e.g.*, W. LaFAVE & A. SCOTT, HANDBOOK ON CRIMINAL LAW 611-12 (1972).

35. *See, e.g.*, WEBSTER'S THIRD NEW INTERNATIONAL DICTIONARY, "terrorism," at 2361 (1966) ("use of terror as a means of coercion").

36. *See generally* Lasswell & McDougal, *supra* note 4; Gurr, *supra* note 7; H. LASSWELL, A PRE-VIEW OF POLICY SCIENCES (1971). *See also* Kerstetter, *Practical Problems of Law Enforcement*, ch. 11 of this report, at 535.

37. Texas Penal Code, § 22.07(a) (effective Jan. 1, 1974).

38. *Id.* § 22.07(b).

39. *See* analysis in Paust, *Private Measures of Sanction*, ch. 13 of this report, at 613-614, n. 7.

40. *See also* Nicaraguan Penal Code, art. 499(a)(b)(d), which makes a person who possesses tear gas or who *threatens* "to harm" persons or organizations by mail, phone or other media a "terrorist criminal," Summary of Responses to the Department of State Circular Airgram Regarding Law and Practice on Terrorism, Nicaragua, 1 (Feb. 1976) [hereinafter cited as Circular, name of country, page, and date of summary] : USSR Penal Code, special pt., ch. 1 (Crimes Against the State), art. 66 ("Terrorist Act"), killing or causing grave bodily injury to authority figures "for the purpose of subverting or weakening the Soviet regime," and art. 67, killing or causing grave bodily injury to a representative of a foreign state "for the purpose of provoking war or international complications," *see* Circular, USSR, 1-2 (May 10, 1976).

41. *See, e.g.*, Decree Law No. 898, Sept. 1969, art. 28, summarized in Circular, Brazil, 1 (Jan. 1976); Circular, Chile, 1-4 (Oct. 1975); Circular, Costa Rica, 3 (Oct. 1975) (title XVII, art. 372); Circular, France, 1 (May 1976); Circular, Italy, 1-2 (May 1976); Circular, Federal Republic of Germany, 1 (Sept. 1975); Circular, South Africa, 1-2 (Oct. 1975); Circular, Spain, 1-3 (Oct. 1975) & 1-2 (Feb. 1976); Circular, United Kingdom 1-2 (Nov. 1975). Many have antiterrorist decrees, statutes, and acts *without* a definition of terrorism. *But see* Spanish Penal Code, art. 261, "with the intention of terrorizing the inhabitants. . . ." Circular, Spain, 3 (Oct. 1975), *supra* note 40.

42. *See* CSSR Penal Code § § 93/94 summarized in Circular, Czechoslovakia, 1 (Jan. 1976), *supra* note 40.

43. *See* El Salvador Criminal Code, art. 400 (utilizing weapons, explosives, etc.), Circular, El Salvador, 2-3 (Jan. 1976); Austria Penal Code, art. 99 (threat with intent to create "fear and alarm"), Circular, Austria, 2 (Sept. 1975); Bolivia Penal Code, bk. II, tit. 1, ch. 3, art. 133 ("intimidate or terrorize . . . stir up uprisings and disorders . . . raise shouts of alarm . . . "), Circular, Bolivia, 1 (Feb. 1976); Lebanese Penal Code, art. 314 ("all deeds the objective of which is to create a state of alarm" committed with use of certain weapons, toxins, etc.), Circular, Lebanon, 1 (Jan. 1976); Mexican Penal Code, ch. VI (alarm, fear or terror by violent means, certain weapons, toxins, etc.), Circular, Mexico, 1 (Aug. 7, 1975) (prepared by J.F. Murphy); and Nicaraguan Penal Code, art. 499 (for the purpose of disturbing public order, or sowing or causing unrest), Circular, Nicaragua, 1 (Feb. 1976), *supra* note 40. *See also* Criminal Code of Canada (crime of intimidation), Circular, Canada, 1 (Oct. 1975), *supra* note 40. This broad approach has been utilized here as well. *See* Mann, *Personnel and Property of Transnational Business Operations*, ch. 7 of this report, at 400.

44. USSR Penal Code, special pt., ch. 1, art. 66, Circular, USSR, 1 (May 10, 1976), *supra* note 40. Furthermore, the restrictive focus on state or public figures as targets is nearly outside the scope of this paper—no attention is paid to attacks on property or to the vast majority of other nonprotected persons.

45. Not included here are Austria, Bolivia, Czechoslovakia, and the Soviet Union.

46. Included here are Lebanon, Mexico, Nicaragua, and El Salvador.

47. *See also* Mexican Penal Code, ch. VI ["any *other* violent means" (emphasis added)], Circular, Mexico, 1 (Aug. 7, 1975) (prepared by J.F. Murphy), *supra* note 40.

48. Even if another provision regulates attempts to violate the USSR Penal Code, special pt., ch. 1, art. 66, it would appear that a "threat" not amounting to an actual attempt to kill or injure would not be proscribed. *See* note 44 *supra*.

49. *See* note 43 *supra*.

50. *See* note 48 *supra*.

51. *Compare* the Mexican Penal Code, ch. 6, *supra* note 47, *with* Appendix 6A and definitional factors identified in Paust, *Some Thoughts on "Preliminary Thoughts" on Terrorism*, 68 AM. J. INT'L L. 502 (1974).

52. *See e.g.*, U.N. Doc. A/C.6/418, *supra* note 23, at 7, 41. Even in time of war, when power struggle is at its greatest intensity, it has long been a basic expectation of man that there are limits to allowable death and suffering and that certain normative protections are peremptory. *See, e.g.*, Hague Convention No. IV, Respecting the Laws and Customs of War on Land, Oct. 18, 1907, Annex, preamble, & art. 22, 36 Stat. 2277, T.S. No. 539; 1 Bevans 631, 94 L.N.T.S. 2138 [hereinafter cited as H.C. IV]. *See also* R. Rosenstock, *At The United Nations: Extending the Boundaries of Int'l Law*, 59 A.B.A.J. 412, 413 (Apr. 1973); Paust, *supra* note 18, and references cited; U.N. Report of the Secretary General, Respect for Human Rights in Armed Conflicts, 25 U.N. GAOR, (Agenda Item 47) 1, U.N. Doc. A/8052 (1970) [hereinafter cited as U.N. Doc. A/8052]; G.A. Res. 2675, 25 U.N. GAOR, Supp. (No. 28) 76, U.N. Doc. A/8028 (1970); U.N. Report of the Secretary General, Respect for Human Rights in Armed Conflicts, 24 U.N. GAOR, (Agenda Item 61) U.N. Doc. A/7720 (1969) [hereinafter cited as U.N. Doc. A/7720]; G.A. Res. 2444, 23 U.N. GAOR, Supp. (No. 18) 50, U.N. Doc. A/7218 (1969), condemning indiscriminate warfare, attacks on the civilian population as such and refusals to distinguish between "those taking part" in the hostilities and those who are not; FM 27-10, *supra* note 18; Lauterpacht, *The Problem of the Revision of the Law of War*, 29 BRIT. Y.B. INT'L L. 360, 369 (1952) on the peremptory norm against intentional terrorization of the civilian population, as such, not incidental to lawful military operations.

53. Re: the theory that "the ends justify the means." *See* U.N. Doc. A/C.6/418, *supra* note 23, at 41. *See also* OAS Convention to Prevent and Punish the Acts of Terrorism Taking the Form of Crimes Against Persons and

Related Extortion That Are of International Significance, Feb. 2, 1971, art. 2, T.I.A.S. No. 8413, Serie Sobre Tratados [S.S.T.] No. 37, OAS Off. Doc./OAS/ Ser.A/17 [hereinafter cited as 1971 OAS Convention on Terrorism], *reprinted in* U.N. Doc. A/C.6/418, *supra* note 23, at annex V; Convention for the Suppression of Unlawful Acts, against the Safety of Civil Aviation, signed at Montreal, Sept. 23, 1971, arts. 7, 8, 24 U.S.T. 564, T.I.A.S. No. 7570 (binding 73 states as of June 30, 1977) [hereinafter cited as 1971 Montreal Convention], *reprinted in* U.N. Doc. A/C.6/418, *supra* note 23, at annex IV; Convention for the Suppression of Unlawful Seizure of Aircraft, signed at The Hague, Dec. 16, 1970, arts. 7, 8, 22 U.S.T. 1641, T.I.A.S. No. 7192 (binding 80 states as of June 30, 1971) [hereinafter cited as 1970 Hague Conventiona], *reprinted in* U.N. Doc. A/C.6/418, *supra* note 23, at annex III; General Aviation and Policy of the Organization with Regard to Acts of Terrorism and, Especially, the Kidnapping of Persons and Extortion in Connection with That Crime, June 30, 1970, A.G. Res. 4(I-E/70) OAS Doc. OAS/Ser.P/I-E.2 (1970) [hereinafter cited as A.G. Res. 4(I-E/70)], *reprinted in* U.N. Doc. A/C.6/418, *supra* note 23, at 36, *reprinted in* 9 INT'L LEGAL MATERIALS 1084 (1970), stating: "The political and ideological pretexts utilized as justification for the crimes in no way mitigate their cruelty and irrationality or the ignoble nature of the means employed, and in no way remove their character as acts in violation of essential human rights"; Convention on Offenses and Certain Other Acts Committed on Board Aircraft, Sept. 14, 1963, art. 2, 20 U.S.T. 2941; T.I.A.S. No. 6768; 704 U.N.T.S. 219 (binding 87 states as of June 30, 1977), implying an exclusion of any exceptions to prosecution on the basis of purpose or "political" offense [hereinafter cited as 1963 Tokyo Convention], *reprinted in* U.N. Doc. A/C.6/418, *supra* note 23, at annex II. For other relevant references, *see, e.g.*, M. McDOUGAL & F. FELICIANO, LAW AND MINIMUM WORLD PUBLIC ORDER, 72, 80 nn. 194-95, 134-35, 186-88, 521-24 & 529 (1961) [hereinafter cited as M. McDOUGAL & F. FELICIANO]; 2 L. OPPENHEIM, INTERNATIONAL LAW 218 (H. Lauterpacht ed., 7th ed. 1952); FM 27-10 *supra* note 18 at para. 3(a); 4 COMMENTARY, GENEVA CONVENTION RELATIVE TO THE PROTEC-TION OF CIVIL PERSONS IN TIME OF WAR 15-16, 34, 37-40, 225-26 (J. Pictet ed. 1958) [hereinafter cited as J. Pictet, 4 COMMENTARY]; United States v. List, 11 T.W.C. *supra* note 18; United States v. von Leeb, 10-11 *id.*; H. HALLECK, INTERNATIONAL LAW 426 (1861).

54. U.N. Doc. A/C.6/418, *supra* note 23.

55. Early work on terrorism prior to 1937 included drafts that specifically excluded terrorism or related acts from "political" offenses and created a criminal offense where the purpose was to "propound or put into practice political or social ideas" or "commit an act with a political and terroristic" purpose, thus pointing to the exclusion of the offense from the category of "political" crimes for extradition purposes. *See* U.N. Doc. A/C.6/418, *supra* note 23, at 11, 13, 16, 22. Furthermore, many extradition treaties have

excluded terrorism from "political" offenses; *see id.* at 16-21. The Convention for the Prevention and Punishment of Terrorism, Nov. 16, 1937, arts. 1, 9-10, 19, 19 LEAGUE OF NATIONS O.J. 23 (1938) [hereinafter cited as 1937 Convention on Terrorism], would seem to fit within this trend; so would the United States Draft Convention on Terrorism, Sept. 25, 1972, arts. 2-4, 6, 7, U.N. Doc. A/C.6/L.850 (1972) *reprinted in* 11 INT'L LEGAL MATERIALS 1382 (1972). *See also* Declaration of the Conference at St. James' Palace, Jan. 13, 1942, Doc. Inter-Allied Information Comm. (1942), *reprinted in* 37 AM. J. INT'L L. 84-85 (1943) (acts under "regime of terror," including the execution of hostages and massacres, thus inflicted on civilian populations are not political crimes). The U.S.-Cuba Agreement on the Hijacking of Aircraft and Vessels and Other Offenses, Feb. 15, 1973, arts. 1, 4, 24 U.S.T. 737, T.I.A.S. No. 7579, also seems to exclude the offense listed from the category of "political" crimes for purposes of extradition (and this seems to be the whole purpose of the agreement).

56. For example, even though the European Convention on Human Rights allows certain derogations under specified conditions, it affirms that no derogation is permissible from articles 2 (except "lawful" acts of war) and 3 or from other international obligations (such as H.C. IV, *supra* note 52, or the 1949 Geneva Conventions). The convention adds that nothing shall imply any right for any state, group, or person to derogate from the rights and freedoms of persons set forth in the convention or to limit such rights to a greater extent than is provided in the convention. *See* European Convention for the Protection of Human Rights and Fundamental Freedoms, Nov. 4, 1950, arts. 15, 17, 213 U.N.T.S. 221 (1950) (arts. 2 & 3 prohibit conduct most often connected with terrorism). Similar absolute prohibitions against conduct that includes terroristic acts appear in other human rights instruments. *See* American Convention on Human Rights, Nov. 22, 1969, arts. 4-5, 8, 25, 27, 29, 32 (not yet in effect), OAS/Ser.K/XVI/1.1, Doc. 65 Rev. 1 Corr. 2 (1970), *reprinted in* 65 AM. J. INT'L. L. 679-702 (1971); International Covenant on Civil and Political Rights, Dec. 16, 1966, arts. 6, 7, 4(1)(2), adopted by G.A. Res. 2200, 21 U.N. GAOR, Supp. (No. 16) 52-58, U.N. Doc. A/6316 (1966) (vote: 106-0-0) (not yet in effect); G.C., *supra* note 18, at arts. 3, 4, 13, 16, 27-33, 147. Note also that these prescriptions do not depend on reciprocity between contending participants in a particular arena for their force and effect, but are obligations to mankind (or at least to regional persons), and state provisional characterizations of persons and protections are subject to community review. *See* M. Mc-DOUGAL & F. FELICIANO, *supra* note 53, at 218-19; U.N. Doc. A/C.6/418, *supra* note 23, at 6-7, 40-41; U.N. Doc. A/7720, *supra* note 52, at 31; J. Pictet, 4 COMMENTARY, *supra* note 53, at 15-17, 21, 23, 34, 37-40, 225-29.

57. The concept of law adopted here recognizes the interplay between patterns of authority and patterns of control and that "authority" is ultimately based in the shared expectations of all members of the living human community. Decisions that are controlling but not based at all on authority are not law but

naked power. *See* Lasswell & McDougal, *Criteria For A Theory About Law*, 44 S. CAL. L. REV. 362, 384 (1971) and references cited at 380 n.36 & 390 n.40. *See also* Moore, *Prolegomenon to the Jurisprudence of Myres McDougal and Harold Lasswell*, 54 VA. L. REV. 662 (1968), and references cited at 664 n.3. Terrorism motivated by "blind fanatacism, or . . . the adoption of an extremist ideology which subordinates morality and all other human values to a single aim" or the dominance of parochial political dogma by coercive violence is, of course, rejected. *See* U.N. Doc. A/C.6/418, *supra* note 23, at 9, para. 18; and *Air Piracy Curb Signed by Nixon*, Washington Post, Nov. 2, 1972, at 7, col. 3, quoting the former president: "A civilized society cannot tolerate terrorism. . . . Any action which makes a diplomat, a government official or any innocent citizen a pawn in a politically motivated dispute undermines the safety of every other person." *See also* Rogers, *A World Free of Violence*, 67 DEP'T STATE BULL. 425, 429 (Oct. 16, 1972), stating that terrorist acts "must be universally condemned, whether we consider the cause the terrorists invoke noble or ignoble, legitimate or illegitimate"; Convention To Prevent and Punish Acts of Terrorism, Dep't of State Executive Report No. 92-93 to Senate Comm. on Foreign Rel., 92d Cong., 2d Sess. 4 (1972) (statement of M. Feldman, Assistant Legal Adviser for Inter-American Affairs, Department of State).

58. *See, e.g.*, Lawrence, *The Status Under International Law of Recent Guerrilla Movements in Latin America*, 7 INT'L LAW. 405-08, 413, 420 (1973); Rubin, *The Status of Rebels Under the Geneva Conventions of 1949*, 21 INT'L & COMP. L.Q. 472, 481 (1972); T. FARER, THE LAWS OF WAR 25 YEARS AFTER NUREMBERG 42-43 (1971); Falk, *Six Legal Dimensions of the United States Involvement in the Vietnam War*, 2 THE VIETNAM WAR AND INT'L LAW 216, 240 (R. Falk ed. 1969), stating that the insurgent-guerrilla has no alternative other than terror to mobilize an effective operation. For a different view, *see* Paust, *supra* note 18, at 128-46. *See also* Rosenblad, *Starvation as a Method of Warfare–Conditions for Regulation by Convention*, 7 INT'L LAW. 252, 258, 267 (1973); Schwarzenberger, *Terrorists, Guerrilleros and Merce-naries*, 1971 UNIV. OF TOLEDO L. REV. 71 (1971); T. MERON, SOME LEGAL ASPECTS OF ARAB TERRORISTS' CLAIMS TO PRIVILEGED COMBATANCY 1-10, 25-28 (1970); T. TAYLOR, NUREMBERG AND VIET-NAM: AN AMERICAN TRAGEDY 17, 22, 39-41, 136-37, 145, 192-95 (1970); Wales, *Algerian Terrorism*, 22 NAVAL WAR COLL. REV. 26 (1969); W. FORD, RESISTANCE MOVEMENTS AND INT'L LAW (ICRC reprint 1968) (reviewing several customary trends, opinions of scholars, and relevant cases); U.N. Doc. A/C.6/418, *supra* note 23, at 7, 41; J. Pictet, 4 COMMENTARY, *supra* note 53, at 15-16, 31, 34, 37-40, 225-26 (concerning the peremptory prohibition of terrorism); P. BORDWELL, THE LAW OF WAR BETWEEN BELLIGERENTS 229-31 (1908); H. HALLECK, INTERNATIONAL LAW 386-88, 400-01, 426-27 (1861); G. VONMARTENS, THE LAW OF NATIONS 287 (Cobbett trans., 4 ed. 1829). This is not the place for a more elaborate exploration, but it

should be noted that Lawrence's conclusions about the general "humanitarian" nature of Latin American guerrillas and their "discriminating" tactics (*see* Lawrence, *supra* at 406, 418-19) can be questioned, and he deleted certain references in Che Guevara's cited work (*id.* at 406 n.2) concerning the harassment of cities with concomitant paralysis and distress to the entire population and certain "ruthless" tactics therein elaborated. On this point he also ignored the 1970 resolution of the OAS Inter-American Commission on Human Rights, which condemned acts of political terrorism and of urban or rural guerrillas as being grave violations of human rights and fundamental freedoms. Terrorism for Political or Ideological Purposes, OAS Doc. OAS/Ser.L/ V/II.23, Doc. 19, Rev. 1 (Apr. 30, 1970) (Resolution approved by the Inter-American Commission on Human Rights at the 9th meeting of its 23d sess. held Apr. 16, 1970). *See also* U.N. Doc. A/C.6/418, *supra* note 23, at 35-39.

59. *See, e.g.*, PROPHETIC POLITICS: CRITICAL INTERPRETATIONS OF THE REVOLUTIONARY IMPULSE (M. Cranston ed. 1970). This work is useful for a concise reference to relevant claims by Che Guevara, Frantz Fanon, Jean-Paul Sartre, Herbert Marcuse, Ronald Laing, and others, and for a critical analysis of those claims from political, sociological, historical, and philosophical perspectives. *See also* G. SOREL, *supra* note 6.

60. *See* G. SOREL, *supra* note 6; at 11; H. MARCUSE, FIVE LECTURES 89-90, 93, 103-04 (1970); *cf. id.* at 79. For a related claim by the state (the Soviet Union), *see, e.g.*, CONTEMPORARY INTERNATIONAL LAW 6 & 13 (G. Tunkin ed. 1969). For recent evidence of insurgent practice along these lines, *see Argentine Guerrillas Vow More Attacks*, N.Y. Times, May 28, 1973, at 3, col. 6. In H. MARCUSE, SOVIET MARXISM—A CRITICAL ANALYSIS 199, 209 (1961), Marcuse seemed highly critical of this approach, stating that "the means prejudice the end" and that the "end recedes, the means becomes everything; and the sum total of means is 'the movement' itself. It absorbs and adorns itself with the values of the goal, whose realization 'the movement' itself delays." *Id.* at 225. *See also* M. OPPENHEIMER, THE URBAN GUERRILLA 50, 57, 59-60, 63-64, 66, 69, 161 (1969); A. CAMUS, THE REBEL 209, 292 *passim* (1956).

61. *See* U.N. Doc. A/C.6/418, *supra* note 23, at 9, 41; Schwarzenberger, *supra* note 58, at 76. *See also* McDOUGAL & FELICIANO at 79-80, 652, 656-58; authorities cited *infra* note 73.

62. *See also* pp. 354-356 *infra* regarding self-determination.

63. *See* Paust, *supra* note 33, at 431-33.

64. *Id.*

65. *See* United States Draft Convention for the Prevention of Certain Acts of International Terrorism, art. 1, 67 DEP'T STATE BULL. 431 (1972) (note the necessity for killing, serious bodily harm, or kidnaping or an attempt to do such). Not only are other types of conduct that could produce a terror outcome missing, but "attempt" does not include various forms of threat that may cause a terror outcome or effect.

66. *Id.*; *see also* Paust, *supra* note 33, at 431-33.

67. *See* Project of an International Declaration Concerning the Laws and Customs of War, Adopted by the Conference of Brussels, Aug. 27, 1874, arts. 9(4), 12, *reprinted in* 1 AM. J. INT'L L., SUPP. 96, 97-98 (1907). These expectations of law and custom were reiterated in the 1899 and 1907 Hague conventions. *See* Hague Convention with Respect to the Laws and Customs of War on Land, July 29, 1899, arts. 1(4), 2, 22, *reprinted in* 1 AM. J. INT'L L., SUPP. 129, 134-35, 142 (1907); H.C. IV, *supra* note 52, at annex, art. 22.

The Hague conventions were considered customary at Nuremberg; *see* FM 27-10, *supra* note 18, para. 6; Judgment of the I.M.T., I.T.M.W.C. *supra* note 18, 221, 254 (1947). *See also* WINTHROP, MILITARY LAW AND PRECEDENTS 778-79 (2d ed. 1920).

68. *See* Wright, *The Bombardment of Damascus*, 30 AM. J. INT'L L. 263, 273 (1926); Report of Subcomm. No. 1 of Comm. for Advancement of Int'l L. (1921), PROCEEDINGS AM. SOC'Y INT'L L. 102, 104 (1921), stating that "treacherous killings, massacres and terrorism are not allowed by the laws of war" [hereinafter cited as Report of Subcomm. No. 11; 1. J. GARNER, INTERNATIONAL LAW AND THE WORLD WAR 283 (1920); E. STOWELL & H. MUNRO, INTERNATIONAL CASES 173-76 (1916); 2 WHEATON's ELEMENTS OF INTERNATIONAL LAW 789-90 (6th ed. 1929). *See also* the 1818 trial of Arbuthnot and Ambrister, 3 WHARTON's DIGEST OF THE INTERNATIONAL LAW OF THE U.S. 326, 328 (1886); the Code of Articles of King Gustavus Adolphus of Sweden, art. 97 (1621), *reprinted in* WINTHROP, *supra* note 67, at 907, 913, stating that no man shall "tyrannize over any Churchman, or aged people, men or women, maides or children, unless they first take up arms. . . ." This prohibition grew into the customary prohibition of any form of violence against noncombatants. *See id.* at 778, 843 (concerning the case of the "anarchist" Pallas, tried by a court-martial at Barcelona in September 1893).

69. *See* Report Presented to the Preliminary Peace Conference by the Commission on the Responsibility of the Authors of the War and on Enforcement and Penalties, List of War Crimes, items no. 1, 3, 17 (1919) (copy at United States Army TJAG School) (members were: United States, British Empire, France, Italy, Japan, Belgium, Greece, Poland, Romania, and Serbia); Report of Subcomm. No. 1. It was not clear whether all forms of violent terrorism (including terrorization of combatants not in force control) were denounced, but a general ban on terrorism was affirmed along with other strategies generally utilized only against combatants or against both combatants and noncombatants (*i.e.*, assassination, use of prohibited weapons, treachery, etc.).

70. *See* Report of the Bryce Committee, 1914, *extract* in E. STOWELL & H. MUNRO, INTERNATIONAL CASES 173 (1916). The Bryce Report added that the murder of large numbers of innocent civilians is "an act absolutely forbidden by the rules of civilized warfare"; *id.* at 176.

71. For a brief consideration of the German jurists and the Prussia

War-book *see* T. BATY & J. MORGAN, WAR: ITS CONDUCT AND LEGAL RESULTS 176, 180-81. Karl von Clausewitz in 1832 had favored terrorizing the occupied populace including a spread of the "fear of responsibility, punishment, and ill-treatment which in such cases presses like a general weight against the whole population . . . ," *see id.* at 180 n.1; J.W. GARNER, INTERNATIONAL LAW AND THE WORLD AT WAR 278-82, 328 (1920). Garner added that it was "entirely in accord with the doctrines of the German militarists that war is a contest . . . against the civil population as well, that violence, ruthlessness, and terrorism are legitimate measures, and that whatever tends to shorten the duration of the war is permissible"; *id.* at 328. It is not clear whether Baty and Morgan repudiated the German views; but most other writers did. *See id.* at 283.

72. *See, e.g.*, E. STOWELL & H. MUNRO, *supra* note 70, J.W. GARNER, *supra* note 71, at 283; 2 WHEATON'S ELEMENTS OF INTERNATIONAL LAW, *supra* note 68, at 789-90; FRANCE, MINISTRY OF FOREIGN AFFAIRS, GERMANY'S VIOLATIONS OF THE LAW OF WAR, 1914-1915 at 77-215 (J. Bland trans. 1915). *Cf.* E. STOWELL, INTERNATIONAL LAW 523-26 (1931), arguing for a reconsideration of the German claim of permissible terror in cases where the principle of military necessity applies and warning of a "precedent" for a World War II calamity that he could only dimly envision and would not deny. The 1949 Geneva Conventions would prohibit all acts of terrorism against protected persons regardless of military necessity claims, but Stowell's remarks were significant with respect to certain World War II bombardments that were most likely permissible then but would be condemned today. *See* M. McDOUGAL & F. FELICIANO, *supra* note 53, at 79-80, 652-57.

73. *See* Lauterpacht, *The Problem of the Revision of the Law of War*, 29 BRIT. Y.B. INT'L L. 360, 378-79 (1952); McDOUGAL & FELICIANO, *supra* note 53, at 79-80, 652-58; CARNEGIE ENDOWMENT FOR INTERNATIONAL PEACE, REPORT OF THE CONFERENCE ON CONTEMPORARY PROBLEMS OF THE LAW OF ARMED CONFLICTS 39, 42 (1971); J. GARNER, RECENT DEVELOPMENTS IN INTERNATIONAL LAW 174 (Calcutta 1925). *Cf* E. STOWELL, *supra* note 72, at 524-26. Present support for a peremptory prohibition of intentional terrorization of noncombatants would also seem to come from R. Baxter, G.I.A.D. Draper, Professor J. Freymond, M. Greenspan, H. Levie, T. Meron, J. Pictet, G. Schwarzenberger, H. Meyrowitz, Y. Dinerstein, and others. *See* T. MERON, *supra* note 58; 1 & 3 ISRAEL Y.B. ON HUMAN RIGHTS (1973); Schwarzenberger, *supra* note 58, at 73-76.

74. *See id.*

75. G.C., art. 33. *See also* J. Pictet, 4 COMMENTARY, at 225-26, 594. This article is technically applicable only to noncombatants in the terror process since "protected persons" are defined in article 4. The article is also specifically applicable in case of an armed conflict of an international character including a civil war between "belligerents" (an article 2 conflict). *See* FM 27-10, *supra* note

18, para. 11(a); 2 L. OPPENHEIM, *supra* note 53, at 370 n.1; HALLECK, ELEMENTS OF INT'L LAW AND LAWS OF WAR 151-53 (1866) concerning the applicability of the law of war to civil war between "belligerents." Respected authority states that terrorism is also prohibited in an article 3 conflict (not of an international character), and it seems sufficiently clear that those who follow article 3 will not commit acts of terrorism against noncombatants. *See* J. Pictet, 4 COMMENTARY, at 31, 40.

76. *See, e.g.*, G.C., *supra* note 18, arts. 3, 16, 27, 31-34, 147; GPW, *supra* note 18, arts. 13, 17, 130. Common article 3 contains each of these.

77. *See* G.C., art. 31; J. Pictet, 4 COMMENTARY, at 219-20. *See also* GPW, arts. 13, 17, 99. Permissible derogations from this ban must serve other Geneva policies. *See* J. Pictet, 4 COMMENTARY, at 219-20.

78. *See, e.g.*, INT'L COMM. OF THE RED CROSS, I BASIC TEXTS, Protocol I, art. 45, Protocol II, art. 5 (Jan. 1972) (proposed draft Protocols to the Conventions, Conference of Governmental Experts, Geneva 3 May-3 June 1972), concerning specific prohibitions of "terrorization attacks" and "acts of terrorism." These prohibitions appear in articles designed to protect the general population and individual noncombatants against the dangers of armed conflict in both article 2 and 3 types of conflict (international and noninternational).

79. It is doubtful that the "and" is meant as a condition or that attacks with distinction or discriminate attacks on civilians are meant to be approved.

80. Again, it is doubtful that this sloppy draftsmanship contains an intended permissibility of discriminate attacks on noncombatants.

81. It should be noted that most of those protected by G.C., art. 4 are those in force control ("protected persons"); however, article 4 also refers to Part II of the convention and to a broader group of persons protected by arts. 13, 16, for example ("persons protected"). *See* J. Pictet, 4 COMMENTARY, at 50-51, 118-37; Paust, *Legal Aspects of the My Lai Incident: A Response to Professor Rubin*, 50 ORE. L. REV. 138 *reprinted in* 3 THE VIETNAM WAR AND INTERNATIONAL LAW (R. Falk ed. 1972). No such "in the hands of" or control limitations attach to common article 3 of the conventions and its prohibitions apply "in all circumstances" including "any time" and "any place" whatsoever. *See also* J. PAUST & A. BLAUSTEIN, WAR CRIMES TRIALS AND HUMAN RIGHTS: THE CASE OF BANGLADESH (1974).

82. *See* United States v. von Leeb, 10 T.W.C. at 1, and 11 T.W.C. at 528, adding that it might be impermissible to execute hostages under any circumstances. *Cf.* United States v. List, *supra* note 18, *id.* at 757, 1250, applying pre-1949 Geneva Convention norms.

83. *See* G.C., arts. 3, 34, 147; GPW, arts. 13, 84-85, 130; J. Pictet, 4 COMMENTARY, at 35-40, 229-31, 596-601.

84. *See* G.C., arts. 27, 33; J. Pictet, 4 COMMENTARY, at 199-202, 205, 224-29. These prohibitions arguably are applicable to an article 3 conflict as well, even though no specific mention of reprisals or collective penalties exists in

the article. *See id.* at 34, 39-40. In any event, it would be a very limited type of "reprisal" or "collective penalty" that could survive the absolute ban on hostages, murder, cruel treatment, torture, outrages upon personal dignity, other forms of inhuman treatment, and summary executions or the "passing of sentences" without regular court proceedings. Indeed, in view of the purpose of the article and the last mentioned form of prohibition, it would seem that collective "penalties" are also prohibited unless such is actually beyond the connotation of the phrase in that a personal guilt of each accused has been somehow determined by an authoritative judicial body utilizing fair procedure. *See also id.* at 225.

85. 1948 Universal Declaration of Human Rights, arts. 3, 5, G.A. Res. 217 A, U.N. Doc. A/810, at 71, (1948) [hereinafter cited as 1948 Universal Declaration]. This is the thirtieth anniversary of the declaration, and many scholars view it as an evidence of customary law. *See* J. CAREY, U.N. PROTECTION OF CIVIL AND POLITICAL RIGHTS 13-14 (1970), *citing* the 1968 Montreal Statement. *See also* G.A. Res. 3059, 28 U.N. GAOR, Supp. (No. 30) 74, U.N. Doc. A/9030 (1973) [hereinafter cited as G.A. Res. 3059] (adopted unanimously), rejecting "any form of torture and other cruel, inhuman or degrading treatment or punishment"—apparently also rejecting, then, any excuse.

86. This type of language appears in common article 3 of the Geneva Conventions, and respected authority asserts that it is broad enough to cover acts specifically prohibited in other articles such as acts of terrorism. *See* J. Pictet, 4 COMMENTARY, at 3, 40. Detailed prohibitions contained in G.C., art. 3, but not necessarily in the 1948 Declaration as such include the taking of hostages and mutilation. *See also* 1948 Universal Declaration, at arts. 2, 10, 11; G.A. Res. 3059.

87. G.A. Res. 2200 A, at arts. 6(1), 7. Note that article 4(2) prohibits all derogations from this basic expectation. One wonders, however, if some claims to terrorize combatants not in force control could survive this blanketing prohibitory language through policy inquiry and a comparison with developed expectations concerning the law of war (note that the law of war may not forbid *all* terrorism). Since the human rights provisions apply to all persons and no derogation is allowed from relevant articles even in times of war or grave public danger, the presumption may lie with a peremptory prohibition (with respect to all participants).

88. *See* 1950 European Convention on Human Rights, arts. 2, 3; 1969 American Convention on Human Rights, arts. 4, 5, 7(1), 11(1). These regional human rights conventions also prohibit all derogations from the listed articles; *see* arts. 15(2) & 27(2) respectively.

89. A.G. Res. 4 (I-E/70), U.N. Doc. A/C.6/418, also *citing* the 1970 Inter-American Commission on Human Rights resolution on terrorism.

90. U.N. Doc. A/C.6/418, at 41. *See also id.* at 6.

91. G.A. Res. 3034, 27 U.N. GAOR Supp. (No. 30) 119, U.N. Doc. A/8730 (1972) [hereinafter cited as G.A. Res. 3034] [vote: 76-35, −17]. The writer feels that the split of votes was not due to the perspective outlined here. *See* Bennett, *U.S. Votes Against U.N. General Assembly Resolution Calling for Study of Terrorism*, 68 DEP'T STATE BULL. 81, 87-89 (1973). It should be noted that the word "innocent" is not a very useful criterion for distinction; nor does terrorization of the "guilty" leave mankind much better off. *See* note 69 *supra.*

92. *See* Resolutions Adapted by the XXIst International Conference of the Red Cross, Res. XIX (Istanbul Declaration), 9 INT'L REV. OF THE RED CROSS, 608, 620-21 (1969). *See also* J. PICTET, THE PRINCIPLES OF INTERNATIONAL LAW 34-36 (1966); Final Act of the International Conference on Human Rights, Teheran, April-May 1968, Res. XXIII, at 18, U.N. Doc. A/CONF. 32/41 (1968).

93. *See* 1948 Universal Declaration of Human Rights, 18-19, 21; 1966 Covenant on Civil and Political Rights, *supra* note 56, arts. 18-19, 25; 1950 European Convention on Human Rights, arts. 9-10 (*cf.* art. 16), Protocol I, art. 3; 1969 American Convention on Human Rights, arts. 6(1), 12-13 16(1), 23.

94. *See* 1948 Universal Declaration of Human Rights, arts. 1-2; 1966 International Covenant on Civil and Political Rights, arts. 2(1), 3, 18(2); 1950 European Convention on Human Rights, arts. 1, 14; 1969 American Convention on Human Rights, arts. 1, 24.

95. *See* A.G. Res. 4, *supra* note 53, stating that acts of terrorism constitute crimes against humanity, serious violations of the "fundamental rights and freedoms of man" or "essential human rights," and flagrant violations of "the most elemental principles of the security of the individual and community as well as offenses against the freedom and dignity of the individual"; U.N. Doc. A/C.6/418, at 7, 9, 41, stating that "terrorism threatens, endangers or destroys the lives and fundamental freedoms of the innocent"; J. IRWIN II, LETTER OF SUBMITTAL, MESSAGE FROM THE PRESIDENT OF THE UNITED STATES TRANSMITTING THE CONVENTION TO PREVENT AND PUNISH THE ACTS OF TERRORISM TAKING THE FORM OF CRIMES AGAINST PERSONS AND RELATED EXTORTION THAT ARE OF INT'L SIGNIFICANCE, Exec. D, Senate, 92d Cong. 1st Sess. 3 (1971). *See also* Bennett, *supra* note 91, at 81-83, 92; G.S. Res. 3034, *supra* note 91 (*re:* governmental terrorism and human rights); Rogers, *supra* note 57, at 429.

96. *See* 1970 Declaration on Principles of International Law Concerning Friendly Relations and Co-operation among States in Accordance with the Charter of the United Nations, G.A. Res. 2625, 25 U.N. GAOR, Supp. (No. 18), 122-24, U.N. Doc. A/8028 (1970) [hereinafter cited as G.A. Res. 2625]; 1948 Universal Declaration of Human Rights, arts. 21(1), 21(3); G.A. Res. 2131, Declaration of the Inadmissibility of Intervention in the Domestic Affairs of States and the Protection of Their Independence and Sovereignty, 20 U.N.

GAOR, Supp. (No. 14), 11-12, U.N. Doc. A/6014 [hereinafter cited as G.A. Res. 2131] (1965) [vote: 109-0-1 (U.K.)]; 1966 Covenant on Civil and Political Rights, *supra* note 56, arts. 1, 25(a)(b).

97. G.A. Res. 2625, *supra* note 96 [elaborating expectations connected with U.N. CHARTER, art. 2(4) and adding: "when the acts referred to in the present paragraph involve a threat or use of force"]. *See also* Draft Convention on Terrorism, *supra* note 65, preamble art. 10(1); 1971 OAS Convention on Terrorism, art. 8(a); 1971 Montreal Convention, *supra* note 53, art. 10(1); 1937 Convention on Terrorism, *supra* note 55, arts. 1(1), 3; G.A. Res. 2131, Draft Code of Offenses Against the Peace and Security of Mankind, arts. 2(4), (5), (6), (13), 9 U.N. GAOR, Supp. (no. 9), at 11-12, U.N. Doc. A/2693 (1954) (adopted by the U.N. ILC). *See also* LEAGUE OF NATIONS COVENANT, art. 10; 1 L. OPPENHEIM, INTERNATIONAL LAW 292-93 (H. Lauterpacht ed., 8th ed. 1955); 2 L. OPPENHEIM, *supra* note 53, at 698, 704, 751-54. For comments on the 1970 Declaration Concerning Friendly Relations, *see, e.g.*, U.N. Doc. A/C.6/418, at 27-29; Rosenstock, *The Declaration of Principles of International Law Concerning Friendly Relations: A Survey*, 65 AM. J. INT'L L. 713 (1971).

98. G.A. Res. 2625. This prescriptive elaboration is listed under a section on U.N. CHARTER art. 2(7).

99. *See* U.N. Doc. A/C.6/418, at 26. This would include individual criminal sanctioning, and such individual responsibility can be found in numerous examples of current expectation or traced to customary law, as is the 1818 case of Arbuthnot and Ambrister. *See* 3 WHARTON, DIGEST OF INTERNATIONAL LAW 326 (1886).

100. *See e.g.*, U.N. Doc. A/C.6/418, at 30; *supra* notes 97-98; 2 L. OPPENHEIM, *supra* note 53, at 656, 678-80, 698, 704, 751-54, 757-58; Wright, *Subversive Intervention*, 54 AM. J. INT'L L. 521, 533 (1960); 2 G. HACKWORTH, DIG. OF INT'L L. § 155, at 334-36 (1941); United States v. Arjona, 120 U.S. 479 (1887).

101. If this is true, then the main focus of this chapter and Paust, *supra* note 1, should allow the reader to test the new efforts put before the United Nations in terms of convention proximity to implementary needs and realistic possibilities.

102. These are the 1963 Tokyo, 1970 Hague and 1971 Montreal Conventions. *See also* Evans, *Aircraft and Aviation Facilities*, ch. 1 of this report.

103. *Supra* note 53. Note that article 1 articulates the undertaking of the contracting parties to prevent and punish all acts of terrorism, athough the convention's main aim seems to lie in the protection of "persons to whom the State has the duty to give special protection according to international law" (notably diplomatic personnel). Do protected persons under the Geneva Conventions qualify? It would not seem to matter in view of the Geneva prohibition of terrorism and the Geneva obligations upon all signators and parties to take affirmative protective measures. *See* J. Pictet, 4 COMMENTARY, at 45-51,

133-35, 201-05, 225-26 on this point. *See also* Murphy, *Protected Persons and Diplomatic Facilities*, ch. 5 of this report, at 000 ff.

104. *See* U.N. Doc. A/AC.160/1 & Adds. 1-5. Included here (with some uncertainty as to actual position) are: the Byelorussian Soviet Socialist Republic (?), Cyprus, Czechoslovakia, Greece (?), Italy (?), Lebanon, Nigeria, Norway (?), Romania (?), the Syrian Arab Republic, the Ukranian Soviet Socialist Republic, the Soviet Union, the Yemen Arab Republic, and Yugoslavia. Sweden would seem to wish to exclude this context as well by its unacceptable, conclusionary definition of what is "international" [in apparent disregard of U.N. CHARTER, art. 2(7) consequences for human rights efforts] . *See id.* at 32-33.

105. It should be noted that the Nonaligned Group in the *Ad Hoc* Committee (Algeria, Congo, Democratic Yemen, Guinea, India, Mauritania, Nigeria, the Syrian Arab Republic, Tunisia, the United Republic of Tanzania, Yemen, Yugoslavia, Zaire, and Zambia) expressed the view that the ban on terrorism "*should not affect* the inalienable *right to* self-determination and independence . . . *and the legitimacy of their struggle*, in particular the struggle of national liberation movements, in accordance with the purpose and principles of the Charter. . . ." [emphasis added] . Some of the members of the Nonaligned Group seem to actually have taken a much stronger position elsewhere; see note 104 *supra* (*i.e.* Nigeria, the Syrian Arab Republic, and Yugoslavia). Note that a struggle "in accordance with the purposes and principles of the Charter" would most certainly seek to respect and to ensure respect for human rights in times of armed conflict (plus general human rights). *See* U.N. CHARTER, preamble, arts. 1(2)(3), 2(4), 55(c), 56.

106. Note that a claim that an otherwise permissible process of political change should not itself (as a whole) be banned because of its terror impact is far different from a claim that any means utilized during such a process should be legitimate when they are analyzed as separate strategies. It seems quite likely that most states that mention self-determination or national liberation movements wish to claim only that the overall process should not be impermissible because of some terror impact. The author notes that the mere accumulation of terror producing strategies that are separately impermissible into a movement should not result in a conclusion of permissibility. Thus the author wishes to reserve judgment on self-determination processes with the remark that they should not be impermissible *per se* because of some terror impact. Each process would have to be examined in terms of all relevant goal values and the actual context. *Contra* U.N. Doc. A/C.6/418, at 7, stating: "The subject of international terrorism has . . . nothing to do with the question of when the use of force is legitimate. . . ." Moreover, because of the author's concept of authority and legitimate self-determination (by all participants in a freely determined process), *see supra*, the author finds the remarks of Czechoslovakia that condemn acts of "individual" terrorism "as a means to achieve revolutionary aims" quite compatible with his own view. *See* U.N. Doc. A/AC.160/1/Add. 2,

at 3. *See also id.* for the apt statement of Austria that "acts of individual violence should be condemned . . . since they, by their very nature, infringe upon the right of self-determination of those peoples whose Governments become the object and aim of such terroristic acts and jeopardize peaceful and constructive relations between States."

107. *See, e.g.*, M. McDOUGAL & F. FELICIANO, *passim*; *supra* note 57. *See also* U.N. G.A. Res. 3166 (XXVIII) (Dec. 14, 1973), adopting the new Convention on the Prevention and Punishment of Crimes Against Internationally Protected Persons, Including Diplomatic Agents, recognizing that the convention "could not in any way prejudice the exercise of the legitimate right to self-determination. . . ."

108. *See* U.N. Doc. A/AC.160/1 & Adds. 1-5, *supra* note 17. They have left no other feasible interpretation. Included are: Cyprus, Czechoslovakia, Lebanon, Nigeria, the Syrian Arab Republic, the Ukranian Soviet Socialist Republic, the Soviet Union, the Yemen Arab Republic, and Yugoslavia. Note that the Soviet Union is included here while the Byelorussian Soviet Socialist Republic is not (surely an oddity) because of the Byelorrusian use of general terms such as movements, opposition, and assertion of rights, whereas the Soviet Union refers to acts and action (presumably any acts or means within the struggle, opposition, or assertion of rights). More specifically, Yugoslavia refers to an exclusion of interference "in any way" with struggles and an approval of the carrying on of a struggle "with all means at their disposal" (similar statements come from Cyprus, Czechoslovakia, Lebanon, Nigeria, the Syrian Arab Republic, and the Yemen Arab Republic).

109. Made only by three entities: Czechoslovakia, the Ukranian Soviet Socialist Republic, and the Soviet Union.

110. *See* U.N. Docs. A/AC.160/1/Add. 1 & Add. 2. Close positions are those of Lebanon and the Syrian Arab Republic, which refer to a situation where a people is fighting "to reconquer usurped territories, to drive out an invader," or to seek "the liquidation of foreign occupation."

111. *See, e.g.*, notes 52, 53, 56, & 105 *supra.*

112. *See* U.N. Doc. A/AC.160/1/Add. 1 & Add. 2. Advocates include: the Byelorussian Soviet Socialist Republic, the Ukranian Soviet Socialist Republic, and the Soviet Union.

113. *See* notes 58 & 60, *supra*; U.N. Doc. A/8052, at 56-57 (view of "some of the ICRC experts").

114. *See id.*

115. *See id.*

116. *See* Paust, *supra* note 18 Annex A; *id.* at 138-46; Paust, *Law in A Guerrilla Conflict: Myths, Norms and Human Rights*, 3 ISRAEL Y.B. ON HUMAN RIGHTS (1973). *See also* U.N. Doc. A/7720, at 54-55, 118-28; U.N. Doc. A/8052, at 56-73; and ICRC, I BASIC TEXTS, *supra* note 78, Protocol I, art. 38 at 15, Protocol II, art. 25 at 40.

117. *See supra* note 7, at 16-17. The percentage figure is, however, only 11 percent; but it ranged from 13 to 14 percent of the human targets in Europe and Latin America. Compare with these the frequency of reported attacks on police in Appendix 6A.

118. *See id.* at 17. Adding these together, the total is some 49 percent of the human targets.

119. *Id.* at 1 (emphasis added). *See also id.* at 19, stating: "Only 8 percent of all episodes and campaigns had as an explicit, primary objective the seizure of power or the advancement of a particular revolutionary ideology." *Cf.* E. Mickolus, Statistical Approaches to the Study of Terrorism, paper delivered at the New York Conference on International Terrorism, June 11, 1976, at table 7.

120. *See supra* note 1.

121. *See, e.g.*, Kelly, *Assassination in War Time*, 30 MIL. L. REV. 101 (1965); Paust, *supra* note 18, at 143-46.

122. *See* Appendix 6A.

123. For evidence of a distinction between terror assassination and mere elimination assassination, *see* M. HAVENS, C. LEIDEN, & K. SCHMITT, THE POLITICS OF ASSASSINATION (1970); NATIONAL COMMISSION ON THE CAUSES AND PREVENTION OF VIOLENCE, REPORT, ASSASSINATION AND POLITICAL VIOLENCE (1969).

124. For guidance, *see* W.M. REISMAN, NULLITY AND REVISION 836-51 (1971) (self-help); *cf.* Paust, *supra* note 4. *See also* Reisman, *Private Armies in a Global War System: Prologue to Decision*, 14 VA. J. INT'L L. 1 (1973).

125. *Supra* note 7, at 12. These trends seem confirmed for the 1970s. *See* E. Mickolus, *supra* note 119; D.L. Milbank, International and Transnational Terrorism: Diagnosis and Prognosis, paper delivered at the Department of State Conference on Terrorism, March 25, 1976 (newly declassified); *see* N.Y. Times, June 18, 1976, at 3, col. 6.

126. Gurr, *supra*, note 7.

127. *See, e.g.*, U.N. CHARTER, preamble, arts. 1, 55(c) and 56; Paust, *Human Rights and the Ninth Amendment: A New Form of Guarantee*, 60 CORNELL L. REV. 231 (1975); McDougal, *Human Rights and World Public Order: Principles of Content and Procedure for Clarifying General Community Policies*, 14 VA. J. INT'L L. 387 (1974).

128. *See* Paust, *Private Measures of Sanction*, ch. 13 of this report.

129. *See id*; Paust, *An International Structure for Implementation of the 1949 Geneva Conventions: Needs and Function Analysis*, 1 YALE STUD. WORLD PUB. ORDER 148 (1974).

130. *See also id.*; Paust, *supra* note 128.

131. The responsibility should rest within the Department of State as oppposed, for example, to Health, Education, and Welfare because of interconnected international legal aspects and effort. Further, there are relevant treaty

obligations, *see* Paust, *supra* note 129, which clearly make such efforts of great concern to the Department of State. Although the law of war is also relevant, the Department of Defense does not seem a proper entity for the ultimate control of such an effort. Certainly useful, however, would be past Department of Defense and Army J.A.G. efforts to implement the law of war in the military. *See also id.*

132. *See also supra* note 129 for more detailed approaches.

133. *See* N.Y. Times, June 9, 1976, at 1, col. 4; June 7, 1976, at 3, col. 3.

134. *See id.* (both articles).

135. *See* N.Y. Times, June 9, 1976, at 1, col. 4. *See also id.*, June 20, 1976, at 15, col. 1 (OAS).

136. *See* N.Y. Times, May 28, 1976, at 2, col. 1.

137. N.Y. Times, June 9, 1976, at 1, col. 4. *See also* Paust, *supra* note 127, at 250, *passim*; N.Y. Times, June 19, 1976, at 1, col. 6 (South Africa).

138. *See* Paust, *Private Measures of Sanction*, ch. 13 of this report.

139. *See generally*, N.Y. Times, Aug. 17, 1975, at E3, col. 4; July 14, 1975, at 6 col. 3; July 11, 1975, at 1, col. 2.

140. *See* Paust, *supra* note 138. *See also* Paust, *supra* note 33.

141. *Id.*

142. *See id.* Presently, the U.S.-Swiss treaty on Mutual Assistance in Criminal Matters seems limited generally to exchanges of information; *see* 12 INT'L LEGAL MATERIALS 916 (1973).

143. *See also What Should Be Given Up In Order to Save Hostages,* N.Y. Times, Mar. 20, 1977, at E3, col. 3; *Police Toughening Antiterrorist Tactics, id.*, Dec. 25, 1975, at 1, col. 5; *Patience Key to Method in Handling Terrorists,* Houston Post, Jan. 18, 1975, at 4, col. 5 (UPI); Murphy, *supra* note 3; Paust, *supra* note 33, at 448-58. It is worth noting that a McDougal-Lasswell approach to decision would not attempt to impose static rules on police or businessmen for negotiation with terrorists, but would instead seek a flexible strength through awareness of variations in actual context and the general policies sought to be served in each specific instance.

A separate question concerns "agreements" with terrorists holding hostages. Clearly such "agreements" are void at law due to illegal coercion and duress. However, another aspect of the problem relates to overall law enforcement strategy and the question whether governmental groups might abide by nonbinding agreements in order to facilitate wider human protections through time.

144. *See e.g.*, Paust & Blaustein, *The Arab Oil Weapon—A Threat to International Peace* 68 AM. J. INT'L L. 410 (1974); *International Law and the Food Crisis,* 1975 PROCEEDINGS AM. SOC'Y INT'L L. 39, 45-52, 57-58, 60 (Remarks by Jordan Paust).

145. The following draft prohibition is offered: Any terroristic threat or attack upon children, medical personnel and facilities, food complexes, and energy complexes constitutes an international crime over which there is universal jurisdiction. "Terrorism" can be defined as it is in Appendix 6B.

146. *See* note 7, *supra* at 16-17.

147. *Id.*

148. *Id.*

149. A proposal is offered in footnote 145 *supra.*

150. Declaration of the Rights of the Child, G.A. Res. 1386, 14 GAOR, Supp. (No. 16) 19, U.N. Doc. A/4354 (1959), *reprinted in* I. BROWNLIE, BASIC DOCUMENTS ON HUMAN RIGHTS 188 (1971).

151. *See* note 33 *supra.*

152. *See also* Treaty of Mutual Assistance in Criminal Matters, May 25, 1973, United States-Switzerland, T.I.A.S. No. 8302; Bassiouni, *An International Control Scheme for the Prosecution of International Terrorism: An Introduction*, ch. 8 of this report, at 485-486.

153. *See also* Houston Post, June 5, 1976, at col. 2 (UPI) (new European accord); Bassiouni, *supra* note 152, at 6; Bassiouni, *Criminological Policy*, ch. 10 of this report, at 530-531; Barcelona Traction Light and Power Co., Ltd. [1970]. C.J. Rep. 4, at paras. 33-34 (1970).

154. *See* N.Y. Times, Jan. 16, 1976, at 6, col. 2.

Appendix 6A
Targets of Terrorism

1. *Children:* See N.Y.T., May 28, 1976, at 2, col. 3 (16-year-old daughter of Belgian Ambassador to Mexico); N.Y.T., Feb. 5, 1976, at 11, col. 1 (30 French children held in East Africa); N.Y.T., March 3, 1975, at 3, col. 5 (Kenyan bus carrying women and children, 27 killed, 90 injured); N.Y.T., Dec. 23, 1974, at 1, col. 1 (U.S. 16-year-old Christian pilgrim injured in attack on bus in Israel); N.Y.T., May 16, 1974, at 1 and 18 (school in Maalot, Israel); N.Y.T., April 12, 1974, at 1, col. 2 (Qiryat Shemona, Israel); N.Y.T., Nov. 20, 1974, at 1, col. 1 (Beit Shean, Israel); N.Y.T., May 15, 1973, at 4, col. 5 (Belfast nursery school).

2. *Shoppers:* See N.Y.T., Jan. 14, 1976, at 3, col. 3 (shopping arcade in Belfast); N.Y.T., Nov. 14, 1975, at 1, col. 2 (Jerusalem); N.Y.T., Sept. 23, 1975, at 5, col. 1 (9 towns in N. Ireland); Houston Post, Aug. 16, 1975, at 6, col. 4 (Belfast); Houston Post, Aug. 13, 1975, at 1, col. 3 (Mexico); N.Y.T., July 5, 1975, at 1, col. 1 and at 3, col. 6 (Jerusalem); N.Y.T., June 15, 1975, at 37, col. 1 (U.S.); N.Y.T., April 19, 1974, at 3, col. 1 (Arab shoppers killed in Tel Aviv); N.Y.T., Sept. 19, 1974, at 3, col. 1 (Paris).

3. *Hotels, Restaurants, and Bars:* See N.Y.T., May 16, 1976, at 7, col. 1 (crowded Catholic bar in Belfast); N.Y.T., Jan. 31, 1976 at 10, col. 5 (crowded Protestant bar in Belfast); N.Y.T., Nov. 15, 1975, at 7, col. 2 (London hotels, restaurants and other targets); N.Y.T., Sept. 23, 1975, at 22, col. 6 (London hotel); N.Y.T., Sept. 6, 1975, at 1, col. 4 (London Hilton); Houston Post, Aug. 31, 1975, at 14, col. 1 (Belfast bar); N.Y.T., March 25, 1975, at 10, col. 2 (Spain); N.Y.T., April 7, 1975, at 21, col. 2 (Belfast); Houston Chronicle, March 17, 1975, at 2, col. 4 (N. Ireland); N.Y.T., March 9, 1975, at 2, col. 3 (Tel Aviv hotel); Houston Chronicle, March 8, 1975, at 14, col. 1 (Kenya); Houston Chronicle, Feb. 21, 1975, at 3, col. 1 (Belfast bars); Houston Chronicle, Jan. 23, 1975, at 4, col. 4 (Belfast hotel). See also Houston Chronicle, Feb. 27, 1975, at 8 (theater in Philippines); N.Y.T., Dec. 12, 1974, at 11, col. 1 (Tel Aviv theater).

4. *Workers:* See N.Y.T., Feb. 10, 1976, at 17, col. 1 (truck carrying five men to work at a lumber company in Belfast); N.Y.T., Sept. 3, 1975, at 16, col. 1 (N. Ireland); N.Y.T., Aug. 1, 1975, at 3, col. 7 (N. Ireland); N.Y.T., July 27, 1975, at 2, col. 7 (students in Tanzania held in Zaire). Also see Houston Post, Dec. 23, 1975, at 6, col. 2 (mother of eight children killed in Belfast putting Christmas decorations on her home); neo-fascist bombing of Italian trade union rally on March 28, 1974 (6 killed, 100 injured; see ASIL summary, Italy, at 4).

5. *Post Offices:* See N.Y.T., Feb. 17, 1976, at 4, col. 6 (main post office in Belfast).

6. *Trains:* N.Y.T., June 2, 1976, at 8, col. 5 (London subway); N.Y.T., March 16, 1976, at 3, col. 1 (subway in London); Houston Post, March 5, 1976, at 11, col. 6 (bombing of a passing train in London); N.Y.T., Jan. 14, 1976, at 4,

col. 4 (train near Buenos Aires); Houston Post, Dec. 15, 1975, at 1, col. 2 (Dutch train); Houston Post, Sept. 14, 1975, at 13, col. 1 (crowded West German train station); Houston Post, Sept. 21, 1975, at 3, col. 2 (Japanese Emperor's special train); Houston Chronicle, March 8, 1975, at 14, col. 1 (Kenyan freight train); neo-fascist bombing of Italian train on Aug. 3, 1974 (see ASIL summary, Italy, at 4); N.Y.T., Sept. 29, 1973, at 1, col. 1; N.Y.T., Sept. 30, 1973 at 1 (Train carrying Jewish emigres in Austria); N.Y.T., Sept. 11, 1973, at 3, col. 5 (London railroad stations). The frequency of these types of targetings may require certain precautions borrowed from attempts to combat air hijacking, although different problems are posed by air hijacking attempts and train bombings.

7. *Civil Aircraft:* See, *e.g.*, pp. 67-147 in this book; N.Y.T., March 2, 1975, at 12, col. 4 (Iraq); Houston Chronicle, Feb. 23, 1975, at 5, col. 3 (Brazil). See also N.Y.T., Aug. 29, 1975, at 2, col. 1 (military aircraft in Argentina); N.Y.T., Aug. 23, 1975, at 3, col. 7 (Argentine naval frigate); N.Y.T., Feb. 4, 1974, at 3, col. 1 (Greek ship held in Pakistan); N.Y.T., Feb. 5, 1974, at 2, col. 2 (ferry boat in Singapore).

8. *Athletes:* N.Y.T., Sept. 7, 1972, at 1; The Evening Star (Washington), Sept. 6, 1972, at 1.

9. *Historic Sites:* See L.A. Times, Feb. 22, 1976, at 1, col. 7 (Hearst Castle); Communist bombing of the Malaysian National Monument on August 26, 1975 (see ASIL summary, Malaysia, at 4).

10. *Leftists:* N.Y.T., June 12, 1976, at 3, col. 5 (Argentina); N.Y.T., June 11, 1976, at 3, col. 1 (Argentina); N.Y.T., June 7, 1976, at 3, col. 1 (Brazil); Houston Post, June 27, 1976, at 20, col. 1 (Spain); N.Y.T., June 25, 1976, at 6, col. 4 (Argentina); N.Y.T., May 28, 1976, at 1, col. 2 (sister of Moslem leader assassinated in Beirut); N.Y.T., March 22, 1976, at 6, col. 1 (Argentina, adding that some 5,000 people are being held); Houston Post, Feb. 21, 1976, at 4, col. 3 (Argentina); Houston Post, Jan. 18, 1976, at 2, col. 5 (Portugal); Houston Post, Dec. 5, 1975, at 8, col. 1 (UPI, Argentina); N.Y.T., Sept. 7, 1975, at 7, col. 1 (Argentina); N.Y.T., Aug. 6, 1975, at 3, col. 1 (Spain—bookstores and homes); N.Y.T., April 20, 1975, at 1, col. 5 (S. Vietnam); N.Y.T., March 23, 1975, at 14, col. 3 (Argentina); Houston Chronicle, March 21, 1975, at 6, col. 8 (Argentina). An International Committee of Jurists report prepared by Dr. H.C. Fragoso of Brazil in 1975 also discloses threats against and murders of any Argentine lawyers and at least one judge, with the result that lawyers are refusing to defend political prisoners in Argentina. See ASIL summary by C. Cerna, Argentina, at 6.

11. *Party and Union Offices:* See N.Y.T., Jan. 30, 1976, at 7, col. 1 (Portugal); Houston Post, Aug. 23, 1975, at 1, col. 1 (Portugal); Houston Chronicle, Feb. 21, 1975, at 3, col. 1 (Argentine labor leader).

12. *Businessmen:* See N.Y.T., June 16, 1976, at 3, col. 3 (Italian meat wholesaler); N.Y.T., June 17, 1976, at 13, col. 1 (Italian poultry wholesaler); N.Y.T., May 16, 1976, at E 11, col. 3 (French bank president); N.Y.T., April 12,

1976, at 18, col. 1 (U.S. businessman in Venezuela); N.Y.T., Jan. 30, 1976, at 7, col. 1 (Argentina); Houston Post, Oct. 4, 1975, at 24, col. 1 (Dublin); N.Y.T., Sept. 16, 1975, at 2, col. 4 (London); N.Y.T., August 7, 1975, at 12, col. 1 (Colombia); N.Y.T., August 1, 1975, at 3, col. 6 (Argentina); N.Y.T., May 20, 1975, at 6, col. 1 (Tokyo); N.Y.T., April 4, 1975, at 14, col. 3 (New York); Houston Chronicle, Feb. 22, 1975, at 8, col. 1 (Argentina); N.Y.T., Jan. 1, 1974, at 1, col. 3 (Jewish leader killed by Arabs in London); N.Y.T., Oct. 15, 1974, at 9, col. 1 (Tokyo). See also Houston Post, Dec. 31, 1975, at 3, col. 7 (OPEC headquarters); Houston Post, Aug. 31, 1975, at 3, col. 7 (London bank); N.Y.T., April 26, 1976, at 3, col. 4 (Mexican bank and supermarket robberies).

13. *Mayors and Other Civic Leaders:* See N.Y.T., June 22, 1976, at 8, col. 4 (Guatemala); N.Y.T., June 12, 1976, at 3, col. 5 (Argentina); N.Y.T., Feb. 10, 1976, at 7, col. 1 (Spain); Houston Post, Feb. 11, 1976, at 11, col. 2 (Spain); N.Y.T., Jan. 15, 1976, at 7, col. 1 (homes of British officials in Ulster); N.Y.T., Sept. 10, 1975, at 3, col. 1 (West German opposition political leader); Houston Post, June 9, 1975, at 20, col. 1 (a black nationalist leader in Rhodesia); N.Y.T., June 4, 1975, at 7, col. 1 (Kenya); N.Y.T., March 19, 1975, at 8, col. 3 (Rhodesian black leader and aide killed in Zambia); N.Y.T., March 23, 1975, at 14, col. 3 (Argentine city councilman); N.Y.T., March 9, 1975, at 7, col. 1 (West German political leader); N.Y.T., June 4, 1964, at 14, col. 1 (Argentine politicians and military elites).

14. *Policemen:* N.Y.T., June 25, 1976, at 6, col. 4 (42 in Argentina since March 24 coup); N.Y.T., June 19, 1976, at 7, col. 3 (Argentine Chief of Fed. Police); N.Y.T., June 5, 1976, at 5, col. 3 (9 police in Mexico City machine-gunned to death, 6 others injured); N.Y.T., May 25, 1976, at 2, col. 4 (two wounded, N. Ireland); N.Y.T., May 16, 1976, at 2, col. 4 (3 killed N. Ireland); N.Y.T., March 22, 1976, at 6, col. 1 (Argentina); N.Y.T., April 8, 1976, at 21, col. 6 (nine police slain in two weeks, Argentina); Houston Post, Sept. 18, 1975, at 6, col. 1 (Mexico); N.Y.T., Sept. 19, 1975, at 11, col. 1 (Spain); N.Y.T., Sept. 23, 1975, at 5, col. 1 (N. Ireland); Houston Post, Sept. 23, 1975, at 9, col. 1 (N. Ireland); N.Y.T., August 31, 1975, at 12, col. 1 (Mexico); N.Y.T., Aug. 21, 1975, at 10, col. 1 (Argentina); Houston Post, Aug. 13, 1975, at 1, col. 3 (Mexico); N.Y.T., May 25, 1975, at 7, col. 1 (Belfast); Houston Post, March 30, 1975, at 13, col. 4 (Spain); see also N.Y.T., Sept. 18, 1975, at 10, col. 1 (Argentine intelligence chief); N.Y.T., July 11, 1975, at 3, col. 1 (U.S. Army Colonel seized by PLO in Beirut); General Public Prosecutor kidnapped in Italy, April 1974 (see ASIL summary, Italy, at 4); N.Y.T., June 2, 1976, at 16, col. 2 (U.S. military headquarters in W. Germany).

Appendix 6B
Proposed Federal Legislation to Acquire Jurisdiction Over and Prosecute Acts of International Terrorism

A BILL

To amend title 18, United States Code, to provide a penalty for the commission of acts of international terrorism at home or abroad.

Be it enacted by the Senate and House of Representatives of the United States of America in Congress assembled, That Chapter 7 of title 18, United States Code, is amended by adding after section 114 the following new section:

"§ 115. Commission of International Terrorism

"(a) Whoever assaults, strikes, wounds, kidnaps, imprisons, or threatens violence to another human being within the ordinary jurisdiction, and special maritime and territorial jurisdiction of the United States, or whoever does so abroad, and thereby commits an act of terrorism against a U.S. citizen or in any manner contrary to international law, shall be fined not more than $10,000, or imprisoned for not more than ten years, or both.

"(b) Whoever commits an act of terrorism proscribed above which leads to the death of another human being shall be subject to a penalty of death or life imprisonment.

"(c) As used in subsection (a), the term—

"(1) 'terrorism' means any intentional use of violence or a threat of violence by the accused against an instrumental target in order to communicate to a primary target a threat of future violence so as to coerce the primary target through intense fear or anxiety;

"(2) 'in any manner contrary to international law' means in any manner contrary to treaty law to which the United States is a party or customary international law, e.g., treaty and customary law prohibiting terrorism against the civilian population in time of armed conflict or in a manner prohibited by general human rights law;

"(d) As used in subsection (c), the term—

"(1) 'instrumental target' means a human or nonhuman target which is assaulted, struck, wounded, kidnapped, imprisoned or detained, or threatened with violence in order to communicate the threat of future violence to and coerce some primary target. In some cases, the instrumental target and the primary target could be the same person.

"(2) 'primary target' means a human target which is the intended victim of terroristic coercion.

393

Comment:

Jurisdiction is now obtained over acts of terrorism committed against United States citizens abroad for which there had previously been no federal jurisdiction. Jurisdiction, under international law, is permissible under the nationality and protective theories of jurisdiction; while passive personality theory is not specifically adopted, it would also support such a jurisdictional basis under international law. There can be no doubt that with increasing terroristic threats against United States citizens abroad, that the United States has significant security and protective interests at stake.

Reference to international law in supplementation of jurisdiction over acts of terrorism committed against United States citizens will assure United States ability to effectively implement several international treaties relating to this crime and the general customary international norms which are also violated by acts of international terrorism. Other federal provisions use international law as a standard; for example, federal law punishing acts of piracy and war crimes.

Reference to "international" terrorism is necessary so as to assure that the United States does not impermissibly interfere with some activity which is *primarily* within the domestic jurisdiction of another state. The term "international" does not have to be defined, but would refer to acts with international impact or effect such as attacks against United States citizens within a foreign country, attacks against foreign diplomats in a foreign country (using international treaty and customary law as a jurisdictional base), significant acts of terrorism committed abroad but with significant international impact or effect, significant acts of terrorism committed abroad against foreign nationals but in violation of international treaty law which authorized universal jurisdiction over prosecution of the offense, and so forth.

Appendix 6C
Passive Personality
Legislation

The federal district courts are competent to try under U.S. law any person who has committed an act abroad which would be an offense if it had been committed in the United States, provided that the act was committed against a U.S. citizen.

Comment:

The problem with this approach to solution is that it adopts a U.S. attempt to exercise jurisdiction over acts committed abroad when the only justification seems to be injury to a U.S. national. This would be an instance of adoption of the passive personality theory under international law—a theory that the U.S. has traditionally opposed [see U.S. Department of Army Pamphlet No. 27-161-1, I *International Law* 80-81 (1964)]. Such a measure would be highly questionable under international law and would subject the United States, particularly U.S. military forces, tourists, and businessmen, to reciprocal treatment abroad—a cost that I feel the United States does not really wish to pay.

I feel that this approach to solution is unwise and unrealistic. Congress is not about to subject tourists, military personnel, and business persons to similar treatment abroad, or to open up acceptance of the passive personality principle under international law—nor will the Pentagon be willing to do so. We cannot seek to prosecute foreign acts committed against our citizens without opening ourselves up to similar prosecutions of our people in foreign countries.

An alternative approach is to extend extraterritorial jurisdiction on the basis of nationality. This would entail adoption of a restriction making the legislation applicable only to U.S. citizens for acts committed against U.S. citizens or others abroad. Such legislation would have a useful function in plugging a present gap in U.S. jurisdiction, but again there are costs to be taken into consideration, especially with regard to military SOFAs and general reciprocity. Further, such an approach would not allow jurisdiction to obtain over foreign terrorists.

There seems no avoidance of the need to adopt alternative (a) in Appendix 6B. Failure to condition extraterritorial jurisdiction with the term "terrorism" and its definition would result in exercise of too broad a jurisdictional claim and subject the United States to reciprocal treatment that I believe would not be policy-serving in the long run. We do *not* seek to prosecute every assault committed against a U.S. tourist abroad; what we seek to sanction are special crimes or *terrorism*! There can be no avoidance of the need to define the term and to condition the exercise of extraterritorial jurisdiction by use of the term in new legislation.

There will be greater difficulties posed for the prosecutor who must prove political motive and terror outcome, or the attempt at terrorism, but the alternative—to allow the prosecutor merely to prove normal assault, kidnaping and so forth—will have tremendous costs for the State Department, the Department of Defense, and overall U.S. interests. To make the job easier for the prosecutor and ignore these interests at stake is to be unresponsive to the need to maximize the serving of all policies at stake.

Appendix 6D
Protocol, for Bilateral and Multilateral Adoption As Such or in Conjunction with Other Human Rights Covenants, Treaties, etc.

Protection of Children

Any terroristic threat or attack upon children, under any circumstances, constitutes an international crime over which there is universal jurisdiction. (Terrorism or terroristic threat or attack should be defined as in Appendix 6B.)

Protection of Children, Medical, Food, and Energy Facilities

Any terroristic threat or attack upon children, medical personnel and facilities, food complexes, and energy complexes constitutes an international crime over which there is universal jurisdiction. (Terrorism or terroristic threat or attack should be defined as in Appendix 6B—especially so far as the Department of Defense is concerned with regard to the targeting of food and energy complexes in time of armed conflict—thus leaving the targeting of enemy energy complexes permissible when necessary under the circumstances and when no terrorist motive is intended and no terror outcome is readily foreseeable.)

7 Personnel and Property of Transnational Business Operations

Clarence J. Mann

Introduction

The transnational business operation has become a frequent target of terrorist activities over the past few years. Increasingly, attacks have been mounted by relatively large, well-organized, and highly disciplined groups in order to achieve political ends. As a natural ally of political stability, a very effective mode for the organization of capital and technology, and as an extension of foreign economic interests, the transnational enterprise has become a highly symbolic and lucrative target of terrorists whose ultimate objective is to embarrass the host government, erode its authority, and force political change. The costs to the enterprise, both visible and hidden, may far exceed the payments exacted by terrorists. The international investment climate as a whole also suffers, and with it international commerce. The threat of terrorism is forcing the transnational enterprise to rethink its traditional approach to security and to develop new modes of cooperative action with governmental authorities as well as within the private sector. Because terrorism represents a comprehensive threat to transnational business operations, it requires an equally broad-gauged response. This chapter focuses on the nature of this response, both public and private, from a policy perspective.

For purposes of this chapter, terrorism qualifies as "international" when the interests of more than one state are involved.[1] This may be true because of the parties involved, the nature of the terrorist acts, or the effects of the terrorist acts. Of course, before a state can act legally to protect these interests, they must be translated into principles of jurisdiction.

As to parties, the acts of violence may be directed against a foreign-owned business or against specially protected persons such as diplomats. They also may be perpetrated by terrorists with a foreign nationality. Second, the acts themselves may cross state boundaries where the attack is launched from the territory of another state or where the instrumentality used or attacked by terrorists performs an international function, as in the case of the postal service (letter bombs) or international flights.[2]

Third, the acts of terrorists may have an international effect even though they are committed wholly within a state's territory. This may occur, for instance, when extortion is used to influence the policies of foreign governments

This chapter reflects solely the views of the author, and does not necessarily represent those of his employer, Sears, Roebuck and Co.

or when terrorists flee into the territory of another state. It may also occur when the flow of international commerce is interrupted or endangered. The growing interdependence of national economies, as well as the importance of highly integrated transnational business operations to the global economy, suggest that economic effects will become increasingly important in measuring "international" concern over terrorism.

Moreover, as used in this chapter, "terrorism" refers to the threat or use of violence—whether *ad hoc* or on a systematic basis—which is designed to instill fear, alarm, or terror in a target audience. It is, as Brian Jenkins well notes, "violence for effect" or "violence aimed at the people watching,"[3] for the target audience often bears only a symbolic relationship to the target victim. Witness the massacre at Lod Airport in May 1972, where the choice of the victims was completely arbitrary. The 25 persons killed by gunfire and grenades were "guilty" of simply being there.[4] The same arbitrariness appears also for business executives who are kidnaped simply because of their employment with a large foreign enterprise. In both instances, however, there is one common denominator: the terrorism is designed primarily at obtaining political ends, whether to alleviate the plight of, say, the Palestinians or to embarrass the government and drive out foreign business interests. Such political motivation is often the defining characteristic of "international terrorism" today.

Finally, as used here, "terrorism" refers to acts or activities that normally are not performed by or under the control of a recognized government or governmental agency. Terrorist groups may receive substantial training, financial support, and other types of aid from foreign governments, but most groups remain essentially in control of their overall strategy and implementing activities. Indeed, as is evidenced by the Irish Republican Army (IRA), the Palestine Liberation Organization (PLO), and the Montoneros or the People's Revolutionary Army (ERP) of Argentina, such groups often achieve a high degree of political autonomy within a society. So-called state terrorism, where state agencies control the terrorist activities, will not be considered here. Its exclusion, however, is not intended to belittle its importance to the international community or the need to deal with it in keeping with the requirements of the United Nations Charter and the various applicable international conventions, covenants, and declarations for the protection of human rights.

This chapter will deal as practically as possible with the nature of terrorist activities faced by transnational business operations in order to arrive at useful recommendations for combating this problem. To assist in doing this, a sample survey was taken of 12 corporate security officers and 8 security consultants.[5] The survey was based on questionnaires and telephone interviews. In addition, officials of the U.S. Department of State have been interviewed. These interviews form the basis of some of the conclusions in this paper. (In all cases, however, the conclusions are those of the writer.) Further, the sources were assured that their remarks would be kept confidential and that their comments were not for attribution.

The next section of this chapter analyzes the characteristics of transnational business operations as they relate to the problem of international terrorism. Next, the nature of the terroristic threat that these operations face today is identified, and then the immediate and long-term impact that terrorism has on their conduct is assessed. Based on this analysis, various responses of the business community to this terroristic threat are considered and then national and international governmental measures to combat terroristic activities against transnational enterprises are covered. Finally, the chapter concludes with recommendations of policies and approaches by which the U.S. government, in conjunction with transnational enterprises and the news media, may combat terrorism more effectively.

The Critical Characteristics of Transnational Business Operations

Among the many defining characteristics of transnational business operations today, the following five depict the importance of the operations and their sensitivity to international terrorism.

1. Transnational business operations are a critical component in the continuing evolution and growth of a global economy.
2. National groups and host governments frequently perceive a major conflict between the operating objectives of transnational enterprises and the developmental goals and cultural values of their host countries.
3. The transnational enterprise has become a conspicuous symbol in host countries of foreign interests and foreign control, which are both anathema to and highly exploitable by terrorist groups.
4. The discipline of the international marketplace makes transnational business operations highly sensitive to disruptive acts and threats of terrorism.
5. Transnational business operations, with the exception of commercial aircraft operations, possess no special protection under international law or treaty.

Evolution and Growth of a Global Economy

Over the past three decades, transnational business operations have become the keystone of an evolving global economy. Two hundred major transnational enterprises, for instance, account for approximately 25 percent of total world exports.[6] This evolution has been fostered through the spectacular growth of foreign investment. Thus during the 25 years between 1950 and 1975, the value of private U.S. long-term direct investments abroad increased over elevenfold, from $11.8 billion to $133 billion. During the same period, foreign long-term investments in the United States multipled almost eightfold, from $3.4 billion to $26.7 billion.[7] While perhaps 300 major transnational enterprises, 200 of which are U.S.-based companies, account for 75 to 80 percent of all foreign direct investment, several thousand companies conduct transnational business operations through many more thousands of affiliated companies around the world.[8]

What made this evolution and growth possible, however, was not the concept of the multinational or transnational enterprises nor the perception of a common corporate strategy. The modern history of these enterprises goes back many decades.[9] Instead, the critical innovation that occurred over the past three decades has been "the capability of having the management of that strategy take place at a common nerve center based on a flow of common information."[10] This capability is founded on the technological revolution that is taking place in communications, transportation, and data storage and analysis. This in turn has spawned a new management consciousness and a new generation of management techniques, which make it possible today to speak of a company's "global operations."

If the past three decades are any indication of the future, therefore, some form of the transnational enterprise is critical to the continuing evolution and growth of a global economy. Increasing and varying national regulation is changing the patterns of control and ownership of these enterprises. Present trends suggest that their control and ownership, like their operations, also are becoming multinational. Nevertheless, their "nerve centers" and those of their successors must be enabled to function effectively. On this depends the future of world commerce and, in large part, the successful economic development of individual countries.

Conflict between Transnational Business
Operations and National Interest

While transnational business operations since World War II have contributed significantly to economic development in many parts of the world, they also have contributed to a growing conflict within host countries. In part, this conflict stems from the integrated global approach of transnational enterprises, whose priorities and mobility transcend national boundaries. Consequently, this impinges on the rising nationalism within many countries who fear that foreign investments threaten their sovereignty and enhance foreign dependence. "It is hard to overestimate," counsels Mira Wilkins, "how much less-developed countries desire economic and political independence from all great powers."[11]

This conflict has been reinforced further by the fear among many host countries that the advanced management methods and technology of large foreign enterprises will subvert the traditional values and patterns of their cultures. They also may threaten governing elites by tending to undermine the privileged economic status of traditional groups and classes.[12] This basic conflict and the fears behind it are amply reflected in the panoply of foreign investment regulations in many countries, the United Nations "Charter of Economic Rights and Duties of States," and the UNCTAD debate on a "Code of Conduct" for transnational enterprises.

Conspicuous Symbol for Terrorist Exploitation

The very economic success of the transnational enterprise in recent years has made it an attractive target for forces opposing the established order. This is true for at least four reasons. First, the assets of these enterprises are sizable by comparison with national companies. Therefore the enterprise is a "deep pocket" that may be exploited for financing terrorist activities, and a symbol of wealth that may have propaganda value among the poorer segments of the population. A large company is hard pressed to plead that it has no resources to pay ransom.

Second, the long-term interest of the transnational enterprise normally lies with the established order and with political stability, as far as the latter safeguard a favorable business climate and fundamental human rights. Their investments normally are long-term decisions of 10 to 20 years, often involving very sizable fixed assets. Once made, an enterprise cannot abandon its position with changes in the government or government philosophy or policy except at a heavy cost. Further, the successful operation of a major business entails a certain amount of interchange and cooperation with the government, whether or not management approves of the government's policies. For their own protection, transnational enterprises as a rule studiously avoid becoming embroiled in the politics of the host country. Terrorists, on the other hand, are seeking to overthrow or to change radically the established order. Undermining the position of the transnational enterprise can embarrass the existing regime and adversely affect the business climate for foreign investment as a whole.

Third, the transnational enterprise represents a foreign presence. Its name, which often copies the foreign parent name, may have been promoted vigorously in the host country. This permits the terrorist, through propaganda, to identify the economic power of the enterprise readily and to assert the presence of foreign domination and control. Finally, and largely as a result of the foregoing, the transnational enterprise possesses a relatively high profile in the host country. This presence may be highlighted by resident foreign executives and their families in the country and their patterns of conspicuous consumption.

Discipline of the International Marketplace

From the business perspective, the discipline of the international marketplace requires that the earnings of a particular foreign operation compare favorably over time with similar operations in other countries and areas of the world. Should opportunity costs be greater and benefits fewer in one country than at other comparable available locations, the transnational enterprise will be disinclined to invest or to reinvest further in that country at that time. Within this context, the threat level of terrorism may add substantially to security costs or increase the risks of making a profit.[13]

Moreover, the arbitrary impact of terrorist activities has an inordinately disruptive effect on business operations. These effects may be on executive morale as well as on management continuity, as when executive expatriates are forced to leave the host country. These effects may also be felt, for instance, on corporate planning. Where substantial long-term investment or start-up costs are involved in establishing or expanding an operation, corporate planning may require a 10- to 20-year amortization term. The arbitrariness of the terrorist threat is difficult, if not impossible, to compute. Indeed, as an emotional matter, it may well dominate a more rational analysis by management.

No Special Protection under International Law or Treaty

Several international conventions presently grant special protection against terrorist attack to aircraft and to diplomatic officers and related persons. These include the 1963 Tokyo Convention on Offenses and Certain Other Acts Committed on Board Aircraft, the 1970 Hague Convention for the Suppression of Unlawful Seizure of Aircraft, and the 1971 Montreal Convention for the Suppression of Unlawful Acts Against the Safety of Civil Aviation. The latter two conventions amplify the Tokyo Convention in certain respects by classifying air piracy as an international crime and providing for the extradition or prosecution of hijackers. Additionally, the OAS adopted in 1971 and the U.N. General Assembly approved in 1973 conventions protecting diplomats and other internationally protected persons from terrorism.

While various countries, including the United States, have submitted draft conventions in the United Nations to prohibit the export of violence generally to third countries, none as yet has been approved. These proposals did not survive the debate on whether terrorism is justifiable, as Syria and Algeria affirm, when it is employed against "state terrorism" and colonialism for the purpose of national liberation.[14] Transnational enterprises and their employees, therefore, fall within the general category of persons who do not enjoy special protection against terrorist attack under customary or conventional international law.

The Nature of the Terrorist Threat toward Transnational Business Operations

Increasingly, over the past decade, international terrorism has become an indigenous threat to transnational business operations. Terrorists are seeing utility in weaving attacks on business operations into their overall strategies. Of 913 terrorist incidents carried out internationally by individuals or groups between 1968 and 1975, 330 are reported to have been directed against U.S. citizens or property.[15] This figure does not reflect numerous cases of attempted extortion, threats of violence, and other acts of violence that have gone unreported. While the majority of these recorded incidents occurred in Latin America and Western and NATO Europe, a substantial number (largely bombings) also took place in the United States.

The figure itself is not large, considering the vast number of transnational business operations. However, the incidents carry a disproportionately high impact on business, as will be shown later. If, as appears probable, the threat of terrorism will become an increasing risk of doing business in the foreseeable future, especially for larger transnational businesses operating outside the United States, then this fact may entail the necessity, as one author puts it, of "living with terrorism."[16] This conclusion need not imply a permissive or tolerant attitude toward terrorism, but simply the realization that causes of terrorism may to an important degree be a function of increasingly complex, rapidly changing, and densely populated societies. Every deep-seated value conflict of major proportions that remains unresolved creates a potential for frustration that may give rise to terrorist activity. And the more democratic the government, the more vulnerable it may be to political violence.[17]

For purposes of analysis, it is important to define the nature of the terrorist threat toward transnational business operations. This threat will be considered with regard first to the motives and, then, the targets and modes of attack that are most characteristic at this time in terrorist activities. The typologies employed in each case are not new. They have been selected because they help clarify the sociological reality that transnational enterprises face in the form of terrorism and because they raise relevant questions for investigation. As such, they shed light on how business fits into the terrorist's rationale and on the possible means for combating terrorist activities.

Motives of Terrorists

Motives reveal much about the operating dynamics of terrorist activities. An understanding of motives not only instructs the transnational enterprise why it has been chosen as a target of terrorism, but also assists it in fashioning an appropriate response to terrorists' attacks either as a matter of corporate policy or of negotiating strategy. A catalogue of violent threats and acts against transnational business operations would reveal at least four major types of motives at play: political, personal gain (common criminal), psychotic, and cultic.[18] Political motivation, which is the sole concern of this chapter, creates the greatest concern at this time among transnational enterprises because of the intensity, dedication, and organizational capacity of the actors. Further, politically motivated terrorism may awaken and be exploited by the common criminal.

The political motive, of course, may overlap with other motives, depending on the terrorist group's internal dynamics and needs. Undoubtedly, personal gain and psychotic behavior are mixed into the complex personalities of terrorists who are able to justify the routine death of innocent persons as necessary revolutionary deeds. And certainly revolutionary-oriented terrorists, although they may never adopt a "Bonnie and Clyde" lifestyle or establish a "Manson" cult,[19] understand that their long-term survival demands at least to some extent a ritualized and well-disciplined organization. Properly speaking, the pure political motive may be as rare as the pure terrorist. Nevertheless, as Bowyer Bell points out, politically motivated terrorists share in common a tunnel vision, "see their options as Liberty or Death," and are committed to "violence as the only viable route to power."[20]

Political motivation is defined by the political ends of terrorism. These ends may be limited to a particular cause or issue, such as an antiwar campaign, labor legislation, a protest against nuclear testing, or the exclusion of foreign business from a country. The kidnaping of U.S. business executives in Latin America has often been justified by accusations that the company "plunders the country" and "interferes with its internal affairs."[21] On the other hand, political ends may encompass an overall revolutionary strategy leading to the overthrow of the government and of the established economic and social system. Whether this strategy stems from the classical Marxist-Leninist view of class warfare, from the Maoist reliance on rural peasantry and staged guerrilla warfare, or from the Guevarist emphasis on guerrilla *focos* to catalyze revolutionary conditions, there remains a place in each for terrorist activity. The difference between these strategies lies not so much in whether terrorism is a legitimate form of revolutionary struggle, but rather in the timing and conditions under which it should be employed and the degree of central control by the political party.[22]

The political category also includes such anarchistic groups as the Movimiento Ibérico Libertario (MIL) of Spain or, perhaps, the Angry Brigade in the United Kingdom.[23] Within that category may be placed ethnic, religious, or linguistic causes of minorities, such as the Official and Provisional IRA in Ulster, the Basque Euzkadi ta Azkatasuna (ETA) of Northern Spain, and the Croatian nationalist emigrés, the Palestine Liberation Movement, and Fatah.[24] Further, although they have not proved so threatening to business, radical groups of the right also may be committed to terrorism for political purposes, *e.g.*, the Argentine Communist Alliance (AAA). Formed in 1973, its death squad has taken "credit" for a number of political murders, including those of two Argentine journalists.[25] Although terrorist organizations of this latter type have objectives that are less global than the revolutionary groups mentioned above, their fanaticism reveals a distinct ideological direction.

However the political ends of terrorists are defined, the political motive itself may assume any one or more of three forms: ideological, supportive, or organizational. A closer review of each of these not only will offer insight into the nature of terrorist activities, but also will demonstrate the unique role that transnational business operations play in terrorist strategy.

Ideology. Terrorism today, almost by definition, occurs within an ideological framework, and terrorist acts are designed to embody those values. The ideology furnishes the terrorist with an all-encompassing rationale. It may dictate kidnaping in order to obtain specific concessions, assassination in an attempt to coerce the legislature to pass desired legislation, or absurd violence as a means to provoke political repression, reprisals, and counterterrorism, and to demonstrate the brutality and fear of the existing government.[26] Ideology also imposes a judgment on every facet of society. There are no innocent bystanders for the terrorist, neither the foreign-owned corporation that follows the most scrupulous standards of business conduct nor the tourist who stops by chance in a cafe where a bomb explodes. Whoever is not an ideological friend is either an enemy or an unwitting tool of the enemy.[27]

Terrorism serves ideology through the use or manipulation of symbols, publicity, and the distribution of economic benefits. Threats and attacks on foreign businesses operating within the country, especially when they are subsidiaries of large multinational companies, have triple symbolic value for the terrorist. They strike a blow against "economic imperialism," waive the banner of nationalism, and undermine the established regime by revealing the fragility of domestic order. One writer reports that between 1961 and 1970, "just over a quarter of all terrorist episodes and campaigns had some anti-foreign element, in purpose or target or both." Of these, half were primarily antiforeign.[28] "The urban guerrilla," states Carlos Marighela, "is an implacable enemy of the government, and systematically works against the authorities, and those who rule the country and wield power." The terrorism he advocates includes "kidnaping American personalities" and "setting fire to North American business establishments." The North American, he proclaims, "must be expelled from the country."[29]

Terrorism may also be staged to heighten the dramatic effect of an act and thereby to gain increased press coverage. Revolutionary terminology refers to this as "armed propaganda." Thus, upon imprisoning Victor Samuelson of Exxon, the ERP announced that he would be "tried" for the "crimes" of the multinational corporation. Exxon, they said, owed the Argentine government $10 million in back taxes, which they intended to collect.[30] Apparently building on this example, the Revolutionary Command group that kidnaped William Niehous charged Owens-Illinois with "political interference" and "economic administrative meddling" in Venezuela. They alleged acts of bribery and "embezzlement in all forms of administrative corruption," which "form a deceitful current that runs from foreign capital into the administrative structure of the State," and stated that Niehous would be tried as "an enemy of the people."[31] Their apparent attempt to use the press to present their case, however, was foiled by a governmentally imposed "blackout" on press coverage in Venezuela.

Finally, the extortion of economic benefits from business not only neatly combines symbolic and publicity values, but also may be aimed at creating fraternal bonds between the terrorists and the poorer classes. To a guerrilla movement, this Robin Hood image may be critical for survival. The ERP has followed this tack against transnational businesses on several occasions in Argentina. Thus in March 1972, Fiat of Argentina was required to pay $1 million in the form of school supplies and shoes to children in poor areas of the country and, in addition, to reinstate 250 workers who had been fired in a labor dispute.[32] Two years later, in May 1973, Ford paid $1 million for the purchase of ambulances and medical supplies for provincial hospitals and of other goods for the poor in order to avoid further attacks by the ERP on its employees.[33] A similar demand was also part of the kidnaping of Exxon's Samuelson in December 1973.[34] More recently, the Revolutionary Command group in Venezuela required Owens-Illinois to pay its Venezuelan employees as a whole a wage supplement of over $120,000 as a condition for the release of Niehous, its vice president. Additional amounts were demanded for charitable purposes.[35]

Economic Support. Because the politically motivated terrorist operates out of an integrated rationale, the ideological attack must be supported by an economic strategy. At times, these support activities may appear to be simply criminal banditry motivated by personal gain. Certainly much of the kidnaping that goes on almost daily in many countries of Latin America is of this type. During the period 1971-1973 in Argentina, domestic and transnational companies reported over 250 cases in which their employees were kidnaped.[36] On the other hand, it is also clear that a revolutionary group of any size that is engaging in guerrilla warfare or other types of insurrectional activities requires substantial funds for its livelihood, the purchase of arms and ammunition, and international travel and communication. Terrorism is a tactic designed to gain these economic ends.

Based on one chronology of international terrorism, foreign companies operating in Argentina paid at least $35 million to $55 million in ransom from 1970 to 1974. Approximately two-thirds of this amount was collected by the ERP.[37] This amount does not account for the ransoms collected from purely domestic kidnapings, such as the more than $60 million ransom paid to the Montoneros organization in 1975 for the kidnaping of the co-owners of Bunge and Born Ltd.[38] That is the largest ransom reportedly paid to date by a business. Nor does this amount include money from bank robberies or narcotics trafficking and arms stolen from military or police authorities that are utilized in the guerrilla campaigns of revolutionary groups. The Association of Colombian Banks in Bogota reported that 60 armed robberies of member banks occurred during 1975, costing the banks nearly $10 million.[39] The report does not indicate how much of this money was stolen by politically motivated groups.

Beyond the uses mentioned, these illegal gains may also be directed toward expanding and reinforcing the scope of revolutionary activities. Thus in 1973, the ERP reportedly established a Revolutionary Coordination Board under a four-part agreement with the Tupamaros of Uruguay, the Movimiento de Izquierda Revolucionaria (MIR) of Chile, and the Ejército de Liberación (ELN) of Bolivia. Following Exxon's payment of the Samuelson ransom, ERP reported that $5 million would be distributed among the other members of the Coordination Board for use in establishing rural guerrilla movements to mobilize and organize the masses and to complement the operations of the existing urban terrorist units.[40] Furthermore, following a series of kidnapings in Colombia, including Don Cooper of Sears, there was speculation that the well-publicized election campaigns of left-wing parties in that country during spring 1976 were being financed, at least in part, from the criminal activities of terrorist groups. This was denied by the two parties in question.[41]

Organizational Strengthening. Any group, particularly those living under the parole of "Liberty or Death," faces the question of organizational allegiance, effectiveness, and survival. Not surprisingly, therefore, groups that are dedicated to terrorism use terror as a tool to maintain internal discipline, to encourage loyalty to the cause, and to punish for disobedience and defection.[42] The examples they set can be as swift and harsh as the lynchings by the Japanese Red Army[43] and as brutal as the kneecapping practiced by the IRA.[44] While purely disciplinary activities of terrorists need be of little concern to transnational enterprises, there are other organizational aspects, both internal and external, of the political motive that may affect them directly. In contrast to the ideological and economic aspects described above, however, the organizational component is less visible and therefore more difficult to demonstrate.

From an internal perspective, attacks on businesses operate to train the revolutionary, maintain group morale, and harden discipline. Brian Crozier calls this "muscle-flexing," for the terrorist group is demonstrating its capacity and will to act.[45] By comparison with actions against military targets or state officials, the risks of failure in attacking enterprises are lower and the reaction of the authorities may be less severe, especially where the target is foreign-owned and nationalistic feeling is strong. At the same time, the careful planning, which is required for such assaults, offers terrorists a useful exercise in tactical thinking and combats boredom. Further, group morale is strengthened when, as in several instances, the ransom for a business executive includes the release of prisoners.[46] Aside from the aircraft hijacking cases, however, only seldom has this attempt proved successful.[47]

Viewed externally, terrorism may be employed as an instrument of intergroup rivalry. It also may be used to radicalize the atmosphere where a splinter group determines that the existing leadership has failed in its objectives or is following too moderate a course. An instance of this intergroup dynamic is reflected in the response of the Black September Organization to the outrage of the West at the attack on the Israeli Olympic team. In an interview, one Palestine spokesman stated, "Call us what you may but it's good for our morale, and it may help the moderate elements in the movement to take a more militant position. After all our defeats, this comes as an uplift. We feel we have to do something. What does the world expect of young Arabs these days? We have seen too many defeats."[48] Sufficient information is not available, however, to say in which cases or to what extent such considerations have motivated terrorist attacks on transnational business operations.

From several perspectives, therefore, terrorist attacks on transnational business operations appear to be politically motivated. This is especially true for the ideology and economics of revolutionary strategy. Additionally, there is concern that the common criminal and the deranged may mimic these terrorist tactics and exploit the climate of fear that terrorism creates.[49]

More importantly, the militancy and fanaticism that are so often associated with the political motive may be brought to bear against the transnational enterprise through a wide spectrum of strategies. Because motives overlap, the moving cause of any particular terrorist group may be difficult for business to discern and to combat. Where the terrorist attack is an occasion for promoting revolutionary change, companies will be faced with lengthy complex negotiations and at times cumulative and changing demands. Further, as long as obvious poverty and deprivation exist, there remains great potential for political exploitation of the issues and for mobilizing opinion against transnational business operations. The political motivation behind terrorism will not easily be dissipated in the foreseeable future.

Targets and Means

Within the context of the political motivation just described, terrorist attacks against transnational business operations take on a highly rational pattern. This can be shown by a closer look at the types of business targets selected and the means most frequently employed by terrorists against them. This is not to say that terrorists have been even moderately successful in achieving their ultimate political ends. Indeed, even their short-term tactical triumphs, as in the destruction of the three airliners in Jordan in 1970 and in the kidnaping of William Niehous in Venezuela in February 1976, may result in strategic reverses. Nevertheless, on a case-by-case basis, they have fared well in their numerous attacks on transnational enterprises.

Emerging Patterns. The immediate targets of terrorist attacks against transnational business may be broadly divided between persons and property. Due to the paucity of statistical studies and of common criteria for defining the two categories, the incidence of attacks in each case can be only roughly approximated. One source of statistics is the Milbank Study, recently published by the Central Intelligence Agency.[50] Of the 330 international terrorist incidents cited there, which directly affected U.S. citizens or property from 1968 to 1975, over one-third were attacks on persons. In these 115 attacks, the following means were employed by terrorists in the frequency indicated: kidnaping (59), armed assault or ambush (37), assassination (15), and hostage and barricade (4). Another 169 incidents, which are identified as bombings (136) and incendiary attacks or arson (33), may be attributed largely (although certainly not exclusively) to attacks on property. A remaining 29 incidents were designated "hyjacking [sic] (air and non-air)" and 17 were identified as "other."

Unfortunately, the Milbank Study does not provide figures relating to international terrorist attacks on business personnel and property. By use of available chronologies, however, kidnapings and bombings directed at U.S. businesses operating abroad can be roughly approximated. During the period 1968-1975, there were at least 27 reported incidents of kidnaping involving U.S. business executives or employees of U.S. companies operating abroad.[51] Of these, 21 occurred in Latin America and 15 in Argentina alone. During the same period, there occurred at least 48 bombings and 4 incendiary attacks on the offices, plants, or pipelines of U.S. companies operating abroad. Of these 52 incidents, 37 occurred in Latin America—27 in Argentina alone. Looking solely at kidnapings and bombings involving U.S. businesses operating abroad, therefore, 74 percent of the incidents took place in Latin America and 54 percent in Argentina.

Even though bombings and incendiary attacks outnumber kidnapings two to one, U.S. business perceives kidnaping presently to be the primary threat of terrorism overseas. Latin America remains the most critical area, but the danger varies from country to country and from time to time depending on the political situation. While the range of kidnaping targets encompasses executives as a group, executives of higher rank who reside in the foreign country have been the more likely targets. This is because of their importance to the operations of the company, their symbolic positions in the country as representatives of foreign interests, and their relatively high profiles and hence publicity value to the terrorists. In addition, since they are residents in the country, their work schedules and travel patterns can be calculated more easily.

Some concern has been expressed that kidnap targets may be expanded by terrorists to include not only higher-level executives, but also their families and perhaps a much broader range of employees. Would a transnational corporation show less compassion for the wife or child of an executive or for a secretary or foreman than for a top executive? Most probably, its response would be the same. Nevertheless, politically motivated terrorists would be disinclined in this direction because of a sympathy factor. Terrorists must be able to link their attacks with the justice of their cause. Kidnaping a top-level executive can be

justified by the misdeeds of the company and the symbolic or actual responsibility of the executive for the actions of the foreign owners. As the public would
not readily believe this of the family or of an average employee, the ideological
position of the terrorists would be undercut. On the other hand, public opinion
may have little influence on terrorists whose choice of targets derives primarily
from personal gain, psychotic, or cultic motives. The sympathy factor also may
be overridden by a political strategy calling for shock tactics.

The sympathy factor may help explain why assassination is little used
against executives. Certainly, as a shock tactic, a serious effort at assassination
would be difficult to thwart and would quickly drive foreign executives and,
perhaps, foreign companies from the country. Within 10 days after the bloody
ambush of John Swint, the general manager of Ford's parts subsidiary, 25 Ford
executives and their families left Argentina.[52] However, it is difficult to justify
such extreme violence to the public. Further, a concerted use of assassination
would call forth a much stronger reaction from the host government. Shortly
after the Swint murder, the late President Juan Perón personally met with Ford's
vice president in Argentina and offered the use of national patrolmen for plant
protection.[53]

While businesses view kidnaping as the primary threat of international
terrorism today, bombings and incendiary attacks remain a matter of great
concern. If employed concertedly by terrorists, they could prove extremely
costly to the continued profitable operation of business. Within the United
States, by contrast to Latin American countries generally, business ranks
bombings and incendiary attacks as the primary threat of terrorism. During the
first eight months of 1976, for instance, there were 1068 incidents of this type
in the United States (an average of 134 per month), causing 157 personal
injuries, 32 deaths, and property damage of about $9 million. By far the most
prevalent targets were residences (284 cases) and commercial operations and
office buildings (240 cases). This is a decline from an average of 175 bombings
and incendiary incidents per month during the same period in 1975, and
considerably less than the monthly average of 433 for 1971. Of this number,
based on 1975 statistics, only 1.2 percent of the incidents were reported to have
"foreign political" as the apparent motive. An additional 7.5 percent could be
classified as having some other type of political motive.[54]

By stark contrast, only 118 hostage cases[55] were reported to the FBI during
the entire first six months of 1976. This is considerably less than the monthly
average reported during the same period for bombings and incendiary attacks.
None of the hostage cases was reported to have a political motive. The total
ransom demanded was $3,257,000, of which $1,041,300 was paid and $807,240
was recovered by authorities.[56] Further, this contrast is highlighted when
compared with statistics from Colombia, which appear to reflect the pattern for
much of Latin America. Whereas during 1975 only 6 terrorist bombings were
recorded, 64 incidents of kidnaping occurred, for total ransom payments of

$8,361,791. Various terrorist groups took public "credit" for most of these kidnapings; however, it is believed that many kidnapings by common criminal groups in Colombia are not reported.[57]

With some important exceptions, terrorists have directed their bombings of U.S. businesses overseas primarily against administrative and sales offices rather than against manufacturing plants and other operating facilities. The target companies typically are high profile, whose names are well known and, therefore, will generate publicity for the terrorists. Applying this same "publicity rationale" to the future, concern is expressed by corporate security officers that terrorists will begin to look for more sensational targets such as supertankers, chemical carriers, ocean drilling rigs, nuclear power plants, and pipe-and-slurry lines. A number of bomb threats against supertankers owned by oil companies have been reported, but they have turned out to be hoaxes. However appealing these targets may appear at first blush, terrorists also must weigh the political backlash that such bombings may have on their political goals. At the same time, it must be remembered that terrorists trapped into a hopeless cause may just decide to take a suicidal route.

Those interviewed ranked the seriousness of extortion just behind kidnaping, bombings, and incendiary attacks. While extortion may be based on any threat of violence, threats of assault, assassination, and bombing appear to be the most prevalent. The extortionist may force expatriates to leave the country, as happened with Ford in Argentina in November 1973,[58] may require the company to increase the wages of employees or to hire additional employees, or may seek money payments either in a lump sum or on a regular basis.[59] Extortion, of course, is only as effective as the company's belief that the threat will be acted on. One police official estimates that the ratio of bombing threats to explosions is 200:1 in New York City.[60] Because extortion threats and payments are not regularly reported in either the United States or foreign countries, there is no way to estimate the extent of their use or the frequency of their success.

Aside from targets of persons and property, the very name and function of the transnational business may also be the target of terrorist attacks. That is to say, terrorists may seek to defame or to discredit the company in order to undermine its position in the foreign country. Such efforts often accompany the publicity surrounding a bombing or kidnaping. During the kidnaping of Victor Samuelson, the ERP charged that Exxon owed $10 million in back taxes to the Argentine government.[61] Similarly, when guerrillas threatened the systematic murder of all Ford executives and their families in Argentina in November 1973, they asserted that the company had "pillaged the country by super-exploitation of workers."[62] Further, the Revolutionary Commander Argimiro Gabaldon sought to use stolen documents from Owens-Illinois' subsidiary in Venezuela as means to demonstrate how the company had opposed the social and economic goals of the country, including the entry of Venezuela into the Andean Pact in 1972.[63]

This same end also may be pursued purely through propaganda attacks that subvert the loyalty of employees and the support of the populace. As a result, it is difficult for local and national governments to stand behind the transnational enterprise when the need arises. In some cases, labor unions also may be exploited for this purpose. Strictly speaking, such propaganda is not terrorism; yet when it is employed in a planned and sophisticated manner, it can have insidious effects on a company's operation.

Criteria of Selection. Three interrelated criteria appear to be involved in the selection by terrorists of targets and means of attacks against transnational business operations.

Suitability to Terrorist Ends. As terrorism is essentially a tactic of the weak designed to achieve broad political ends with a small investment of time and energy, shock tactics that address the public consciousness are of critical importance. If at the same time these tactics fund the revolution, so much the better for political terrorists. Kidnapings, bombings, and incendiary attacks, which are directed at transnational corporations, suit both purposes well. Not only do they have high impact value, but they also play on the widespread rhetoric of "exploitative, monopolistic, foreign intervention" and fully utilize the modern capacity for rapid mass communication, which publicizes sensational events around the world. Where the primary objective of the attack is extortion, however, executive kidnaping appears to be much more lucrative for terrorists than bomb threats against transnational companies. For the reasons mentioned above, assassination appears to have a serious ideological weakness.

Vulnerability of the Target. By comparison with the existing regime, which is the ultimate target of revolutionary groups, the transnational enterprise is easy prey both to propaganda and to violent attack. It lacks the resources and comprehensive authority of the state, yet it may be made to symbolize the established order. As between targets of persons and property, fixed facilities can be more easily guarded and defended, although a substantial investment in equipment and security personnel may be required. Personnel and vehicles are much more exposed outside company offices and facilities. This is especially true of top executives in residence, whose movements can be monitored over a period of time, whose positions require them to make frequent public appearances, and whose own morale and that of their family would seriously suffer by stringently limiting their movements. For these reasons also, kidnaping becomes more attractive to the terrorist than bombings.

Risks and Costs to the Terrorists. At this point, the scale tends to weigh more heavily in favor of bombings and assassinations. They are relatively easy to plan and execute, their cost can be quite low, and the chances of escaping capture very high. Most risky, on the other hand, would be barricade-and-hostage tactics. Except in some bank robberies, they have scarcely been used against businesses.[64] However, they give the terrorists on-the-spot intensive media exposure and the opportunity to obtain immediate compliance with their demands. Thus on October 18, 1973, the Lebanese Socialist Revolutionary Organization raided the Bank of America in Beirut, holding 40 persons hostage. Their demands for release of prisoners and $10 million to finance the Arab war effort against Israel were rejected. After the terrorists were captured or killed in a direct assault by police and army commandos, one U.S. national was found executed.

Somewhere between these two extremes of cost and risk lies kidnaping.[65] As with bombings and assassinations, a kidnaping can be well planned in advance. In contrast to barricade situations, it requires only a brief initial exposure to danger at the time the victim is captured, and the entire operation can be aborted at any time with a good chance of escape. Further, the timing and direction of all phases in the kidnaping, from the capture to the release of the victim, remain essentially within the terrorists' control. Demands can be tailored as the situation evolves in order to play to the media and still obtain a ransom. By comparison with bombings and assassination, however, kidnaping requires substantial and sometimes complex organizational and logistical support in order to guard the secrecy of the victim's location, maintain the kidnapers' anonymity, and gain time and leverage in negotiations.

Based on this analysis of the nature of the terrorist threat, it appears that transnational enterprises fit well the motives, the targets, and the means of terrorists today. Further, among the various targets and means available to terrorists, the kidnaping of top-level executives of these enterprises promises to remain a major danger. This is particularly true of transnational enterprises, especially U.S. enterprises, operating in Latin America because of the nationalistic reaction toward foreign business ventures and of the numerous revolutionary groups operating throughout the area. The political instability of regimes can only heighten this danger. Finally, the high degree of success that terrorists have had in recent years with transnational enterprises will surely encourage them to pursue the transnational enterprise as a target in the future.

In light of this prospect, transnational enterprises must develop carefully the means to discern the operating principles and strategic objectives behind the terrorist threat. From even this brief analysis of terrorism, it is clear that ideology plays a key motivational role. It is the organizing principle that determines the long-term strategy of a terrorist group. Yet within this strategy there is room for great flexibility relating to the current political situation in a country and the economic and organizational needs of the group. Furthermore, the selection of targets and means may shift widely from time to time, depending on their suitability to achieve the political ends of terrorists, the vulnerability of the enterprises to terrorist demands, and the costs and risks to the terrorists. While it may be that traditional criminal groups will mimic the tactics of terrorism more and more, the two must not be confused. Different methods and approaches will probably be necessary to deal with the militant ideological motivation of the terrorist and the personal gain motive of the common criminal. The challenge for the transnational enterprise is to create the sophisticated analytical tools for making these distinctions and for drawing the proper conclusions as they relate to security policy, to negotiating strategy, and ultimately, to the requirements of public policy.

The Impact of Terrorism on Transnational Business Operations

As a tactic, terrorism has the value of achieving disproportionately large effects at a minimum cost to the perpetrators. The 507 incidents of international terrorism that occurred between 1968 and April 1974 took a toll of 520 lives, including terrorists, and wounded 850. Though these numbers do not exceed the annual homicide rate of a major city today, the attention given them in the news media far exceeds their statistical importance.[66] Detonating one well-placed bomb in corporate offices or kidnaping or ambushing one executive can set off a chain reaction of security measures and introduce a climate of apprehension throughout the foreign operations of a transnational enterprise. Its effects also may reach into the home office thousands of miles away. One corporate security officer estimates that one bomb explosion may be rewarded in numerous subsequent extortion threats. The costs to the enterprise, both visible and hidden, may far exceed the payments exacted by the terrorists.

Any attempt to assess terrorism's impact on transnational enterprises is clouded by the impingement of other economic and political circumstances. Except in extreme situations, terrorism becomes simply one of many factors that affect the operations and the success of a business operation. On the other hand, few would deny that at least from the viewpoint of business, it has become a factor of increasing importance and promises to continue being so for the foreseeable future. While there are scarcely any instances of transnational enterprises withdrawing their operations from a country because of the threat of terrorism, there are equally few cases in which such enterprises have successfully resisted terrorist demands. An appraisal of the impact lies somewhere between withdrawal and capitulation. The four factors identified below—employee morale, operating expenses, business climate, and investment decision—offer some insight on the impact of terrorism. The data, however, are far from conclusive.

Employee Morale

It can be argued that the morale factor has been exaggerated, that terrorism is simply a vocational obstacle or, as one Foreign Service officer put it, "one of the things you live with." If so, then the personnel policy of transnational enterprises, which has been fashioned largely out of each company's own experience, is completely mistaken. There are no reported kidnap cases in which a transnational enterprise has refused to reach a settlement with terrorists where a life was believed to be seriously at stake. Indeed, corporate security officers and security consultants who were interviewed unanimously agreed that a company could not refuse to do everything possible to negotiate an employee's release. An enterprise, especially a large one, would be hard pressed to plead that it had no resources to pay ransom, and would not want to be placed in the position of causing the death of an employee.[67] A failure to respond to terrorist demands would not only make foreign assignment unacceptable, but it also could lead to the company's crucifixion in the press and severely undermine its public image.[68]

Moreover, some of those interviewed distinguished the position of the corporate executive from that of a State Department officer. Whereas the executive is essentially an "economic man" doing his job for pay, the State Department officer, like the soldier, is an agent of the government who serves a political purpose and understands the risks he takes. While this comparison is open to dispute,[69] there may be an idealistic or other vocational attraction to the Foreign Service that is not present for transnational enterprises.[70] Insofar as this is true, the State Department becomes a unique institution with a special advantage in the labor market. It can uniformly implement a policy of "no ransom" on a worldwide basis without fear that its employees will defect to a competitor. Transnational enterprises do not enjoy this privileged position and have no serious possibility, short of legislation, of getting the private business sector to accept a uniform "no-ransom" policy.

Not surprisingly, therefore, terrorism has had visible effect on the personnel policies of transnational enterprises. Where threats of violence have become serious, as in Argentina since 1969, corporate executives and their families have been moved to safer locations. Even executives who are nationals of the host country have had to be posted to assignments in other countries for their own protection. During the 18 months between mid-1972 and the end of 1973, when the ransom payments to kidnapers in Argentina escalated from $200,000 to $14.2 million, the expatriate population reportedly fell from 1000 to 300.[71] In many cases, the corporate offices were simply moved to a neighboring country like Brazil. This results in an abrupt loss of talent, which can be replaced only slowly and at considerable cost. It may also reduce transnational control over the affiliate's operation, as host country nationals assume top management positions and become more responsive to national interests than to the global priorities of the transnational enterprise.

The less obvious effects of terrorism are equally critical. Stringent security precautions may make life in the host country both inconvenient and less interesting than anticipated for both executives and their families. Bodyguards detract from privacy, inhibit spontaneity, and attract notice. Avoiding publicity may interfere with social life as well as with participation in useful business organizations. Finally, a state of apprehension can have debilitating psychological effects that permeate the entire business organization and undermine morale.

Operating Expenses

Since 1970, the threat of terrorism has added to the operating expenses of transnational enterprises. This is obviously true if ransom payments are carried as operating costs. As noted earlier, ransom payments by transnational enterprises operating in Argentina amounted to at least $35 million to $55 million during the years 1970 to 1974. Or, to use another standard, the $1.5 million ransom that Kodak paid guerrillas for the release of its technical operations manager, Antony DaCruz, in April 1973, reportedly exhausted its profits for the previous several years.[72] In that sense, however, ransom payments are not "just another" operating expense. The same can be said of losses suffered from the destruction of property of transnational enterprises although the amounts involved thus far have not reached the level of ransom payments.

Another obvious increase in operating expenses can be attributed to the additional security measures that transnational enterprises must undertake. This includes the cost of additional and often highly sophisticated equipment as well as enlarged personnel requirements. One transnational enterprise reports spending close to $1 million per year for executive protection in Mexico. Another, a medium-sized firm, paid $500,000 for guards and other protection in 1973.[73] Further, an oil company that had no security department in 1974 now has a security department with a staff of five, which was increased to seven in 1977. Overall, the security costs of transnational enterprises may have doubled or tripled over the past few years.[74]

There also are many hidden costs that result from the threat of terrorism. Some of these are administrative. Others appear less subtly in the salary negotiations with employees for foreign assignments. In 1974, Coca Cola reclassified Buenos Aires as a "hardship post" and increased "environmental allowances" by 10 percent of the base salary.[75] Another company had to commit itself to fly the employee's family to Bangkok to assure them a safe haven each time that the executive leaves Bangladesh for a few days. Additionally, executives may well work less productively under security constraints and the accompanying psychological pressures. They also are likely to request transfer more frequently from "hardship posts."

Business-Government Relations

Although it is not always easy to demonstrate, terrorism can strain the relations of transnational enterprises with host country governments if it is combined with a sophisticated and carefully orchestrated propaganda attack. As pointed out earlier,[76] attacks on foreign-owned enterprises have a nationalistic appeal and at the same time embarrass the existing regime by revealing the fragility of domestic order. Further, while governments in many developing countries are painfully aware of their economic dependence on the capital and technology of transnational enterprises, they also are highly critical of the ownership and management practices of these enterprises, which allegedly subordinate host country operations to foreign priorities. In addition, they suspect and occasionally charge these enterprises with manipulating world prices, revenue flows, and technology transfer contrary to the host country's national interests.

In the event of terrorist attack, however, the government finds that it must come to the aid of the transnational institution, which on other occasions it has vilified. The embarrassment is all the greater if the case is highly publicized and particularly, if through this publicity, the government and the enterprise in question are charged with corrupt dealings. This tack began to emerge in late 1973, when both the ELN in Colombia and the ERP in Argentina announced their intentions to "try" their kidnap victims for the crimes of the enterprises.[77] It took on monumental proportions in Venezuela with the kidnaping of William Niehous.

During the first month of the Niehous kidnaping, the Revolutionary Command Argimiro Gabaldon focused on only one demand: the publication by Owens-Illinois of a five-page document accusing the glass company of interfering in the domestic affairs of the country through illegal transactions with prominent officials of the ruling Accion Democratica Party. As proof of this charge, the terrorists attached 22 photocopies of company telexes, memorandums, and business reports, some of which reportedly had been falsified.[78] Although at first the Revolutionary Command demanded that the document be published in major national and foreign newspapers and be given a half-hour radio coverage by a local station, a government-imposed "blackout" on news coverage ruled this out.[79] When Owens-Illinois then published the document, limiting publication to the *New York Times, The Times* (London), and *Le Monde*, the Venezuelan government announced that it would "acquire" the Venezuelan assets of the company for "violating Venezuela's legal constitutional norms." The government charged that Owens-Illinois had defamed Venezuela by publishing "a communique produced by subversive groups."[80] In response to an expression of concern by the U.S. State Department that "expropriation" was being used as a criminal sanction, the Venezuelan government countered that Owens-Illinois was being declared *persona non grata* for allegedly violating the laws of Venezuela. Although the Venezuelan government stated that it would pay Owens "just compensation," the foreign business community expressed great dismay at what was said to be "a terrible overreaction."[81]

The Owens-Illinois case vividly demonstrates how terrorists can use the media to undermine business-government relations as well as to damage the business climate overall. Indeed, despite the reportedly rather unsophisticated documentation that the Revolutionary Command submitted to support its position, the strategy yielded an enormous dividend of embarrassment to the government and an intense suspicion of the government on the part of foreign business. Further, while the debacle also can be attributed in part at least to misjudgments, misunderstandings, and overreactions by both the government and the company, the business-government tension portrayed there is potentially present in many cases where terrorists skillfully employ propaganda and publicity. The irony of the Owens-Illinois case is that after the Revolutionary Command achieved its ideological mission of embarrassing the government and poisoning the business climate, it shifted its tactics to place monetary demands on the company in the amount of $3.5 million.[82]

Investment Decisions

Beyond the effects described above, terrorism also has become a factor over the past five years in the investment decisions of transnational enterprises. This is especially true for enterprises operating in developing countries of Latin America and the Middle East. At the same time, the degree of impact that terrorism has on investment decisions is difficult to assess, for terrorism is only one, and normally not the most important, factor in such decisions.

For example, the book value of U.S. investment at year end in Argentina increased from $1022 million in 1970 to $1144 million in 1973 and then fell to $1122 million in 1975.[83] As the decrease became apparent in 1974, it is tempting to argue that this decline in U.S. foreign investment resulted from the 18-month terrorist splurge from mid-1972 to the end of 1973, when a number of executives of foreign companies were kidnaped and ransoms escalated from $200 thousand to $14.2 million. However, during the same period of intensified terrorism, Argentina also passed highly restrictive foreign investment laws and experienced considerable political instability. Indeed, the increase in terrorism may well be attributed to this lack of political stability, for terrorist attacks certainly were not at all limited to transnational enterprises. In 1973 alone, 190 kidnapings were reported in Argentina.[84] The impact of terrorism on the investment decision, therefore, cannot be separated from other political and economic conditions in the host country.

The question remains: In what way and to what extent has the threat of terrorism affected the investment decision of transnational enterprises? There is little evidence that terrorism has caused transnational enterprises to disinvest and leave the host country. While some U.S. companies such as Koppers and A.E. Staley have pulled out of Argentina, their decisions do not appear to be the result of the threat of terrorism.[85] On the other hand, companies such as Otis Elevator, IBM, ITT, Alcan, John Deere, and Coca-Cola moved their corporate offices or regional headquarters in 1973 to 1974 from Buenos Aires to the safer havens of Madrid, Coral Gables, Rio de Janeiro, and Sao Paulo. These moves were a direct result of increased kidnaping of foreign executives. Although the divestment impact of terrorism appears not to reach below the level of the top corporate offices, the shift of corporate and regional officers can disrupt decision-making and result in a loss of productivity at least temporarily.[86] The shift also may create problems of management coordination for the future.

The impact of terrorism on reinvestment is less easily discerned. The decrease in total book value by $122 million of U.S. investment in Argentina during 1974 and 1975 suggests, at least, that capital is not being replaced as rapidly as it is being exhausted.[87] Once again, the exact cause for this is difficult to isolate. Several security consultants stated that in their private conversations with transnational companies, several reported that their decisions to postpone future expansion plans in two or three countries or to shift them to other countries primarily because of the problem of terrorism. One consultant pointed out that out of 30 U.S. industrialists with whom he had recently spoken, 5 executives indicated that their companies had shifted their investment decisions considerably over the past year as a result of the threat of terrorism. Of course, not every transnational enterprise possesses such flexibility either due to the importance of the market, the sources of raw materials, or the substantial investment already in place. For this reason, any reluctance toward reinvestment may be attributed more to a wait-and-see policy rather than to a longer-term investment decision. If the political and economic climate stabilizes, the normal pattern of reinvestment may well be resumed.

While the threat of terrorism has become an important factor in investment decisions, it is only one of several factors affecting investments, and rarely is it the most critical. Contrary to a popular belief that transnational enterprises possess great flexibility, business opportunities are not highly fungible. Before deciding not to invest or reinvest, and certainly before deciding to disinvest, in a country that offers a business opportunity, an enterprise will explore every other avenue for dealing with terrorism. In fact, transnational enterprises apparently are willing to accept enormous inconveniences and substantial additional costs and risks, if the "bottom line" (however defined for a particular country) warrants the investment decision. As one U.S. executive put it in reaction to the attack on Ford in Argentina on May 21, 1973: "Companies will just have to figure out whether the profits are worth the investment in security, blackmail and worries. This has become the price of doing business here."[88]

On the other hand, terrorism clearly has become a material risk factor in planning foreign investment and in arriving at the foreign investment decision. This risk will be calculated not only in the financial losses and added costs that may result from the anticipated level of the terrorist threat, but also in the reluctance of high-caliber management personnel to oversee the investment or expansion. In some cases, this risk factor may simply dictate the postponement of an investment or reinvestment. In others, it may require an increase in the expenditures for security measures or "overseas pay." In still others, it may tip the scales for a safer location. In any case, the results of increased risks to investment, for whatever reason, may be expected to increase the rate of return that the enterprise requires and may cause it to shorten its time line for recouping the value of its foreign investment.

Private Sector Responses to the Threat of Terrorism

The response of the transnational enterprise to the threat of terrorism will differ obviously from the response of government. This difference, as well as the nature of the response, depends on the number of variables, *e.g.*, the perception that each has of terrorism and the threat that it presents, the prevailing social conditions in which terrorism occurs, the tactical and technical means available for combating terrorism, the apparent urgency to deal with terrorism, and the authority to act within a given legal framework. Certainly, a government fighting for survival against revolutionary guerrillas will react differently from a foreign enterprise that faces infrequent ransom demands or occasional extortion. A detailed examination of these variables lies well beyond the scope of this chapter, although the previous section attempted to describe in a limited way certain parameters of the terrorist threat to transnational enterprises. The discussion that follows offers an overview within the business context of the types of responses by the private sector and government to this threat. Out of this analysis will emerge recommendations of approaches for combating terrorism directed against transnational enterprises.

Existing private sector responses against the threat of terrorism fall roughly into four groups: the internal security of the enterprise, cooperative relationships within the private sector and between government agencies and other enterprises, modes of self-restraint by the news media, and risk-pooling through insurance.

The Internal Security of the Enterprise

In response to the threat of terrorism, transnational enterprises place primary emphasis on updating, expanding, and improving their internal security programs. While the specifics differ depending on the company and its own threat analysis, major companies find it necessary (1) to institute comprehensive security programs, (2) to introduce special procedures for the protection of executives and their families, (3) to pursue a concerted policy of "low profile" for the company and its executives, and (4) to adopt special methods and policies of contingency planning.[89]

On the whole, these approaches constitute tactical responses that are essentially reactive in nature and limited to the enterprise and its employees. They are designed to reduce the marginal exposure of the company to terrorist attack in favor of more likely targets. In the words of one security company, its individual enterprise analyses are intended to make "protected persons less desirable targets for guerrilla groups than executives of other industries."[90] In effect, enterprises are addressing the second and third criteria[91] that terrorists employ in target selection—namely, target vulnerability and risk/cost analysis. They are using risk management within a business setting to obtain certain limited objectives. A brief review of these approaches will offer some insight into this emerging concept of risk management and the weaknesses inherent in the "marginal exposure" strategy of transnational enterprises to combating terrorism.

Comprehensive Security Programming. Increasing terrorist activity in recent years is forcing transnational enterprises to review their security programs. This is due not only to the increasing real and potential losses arising from terrorism, but also to the brazenness, unpredictability, armed intensity, and organized sophistication of terrorist attacks. For this reason, companies have placed increasing emphasis on systematic threat analysis and assessment, whether through the use of outside consultants or in-house capability. This approach entails a thorough analysis of the entire business operation from the physical protection of plants and property through to top management procedures. Close examination must be made of manpower organization, personnel management and practices, internal and external communication facilities, guard force and armament, executive travel and work schedules and procedures, and the selected use of alarm systems and security devices. Based on the conclusions of such studies, management determines the degree of protection needed after taking into consideration such factors as budgetary constraints, employee morale, business operating requirements, and the anticipated level and nature of the terrorist threat. The resulting security program is a strategic choice by management that melds together these and other critical decisional factors.

The resulting program, of course, will vary enormously from company to company. For instance, banks and manufacturers of volatile products and munitions obviously have special concerns about asset protection that do not exist for other businesses.[92] There are, however, a number of program elements that appear with frequency in comprehensive security planning. A sample list was published recently by a security consultant in *Security Management*:[93]

1. Train management and security and safety personnel in effective handling of emergency situations so that they can, within their own organization, set up the necessary plans. Such plans must be tailored to their specific needs and requirements, so that all emergency situations can be handled effectively and safely by their own personnel.
2. Establish a communication link with local law enforcement so that emer-

gency programs can be effectively set up in order to establish proper communication in connection with these vital problems.

3. Establish within each department of industrial concerns, factories, offices, etc., an assistant security official who would be responsible for security in that particular department. Such individuals must receive a certain amount of security training, and should attend security meetings and briefings at which potential problems will be discussed. This is a key unit which can make internal security programs effective.

4. Provide for management control; for example, use of undercover services to guard against industrial espionage and sabotage.

5. Conduct an up-to-date security survey and include residences of V.I.P.'s and executives.

6. Conduct an up-to-date personnel security check on all employees, regardless of length of service with company, including guard force if "in-house" guards are utilized. If an outside agency is employed, the matter should be discussed with the head of the security company.

7. Conduct, on an irregular basis, monthly security checks to assure that maximum security is implemented. Include homes and offices of V.I.P.'s as well.

8. Establish security duties for certain employees in case emergency situations arise. Hold briefings for such employees.

9. Provide security guidelines for American employees working overseas.

10. As political or emergency situations arise, provide lecture programs on specific problems. Such briefings to include:
    (a) The political situation.
    (b) Information on terrorist groups that operate in the area or country.
    (c) Briefing on explosives and explosive devices, if bombings are involved.

11. If overseas, have all executives adopt a low profile and blend in with local conditions.

The Niehous kidnaping has aroused special concern for maintaining the confidentiality of company matters, as reflected in points 4 and 6 in the list. In that case, working documents stolen from the files of the Owens subsidiary in Venezuela were used to support public allegations that the company had interfered improperly in the country's internal affairs.[94] For reasons such as this, corporate security officers believe that much more emphasis must be placed on screening personnel, especially those with access to sensitive documents, and on tailoring, routing, and handling procedures in order to limit the circulation of sensitive documents and papers.

Executive Protection. Because of the increased concern for kidnaping, executive protection has become a major component of the corporate security program. Normally, it becomes a central focus in any threat analysis. Two parallel, and sometimes competing, viewpoints tend to predominate: the hardware and bodyguard approach *versus* the stance of alertness, flexibility, and mobility. In high-risk areas, such as Argentina, bodyguards are frequent, and homes and offices are equipped with sophisticated surveillance and alarm systems. Security companies report that the demand for executive protection of one type or the other has doubled and tripled over the past year alone.[95] Confinement and surveillance, however, may not be conducive to job effectiveness. They can be quite expensive, and they take a toll in convenience and morale, especially for the executive's family. Indeed, in some cases, armed guards may only invite attack, for they signal the location of the executive. For this reason, many companies emphasize the second option and take pains to keep the movements of their executives and their families unpredictable and unobtrusive. A number of checklists have been designed to maintain the alertness of executives to traps and surveillance and to break up any pattern as to their schedules that would make their movements foreseeable.[96]

However these two approaches are combined, their effectiveness depends on a high and continuing degree of executive preparedness. This requires not only furnishing executives and their families with checklists and other cautionary material and collecting from them personal information for identification purposes, but also giving them the necessary training, psychological orientation, and value context so that they can deal effectively with their new "siege environment." Dealing effectively in this case entails an adequate understanding of the problem and its implications, knowledge of how to deal with it concretely, and the motivation to implement "what you know" on a daily basis. Films, such as those produced by Motorola Teleprograms, help to dramatize the problem as well as to demonstrate useful avoidance techniques in action. Additional films are being produced on hostage survival and coercive bargaining.[97]

It may be, however, that personal discussions with executives and their families will prove most effective in maintaining executive preparedness. One transnational enterprise reports excellent results in having a middle-aged female psychologist[98] sit down periodically with executives and their families in their homes to talk through the terrorist problem and the executive protection program. This makes their daily routines more than a matter of professional concern of the company. Each member of the family becomes a constant reminder to the other members of the need for caution, alertness, and varying schedules.

Corporate Profile. A third group of countermeasures to terrorism requires the enterprise to reduce its corporate profile toward the public. For many companies this is virtually impossible, either because the nature of their business requires a high profile or because their name already has become well known as a result of investing years of effort and millions of dollars. Nevertheless, a number of attempts are being made in this direction by replacing foreign executives with host country nationals; changing the name of the subsidiary; removing the name of the foreign company from buildings, trucks, and shipping crates; contracting out high-profile activities to host country nationals; delisting telephone numbers of executives; and keeping company executives out of the limelight. At the height of the kidnaping spree in Argentina in 1973, one transnational enterprise even refused to report publicly the name of the new president of its subsidiary.[99] Conceivably, a transnational enterprise might also decide to undertake a joint venture or to license its technology, instead of being the controlling investor, in order to lower its profile. However, no examples of this approach have come to light. Such an approach would be an extreme response and would more likely be dictated by other overriding business considerations.[100]

Low profile also is maintained by avoiding all publicity related to terrorism. This applies to specific incidents, company policies, and even the company's participation in cooperative efforts with other companies to combat terrorism. Companies tend to believe that any press on these matters will increase their marginal attractiveness as a target by comparison with other firms. Thus a number of enterprises which considered themselves vulnerable to terrorist attack, declined to testify at hearings on terrorism held in 1974 by the House Committee on Internal Security. They took the position "that any public identification and testimony by them would invite incidents against their firms and create serious problems for them."[101]

Ransom policy illustrates this concern. From the viewpoint of the enterprise, a pre-announced willingness to negotiate or a categorical refusal to pay would either invite kidnaping or provoke a terrorist attack in order to "put down" the enterprise and set an example for others. In addition, a "hard line" against ransom payment may be circumvented easily by assaults combined with extortion demands. The ERP successfully followed this tack against Ford in Argentina by threatening to shoot additional employees if the ransom were not paid.[102] Furthermore, for the reasons stated above in discussing employee morale, the transnational enterprise does not wish to go on record as resisting ransom payments; yet neither does it want to indicate that ransom would be paid. Consequently, companies generally refuse to reveal or to comment on their ransom policies, including whether payments were made in specific cases. This keeps the terrorist guessing and allows the company maximum flexibility in negotiations.[103]

Overall, these "low-profile" tactics are likely to have only marginal value. The activities of large foreign companies are not easily veiled. Their profitable operation almost certainly demands some visibility. Nor are the tactics themselves necessarily effective, even in a limited way. Host country nationals in top management positions, for instance, may not insulate an enterprise from attack. Indeed, some have had to be removed from the host country for their own protection. Further, while companies may resist acknowledging ransom payments, terrorists may, as in the 1973 kidnaping of Exxon's Victor Samuelson, require the enterprise to concede publicly that all ransom demands have been met in order to demonstrate their victory.[104]

Contingency Planning. This fourth approach focuses the various tactics of an enterprise into one cohesive strategy. It establishes the security priorities through clear policy guidelines; ensures the comprehensive functioning of the overall security plan through periodic re-evaluation; locates clear, direct lines of authority and the persons responsible; provides for the necessary intelligence and an appropriate interfacing with local authorities; and designates a management team and the procedures for dealing comprehensively with crisis situations. Terrorism has taught the transnational enterprise that its response to terrorist attacks must be not only professional but also related to all aspects of the business. In times of crisis, responsible decisions must be fashioned rapidly from numerous technical, sociological, psychological, media, and business policy viewpoints. This assumes thorough preparation and planning before the fact.

While crisis management is quite advanced in theory, its practical application even within major enterprises is still in the formative stages. Few if any companies believe as yet that they have an adequate response to terrorism. Considerable research, experimentation, and training remain before crisis management becomes a thoroughly tested mode of business operation. A number of security companies and consultants offer courses in the design and implementation of crisis management programs. Twelve major U.S. enterprises have united around the initiative of Motorola to conduct practical interdisciplinary research and to develop business strategies in crisis management and coercive bargaining. This program will be discussed later in this chapter.

These four approaches to internal security rely essentially on the enterprise's own resources, plus some personnel and planning assistance from outside consultants and security companies. They have one view in common: that terrorism is a problem to be avoided rather than one to be solved. And the best way for the enterprise to avoid the problem is to improve and better manage its internal security systems. Where feasible, executives may even withdraw from participation in business and social organizations that give them public exposure.

There was consensus among those interviewed that each of these approaches offers the enterprise and its personnel some significant degree of protection against terrorist attack. There was also consensus, however, that the degree of protection was relative, both as to the effectiveness of the security programs adopted by alternative target enterprises, and to the determination of terrorists to make good on their threats. Where this determination exists, terrorists have a clear advantage over the security forces of an enterprise, due to the element of surprise and to their ability to mobilize armed squads or to plant a bomb at a location of their choice.[105]

This traditional and somewhat individualistic view of security, therefore, tends to overlook or to neglect the fact that terrorism is a "social disease." For the most part, terrorists are not motivated by personal greed, but by a political fanaticism that is willing to turn society upside down to achieve social change. The transnational enterprise has particular relevance for terrorists because it is so symbolic of the established order. Terrorism, therefore, is a distinctly social challenge that must be countered in large part by a concerted social effort. This is not to say that transnational enterprises can or should lead in this effort.

Indeed, where they are operating as foreigners in a host country, a certain reserve is indicated. Nevertheless, transnational enterprises still have considerable leeway to fashion counterterrorist measures out of cooperative relationships with other enterprises and other institutions of society.

Cooperative Relationships

An effective response to terrorism cannot be limited to the internal security programs of transnational enterprises. It must have a breadth and depth that match the challenge. Where the social system or the governmental regime itself is under attack, the stakes are high, and the adversary often well armed and organized. The foreign enterprise becomes simply a pawn in a larger game. For this reason, the transnational enterprise must expand its security horizons to encompass a broad range of cooperative working relationships in the society. Some of these, as with local police authorities, are rather traditional and must be intensified. Others, although traditional, must be reshaped, as with intercompany and press relationships. Still others, as with the U.S. missions and the Department of State, are relatively new and must be given a useful form. Great potential value lies in developing these cooperative relationships. They can provide the transnational enterprise with accurate and current sources of intelligence on terrorist movements, accelerate practical research in providing more effective preventive systems and techniques, and achieve a balanced media reporting that can educate the public and undercut the terrorists' position.

In a number of cases, significant initiatives have already been undertaken in these areas. In others, there is considerable experience that has yet to be drawn together, formulated, and brought to bear on the problem. The following discussion is aimed at ferreting out the most promising courses of action. The first part considers cooperative relationships with governmental authorities, while the second deals with interfirm cooperation.

Governmental Authorities. In its foreign operations, the U.S. transnational enterprise has recourse to three types of governmental agencies in dealing with terrorism. In the foreign country, cooperative working relationships are developed with local and national law enforcement authorities as well as with the U.S. mission. Especially in times of crisis, enterprises also will look to the U.S. Department of State. In the host country, one basic principle of a corporate security program, as pointed out previously,[106] calls for the enterprise to establish a communications link with the *law enforcement authorities.* Depending on the capabilities of these authorities, this link should provide the enterprise with a current source of intelligence on terrorist strategies, movements, and target priorities. These authorities also can assist the enterprise in screening personnel to avoid sabotage, security leaks, and terrorist intelligence gathering on the inside. Further, when the threat of attack increases or a crisis occurs, this link will enable the enterprise to receive early warnings as well as the serious support and cooperation of these authorities.

While this relationship with law enforcement authorities often occurs as a matter of course in the United States, it cannot be taken for granted in foreign countries.[107] The different customs, practices, and expectations of their cultures and their governmental forms require the enterprise to carefully and thoughtfully nurture a communications link. It is important to know, for instance, not only how and within what jurisdictional framework these authorities operate, but also whom to contact in order to receive efficient and confidential treatment and what level of competency to expect. As personal contacts often are critical, these relationships must be cultivated continuously and not left for crisis situations. Corporate security officers have been aided in making and developing these contacts by the U.S. mission in a given country, the FBI, and the International Criminal Police Organization (Interpol).

The value of this relationship with law enforcement authorities, of course, will vary enormously from country to country. In some countries, due to the lack of training or to the disaffection of local security forces, an effective and confidential communications link can be established only with national authorities or perhaps with the military. Companies frequently are reluctant to confide in host country authorities, especially at the local level, due both to lax security procedures and to the exposure of these authorities to infiltration. On the other hand, the relationship may have useful rewards. Shortly after the assassination of Ford's general manager in Argentina in November 1973, President Juan Perón met with Ford's vice president and offered guards to any company that wanted them. Eighty armed border patrolmen soon arrived at Ford's plants in Argentina.[108] Later, on May 29, 1974, the Argentine government reportedly set up a special Industrial Police Organization under the jurisdiction of the federal police to guard industrial plants throughout the country.[109] No assessment of the success of this governmental measure is available.

A second set of relationships runs from U.S. foreign affiliates to the U.S. mission in the host country. While U.S. companies operating in foreign countries maintain contact with the U.S. mission, only in the last three or four years has there been a concerted attempt by the State Department or a serious concern by U.S. business to focus on security matters. With the increasing threat from terrorism, U.S. missions have organized Security Watch Committees, consisting of the deputy chief of mission, the head political officer, the security officer, and other appropriate staff, which meet regularly to assess terrorist activity in the country and the region in respect to the mission and the resident U.S. community. As transnational enterprises have been forced to do for their expatriates, U.S. missions also have developed Emergency and Evacuation Plans for all U.S. nationals and their families residing in the country. As appropriate, U.S. enterprises are kept informed on a need-to-know basis about terrorist activity. In some cases, the Security Watch Committee also holds monthly information meetings for the U.S. business community.

Nevertheless, almost without exception, the U.S. enterprises that were interviewed believe that a much closer working relationship must be developed between them and the U.S. missions on security matters. In particular, there is need for better quality, current intelligence on terrorist activities from the missions and for periodic meetings of U.S. companies with the missions in order to assist in the development and coordination of contingency planning. Some of those interviewed advocate the establishment of a Command Center within the U.S. mission to coordinate all information and to serve as a focal point for message clearance and planning. The mission would have access to information from both Washington and the host country authorities and could best guard its confidentiality.

The State Department has moved recently to meet this need, at least in part, by directing its regional security supervisors, regional security officers, and regional technical officers to assist U.S. business firms overseas "in every way possible." In a memorandum of May 21, 1976, the deputy assistant secretary for security, Victor Dikeos, noted the sharp increase in international terrorist activity aimed at U.S. business firms operating abroad and set forth the types of assistance that the more than 100 security officers abroad could "usefully" provide:

These include the identities of appropriate police contacts with whom the businessman or his company might effect working liaison; the names of reliable local firms providing guard services, security hardware or other security assistance; general guidance on the preparation of emergency and evacuation, bomb threat and other contingency plans; travel advisories where domestic security conditions dictate; and briefings to social and security planning groups of the local U.S. business community regarding practical security precautions to be taken at home, when traveling, and other related matters.[110]

A conscientious implementation of this State Department directive will assist greatly in establishing a closer working relationship with the U.S. business community. There was general agreement among those interviewed that the move is clearly in the right direction. Concern was voiced, however, whether the security officers in the U.S. missions generally have an adequate business perspective to offer practical, useful advice. Security officers also were urged to take a more "professional" approach although it was granted that the qualities of practicality and professionalism depend very much on the security officer in question. These gaps might be overcome by close coordination between security officers and commercial attachés and by giving security officers additional training in respect to the security needs of business.

Further, the mission's ability to bridge the "intelligence gap" of U.S. companies remains a delicate question. Significantly, while pointing out that "senior elements in the Department place heavy emphasis on assisting American citizens abroad in every way possible," Dikeos reminded the security officers to observe "propriety and good judgment in these relationships, and the strictures imposed on the disclosure of classified and sensitive information."[111] Not only does the security officer often possess sensitive or classified information whose disclosure could prove embarrassing to the host country government, but also by becoming a conduit for counterinsurgency intelligence, the mission could jeopardize its diplomatic status with the host country. Additionally, there are the usual problems of protecting the source and respecting the confidentiality of the information.

While these are delicate matters that deserve full consideration, they should not serve as an excuse for unduly classifying intelligence of value to U.S. enterprises. As a first step in resolving these issues, corporate officers could well sit down with the Security Watch Committee of a given U.S. mission and define the types of intelligence that are critical to the corporate security programs. It might then be feasible to establish a formula, based on the relevance, urgency, and reliability of the intelligence, for determining when and in what form it should be communicated to the enterprise.

The cooperative relationship of the parent offices of transnational enterprises with the Department of State constitutes a reverse side of the relationship of the foreign affiliates to the missions. While the operations of the latter are focused at the state and regional level, the perspectives of the former are, relatively speaking, global. Further, much of the intelligence that the missions receive comes from the State Department and the various intelligence agencies located in Washington, although the missions themselves contribute to that intelligence system. In certain respects, therefore, the Department of State offers a more appropriate site for an intelligence center on terrorism than do the missions. A broader spectrum of data and expertise is available, which in the future may result in a more thorough analysis of terrorist activities and projection of trends for countries and regions. Further, a central location better ensures the coordination of intelligence distribution and the preservation of confidentiality.

It also may increase the overall access of transnational enterprises to critical intelligence, for the intelligence can be more easily "packaged" and made available to parent offices on a need basis with less likelihood of compromising the missions' positions in the host countries.

The Department of State already has begun to develop its capability in this direction. Its counterterrorism effort is centered in two offices with overlapping responsibilities: the Office of Security (SY) and the Office of the Coordinator for Combating Terrorism (CCT). The former, which is responsible for protecting U.S. missions and their personnel around the world, has expanded its capacity to protect visiting foreign dignitaries[112] and certain State Department officials and their families traveling abroad. SY in turn has had to increase its coordination with other U.S. intelligence agencies and to improve its threat analysis and evaluation capabilities in order to deal with terrorism more effectively.

CCT, on the other hand, was established relatively recently as the result of a presidential directive of September 1972, requesting the Secretary of State to create a Cabinet Committee for Combating Terrorism to consider "the most effective means to prevent terrorism here and abroad." Under this committee was formed a working group, which is chaired by the CCT coordinator and the former special assistant to the secretary of state, L. Douglas Heck. Although the CCT is concerned with intra-agency coordination and the cabinet committee/ work group concentrates on interagency matters, the focus of both is protecting U.S. nationals abroad and internationally protected foreign persons in the United States.[113] Their assistance to U.S. businessmen operating abroad has been largely case-by-case advice on security techniques and experiences, including official contacts with host governments, available intelligence on terrorist operations, and the formulation of "General Security Tips for U.S. Businessmen Abroad."[114] The advice and intelligence, however, has been limited by the amount and quality of the experience and of the data available.

Recognizing this limitation, in October 1975 the offices of SY and CCT in the Department of State formed a task force with the following duties: "[To] review the Department's needs for terrorism information, to examine the procedures being used to collect, store, retrieve and analyze such information, to look at the mechanisms for making such information available to both top management and operational counter-terrorism elements in the Department and to recommend changes and improvements to the present system."

They concluded that the department's counterterrorism measures have been largely reactive to specific terrorist acts and threats; that the data base is widely fragmented and uncoordinated among a number of intelligence agencies; that in many cases data are incomplete, especially as to transnational terrorist groups, their activities, and their targets; and that insufficient resources have been committed "to develop the personnel capability to perform meaningful, user-oriented analysis and evaluations of terrorism data."[115]

The task force recommended a two-phase program to deal with these weaknesses. Phase I is designed to upgrade the present intelligence system of the State Department through the establishment of an operations coordination center within SY, combined with a communications network among the various intelligence agencies. It will include data bases that centralize and improve the collection, retrieval, and dissemination of current intelligence information. While the data systems are to be phased in over a five-year period, a Command Intelligence Center (CIC) has been functioning since July 1, 1976. It consists of a Watch Officer Group to coordinate alerts and respond to information requests on a 24-hour basis, and a Threat Analysis Group to conduct situation analysis of immediate threats and, over the longer term, to track terrorist movements and threat levels by country. Since January 1, 1977, the CIC has been in a position to track and locate security details and security officers around the globe to put any one of them—*e.g.*, a bomb disposal specialist—on site at crisis points.[116] The services of the CIC also may be utilized by transnational enterprises.

Building on Phase I, and commencing within the next two to three years, Phase II will provide the automated systems in support of the intelligence networks described above. This should improve both the timeliness and comprehensiveness of the intelligence. Further, these systems will permit a more current and accurate tracking of terrorists and their movements, activities, and targets, which can be matched with movements of persons within the protective oversight of the U.S. government. This will go hand in hand with the development of a more rational methodology for analyzing and assessing terrorists' threats, including long-term trends, as well as for allocating available security resources worldwide in order to increase the effectiveness of counter-terrorist measures.[117] In interviews, corporate security officers and the security firms repeatedly stressed the importance of having access to the systems proposed for Phase II. However, it is not at all clear at this time whether the confidential nature of the data involved will permit this.

Three points of importance emerge from this analysis of governmental relationships. First, transnational enterprises normally should establish close working relationships with local, regional, and national law enforcement authorities of the host country. The U.S. missions can be of considerable value in assisting these enterprises to establish and maintain productive contacts with host country governments. While the initiative and the responsibility for making and maintaining these contacts, especially at the local law enforcement level, remain with the enterprise, the mission can offer guidance and insight.

Second, both at the level of the mission and of the Department of State, an understanding must be reached with transnational enterprises and their foreign affiliates of which intelligence is critical to the effective operation of the latter's security programs. Based on this determination, an effort must be made to "package" the intelligence and to develop channels for its delivery to enterprises in ways that do not compromise the missions' diplomatic position in the host countries. It may be that the "packaging" and dissemination of intelligence could be facilitated through a bureau in the Department of Commerce.

Finally, while the creation of a sophisticated data center and communications network in the Department of State constitutes a very positive initiative, ways must be found for using this data base to develop new techniques and approaches for the security systems of transnational enterprises, for threat analysis and evaluation, for hostage survival, and for negotiation strategy. This should be undertaken on an accelerated basis and in a close working relationship with these enterprises. Indeed, the government could be a useful catalyst in promoting greater interfirm cooperation and experience sharing on these matters.

Interfirm Cooperation. There exists a large potential for interfirm cooperation, which thus far remains relatively untapped. A concerted effort in this direction not only might produce substantial savings in security expenditures, but also might accelerate practical research in counterterrorist methods and techniques and the formation of centralized systems for intelligence exchange and crisis management that otherwise will evolve more haltingly and with less accuracy. Although highly fragmented, existing efforts bear the seeds of a fruitful beginning.

At present, these efforts are confined largely to private associations of security professionals. By far the largest of these is the American Society for Industrial Security (ASIS), with a membership of over 9000 covering more than 3000 businesses in the United States. ASIS also has 10 foreign chapters with a membership of 400 security professionals. Other associations of this type have developed along industry lines, such as the National Industrial Security Organization (NISO), consisting essentially of defense contractors, and the Security Committees of the Air Transport Association (ATA) and the International Air Transport Association (IATA). In addition, the International Association of Chiefs of Police (IACP) publishes a service, entitled "Clandestine Tactics and Technology," and a number of private security consultants, security companies, and criminology institutes offer training courses for security officers to deal in depth with a broad range of topics, including terrorism. These associations, committees, and security consultants and companies, as well as *ad hoc* groupings of corporations, have been carrying on discussions and some research into counterterrorist measures. Their efforts, however, have no overall coordination or direction.

Without attempting to deal in any detail with these diverse efforts, three types of interfirm cooperation bear consideration. They relate to common security measures, practical research, and comprehensive resource centers. As to the first, *common security measures* among two or more enterprises in a host country offer one of the most direct means to cut security costs and to improve security measures. One company, for instance, reports that it has located new facilities in three different industrial parks over the past four years. This allows for a common defense perimeter and alarm system and the employment of sophisticated security devices that otherwise might not be cost-justified. The same concept may be applied to the protection of executives and their families through the use of residential compounds and of a common base station equipped with a radio transmitter and receiver for tracking selected personnel and families around the clock.[118] Companies also point out that informal but regular interchanges among their corporate security officers, *e.g.*, in Japan, have proved quite useful. The list of possible common measures that companies can adopt is long and varied, but these measures require that enterprises give up some of their individualistic approach to security, described earlier.[119] Further, morale requirements, geography, and the nature of the business, as well as the existing configuration of installations, may be practical barriers to such measures.

Second, valuable *practical research* is being conducted through intercompany cooperation. For instance, a Terrorist Activities Committee within the ASIS has been formed to bridge the gap between law enforcement agencies in the United States and security officers and consultants. While freely acknowledging the support that companies receive from these agencies when a crisis arises, the committee emphasizes the longer-term need to develop more sophisticated intelligence, more effective preventive measures, and crisis management concepts and methodologies. Similarly, the Airline Security Committee of the ATA and the Security Advisory Committee of IATA have become conduits of data exchange and sounding boards for examining new security problems and techniques.[120] The former, for example, is assisting the Federal Aviation Agency to develop profiles for spotting terrorists.

An ambitious intercompany program has been initiated by Motorola through its subsidiary Motorola Teleprograms. During 1975, with the encouragement of the Department of State, Teleprograms brought together a small group of transnational enterprises to sponsor the production of two 25-minute films on executive protection under the rubric "The Anatomy of Terrorism."[121] The first, a motivational training film entitled "Executive Decision," is designed to develop the awareness and security consciousness of the executive and the security director. The second, entitled "Personal and Family Security," continues the theme of the first but adds substantial specific security details for the executive and his family, including many of the common sense guidelines for executives contained in such security checklists as that produced by the State Department. This effort also resulted in a 300-page "Executive Protection Manual," which provides directors and general managers who are involved in executive protection with an in-depth information resource.

Building on the success of its first endeavor, the project was expanded in 1976 to deal more comprehensively with the task of crisis management. Additional transnational enterprises joined the effort, bringing the total sponsorship to 12. Each sponsor committed both $13,000 in seed money and the participation of its security officer in think-tank seminars in order to sort through the critical issues, to pool experiences, and to brainstorm effective responses to the many facets of the terrorist threat. This effort was assisted by a multidisciplinary group of specialists, research by the Rand Corporation, interviews with former hostages, and advice from the FBI and other federal agencies. Out of this endeavor will come two more films, "Hostage Behavior" and "Hostage Negotiation," as well as a full-blown program on crisis management, including a multimedia top management briefing package, a crisis management team training program for a selected group of executives in each corporation, and a hostage survival training component for all high-risk executives. Through this program (to have been completed in 1977) an enterprise will be able to establish a crisis management team that can deal with all aspects of a terrorist attack—negotiations, financing ransom payments and other kinds of extortion, legal implications, media relationships, medical treatment, family concerns, informants, technical experts, etc.—and arrive at informed management decisions rapidly. Further, potential hostages and their families will have a clearer understanding of their situations and the tools for dealing with them.

Beyond these various efforts at practical research, interfirm cooperation exists only in proposal form. A number of those interviewed urged that centralized systems for intelligence exchange and crisis management services be established within a privately funded entity.[122] It might be organized, in part, like a credit information bureau that merchants support with an annual membership fee and their own credit experience and that, in turn, supplies them with credit data and services for their business needs. Analogous also would be the Airline Security Committee of ATA, which works closely with the federal government on the collection, evaluation, and dissemination of intelligence. The intelligence agencies of the U.S. government deliver all intelligence that is relevant to and needed by airline operations to the Federal Aviation Administration. The FAA in turn reviews it in light of existing information, "sanitizes" the data (if it is classified), and distributes it to the director of security for the ATA or, in emergencies, may transmit it directly to individual airlines.[123]

One such proposal for centralized security services has been designed by James Kelly of the Institute for Systematic Security Strategies. He envisions the establishment of a Comprehensive Resource Center for corporations, and estimates an annual operating budget of $2 million to be raised through retainers of $10,000 from 200 corporations.[124] The center would offer its membership a broad range of services, including threat analysis, contingency planning, and crisis management. These would be implemented through training programs, interdisciplinary consultant services, and a clearinghouse of security related documents, procedures, equipment, techniques, and intelligence. The center also would have crisis management capability. Multidisciplinary teams of experts would provide assistance and on-site consultation on request.[125]

A center of this type would bring both program continuity and a concentrated professional effort to bear on solving critical counterterrorist issues. Through a more permanent organization, it would expand and intensify the practical research and the interchange of experience among enterprises as have occurred through the more limited Motorola effort. Such concerted effort among a large sample of enterprises could rapidly evolve crisis management into a practical multidisciplinary science. This could benefit the enterprise significantly through resource savings and easing the plight of executives and their families who are faced daily with the threat of terrorism. Finally, the center would operate an intelligence system that could service the special needs of transnational enterprises without overly relying on governmental intelligence sources. Much of the data would come from member enterprises,[126] field agents of the center, and other public and private institutions and publications. This data then would be processed for business analysis, governmental profiles, law enforcement evaluations, trend projections, and so on, as well as periodic updates on terrorist movements and tactics.

Despite the apparent attractiveness of the Motorola initiative and the Kelly proposal, transnational enterprises have not demonstrated much interest in them. To find 12 firms to sponsor the second phase of the Motorola project, which required a commitment of just $13,000, a participation in the think tanks and a willingness to test the products of the program in their organizations, Teleprograms had to approach 200 of the largest enterprises in the United States. Part of the reluctance may stem from a failure to appreciate the magnitude of the problem and a general unwillingness to deal strategically with terrorism as a long-term issue. This reluctance also may be the individualistic approach of companies to security, which was described earlier.

In large part, moreover, the reluctance to join in such cooperative efforts appears to flow from any publicity that might connect an enterprise with the subject of terrorism, even though the thrust of the project is clearly to combat terrorism. It must also be expected that enterprises participating in a center, as just described, would be extremely concerned about maintaining the confidentiality of their security policies and programs. These issues, however, should be manageable, for they are not different in kind from those successfully faced by security consultants in their dealings with client enterprises. Procedures and techniques exist for structuring, "washing," or "sanitizing" data in a way that protects the confidentiality of the sources.[127] Indeed, it can be argued that because of information disclosure requirements that often are imposed on data in government files, only a privately funded and operated intelligence system would gain the trust of participating enterprises. The center, in effect, would act as a buffer among participating enterprises as well as between enterprises and government intelligence agencies, encouraging a flow of intelligence that otherwise would be hampered through mistrust or government classification. Perhaps, as its greatest contribution, the Motorola initiative stands as a sign to the private sector that interfirm cooperation in the security field can work and achieve useful results.

Media Self-Restraint

The role of the mass media in combating terrorism remains largely unclarified. Yet undeniably, as previously discussed in the context of motives,[128] publicity and "armed propaganda" constitute an important element of terrorism today. Indeed, Bowyer Bell asserts that the media are "the transnational terrorists' greatest single asset."[129] Terrorism, says Brian Jenkins, is "theater." Most would agree with him that "terrorists want a lot of people watching and a lot of people listening. . . ."[130] Their moral outrage at society, and, particularly, at the governing elites, must be vented and their moral superiority clearly established.

This helps to explain, for instance, why executives are "tried" for the alleged "crimes" of their companies,[131] why ransom often must be paid at least in part to the poor, why Firestone was required to conduct open ransom negotiations with the ERP in a hotel in Buenos Aires,[132] why ideological tracts of the terrorists must be printed not only in national but also in international newspapers,[133] and why Exxon was required to publish an ad in Argentine newspapers stating the amount that it paid as ransom for the release of Victor Samuelson.[134] Not only does such publicity serve the ideological purposes of terrorists, but it also offers an organizational advantage by allowing one group to demonstrate its strength and courage in comparison with its rivals.[135]

Because publicity appears to be so important to terrorism, it is tempting to oversimplify the diagnosis. Surely the media are guilty of sensationalizing, romanticizing, or simply dramatically reporting terrorist activities and, therefore, of further reinforcing the motivation for terrorism. Is this not obvious when leading newspapers print ads containing propaganda of terrorist groups,[136] when a news magazine runs the story of a reporter who accompanies part of the Meinhof group on a sacking expedition of a Hamburg house,[137] when British media grant exclusive interviews and attend clandestine press conferences of IRA leaders[138] or present a television documentary showing IRA gunmen loading a car with explosives and then driving it to a corner where it is to be detonated,[139] and when a Los Angeles radio station broadcasts tape recordings of propaganda produced by members of the Symbionese Liberation Army?[140]

On the other hand, if publicity is a major motivating factor for terrorism, will news suppression have a substantial preventive effect? Is it not as likely to provoke even more visible forms of terrorism that cannot be ignored, such as more frequent bombings of public places, barricade-and-hostage incidents such as that at the Munich Olympiad, public assassinations, and attacks against critical public facilities?[141] Moreover, even if news suppression would be an effective measure, would protection against terrorism be worth the loss in individual freedom?

Policy Considerations. Rather than debate the issue of "free press" or belabor alleged media abuses, the policy question should be considered within the existing constitutional framework of the United States and its First Amendment freedoms. There is no indication that this framework would prevent a free press (including the broadcasting industry) from addressing in a fully responsible manner the question of publicity in respect to terrorism. Within this framework, there are five basic and, to some extent, competing policy considerations. They are set forth below in descending order of the need to publicize terrorist activities.

The Public. The public's need to know must be satisfied by a free press. While what is "newsworthy" must remain within the good judgment of editors and reporters, the exercise of this decision is by no means a private matter. Because terrorism greatly affects the public order, the public must be advised of the issues involved, the response of law enforcement authorities, and the disposition of the case. Even as embodied in the First Amendment, however, the right of free speech cannot be used to justify performance of a criminal act so long at least as the law that is violated does not itself constitute a suppression of free expression.[142] Thus it would be no defense for a hijacker to contend that his crime was actually "symbolic speech" and was perpetrated simply to place his political views before an audience with whom he otherwise could not communicate.[143]

Target Victims. The safety and well-being of the target victims must be respected. In the past, this has required responses varying from a temporary news blackout to front-page publication of terrorist demands. Obviously, in the Niehous kidnaping, political publicity was a major objective of the terrorist.[144] In some cases, where the threat is directed against part or all of a community, its seriousness must be assessed and the type of media communication carefully selected, so as not to unduly alarm the public and yet give ample warning to the target victims.

Law Enforcement. Law enforcement efforts must not be unduly hampered, for the public also has an interest in preserving domestic order. Full disclosure in the media could either interfere with these efforts or reveal useful techniques or strategies of surveillance, investigation, and pursuit that will impede counterterrorist efforts in the future. In the Kronholm kidnaping (a classic kidnaping, for ransom, of the wife of a Minneapolis executive), for instance, the Minneapolis Press Council charged that "irresponsible journalism" by the *Minneapolis Tribune* not only endangered the life of the victim, but also caused the FBI to withdraw surveillance and to arrest a primary suspect prior to the victim's release. The newspaper monitored police radios and relayed information to a reporter who attempted on-the-scene coverage of the ransom drop.[145]

Future Acts of Terrorism. A real concern also exists that publicity will encourage future acts of terrorism. The Rand study of 77 hostage cases concludes: "In almost all cases . . . terrorists at least attracted substantial public attention to their cause and identity, a major goal that was explicit or implicit in their actions."[146]

Instantaneous worldwide publicity, based on television coverage and the capabilities of global satellite communications systems, not only may create a climate of permissiveness toward the counterculture hero, but also "leads to a contagion or imitation effect, which can in turn become a direct cause of subsequent acts of terrorism."[147] As a result, terrorist techniques are disseminated, stories of daring and success against authorities are created, and highly diverse motivations may be attracted to the banner of terrorism.

Protection of Privacy. At the opposite end of the spectrum, the privacy of the victims, their families, and the enterprises that employ them counsels against all publicity. The invasion of privacy by the media both during and following a kidnaping, for instance, can be as traumatic to victims and their families as the kidnaping experience itself. From the viewpoint of the enterprise, there exists concern that any media exposure could complicate, impede, or extend negotiations with the terrorists as well as endanger the life of the victims. Even dickering about ransom, especially in a climate of apprehension and extended negotiations, may suggest that company management is insensitive or materialistic in its concern.[148] The enterprise, however, must not only fear that publicity will increase its profile as a target of terrorism, but also must realize the impact that ransom decisions can have on executive morale and exposure to future terrorist attacks.

As this spectrum of policy considerations suggests, there can be no single formula for determining appropriate media response to incidents of terrorism. Within the constitutional framework of First Amendment freedoms, consideration at first weighs heavily in favor of media coverage, while the latter three caution decidedly against publicity. Depending on the circumstances, the safety of the victims may be considerably enhanced or obstructed by media reporting. Further, while responsible editors and reporters would probably agree with little difficulty that media coverage of terrorist incidents should not be sensationalized, at the same time they would vigorously defend their right to determine how any particular incident should be reported. The tension that exists between these opposing considerations and viewpoints raises anew the perennial question of responsible journalism.

Toward Standards of Media Reporting. At the outset, it is important to note that the news media have no set policy for reporting terrorist incidents. Their reporting is governed by the overall responsibility of the press, as the *Long Island Press* recently put it, "to publish the news, and to use its resources to get the whole truth."[149] The Television Code of the National Association of Broadcasters, however, is not so categorical about its news function. In keeping with the mandate of the Federal Communications Act of 1934, the broadcaster measures its news reporting responsibility in terms of serving the "public interest" while avoiding all forms of government censorship.[150] As air time and available frequencies are limited, the code emphasizes "high standards of professional journalism" and news reporting that is "adequate and well-balanced," is "factual, fair and without bias," and provides "coverage consonant with the ends of an informed and enlightened citizenry."[151] Nevertheless, the code is clear, as are the courts,[152] that the broadcaster may not delegate "to others [its] responsibility as to judgments necessary in news and public events programming."[153]

Nevertheless, within this framework the media have delineated their responsibility to select and tailor the news in certain respects. The *Long Island Press*, in the above instance, went on to point out that "publishing the news is not the media's only role. There are times when not publishing the story can be just as important." Examples of this are "when a defendant's right to a fair trial might be compromised" and when the life of a kidnap victim might be jeopardized.[154] The code, too, cautions broadcasters to "exercise due care in the supervision of content, format and presentation of newscasts . . . , and in the selection of newscasters, commentators and analysts." This requires, for instance, avoiding "morbid, sensational or alarming details not essential to the factual report, especially in connection with stories of crime." Further, "news should be telecast in such a manner as to avoid panic and unnecessary alarm."[155]

Stated strategically, from a counterterrorist viewpoint, the very importance of publicity to the success and spread of terrorism gives the media a powerful means to combat terrorism without relinquishing its responsibility "to get the whole truth." As Richard Clutterbuck suggests, "the television camera is like a weapon lying in the street. Either side can pick it up and use it." And if it is used well, "it is far more effective than any kind of censorship or government control."[156] The same is true of the press in general.

What responsible means are available to the media to combat terrorism? The four approaches presented below are not new. They relate to news timing, balanced coverage, news tailoring, and public education. However, they could be given more conscious consideration by the media in dealing with terrorist incidents. They certainly deserve more attention by the media in establishing professional guidelines for the industry as a whole.

News Timing. Numerous instances exist in the United States and the United Kingdom undoubtedly as well as in other free societies of media temporarily withholding the publication of a kidnaping or extortion threat until the incident has been solved. This was the subject of the justification statement quoted above from the *Long Island Press*. As in other kidnaping cases, the press agreed to postpone publication of the story until the victim was released, but always subject to the understanding that the "blackout" was voluntary and that the media would be kept informed of all developments. "Pacts of silence of this kind are proper," said *The Times* (London) in an editorial, "so long as it remains a matter of unfettered discretion for the media whether to cooperate, and for how long."[157] The rationale for the action varies with the case, emphasizing at times the safety of the victim and, at other times, support of law enforcement investigation.

Transnational enterprises can employ the same policy in their relationships with the media. To do so, they must centralize all press releases and responses to all inquiries. Further, they must enlist the cooperation of local law enforcement authorities. In some cases, such as bombings and other highly visible terrorist attacks, an understanding may have to be worked out with the media, which in turn may require the company to keep the media advised of new developments. In other cases, such as kidnapings, the company may be able to avoid all comment and, in addition, to remove the family from the area or the country and out of sight of reporters until the case is resolved. The failure to follow this approach in the Niehous case appears to have reinforced media preoccupation with the incident, and may have exacerbated the relationship between Owens-Illinois and the Venezuelan government.[158] Of course, as was true in the Niehous case, the company cannot control the terrorists' demands for publicity. It can only attempt to moderate them. Neither can it force a victim's spouse or family to leave the country or to avoid press statements if they decide otherwise.

Balanced Coverage. The media have great leeway in balancing their coverage of terrorist incidents. They can, for instance, avoid sensationalizing the story and reporting all the brutal details. Further, they have discretion to determine how to allocate limited news time or news space and where to place it on the program or in the newspaper. They can also present the same event from a variety of different viewpoints and, in so doing, reduce the drama or poignancy of the terrorist incident. However, as Brian Crozier points out, the very nature of terrorist activities usually makes balanced coverage quite difficult.[159] The incident may be carefully tailored by the terrorists to highlight their cause, and ordinarily will not reveal the violent presuppositions that run through their organization and frame of mind or the alternatives that are available to them within the existing structures of society to make their case and to work constructively toward a nonviolent resolution of social problems. For this reason alone, the media must make a special effort to present a balanced news coverage.

News Tailoring. On a daily basis, the media tailor their news coverage. That is, they decide not only the amount of space and the location to be given a particular item in overall news coverage, but also select which items are "newsworthy" and determine how to report them. For instance, the media normally will not report the techniques used by terrorists in order not to be instructional.[160] By the same token, they should not reveal the details of law enforcement strategy nor the means available to circumvent the law, except where this is necessary to a better understanding of critical social issues, such as abuses of authority or the protection of individual rights. At the same time, however, prominent coverage should be given to the prosecution and sentencing of terrorists, especially where the terrorist event itself has received widespread public attention.

Furthermore, not every event finds its way into a newscast or newspaper. The decision is not arbitrary, as the *Long Island Press* noted in its editorial. For instance, when four major U.S. newspapers—the *Chicago Tribune*, the *New York Times*, the *Washington Post*, and the *Los Angeles Times*—received a demand on September 11, 1976, from the Croatian hijackers to print "An Appeal to the American People," they followed instructions. In a subsequent editorial, the *Tribune* explained: "Ordinarily, when anyone demands this kind of action from a newspaper, we tell them to go to hell." In this case, the *Tribune* and each of the other newspapers, acting independently, acceded to the demand out of "an instinctive desire to protect the hostages." Nevertheless, the *Tribune* eschewed "a set policy for responding to this kind of crisis," because of the impossibility "to foresee every contingency, every emergency."[161]

Similarly, on April 6, 1976, the *New York Times* published a half-page proclamation of the Revolutionary Command of Venezuela at the request of Owens-Illinois. In doing this, it noted, the *Times* "waived some of its usual requirements" because the ad could be instrumental in saving someone's life.[162] On the other hand, news suppression apparently has occurred on a permanent, though voluntary, basis in the United Kingdom. It was done, for example, in response to threats by Ugandan President Idi Amin "to slaughter Britons living in Uganda if British news media published about his regime what he did not want to have published."[163] There have been other occasions where news of terrorist activities or propaganda tracts have been suppressed under the democratic governments of Colombia and Venezuela. In these cases, however, the media acted specifically at the behest of the national government.[164]

In all but these last cases, the newspapers acted voluntarily in response to immediate and apparently serious threats to life. The responsibility of the media, however, goes beyond this. The media must find approaches to news reporting that allow them to be equally affirmative and circumspect in dealing with terrorist incidents, even when they are not addressed with specific demands of terrorists. For instance, should not stories on isolated bombings and kidnapings be reported tersely and buried in the back pages? In other cases, where terrorists' craving for publicity must be assuaged for the sake of the victims, cannot the story be held to a factual report to avoid unnecessary dramatization? In still other cases, as one psychologist suggests, the media may perform a useful reporting function if their approach serves to stabilize the situation, then gradually confronts the terrorists with the reality and difficulty of their position and, at the same time, prepares the public for possible outcomes of the incident.[165]

Public Education. The media have the longer-term responsibility of educating the public to the import of terrorism for society. Above all, they must make clear that even legitimate grievances can not justify the taking of innocent lives. This is all the more true where social grievances can be espoused through democratic processes. Further, terrorism must be stripped of its romantic veneer, and its violent underpinnings must be exposed to public scrutiny.[166] The impact of such violence on democratic institutions should be discussed, including the difficulties that law enforcement authorities face in being effective and yet safeguarding due process rights. Equally, terrorist methods by governmental authorities must be brought to light, for terrorism in any form tends to brutalize society. By setting this broadened context, the media can mobilize public opinion against unnecessary violence and bring isolated incidents of terrorism into sober perspective.

Within the context of terrorism, the media function as a two-edged sword. They assure terrorists that their grievances will receive public attention; yet they also can mobilize public opinion against the arbitrary use of violence. The use of the media in the Niehous case, both by the terrorists to attack the Venezuelan government and the company, and by the company and the Niehous family to gain the sympathy of the Venezuelan people, amply demonstrates that publicity is not simply a captive of terrorists. Nevertheless, as Owens-Illinois later learned with the expropriation of its assets, the use of the media can have unfortunate unforeseen consequences.[167] Enterprises, therefore, must carefully weigh and plan their use of the media when countering the activities of terrorists.

From the viewpoint of the media themselves, similar caution is required. While the media have great power to mobilize public opinion against terrorism, in specific incidents this power must be exercised with great care. A miscalculation could endanger the lives of hostages or hamper the efforts of law enforcement authorities. At the same time, to use this power only to suppress the news would ignore the constructive potential of the media during the course of a terrorist incident and over the longer term. Perhaps, more importantly, any injudicious or prolonged suppression of the news could ultimately undermine the media's credibility.

The major difficulty with the concept of self-restraint is that the media, collectively, appear to lack a thoroughly considered view of their role in dealing with terrorism. Considering the importance of publicity to terrorist motivation, it is incumbent on the media to review these issues carefully, to conduct the necessary practical research into the relationship of the media to terrorism and to arrive at some practical guidelines for the industry. These tasks could be pursued through a number of professional and industry organizations, such as the International Press Institute, the Radio and Television News Directors Association, and the American Society of Newspaper Editors.[168] Finally, the media must also be prepared to review their own news treatment of terrorist events and to censure where news reporting is irresponsible. For this reason, consideration should be given to such ombudsman-type structures as the Minneapolis Press Council, noted above, and the Television Code Review Board and Television Board of Directors established in the Regulations and Procedures of the Television Code.

Hostage Insurance

Insurance is a form of risk management that traditionally has allowed the insured to spread losses or damages arising out of specified risks among a number of parties or units exposed to the same risks. As such, it facilitates the planning function of an enterprise, as potential losses from such risks can be estimated on the basis of experience and budgeted for over a period of time among the various parties or units. This is true whether the resulting charges are then pooled through periodic payments to a commercial underwriter or to a captive insurance subsidiary or are simply reserved on the company books as a form of self-insurance. Despite the special "political" characteristics of terrorism, the same principles can be applied to losses and damages arising from bombings, incendiary attacks, and kidnapings. For instance, criminal loss insurance is well known, and "bankers blanket bond" policies have for some years in some cases included kidnaping insurance coverage as a separate rider. Such addendums insure against financial loss that the bank incurs "through the surrender of property as a result of a threat to do bodily harm to an employee, or one of his relatives."[169]

More recently, hostage insurance has become a serious concern generally for business, especially for transnational enterprises and their executives. Policies may be obtained individually by executives for themselves and for their families. The premium rates will vary widely, depending on the underwriter's evaluation of the individual's exposure. One survey, apparently limited to North American residents, reports that these rates may vary between 0.12 percent and 0.15 percent of the pay-out amount, or $1200 to $1500 in annual premiums on a policy of $1 million with a deductible of perhaps $10,000.[170] Normally, however, the policy will be carried by the enterprise because of the growing tendency to make corporations the targets of kidnapings, rather than executives as such. Further, where the policy is owned by the enterprise, whether issued by a commercial underwriter or by a captive insurance subsidiary, premiums as well as ransom payments not covered by insurance are deductible as ordinary and necessary business expense.[171] While individuals can deduct ransom payments as losses "arising from theft,"[172] they may have difficulty bringing premiums or kidnap insurance within the cost-of-business doctrine. Self-insurance allows a company to retain insurance reserves for its own use, but it restricts tax deduction to amounts paid at the time of the loss.

Hostage insurance purchased by larger enterprises is often designed for group coverage. The more expensive type covers an unspecified number of employees based on defined job classifications or categories. A less expensive version limits the group to designated employees or to positions that the enterprise determines have a high risk of kidnaping. In either case, absolute secrecy is normally required by the policy, both as to the existence of insurance and as to who is insured. Code numbers may even be used to assure that secrecy is maintained.[173] Indeed, because of a fear that kidnaping might be encouraged if hostage insurance is believed to be widespread, underwriters are reluctant to talk about it or to discuss whether its use is common. For this reason, underwriters were particularly chagrined by advertisements for kidnap insurance that appeared in two suburban Detroit newspapers.[174] For the same reason, as well as to encourage caution, insurance may be cancelled if its existence becomes known during the course of kidnap negotiations. Most underwriters refuse to become involved in the negotiations themselves.

The cost of hostage insurance to corporations also varies widely, depending on the size of the enterprise, its public profile, the states or regions to be covered, the amount of coverage, and the group insured. In the United States, where the FBI's solution rate on kidnaping exceeds 90 percent, premiums can be relatively modest and fairly uniform throughout the country. In 1974, it was estimated that a $500,000 ransom policy could cost an enterprise with sales under $1 million about $1000 per executive insured, while a major company with sales over $500 million might pay $5000 for the same coverage.[175] A more recent estimate places an annual premium of $10,000 on a $1 million policy with a $100,000 deductible. For coverage outside the United States, and especially in Latin America and other developing countries, the premium multiplies and in some cases may well be prohibitive in amount. One security consultant estimates that $1 million coverage in Mexico and Central America today would bear an annual premium of $100,000 per executive insured. These premiums may vary on an almost daily basis, however, depending on the stability of the political and social climate in the insured territory and on the frequency and success of terrorist activities.

For reasons given above, no reliable estimate can be given of the prevalence of hostage insurance. Some of those interviewed believe that it is being used "to a large extent," and others that a majority of transnational enterprises do not carry it. In some countries, such as Italy and France, hostage insurance reportedly is not legally permitted because of the view that it would encourage kidnaping. In others, such as Argentina, Colombia, the United Kingdom and Venezuela, the payment of ransom may be discouraged or prohibited as a matter of government policy.[176] Certainly, any attempt by governments to subsidize hostage insurance or ransom payments directly or through special tax treatment could have undesirable effects. Not only would terrorists then be offered a short-cut to the public treasury, but in the terrorists' minds the policy would strengthen the symbolic link that the terrorists already see between the transnational enterprise and the target government.

On the other hand, unless governments are willing to ban all ransom payments, there is little basis for prohibiting hostage insurance as such.[177] Further, where ransom payments are not prohibited, as in the United States, the availability and cost of hostage insurance should be left for determination by the marketplace. From a public policy viewpoint, the critical factor in such cases is that the use of insurance be kept confidential. Moreover, consideration should be given to means for reducing the impact of ransom payments on the operations of transnational enterprises. Enterprises operating within high-risk countries or regions, for instance, should investigate various techniques of risk management. For instance, could the captive insurance subsidiary, which is being used increasingly as a mode of risk management, be adapted to alleviate hardship arising from hostage payments? Could it be utilized on a joint venture basis among several enterprises in a high-risk area? This type of risk pooling could not only serve the risk-spreading and planning functions of enterprises, but also encourage cooperation among corporations in combating terrorism.

Additionally, U.S. tax law should be changed to provide that individuals may deduct premiums paid for hostage insurance and that companies may fully deduct ransom payments as ordinary and necessary business expenses even when such payments are made on behalf of a foreign subsidiary. Such practices should not subsidize ransom payments nor create special advantages for the business executive or the enterprise. Rather, they should be limited to enabling legitimate risk-spreading techniques and to ensuring that ransom payments are fully deductible to the extent that they are actually paid by the taxpayer for sound business reasons.

Finally, in their own interests, transnational enterprises should carefully formulate with counsel a company policy on hostage insurance. Depending on the circumstances, management may need to justify its position on ransom payments to shareholders at some future date.

Governmental Measures for Combating Terrorism

Contrary to the overriding purpose of this report, little has been said thus far in this chapter about the legal aspects of international terrorism. The reasons for this are threefold. First, terrorist attacks on transnational enterprises at their present scale constitute a relatively new phenomenon. Since international terrorism today is primarily political in nature, it has been necessary first to define the "political" qualities of these essentially private business targets before undertaking a legal assessment. As earlier sections of this chapter make clear, the targeting of transnational enterprises, especially in Latin America, fits in most respects the political rationale of a wide spectrum of revolutionary terrorist activity.

Second, it may be doubted that new legal measures, either national or international, are necessary. Except for the aggravating element of terror, acts of terrorism fall within the normal purview of criminal laws in force in almost every society. While the crimes of homicide, theft, robbery, kidnaping, and extortion are common to most countries, they are not yet "international crimes"—such as piracy or slave trade—over which any state that apprehends the offender has jurisdiction to prosecute and punish without regard to the nationality of the offender or to the situs or effect of the unlawful act. Further, even where jurisdiction exists, law enforcement may be weak or lacking. The question, therefore, is not so much the substance of the law, but how to give it efficacy. This is largely a matter of improved law enforcement and of expanding the authority of states to take jurisdiction over acts of terrorism.

Third, while law is an important instrument for combating terrorism, it is by no means a panacea for halting the impassioned acts of terrorists against transnational business operations. As in dealing with common crime in any community, the success of national and international measures to counter terrorism will require the close and continuing cooperation of all members of the community, including transnational enterprises. Because of their foreign control, however, the common efforts of these enterprises must be carefully tailored to the needs, circumstances, and policies of the host country. Some initiatives have been discussed earlier in this chapter.

With this in mind, what then ought the response of government be to international terrorism as it affects transnational enterprises? These responses will be treated in two sections, one relating to national measures and the other to international measures. Care will be taken, however, not to duplicate what already has been discussed by others in other chapters of this report. Rather, attention will be paid primarily to measures that governments and the international community might take especially with respect to protecting transnational enterprises.

National Measures

From the viewpoint of international law, the transnational enterprise exists only as a grouping of separate business entities, each of which is governed by the laws of the state(s) in which it does business. Aside from treaties of friendship and commerce and other special treaties, such as those among the members of the European Economic Community,[178] each state, because of its territorial supremacy, has the right to exclude aliens and their property from all or any part of its territory.[179] Nevertheless, once aliens are permitted to enter to do business, the host state must protect their persons and property under standards that not only are equal to those accorded its own citizens but that meet minimum requirements of international law even though this protection is not extended to its own subjects.[180] As under international law states claim plenary jurisdiction over their internal affairs, they likewise must incur plenary responsibility for the aliens and their property that they admit.[181] Subject to these general principles, states possess great discretion in the treatment of aliens and may regulate their right to do business in many respects.[182]

Arguably, Chapter II of the Charter of Economic Rights and Duties of

States challenges these traditional principles of international law.[183] The charter denies "privileged treatment" for foreign investors. It claims exclusive jurisdiction for the host state in regulating and supervising the activities of "transnational enterprises within its national jurisdiction."[184] Whatever the merits of this view, the charter should not affect the principles just stated. The charter's history makes clear that it is not intended to state binding principles of law. Indeed, resolutions of the United Nations General Assembly are not legally binding on member states,[185] except with respect to certain internal organizational matters of the United Nations, which are not relevant here. Further, nowhere does the charter state that it contravenes existing principles of international law or even that it is intended to alter such principles. Absent an express intention to this effect, General Assembly resolutions should not be presumed to contradict long-established rules of international law. In any case, the charter is addressed exclusively to matters of economic regulation and cooperation. It does not pretend to consider the protection that international law affords aliens and their property against criminal attack in host countries.

Limiting the application of these principles to this chapter, international law requires the state to "have a system of law and administrative facilities adequate under normal circumstances to secure the freedom and safety of aliens and their property."[186] While international law may not require a remedy for every wrong, at the minimum the state must provide for the maintenance of internal order under normal circumstances through an adequate police force, must take precautionary measures with respect to aliens and their property where circumstances require it,[187] and must provide a means for redress and punishment of the offender where aliens are assaulted or their property willfully damaged.[188] Where the state meets these objective standards, even if injury might have been averted through more competent handling, the state normally has met its responsibility under international law and aliens must be satisfied with the law enforcement administration and the municipal law remedy of the host country.[189]

These principles leave much to be decided by the circumstantial rule of reasonableness.[190] Further, where injury to aliens is accompanied by a partial or general breakdown in the domestic order, a state may attempt to disclaim responsibility on the basis that any injury to aliens was caused by violent actions of insurgents beyond its reasonable control.[191] Consideration of this point, however, would go outside the scope of this chapter. Suffice it to say that short of a state of insurgency, a state has an affirmative duty under international law to provide for the protection of aliens and their property in its territory against criminal acts. Normally, this will include the threats and attacks of terrorists. By the same token, where terrorist activities become more than infrequent occurrences in a country, this duty requires the host state to increase its enforcement activities, including the special training, equipping, and expanding of security forces necessary to deal with the intensified threat of violence.[192] President

Perón's creation of a special Industrial Police organization early in 1974 for guarding industrial plants in Argentina against terrorist attack,[193] for instance, can be viewed as a measure designed to meet this duty.

Some of those interviewed complained that host state law enforcement authorities, especially at the local level, have shown disinterest in making their assistance available to transnational enterprises. Other U.S. companies, on the other hand, have stated that the flow of intelligence, at least from law enforcement authorities and governmental agencies, is better in foreign countries than in the United States.[194]

The practice either way is not clear; it would depend on the particular country. Whatever the practice is in fact, host states should be highly motivated to combat terrorism against transnational enterprises. Not only can terrorism dampen the business climate among international investors for loans as well as equity capital, but terrorist attacks against transnational enterprises normally are perpetrated by indigenous groups who also have designs on the host state government. Nevertheless, where obvious laxity exists in combating terrorist activities against transnational enterprises, the home state of the enterprise can exercise its right of protection over nationals abroad and demand that the host state take all reasonable steps to secure its nationals and their property against terrorist attack.[195]

Law Enforcement. In fact, the overall record for apprehending terrorists and bringing them to trial has not been very encouraging. Within the United States, the solution rate of the FBI for kidnapings has exceeded 90 percent over the past 30 years.[196] In many other countries, however, governmental efforts to combat terrorism have met with widely varying results. In some cases, this spotty record may be due to the government's unwillingness to deal forcefully with terrorists. International terrorists have an 80 percent chance of escaping death or capture. Of the 267 terrorists apprehended in international incidents between 1970 and 1975, 39 were freed without punishment; 58 escaped punishment by receiving safe conduct to another country; 16 were released from confinement on demand of fellow terrorists; 50 were released after serving prison terms; and 104 were still confined in mid-September 1975.[197]

While these statistics offer no insight into the causes of this distinctly unimpressive record, they underline the conclusions of other studies that tough antiterrorist measures and law enforcement policies at the state level are critical for effectively combating terrorism.[198]

If this is true, then the first step in combating terrorism is for states to improve their records in apprehending and punishing terrorists. They must not only commit the additional resources necessary to do this but also see that existing criminal laws applicable to acts of terrorism are stringently enforced. States must communicate uncompromisingly to all who seek social change, in the words of a United Nations study, that "even when the use of force is legally and morally justified, there are some means, as in every form of human conflict, which must not be used; the legitimacy of a cause does not in itself legitimize the use of certain forms of violence, especially against the innocent."[199] At the same time, state action must studiously avoid a regressive crackdown that jeopardizes due process of the law. While such efforts may lead to a defeat of terrorism, the cost may be the long-term loss of individual freedom.[200]

Crime Prevention. In addition to the apprehension and punishment of terrorists, law enforcement strategies must also focus on crime prevention. The installation of the costly airport security system by the United States in January 1973 is a striking example of crime prevention. It has been credited with substantially deterring hijackings.[201] Whereas there were 83 hijackings and 43 attempted hijackings of commercial aircraft in the United States during the four years (1969 to 1973) preceding the introduction of preboard screening, only 3 hijackings and 6 attempted hijackings occurred in the almost four years ending December 1976.[202] In addition, the United States has tightened visa regulations, introduced further screening of foreigners seeking admission to the country, alerted customs and postal employees to detecting letter bombs, and improved interagency coordination and intelligence collection and analysis through the Cabinet Committee/Work Group for Combating Terrorism discussed previously.[203] Other initiatives are being pursued through the support of the Law Enforcement Assistance Administration.[204]

In respect to the protection of transnational enterprises, states could perform equally useful counterterrorist functions. First, just as in the case of aircraft security, law enforcement authorities could receive special training so that they can identify and coordinate more effectively with the security needs of business. This should include instruction both as to the security context of business in general and as to security techniques. In addition, effective coordination requires ongoing liaison through periodic meetings at the local level of law enforcement authorities, security companies, and enterprises. One security consultant refers to these as "local councils on law enforcement."

Second, law enforcement authorities could establish multidisciplinary crisis management teams to support the enterprise in dealing with crisis situations. As discussed in the 1974 hearings of the House Committee on Internal Security, these teams could be located at various centers around the country and consist of law enforcement officials, psychiatrists, criminologists, and specialists in other disciplines.[205] While these teams should maintain close liaison with the news media in times of crisis, members of the press should not be integrated into the team.[206] It is important to preserve both the independence of the press and the prerogatives of public officials and enterprise management to keep certain data confidential.

Law enforcement crisis management teams could offer the enterprises on-the-scene advice. Where the enterprise has a crisis management group, the "multidisciplinary" teams could assist in coordinating the efforts of the team with local and national law enforcement authorities and the news media. While some representatives of transnational enterprises have expressed concern that these teams of experts "might be 'in the way' and create problems of jurisdiction," others would welcome such assistance because it would be "more effective than local experts."[207] One airline testified that it arranges for members of the FBI, FAA, U.S. Customs, U.S. Marshals Office, and airline pilots associations, as well as psychiatrists, to be present at the crisis table to assist and consult on what action to take.[208] Further, these crisis management teams could serve as teaching units both for law enforcement officials and business management.[209] For these teams to be acceptable to business management, however, they must serve only as consultants to business and not attempt to dictate policy.[210]

Third, as discussed previously,[211] governmental authorities can assist transnational enterprises through the increased flow of needed intelligence and through the support of practical research on threat and profile analysis, crisis management, negotiations strategy, and hostage survival. This assistance and support need not replace, but instead could supplement, the activities of a Comprehensive Resource Center as outlined above. For the intelligence to be useful, however, it must be refined to fit the needs of the transnational enterprise, e.g., country and industry profiles of terroristic activities. Further, because intelligence of this type is highly perishable, it must be systematically updated and communicated on a regular basis. This refining and "packaging," as well as the "washing" that is necessary to preserve the confidentiality of sensitive data, could be undertaken by a special bureau in the Department of Commerce working closely with the professional staff of the center.

The practical research, on the other hand, could be undertaken largely through the Comprehensive Resource Center with the assistance of the Department of Commerce. Very recently, Commerce has established an Intra-Agency Work Group to initiate studies of this type. The practical utility of this research to business, however, will depend on involving transnational enterprises in the research process itself. Not only do these enterprises possess an almost untapped fund of experience upon which any realistic research must be based, but their direct involvement in the research process would uncover a host of useful techniques and test the practicality of others. It must be remembered also that counterterrorist techniques and strategies do not exist in a vacuum; rather, they must be costed out and fit into the management styles, policies, and strategies of the enterprise. And conversely, counterterrorist techniques and strategies may require a change in an enterprise's management policies and strategies.

At least initially, some government funding of a center may be necessary to launch its pilot stage and to evidence the cooperation of federal intelligence agencies. Perhaps this could be done through the Law Enforcement Assistance Administration (LEAA), although a question has been raised whether the research, training, and intelligence functions of an essentially private institute would fall within the LEAA's legislative mandate. From a purely policy point of view, such funding should be justified, as overall public security depends to a significant degree on the effectiveness of private security forces. The annual budget for private security in the United States and the number of personnel involved equal or exceed these figures for the public sector.[212] In any case, the counterterrorist techniques and strategies developed through a center would be as applicable by transnational enterprises within the United States as by their foreign affiliates.

Furthermore, Congress has authorized LEAA to concern itself both with terroristic and international crime. With this in mind, LEAA chartered the Private Security Advisory Council in 1972 to review private sector security problems in these areas. It established the National Criminal Justice Reference Service to act as its research arm and an information clearinghouse. It has funded research and studies in international terrorism by the United Nations Social Defense Research Institute. However, none of these is designed to develop counterterrorist techniques and strategies, to undertake intelligence analysis, or to prepare operational intelligence that could be used by the private sector.[213] There appears to be a gap, therefore, between legislative policy and practice in developing effective measures to combat terrorism. A resource center along the lines described could be of great practical value to the private sector, both domestically and internationally.

Government Subsidies. A separate policy issue arises as to government subsidies for the security costs of private enterprise. Should the government, as a means of combating terrorism, provide tax incentives or matching fund grants to assist companies in modernizing and expanding their security capability? It can be argued in favor of subsidies that, as pointed out above, private security measures are a significant and critical supplement to public security forces. Further, the monetary gains of terrorists as well as of common criminals may be used to finance further criminal activity. Even slight increases in terrorist activity require substantial investment in new equipment and security payroll. The causes for these increased expenditures arise primarily from the state of the public order and not from the activities of private enterprise. Should not the state help absorb these increased security costs and encourage additional private security measures?

While these considerations must not be dismissed lightly, government subsidies of private security measures in whatever form should be based on an extraordinary, demonstrated social need. In the United States at least, this need does not appear to exist. Only approximately 9 percent of all bombing incidents and rarely a kidnaping are attributable to terrorist activities.[214] Further, even if these percentages were to increase to a critical point, the basic issues would still remain of whether public policy should promote public or private security forces and of where the emphasis should be placed, *e.g.*, on hardware, manpower training, new strategies, and techniques. At what point in growing levels of terroristic activity should the state encourage private armament? These are crucial value choices for a democratic society.

Another, more delicate question arises as to security subsidies for the foreign operations of transnational enterprises. Here the issues are different in kind, for the impact of the fiscal measures would be intended to have effect in a foreign country. It can be argued that these transnational operations are critical to the U.S. balance of payments and to the supply of needed goods and resources, and that the United States has a duty to protect U.S. nationals and assets abroad. However, because an effective counterterrorist effort depends so much on the will and the measures of the host government, it is doubtful that such subsidies could have more than a very marginal effect. It is even more doubtful that the U.S. government should either encourage U.S. enterprises to continue operating in countries where terrorism has reached such a critical stage or grant subsidies when the foreign government itself is unwilling to grant them. Indeed, such subsidies might be viewed as interference in the internal affairs of the foreign country. For these reasons, U.S. assistance to its transnational enterprises should more appropriately be limited to the research, training, and intelligence functions discussed above. Except for some aspects of intelligence exchange, this assistance can be rendered in the United States.

Ransom Policy. Governmental responses to ransom demands is another major issue of national policy. As securing ransom payments is an important objective of kidnaping and other types of extortion, would not a law that generally prohibits compliance with these demands undercut the advantage of extortion and significantly reduce the incidence of terrorism? Certainly, all those interviewed agree that transnational enterprises would be able to resist ransom demands only by virtue of a generally applicable legal prohibition.

Some states have adopted a no-concessions policy where the ransom demands are directed at the government. U.S. Government Policy Guideline No. 6 states: "The U.S. Government does not pay ransom, release prisoners or otherwise yield to blackmail by terrorist groups."[215] As to third-party responses, however, U.S. policy is more conciliatory: "The U.S. Government generally opposes but cannot prevent foreign governments, private individuals, or companies from meeting terrorists' demands, including payment of ransom."[216] Other states—such as Argentina, Colombia, the United Kingdom, and Venezuela—have prohibited compliance with ransom demands of terrorists both by public authorities and by private parties. This prohibition may be simply a matter of government policy,[217] or it also may be reinforced by statutory or decree authority.[218] In addition, as in Argentina and Colombia,[219] the government may forbid any public announcement that ransom has been paid.

The merits of a general prohibition on meeting ransom demands must be weighed carefully from several perspectives: (1) the individual victims and their families, (2) the enterprise and its employees, and (3) society as a whole. In making this analysis, no attempt will be made to evaluate a no-concessions ransom policy of the government as set forth in Guideline No. 6. It will be assumed, however, that any affirmation of a general prohibition would include an identical policy by the government. Further, because of the nature of terrorism, the prohibition must extend to all types of ransom demands, including the publication of terrorists' views, charitable contributions to third parties, as well as monetary and in-kind payments to extortionists. Not to preclude these possibilities would simply allow terrorists to redirect their demands. By the same token, to be reasonably effective, the prohibition must be applied alike to individuals and to private institutions of all kinds, including businesses.

Perspective of Individual Victims. From the perspective of the individual victims and their families, the short-term value of saving a life by meeting ransom demands must be weighed against the longer-term potential of saving many lives by making extortion an unprofitable venture. This evaluation pits the individual and the family against the common good, or the human drive for self-preservation against social morality. It is immoral and destructive of the legal order, it may be argued, to capitulate to coercion and threats of violence, to allow society to indulge arbitrary demands of terrorists, and to silently stand by and permit payments to be made to groups who will use the money only to further their ends of revolutionary violence. "The policy of permissiveness," the Colombian minister of justice stated in announcing the government's no-ransom policy, "has resulted in an increase in kidnaping and in a growing temerity and ambition of the kidnapers." Further, "the preservation of life is very precious, but the price which society has had to pay has been excessive, for many more lives have been placed in danger and numerous persons have been sacrificed." Ransom payments can no longer be permitted when society "faces an uninterrupted chain of kidnapings which were produced by and arose precisely out of the success of those which preceded them."[220]

The validity of this reasoning depends on two crucial assumptions: (1) that there is a causal link between the ransom prohibited and the acts of extortion, and (2) that a legal prohibition would be applied uniformly and contain no loopholes. As to the first assumption, a causal link is believable on its face because where ransom demands are met, the victims almost always are returned alive.[221] *Ipso facto,* by removing the fruit, the tree should lose its attractiveness.

This fact, however, is in dispute. In the Rand study of 77 international hostage episodes, where either government officials were victims or demands were made on governments, the authors conclude that "tough anti-terrorist campaigns, not tough anti-concessionary policies toward specific kidnapings, seem to account for the demise of kidnaping tactics over time." A no-concessions policy, the authors continue, "may affect the form more than the frequency of kidnaping—that is, the kidnapers may make propaganda rather than concessions their main objective."[222]

The authors of the Rand study, however, base their conclusions on a relatively small sample of incidents covering 11 countries and 29 guerrilla or terrorist groups. In any case, they have no way of ascertaining how many opportunities terrorists have foregone because of no-concessions policies. Indeed, they admit that in Argentina a no-concessions policy toward diplomats led the terrorists to find other targets, including foreign businessmen.[223] Further, "in almost all cases," publicity was "a major goal that was explicit or implicit" in the terrorists' actions against governments and their officials. While publicity was not classified as a ransom demand in the study, the authors admit that "it is generally difficult to tell whether many terrorists were more interested in concessions to specific demands, or in public recognition and front-page publicity."[224] Since with a few notable exceptions publicity has not played nearly as prominent a role as monetary demands in the kidnaping of private individuals, the study loses considerable weight when applied to the private sector. To date, therefore, the case has not been proved either way with respect to a general no-ransom prohibition. The presumption of a causal link, however, has been placed in question.

Assuming *arguendo* that a causal link exists, the effectiveness of a ransom prohibition depends on its credibility among terrorists. Any weakness will be exploited by terrorists, as the Rand study points out, through a shift in the form of extortion. It is here that the human factor takes hold. Are states willing to embody the no-ransom policy in their criminal codes, and will judges and juries be willing to convict those who violate these codes to save members of their families? Will the government arrest those who receive in the mail and do not return a bonus from their employer, or who receive and do not return free food packages, when these are sent in response to ransom demands? Will governments follow the same hard line when high officials are kidnaped, or will they permit private arrangements? Will 200 passengers on a jumbo jet be abandoned or be forced to endure a frontal assault as the only alternatives? And, finally, will governments forbid the printing of political advertisements, the reporting of political views and front-page publicity if these are the fruits of extortion?

Thus far, few governments have demonstrated a willingness to cast their ransom prohibitions so uncompromisingly and comprehensively. Argentina, for instance, has prohibited ransom payments altogether;[225] however, the escalation in the general level of violence during 1976 makes it difficult to determine the impact of this policy on extortion demands. In other jurisdictions, such as Colombia[226] and California,[227] legislative proposals would limit the prohibition to business entities and private foundations and to persons or entities unrelated to the immediate family of the victim. Indeed, the Colegio de Abogados Penalistas de Bogota reported recently to the Minister of Justice its opposition to making the payment of ransom by a family member a criminal offense. Due to the presence of coercion in extortion demands, it explained, the payment of ransom by a member of the immediate family would lack the element of "will" in proving culpability as required by the penal code.[228] As a result, serious doubt is thrown on the willingness of states to enact a comprehensive no-ransom policy.

Perspective of the Enterprise. From another perspective, that of the transnational enterprise, a ransom prohibition appears equally dubious. Within this context, the advantage to the enterprise in avoiding all ransom demands by force of law competes with the injury to its image and to the morale of its employees when the latter are abandoned in the hands of terrorists. Corporate management might well be relieved at first blush as the company no longer would be burdened with ransom negotiations and decisions. Further, all enterprises would be in the same position, so that terrorists could not play one off against the other. No longer could the deep pocket of the corporation be used to finance further acts of terrorism. More importantly, perhaps, employees would be assured that they no longer would be of value to terrorists, at least as hostages. Terrorists would have to seek their fortune elsewhere.

Unfortunately, the implications of a ransom prohibition for the enterprise raise some difficult issues. In the first place, the enterprise must operate on the premise that absolute security for its employees and its property is virtually impossible. For this reason, an enterprise normally follows several complementary security strategies.[229] If these strategies fail and an executive is kidnaped, as matters stand now, it can negotiate and pay the ransom with some assurance from experience that extortions succeed only infrequently. From the enterprise's viewpoint, this may be the most cost-effective way to view terrorism.[230] On the other hand, if negotiation is impossible because ransom payments are prohibited, the enterprise loses an important escape hatch. This may well require that security provisions be increased substantially, and this means increased costs.

Second, in the case of a ransom prohibition, executives suddenly are faced with an all-or-nothing situation. As they no longer can count on the support of their employers in case of kidnaping, their only hope is that the ransom prohibition successfully deters terrorists. However, as Paul Wilkinson points out, "revolutionary terrorists make war on legality and hence their 'criminality' is an essential part of their self-definition."[231] It is unlikely that a group steeped in "criminality" and dedicated to the destruction of the established order will be deterred by legal restraints on others,[232] particularly if there is any hint either that the law might be circumvented or that it might not be enforced. This fatal flaw already is indicated in states' unwillingness to embody a no-ransom policy in their criminal code and their seeking instead to limit its application to private enterprises.

Under these circumstances, terrorists are likely to pursue one or two alternatives. On the one hand, their initial reaction might well be to test the resoluteness of the enterprise and the strength of the law by carrying out a number of kidnapings and then executing particular hostages when their ransom demands are not met. The shock of executions could prove devastating to the enterprise[233] and force it to find some way to appease the terrorists. On the other hand, where the ransom prohibition is limited to enterprises, terrorists could simply direct their demands to the executive's family. Either the family would have to suffer the burden alone or, once again, the company would have to find some way to assist it. For this reason, hostage insurance would become quite popular unless it also is made illegal. Whether the policy premiums are borne by the enterprises directly or through a commensurate increase in executives' salaries, a widespread practice of insuring executives might well encourage kidnaping, for it would be difficult to keep it confidential. As a net result of these alternatives, either employee morale would suffer because the company's hands would be tied in the event of kidnaping, or the law would suffer because ways would be found to appease the terrorists.

Third, if the ransom prohibition is limited to enterprises, the image of the enterprise also is likely to suffer. The company, it could be said, was being protected at the expense of the employee. Indeed, the ransom prohibition might be used as evidence of an alliance between the host government and the transnational enterprise. Further, should the employee be killed because of the company's failure to meet the ransom demand, the terrorists would have demonstrated quite clearly that the transnational enterprise "values money more than life, that people can be sacrificed but profits cannot, that such laws are part of the ... capitalist system."[234] Public sympathy is not a rational matter. Among the impoverished and underprivileged, the large profitable foreign enterprise must always bear the burden of proof.

Perspective of Society. Finally, from the perspective of society, the deterrence value of a ransom prohibition must be weighed against the likelihood of its circumvention. At issue is the efficacy of the law itself when applied to ransom demands. For the sake of this analysis, it will be assumed that a causal link exists between a ransom prohibition and ransom demands, although this has been disputed as previously discussed. Further, it will be assumed that the prohibition is enforced uniformly and generally across the board to all public officials and private individuals and enterprises alike. Even then, serious doubts arise about the effectiveness of the prohibition and, therefore, its deterrence value.

In the first place, successful law enforcement against extortion requires close cooperation from the family or enterprise. If it appears that the victim's life will be jeopardized or that the family or enterprise will be exposed to legal liability in taking measures to save the victim's life, then the authorities will not be informed about the demands. This result reportedly has been and continues to be a serious problem in Argentina, where the government has attempted to enforce a ransom prohibition.[235] Further, in Colombia the government enforces its ransom prohibition by seizing bank accounts;[236] as a result ransom payments simply are arranged outside the country.[237] Even within a country, it will be difficult to supervise adequately bank transfers by holders of large and diversified assets in order to prevent ransom payments.

The absence of valuable information will seriously interfere with the prevention of extortion. Rumor will replace reliable data. The victims of extortion, their families, and employers will be pitted against the authorities. Ironically, the terrorist could collect twice or more for his crime: first by virtue of extortion and second by blackmailing the family or enterprise on the basis of having made an illegal ransom payment. Further, since by definition the authorities will be excluded from any ransom negotiations, they will miss a valuable opportunity to identify and apprehend the criminals. A ransom prohibition, therefore, would not only interfere with, but could be counterproductive to, the prevention of extortion.

Finally, society must also decide whether it will pay the high price of a comprehensive ransom prohibition by suppressing publicity of extortion incidents. To be effective, this policy would entail not only preventing the publication of propaganda tracts, but also ensuring that news reporting is limited to the briefest announcements. In Colombia, the government announced that it would "make use of its legal and constitutional prerogatives to prohibit every type of news and news comments relating to kidnaping by television and radio";[238] and, in Venezuela, the government reportedly suppressed the publication of propaganda tracts by the Niehous kidnapers by closing a television station for 72 hours and seizing the press run and printing plates of a Caracas daily.[239] While these measures extend well beyond the bounds of media self-restraint, both governments have had to weigh the necessity for these responses against their constitutional guarantees of press freedom.

Unless the incidence of terrorist extortion were to increase dramatically, similar measures could not be justified in the United States. Restrictions on publicity relating to terrorism, therefore, must remain a matter for media self-restraint. In the present state of media standards, these offer only a sometime and uncertain means to publicity control.

From this overview, it is clear that the imposition of a ransom prohibition has widespread implications for a democratic society. These range from media control to family relationships, employee morale, the image of the transnational enterprise, the efficacy of the law, and the basic concept of criminality in respect to recipients of terrorist demands. While the existence of a causal link between a ransom prohibition and ransom demands cannot be confirmed or denied at this point, the prohibition probably would not have a significant deterrent value as a practical matter. Not only would the prohibition be difficult to enforce, but it would be counterproductive generally with regard to law enforcement efforts against extortion.

A ransom prohibition, therefore, must be rejected in respect to the private sector. As applied to individual victims and their families, it would be difficult to enforce even in the courts. As applied to enterprises, it would place them under enormous social pressure to circumvent the law, for otherwise executives and their families would be left to fend for themselves. Society, too, would suffer because the prohibition would engender suspicion toward law enforcement authorities. The victims' families and their employers would be reluctant to communicate and to cooperate with these authorities. Further, if media control or self-restraint were pressed to the point of suppressing critical data about terrorist events, not only would the public be uninformed but the press would soon lose its credibility. In any case, absent relatively high levels of terrorist incidents, democratic societies will be reluctant to enact and enforce rigorously the type of comprehensive legal prohibitions that would be required to counter ransom demands effectively.

International Measures

From the viewpoint of the international community, any attempt to combat terrorism must recognize two points. First, the primary responsibility for the apprehension and punishment of terrorists lies with the individual states and their law enforcement authorities. International measures can offer only supplemental assistance and remedies and establish minimum legal principles, which in turn must be implemented for the most part by state authorities. Second, terrorism as yet has had a relatively marginal impact on the international order.[240] Beyond their temporarily disruptive impact, terrorists have not in themselves overthrown any governments or managed to escalate their violence and political authority to a state of insurgency. Mostly, they have achieved a worldwide publicity far in excess of their strength and claims and, quite often, triggered regressive governmental responses, which have resulted in general restrictions on individual freedoms. Preoccupied with other concerns, therefore, the international community will not be rushed into adopting new international measures, particularly if they appreciably restrict state sovereignty.

Nevertheless, terrorism raises a number of issues of international concern that escape the effective control of individual states:

1. There is increasing incidence of international contact and cooperation among terrorist groups, including the flow of arms and coordinated actions.
2. Instrumentalities of international communication and travel have proved to be both useful and vulnerable to terrorism.
3. Absent common agreement on "international crimes," states may become sanctuaries for terrorism committed in other states.
4. In some cases, terrorism becomes an instrument in the hands of small groups

to aggravate or to disrupt the resolution of major international tensions and conflicts.

5. The potential impact of terrorism on world order is increasing, due both to the proliferation of weapons capable of mass destruction and to the erosion of authority at the state level in recent years. The latter often provides fertile ground for insurgent activity.

6. Finally, terrorism has been tried and proved to be a frequently successful tactic for extorting money and for gaining a substantial amount of worldwide publicity.

For these same reasons, U.S. nationals and institutions, both public and private, promise to be frequent targets of terrorism, at least for the foreseeable future.[241]

Complements to National Jurisdiction. Transnational enterprises as well as states should have a serious interest in the enactment of international measures that will assist states to combat terrorism more effectively. Without entering into the debate of justifiable versus illegal political violence, which has stalled international action to date,[242] transnational enterprises could endorse without reservation four measures of international cooperation set forth in the Working Paper of the Secretariat at the Fifth United Nations Congress on the Prevention of Crime and the Treatment of Offenders, which was held in Toronto in September 1975.[243] Proceeding from the premise, announced in a previous study, that "certain forms of violence, especially against the innocent," should not be permitted under any circumstances,[244] the secretariat proposed an "interim solution" to permit the international community to deal more forcefully with the problem of terrorism.

The four measures, together with some elaboration, are as follows.

Universal Jurisdiction. Terrorism would be constituted a "crime" under international law, so that the state in possession of an alleged offender would be required to prosecute that person under its own national law. Defining "crime" is the critical factor. Transnational enterprises would be served if broad agreement could be reached initially upon a very limited number of specific acts, such as kidnaping and letter bombs. As the international community gains confidence in this approach, additional acts might be added to the list.

Extradition. A state may determine not to prosecute an alleged offender as required under the universal jurisdiction measure, but to extradite the person to a requesting state, especially one with preferred jurisdiction. This measure would require, in effect, an exception to the "political offense exception" to which extradition obligations are presently subject.[245] It must be carried out, however, "subject to international concern for the safeguards on human rights."[246] This means at least that the extraditing state must be assured that the requesting state will grant the alleged offender due process. Often, considerations of fairness will dictate that a person should not be extradited to the state that was the object of the terrorist attack. If, for whatever reason, a state does not extradite the alleged offender, however, it should be obligated to prosecute the person itself.

International Criminal Court. The establishment of an International Criminal Court would form an important adjunct to the principles of universal jurisdiction and extradition just discussed. The First International Criminal Law Conference, held at Wingspread, Wisconsin, in 1971, for instance, proposed a draft statute that would authorize the court "to try persons accused of crimes generally recognized under international law."[247] The court would have full powers of investigation, prosecution, and sentencing. It would be composed of a panel of independent judges who are both eminent jurists and "represent the main forms of civilization and the principal legal systems of the world."[248] The court would offer an alternate jurisdiction for the prosecution and punishment of defined crimes. It would permit a state, which could not prosecute an alleged offender because of internal political pressures and could not extradite the person to the requesting state for reasons of fairness, to bind the person over to the International Criminal Court for trial.

Mutual Assistance. The secretariat recommends the "exchange of technical information on the protection of persons and property against acts of transnational violence."[249] This measure might require states to exchange information relating to their responsibilities in protecting international services such as the mail, to criminal proceedings instituted against alleged offenders, and to offenses that a state has reason to believe will affect or be committed in the territory of another state. This exchange of information could be assisted through Interpol.

Special International Protection. The international measures for combating terrorism just discussed apply equally to all victims of terrorist attack. They offer no special protection to the transnational enterprise. For this reason, it might be asked whether transnational enterprises and other transnational business operations should receive special protection under international law as is afforded diplomats and other governmental representatives. It may be granted that transnational enterprises contribute uniquely to the world economy and have been singled out by terrorists as targets. Nevertheless, special protection appears on balance to be neither appropriate nor desirable.

The reasons for this are several. In the first place, the definition of the protected subject will be difficult. When is a business operation "transnational" and when is it simply "domestic"? Is this determined by criteria of ownership, control, nationality of the executives, location of production facilities, markets, or of product content?

Second, why should international economic intercourse be given preferred status over international cultural relations (*e.g.*, the academic community or tourism), or over purely national business? In most countries where terrorists have targeted transnational enterprises, they have shown similar interest in nationally owned businesses. Indeed, terrorist attacks against transnational enterprises appear to originate almost exclusively within the host state. The international component of these attacks, therefore, is limited for the most part to foreign ownership and control of the enterprise and the foreign nationality of the executives.

Third, to the extent that transnational enterprises deserve special protection under international law, it can be argued that they and their foreign national employees already have such protection by virtue of their alien status in the host state.[250] As a result, any attempt to obtain special protection for transnational enterprises could detract from the existing international responsibility of the host state for aliens in general. It would be better to reinforce existing general responsibilities of states under international law rather than create special classes.

Fourth, any effort at this time to obtain special protection for transnational enterprises would probably not be well received by states in general. The Charter of Economic Rights and Duties of States clearly evidences the intent of most states not to grant foreign investors "privileged treatment."[251] At the same time, home states are beginning to show a disenchantment with the foreign operations of their own enterprises, alleging that jobs are being exported and that technology transfer is undermining their own economic growth. Within this political climate, any suggestion that transnational enterprises deserve special protection under international law could simply exacerbate the already difficult position of these companies, and yet offer little chance of success. In the absence of highly persuasive reasons for special protection, transnational enterprises and the international community as a whole would be better advised to emphasize the general responsibility of states both to protect aliens and their property in accordance with minimum international standards as well as to grant them equal treatment with nationals of the host state.

Finally, as a corollary to this reasoning, it must be concluded that state liability for injury to the personnel or property of transnational enterprises should also be governed by general principles of international law. These are derived from the responsibility of states to maintain internal order. Pursuant to these principles, a state can not be expected to prevent or even to punish all criminal acts, including those of terrorists. However, should a state fail to provide for an adequate police force or to take reasonable precautions in training, equipping, and deploying this force to deal with the threats and acts of terrorists of which it has knowledge or that it can reasonably be expected to anticipate, and should this failure result in or contribute to the injury of a foreign-owned business or its personnel, the state may be negligent in its international duty to protect aliens and their property.[252] By the same token, a state may also fail in its international duty if it makes no attempt or takes inadequate measures to apprehend, prosecute, and punish the offender.[253] The standard to be applied, therefore, is negligence and not strict liability. There appears to be no basis for increasing this standard with respect to terrorist acts perpetrated against transnational businesses and their personnel.

Conclusions and Recommendations

The transnational business operation has become a frequent target of terrorist activities over the past few years. Increasingly, attacks have been mounted by relatively large, well-organized, and highly disciplined groups in order to achieve political ends. The transnational enterprise, as a natural ally of political stability, a very effective mode for the organization of capital and technology, and an extension of foreign economic interests, has become a highly symbolic and lucrative target of terrorists whose ultimate objective is to embarrass the host government, erode its authority, and force political change. The costs of the enterprise, both visible and hidden, may far exceed the payments exacted by terrorists. The international investment climate as a whole also suffers, and with it international commerce. The threat of terrorism is forcing the transnational enterprise to rethink its traditional approach to security and to develop new modes of cooperative action with governmental authorities as well as within the private sector. Because terrorism represents a comprehensive threat to transnational business operations, it requires an equally broad-gauged response.

The first line of defense against terrorist attack lies within the enterprise itself. Generally speaking, this consists of comprehensive security programming, executive protection, low corporate profile, and contingency planning. These strategies, however, are not sufficient in themselves. They have only relative value in preventing terrorist attack. They may cause the terrorist to choose a more accessible target, either among enterprises or within a particular enterprise. They may cut losses arising from terrorism, but they will rarely ward off the determined efforts of a terrorist group. Finally, they cannot deal with the longer-term challenge of terrorism to the business sector as a whole.

Transnational enterprises, therefore, must begin to develop intelligence networks, crisis management planning, and preventive systems that deal long-range and more comprehensively with the programming among enterprises. These require close working relationships between enterprises and government intelligence agencies and law enforcement authorities. Through such efforts, enterprises may develop more effective management forms, organizational procedures, and security strategies and techniques. Further, enterprises must find ways to counteract and to undercut the ideological attacks of terrorists. As the transnational enterprise by definition must operate and compete in a foreign environment, it must be able to demonstrate most forcefully to the public and to the government of the host country its unique contribution to the economic and social development of that society.

This chapter, however, has touched only tangentially on the security strategies, methods, and techniques of individual enterprises. Its major focus has been to analyze and to evaluate the nature and level of the terrorist threat to transnational business operations and, as a result of this analysis, to recommend policies and practical measures that the U.S. government might take the better to combat the terrorist threat. Some of the recommendations require direct government action, while others are designed to encourage and enable cooperative action within the private sector. In either case, the development and implementation of effective measures to combat terrorism require a concerted effort by both the public and private sectors.

The recommendations are grouped under four major categories as follows: U.S. policy, research, data exchange, and the private sector resource center: Although these recommendations are directed toward policy or action by the U.S. government, they presume that the private sector itself must initiate and be prepared to take cooperative action of its own. Furthermore, these recommendations deal primarily with national rather than international policies and measures. In part, this is because traditional principles of international law and the conclusions of this chapter do not support special protective status for transnational business operations. Additionally, a number of the recommendations having international significance are covered in the Appendix to this book and therefore will not be treated separately here.

U.S. Policy

To combat international terrorism directed against the transnational business operations of U.S. companies more effectively, the U.S. government should adopt the policies set forth below relating to national and international issues. These policies are designed to give enterprises maximum flexibility in dealing with terrorism, recognizing that hard-line responses are as likely to provoke attacks as to deter them, and that they may well not be cost-effective. At the same time, governmental policies must be based on a realistic understanding of the limits on legal norms in combating terrorism, as well as of the need for cooperative and innovative responses within the private sector to complement governmental measures. Further, governmental policies must carefully balance the short-term urgency for effective deterrents against the longer-term preservation of constitutional values and general principles of international law.

A number of policy recommendations are not presented here because they have general application to several aspects of terrorism covered in this report. Thus the need for the media to adopt their own industry standards applies across the board to all terrorists' acts, whatever their targets. Furthermore, some recommendations are directed generally to the efforts of the United States to obtain the adoption of international conventions. These concern the establishment of universal jurisdiction over terrorist crimes, expanding the scope of extradition, the establishment of an International Criminal Court, and measures of mutual assistance among states in apprehending and prosecuting persons accused of terrorist acts. Although these policy recommendations are covered in the Appendix, they also retain their importance as useful measures for combating terrorists' acts against transnational business operations.

Ransom Policy. The U.S. government should not foster a "no-ransom" approach by business enterprises in their dealings with terrorists. Nor should it support efforts to establish such a policy by other states. Such an approach cannot be justified from the point of view either of the individual victim, or of the business sector, or of society as a whole. It would place business in an impossible personnel position, a classic "double-bind." Furthermore, it would be extremely difficult to enforce and could well work counterproductively in preventing extortion. At the same time, the United States should respect the decisions of other states to prohibit ransom payments within their jurisdictions.

Hostage Insurance. The U.S. government should take the position that hostage insurance is a private business matter to be regulated by supply and demand within the insurance industry. It should neither encourage the use of hostage insurance—for to do so could well increase the ransom expectations of terrorists—nor should it prohibit hostage insurance, because as recommended above, a ransom prohibition should not be applied to the private sector.

Risk Pooling. The U.S. government should investigate ways in which changes and clarifications in U.S. tax law could reduce the impact of ransom payments of U.S. enterprises operating in high-risk areas. Such changes or clarifications, however, should not subsidize ransom payments nor create special advantages for the enterprise. Rather, they should be limited to enabling legitimate risk-spreading techniques and to ensuring that ransom payments may be fully deducted as ordinary and necessary business expenses to the extent that they are actually paid by the taxpayer for sound business reasons.

Government Subsidies. The U.S. government should not at this time undertake a program to subsidize the security costs of private enterprise. In the United States, terrorist activity against business enterprises has not reached a point that would justify such extraordinary measures. Even if it did, serious questions would arise as to whether, to what extent, and what type of private security forces should be encouraged. Moreover, no subsidy should be granted for the security programs of the foreign operations of U.S. enterprises. Such subsidies could be interpreted as interference in the internal affairs of the host country and, in any case, should be granted (if at all) by the host government that has an immediate interest in encouraging such expenditures.

International Protection. The United States should support and reinforce, where appropriate, the general responsibility of states under international law to protect the person and property of aliens doing business within their jurisdiction against injury, including injury arising from the acts and threats of terrorists. Nevertheless, the United States should not attempt to establish a higher or special standard of protection under international law with respect to acts and threats of terrorists directed at transnational business operations or their personnel. There is no clear basis for drawing a distinction between business and any other victim category, nor between transnational and purely domestic commerce. Further, any effort to obtain such protection would probably not be well received by foreign governments and could well detract from the general principle of international law applicable to the protection of all aliens. By the same token, the United States should not seek the adoption of a standard of liability under international law with respect to terrorist attacks or transnational business operations that is more strict than the general standard for aliens based on the fault of a state and its authorized personnel.

Research

The U.S. government should foster research on a wide variety of subjects dealing with the analysis of terrorist activities, their strategies, and the means of prevention in respect to transnational business operations. This research should be undertaken both within the intelligence agencies of the government, especially with respect to the analysis of highly sensitive data, as well as within the private sector. In the latter case, it should be supported by government funding. The research should emphasize practical methods, techniques, and measures for combating terrorism by U.S. business enterprises within the United States and in foreign countries. It should be aimed at developing practical training models and immersion courses as well as strategy alternatives that can be utilized by U.S. business. For this reason, it is critical that much of the research be undertaken with the cooperation and direct participation of representatives from business who have practical experience in security management and in dealing with terrorist activities. This research should be to a large extent interdisciplinary, including such fields as security analysis, sociology, psychology, criminology, law, and political science. It also should cross-fertilize the experience of government intelligence agencies; law enforcement authorities on the federal, state and local levels; and representatives of business enterprises.

Threat and Risk Analysis. Strategies and methods should be developed to assist management in determining the type and degree of risks involved in locating plants, offices, and other facilities and in securing them and their personnel against attack.

Screening Methods. Methods should be developed for use in personnel hiring and in executive and facility protection to spot terrorists who attempt to infiltrate a company or an executive's household or who make deliveries or visits to company facilities. In many respects, these methods may be similar to the efforts of the airline industry for screening passengers and personnel.

Profile Analysis. Methods should be developed for identifying the activities of terrorists in terms of their likely targets, the means of terror employed, their motives, and the nature of their internal organization. These methods should enable the preparation of individual, group, and country profiles of terrorist activities, as well as their movements and international relationships that are operationally useful to business.

Negotiation Strategy. Alternative strategies must be developed for negotiating with terrorists depending on the motives involved and the strengths and weaknesses of the parties. These strategies should assist in clarifying the key issues, allow management the greatest degree of flexibility possible, assure a smooth working relationship with the media and with law enforcement and other governmental authorities, and assist in defusing the emotional and ideological pressures at work in the situation.

Hostage Survival. Executives and their families must have a better understanding of the situation that they face as potential hostages and when confronted with the fact of kidnaping. This requires research into psychological stresses to which hostages and their families are subjected during and subsequent to kidnaping, and the development of techniques for dealing with those situations.

Crisis Management. Comprehensive methods and techniques must be developed for managing crises within enterprises faced with terrorist threats, acts, and negotiations. These may require a coordinated interdisciplinary approach such that a team of executives can deal with all aspects of terrorist threats or attacks, including matters relating to negotiations, financing of ransom payments, legal relationships, media relationships, medical treatment, family concerns, informants, and technical experts. These methods and techniques also should permit management to arrive rapidly at informed decisions under pressure.

Data Exchange

The U.S. government should establish a data base through which the private sector is kept informed on a current basis about the activities, movements, and organization of terrorist groups around the world. Such a resource base might be placed within the Department of Commerce, but it should have access as needed to the information of the various intelligence agencies of the government. To preserve the confidentiality of sensitive information and sources, the data could be evaluated and screened before disclosure. In some cases, such as country and terrorist group profiles, the data should be made available on a regular basis to U.S. business enterprises. In other cases, where the data are more sensitive, their disclosure could be limited to the special needs of an enterprise. The flow of data in the United States could be coordinated through the Department of Commerce, while in foreign countries it could be coordinated through security officers and commercial attachés of the U.S. missions to the extent that this does not create embarrassment for or compromise the diplomatic positions of these missions. In addition, the use of these data could be made more effective if security officers and commercial attachés of the missions were trained in the security needs of the foreign operations of U.S. companies.

Private Sector Resource Center

The U.S. government should foster the establishment of a resource center for the private sector, which would be owned and controlled by subscribing businesses and would work in cooperation with government intelligence and law enforcement agencies. In contrast to the more traditional services offered by private security companies and consultants, its purposes would be to (1) undertake practical research of the type described in the research recommendations above; (2) design and conduct training programs on such matters as hostage survival, negotiation strategy, and crisis management; (3) develop a data system in cooperation with government agencies for keeping businesses currently informed of terrorists' movements and strategies; and (4) offer a crisis management service for businesses in conjunction with law enforcement agencies. While the center would be located in the United States, it could furnish services worldwide to transnational business operations. Much of the research undertaken, programs developed, and data accumulated would come out of the experience of the private sector and require active private sector participation for their success. However, government funding might be necessary in the beginning phase of the center. A pilot project might be launched to determine the workability and operating principles for the center. As a privately owned center, it would act as a buffer in data collection and dissemination among the participating enterprises and between the private sector and government intelligence agencies. Furthermore, the center would provide the government with valuable insight into the security needs of business as well as the opportunity to analyze and test the practicality and effectiveness of security programs.

Notes

1. U.N. Report of the Secretary-General, Measures to Prevent International Terrorism Which Endangers or Takes Innocent Human Lives or Jeopardizes Fundamental Freedoms, And Study of These Forms of Terrorism and Acts of Violence Which Lie in Misery, Frustration, Grievance and Despair and Which Cause Some People to Sacrifice Human Lives, Including Their Own, in an Attempt to Effect Radical Changes, 27 U.N. GAOR, C.6 Annexes (Agenda Item 92) 6, U.N. Doc. A/C.6/418, Annex I (1972) [hereinafter cited as U.N. Doc. A/C.6/418].

2. Terrorist attacks on aircraft will not be treated in this chapter.

3. B. JENKINS, INTERNATIONAL TERRORISM: A NEW MODE OF CONFLICT 1 (1975).

4. *Id.* at 8.

5. The author is indebted to discussions with representatives of the following security companies: Burns International Security Services, Inc.; Harris & Walsh Management Consultants; Pinkertons, Inc.; Rayne International, Inc.; The Security Institute; Wackenhut Corporation. The author also gratefully acknowledges the assistance of the American Society for Industrial Security.

6. *Hearings on Multinational Corporations Before the Subcomm. on International Trade of the Senate Comm. on Finance*, 93d Cong., 1st Sess., at 298 (1973).

7. U.S. DEP'T OF COMMERCE, HISTORICAL STATISTICS OF THE UNITED STATES: COLONIAL TIMES TO 1970, pt. 2, at 868-69 [hereinafter cited as U.S. HISTORICAL STATISTICS]; SURVEY OF CURRENT BUSINESS, Aug. 1976, at 32.

8. Stobaugh, *U.S. Multinational Enterprises and the U.S. Economy* in U.S. DEP'T OF COMMERCE, THE MULTINATIONAL CORPORATION: STUDIES ON U.S. FOREIGN INVESTMENT, at 2 and 4 (1972); M. WILKINS, THE MATURING OF MULTINATIONAL ENTERPRISE vi (1974).
(1974).

9. *See, e.g.*, M. WILKINS, *supra* note 8.

10. U.S. Department of Commerce, Staff Study, "Policy Aspects of Foreign Investment by U.S. Multinational Corporations," in U.S. Department of Commerce, *The Multinational Corp.: Studies on U.S. Foreign Investment* at 3 (1972).

11. M. WILKINS, *supra* note 8, at 352; U.S. Department of Commerce, Staff Study, *supra* note 10, at 81-84.

12. *See* Wionczek, *A Latin American View*, in HOW LATIN AMERICA VIEWS THE U.S. INVESTOR 5 (R. Vernon ed. 1967); M. WILKINS, *supra* note 8, at 401; U.S. Department of Commerce, Staff Study, *supra* note 10, at 81-84.

13. *See* TIME, Jan. 14, 1974, at 25.

14. *See* G.A. *Ad Hoc* Committee on International Terrorism, Observations

of States Submitted in Accordance with General Assembly Resolution 3034 (XXVII), U.N. Doc. A/AC.160/1, at 36 (1973) (observations submitted by the Syrian government); *id.* U.N. Doc. A/AC.160/L.31 Add.1/Corr.1, para. (3) (1973) (observations submitted by the Algerian government). *See also* more recent statement of Colonel Muammar Qaddafi of Libya, speaking at the Fifth Summit Conference of Non-Aligned Nations in Sri Lanka, Chicago Tribune, Aug. 19, 1976, § 1 at 12, col. 1.

15. D. MILBANK, INTERNATIONAL AND TRANSNATIONAL TERRORISM: DIAGNOSIS AND PROGNOSIS 43 (1976) (CIA Research Study, PR 76 10030).

16. *See* R. CLUTTERBUCK, LIVING WITH TERRORISM 15, 148-50 (1975).

17. These factors are described in the writings of MILBANK, *supra* note 15, at 3-4, 18-22; Gurr, Characteristics of Contemporary Terrorism, 6-9 (unpublished paper, 1976). THE POLITICS OF TERRORISM: A READER IN THEORY AND PRACTICE (M. Stohl, ed., forthcoming).

18. *See, e.g.*, J.B. BELL, TRANSNATIONAL TERROR 10-19 (1975); B. Crozier, Terrorism: The Problem in Perspective, 18-19 (unpublished paper 1976); C. Johnson, Perspectives on Terrorism, 11-13 (unpublished paper, 1976).

19. *See* Crozier, *What Terrorists Hope to Gain by Murdering Americans*, U.S. NEWS & WORLD REP., June 28, 1976, at 34; P. Wilkinson, A FATALITY OF ILLUSIONS: DOMINANT IMAGES OF INTERNATIONAL TERRORISM, 7, 14f, 29f (unpublished paper, 1976).

20. Bell, *The Profile of a Terrorist*, INTERNATIONAL TERRORISM 10, 13 (C. Baumann ed. 1974).

21. Revolutionary Command Argimiro Gabaldon, *To the People of Venezuela*, N.Y. Times, Apr. 6, 1976 at 59, col. 1 (an advertisement published as part of kidnaping demands).

22. STAFF OF HOUSE COMM. ON INTERNAL SECURITY, 93d Cong., 2d Sess., STUDY ON TERRORISM 192-94 (Comm. Print 1974) [hereinafter cited as STAFF STUDY].

23. See *Terroristic Activity, International Terrorism: Hearings Before the Subcomm. to Investigate the Administration of the Internal Security Laws of the Senate Comm. on the Judiciary*, 94th Cong., 1st Sess., at 182-83 (1975) [hereinafter cited as *International Terrorism Hearings*].

24. *See id.*, at 182-83; STAFF STUDY, *supra* note 22, at 42-44, 66-70; BELL, *supra* note 18, at 27-37, 56-68.

25. *See* ECONOMIST, Oct. 5, 1974, at 46, 48.

26. *See* BELL, *supra* note 18, at 17; JENKINS, *supra* note 3, at 4-7.

27. *See* JENKINS, *id.*, at 6, with reference to the Lod Airport massacre.

28. Gurr, *supra* note 17, at 21.

29. C. MARIGHELA, FOR THE LIBERATION OF BRAZIL 37f, 44, 47, 63, 71, 78-80, 87-89, 107, 120 (1971).

30. *See* BUSINESS WEEK, Mar. 9, 1974, at 40-42. *See also* the kidnaping

of two U.S. employees of International Mining Co. in Colombia, in STAFF STUDY, *supra* note 22, at 20-21.

31. *See* note 21 *supra.*

32. *See* B. JENKINS & J. JOHNSON, INTERNATIONAL TERRORISM: A CHRONOLOGY, 1968-1974, 31 (1975).

33. *Id.* at 44. *But cf.* MARIGHELA, *supra* note 29, at 118: "When we expropriate money we must never distribute it to the people, because this will give the masses the false idea that we can replace them in the struggle for power.... This would be a paternalistic attitude."

34. *Id.* at 51.

35. N.Y. Times, Apr. 6, 1976, at 57, col. 4. *See also* El Nacional (Venezuela), Mar. 30, 1976, at D-13 (public reply of Owens-Illinois to terrorist demands).

36. BUSINESS WEEK, Sept. 29, 1973, at 93.

37. B. JENKINS & J. JOHNSON, *supra* note 32. The figures are the author's calculations.

38. *See* MILBANK, *supra* note 15, at 14.

39. Private study by major security firm.

40. STAFF STUDY, *supra* note 22, at 10-11, 15; CLUTTERBUCK, *supra* note 16, at 44-45.

41. El Universal (Venezuela), Mar. 23, 1976, at 2, cols. 5-7.

42. *See* BELL, *supra* note 18, at 15-16; JENKINS, *supra* note 3, at 5-6; Wilkinson, *supra* note 19, at 30-33.

43. *See* BELL, *supra* note 18, at 62.

44. *See International Terrorism Hearings, supra* note 23, at 189, 206 (testimony of B. Crozier).

45. B. Crozier, *supra* note 19, at 33. *See also* MARIGHELA, *supra* note 29, at 96, 116f.

46. *See* B. JENKINS & J. JOHNSON, *supra* note 32, at 22, 31, 50, 56 (incidents: No. 141, ELN, Bolivia, July 1970; No. 252, ERP, Argentina, Mar. 1972; No. 455, Lebanese Socialist Revolutionary Organization, Lebanon, Oct. 1973; No. 507, IRA, Ireland, Apr. 1974).

47. *See id.* at 22 (incident No. 141).

48. N.Y. Times, Sept. 20, 1972, at 12, col. 6.

49. *See* B. JENKINS & J. JOHNSON, *supra* note 32, at 44 (incident No. 400, where hijackers of a Colombian airliner admitted upon capture that contrary to their statements during the hijacking, their real motives were not political).

50. *Supra* note 15, at 43.

51. *See* B. JENKINS & J. JOHNSON, *supra* note 32, at 29, 33, 37, 39, 40, 41, 44, 45, 49, 50, 51, 52, 53, 55 [incident Nos. 216, 218, 277, 317, 318, 338, 357, 359, 397, 398, 408, 409, 415, 451, 455 (barricade and hostage), 459, 468, 472, 479, 500]. In addition, kidnapings of employees of the following

companies occurred after the close of the chronology: Collins International (Ethiopia, July 14, 1975), Sears, Roebuck (Colombia, Aug. 5, 1975), Boise-Cascade (Philippines, Aug. 30, 1975), Trans-Mediterranean Airlines (Lebanon, Oct. 29, 1975), Collins International (Ethiopia, Dec. 21, 1975), and Owens-Illinois (Venezuela, Feb. 27, 1976). The calculations are the author's.

52. *See* STAFF STUDY, *supra* note 22, at 14-15.

53. *See* TIME, Jan. 14, 1974, at 25.

54. *See* FBI, BOMB SUMMARY 16 (1975); McGuire, *Terrorist Bombings Sputter Back to Normal*, CONFERENCE BOARD RECORD, Oct. 1973, at 6-7. The 1976 figures were obtained in an interview with an FBI agent.

55. For statistical purposes, these hostage incidents include not only conventional kidnapings but also cases in which, for instance, a bank teller is abducted by robbers to support their escape.

56. Interview with FBI agent.

57. Private study by major security firm, relying on statistics furnished by the Colombia National Police.

58. Following the Swint murder, discussed in STAFF STUDY, *supra* note 22, at 14-15, Ford was notified that its executives and their families would be murdered one by one and that the Ford plant in Buenos Aires would be bombed.

59. After wounding a Ford employee resisting a kidnaping attempt, the ERP warned that the kidnaping of Ford's Argentine executives would continue unless Ford paid $1 million in ransom. The amount was paid.

60. *See* McGuire, *supra* note 54, at 8.

61. TIME, Jan. 14, 1975, at 24.

62. STAFF STUDY, *supra* note 22, at 15.

63. *See* note 21 *supra*.

64. B. JENKINS & J. JOHNSON, *supra* note 32, at 49 (incident No. 455).

65. *See* B. JENKINS J. JOHNSON, & D. RONFELDT, NUMBERED LIVES: SOME STATISTICAL OBSERVATIONS FROM 77 INTERNATIONAL HOSTAGE EPISODES 10-14, 19-22 (1975), comparing the advantages and disadvantages of kidnaping and hostage-and-barricade situations.

66. B. JENKINS & J. JOHNSON, *supra* note 32, at 4. MILBANK, *supra* note 15, at 23, estimates that as of April 1976 the human casualties resulting from terrorism amounted to 800 killed and 1700 wounded, including terrorists.

67. McGuire, *Safeguarding Executives Against Kidnapping and Extortion*, CONFERENCE BOARD RECORD June 1974 at 56.

68. *See Terrorism: Hearings Before the House Comm. on Internal Security* 93d Cong., 2d Sess. 4025, 4477 (1974) [hereinafter cited as *Terrorism Hearings*].

69. B. Howard, *Living with Terrorism*, Washington Post, July 18, 1976, at C4, col. 1.

70. *See id.*, at C4, col. 3, pointing out that despite the increased hazards of

the diplomatic job, the number of foreign service applicants has increased from 6700 in 1969 to more than 20,000 in 1976.

71. *See* BUSINESS WEEK, Mar. 9, 1975, at 40.

72. NEWSWEEK, June 11, 1973, at 94.

73. U.S. NEWS & WORLD REPORT, Mar. 11, 1974, at 60.

74. *See Terrorism Hearings, supra* note 68, at 4026; MILBANK, *supra* note 15, at 26, n.

75. *See* note 70 *supra.*

76. *See* p. 407 *supra.*

77. *See* pp. 407-408 *supra.* STAFF STUDY, *supra* note 22, at 21.

78. Daily Journal (Venezuela), Mar. 25, 1976, at 1; Mar. 28, 1976, at 1; El Nacional (Venezuela), Mar. 17, 1976, at D14, cols. 3-4.

79. Daily Journal (Venezuela), Mar. 30, 1976, at 23, col. 1; N.Y. Times, Apr. 7, 1976, at 57, col. 4.

80. El Nacional (Venezuela), Apr. 7, 1976, at 1, col. 3; N.Y. Times, Apr. 7, 1976, at 55, cols. 1-3; Christian Science Monitor, May 6, 1976, at 12, cols. 1-2.

81. N.Y. Times, Apr. 7, 1976, at 55, cols. 1-3; at 60, col. 4. Subsequent embarrassments in the Niehous case have continued to plague the government-business relationships. *See, e.g.*, LATIN AMERICA, Mar. 19, 1976, at 94; July 30, 1976, at 233-34; Aug. 6, 1976, at 244; Oct. 6, 1976, at 305-06. *See also* THE MONTHLY REPORT (Venezuela), Aug. 29, 1976, at 19-22.

82. THE MONTHLY REPORT (Venezuela), Aug. 29, 1976, at 19.

83. SURVEY OF CURRENT BUSINESS, Aug. 1976, at 48; U.S. DEP'T OF COMMERCE, REVISED DATA SERIES ON U.S. DIRECT INVESTMENT ABROAD 1966-1974, at 1-8 (1975).

84. BUSINESS WEEK, Mar. 9, 1974, at 40.

85. *See* BUSINESS LATIN AMERICA, Jan. 29, 1975, at 35; Mar. 10, 1976, at 70.

86. U.S. NEWS & WORLD REPORT, Mar. 11, 1974, at 60.

87. *See id.*

88. N.Y. Times, May 25, 1973, at 3, col. 1.

89. These four categories, which emerged from the various interviews of the author with corporate security officers and security consultants, closely parallel the categories of countermeasures identified in the monograph of K. JACOBSON, THE MOUNTING CHALLENGE OF INTERNATIONAL TERRORISM 9-12 (1976) (Stanford Research Institute, Business Intelligence Program, Guidelines No. 1002).

90. Private study by major security firm.

91. *See* pp. 414-415 *supra.*

92. *See generally* T. WALSH & HEALY, PROTECTION OF ASSETS MANUAL (1975), esp. ch. 18; CLUTTERBUCK, *supra* note 16, at 61-64, for an overview.

93. Rayne, *Protecting the Executive*, SECURITY MANAGEMENT 16 (Mar. 1976).

94. *See* pp. 408, 413-14 *supra.*

95. Christian Science Monitor, Sept. 10, 1976, at 3, col. 3.

96. *See, e.g.*, BUSINESS INTERNATIONAL, Apr. 20, 1973, at 121-22; the five-page "Security Suggestions for U.S. Businessmen Abroad" published June 1975 by the Department of State; BURNS INTERNATIONAL SECURITY SERVICES, INC., THE BURNS INTERNATIONAL INVESTIGATION BUREAU, EXECUTIVE PROTECTION HANDBOOK, *reprinted in Terrorism Hearings, supra* note 68, at 3234-59.

97. *See* p. 435 *infra.*

98. These characteristics were said to be essential.

99. BUSINESS WEEK, Mar. 9, 1974, at 40.

100. *See* pp. 419-420 *supra.*

101. *Terrorism Hearings, supra* note 68, at 4025. *See also* pp. 436-437 *infra.*

102. B. JENKINS & J. JOHNSON, *supra* note 32, at 44 (incident No. 398).

103. *See Terrorism Hearings, supra* note 68, at 4025.

104. *See* STAFF STUDY, *supra* note 22, at 15.

105. *See* Testimony of Braniff International Security Director, H. Pizer, in *Terrorism Hearings, supra* note 68, at 3951: "Regardless of how stringent a security program is implemented, an organized terrorist group especially if they are the ERP . . . more than likely will succeed." *See also* MARIGHELA, *supra* note 29, at 74f, 80-82.

106. *See* pp. 423-424 *supra* (point 2).

107. Some U.S. enterprises think that the exchange of intelligence data between industry and law enforcement authorities is better in foreign countries than in the United States. *See Terrorism Hearings, supra* note 68, at 4026.

108. TIME, Jan. 14, 1974, at 25.

109. *See* STAFF STUDY, *supra* note 22, at 14.

110. DEP'T OF STATE NEWSLETTER, June 1976, at 27, col. 3.

111. *Id.*, at 27, cols. 2-3.

112. Visiting foreign heads of state remain within the jurisdiction of the Secret Service.

113. *See International Terrorism Hearings, supra* note 23, at 212-14, 247-48 (testimony of the former CCT coordinator, R. Fearey, and of his predecessor, Ambassador Hoffacker).

114. *See id.* at 214; *reprinted in Terrorism Hearings, supra* note 68, at 4125-30.

115. DEP'T OF STATE, TASK FORCE REPORT RE INFORMATION SYSTEMS AND THE DEPARTMENT OF STATE'S COUNTER-TERRORISM PROGRAMS, §§ I, V (1976).

116. Interview with Department of State official.

117. *Id. See also* note 115 *supra*, at §§ I, VI.

118. *See* BUSINESS WEEK, Sept. 29, 1973, at 93.

119. *See* pp. 422-423 *supra* and conclusions to the previous section on internal security.

120. The ATA Security Committee apparently was not used initially, however, to develop the preboard screening procedures.

121. *See* Chicago Tribune, Aug. 15, 1976, at 18, cols. 1-3.

122. *See also Terrorism Hearings, supra* note 68, at 4026, 4028.

123. *See id.* at 4011 (testimony of H. Murphy, director of security, ATA).

124. J.A.F. Kelly, A Resource to Counter Criminal Threats and Attacks Against the Security Environment of Corporations and Institutions (unpublished proposal, 1974).

125. The formation of multidisciplinary study-action teams for consultation in crisis situations is supported throughout the Terrorism Hearings, *supra* note 68, *e.g.*, at 2959, 2995-99, 3008f, 3957, 4163f.

126. *See id.* at 3956, 3959 (testimony of H.L. Pizer, director of security for Braniff International). *See also id.* at 3984, 4026.

127. *See id.* at 3959 (testimony of Pizer).

128. *See* pp. 407-408 *supra.*

129. J.B. Bell in panel discussion of International Press Institute, Christian Science Monitor, May 18, 1976, at 16. *See also Terrorism Hearings, supra* note 68, at 2986, 4027.

130. B. JENKINS, *supra* note 3, at 3; MILBANK, *supra* note 15, at 3.

131. *See* pp. 407-408 *supra.*

132. *See* STAFF STUDY, *supra* note 22, at 13.

133. *See, e.g.*, Washington Post, June 19, 1975, at A28 (Montoneros's statement re Bunge & Born Ltd. kidnaping in Argentina); and N.Y. Times, Apr. 6, 1976, at 59 (Revolutionary Command Argimiro Gabaldon's statement re Owens-Illinois kidnaping in Venezuela).

134. *See* STAFF STUDY, *supra* note 22, at 15.

135. *See* pp. 409-410 *supra.*

136. *See* note 133 *supra.*

137. *Terroristic Activity, Hostage Defense Measures: Hearings Before the Subcomm. to Investigate the Administration of the Internal Security Act and Other Internal Security Laws of the Senate Comm. on the Judiciary*, 94th Cong., 1st Sess., 261, 273f (testimony of Brooks McClure) [hereinafter cited as *Hostage Hearings*].

138. *Id.*

139. *Id.* at 275f.

140. *Terrorist Activity Hearings Before the Subcomm. to Investigate the Administration of the Internal Security Act and Other Internal Security Laws of the Senate Comm. on the Judiciary*, 93rd Cong., 2d Sess., 155, 158 (testimony of Dr. Frederick Schwartz) [hereinafter cited as *Schwartz Testimony*].

141. *See Terrorism Hearings, supra* note 68, at 2971.

142. *See* the Draft Card Burning Cases: United States v. O'Brien, 391 U.S. 367, 20 L.Ed 2d 672 (1968); and United States v. Kiger, 297 F. Supp. 339 (S.D.N.Y. 1969), *appeal denied*, 421 F.2d 1396 (2d Cir. 1970), *cert. denied*, 398 U.S. 904 (1970).

143. *But cf.* the separate opinion of Justice Harlan in *O'Brien, id.*, at 388f, who did not wish to foreclose consideration of a First Amendment claim "in those rare instances when an 'incidental' restriction upon expression imposed by governmental regulation . . . has the effect of entirely preventing a 'speaker' from reaching a significant audience with whom he could not otherwise *lawfully* communicate" [emphasis added]. *See* J. BARRON, FREEDOM OF THE PRESS FOR WHOM? 117-125 (1973).

144. Not only have the terrorists attempted to exploit the media to their advantage, but the Niehous family and Owens-Illinois have used it to air their views and, indeed, to undercut the position of the terrorists in the public mind. *See* pp. 419-420 *supra; e.g.*, El Nacional (Venezuela), Mar. 13, 1976, at D16; Mar. 17, 1976, at D14-16; Mar. 25, 1976, at D20; Mar. 30, 1976, at D13, 16; Apr. 7, 1976, at A1.

145. *See* EDITOR AND PUBLISHER, June 22, 1974, at 16. The *Tribune* acknowledged that "its activities in gathering the facts for the story in question may have been overzealous"; *see also, How Not to Cover a Kidnapping*, 103 TIME 44 (April 18, 1974).

146. JENKINS, JOHNSON, & RONFELDT, *supra* note 65, at 22.

147. Johnson, *supra* note 18, at 17, 21. *See also* MILBANK *supra* note 15, at 30, col. 2; *id.* at 32, col. 2; Crozier, *supra* note 18, at 17; *Terrorism Hearings, supra* note 68, at 3025 (testimony of Frederick J. Hacker).

148. *See* CLUTTERBUCK, *supra* note 16, at 24; *Terrorism Hearings, supra* note 68, at 4025.

149. EDITOR & PUBLISHER, Nov. 30, 1974, at 15.

150. *See* 47 U.S.C. § § 303, 306-07, 326 (1976); Brenner, *The Limits of Broadcast Self-Regulation Under the First Amendment*, 28 FED. COMMUNICATION BAR J. 1, 2 (1975).

151. NATIONAL ASSOCIATION OF BROADCASTERS, THE TELEVISION CODE 7 (19th ed. 1976) [hereinafter cited as NAB CODE].

152. *See* Mass Universalist Convention v. Hildreth, 87 F. Supp. 822 (D. Mass. 1949), *aff'd* 183 F.2d 497 (1st Cir. 1950) (broadcaster may not delegate the program selection duty to a network or indirectly to an advertising agency). *See also* CBS v. Democratic Nat'l Comm., 412 U.S. 94, 105 (1973).

153. NAB CODE, *supra* note 151, at 7, ch. V. *Cf.* Brenner, *supra* note 150 at 40-62, challenging the constitutionality of the programming prescriptions in the code; and the recent decision in Writers Guild v. F.C.C. (C.D. Cal., 1976), concluding that the adoption of the "family hour" viewing provisions in the NAB code violated the First Amendment because it was done in response to FCC pressure.

154. EDITOR & PUBLISHER, Nov. 30, 1974, at 15.

155. NAB CODE, *supra* note 151, at 7-8 (ch. v).

156. CLUTTERBUCK, *supra* note 16, at 147.

157. EDITOR & PUBLISHER, Dec. 27, 1975, at 32.

158. *See* pp. 419-420, 439 *supra.*

159. *International Terrorism Hearings, supra* note 23, at 189 (testimony of Brian Crozier).

160. *See Terrorism Hearings, supra* note 68, at 3988; NAB CODE, *supra* note 151, at 4 (ch. IV-1).

161. Chicago Tribune, Sept. 19, 1976, at F-4, col. 1.

162. N.Y. Times, Apr. 7, 1976, at 57, col. 4.

163. EDITOR & PUBLISHER, Dec. 27, 1975, at 36.

164. *See* El Tiempo, May 16, 1976, at 6-A, cols. 3-4 (Colombia); N.Y. Times, Apr. 7, 1976, at 60, col. 4.

165. *See* comments of R. Mulder at Seminar of International Press Institute, Christian Science Monitor, May 18, 1976, at 16.

166. *See International Terrorism Hearings, supra* note 23, at 206 (testimony of Brian Crozier).

167. *See* pp. 419-420, 439 *supra.*

168. *See Terrorism Hearings, supra* note 68, at 4002.

169. McGuire, *supra* note 67. *See also* BUSINESS WEEK, Apr. 20, 1974, at 95.

170. McGuire, *supra* note 67. BUSINESS WEEK, *supra* note 169, at 95-96 95-96.

171. Treas. Reg. § 1.162-1 (1975).

172. *See* Rev. Rul. 112, 1972-1 C.B. 60.

173. BUSINESS WEEK, Apr. 20, 1974, at 95.

174. See *id.* at 96.

175. *Id.* at 95.

176. *But cf.* pp. 456-457, *infra.*

177. *But cf.* C. Johnson, *supra* note 18, at 26.

178. *See* Treaty Establishing the European Economic Community, signed at Rome, Mar. 25, 1957, arts. 52-66, 295 U.N.T.S. 2.

179. 1 OPPENHEIM'S INTERNATIONAL LAW 675-76 (8th ed., H. Lauterpacht ed. 1963) [hereinafter cited as 1 OPPENHEIM]; *but cf.* 2 D.P. O'CONNELL, INTERNATIONAL LAW 753-54 (1965).

180. 1 OPPENHEIM, *supra* note 179, at 686-88; O'CONNELL, *supra* note 179, at 1019-25.

181. *See* O'CONNELL, *supra* note 179, at 1021; Affaire des biens Britanniques au Maroc Espagnol (Espagne v. Royaume-Uni), 2 R. INT'L ARB. AWARDS 615 (1925).

182. 1 OPPENHEIM, *supra* note 179, at 1022; *see generally id.* at 751-65.

183. *See, e.g.*, Brower & Tepe, *The Charter of Economic Rights and Duties: A Reflection or Rejection of International Law*, 9 INT'L LAWYER 295, 302ff (1975); remarks of Rubin, Garcia Robles, & Brower, *The Charter of Economic Rights and Duties of States*, AM SOC'Y INT'L L. PROC. 227-34 (1975).

184. Charter of Economic Rights and Duties of States, arts. 2 (a)(b), G.A. Res. 3281, 29 U.N. GAOR, Supp. (No. 31) 50, 52, U.N. Doc. A/9631 (1974).

185. *See* J.L. BRIERLY, THE LAW OF NATIONS 110 (6th ed. 1963) (recommendatory force); R. HIGGINS, THE DEVELOPMENT OF LAW THROUGH THE POLITICAL ORGANS OF THE UNITED NATIONS 5 (1963) ("rich source of evidence"); Falk, *On the Quasi-Legislative Competence of the General Assembly*, 60 AM. J. INT'L L. 782, 790 (1966) (contribute to a process of norm-creation).

186. O'CONNELL, *supra* note 179, at 1035. *See also* 1 OPPENHEIM, *supra* note 179, at 687f.

187. *See* Sarropoulos v. Bulgarian State, 4 Ann. Dig. 263 (Greco-Bulgarian Mixed Arb. Trib. 1927) (special obligation on state to protect aliens from rioters may arise where persons of one nationality are singled out for injury). *See also* O'CONNELL, *supra* note 179, at 1049.

188. *See* O'CONNELL, *supra* note 179, at 1035 [point 2(b)] ; 1 OPPENHEIM, *supra* note 179, at 689.

189. *Id.*; O'CONNELL, *supra* note 179, at 1019f.

190. *See* Affaire des biens Britanniques au Maroc Espagnol, *supra* note 181, where the Claims Commission pointed out that "the State must be considered as obliged to exercise vigilance of a superior order to prevent crimes committed in violation of military discipline." At the same time, the commission had to look at "what was the duty of a commanding officer under the circumstances. . . ." *See also* O'CONNELL, *supra* note 179, at 1021, 1023, 1047.

191. *See generally* O'CONNELL, *supra* note 179, at 1047, 1049-51.

192. *See id.* at 1048; the cases listed Harvard Law School, *Research in International Law, Responsibility, States*, 23 AM. J. INT'L L., SP. SUPP. 192 *et seq.* (1929).

193. *See* STAFF STUDY, *supra* note 22, at 14.

194. *See Terrorism Hearings, supra* note 68, at 4026.

195. *See* 1 OPPENHEIM, *supra* note 179, at 686ff; O'CONNELL, *supra* note 179, at 1113-17, 1124-34. "U.S. Government Policy Guidelines for Dealing With Terrorism Involving American Citizens Abroad" states: "If terrorists seize Americans abroad, our Government reminds the host government of its primary responsibility to cope with such terrorists and to effect the safe release of the American hostages, whether they enjoy diplomatic status or otherwise." *See International Terrorism Hearings, supra* note 23, at 231.

196. *See Terrorism Hearings, supra* note 68, at 4475 (testimony of Brian Jenkins), based on 647 cases of ransom kidnaping over the previous 30 years; and McGuire, *supra* note 67.

197. Fearey, *Terrorism: Growing and Increasingly Dangerous*, U.S. NEWS & WORLD REP., Sept. 29, 1975, at 79. *See also* JENKINS, JOHNSON, & RONFELDT, *supra* note 65, at 25.

198. JENKINS, JOHNSON, & RONFELDT, *supra* note 65, at 30. *See also* B. Crozier, *supra* note 18, at 22-27, and C. Johnson, *supra* note 18, at 25-28.

199. *See* note 1 *supra* at 7.

200. *See* B. Crozier, *supra* note 18, at 22-27; C. Johnson, *supra* note 18, at 25-28.

201. *See* Evans, *Aircraft and Aviation Facilities* ch. 1 of this report, at 11. The decrease in hijacking incidents was helped also by the U.S.-Cuban accord, which denied hijackers asylum in either country, and the Anti-Hijacking Act of 1974, which provides for sanctions against countries that harbor hijackers.

202. Based on an update of U.S. Department of State figures, which are reported in BELL, *supra* note 18, at 83.

203. *See* International Terrorism Hearings, *supra* note 23, at 213f, 227-29, 235f, 247f, 254f.

204. *See id.* at 212-14, 228, 240, 248, 254.

205. *See* various proposals in *Terrorism Hearings, supra* note 68, at 2995-99, 3008f, 4163f.

206. *But cf. id.* at 3988.

207. *See id.* at 4027.

208. *Id.* at 3957 (testimony of Braniff International director of security).

209. *See id.*, but limited to the instruction of law enforcement officers.

210. *Id.*

211. *See* pp. 429-433 *supra.*

212. *See Terrorism Hearings, supra* note 68, at 4134f, citing results of a study by the Rand Corporation.

213. *See id.* at 4134-36, 4141, 4149, 4340f.

214. *See* p. 412 *supra.*

215. *International Terrorism Hearings, supra* note 23, at 231.

216. *Id.* It is quite possible, however, that legislation related to "improper payments" or the national emergency powers of the president under the Trading with the Enemy Act of 1917, as amended, could be construed at some point to prohibit ransom payments to terrorist groups.

217. As to Venezuela, *see* N.Y. Times, Apr. 7, 1976, at 55, col. 4; Summary of Responses to Department of State Circular Airgram Regarding Law and Practice on Terrorism, Venezuela, 2-4 (Oct. 1976); as to Colombia, *see* El Tiempo, May 16, 1976, at 1-A, 6-A.

218. This is believed to be true of Argentina. *See* LATIN AMERICA, Oct. 8, 1976, at 306.

219. *See* notes 217 and 218 *supra.*

220. El Tiempo, May 16, at 1-A, 6-A.

221. *See Terrorism Hearings, supra* note 68, at 3973 (testimony of Claude Fly). *See also* JENKINS, JOHNSON, & RONFELDT, *supra* note 65, at 26-29.

222. *Id.* at v, 30.

223. *Id.* at 32.

224. *Id.* at 22.

225. *See* notes 217-218 *supra.*

226. *See* El Tiempo, June 21, 1976, at 2-A, cols. 4 & 5.

227. *See* Jenkins, *Should Corporations Be Prevented From Paying Ransom? reprinted in Terrorism Hearings, supra* note 68, at 4470. Not only was the proposed legislation defeated, but most California corporations themselves apparently opposed it. *Id.* at 4477.

228. *See* El Tiempo, June 22, 1976, at 3-A, cols. 1 & 2.

229. *See* pp. 416-418 *supra.*

230. *See* Editorial, *The Pros and Cons of Paying Ransom*, 1 ASSETS J. 30 (No. 2, 1975).

231. P. Wilkinson, A Fatality of Illusions: Dominant Images of International Terrorism, 14ff. (unpublished paper, 1976).

232. *See* Jenkins, *supra* note 227, at 4473.

233. *See, e.g.,* the Swint murder and its impact on Ford, discussed on pp. 412-413 *supra.*

234. Jenkins, *supra* note 227, at 4477.

235. *See id.* at 4476; LATIN AMERICA, Oct. 6, 1976, at 307.

236. *See* El Tiempo, June 21, 1976, at 2-A, col. 6, where the government acknowledged this practice but denied that the act is confiscatory. The seized funds simply are held by the court for the duration of the investigation.

237. *See* El Tiempo, June 16, 1976, at 1-A, col. 5; 6-A, cols. 1 & 7.

238. El Tiempo, May 16, 1976, at 6-A, col. 4.

239. *See* N.Y. Times, Apr. 7, 1976, at 57, cols. 2 & 4.

240. *See* JENKINS, *supra* note 3, at 14; MILBANK, *supra* note 15, at 23, 26.

241. *See* MILBANK, *supra* note 15, at 12, 33.

242. *See* the analysis of Franck & Lockwood, *Preliminary Thoughts Towards an International Convention on Terrorism*, 68 AM. J. INT'L L. 69, 72-74, and 87ff (1974).

243. U.N. Doc. A/CONF.56/3, at 35f (1975) [hereinafter cited as Fifth U.N. Congress].

244. U.N. Doc. A/C.6/418, *supra* note 1, at 7.

245. *See generally* M.C. BASSIOUNI, INTERNATIONAL EXTRADITION AND WORLD PUBLIC ORDER 368-434 (1974).

246. Fifth U.N. Congress, *supra* note 243, at 35. *See also* Franck & Lockwood, *supra* note 242, at 84f.

247. Draft Statute for an international criminal court, art. 1, in R. WOETZEL, THE ESTABLISHMENT OF AN INTERNATIONAL CRIMINAL COURT, 13 (1971).

248. Draft Statute, arts. 1 and 10, *id.* at 13ff.

249. Fifth U.N. Congress, *supra* note 243, at 36, referring to Hague (1970) and Montreal (1971) conventions against aircraft hijacking and violence on board aircraft.

250. *See* pp. 448-450 *supra.*

251. *See* pp. 448-449 *supra.*

252. *See* O'CONNELL, *supra* note 179, at 1035, 1047ff.

253. *Id.*

**Part II
Prevention and Control
of Terrorism:
International
Responses**

8

An International Control Scheme for the Prosecution of International Terrorism: An Introduction

M. Chérif Bassiouni

A Working Definition of International Terrorism

Violations of the law of armed conflicts are not subject to the law of peace. Even though such violations would be in the nature of war crimes and subject to special prescriptions, their prevention and suppression relies on the same control scheme covering other international crimes.[1] The definition of international terrorism used in this chapter is designed, therefore, to include terror-violence activities committed by individuals acting for or on behalf of a state as well as individuals whose activities are regulated by the law of armed conflicts, including conflicts of a noninternational character such as certain wars of national liberation. Thus for the purposes of this chapter, "international terrorism" will be defined as a strategy of terror-inspiring violence containing an international element and committed by individuals to produce power outcomes.

International terrorism occurs when an unlawful act of violence is directed against an internationally protected target or person or when a crime of violence defined by municipal law is committed in a manner that affects the interests of more than one state. Existing national and international prescriptions, which fall into the same two categories as above, were developed to regulate international cooperation for the prevention and control of international terrorism with the objective of bringing persons accused of such offenses to trial. The guiding principle, therefore, has been *aut dedere, aut judicare*, as developed by Hugo Grotius in 1624.[2] In this frame of reference, the nature and function of an international control scheme for the prosecution of international terrorists will be examined as an introduction to the subsequent chapters on the prevention and control of international terrorism.

Prosecuting Terrorists: An International Control Scheme[3]

At present, international cooperation for the control and prevention of international criminal activity is indirect. No international body or structure can promulgate, or enforce, laws against existing international crimes. A semblance of international control is achieved only through the voluntary cooperation of states that, by becoming parties to certain treaties, pledge to use their domestic processes to prosecute or assist another state in prosecuting an accused offender by providing extradition.[4]

Beyond extradition, existing international treaty obligations require only the most rudimentary international cooperation in penal matters concerning protected targets and persons,[5] or municipal crimes of terror-violence that have an international element.[6] In both cases, cooperation, if it exists at all, usually is based on multilateral or bilateral treaties and on the national laws and practices of the states in question.

International judicial assistance and cooperation in penal matters other than extradition cover a wide range of techniques, but their application is limited even with respect to countries that engage in them.[7] Several methods of cooperation that should be encouraged include:

1. direct exchange of information by law enforcement agencies
2. sharing information through Interpol
3. taking testimony abroad
4. recognizing foreign penal judgments
5. executing sentences abroad
6. transmitting criminal proceedings
7. supervising the conditionally released abroad
8. securing evidence by one country in favor of another and transmitting it thereto

If applied, these methods could facilitate the effective prosecution of accused terrorists; however, such international cooperation depends on the good will of the states involved. To illustrate that point, it is important to examine its application to the two categories of international terrorism referred to above.

Internationally Protected Targets and Persons and the Duty To Prosecute or Extradite

This category of international prescriptions usually covers activities that constitute a common crime in the domestic criminal laws of all countries of the world in addition to being criminalized by the relevant international treaties. Thus there is little need for substantive criminal law in these areas, even though special legislation may have its advantages in some legal systems. This category of internationally defined crimes does not rely on a direct international enforcement scheme; instead, it employs an indirect enforcement scheme that relies on the municipal criminal processes of the states that adhere to the international treaty or practice the international customary law in question. This category is presently limited to three subjects: (1) hijacking and its related offenses;[8] (2) kidnaping of diplomatic personnel;[9] and (3) protected persons and targets under the Four Geneva Conventions of August 12, 1949, and the Laws and Customs of War.[10]

All these treaties prohibit *inter alia* violence against certain internationally protected targets and persons and require states to "prosecute or extradite" (*aut dedere, aut judicare*). This indirect enforcement scheme requires a state to use its domestic processes (criminal and administrative) to prosecute a violator under its municipal criminal laws (but without requiring any specific penalty) or to extradite the offender to another state for prosecution in accordance with the legal processes of the prosecuting state. As the principle of universality of jurisdiction is implicitly recognized with respect to all three subjects listed above, there is no problem with respect to subject-matter jurisdiction.[11] *In personam* jurisdiction, however, can be assured only through extradition with that process's manifold cumbersome procedures and limitations. Indeed, in all international treaties in force that contain an extradition provision, the duty to extradite is not absolute but is subject to the limitations contained in the laws and practices of the requested state. Among the relevant limitations that exist in various legal systems are (1) the prohibition of extradition of nationals, (2) the prohibition of extradition where the death penalty could be imposed by the requesting state, and (3) the "political-offense exception." The first two limitations may be found in the constitutions, laws, and practices of many states, but the third one—namely, the "political-offense exception"—is universally recognized.[12]

Ideally, the thrust of an international "duty" to extradite, in the absence of the prosecution of those who commit international crimes, should not allow such unbridled limitations, particularly the political-offense exception.[13] This latter limitation is the main impediment to the effective fulfillment of the relevant treaty obligations and of the customary duty to extradite violators of international criminal law so that they may stand trial for their conduct. To that extent, there is a conflict between the duty to extradite such offenders and the right of the requested state to refuse to do so on grounds of the political-offense exception. A question arises, therefore, as to whether the duty to extradite in the case of international crimes does not limit a state's right to deny extradition on the grounds of the political-offense exception. Such a norm would derive from the doctrine of the "exception to the exception," which holds that international crimes should not benefit from being characterized as political offenses, but should be the object of mandatory extradition for prosecution in the requesting state in the absence of prosecution in the requested state.[14] While there is a growing international trend toward the recognition of this doctrine, it is debatable whether it has been incorporated in the treaties protecting certain international targets and persons. It is also questionable whether the doctrine constitutes customary international law as evidenced by the consistent practice of states, although support for such a conclusion may be found in the writing of distinguished publicists.

Thus in this category of international prescription for the prevention and control of international terrorism, the international enforcement scheme relies almost exclusively on the extradition laws and practices of interested countries. Although extradition is supposed to be the principal instrument of mutual cooperation between states for the prosecution of accused terrorists, its cumbersome practice has paradoxically become the means by which such prosecution is thwarted. As a consequence, there has been an increasing reliance by some states, including the United States, on alternative means to secure *in personam* jurisdiction of the person sought to be prosecuted, namely, misuse of immigration laws and resort to unlawful seizures of persons.[15] Both practices are incompatible with the concept of fairness, and the second practice violates international due process of law and should not be encouraged. To prevent such practices, more flexible extradition procedures should be established by interested states.

It is also noteworthy that up to this point, no international treaty that covers any of the three subject matters of this category of international terrorism includes a duty of judicial assistance and other forms of cooperation in penal matters. Such a duty, if it exists, is based on other multilateral or bilateral treaties or customary practices whenever they apply.

Municipal Crimes of Violence Having an
International Element

This type of activity is not directed against internationally protected targets and persons as defined by the relevant international treaties, referred to earlier. Instead, it constitutes almost exclusively a violation of the municipal criminal laws of a given state but in addition thereto contains an international element. Such an international element exists when:

1. the conduct in question takes place in more than one state
2. the conduct in question affects nationals of more than one state
3. the conduct in question affects the security or economic interests of more than one state

In these cases, an international interest exists, which should be translated into an international *civitas maxima* to cooperate in the prevention and control of such activities.[16] The methods of cooperation between interested states manifest themselves in the practice of extradition and other forms of judicial assistance and mutual cooperation in penal matters. In this category of violations, as in the category discussed above covering conduct affecting internationally protected targets and persons, the national laws and practices of states with respect to extradition and other forms of judicial assistance and cooperation in penal matters are controlling. However, this category of offenses, unlike the first one, does not carry an international duty to prosecute or to extradite. The practice of extradition, as well as other modalities of cooperation in penal matters, exclusively depends on the bilateral relations of the interested states. In this category of offenses, as in the first one, the limitations to extradition are the same, and the political-offense exception remains the principal obstacle to extradition. Thus the goal of prosecuting such offenders is thwarted by considerations that are unrelated to the criminal activity sought to be prevented and controlled.

Conclusions

1. The processes of extradition are cumbersome and need to be streamlined.
2. The political-offense exception is a serious impediment to the effectiveness of that process and a limitation thereto has to be developed.
3. Judicial assistance and other forms of cooperation in penal matters are varied but seldom employed.
4. Increased cooperation in penal matters is a more viable policy alternative than the attempt to elaborate substantive international treaties on terrorism.
5. Few international treaties in the field of international criminal law contain provisions on judicial assistance and other forms of cooperation in penal matters, and that gap should be filled.
6. There are multiple agencies in the United States interested in the enforcement of international criminal law. Their interests and activities are overlapping and uncoordinated. The United States is insufficiently involved, at the governmental level, in international criminal law activities throughout the world, particularly with respect to its representation at international conferences.

Recommendations

On the basis of the preceding conclusions, the following recommendations are made:

1. The elaboration of a multilateral treaty on the establishment of the doctrine of "exception to the political-offense exception" in extradition, which would list the internationally recognized crimes that are to be excluded from the political-offense-exception existing in the treaties, laws, and practices of states.

2. The convening of an international conference of government legal experts on the topic of judicial assistance and other forms of cooperation in penal matters. Such a conference should prepare a Draft Treaty on Judicial Assistance and Other Forms of Cooperation in Penal Matters.

Notes

1. M.C. BASSIOUNI, INTERNATIONAL TERRORISM AND POLITICAL CRIMES xi-xxii (1975) [hereinafter cited as INTERNATIONAL TERRORISM].

2. This maxim is attributed to Hugo Grotius, *De Jure Belli ac Pacis* (1624). It has often been erroneously referred to as *aut dedere, aut punire.*

3. Bassiouni, *The Growth and Developing Trends of International Criminal Law*, 45 REVUE INTERNATIONAL DE DROIT PENAL 405 (1974). For an examination of this scheme with respect to international control of drugs, *see* Bassiouni, *The International Narcotics Control System: A Proposal.* 46 ST. JOHN'S L. REV. 713 (1972); Maas, *Alternatives to Indirect Control of International Narcotics Traffic*, 8 N.Y.J. INT'L & POL. 241 (1975).

4. *See* M.C. BASSIOUNI, INTERNATIONAL EXTRADITION AND WORLD PUBLIC ORDER (1974) [hereinafter cited as EXTRADITION]; I.A. SHEARER, EXTRADITION IN INTERNATIONAL LAW (1971).

5. *See* pp. 486-488 *infra.*

6. *See* pp. 488-489 *infra.*

7. Grützner, *International Judicial Assistance and Cooperation in Criminal Matters*, in 2 A TREATISE ON INTERNATIONAL CRIMINAL LAW 189-249 (M.C. Bassiouni & V. Nanda eds. 1973) [hereinafter cited as TREATISE], and his multivolume series, INTERNATIONALER RECHTSHILFEVERKEHR IM STRAFRECHT, continued by P.G. Potz.

8. *See* Evans *Aircraft and Aviation Facilities*, ch. 1 in this report; Evans, *Aircraft Hijacking—What is Being Done*, in INTERNATIONAL TERRORISM, *supra* note 1; L. BLOOMFIELD & G. FITZGERALD, CRIMES AGAINST INTERNATIONALLY PROTECTED PERSONS (1975).

9. *See* J.F. Murphy, *Protected Persons and Diplomatic Facilities*, ch. 5 in this report; James Murphy, *Role of International Law in the Prevention of Terrorist Kidnaping of Diplomatic Personnel*, in INTERNATIONAL TERRORISM, *supra* note 1, at 285.

10. *See* Toman, *Terrorism and the Regulation of Armed Conflicts*, in INTERNATIONAL TERRORISM, *supra* note 1, at 133. For the Amendments to the Four Geneva Conventions of August 12, 1949, *see also* Draft Protocol Additional to the Geneva Conventions of August 12, 1949, and Relating to the Protection of Victims of International Armed Conflicts, June 1973, arts. 74-79, INTERNATIONAL COMMITTEE OF THE RED CROSS, DRAFT ADDI-

TIONAL PROTOCOLS TO THE GENEVA CONVENTIONS OF AUGUST 12, 1949, at 3 (1973), and for a commentary thereon *see* Bassiouni, *The Enforcement Provisions of the Draft Additional Protocol, Protocol I, to the Geneva Conventions of August 12, 1949*, in 8 RUTGERS-CAMDEN, L.J. 185 (1976).

11. Feller, *Jurisdiction over Offenses with a Foreign Element*, in TREATISE, *supra* note 7, at 5 *et seq.*; DeSchutter, *Problems of Jurisdiction in the International Control and Repression of Terrorism*, in INTERNATIONAL TERRORISM, *supra* note 1, at 377.

12. EXTRADITION, *supra* note 4, at 370-488.

13. This theory was advanced by this writer at the 1968 Preparatory Colloquium to the Tenth International Congress on Penal Law and first appeared in print in 47 REVUE INTERNATIONALE DE DROIT PENAL (1968) and thereafter in TREATISE, *supra* note 7, at 416-25. *See also* the European Convention on the Suppression of Terrorism, Jan. 27, 1977, E.T.S. No. 90.

14. O'Higgins, *Unlawful Seizure of Persons by States*, in INTERNATIONAL TERRORISM, *supra* note 1, at 336-42. *See also Enforcement Provisions, supra* note 10, at 121-201; United States v. Toscanino, 500 F.2d 267 (2d Cir. 1974); *In re David*, 390 F. Supp. 521 (E.D. Ill. 1975); *In re Extradition of David*, 395 F. Supp. 803 (E.D. Ill. 1975); United States v. Lira, 515 F.2d 68 (2d Cir. 1975); United States v. Quesada, 512 F.2d 1043 (5th Cir. 1975); United States v. Caramainan, 468 F.2d. 3170 (5th Cir. 1972); United States v. Vicars, 467 F.2d. 452 (5th Cir. 1972); Frisbie v. Collins, 342 U.S. 519 (1952); Ker v. Illinois, 119 U.S. 436 (1886).

15. *See* Feller, *supra* note 11.

16. Bassiouni, *World Public Order and Extradition: A Conceptual Evaluation*, in AKTUELLE PROBLEME DES INTERNATIONALEN STRAFRECHTS 107 (D. Oehler & P.G. Potz eds. 1970).

The Apprehension and Prosecution of Offenders: Some Current Problems

Alona E. Evans

Apprehension

Practice

The Apprehension and prosecution of offenders is the one means of control of international terrorism that has the advantages of being easily comprehended and apparently relatively uncomplicated. In fact, the injunction to "extradite or submit to prosecution" persons accused of international terrorist acts is appearing in an increasing number of multilateral and bilateral treaties.[1] The question is whether this injunction is balanced by consideration of the realities of the situation that it comprehends or whether it is simply a convenient rule of thumb for treaty draftsmen. Before this rule becomes a maxim for treaty texts concerning matters of international criminal law relative to international terrorists, it would be well to make sure that the injunction is meaningful from a practical point of view. That is, whether in contemplating the apprehension of offenders, "extradition" is the term that is wanted or whether the concern is for "lawful return," and whether, in supplying an alternative to apprehension, "submit to prosecution" is recognized as being a concept that is open to widely varying interpretations reflecting particularist moral principles, legal precepts, political practices, and other considerations. If the scope and limits of these expressions are not appreciated, the results, in practical terms, may make for unnecessarily strained relations among states, while within states having a strong emphasis on individual rights and guarantees, there will be a fomentation of litigation as apprehended offenders object to alleged infringements of these rights and guarantees.[2]

In international practice, the apprehension of offenders comprehends formal and informal processes as well as illegal methods of return. Extradition may be denominated as the only "formal" or "legal" method of apprehension. The extradition process, which is spelled out in treaties, statutes, or codes of criminal procedure,[3] operates within a framework of customary rules regarding such matters as double criminality, *non bis in idem*, specialty, provisional detention, evidentiary requirements, third-party requests, prescription, expenses, as well as various kinds of exemptions, *e.g.*, nationals of the requested state or political offenders. The treaty texts, statutes, or codes of criminal procedure may vary as to details; however, essentially, there is a "common law" of

493

extradition.[4] But extradition is by no means the most practical method for the international apprehension of offenders. Without dwelling at this point on the operation of extradition, suffice it to say that from the moment that an accused is discovered to be within the requested state to the dispatch of the accused to the requesting state in the custody of agents of that state, there is ample opportunity for the extradition process to fail, and fail it does with ordinary offenders.[5] Where the apprehension of an international terrorist is the objective, factors of foreign and domestic politics impinge upon the extradition process and often outweigh any concern for extradition as a means of carrying out a state's obligation as a member of the international community to enforce its commitments with respect to this aspect of international criminal law.[6]

What are the alternatives to extradition? Where there is concern for legal niceties, "informal" methods of return—*i.e.*, by exclusion or expulsion (deportation)—furnish the most convenient procedures, due allowance being made for the particularities of national immigration laws[7] and the strictures of the Convention and Protocol on the Status of Refugees.[8] That deportation is an administrative process, essentially civil in nature, that has not been designed as a surrogate for extradition, which is a criminal process, is an argument that does not outweigh its convenience in practice.

Classifying extradition and deportation as "lawful" methods of apprehension and recognizing that lawfulness of apprehension is a matter of concern in countries such as the United States where the accused may challenge the circumstances of his return as a defense to prosecution,[9] the only other method of apprehension is unlawful, *i.e.*, resort to kidnaping, violence, or "voluntary" return that has been induced by threats of force, blackmail, and similar acts. Depending on the level of the criminal justice systems in the deporting state and the state of destination, these methods are hardly viable alternatives. And their negative impact on relations between the states concerned may be of greater international significance than the affirmative impact of bringing an accused to trial.[10]

An examination of 86 instances of efforts to apprehend international terrorists—including persons accused of such offenses as aircraft hijacking, sabotage of aircraft, attacks on urban airline offices, attacks on air terminals, an attack on an embassy, urban terrorism, and escape *qua* extortionate release from prison—indicates that deportation rather than extradition has been commonly used to acquire custody of such offenders.[11] This is not to suggest, however, that extradition is in desuetude. Between January 1, 1961, and June 30, 1977, 20 states requested the extradition of 87 persons from 21 states.[12] Requests for 6 persons were granted.[13] Requests for the extradition of 75 other persons were denied; it should be added, however, that more than half of these offenders were subsequently submitted to prosecution in the requested state.[14] Extradition is not generally in desuetude, but with regard to international terrorist offenses, it is certainly not an effective means of rendition.

Between January 1, 1961, and June 30, 1977, 145 persons wanted for the commission of international terrorist acts, and many of them wanted on other criminal charges as well, were deported by 28 states to 25 destinations.[15] The grounds for deportation can only be surmised for the most part; certainly many of the deportations simply amounted to ridding the territorial state of an undesirable alien.[16] In one instance, deportation was ordered as part of a terrorist extortion scheme.[17] Even allowing for the scanty data base, deportation is clearly preferred to extradition as the method for apprehending international terrorists. It may be asked why deportation is preferred and why the method of rendition should be a matter of any interest as long as rendition is achieved.

Policy

Extradition versus Deportation. Extradition is part of the criminal justice process, *i.e.*, acquisition of custody of the accused for trial or, where the person has escaped from prison, for completion of his sentence.[18] As mentioned earlier, the extradition process is generally spelled out in bilateral treaties supplemented by statutes or provisions in codes of criminal procedure. The United States, for example, may by law extradite or request extradition only by treaty.[19] Where a state grants extradition to the United States in the absence of a treaty, pursuant to its own laws, such state cannot expect the United States to return the favor by comity or reciprocity.[20] Although the ultimate decision of whether an accused should be surrendered is, generally speaking, a matter for the executive branch, the actual determination of whether a valid claim for surrender has been made by the requesting state is usually a matter for the courts, so that the factor of a strict or moderate interpretation of a given treaty may advance or inhibit the grant of extradition.[21]

Policy considerations can be a substantial bar to extradition. Even where a treaty exists and diplomatic relations obtain between the parties, extradition may be denied on the ostensible grounds that the charge against the accused is political in nature[22] or that extradition formalities have not been complied with[23] or that the accused is being tried in the requested state,[24] whereas the real grounds for the denial of extradition may lie in the Byzantine permutations of daily relations between the requesting and requested states as well as the relations between the requested state and other countries with which it desires to be on cordial terms. The latter point comes to mind in analyzing a French court's denial of the U.S. extradition request in the Holder-Kerkow case on the grounds that their act was political in nature. (Holder and Kerkow had hijacked an aircraft from the United States to Algeria in 1972 and about three years later, the two fugitives had arrived in France from Algeria, voluntarily or otherwise.) Policy considerations also include economic considerations, ranging from concern for the protection of air transport franchises and other trade advantages in a given geographical region to maintaining a bargaining position in regard to foreign economic, technical, and military assistance.

The difficulties inherent in the extradition process cannot be ascribed wholly or in substantial part to policy factors. The extradition process is fraught with opportunities for carelessness or genuine error in the paperwork and in communications between the requesting and requested states. The accused may be inadequately identified; the formal extradition request may be delayed past the time when the accused may be provisionally detained; the formal request may not contain adequate supporting material, such as a description of the offense, the texts of relevant laws, the warrant of arrest, or supporting evidence.[25] The factor of expense may be a deterrent, especially where one of the states of the United States is, in fact, the requesting state. While the recent extradition treaties of the United States with common law countries, following the form of treaties with civil law states, provide for reciprocal assistance by the "appropriate legal officers of the [requested] State" in the extradition process,[26] such expenses as the ascertainment of the whereabouts of the accused, preparation of the request, and transportation of the accused to the requesting state in the company of its authorities become costly. When balanced with consideration of the cost of the subsequent trial process, the expenses may lead to the conclusion that extradition is not worth the effort.[27] It may be added that for his part, a fugitive returned to the United States will have little success in challenging the extradition process in the requested state, as U.S. courts have taken the position that a foreign extradition process cannot be reviewed.[28] Nor can he complain, in contemplation of surrender to a foreign state, that its criminal justice system does not provide the safeguards of the U.S. system.[29]

Deportation provides a useful alternative to extradition in which time and expense are reduced in significance. An alien designated as undesirable or an illegal entrant can be removed from a country in a very short time and without inquiry as to whether the individual is, in fact, "wanted" in the state of destination on criminal charges.[30] Although cordial relations between the deporting state and the state of destination are desirable, strained relations do not necessarily bar the use of deportation, as, for example, where Cuba deported several hijackers to the United States in 1962 and 1970.[31] Moreover, considerations of comity and reciprocity can operate where the United States is involved in deportation as they could not with respect to extradition.[32] Because deportation is a civil proceeding designed to remove from a country an alien who has violated its immigration laws, the thrust of the proceeding is not directed to considerations of criminal law as in extradition. It is difficult for the alien to challenge the procedure and purpose of his deportation. As Circuit Judge Kaufman observed in *United States ex rel. Lujan* v. *Gengler* (where the petitioner sought his release from jail on the ground of rendition by forcible abduction):

In sum, but for the charge that the law was violated during the process of transporting him to the United States, Lujan charges no deprivation greater than that which he would have endured through lawful extradition. We scarcely intend to convey approval of illegal government conduct. But we are forced to recognize that, absent a set of incidents like that in *Toscanino*, not every violation by prosecution or police is so egregious that *Rochin* and its progeny requires nullification of the indictment.[33]

The Defense of the Political Offense. Policy considerations may appear in a different context, *i.e.*, where the accused seeks to block extradition by offering the defense of the political offense. This defense is based on the contention that the act for which the surrender of the accused is sought was a political act; or if such an act had the appearance of a common crime, it was politically motivated; or that while the accused is ostensibly being sought on a charge of a common crime, in fact, he will be tried on political charges in the requesting state. While this is not the place for a disquisition on the nature and scope of the political defense, some aspects of the problem will be examined briefly.

Conventional International Law. Extradition treaties, bilateral and multilateral, as well as extradition statutes and codes of penal procedure, and in some states, constitutional provisions, generally, if not universally, exempt the political offender from extradition. They do not, however, define the political offense affirmatively if at all. Increasingly, treaties and statutory provisions are defining it negatively, *i.e.*, by declaring that certain offenses cannot be classified as "political" offenses. The earliest such exception was made for an attempt on the life of a head of state.[34] In recent years, exceptions have been made for willful crimes against human life,[35] genocide,[36] attacks on internationally protected persons,[37] aircraft hijacking,[38] and violations of the laws of war.[39]

The European Convention on the Suppression of Terrorism, which was adopted by the Council of Europe on November 10, 1976, and signed by 17 of the 19 member states on January 27, 1977,[40] makes a far-reaching statement of exclusion from the classification of "political offense" by providing:

For the purposes of extradition between Contracting States, none of the following offences shall be regarded as a political offence or as an offence connected with a political offence or as an offence inspired by political motives:

a. an offence within the scope of the Convention for the Suppression of Unlawful Seizure of Aircraft, signed at The Hague on 16 December 1970;
b. an offence within the scope of the Convention for the Suppression of Unlawful Acts against the Safety of Civil Aviation, signed at Montreal on 23 September 1971;
c. a serious offence involving an attack against the life, physical integrity or liberty of internationally protected persons, including diplomatic agents;
d. an offence involving kidnaping, the taking of a hostage or serious unlawful detention;

e. an offence involving the use of a bomb, grenade, rocket, automatic firearm or letter or parcel bomb if this use endangers persons;

f. an attempt to commit any of the foregoing offences or participation as an accomplice of a person who commits or attempts to commit such an offence.[41]

The convention invites additional exclusions of acts of violence against persons or property.[42] At the same time, it retreats from the vigor of articles 1 and 2 above by allowing a requested state to weigh the political factor in its consideration of an extradition request:

Nothing in this convention shall be interpreted as imposing an obligation to extradite if the requested state has substantial grounds for believing that the request for extradition for an offence mentioned in Article 1 or 2 has been made for the purpose of prosecuting or punishing a person on account of his race, religion, nationality, or political opinion, or that the person's position may be prejudiced for any of these reason.[43]

This tenor of restraint is followed in respect to the provision for mutual assistance in criminal matters, which may be denied if the requested state has "substantial grounds" for concluding that an extradition request is motivated by political considerations.[44] Restraint is further evidenced in the provision for reservations to extradition for article 1 offenses that a state may consider to be political in character:

[P]rovided that it undertakes to take into due consideration, when evaluating the character of the offence, any particularly serious aspects of the offence, including:

a. that it created a collective danger to the life, physical integrity or liberty of persons; or

b. that it affected persons foreign to the motives behind it; or

c. that cruel or vicious means have been used in the commission of the offence.[45]

It is too soon to know what the fate of this particular treaty will be, *i.e.*, whether member states of the Council of Europe will ratify or approve it with or without reservations to article 1 or whether it will be the prototype for a general treaty for the suppression of international terrorism. The prospects are not promising. The Republic of Ireland, for one, is reported to have refused to sign the convention on the grounds of a constitutional conflict.[46] Apparently, the position was that the convention's provisions regarding political offenses conflicted with the general practice of states that political offenses are not extraditable, which practice is part of the *corpus* of international law to which the Republic is committed under its constitution.[47] While one may understand the political milieu reflected in this point of view, nonetheless it does represent a narrow conception of the nature of international law and the process of its growth.

The French reaction to the convention will be of particular interest, given the controversy over the arrest and subsequent release and expulsion of Abu Daoud, a sometime leader of Al Fatah, who was reported to be implicated in the murders of the 11 Israeli athletes at the Olympic Games in Munich in September 1972.[48]

U.S. Practice. In U.S. practice, the "political offense" is narrowly defined for purposes of extradition. As Circuit Judge Coleman pointed out in *Garcia-Guillern* v. *United States*:

A political offense under the extradition treaties must involve an "uprising" or some other violent political disturbance. Moreover, the act in question must have been incidental to the occurrence in order to justify the exclusion . . . The status of the offense committed, whether a political offense or not, is to be determined by the circumstances attending the alleged crime at the time of its commission. . . .[49]

Where exclusion and expulsion are concerned, a *soi-disant* political refugee has certain options under the U.S. immigration laws, but their availability as a defense of a political nature has been circumscribed in administrative and judicial practice. Following the same rule that obtains in extradition, the alien pleading a political offense must show that his act was "related to a concerted action for a political purpose" and not an independent, individual act.[50] A refugee who has been found to be a deportable alien can petition the attorney general for the withholding of deportation to a destination in which the alien would be "subject to persecution on account of race, religion, or political opinion. . . ."[51] The evidence offered by the petitioner in support of this contention will be weighed against information about political conditions in the state of destination and the alien's particular prospects there, which is known to the Immigration and Naturalization Service or which they may be supplied by the Department of State.[52] The decision is discretionary with the attorney general. It may be asked whether a person accused, for example, of aircraft hijacking, who had entered the United States and had been found to be a deportable alien could successfully seek relief as a refugee from deportation to the state of registration of the aircraft[53] on the contention that he acted for political reasons. Proving prospective persecution as against prospective prosecution for an international terrorist act would be a rather difficult task for the alien and one that would be affected by the current U.S. attitude toward the state of destination.[54] In the case posited, the alien would be caught between Scylla and Charybdis in that he would be liable to prosecution for the offense in the United States under the limited universality jurisdiction provision of the

1970 Hague Convention, assuming that the state of destination was also bound by this convention.[55]

In the threshold or exclusionary situation under U.S. law, an alien can seek classification as a political refugee under § 203(a)(7) of the Immigration and Nationality Act of 1952 as amended in 1965 [8 U.S.C. § 1153(a)(7)].[56] The application, however, must be made elsewhere than in the United States,[57] and it must show that the alien had recently fled a Communist or Communist-dominated state or a state within a designated part of the Middle East for reasons of political, racial, or religious persecution; that he feared to return to this state for the same reasons; and that he had not "firmly resettled" elsewhere before making the application.[58] The burden of proof is on the applicant, and it is not easily carried, so that the political defense would not seem to have much significance in this situation.[59]

Considering the defense of the political offense generally, it is an obvious tactic in a case in which there is an attempt to extradite a person accused of an international terrorist act. The burden of choice of the weight to be given to the plea rests on the requested state and may be affected by considerations ranging from humanitarianism to the dictates of current foreign policy. As suggested above, however, deportation is less responsive to the political offense defense than extradition. But deportation must be consonant with the relevant requirements of the Protocol Relating to the Status of Refugees.

Impact of the Protocol Relating to the Status of Refugees. With respect to the ouster of a refugee, article 32(1) of the Protocol provides that "[t]he Contracting States shall not expel refugees lawfully in their territory save on grounds of national security or public order."[60] It further requires that expulsion be made in accordance with due process of law and that the refugee be granted sufficient time to find a safe destination. The general admonitions of article 32 are strengthened by Article 33(1): "No Contracting State shall expel or return ('refouler') a refugee in any manner whatsoever to the frontiers of territories where his life or freedom would be threatened on account of his race, religion, nationality, membership of a particular social group or political opinion."[61] But a person whom the territorial state deems to be a "danger to ... [its] security ... or ... a danger to the community" cannot benefit by article 33(1).[62]

That the protocol is "consistent with the relevant provisions of the U.S. immigration laws was asserted by the Department of State when this agreement was before the Senate for approval.[63] But the existence of the protocol once it had come into force for the United States did not become a matter of general concern until the Kudirka incident in November 1970. The protocol was not applied in the situation of a Lithuanian seaman, a member of the crew of a Soviet fishing ship, who endeavored to take political asylum on a Coast Guard cutter in U.S. waters.[64] Following this incident, the Department of State formulated a policy regarding the grant of political asylum to refugees for the use of U.S. government personnel faced with such requests in this country or abroad.[65] Among the items of information about the refugee that must be sent to the Department of State are a "[d]escription of any criminal charges known or alleged to be pending against the asylum seeker . . . also any piracy at sea, air piracy, or hijacking background" and "[a]ny Communist Party affiliation or affiliation with other political party; any government office now held or previously occupied."[66] There is no indication as to how this information would be used by the Department of State or the Immigration and Naturalization Service, the latter of which would have jurisdiction over a refugee attempting to enter or found within the United States. The regulations respecting the authority of special inquiry officers in deportation proceedings were amended in 1974 to take specific cognizance of the protocol, but with the proviso that this amendment was "not intended as a concession that in any particular situation Article 32 or 33 enlarges or adds to the rights of an alien under the immigration laws of the United States."[67] It may be added that a similar stringency respecting the protocol was evident in two immigration cases in Canada, in which it was held in administrative proceedings that the term "refugee" should be strictly defined and that the alien had the burden of proof to show that she would suffer "unusual hardship" in being deported to the United States.[68]

The few judicial decisions in which the protocol has been considered in the United States have contributed little to the elucidation of its impact on U.S. extradition or immigration policy or practice with reference to the defense of the political offense. *Nicosia* v. *Wall* would suggest that it may be invoked with respect to extradition; however, the legal effect of the protocol in such proceedings is not clear, as the case was not reheard at the trial level, a failure that may constitute a positive answer.[69] The protocol does not apply in regard to expulsion where an alien becomes deportable on the ground that he is not lawfully in the United States.[70] Neither does it apply in regard to exclusion where a refugee can be shown to have resettled in another country before applying for admission to the United States under conditional entry [203(a)(7); 8 U.S.C. 1153(a)(7)].[71] That the protocol neither endows refugees with full rights under the due process clause of the Fifth Amendment nor abrogates the attorney general's discretionary power to exclude refugees from the country has been recently held by the Court of Appeals for the Fifth Circuit.[72]

Judicial Assistance in Criminal Matters. The term "judicial assistance" will be used here to comprehend arrangements between states for the exchange of information regarding criminal investigations, service of documents, interrogation of witnesses, transfer of criminal proceedings, enforcement of criminal judgments, and transfer and supervision of offenders convicted in the other country. Provision for judicial assistance in criminal matters is well developed in Western Europe,[73] and there is an extensive literature on the subject.[74]

Moreover, certain multilateral agreements concerned with the control of international terrorism specifically refer to the use of judicial assistance among the parties.[75] Apart from some interest in judicial assistance with regard to civil and commercial matters,[76] the United States has not been particularly receptive to international agreements looking to judicial assistance, especially with regard to criminal matters.[77] A change in this attitude, however, can be seen in U.S. conclusion, during 1977, of international agreements for judicial assistance in criminal matters as well as in certain judicial decisions.

The 1973 Treaty on Mutual Assistance in Criminal Matters with Switzerland,[78] which entered into force January 23, 1977, has been described as the "first major international agreement" that the United States has entered for the purpose of "obtaining information and evidence needed for criminal investigations and prosecutions."[79] This treaty provides for assistance in locating the whereabouts of witnesses, taking of testimony, service of judicial and administrative orders, and authentication of records, and it makes special provision for assistance in uncovering organized crime. It is not an extradition agreement, nor does it provide for the execution of penal judgments; rather, it facilitates the acquisition of relevant information about crime, and it facilitates the building of a case against the accused. The treaty exempts from investigation, however, any offenses that the requested state deems to be political in nature or connected therewith unless such offenses can be ascribed to an organized criminal group that uses violence as one of its techniques of action.[80]

Another recent type of judicial assistance agreement is that which is limited to a particular subject of criminal investigation, for example, the agreement concluded by the United States with Canada on March 15, 1977, for the investigation of the Boeing Company's activities.[81] A landmark agreement of a third type was concluded by the United States with Mexico on November 25, 1976. This Treaty on the Execution of Prison Sentences will enable a national and domiciliary of one state who is a prisoner in the other state to return to his own state to serve his sentence. No exchange will be made, however, where a prisoner is serving time for "a political offense within the meaning of the Treaty of Extradition of 1899 between the parties, nor an offense under the immigration or the purely military laws of a party."[82] A similar treaty was concluded with Canada on March 2, 1977.[83]

As a general rule, U.S. courts do not enforce foreign penal judgments,[84] and U.S. law has little reach to judicial assistance in respect of criminal matters.[85] The United States District Court for the Eastern District of Michigan held in 1974, however, that the provision in 28 U.S.C. § 1782 for the issuance of letters rogatory was as much applicable to criminal proceedings as to civil in the absence of any statement to the contrary in the law.[86] In the following year, the Court of Appeals for the Tenth Circuit recognized a penal judgment of an Iranian court as a bar to the payment of Social Security benefits to a survivor who had been convicted in Iran of the murder of the insured.[87]

Extended development and use of various methods of judicial assistance will hardly solve all the problems involved in the apprehension and prosecution of international terrorists. But these methods can serve not only to supplement present lawful means of apprehension and prosecution in practical terms, but more importantly, they may contribute to the development of a positive climate in which such controls of international terrorism can be effectively undertaken. That is, judicial assistance can help to reduce one state's suspicion of another's motives for requesting rendition of an offender or one state's suspicion of another's standards of criminal procedure and penology. Both views inhibit mutual cooperation in carrying out international obligations with regard to the control of international terrorism.

Prosecution

Variations on Prosecution

The purpose of the injunction "extradite or submit to prosecution" is to initiate and carry out criminal proceedings against the international terrorist whether in the requesting state to which he has been extradited or in the requested state that for whatever reason has declined to extradite the offender. Prosecution is the *duty* of states bound by international agreements that contain this formula.

An examination of the several instances of efforts to apprehend international terrorists, to which reference has been made above, shows that although requests for the extradition of 75 offenders were denied, 46 of those accused were subsequently prosecuted or submitted to prosecution in the requested state on international terrorist or related criminal charges.[88] Of the 145 offenders who were deported, 114 were convicted in the state of destination on international terrorist or other criminal charges.[89] Even allowing for the limited statistical base, these figures are probably not out of line with rates for clearances and prosecutions of other offenders charged with serious crimes.[90]

A skeptical attitude is often taken, however, toward the state having custody of a terrorist that refuses extradition, or refrains from deportation, while announcing or intimating that it will prosecute the offender. This skepticism is founded on the reasonable surmise that prosecution, if it takes place at all, will be only *pro forma*. Certainly, this view can be supported by an examination of state practice, *e.g.* the French court's acceptance of a political defense in the *Holder-Kerkow* case, followed by prosecution on the relatively minor charge of passport fraud,[91] or Pakistan's release of six hijackers of an Indian aircraft on the reported grounds that "[t]here ... [was] not sufficient evidence to justify criminal proceedings against the persons involved,"[92] or Libya's apparent reluctance to act on its reported commitment to "[hold] answerable for their activities" two Arab terrorists who had been sentenced to death for their attack on the Athens airport in August 1973, and who were expelled by Greece to Libya as the aftermath of an extortionist attack by three members of the Muslim International Guerrillas against a Greek freighter at Karachi in February 1974.[93]

Not surprisingly, the decision to prosecute an international terrorist is subject to the influence of political pressures arising from concern for the exigencies of current foreign or domestic policy commitments, often compounded by the offender's well-publicized resort to the political defense or by extortionate demands made on the prosecuting state by the accused's foreign or domestic sympathizers, as happened, for example, in the *Pohle* case.[94] That terrorists are prosecuted, however, can also be demonstrated by the record of state practice.

The extended trial in the Federal Republic of Germany of the three principals in the Baader-Meinhof gang is a case in point. The accused were part of an extensive group of "urban guerrillas" whose terrorist activities were by no means confined to West Germany.[95] The three principals, however, were charged with bomb attacks in 1972 on U.S. Army installations as well as on German police stations and businesses, all of which resulted in a number of deaths. The accused were found guilty after 23 months of proceedings, including an unsuccessful application on their part to the European Commission of Human Rights. The commission held as "manifestly ill-founded" the applicants' complaint that as political prisoners they had been deprived of their rights under the Bonn Basic Law and the 1953 European Convention of Human Rights.[96] Rejecting their argument that in killing four U.S. servicemen they were fighting on behalf of North Vietnam, the chief judge of the Stuttgart Court said: "[n]ot everyone can declare himself a subject of international law and declare war on his own."[97] He sentenced them to life imprisonment.[98]

Three terrorists who raided the Syrian Embassy at Rome in October 1976 as a protest against the Syrian attack on Lebanon received a brisk trial before the Corte di Assise of Rome, in which due regard was given to the international responsibility of the state for the protection of diplomats and foreign missions and to the rights of the accused.[99] The trial moved rapidly because the offenders, who were of Lebanese, Syrian, and Palestinian origin, were caught *in flagrante delicto*. They were charged with an offense against the personal freedom of the ambassador, taking of hostages in the embassy, injury to a member of the embassy staff, introduction into the country and possession of illegal arms, and false identification. At their trial, the defendants contended that their acts came within the purview of articles 51 and 52 of the penal code, concerning fulfillment of a duty or exercise of a right, in that they were soldiers engaged in a war or, in the alternative, that they were engaged in the defense of the Palestinian people who were being harassed by the Syrians. The court pointed out that their attack could not be justified as an act of war because it was carried out in a neutral state, nor could it be justified as reaction to acts by

Syria elsewhere. The court observed that although the political motives of the accused were understandable, such motives did not warrant their attack on the public order with "barbaric ferocity" when they could have used more moderate means of expression.[100] The offenders were sentenced to 15 years imprisonment, of which 13 years and 4 months were for the attack on a foreign embassy and an attempt on the life of an ambassador (articles 298, 299, 300, Penal Code).

In the period from March 1973 to February 1977, there were 276 terrorist incidents in England and Wales, involving death or injury to 685 persons.[101] For the most part, these incidents have been charged to or admitted by the Provisional Wing of the Irish Republic Army (Provos). One of the most serious incidents involved two bomb attacks in Birmingham in November 1974, in which 21 persons were killed and some 180 injured. Six Provos were sentenced to life imprisonment without a recommendation of a minimum term following a ten-week trial in 1975.[102] In February 1977, four Provos, charged with committing nine murders in the course of a terrorist rampage in London in 1975, were sentenced to life imprisonment with a minimum term of 30 years.[103] These several instances of prosecution of international terrorists can be multiplied by examples from many countries, including the United States and the Netherlands.[104]

The Problem of Fair Treatment

Whether prosecution of international terrorists can be classified as *pro forma* in some instances or not, there is another problem of much greater concern to the state that contemplates extradition, or it may be deportation, of a terrorist. This is whether the accused will receive "fair treatment at all stages of the proceeding,"[105] or due process of law in U.S. constitutional terms, when submitted to a given country's criminal justice system. There is no doubt that the impact of international terrorism in some countries has resulted in stringent countermeasures that may single out the terrorist for more rigorous treatment in detention or in the judicial process than would be accorded an ordinary offender. For example, the efforts of the United Kingdom to control Irish Republican Army (IRA) terrorism have resulted in the adoption of stringent legislation proscribing membership in the IRA, making fund raising for terrorist purposes an offense, extending the police powers with respect to apprehension of suspects, and establishing limited universal jurisdiction so that courts of Northern Ireland can prosecute terrorists accused of offenses committed in the Republic of Ireland.[106] Moreover, the United Kingdom has admitted that there were grounds for the charges made by the Republic of Ireland before the European Court of Human Rights that the United Kingdom had subjected IRA prisoners in Northern Ireland to torture and other mistreatment in violation of article 3 of the European Convention on Human Rights.[107] The Republic of Ireland, on the other hand, is by no means lenient toward the IRA, which is an outlawed organization; it has established a Special Criminal Court to handle terrorist cases. The number of judges assigned to this court has recently been increased so that the court can sit in two sections.[108]

The Republic of Ireland is not the only state that provides a special court for the trial of terrorists. The first hijacker to be sentenced to death by an Arab state was tried by the State Security Court in Yemen (Sana).[109] The Superior Security Court in Syria took less than 24 hours to prosecute and condemn to death three Iraqi terrorists who had survived their attack on the Semiramis Hotel in Damascus in which 4 of 90 hostages were killed and another 34 wounded.[110] In December 1976, however, Spain abolished its special Court of Public Order, which had had jurisdiction over terrorism and political offenses generally, and placed these offenses within the jurisdiction of the regular courts while giving military courts jurisdiction over offenses by military or paramilitary organizations.[111]

In some states, terrorists are tried before either regular or special military tribunals, where presumably the procedure is more summary than that accorded in the regular courts. Israel uses military tribunals for proceedings involving terrorists, although there is some evidence that the procedures are less than summary.[112] In Iran, nine members of the Islamic Marxists were sentenced to death by firing squad by military courts on charges of murdering three U.S. Army officers and several Iranian nationals as well as other felonies.[113] Military tribunals are also being used for the trials of terrorists in Egypt, the Philippines, and the Central African Republic.[114] Argentina has recently issued a decree giving special military tribunals jurisdiction over "subversives," a term defined as "anyone who wishes to achieve his ideological ends 'by means other than those contained in the rules governing the country's political, economic and social life.' "[115]

The Hazards of Prosecution

Any realistic analysis, skeptical or otherwise, of the prosecution of terrorists, whether in the requesting state or in the requested state that has denied rendition, or in general, must consider the procedural hazards that may arise in any criminal prosecution. In the United States, for example, the factor of discretion on the part of the prosecutor, the defense, and the court dominates the criminal justice system from arraignment through sentencing. The disappearance of witnesses or essential evidence may lead the prosecutor to drop the charges before indictment or information. The accused may turn state's evidence to mitigate his expected punishment, or he may plea bargain for a lesser charge.[116] A defense of temporary insanity may lead to acquittal by a jury. A case fraught with political elements may lead to a hung jury if not to acquittal. Sentencing is as full of variables for the terrorist as for any other offender. In U.S. law, the principal offenses against civil aviation are aircraft piracy, punishable by 20 years of imprisonment up to the death penalty; interference with a flight crew member, punishable by a maximum of 20 years of imprisonment and/or a maximum fine of $10,000; and kidnaping, which is punishable by a maximum sentence of life imprisonment.[117] In practice, the average sentence for aircraft piracy is 22 years; for interference with a flight crew member, 11 years; and for kidnaping, 12 years. Austria, for example, punishes aircraft piracy with sentences of 1 to 10 years or with 5 to 15 years and up to life imprisonment where a death or serious bodily injury occurs during the incident or where a large number of people are involved in it.[118] In February 1977, Austria, while denying the extradition request of Poland for the surrender of a hijacker of a Polish aircraft prosecuted the offender on a charge of aircraft piracy. He was convicted and sentenced to 4 years of imprisonment.[119] In the Netherlands, which has also had considerable experience with aircraft hijacking, the offense is punishable by a maximum sentence of 12 years of imprisonment unless a death occurs during the incident, in which case the sentence can range from 20 years to life.[120] The general range of sentences for aircraft hijacking in states other than the United States is from 3 months to 12 years. The death penalty for aircraft hijacking has been exacted by Cuba, Iran, Jordan, the Philippines, and the Soviet Union.[121] The punitive or deterrent effect of some of these sentences is open to question, but the wide range is simply another illustration of the variables in states' concepts of criminal justice.

The problem is less one of legal controls over a particular offense, *i.e.*, international terrorist acts, than establishing a meeting of minds for the practical enforcement of these legal controls. A greater knowledge of the practical operations of the criminal justice systems of various states, coupled with the widespread development of judicial assistance procedures in criminal matters, would allay much of the reluctance of states to surrender international terrorists by extradition or deportation or to undertake prosecution themselves. Increasing international cooperation in these matters, supported by private as well as governmental research into feasible ways of developing international criminal law and arriving at a minimum standard of criminal justice, is clearly needed before "submit to prosecution" is a widely meaningful part of the treaty formula.

Conclusions

The antiterrorist treaties enjoin member states to extradite offenders or to submit them to prosecution. State practice indicates that deportation is the more common method of rendition of offenders than extradition. Present policies and practices of states with regard to extradition, exclusion, and expulsion should be reviewed for the purpose of establishing a common standard of international rendition. Historical, philosophical, and jurisprudential considerations may prevent states from arriving at an affirmative definition of the political offense, but the defense of the political offense as an obstacle to legal control of international terrorism can be curtailed by selective elimination of offenses from this category in absolute terms, *i.e.*, without exception. Submission of an international terrorist to prosecution is the duty of the state to which he has been surrendered or of the state that, denying rendition, has retained custody of the offender. Where a state has failed to prosecute or has apparently prosecuted *pro forma*, a realistic appraisal of the situation with a view to a policy determination directed against the delinquent state—*e.g.*, the institution of an economic boycott—can be made only on the basis of knowledge of the meaning of "submit to prosecution" in the criminal justice system of the delinquent state. Consequently, there is a need for concerted development of a fund of information about policy and practice regarding the criminal justice systems of civilized states. The grant of political asylum to an offender is a distinctly separate matter from the obligation to submit an offender to prosecution; it must be considered subsequently to prosecution and on different terms. A greater knowledge of the practical operations of the criminal justice systems of various states, coupled with widespread development of judicial assistance procedures in criminal matters, would allay much of the reluctance of states to surrender international terrorists for prosecution or to undertake prosecution themselves. International cooperation looking to the establishment of an international minimum standard of criminal justice is needed before "extradite or submit to prosecution" becomes a widely meaningful formula for the legal control of international terrorism.

Recommendations

1. A study of contemporary policy and practice of states with respect to the use of extradition, exclusion, and expulsion of international terrorists should be undertaken under private or governmental auspices. The study should determine (a) the extent of use of each method as a means of international rendition of such offenders to states where they are wanted for prosecution, and (b) the reasons why extradition appears to be used less frequently than exclusion and expulsion as a means of international rendition. A clearinghouse of information about instances of extradition, exclusion, and expulsion of international terrorists should be established. A suggested location would be the Criminal Justice Division of the Department of Justice.

2. A multilateral convention should establish a common standard regarding the

use of exclusion and expulsion for purposes of international rendition with procedural safeguards for the interests of the offender as well as those of the states involved. Once such a common standard has been established, "lawful return" should be substituted for "extradition" in the treaty injunction "extradite or submit to prosecution."

3. States that are parties to the antiterrorist conventions are under an international obligation to prosecute the offender, whether prosecution follows lawful return or takes place in the state where the offender was found. A clearinghouse of information regarding instances of prosecution of international terrorists should be established with a view to determining (a) the extent to which such prosecution takes place, and (b) the reasons for discrepancies in bringing offenders to trial and in sentencing. A suggested location would be the Criminal Division of the Department of Justice.

4. It should be recognized that the defense of the political offense is historically, philosophically, and jurisprudentially accepted by many states. The need to circumscribe "political offense" by selected elimination of offenses from this category on absolute terms, *i.e.*, without exception, should be emphasized.

5. The formula "extradite or submit to prosecution" should be amended to recognize that prosecution is a separate act from the grant of political asylum to an offender after he has been prosecuted.

6. There should be an emphasis on the need for widespread development of various methods of judicial assistance in criminal matters through bilateral, and, where feasible, multilateral agreements as an inducement to lawful rendition and prosecution of international terrorists by states concerned about the quality of the criminal justice systems in other states.

Notes

1. *See* Convention for the Suppression of Unlawful Seizure of Aircraft (Hijacking) Dec. 16, 1970, art. 7, 22 U.S.T. 1641, T.I.A.S. No. 7192; Convention for the Suppression of Unlawful Acts Against the Safety of Civil Aviation (Sabotage), Sept. 23, 1971, art. 7, 24 U.S.T. 564, T.I.A.S. No. 7570; Convention to Prevent and Punish the Acts of Terrorism Taking the Form of Crimes Against Persons and Related Extortion That Are of International Significance, Feb. 2, 1971, art. 5, T.I.A.S. No. 8413, Serie Sobre Tratados [S.S.T.] No. 37 OAS/Off. Doc. OAS/Ser. A/17; Convention on the Prevention and Punishment of Crimes Against Internationally Protected Persons, Including Diplomatic Agents, Dec. 14, 1973, art. 7, G.A. Res. 3166, 28 U.N. GAOR, Supp. (No. 30) 146 U.N. Doc. A/9030 (1974); European Convention on the Suppression of Terrorism, Jan. 27, 1977, Europ. T.S. No. 90; Agreement on the Hijacking of Aircraft and Vessels and Other Offenses, Feb. 15, 1973, United States-Cuba, art. 1, 24 U.S.T. 737,

T.I.A.S. No. 7579; Agreement between Cuba and Mexico on Illicit Seizure of Aircraft and Seacraft and Other Offenses, Granma Weekly Review (Havana), June 17, 1973, art. 2; Agreement on Unlawful Seizure (Hijacking) of Aircraft and Vessels and Other Offenses, July 6, 1973, Cuba-Venezuela, art. 1, Department of State, Division of Language Services, L.C. No. 40288, T-125/R-xx. *See also* Convention on Offenses and Certain Other Acts Committed on Board Aircraft, Sept. 14, 1963, art. 15, 20 U.S.T. 2941, T.I.A.S. No. 6768, 704 U.N.T.S. 219; Convention on the Prevention and Punishment of the Crime of Genocide, Dec. 9, 1948, arts. V, VII, 78 U.N.T.S. 277; Convention Relative to the Treatment of Prisoners of War dated at Geneva, Aug. 12, 1949, art. 129, 6 U.S.T. 3316, T.I.A.S. No. 3364, 75 U.N.T.S. 135; Treaty on Extradition, France-Israel, signed at Paris, Nov. 12, 1958, art. 3, 805 U.N.T.S. 271 (submission of nationals to prosecution).

2. *E.g.*, East German reaction to acquittal of East German defector by a West German court on a charge of killing two border guards in self-defense. Boston Globe, Dec. 3, 1976, at 7, col. 3. *See* United States v. Toscanino, 500 F.2d 267 (2d Cir. 1974) (irregular recovery by force): Waits v. McGowan, 516 F.2d 203 (3d Cir. 1975) (complaint against extradition, invoking Civil Rights Act, 42 U.S.C. § 1983 *et seq.*).

3. *See* 6 M. WHITEMAN, DIGEST OF INTERNATIONAL LAW, 727 *et seq.* (1968).

4. *Id. See also* I. SHEARER, EXTRADITION IN INTERNATIONAL LAW (1971); M. BASSIOUNI, INTERNATIONAL EXTRADITION AND WORLD PUBLIC ORDER (1974).

5. Evans, *Acquisition of Custody over the International Fugitive Offender—Alternatives to Extradition: A Survey of United States Practice*, 40 BRIT. Y.B. INT'L. L. 77, 94 (1966) [hereinafter cited as *Acquisition of Custody*] ; 6 WHITEMAN 1054, *supra* note 3. *See* Geisser v. United States, 513 F.2d 862 (5th Cir. 1975) (surrender barred by plea bargain).

6. *E.g.*, Abu Daoud Affair, Ambassade de France, Service de Presse et d'Information, 77/4. Interview of Premier Raymond Barre with the Agence-France Presse, Jan. 13, 1977; N.Y. Times, Jan. 10, 1977, at 1, col. 1; Jan. 12, 1977, at 1, col. 1.

7. *See* 1-2 C. GORDON & H. ROSENFIELD, IMMIGRATION LAW AND PROCEDURE (1959); 8 U.S.C. § 1101 *et seq.*

8. Arts. 32, 33, 19 U.S.T. 6223, T.I.A.S. 6577, 606 U.N.T.S. 267 [hereinafter referred to as Protocol] .

9. *E.g.*, United States v. Toscanino, 500 F.2d 267 (2d Cir. 1974); United States v. Quesada, 512 F.2d 1043 (5th Cir. 1975). *See also* United States v. Lara, 539 F.2d 495 (5th Cir. 1976).

10. *See* abduction of Kim Dae Jung, a political opponent of President Park of South Korea, from Tokyo to Seoul, apparently by South Korean agents. N.Y. Times, Aug. 14, 1973, at 1, col. 7. Japanese reaction is reported as having been *pro forma. Id.*, Mar. 11, 1977, at 8, col. 3.

11. Data on the apprehension of international terrorists by extradition, expulsion, or exclusion and on the prosecution thereof are in large measure both uncertain and ambiguous. The data used in this chapter are drawn from such sources as the semiannual compilations of the Federal Aviation Administration, Civil Aviation Security Service; Summaries of Responses to Department of State Circular Airgram Regarding Law and Practice on Terrorism, 1975 [hereinafter cited as Circular, name of country, page, and date of summary] ; court reports; legal journals; and newspapers.

12. The requesting states were Algeria, Argentina, Bulgaria, Canada, Colombia, Cuba, Czechoslovakia, Greece, Hungary, Italy, Japan, Mexico, Poland, Portugal, Romania, the Soviet Union, Sweden, Switzerland, Turkey, and the United States. The requested states were Argentina, Austria, Belgium, Bulgaria, Chile, Cuba, Denmark, Dominican Republic, Federal Republic of Germany, France, German Democratic Republic, Greece, Italy, Kuwait, Libya, Paraguay, Portugal, Spain, Sweden, Turkey, and Yugoslavia.

13. Argentina (2), Belgium, German Democratic Republic, Greece (2), and Paraguay. An extradition request granted by Paraguay is on appeal.

14. Extradition requests were denied by Argentina, Austria, Bulgaria, Chile, Cuba, Denmark, Dominican Republic, Federal Republic of Germany, France, Italy, Kuwait, Libya, Portugal, Spain, Sweden, Turkey, and Yugoslavia.

15. States granting deportation were Albania, Algeria, Bahamas, Barbados, Belgium, Bermuda, Bulgaria, Canada, Costa Rica, Cuba, Egypt, France, Greece, Jamaica, Kenya, Lebanon, Libya, Malawi, Morocco, Netherlands Antilles, Saudi Arabia, Spain, Sweden, Trinidad, Turkey, United Kingdom (Falkland Islands), the United States, and Yugoslavia. The states of destination were Algeria, Argentina, Barbados, Bermuda, Bulgaria, Canada, Czechoslovakia, Dominican Republic, Ecuador, Egypt, Federal Republic of Germany, France, Jamaica, Libya, Mexico, Nicaragua, Senegal, the Soviet Union, Sweden, Syria, Turkey, the United States, Venezuela, Yemen (Sana), Zambia, and three unspecified destinations.

16. Christian Belon, who hijacked a Trans World Airlines aircraft from Paris to Beirut was sentenced to nine months and deported to France three weeks later. N.Y. Times, July 10, 1970, at 38, col. 8; La SEMAINE JURIDIQUE, Edition Générale (Feb. 16, 1972) No. 16994. Chapin Paterson, who hijacked a Western Air Lines aircraft to Vancouver on February 26, 1971, was deported by Canada to the United States on March 2, 1971, as an alien ineligible for immigrant status, as he was charged in the United States with an offense involving moral turpitude (*i.e.*, aircraft piracy). The Sun (Vancouver, B.C.), Feb. 26, 1971, at 1, col. 1; Feb. 27, 1971, at 2, col. 1; Mar. 2, 1971, at 1, col. 6. The deportation hearing was held at the airport.

17. Two Arab terrorists were sentenced to death for their attack on the Athens airport on August 3, 1973, in which 5 persons were killed and 55 injured. The sentence was commuted under pressure of the seizure of a Greek freighter in Karachi on February 3, 1974, by three members of the Muslim

International Guerrillas who held two sailors hostage, and then made a forced flight on a Pakistani aircraft to Egypt, thence to Libya. Greece expelled the two terrorists on May 5, 1974, in response to Libya's "undertaking" that they would be "held answerable for their activities." INTERNATIONAL FEDERATION OF AIR LINE PILOTS ASSOCIATIONS, AIRCRAFT HIJACKING STATISTICS 1974-75; N.Y. Times, May 6, 1974, at 45, col. 2; Christian Science Monitor, May 6, 1974; [1974] KEESING'S CONTEMPORARY ARCHIVES 26916A; [1974] FACTS ON FILE 374E1.

18. *E.g.*, Greece extradited Rolf Pohle, a member of the Baader-Meinhof gang, to the Federal Republic of Germany for completion of his six- and one-half-year sentence, which was interrupted when he was released as one of the extortionate demands made in connection with the kidnaping of Peter Lorenz, Christian Democratic candidate for mayor of West Berlin in 1975. N.Y. Times, July 23, 1976, at 10, col. 5; Aug. 21, 1976, at 11, col. 2.

19. 18 U.S.C. § 3181.

20. *E.g.*, United States v. Paroutian, 299 F.2d 486 (2d Cir. 1962), *aff'd* 319 F.2d 661 (2d Cir. 1963), *cert. denied*, 375 U.S. 981 (1964). *See* Evans, *Legal Bases of Extradition in the United States*, 16 N.Y.L. FORUM 525 (1970).

21. *E.g., Re* Jackson y otra, 15 Jurisprudencia Argentina [J.A.] 561 (July-Sept. 1972) (Cámara Federal de la Plata, Mar. 24, 1972) (denying United States extradition request); *Re* Jackson y otra, 19 J.A. 454 (July-Sept. 1973) (Supreme Court, Dec. 28, 1972); 21 J.A. 383 (Jan.-Mar. 1974) (Supreme Court, Dec. 27, 1973) (affirming Mexican extradition request).

22. William Holder and Katherine Kerkow, who hijacked a Western Air Lines aircraft from Los Angeles to Algiers on June 2, 1972, went to France in 1975. The U.S. request for extradition was denied on the ground that the offense was politically motivated, but the fugitives were convicted and sentenced on charges of using false passports. Holder received three and one-half months imprisonment and a fine of 1000 francs; Kerkow received three months imprisonment and a fine of 800 francs. N.Y. Times, June 4, 1972, at 1, col. 8; Jan. 26, 1975, at 48, col. 4; May 21, 1975, at 48, col. 1; Circular, France, 2 (May 1976), *supra* note 11; Le Monde (Paris), June 4, 1975, at 10, col. 6. For the U.S. position regarding this extradition request, *see* DIG. OF UNITED STATES PRAC. IN INT'L. L. 1975, 168 (1976).

23. *E.g.*, the U.S. denial of Canadian request for extradition of Harold Banks, a maritime union leader. N.Y. Times, Mar. 15, 1968, at 78, col. 1; Ottawa Journal, Nov. 23, 1968, at 7, col. 1.

24. The Federal Republic of Germany denied a Czech request for the extradition of 10 Czech nationals who hijacked a Czech aircraft to West Germany, killing the pilot and injuring the copilot in the process. It was observed when the request was denied that the case had already been submitted to prosecution in a German court. The offenders were convicted and received sentences ranging from three to seven years; one offender committed suicide before sentencing. N.Y. Times, June 9, 1972, at 2, col. 4; Frankfurter

Allgemeine Zeitung, June 12, 1972, at 1; June 16, 1972, at 1; [1972] FACTS ON FILE, 64G3.

25. For a typical statement of procedural requirements, *see* Treaty on Extradition, Dec. 3, 1971, United States-Canada, arts. 9, 10, & 11, T.I.A.S. No. 8237 (in effect 1976). *See also* Petition of Geisser, 414 F. Supp. 49 (S.D. Fla. 1976) (conflict over extraditing or deporting alien due to failure of authorities to communicate a plea bargain).

26. 1971 Treaty on Extradition, United States-Canada, *supra* note 25, art. 17(1).

27. *See Acquisition of Custody, supra* note 5.

28. *See, e.g.*, Johnson v. Browne, 205 U.S. 309, 316 (1907). *See also* McGann v. U.S. Board of Parole, 488 F.2d 39 (3d Cir. 1973), *cert. denied* 416 U.S. 958 (1974), *rehearing denied*, 417 U.S. 927 (1974); Waits v. McGowan, 516 F.2d 203 (3d Cir. 1975).

29. *See* Holmes v. Laird, 459 F.2d 1211 (D.C. Cir. 1972), *cert. denied*, 409 U.S. 869 (1972).

30. *E.g.*, two Egyptian nationals who hijacked an Egyptian aircraft to Saudi Arabia on August 18, 1969, were returned to Egypt on the same aircraft to face charges of aircraft hijacking. N.Y. Times, Sept. 1, 1969, at 16, col. 1. Five Croatian nationalists who hijacked a Trans World Airlines aircraft to France on September 10, 1976, were returned by France to the United States on September 12 to face charges of aircraft piracy and the murder of a policeman in a bomb explosion. *Id.*, Sept. 22, 1976, at 22, col. 2. All have been convicted on federal charges of aircraft piracy and are awaiting sentencing. N.Y. Times, May 13, 1977, at 4, col. 2. Anthony Lambert Fatine, a Trinidad national, who was convicted in the United States of illegal possession of firearms, was deported to Trinidad, where he was wanted for illegal possession of firearms and "inflammatory literature dealing with guerrilla warfare." U.S. Dept. of Justice, REPORT OF THE COMMISSIONER OF IMMIGRATION AND NATURALIZATION 1974, 14 (1975). *See also* British deportation orders against Mark Hosenball and Philip Agee, U.S. nationals, on the grounds of national security, which have been upheld by the Judicial Committee of the House of Lords. The Times (London), Feb. 1, 1977, at 3a; Feb. 17, 1977, at 1a; N.Y. Times, April 29, 1977, at 12, col. 4.

31. *E.g.*, David Healy and Leonard Oeth, who hijacked a General Aviation aircraft to Cuba on April 13, 1962, were returned to the United States on April 20, 1962. N.Y. Times, Apr. 22, 1962, at 7, col. 1. Robert Labadie, who hijacked a Trans World Airlines aircraft from Chicago to Havana on August 24, 1970, was returned to the United States on September 24, 1970; he was found unfit for prosecution on December 28, 1970. Chicago Tribune, Aug. 25, 1970, at 3, col. 7; FEDERAL AVIATION ADMINISTRATION, CIVIL AVIATION SECURITY SERVICE, CHRONOLOGY OF HIJACKINGS OF U.S. REGISTERED AIRCRAFT AND CURRENT LEGAL STATUS OF HIJACKERS, January 1, 1977.

32. The United States is reported to have "formally asked [Algeria

to] . . . return or prosecute locally" Holder and Kerkow. N.Y. Times, June 6, 1972, at 69, col. 2. The United States has no extradition treaty with Algeria.

33. 510 F.2d 62, 66 (2d Cir. 1975), *cert. denied* 421 U.S. 1001 (1975). *See also* United States v. Neustice, 452 F.2d 123 (9th Cir. 1971) (rejecting defendant's complaint that he had been returned from Mexico without formalities of extradition). With regard to *Lujan*, Circuit Judge Kaufman was referring to United States v. Toscanino, 500 F.2d 267 (2d Cir. 1974) and Rochin v. California, 342 U.S. 165 (1952).

34. Belgium amended its extradition law in 1856, making an attempt on the life of a head of state an extraditable offense, when it was found that the offender who had attempted to assassinate Napoleon III could not be extradited to France under the existing law, which excluded political offenses. *See, e.g.,* Treaty on Extradition, Oct. 29, 1883, United States-Luxembourg, art. IV, 23 Stat. 808; 9 Bevans 694.

35. Treaty on Extradition, July 13, 1930, United States-Germany, art. IV, 47 Stat. 1862, 119 L.N.T.S. 247, 8 Bevans 214.

36. 1958 Extradition Convention between France and Israel, art. 4, *supra* note 1. *See also* Additional Protocol to European Convention on Extradition, Oct. 15, 1975, art. 1(2), Europ. T.S. No. 86 (E.T.S.).

37. Treaty on Extradition, United States-Canada, art. 4(2)(i), *supra* note 25.

38. *Id.,* art. 4(2)(ii).

39. 1975 Additional Protocol to the European Convention on Extradition, art. 1(b)(c), *supra* note 36. The European Convention on Extradition, Dec. 13, 1957, E.T.S. No. 24, exempts political offenses or offenses connected therewith from extradition and provides that extradition need not be granted where the requested state has reason to believe that the accused would be prosecuted or punished on charges involving race, religion, nationality, or political opinion [art. 3(1)(2)]. The exception for the political offense does not include an attempt on the life of a head of state or a member of his family [art. 3(3)] nor military offenses in which there is a common crime element (art. 4). The United Nations Draft Convention on Territorial Asylum would bar political asylum *inter alia* to persons who have committed "acts contrary to the purposes and principles of the United Nations" [art. 1(2)(c)]. DIG. OF UNITED STATES PRACTICE IN INT'L L. 1975, 157 (1976).

40. 1976 European Convention on Terrorism, E.T.S. No. 90, *supra* note 1, at 2.

41. *Id.,* art. 1.

42. *Id.,* art. 2(1)(2)(3).

43. *Id.,* art. 5.

44. *Id.,* art. 8(2).

45. *Id.,* art. 13(1).

46. The Times (London), Jan. 26, 1977, at 2e.

47. *Id.*

48. For a criticism of the Convention from a French viewpoint, *see* Soulier, *Contre le terrorisme. Quelle Europe se dessine?* LE MONDE DIPLOMATIQUE 34 (Nov. 1976). Abu Daoud, a leader of Al Fateh, was sentenced to death in Jordan in March 1973. The sentence was commuted to life imprisonment. [1973] KESSING'S CONTEMPORARY ARCHIVES 25806. In September, five Palestinian terrorists invaded the chancery of the Saudi Arabian Embassy at Paris and, taking four hostages, made a forced flight to Kuwait, where they demanded the release of Abu Daoud in exchange for the hostages. Kuwaiti authorities forced them to surrender without accomplishing this objective. Christian Science Monitor, Sept. 7, 1973, at 1, col. 2; N.Y. Times, Sept. 9, 1973, at 1, col. 5. For the French reaction to foreign criticism of the release and expulsion of Abu Daoud in January 1977, *see* Ambassade de France, Service de Presse et d'Information, 77/4, The Abu Daoud Affair. Interview of French Premier Raymond Barre with the Agence-France Presse, Nov. 13, 1977; Abu Daoud Affair, Letter to the Editor of The Washington Post from Jacques Kosciusko-Morizet, French Ambassador to the United States, Published on Jan. 23, 1977, *id.*, 77/8; N.Y. Times, Jan. 10, 1977, at 1, col. 1; Jan. 12, 1977, at 1, col. 1; Jan. 23, 1977, § 4, at 2, col. 3.

49. 450 F.2d 1189, 1192 (5th Cir. 1971), *cert. denied* 405 U.S. 989 (1972). *See* 6 M. WHITEMAN, *supra* note 3, at 799 *et seq. See also In re* Extradition of David, 395 F. Supp. 803 (E.D. Ill. 1975).

50. 1 C. GORDON & H. ROSENFIELD, § 2.43d, *supra* note 7. *See Matter of K*, 4 IMMIGRATION AND NATIONALITY DECISIONS 108 (1950).

51. Section 243(h), 66 Stat. 163; 8 U.S.C. § 1253(h).

52. *See* Zamora v. Immigration and Naturalization Service, 534 F.2d 1055 (2d Cir. 1976). For a general examination of the problem, *see* Evans, *The Political Refugee in United States Immigration Law and Practice*, 3 THE INT'L LAW. 204 (1969); *Political Refugees and the United States Immigration Laws: Further Developments*, 66 AM. J. INT'L. L. 571 (1972). *See also* D. CARLINER, THE RIGHTS OF ALIENS (1977).

53. 1970 Convention for the Suppression of Unlawful Seizure of Aircraft (Hijacking) art. 7, *supra* note 1. *See* 1 C. GORDON & H. ROSENFIELD, *supra* note 7, at § 5.166.

54. *E.g.*, McCaud v. Immigration and Naturalization Service, 500 F.2d 355 (2d Cir. 1974) (prosecution for escape from prison); Schieber v. Immigration and Naturalization Service, 461 F.2d 1078 (2d Cir. 1972) (prosecution for theft).

55. *See* art. 3 (5), *supra* note 1. The convention was implemented by the Anti-Hijacking Act of 1974, Pub. L. No. 93-366, 88 Stat. 409 (1974).

56. 79 Stat. 916 (1965). Refugees may also be admitted under the parole provisions of the 1952 act. Section 212(d)(5), 66 Stat. 163; 8 U.S.C. § 1182(d)(5).

57. 8 C.F.R. § 235.9. *See* Tai Mui v. Esperdy, 371 F.2d 722 (2d Cir. 1966), *cert. denied* 386 U.S. 1017 (1967).

58. *E.g.*, Rosenberg v. Yee Chien Woo, 402 U.S. 49 (1971).

59. Although conviction for a political offense is not necessarily ground for exclusion, where a common crime is also involved, conviction may be an inhibiting factor, as in the Brazinskas's case. Pranas and Algirdas Brazinskas, of Lithuanian origin, hijacked a Soviet aircraft to Turkey on October 15, 1970, killing the stewardess and wounding the two pilots in the process. They were convicted on charges of manslaughter in Turkey and sentenced, the sentences being reduced under a general amnesty in 1974, after which they lived in a displaced persons camp. The United States refused them political asylum in June 1976. N.Y. Times, July 1, 1976, at 13, col. 1. They were apprehended in September 1976 on charges of entering the United States illegally. *Id.*, Sept. 21, 1976, at 24, col. 3. Deportation proceedings are in progress. N.Y. Times, Apr. 17, 1977, at 41, col. 1. *See also* reported action by the Immigration and Naturalization Service to deport Andrija Artukovic, whose extradition was blocked in 1959 on the grounds that he was wanted by Yugoslavia on political grounds. N.Y. Times, Apr. 29, 1977, at 14, col. 3; United States *ex rel.* Karadzole v. Artukovic, 170 F. Supp. 383 (S.D. Cal. 1959).

60. *See* note 8 *supra*. *See generally* 1-3 A. GRAHL-MADSEN, THE STATUS OF REFUGEES IN INTERNATIONAL LAW (1966-76).

61. Art. 33(1), *supra* note 8.

62. *Id.*, art. 33(2).

63. *See* S. EXEC. REP. No. 14, 90th Cong., 2d Sess., 6 (1968); S. EXEC. K, 90th Cong., 2d Sess., viii (1968).

64. *See Attempted Defection by Lithuanian Seaman Simas Kudirka: Hearings before Subcomm. on State Department Organization and Foreign Operations of the House Comm. on Foreign Aff.*, 91st Cong., 2d Sess. (1970).

65. 37 Fed. Reg. 3447 (1972); 66 DEP'T STATE BULL. 124, 125 (1972).

66. *Id.*, items 8 and 9.

67. 8 C.F.R. § 242.8(a). *See* DIG. OF UNITED STATES PRACTICE IN INT'L. L. 1974, 112 (1975).

68. *Re* Marc Georges Severe, 9 Canada Immigration Appeal Cases 42 (1975); *Re* Rebecca Fogel, 8 Canada Immigration Appeal Cases 315 (1975).

69. Nicosia v. Wall, 442 F.2d 1005 (5th Cir. 1971) (rev'd and remanded for consideration of effect of Protocol on Extradition Treaty between Canal Zone and Panama; no further proceedings ensued).

70. Ming v. Marks, 505 F.2d 1170 (2d Cir. 1974), *cert. denied* 421 U.S. 911 (1975) (overstayed permit).

71. *E.g.*, Cheng v. Immigration and Naturalization Service, 521 F.2d 1351 (3d Cir. 1975), *cert. denied* 423 U.S. 1051 (1976). *Cf.* Chinese American Civil Council v. Attorney General, 396 F. Supp. 1250 (D.D.C. 1975). *See also* Rosenberg v. Yee Chien Woo, 402 U.S. 49 (1971).

72. Pierre v. United States, 547 F.2d 1281 (5th Cir. 1977).

73. *E.g.*, European Convention on Mutual Assistance in Criminal Matters, Apr. 20, 1959, E.T.S. No. 30; European Convention on the Supervision of Conditionally Sentenced or Conditionally Released Offenders, Nov. 30, 1964, E.T.S. No. 51; European Convention on the International Validity of Criminal Judgments, May 28, 1970, E.T.S. No. 70; European Convention on the Transfer of Proceedings in Criminal Matters, May 15, 1972, E.T.S. No. 73; 1948 Convention on Recognition and Enforcement of Judgments in Penal Matters, Denmark, Norway, Sweden, 152 BRITISH AND FOREIGN STATE PAPERS 343, pt. III (1948); Convention on Private International Law (Bustamante Code), Feb. 20, 1928, art. 391, 86 L.N.T.S. 111.

74. *See* B. DE SCHUTTER, A BIBLIOGRAPHY ON INTERNATIONAL CRIMINAL LAW (1972). For a succinct analysis of various forms of judicial assistance and relevant state practice, *see* Grützner, International Judicial Assistance and Cooperation in Criminal Matters, in 2 A TREATISE ON INTERNATIONAL CRIMINAL LAW, 189 (M. Bassiouni & V. Nanda eds. 1974).

75. *E.g.*, 1970 Convention for the Suppression of Unlawful Seizure of Aircraft (Hijacking), art. 10, *supra* note 1; 1973 Convention on the Protection and Punishment of Crimes Against Internationally Protected Persons, Including Diplomatic Agents, art. 10, *supra* note 1; 1976 European Convention on the Suppression of Terrorism, art. 8, *supra* note 1.

76. *E.g.*, Convention on Service of Judicial and Extra-Judicial Documents in Civil and Commercial Matters, Nov. 15, 1965, T.I.A.S., No. 6638, 658 U.N.T.S. 163; Convention on Taking Evidence Abroad in Civil and Commercial Matters, Mar. 18, 1970, T.I.A.S. No. 7444. *See also* 28 U.S.C. §§ 1781-84. The United States has agreements with Spain (1901), the Soviet Union (1935), and Sierra Leone (1966) regarding the execution of letters rogatory, T.S. No. 395; 49 Stat. 3840, 167 L.N.T.S. 303; T.I.A.S. No. 6056, 594 U.N.T.S. 47, respectively.

77. The following agreements are among the few U.S. international agreements bearing on the subject until recently: Agreement on Reciprocal Legal Assistance in Penal Matters and Information from Penal Register, Nov. 7, Dec. 28, 1960 & Jan. 3, 1961, United States-Federal Republic of Germany, T.I.A.S. No. 4826, 416 U.N.T.S. 93; 1947 Informal Arrangement with Panama relating to Cooperation between the American Embassy or Consulate and Panamanian Authorities when American Merchant Seamen or Tourists Are Brought before a Magistrate's Court (not printed).

78. T.I.A.S. No. 8302.

79. *Id.*

80. Arts. 2(1)(c)(1)(3), 6(3)(a)(b). An analysis of this treaty from the Swiss viewpoint appeared in 173 N.Y.L.J. 1 (May 22-23, 1975).

81. United States and Canada, Procedures for Mutual Assistance in the

Administration of Justice in Connection with the Boeing Co. Matter, March 15, 1977. The United States is reported to have similar agreements with 11 states relative to the investigation of the Lockheed Aircraft Corporation. N.Y. Times, Mar. 16, 1977, at 58, col. 6.

82. Art. II(4).S. EXEC. D, 95th Cong., 1st Sess. (1977). *See* Treaty on Extradition, Feb. 22, 1899, United States-Mexico art. III(2), 31 Stat. 1818 (offense of purely political character).

83. S. EXEC. I, 95th Cong., 1st Sess. (1977).

84. AMERICAN LAW INSTITUTE, RESTATEMENT OF THE LAW, SECOND, FOREIGN RELATIONS LAW OF THE UNITED STATES, §§ 7(b), 41(1) (1965).

85. *See* 18 U.S.C. §§ 3491-92.

86. *In re* Letters Rogatory from the Justice Court, District of Montreal, Canada, 383 F. Supp. 857 (E.D. Mich. 1974), *aff'd* 523 F.2d 562 (6th Cir. 1975). *See also In re* Letters Rogatory from Tokyo District, Tokyo, Japan, 539 F.2d 1216 (9th Cir. 1976) (taking depositions in California for use in criminal investigation of Lockheed Aircraft Corporation's activities in Japan).

87. Cooley v. Weinberger, 518 F.2d 1151 (10th Cir. 1975). For a discussion of the significance of this decision, *see* Foran-Rogers, *Recognition of Foreign Countries Penal Judgments—Cooley v. Weinberger*, 14 THE GLOBE (Ill. State Bar Ass'n.) 1 (Jan. 1977). This case and note were brought to the author's attention by M.C. Bassiouni.

88. Prosecuting states: Argentina, Austria, Bulgaria, Denmark, Dominican Republic, Federal Republic of Germany, France, Italy, Spain, Sweden, Turkey, and Yugoslavia.

89. Prosecuting states: Algeria, Argentina, Dominican Republic, Ecuador, Egypt, Federal Republic of Germany, France, Israel, Mexico, [Palestine Liberation Organization], the Soviet Union, Sweden, the United States, Venezuela, Yemen (Sana).

90. It has been reported that 68 percent of the terrorist crimes committed between March 1973 and February 1977 in England and Wales have been "solved or cleared up." The Times (London), Feb. 11, 1977, at 1d.

91. *See* note 22 *supra.*

92. N.Y. Times, Jan. 6, 1977, at 12, col. 4. The hijacking took place on September 11, 1976. *Id.*, Sept. 11, 1976 at 3, col. 6.

93. *Id.*, May 6, 1974, at 45, col. 2. Five persons were killed and 55 injured in the airport attack. The terrorists' death sentences were commuted to life imprisonment in response to the seizure of the ship. Subsequently, they were pardoned and expelled to Libya under the terms indicated.

94. *E.g., see* Pohle case, *supra* note 18.

95. Two members of the gang were deported by Sweden to West Germany in April 1977 after being arrested on a charge of conspiring to kidnap the former minister of immigration and hold her hostage for the release of various members

of the gang who were being held in West German prisons. N.Y. Times, Apr. 4, 1977 at 3, col. 1.

96. Council of Europe, European Commission of Human Rights, Application No. 6166/73, decision of May 30, 1975; 23 THE BULLETIN (Bonn) 216 (Sept. 16, 1975). European Convention for the Protection of Human Rights and Fundamental Freedoms, Nov. 4, 1950, 213 U.N.T.S. 221.

97. N.Y. Times, Apr. 29, 1977, at 3, col. 4.

98. They were also sentenced to 15 years on charges of committing three other bomb attacks. Boston Globe, Apr. 29, 1977, at 15, col. 8. Other members of the gang have been convicted on various charges, including complicity in murder, illegal possession of firearms, forgery, and bank robbery. N.Y. Times, Mar. 17, 1976, at 20, col. 6; Sept. 29, 1976, at 24, col. 3. The fourth principal, Ulrike Meinhof, committed suicide in prison in May 1976. 24 THE BULLETIN (Bonn) 136 (May 18, 1976).

99. No. 56/76, Nov. 6, 1976.

100. *Id.* On the other hand, three Arabs who were accused of plotting to shoot down an El Al Aircraft at the Rome airport in September 1973, received prison terms of five years and fines of $2500 and were then freed on bail. N.Y. Times, Feb. 28, 1974, at 8, col. 4.

101. The Times (London), Feb. 11, 1977, at 1d.

102. N.Y. Times, Aug. 16, 1975, at 7, col. 3.

103. The Times (London), Feb. 11, 1977, at 1d.

104. *E.g.*, United States: Four of the five Croatian nationalists who hijacked a TWA aircraft on September 10, 1976, to Paris were found guilty of aircraft piracy in a jury trial; the fifth pleaded guilty to this charge. One defendant was sentenced to 6 to 18 years in prison, the other four defendants await final sentencing, ranging from 20 years to life imprisonment. Chicago Tribune, Sept. 12, 1976, at 1, col. 2; N.Y. Times, Sept. 22, 1976, at 22, col. 2; May 13, 1977, at B4, col. 2 (city ed.). Netherlands: Seven South Moluccan nationalists who attacked the Indonesian Consulate at Amsterdam on December 4, 1975, were sentenced to 6 years' imprisonment. *Id.*, Apr. 9, 1976, at 7, col. 1.

105. 1973 Convention on Prevention and Punishment of Crimes Against Internationally Protected Persons, Including Diplomatic Agents, art. 9, *supra* note 1.

106. *E.g.*, §§ 1, 2, 12, Sched. 1(1), Prevention of Terrorism (Temporary Provisions) Act 1976, c.8, Current Law Statutes Annotated, pt. 1 (1976); Criminal Jurisdiction Act 1975, Current Law Statutes Annotated 1975, pt. 7, 59. *Cf.* Reference under § 48A of the Criminal Appeal (Northern Ireland) Act 1968 (No. 1 of 1975), [1976], 2 All E.R. 937 (House of Lords, July 7, 1976) (whether a soldier firing on an unarmed person whom he believed to be an IRA Provo was using unreasonable force). *See* Report of the Law Enforcement Commission (Cmnd 5627). The Republic of Ireland also has a law extending the jurisdiction of its courts to terrorist acts committed in Northern Ireland. N.Y.

Times, Jan. 3, 1974, at 3, col. 5. Apparently, no action has been taken under either law. The Times (London), Jan. 26, 1977, at 2e.

107. N.Y. Times, Feb. 9, 1977, at 3, col. 1. 1950 European Convention for the Protection of Human Rights and Fundamental Freedoms, *supra* note 96. The first case before the court was an unsuccessful action by a member of the IRA against the Republic of Ireland. *The Lawless Case*, European Court of Human Rights, Ser. A, July 1, 1961. The president of the Irish Republic resigned in October 1976 in a controversy over the government's proposal to adopt stringent legislation respecting the arrest and detention of terrorists and designed to control the activities of the IRA. N.Y. Times, Oct. 23, 1976, at 1, col. 3; Nov. 3, 1976, at 43, col. 4.

108. The Times (London), Feb. 16, 1977, at 6d. David O'Connell, a reputed leader of the Provos in Ireland, was sentenced to one year's imprisonment for his membership in the IRA. N.Y. Times, July 26, 1975, at 8, col. 4.

109. *Id.*, Feb. 26, 1975, at 2, col. 8. The sentence was later commuted to life imprisonment. The hijacker had seized a Yemeni aircraft with the object of going to Abu Dhabi, but the plane landed in Saudi Arabia, which immediately returned, *i.e.*, deported, the hijacker to Yemen.

110. Library of Congress, Congressional Research Service, CRS Issue Brief 7, IB74042 (Oct. 18, 1976).

111. N.Y. Times, Dec. 31, 1976, at 1, col. 1. [1976] KEESINGS' CONTEMPORARY ARCHIVES 27853A.

112. *E.g.*, Kozo Okamoto, the surviving member of the Japan Red Army group that attacked Lod Airport in 1972, was tried before a military tribunal and received a life sentence. N.Y. Times, July 12, 1972, at 3, col. 1. Five Palestinians who attempted to enter Israel clandestinely with the intent of establishing guerrilla organizations in the Gaza Strip were sentenced by a military tribunal to terms of 4 to 12 years. *Id.*, Apr. 29, 1977, at 5, col. 1.

113. Chicago Tribune, Jan. 25, 1976; Christian Science Monitor, Jan. 27, 1976, at 6, col. 1.

114. *E.g.*, three men who hijacked an Egyptian aircraft from Cairo to Luxor received life sentences. N.Y. Times, Sept. 20, 1976, at 10, col. 3. A reputed member of the Democratic Front for the Liberation of Palestine was sentenced to death for the attempted assassination of a former South Yemeni premier then residing in Egypt. *Id.*, Nov. 11, 1976, at 40, col. 4. A Filipino military court sentenced two hijackers to death in December 1976. Washington Post, Dec. 8, 1976, at C10. Eight participants in an abortive assassination plot against the president of the Central African Republic were sentenced to death by a military court. N.Y. Times, Feb. 18, 1976.

115. 10 LATIN AMERICA 373 (Dec. 3, 1976).

116. *See* range of charges on which prosecution has taken place in the United States for offenses against aircraft, Table 1-4; Evans, *Aircraft and Aviation Facilities*, ch. 1 of this report.

117. 49 U.S.C. § 1472(i)(j); 18 U.S.C. § 1201.

118. Library of Congress Law Library, Legislation Dealing with Control of Terrorism in European Countries, Austria, 1-2 (March 1976), [hereinafter cited as L.C. Legislation].

119. The Times (London), Feb. 16, 1977, at 7, col. 8.

120. Netherlands, 2, L.C. Legislation, *supra* note 118.

121. *See* Table 1-5, Evans, *supra* note 116, at 22. The death penalty has been commuted to life imprisonment in several instances, *e.g.*, two Palestinian terrorists who attacked the Istanbul Airport in August 1976. [1976] FACTS ON FILE. A Yemeni national who hijacked an aircraft to Saudi Arabia in February 1975 was sentenced to death in Yemen (Sana); the sentence was then commuted to life imprisonment. N.Y. Times, Feb. 26, 1975, at 2, col. 8.

10 Criminological Policy

M. Chérif Bassiouni

The Terrorist as an Ideologically Motivated Offender

It is commonly accepted that a terrorist is an ideologically motivated offender, a person who engages in acts of terror-violence not for personal gain but to accomplish a power outcome.[1] Such a person rejects in whole or in part the social, political, or economic system of the society of which he is a part.

Random violence is the usual strategy used to accomplish such a power outcome, except when a specific target is chosen for particular reasons related to the actor's strategy or ideology. The choice of the victim and of the means employed will depend on the anticipated psychological effect of the violent action in relation to the ultimate power outcome desired.

The basic vehicle relied on by the ideologically motivated offender to achieve the political objective (whether it be the tactical objective of the action itself or the strategic goal of disseminating the effect of the action or the claims of the actor) is the mass media.[2] The media have the function of diffusing the effects of the terror-inspiring act so that it can have its desired social impact. In this respect, the actor usually deems the risk of being caught to be secondary to the tactical success of publicizing his objectives or of striking terror into society.

Similarly, the prospect of a criminal trial will be weighed as another opportunity for the dissemination of the actor's objectives. Therefore the likelihood of a highly publicized trial becomes a factor in the decision to carry out the violation.

A basic postulate of criminal law is that as an instrument of social control, it employs socially accepted strategies of coercion to obtain certain socially conceived goals.[3] That postulate is predicated on the assumption that society, having made a value judgment about the significance of certain social interests that it seeks to protect and preserve, resorts to certain coercive means to achieve its essential goals of protection and preservation of these social interests. Thus the purpose of criminal law is to attain value-oriented goals by means that conform to certain socially accepted standards.

These social interests reflect certain basic values, namely, the preservation of the social order and the protection of individual members of society from unwarranted harm inflicted by others. But the ideologically motivated offender who is in a basic value conflict with criminal laws that protect the social interests he rejects ignores the question of individual harm and focuses on the issue of

523

social order. Such a person perceives the violation of criminal law as a clash of ideologies, which is warranted, or needed, while conveniently ignoring its consequences, *i.e.*, the individual harm produced. Thus if the victim is a person who has a symbolic or representative capacity in the system attacked, then the harm caused to such a person is "justified," as "punishment" or "self-defense." However, if the victim is an innocent person who has been harmed as a result of the randomness of the violence, then the rationalization is "political necessity" and the system under attack will be blamed for "causing" or "compelling" the violent action that produced the regrettable result. In any event, harm to individuals is deemed secondary to the ends of the ideologically motivated offender because violations of the criminal law and the victimization of individuals are "justified" by the political ends sought.[4]

It must be concluded, therefore, that the ideologically motivated offender is essentially unconcerned with the fact that he is committing a violation of the criminal law that embodies certain social values and that is likely to cause harm to individuals. Consequently, only preventive control measures can provide effective limits on that person's decision to commit a violation or to refrain from it. In that respect, however, the sanction of the criminal law can be effective only if the personal risks that the actor may incur outweigh the importance of the political objective sought.[5] Thus the effectiveness of the criminal sanction is relative to the actor's personal commitment to his ideological purpose in light of the importance that he attributes to the contemplated act. Consequently, attention must be given to the sanctions employed by the criminal law and their application to such offenders in order to assess their effectiveness.

Sanctions Employed by Criminal Law

Strategies of violence, whether they be wholly within a state or transnational in their effect, are subject to the municipal criminal justice system of the state exercising subject-matter and *in personam* jurisdiction. All criminal justice systems invariably utilize two forms of sanctions against violent offenders: the death penalty and imprisonment.

The Death Penalty

The death penalty has been abolished in more than 40 states and is rarely applied in most of the countries that retain it.[6] It has been under attack throughout the world community since the late seventeenth century.[7] For a variety of reasons, seldom has it been employed in cases of international terrorism. Several countries still rely on the death penalty as a deterrent to certain violent crimes.[8] Surely it is an incapacitating sanction, but its irrevocable finality has raised serious moral questions of humaneness. Indeed, whether the death penalty is or is not a cruel, unusual, or inhuman punishment is still debated, and even its deterrent value remains questionable.[9] Its use is ultimately a policy decision.

Several factors argue against the death penalty as a policy choice. Among these considerations are:

1. It is seldom, if ever, employed.
2. It applies only to a limited number of violations.
3. It tends to make martyrs of the executed persons and thus brings sympathy to the deceased and to his movement.
4. It is somewhat offensive to public morality and rejected by a large segment of the elites of the world.
5. It tends to discredit the society that employs it as revenge against individuals.
6. It diminishes the moral authority of the state that seeks to enlist public support against violence.

For these reasons, the death penalty cannot be considered a viable sanction for the prevention and control of terrorism; therefore the focus of this chapter will be on imprisonment.[10]

Imprisonment

Criminologists and penologists as well as other experts and observers of the corrections systems of the world have contended that imprisonment has failed as an instrument of social control and of the resocialization of offenders, and therefore that it should be reconsidered.[11] Some have even maintained that imprisonment should be abolished altogether.[12] Moreover, there is a trend toward reducing prison sentences and developing alternatives to imprisonment, *e.g.*, community-based programs.[13]

The question arises, therefore, as to whether imprisonment is still a valid means of controlling violent behavior.

Imprisonment: Its Role and Effectiveness

The Role of Imprisonment

Imprisonment as an instrument of social control for crimes of violence is a subject of concerned debate in contemporary industrial societies.[14] Indeed, of history's 21 civilizations, contemporary western civilization has recorded the most significant and troublesome increases in this form of social deviance. Its manifestations, however, have spread with almost parallel characteristics to non-Western societies where the same social environment has been duplicated. It now appears that the model of an industrialized, densely populated urban setting provides a more criminogenic social milieu than any other social setting. In these societies, imprisonment has been resorted to as almost the exclusive sanction for crimes of violence; but the result seems to be invariably the same—namely, an increase in (1) the rate of violent offenses, (2) the number of persons imprisoned or likely to be imprisoned, (3) recidivism, and (4) the incidence of transnational violence.

Consequently, all such societies have been considering whether this situation has resulted from the failure of imprisonment as an effective instrument of social control. They have questioned its validity and explored alternatives thereto. In this context certain basic questions may be raised:

1. Is a sanction that deprives a person of liberty an effective instrument of social control as administered by the criminal justice system?
2. Is such a sanction effective as a means for the attainment of the preventive and prophylactic goals of the criminal law?

To answer these two questions, one must first assess the validity of the theories on which imprisonment rests, and second, determine the effectiveness of these theories in their application to the ideologically motivated offender.

Theories of Punishment

Rehabilitation. This theory is predicated on a quasi-medical model that assumes that a person in an institutional setting will be resocialized once released. Irrespective of the merits of this theory, which is now almost uniformly discredited, it is inapplicable to the ideologically motivated offender because such a person will remain antisocial (in that social context) in that he is opposed in whole or in part to the social system into which, it is presumed, he is to be resocialized. Rehabilitation is inapplicable to this type of offender because there can be no success in resocializing one whose basic values are opposed to the preservation of the values of society, or its existing structures and institutions.

Deterrence.[15] The criminal sanction is a deterrent when its general impact outweighs, in the commonly perceived "scale of values" of most people, the benefits of the contemplated transgression of the law. Its "special effect deterrence" is felt when, in the evaluation of a given transgressor, the particular penalty outweighs the personal benefits to be derived from the violation. In the case of the ideologically motivated offender, such evaluation is made in the light of the degree of the personal commitment of that individual to the ideological value sought as weighed against the personal risks involved. In this evaluative framework, two other factors should be taken into account: (1) the tactical importance of the objective to be attained by the commission of the criminal violation, and (2) the risk of neutralization resulting from the actor's apprehension and detention.

The appraisal of the effectiveness of deterrence in the case of the ideologically motivated offender must be made within a different framework from the one that is contemplated in the case of offenders who engaged in criminal activities for personal gain. Furthermore, because of the peculiar reasoning of the ideologically motivated offender, the imposition of a sanction should also be considered from a different perspective. Indeed, the sanction may be an inducement to commit the violation if it will provide an outlet to the mass media that could be used as an instrument for the advancement of the offender's claims.

Imprisonment is not an effective deterrent to the ideologically motivated offender if his commitment to certain goals and objectives outweighs, in such a person's consideration, the effects of the possible sanction. Nevertheless, imprisonment still has some general deterring effect to the extent that it neutralizes the offender who is apprehended and sentenced.

The ideologically motivated offender presents a peculiar problem for deterrence theory because his objective is usually the destruction or alteration in whole or in part of the social, political, or economic system, whereas the common criminal's objective is to take undue advantage of others within the existing system. However, the deterrent effect of imprisonment has always been appraised on the basis of the values of the common criminal and not on the basis of the values of the ideologically motivated offender.

Retribution.[16] Retribution is a discredited theory because it has almost invariably been presented as the embodiment of a purely retributive *Lex Talionis*; this analysis is not entirely accurate, however. Retributive justice is part of social justice in that it redresses an imbalance between victim and aggressor that was caused by the aggressor's action. There can be no effective deterrence in the criminal sanction in the absence of a retributive or punitive element in the sanction. Thus to the extent that a punitive element is indispensable to deterrence, retribution cannot be ignored. Considering that to the ideologically motivated offender rehabilitation is inapplicable and deterrence is largely ineffective unless it contains a punitive element that can outweigh in the actor's mind the gains to be derived from the violation, the punitive theory is indispensable to the effectiveness of the criminal sanction.

The punitive element in the criminal sanction may well be the principal basis on which to mete out punishment to the ideologically motivated offender. It may be the only way to redress an imbalance with respect to the affected rights of the victim. In essence, this is a form of retributive justice and not a form of repressive injustice, as the punitive approach in the criminal sanction is all too often characterized. It is, nevertheless, important to realize that retributive justice, which is a response to instinctual justice, must balance the social and individual need for vengeance and certain standards of humaneness. The values of each society will determine that balance, subject to the overall standards of humaneness achieved by world community standards and mores. As a matter of criminal justice policy, it is better to err on the side of humaneness than on the side of retribution, in order to avoid the martyrdom with which the offender might be endowed by excessively severe punishment. On the other hand, leniency should not reach a level that would remove all retributiveness from the criminal sanction because so far behavioral studies have found retribution to be the principal ingredient of deterrence.

Incapacitation. Incapacitation is the most logical and credible theory. Its premise is that the offender is dangerous, and so he should be neutralized in an institutional setting to prevent him from repeating similar antisocial behavior. The problem is one of predicting the offender's future threat to society. This is assumed all too often from prior facts. There is a seductive yet deluding appeal to this approach of prophylactic punishment whereby dangerous persons are identified among criminal violators and are incapacitated thereafter in prisons. The determination of dangerousness and its future predictability is a hazardous guessing game, all too often based on little more than hunches deriving more from common tales than from scientific data. There is also the problem of the length of time for which an ideologically motivated offender who committed a crime of violence should be imprisoned. This problem is compounded by the fact that penalties have to be meted out for crimes actually committed and not for foreseeable ones. In any event, incapacitation serves as a control only as long as a person is imprisoned. It serves no purpose beyond that.

Is Imprisonment Effective?[1][7]

With respect to the ideologically motivated offender, compliance with the law is not a value to be upheld; on the contrary, such a person's values may even require the contravention of society's laws whenever practical. The principal consideration to be taken into account by such a person before committing a violation is the ability to carry out the criminal scheme successfully, irrespective of the law. As has been pointed out, the sanctions of the criminal law can be effective only if the personal risks that the actor may incur outweigh the benefits of the political objective sought to be achieved. Furthermore, the effectiveness of the criminal sanction is relative to the actor's personal commitment to his ideological purpose in light of the importance he attributes to the contemplated act.

The effectiveness of imprisonment therefore depends on two assumptions: (1) the sanction will be such that it will outweigh, in the actor's mind, the importance of committing the violation; and (2) the sanction will be incapacitative in that it will effectively neutralize the offender while he is in custody.

The first assumption can be made only in terms of general deterrence theory because it presumes to affect the population at large and not a specific person. To apply it to a specific person would be a special deterrent that could be made only in light of an evaluation of that person's motivation. As criminal sentences are legislatively prescribed and require an element of certainty in their formulation, they cannot be so tailored to individuals without giving the judiciary discretionary powers verging on the arbitrary. Furthermore, to have a special deterring effect on a given person requires the identification of such a person, and that occurs only after the violation has been completed.

Thus deterrence can be considered only in its general effect, and its limits are sharply circumscribed in the case of the ideologically motivated offender.

The second assumption is limited by prevailing practices of conditional release (probation and parole) and developing theories of alternatives to imprisonment, such as community-based programs. In addition, indeterminate sentences and the practice of parole prevent prediction of the duration of detention. The unequal application of sentences and their duration has in fact become a major factor of prison unrest and has fed the increasingly accepted belief among prisoners and the general public that the sanction of imprisonment is "unfair." This situation, which is largely supported by the actual disparity in sentencing and the whimsical procedures of parole, has become a focal point of reaction against the very institution of imprisonment. It has also served to highlight the severity of punishment meted out to ideologically motivated offenders who not infrequently enjoy public opinion sympathy, as contrasted with common criminals. Thus minimum sentencing,[18] flat sentencing, and proposals for abolishing parole are now becoming acceptable.[19]

In the absence of an effective general deterrent and significant incapacitative measures, the alluring alternative for society is to revert to a repressive-punitive approach to punishment. The ideologically motivated offender, however, seeks to frustrate the effectiveness of the criminal sanction in order to thrust society into repressive measures that could then lend credibility to the offender's antisocial claims. This becomes part of a strategy of polarization and radicalization, the object of which is to compel society to undertake repressive measures that are likely to elicit negative responses from persons other than those who are part of the ideological movement.

Imprisonment thus has limited effectiveness except insofar as it neutralizes a person who has already committed a violation; consequently, attention must turn away from imprisonment as a presumed deterrent and focus instead on the effectiveness of preventive law enforcement. Ultimately, this may be the more important factor, in that it determines, in the evaluation of the prospective violator, the chances of success or failure of the contemplated criminal scheme. Thus it is the principal factor in his decision to engage in such conduct.

An International Perspective

Treaties, customary practice, and the national laws of states establish the bases for international cooperation in the prevention and suppression of criminality. The maxim commonly referred to in this context is *aut dedere, aut judicare.* The duty of states to cooperate is restricted to the submission of the alleged offender to extradition or prosecution. Consequently, that duty is an extension of the state's criminological policy of prevention and control of violence because a state's failure to carry out such a duty can only frustrate the effectiveness of any domestic crime control scheme. The effectiveness of the international duty to extradite or prosecute becomes a significant factor in assessing the effectiveness of the domestic preventive and enforcement scheme. It should be observed, however, that the principal impediment to this international duty of extradition is the "political-offense exception."

Not all acts of violence, even those that inspire "terror" or those that are committed against an internationally protected target or person or other innocent persons, are done with a view to achieving a power outcome. Indeed, such acts may be committed as a "last resort," by reason of "necessity," or "self-defense." These cases arise whenever the actor's fundamental human rights to personal freedom and safety or those of such other persons whom he feels morally obligated to protect are the object of serious and repeated repression that by "reasonable standards" can be averted only through the commission of such a violation.[20] Such a person is an ideologically motivated offender who could easily satisfy the definition of a "terrorist." Thus persons who commit acts of violence against others only as a means of safeguarding themselves or others for humanitarian or political reasons violate positive law, but they may have a claim to a defense of "necessity" or to a mitigation of punishment. This is the classic reason that states advance for the preservation of the political-offense exception in extradition, *i.e.,* in order that states may provide persons who fall into this category of offender with humanitarian or political asylum. Thus states refuse to limit their prerogative of denying extradition whenever they deem that the political or humanitarian "necessity" was overriding in the actor's motivation for committing the criminal act.

It is essentially in recognition of this consideration, which is both humanitarian and political, that the duty to extradiate in international criminal law is an alternative to the duty to prosecute. However, the trial of an ideologically motivated offender by a sympathizing tribunal could result in exonerating the accused or imposing a slight sentence or a conditional sentence. In these cases the trial and the criminal sanction are not intended to be a deterrent to such a person or others but merely to be a formality designed to appease another state or world public opinion. As such, it is designed, at best, to justify the denial of extradition and to provide the state in which the violation took place and whose request for extradition has been denied with some face-saving device.

All states presently exclude the category of political offender from the scope of their criminological policy, and some states expand the definition beyond that description. Clearly, the problem is one of definition: What constitutes a "political offense" and under what conditions a person can claim a defense of "necessity" that would result in the denial of extradition, or, in the case of a trial, exonerate him from criminal responsibility or be considered a factor in the mitigation of punishment? In the absence of an absolute duty to extradite or prosecute, and in the absence of a clear policy on the defense of "necessity" in exoneration of responsibility or in the mitigation of punishment, the effectiveness of any national criminological policy is bound to be diminished. In fact, the reduction of the effectiveness of a domestic control scheme will usually be commensurate with the opportunities for freedom of movement from that state to others. It must be concluded, therefore, that the weaknesses of any domestic scheme for the control of violence are compounded by the opportunity of evading that scheme altogether by resorting to safe havens or to countries from which the likelihood of extradition is remote or where the prospects of a trial and serious punishment are limited.

Thus to the endemic problems of the ineffectiveness of the criminal sanction in the domestic processes of the prevention and control of violence, we must add those of any international control scheme. The combination of both further weakens the policy of prevention and control of any legal system and may extend to other types and categories of criminal violation. Indeed, the destruction of the credibility of the criminal sanction is pervasive and all-encompassing, and the consequences that derive from the ineffectiveness of the criminal sanction in the control of "terror-violence" are likely to affect other aspects of the criminal control of social deviance.

Conclusions

1. The prosecution of accused terrorists is the basic requirement of an international control scheme, and extradition is one of the means by which one state assists another in securing jurisdiction over the accused who is to be prosecuted.
2. Prosecution is the means by which criminal sanctions are imposed. Its importance is determined more by its substantive outcome than by its *pro forma* conduct, hence the importance of the criminal sanction and its effectiveness.
3. The criminal sanction is not rehabilitative, seldom deterring, and at best incapacitative.
4. The most effective deterrent is preventive law enforcement.
5. Strategies of terror-violence are essentially designed to function through their psychological impact and often seek to polarize and radicalize the

public either by their very nature or by the reaction (or overreaction) that they are likely to engender.

6. Mass media coverage is one of the most important tactical objectives of terrorists.

7. There is no clear statement of policy in human rights treaties concerning the acceptability of "last resort necessity" as a defense to criminal prosecution for acts of violence undertaken to protect one's right to personal freedom and personal safety.

Recommendations

1. The media and responsible public officials should deemphasize the significance of the dangers and threats of terrorism so as to prevent the creation of a climate of fear and apprehension among the general population. Emphasis on such dangers and the helplessness of society makes more effective the psychological impact of terror-violence activities and thus constitutes an inducement to commit such activities. However, the marshalling of public opinion against terror-violence can generate new factors that would have a controlling effect on terrorist activities.

2. Congress should establish a committee to study the possibility of developing certain guidelines for media coverage of terrorist activities. Such guidelines could include some compulsory restraints of coverage of terroristic events while in progress along the lines of restraints applied to media coverage of trials of terrorists.

3. Educators should develop courses for high schools and colleges on the values of law and justice.

4. Federal government law enforcement officials should develop training material and prepare qualified instructors to work with local law enforcement agencies all over the country on the various aspects of the prevention and control of terrorist activities.

5. Law enforcement officials should refrain from resorting to the death penalty against terrorists in order to avoid the attraction to martyrdom.

6. Judicial officials should review the constitutional aspects of bail provisions for accused terrorists with a view to restricting release on bail pending trial (preventive detention).

7. The Department of State should convene an international conference to study means of preventing and suppressing terrorism.

8. The Department of State should urge the world community to recognize a defense of "last-resort necessity" when a person commits an act falling within the definition of "international terrorism" but does so to secure his personal freedom or safety from personal injury. At the same time, the department should urge member states of the world community to require:

    a.   prosecution of such persons by the asylum state

    b.   the denial of the "last-resort necessity" defense whenever the acts charged resulted in the taking of another's life

    c.   that if the accused's perception of the need to engage in violent conduct is rejected as an absolute defense to prosecution, it should nonetheless be taken into account for purposes of mitigation or aggravation of the sentence

9. The Department of State should convene an international conference to study ways of requiring states to impose criminal sanctions of some deterring effect for specific acts of terror-violence, such as hijacking, kidnaping of diplomats, mailing letter bombs to innocent civilians, and so on.

10. The Department of State should urge the world community to make the failure of states to establish and enforce criminal sanctions against international terrorists subject to principles of state responsibility.

Notes

1. E. HYAMS, TERRORISTS AND TERRORISM (1974); G. MCKNIGHT, MIND OF THE TERRORIST (1974); S. SCHAEFFER, THE POLITICAL CRIMINAL (1974); L.C. GREEN, THE NATURE AND CONTROL OF INTERNATIONAL TERRORISM (1974); Bassiouni, *Ideologically Motivated Offenses and the Political Offense Exception in Extradition—A Judicial Standard for an Unruly Problem* 19 DEPAUL L. REV. 217 (1969).

2. Salomone, *Terrorism and the Mass Media*, in INTERNATIONAL TERRORISM AND POLITICAL CRIMES 43-46 (M.C. Bassiouni ed. 1975) [hereinafter cited as INTERNATIONAL TERRORISM]. Cooper, *Terrorism and the Media*, 24-27 CHITTY'S L. J. 226 (Sept. 1976).

3. M.C. BASSIOUNI, SUBSTANTIVE CRIMINAL LAW 73-85 (1978) [hereinafter cited as CRIMINAL LAW].

4. Friedlander, *Terrorism and Political Violence: Do the Ends Justify the Means?* 24-7 CHITTY's L.J. 240 (Sept. 1976); Sewell, *Political Crime: A Psychologist's Perspective*, in INTERNATIONAL TERRORISM, *supra* note 2, at 11. *See also* Letman, *Some Sociological Aspects of Terror-Violence in a Colonial Setting, id.* at 33.

5. J. BENTHAM, PRINCIPLES OF PENAL LAW, pt. 11, bk. J, ch. 6 (Browning ed. 1943). See CRIMINAL LAW *supra* note 3, at 91-105, *discussing* "Theories of Punishment," and references.

6. Patrick, *The Status of Capital Punishment: A World Perspective*, 56 J. CRIM. L.C. & P.S. 397 (1965).

7. C. BECCARIA, DEI DELITTI E DELLE PENE (1746).

8. Gregg v. Georgia, 428 U.S. 153, 96 S.Ct. 2909 (1976); Jurek v. Texas,

428 U.S. 262, 96 S.Ct. 2950 (1976); Proffitt v. Florida, 428 U.S. 242, 96 S.Ct. 2960 (1976); Woodson v. North Carolina, 428 U.S. 280, 96 S.Ct. 2978 (1976); Roberts v. Louisiana, 428 U.S. 325, 96 S.Ct. 3000 (1976).

9. Peck, *The Deterrent Effect of Capital Punishment*, 85 YALE L.J. 359 (1976); Boldus & Cole, *A Comparison of the Work of Thorsten Sellin and Isaac Ehrlick on the Deterrent Effect of the Death Penalty*, 85 YALE L.J. 170 (1975); T. SELLIN, THE DEATH PENALTY IN AMERICA (1959); THE DEATH PENALTY IN AMERICA (H. Bedau ed. 1967). *See also supra* note 3 at 120-127.

10. *See* Proceedings of the Fourth Joint Colloquium of The International Association of Penal Law, International Society of Criminology, International Society of Social Defense, International Penal and Penitentiary Foundation, Bellagio, Italy, April 1975, published by the Centro Nazionale di Prevenzione e Di Difesa Sociale (1975) and distributed to the Fifth United Nations Congress on the Prevention of Crime and the Treatment of Offenders, Geneva, Sept. 1-12, 1975. *See also* Report prepared by the Secretariat, U.N. Doc. A/Conf. 56/10 (1976).

11. *Id.*

12. E. ASPELIN, N. BISHOP, H. THORNSTEDT, & P. TORNUDD, SOME DEVELOPMENTS IN NORDIC CRIMINAL POLICY AND CRIMINOLOGY (1975) (Scandinavian Research Council for Criminology); *See also* K. MENNINGER, THE CRIME OF PUNISHMENT (1968).

13. L. ORLAND, JUSTICE, PUNISHMENT AND TREATMENT (1973); R. SLOVENKO, CRIME, LAW AND CORRECTIONS (1966).

14. *See* notes 10-13 *supra.*

15. Andenaes, *The General Preventive Effects of Punishment*, 114 U. PA. L. REV. 949 (1966).

16. MENNINGER, *supra* note 12; Andenaes, *supra* note 15.

17. N. MORRIS, THE FUTURE OF IMPRISONMENT (1976).

18. *E.g.*, 49 U.S.C. 1472 (i).

19. This has been proposed in Illinois, and a pending bill on the subject is before a special House Committee.

20. J. HALL, GENERAL PRINCIPLES OF CRIMINAL LAW, 415-48 (1952).

11 Practical Problems of Law Enforcement

Wayne A. Kerstetter

Introduction

This chapter focuses on a series of political, legal, and practical impediments to an effective law enforcement response to international and transnational terrorism. It is based on interviews and observations, both in the United States and in several European countries. In each section, after a statement of the problems as perceived by law enforcement officials, one or more alternatives for ameliorating the problems are discussed. With the exception of the early comments about the elimination of sanctuaries for terrorists, the emphasis is on defining specific, achievable advances in the law enforcement response to the problems. The suggestions do not envision any ultimate or final solution in the foreseeable future.

Repeatedly during the interviews, both here and abroad, police officials emphasized that as international and transnational terrorism involves a broad range of political considerations, it is impossible to treat it as just another international crime problem.[1] Beyond the obvious point that a person who is a "terrorist" to one country may be a "freedom fighter" to another, there lie more subtle forms of national interests, both partisan and general, that can have a major influence on a country's response to terrorist situations, and that frequently interfere with the stable pattern of expectations and behavior on which effective international law enforcement cooperation must be based. Repeatedly throughout the discussions, examples arose of how, not the gross ideological differences, but the more narrow calculations of national interest, impeded effective law enforcement actions. The impact that the vigorous prosecution of a terrorist might have on a local election or on trade relations with a country ideologically sympathetic to the terrorist often becomes a consideration in the prosecutorial decision, sometimes with deleterious results.

This is not to underrate the impact that the larger ideological differences have had. Discussions in several countries pointed to the major influence that the Palestinian problem has had on transnational terrorist activity. This influence goes beyond the impact of their direct terrorist acts. The Palestinian movement has been a prototype for the training and equipping of terrorists and a source of ideological support for similarly inclined individuals in many other parts of the world.

To facilitate discussion, issues have been grouped around three major topics:

535

(1) international agreements and treaties, (2) national legal restraints, and (3) the structure and function of law enforcement agencies.

International Agreements and Treaties

The Elimination of Sanctuaries

There is wide agreement among law enforcement agencies that the ultimate resolution to the problem of terrorism does not lie with more effective police work, whether intelligence, detection, or apprehension. Rather, the most effective step would be to remove the territorial sanctuaries that current political and ideological controversies allow. In the police view, the rationale of terrorist activity works only as long as there is a safe haven to offer hope for a successful resolution of the terrorist endeavor. This solution can be realized only through international agreements and treaties.

The Political Crimes Exception to Extradition Treaties

A related but less ambitious point concerns the political crimes exception to extradition treaties. Elsewhere this report discusses the narrowing of the political crime exception so as generally to extend international control.[2] The police, while supporting that effort, focus on a more immediate step of solving the problems that often arise between nations that share a commitment to the prevention of terrorism, but for whom the political crimes exception currently raises both national and international difficulties. Several officials cited recent examples that involved Germany and Greece in one instance, and France and the United States in at least two other instances.

In 1975, the United States sought the extradition from France of William Roger Holder and Mary Katherine Kerkow.[3] These two U.S. citizens had been indicted for the 1972 hijacking of a commercial flight from Los Angeles to Seattle, which was forced to Algeria by way of San Francisco and New York. Holder and Kerkow had not been engaged in political activity in the United States. The defendants resisted extradition under a provision of a 1909 treaty that provided that extradition should not be granted, "if the offense for which the individual's extradition is requested is of a political character, or if he proves that the requisition for the surrender has, in fact, been made to try or punish him for an offense of a political character."[4]

The political motivation claim was based on the defendants' alleged motive to have the hijacked aircraft flown to Hanoi. The evidence cited to support this claim was the fact that Holder asked the hijacked plane to fly to Hanoi. He did not, however, persist in this request when provided with a second plane with the capacity to do so. Holder apparently made references to Angela Davis and Eldridge Cleaver at separate points in the flight. The defendants threatened the lives of the passengers and crew during the incident in order to extort $500,000. The French government denied extradition on the grounds that the crime was politically motivated.[5]

In November 1976, a French court refused a U.S. request for the extradition of four U.S. nationals charged with hijacking an aircraft from the United States to Algeria and the extortion of $1 million.

It is expected that the continued use of the "political-offense exception" to block extradition in cases such as these will spur efforts, already underway, to limit the scope of this "exception" through the modification of various treaties.

The renegotiated Treaty on Extradition[6] between the United States and Canada specifically provides that the political crimes exception shall not be applicable to attacks against "specially protected persons"[7] and to any unlawful seizure or exercise of control of an aircraft.

The Treaty on Extradition between the United States and Argentina[8] provides that "[t]he allegation of a political motive or end shall not impede the extradition if the alleged offense constitutes primarily a common offense. . . ." The Treaty of Extradition with Spain[9] specifically excludes "the attempt, whether consummated or not, against the life of the Head of State or of a member of his family . . . " from the political crimes exception. It further provides, in article V(C), that

an offense committed by force or intimidation on board a commercial aircraft carrying passengers in scheduled air services or on a charter basis, with the purpose of seizing or exercising control of such aircraft, will be presumed to have a predominant character of a common crime when the consequences of the offense were or could have been grave. The fact that the offense has endangered the life or jeopardized the safety of the passengers or crew will be given special consideration in the determination of the gravity of such consequences.

The Council of Europe, in a convention adopted November 10, 1976,[10] provides for an elaborate structure that includes an arbitration clause. In article 5, it requires extradition for an extensive list of offenses unless ". . . the requested state has substantial grounds for believing that the request for extradition for an offense mentioned in Article 1 or 2 has been made for the purpose of prosecuting or punishing a person on account of his race, religion, nationality or political opinion, or that the person's position may be prejudiced for any of these reasons." As with the Hague and Montreal conventions on crimes against aircraft and the U.N. and OAS Conventions on crimes against internationally protected persons, this convention provides that if a country refuses to extradite an offender, it must then "submit the case, without exception whatsoever and without undue delay, to its competent authorities for the purpose of prosecution" (article 7). The force of the convention is reduced by provisions that allow contracting parties to modify their commitment in a number of ways, including the introduction of a somewhat limited political-offense exception.

The convention provides for binding arbitration by an *ad hoc* panel to settle disagreements regarding the interpretation or application of the treaty. The appointment of this panel may be facilitated by the European Court of Human Rights when necessary.

The handling of the Abu Daoud affair underlines the problems discussed in this section and throws into doubt the promise of this recent European initiative.

Restriction in the Interpol Constitution

The need to clarify the meaning of the word "political" arises in another context as well. Article 3 of the International Criminal Police Organization (Interpol) Constitution provides that "[i]t is strictly forbidden for the organization to undertake any intervention or activities of a political, military, religious or racial character."[11] Because of this restriction, Interpol has felt compelled to proceed cautiously in its involvement with law enforcement activities combating terrorism.[12] It feels constrained to provide assistance only in instances where the activities fall under the proscription of the traditional criminal law. Interpol will not involve itself in intelligence activity aimed at preventing terrorist acts; however, once a criminal act has occurred, it will assist in the law enforcement efforts aimed at apprehending the individuals responsible. This policy also has led Interpol to include in its files only those individuals who are directly implicated in a crime. Those individuals only suspected of involvement in terrorist activity are excluded. Even so, it is difficult to define who should be included.

The "solution" adopted by Interpol is not without its problems. First, it greatly limits both the scope of Interpol files and the effectiveness of preventive action by the international police community. Second, the "directly related" standard is itself imprecise. Does it mean only individuals who are actually on the scene of the terrorist act? If not, how widely should the net be cast for co-conspirators, accessories, and sympathizers?

Although there is substantial dissatisfaction in the law enforcement community with the position adopted by Interpol, a strong argument can be made in its support. Interpol serves a necessary and important function in international law enforcement. It assists in a range of law enforcement activities that fall outside the political complexities involved with terrorism. Greater involvement by Interpol in antiterrorist activity might well embroil it in political controversies that would substantially reduce its effectiveness in carrying out its central mission.[13] There is a natural inclination to assign to an organization additional responsibilities that seem similar to its original function. Care should be taken, however, before succumbing to that impulse so that the result is not counter-productive. In this case, it is quite possible that the cost of broader Interpol involvement in antiterrorist activities would be unduly high, especially when alternatives could be developed to fill the gap.

Such alternatives, as an Interpol-type agency focused solely on terrorism or a special regional antiterrorist police force, are not widely favored in the law enforcement community for reasons discussed later. The development of an international working group on terrorism is one alternative, however, that promises to be both practical and effective.[14]

International Documentation and Passports

A great deal of international travel is carried on with relatively few restrictions. Police in a number of European countries have expressed concern about this situation and have suggested a need for greater restrictions, particularly with respect to forged or indiscriminately issued passports. It is of great concern that some countries issue passports to non-nationals, thus facilitating a wide freedom of international movement for these non-nationals.

Several suggestions have been put forward to ameliorate this problem, including the issuance of an international passport or the standardization and verification of national passports. In either case, the key element involves setting standards for passport eligibility, the format of the passport, and the verification of the information in the passport. The receiving country could set a policy enabling individuals with passports that meet the new international standards to travel without additional documentation or visas. Individuals from the countries that do not meet these standards could be subjected to varying degrees of additional scrutiny and documentation before being allowed entry.

None of these solutions, of course, deals with the problem of individuals who smuggle themselves across borders undetected or with the availability to terrorists of professionally forged documents. Nevertheless, the widespread concern with this issue suggests that it is a topic meriting further consideration.

Airport Security

The issue of international standards arises in another area as well. The degree of airport security screening varies greatly from country to country. The use of the electronic and x-ray screening devices is far from universal, and even where it is available, the demeanor, training, and readiness of the security personnel operating these devices suggest that a properly planned attack could easily overwhelm these safeguards.

The International Federation of Airline Pilots Association (IFALPA) has developed standards for airport security. However, the enforcement of these standards at all airports remains a problem. The pilots' association, whose members are always at risk in any hijacking situation, has been willing to impose economic sanctions, but the effectiveness of a boycott is questionable given the competitive international air travel market.

Further, most international airports were not designed with antiterrorist security precautions in mind. As a result, the design of the airport and the architecture of the buildings often impose serious limitations on the security that may be provided.[15]

National Legal Restraints

Antiterrorist Intelligence in the United States

Under the heading of national legal restraints, a number of issues cluster around the gathering, filing, and dissemination of information. Intelligence activity, both domestic and foreign, has been the center of substantial controversy during the last months at federal, state, and local levels. The public concern about domestic intelligence gathering by the army goes back to the early part of the 1970s. It is an issue that all agencies find particularly sensitive.

Despite the difficulties surrounding the collection and use of intelligence, it is clear that it is crucial to an effective law enforcement response to terrorism. Once hostages have been taken or a bomb planted, all that law enforcement officials can do is attempt to limit the amount of damage suffered. Further, these damage control efforts must be carried out in the surroundings and circumstances chosen by the terrorists, no matter how difficult this renders the task.

Thus prevention and interception become the more desirable enforcement strategies. Prevention by means of additional security for possible targets is extremely expensive both in terms of dollars and of interference with the normal movement of people. Possible targets are almost limitless. The consequences of securing all of them is the creation of a fortress society.

As a result, the interception of terrorist activities has a great appeal both in terms of effectiveness and of economic and social costs. But an interception strategy is impossible without the effective collection, collation, analysis, and dissemination of information about terrorist activities.

To be sure, there are real limits to the effectiveness of an interception strategy and social costs in its use. It cannot be totally effective, obviously, but it should reduce the number of incidents. It will entail social costs, but these can be minimized and controlled by proper safeguards. To be effective, these safeguards must provide clear guidance to the officials charged with enforcement and intelligence responsibilities.

In February 1976, Executive Order No. 11905[16] was issued relating to the foreign intelligence agency activity covering U.S. citizens, aliens admitted to the United States for permanent residence, and corporations or other organizations incorporated or organized in the United States. Section 5(b)(7) of this order exempts from the general prohibition against the collection of information the gathering of "information about a United States person who is reasonably believed to be acting on behalf of a foreign power or engaging in international terrorist or narcotics activity."

Unfortunately, Executive Order No. 11905 is a broad statement of policy rather than a document designed to guide operating agencies in the proper exercise of their authority. Key words are simply not defined. Neither "international" nor "terrorism" is given a precise meaning. The order does not indicate what degree of foreign influence, support, control, or activity is necessary before a group of U.S. citizens is deemed to be involved in international terrorism rather than terrorism for home consumption. The same ambiguity plagues the restriction on physical surveillance of U.S. citizens outside the United States. This imprecision leaves CIA, DIA, NSA, and possibly certain elements of the State Department without useful guidance, but at the same time it implicitly imposes obligations on them.

The foreign intelligence guidelines of the Federal Bureau of Investigation[17] deal with this issue in a way that apparently satisfied the FBI's operational needs. These guidelines provide a likely source of assistance in preparing a set of workable standards for the implementation of Executive Order No. 11905. Recent experience teaches the wisdom of involving the appropriate congressional committees in formulating these standards.

Concern was also expressed by operating agencies about possible conflicts between prior executive orders and Executive Order No. 11905. While beyond the scope of this report, the resolution of such concerns should be a high priority of the executive branch.

The Dissemination of Information

Once information is collected, additional issues arise regarding the dissemination of that information to other agencies and the protection of the sources of that information from disclosure.

The provisions of the Privacy Act of 1974[18] raise questions regarding the dissemination of information about terrorist activities to foreign governments. The general authorization for disclosure of information about an "individual" (by statutory definition, a U.S. citizen or an alien lawfully admitted for permanent residence) is 5 U.S.C. § 552a(b)(3), the "routine use" provision. According to § 552a(a)(7), the term "routine use" means "with respect to the disclosure of a record, the use of such record for a purpose which is compatible with the purpose for which it was collected." This could cause complications if the United States decided to disseminate information from a national data base on terrorism. For example, assume the FBI develops information in the course of its enforcement activities regarding John Doe, a U.S. Army veteran, who is reasonably believed to be involved in terrorist activities. The FBI then forwards this information to the Working Group on Terrorism[19] for inclusion in a national data base on terrorism under the authority of § 552a(b)(3) [assuming proper publication of this routine use in the *Federal Register* as required by subsection (D), § 552a(e)(4) and § 552a(e)(11)]. Working group intelligence analysts, noting John Doe's army experience, query the Department of Defense regarding Doe's record, specifically regarding any special training he received. The army files indicate that Doe received special training in explosives. This information, which is crucially important, clearly is incompatible with the "routine use" provision because it was collected by the army for assignment purposes, not for law enforcement.

The statute contains a specific law enforcement subsection, § 552a(b)(7), which provides for disclosure "to another agency or to an instrumentality of any governmental jurisdiction within or under the control of the United States for a civil or criminal law enforcement activity if the activity is authorized by law. . . ."

The working group was given authority by Presidential Memorandum, dated September 25, 1975, to "coordinate ongoing activity for the prevention of terrorism" including "the collection of intelligence and the physical protection of U.S. personnel and installations abroad, and foreign diplomats and diplomatic installations in the United States."[20]

While these are clearly criminal law enforcement activities, the question remains whether a Presidential Memorandum that was not published in the *Federal Register* (as this was not) meets the requirement that 552a(b)(7) imposes of being "authorized by law."[21]

But assuming, for the sake of analysis, that the working group's authority is well founded, the information is conveyed from the army and entered into a data base created pursuant to the executive mandate to collect intelligence on terrorism. Then the U.S. embassy in England receives an inquiry from Scotland Yard regarding John Doe, who is now in London involved in activity that arouses their concern. Under what authority can the working group disseminate the information regarding Doe's explosives training? Section 552a(b)(7) is not available because Scotland Yard is not an agency "within or under the control of the United States." The most likely prospect is the "routine use" provision 552a(b)(3). But as we have seen, the army collected the information for assignment purposes, not for law enforcement. Does the fact that it was transmitted to the working group under 552a(b)(7) expand the purpose for which it was collected, thus rendering transmittal for law enforcement purposes acceptable under the definition of routine use? The argument that it does must face the tension inherent in the fact that the law enforcement exception,

§ 552a(b)(7), speaks only of law enforcement agencies within or under the control of the United States, suggesting a legislative intention not to allow dissemination to foreign law enforcement agencies.

This problem illustrates a concern expressed also by foreign police officials that they be given clear authority to disseminate information, particularly regarding their own nationals, to other countries.

The Protection of Sources

State Department officials have expressed concern regarding their capacity to protect from disclosure confidential information received by the U.S. government from foreign government agencies below the level of a national agency. The problem involved is underlined in the following example. Assume a Stockholm detective, in the course of an investigation of arms and explosives traffic, develops a confidential source who provides information about the activities of an individual that suggests that that individual may be planning an attack on the U.S. ambassador in Stockholm. The detective is instructed by his superiors to notify State Department Security at the embassy. He does so. Can the State Department protect this information under the Freedom of Information Act?[22]

The Freedom of Information Act provides wide access to the records of most federal agencies to all persons, including nonresident foreign nationals. The act provides nine specific exemptions to its disclosure requirements (5 U.S.C. § 552(b)).

Section 552(b)(1) authorizes nondisclosure when secrecy is specifically required by Executive Order in the interest of the national defense or foreign policy. Executive Order No. 11652, effective June 1, 1972, provides in § 4(C) for the security classification of information furnished by a foreign government or international organization that would "assume a degree of protection equivalent to that required by the government or international organization which furnished the information or material."[23]

State Department officials question whether § 4(C) authorizes security classification for information provided by a foreign municipal agency. (Whether the Stockholm Police Department is closely enough associated with the Swedish National Police Board to be considered an agency of the Swedish government is another issue, but the example illustrates the uncertainty that the current law introduces into a matter that can have life-or-death consequences.)

Section 552(b)(7) provides for the exemption of investigative records compiled for law enforcement purposes under one of six specific circumstances. Subsection (d) of § 552(b)(7) provides for an exemption "but only to the extent that the production of such records would . . . disclose the identity of a confidential source and, in the case of a record compiled by a criminal law enforcement authority in the course of a criminal investigation, or by an agency conducting a lawful national security intelligence investigation, confidential information furnished only by the confidential source."

Thus a great deal turns on whether the State Department is legally a "criminal law enforcement authority" and can be said to be conducting either a criminal investigation, or whether it is an agency conducting a lawful national security intelligence investigation. A review of the Conference Report on the 1974 amendments to the Freedom of Information Act raises serious questions in this regard.[24] These examples illustrate the need to review recent statutes and executive orders to ensure that they (1) provide the authority that law enforcement and security officials need to respond to terrorist activities; (2) do not impose unnecessary and undue restrictions on antiterrorist law enforcement activities; and (3) provide adequate guidelines for officials discharging their antiterrorist responsibilities.

The Structure and Function of Law Enforcement Agencies

This section covers a loose collection of issues concerning the structure and function of police agencies, the most prominent being mechanisms to facilitate the exchange of information between the police of various countries.

Conflict of Jurisdiction

In most countries law enforcement and national security agencies are organized to respond to the traditional dichotomy between internal criminal activity and activity against the security of the state and its interests abroad. International and transnational terrorist activity, because it crosses national borders and has political overtones but uses traditional criminal activity, cuts across these established organizational lines. Thus the responsibility for responding to terrorism is often diffused. In the United States, for example, the FBI has a responsibility for law enforcement activity with regard to internal terrorist activity. At the same time, the Cabinet Committee to Combat Terrorism and the Working Group on Terrorism are centered in the State Department because terrorist acts often involve the interests and lives of U.S. citizens in foreign countries. Jurisdictional problems of this kind arise both here and in other countries.

One significant improvement would be the further definition of the relationships between members of the Cabinet Committee to Combat Terrorism and the Working Group on Terrorism. In particular, a clear assignment of authority to direct and coordinate the efforts of federal agencies in responding to a crisis situation is an urgent necessity.

The Need for Information

The consistent and universal theme of the police agencies contacted during the research was the need for more and better information about the individuals and groups involved in terrorist activities. On the international level, an exchange of information is occurring among countries through a variety of channels, including the development of *ad hoc* groups in Western Europe; the Kilowatt System, a teletype information-sharing system; and the informal utilization of relationships developed in the course of NATO and Interpol activities. This exchange, particularly as it relates to Interpol, has not been under the official auspices of that organization. But police officials who have developed international contacts in other contexts have been able to use those contacts for this purpose.

Spurred by the failure of efforts to deal with the problem through the United Nations, the countries of Western Europe have begun approaching the problem on a regional basis. A limited group of these nations has been meeting and exchanging information as an *ad hoc* committee on a regular basis. Both strategic and tactical information have been included; however, accounts vary as to the scope of the interest in this *ad hoc* group and of its effectiveness. Precise information has been unobtainable.

In the United States, the *ad hoc* approach has been formalized around a Cabinet Committee on Terrorism chaired by the secretary of state and supported by a working group composed of representatives from 23 federal agencies involved with the problem. This working group meets regularly and exchanges general or strategic information about trends and developments in terrorism. The group does not exchange tactical information about specific individuals and groups.[25] However, it does serve as a useful forum in which individuals representing the various agencies have an opportunity to meet and work together. This opportunity is important to the development of the trust and respect crucial to the exchange of information between the enforcement officials. The necessity of this personal underpinning to the organizational relationships is universally recognized at all levels of law enforcement both here and abroad. Without it, any attempt to formalize an exchange of information is likely to fail; with it, the necessary exchange of information may succeed despite obstacles. The working group served as a good first step.

Until recently there has been no attempt in the United States to collect and collate information on terrorist activity from various sources and to provide for the systematic analysis and dissemination of that information. This centralization is necessary given the large number of agencies involved in the working group and the need to bring together numerous items of information from many sources into a meaningful whole in order to develop useful intelligence about terrorist activities.

A National Data Base on Terrorism

Efforts are now underway in the Office of Security in the State Department to develop a data base on terrorism. Initially this data base will contain information relevant to the State Department's responsibilities to protect diplomatic personnel and facilities. The intention is to use this data base as the foundation of a more comprehensive effort that would respond to the duties imposed by the Presidential Memorandum creating the Cabinet Committee to Combat Terrorism.

This data base may also contain information developed in the course of handling past terrorist activities, which would help in responding to future incidents. Capacities and limitations of various weapons and studies of behavior patterns of terrorists in hostage situations are examples of this type of information.

In developing this expanded data base, however, care should be taken to ensure that the appropriate legal authority has been established. Two sources of authority are currently available. The Presidential Memorandum of September 25, 1972,[26] establishing the Cabinet Committee to Combat Terrorism, contains a broad statement of duties but provides questionable legal authority. The second is the authority implicit in the responsibilities to the Office of Security for the physical protection of U.S. personnel and installations abroad, and foreign diplomats and diplomatic installations in the United States. The scope of an effective national data base on terrorism must be broader than the protection of diplomatic personnel and facilities would justify.

There is a clear need for a careful review of the authority of all agencies dealing with terrorist activities, and in particular for the authority to establish an expanded data base on terrorism. Furthermore, care should be taken to obtain guidance and support from the highest levels of the executive branch in the development of a realistic and appropriate set of guidelines for the collection, storage, and dissemination of this information. These guidelines should provide a precise standard regarding what information is to be collected and stored, to whom and under what circumstances it will be disseminated, and how long it will be maintained before being purged.

Consideration might be given to establishing judicial review of certain threshold decisions relating to terrorist intelligence. The key element in judicial review would be the articulation of realistic standards for opening a file on an individual and for sealing or purging that file.

These standards must allow for the uncertainty inherent in the intelligence-gathering process and at the same time impose meaningful restrictions on the collection of information. Such standards can be developed only in close cooperation with officials involved in field operations.

Representatives of the Congressional Oversight Committees should be invited to review these guidelines and offer suggestions regarding their content.

Steps should also be taken to police the integrity of the guideline implementation. The Justice Department guidelines for both foreign and domestic activity may help in this effort and should be coordinated with it.

An Interpol Police Force versus an
International Working Group

Little support was expressed by police officials for the establishment of an Interpol-type organization for terrorism. The reason for this lack of enthusiasm is the sensitivity that all the police agencies have to the political variability of governmental attitudes toward antiterrorist enforcement efforts. They assert that governments take different attitudes toward different situations and even vary from time to time in their attitudes toward similar situations. Few police officials believed that any elaborate structure could be built on this shifting sand. Nor did they see the need for such additional resources. Yet they all expressed a need for additional information about terrorist activities.

Substantial support was expressed for establishing a formalized working group concept that would bring together police and national security officials from a group of countries on a regular basis. The support for this notion was not universal. The French government expressed the opinion that such meetings as were occurring were adequate.[27] The West Germans, the Dutch, and the Swedes, however, did not share this opinion. The view was expressed that the current efforts were too narrow, both in the scope of their interest and in the number of nations participating. The German representative indicated that a U.S. initiative to establish a formal working group would be welcome.

While the precise details of the organization and operation of the working group should be left to discussions with participants, several principles might be suggested for its operation. First, the representatives to the conference should be working-level executives. These individuals should have been involved in the antiterrorist activity for some time, and there should be a reasonable likelihood that they would remain in that assignment for some time in the future in order to maintain stable relationships. Second, the group should be kept at a manageable size, perhaps no more than 30 representatives. Both police and security agencies from each country should be represented at the meeting. Third, the discussion should begin with an exchange of general information and then develop into an exchange of tactical information. Perhaps a status report from each participant concerning the events in his country and a prediction of the future course of events would be a useful way to begin the conference. The conference probably would be of one or two days' duration.

In addition to the exchange of information about terrorist activities, there are a number of issues that could usefully be placed on the agenda of this group: a joint definition of mutual assistance and cooperation provisions between participants; the maintenance of an interconnecting telephone and communications network between participating countries to facilitate the rapid mobilization of assistance when a terrorist incident occurs; and the advisability of a name index file, which would facilitate the exchange of information between participant countries without entailing the difficulties that an international data bank would involve. The development of an international data bank is not feasible.

An International Detention Center

Law enforcement officials in a number of countries are concerned with the problems inherent in capturing and holding an individual involved in terrorist activities. The effect of this action has been to make the country a target for terrorist activities aimed at securing the release of such prisoners. It has been suggested that as a result of this risk, a number of countries have been less than vigorous in prosecuting terrorists, preferring rather to expel them to whatever country can plausibly be held responsible for them. The establishment of an international detention center has been suggested as a way of deflecting terrorist pressure from any particular country. Whether this is a workable and internationally acceptable response to this problem is not clear. The problem, as long as it persists, clearly undermines the effectiveness of law enforcement efforts.

Conclusions

This chapter has outlined a series of concerns raised by law enforcement officials in the United States and in Western Europe. Throughout, this chapter has attempted to point in the direction of positive, incremental improvements in the law enforcement capacity to respond to terrorism. These comments should be read within the context of an underlying perception that an ultimate solution to the problem lies in political and not law enforcement action. More importantly, this chapter suggests specific, limited steps that are available to close certain loopholes in the law enforcement response to terrorism. Imaginative initiatives in these areas might find support for a new balance between international order and national freedom, which would aid in making the world safer.

Recommendations

1. The United States should give special emphasis to narrowing the scope of the political crimes exception in extradition treaties with countries that share its commitment to the prevention of terrorism. While ideological

controversies allow territorial sanctuaries for terrorists, the consideration of narrow political interests often frustrates effective law enforcement coordination between countries committed to the prevention of terrorism. Limiting the scope of the political crimes exception in extradition treaties with countries who share the U.S. commitment to prevent terrorism would reduce the impact of these narrow political interests.

2. Recent statutes and executive orders should be reviewed to ensure that they: (1) provide law enforcement and security officials with appropriate authority to discharge their responsibilities to combat terrorist activities; (2) do not impose unnecessary and undue restrictions on antiterrorist law enforcement activities; and (3) provide adequate guidelines for officials discharging their responsibilities to combat terrorism. A review of Executive Order No. 11905 discloses a serious lack of definition of key terms. An analysis of both the Privacy Act of 1975 and the Freedom of Information Act discloses ambiguities of concern to law enforcement officials. The Presidential Memorandum establishing the Cabinet Committee to Combat Terrorism charges the committee with the responsibility to "coordinate, among the governmental agencies, on-going activity for the prevention of terrorism. This will include such activities as the collection of intelligence worldwide. . . ." It is unclear precisely what this memorandum was intended to authorize. In the sensitive area of intelligence, such ambiguity is unwise.

3. The executive branch of the U.S. government should consider developing a data base on terrorism by centralizing the collation and analyses of information about terrorists and terrorist activities currently collected by various U.S. agencies. Realistic guidelines should be adopted defining what information is to be collected, analyzed, and disseminated to ensure that this activity is kept within appropriate limits.

4. If the collation and analysis of terrorism information is centralized, care should be taken to ensure that the appropriate legal authority has been established for this action and that effective guidelines for the activity are promulgated. Whether article II of the U.S. Constitution vests authority in the president to authorize this activity or not, political wisdom suggests that consultation with Congress in the matter is advisable.

Notes

1. Specific officials will be identified only when the view expressed is unique or of overriding importance.

2. *See* Bassiouni, *Criminological Policy*, ch. 10 in this report.

3. DIGEST OF UNITED STATES PRACTICE IN INTERNATIONAL LAW, 1975 198-69 (1976).

4. Convention on Extradition, Jan. 6, 1909, United States-France, art. VI,

37 Stat. 1526, T.S. No. 561, and Supplementary Extradition Convention, Feb. 12, 1970, 22 U.S.T. 407, T.I.A.S. No. 7075.

5. It should be noted that Holder and Kerkow were convicted on June 2, 1975, of using false passports. Holder was sentenced to three and one-half months and a fine of 1000 francs and Kerkow received three months and a fine of 800 francs. Both were released in consideration of their having been in prison since January 1975. [1975] FACTS ON FILE. *See* case of M. and J. McNair, G. Brown, J. Burgess, arrested in France on May 28, 1976.

6. Treaty on Extradition, Dec. 3, 1971, United States-Canada art. 4, and Exchange of Notes, June 28 and July 9, 1974, T.I.A.S. No. 8237.

7. Art. 4(2)(i) provides: "A kidnaping, murder or other assault against the life or physical integrity of a person to whom a Contracting Party has the duty according to international law to give special protection, or any attempt to commit such an offense with respect to any such person."

8. Treaty on Extradition, Jan. 21, 1972, United States-Argentina, art. 7, 23 U.S.T. 3501, T.I.A.S. No. 7510.

9. Treaty on Extradition, May 29, 1970, United States-Spain, art. V(B), 22 U.S.T. 737, T.I.A.S. No. 7136.

10. European Convention on the Suppression of Terrorism, Jan. 27, 1977, European Treaty Series [E.T.S.] No. 90.

11. Constitution and General Regulations of the International Criminal Police Organization (Interpol) as adopted by the XXVth session of the General Assembly at Vienna, Austria, in 1956 and modified in 1962, 1964, and 1967.

12. Interview with Jean Nepote, Executive Secretary of Interpol, Sept. 1976, St. Cloud, France.

13. Note the bombing of the Interpol headquarters apparently by persons protesting the visit of King Juan Carlos to France.

14. *See* p. 547 *infra*.

15. *See generally* Evans, *Aircraft and Aviation Facilities*, ch. 1 of this report.

16. United States Foreign Intelligence Activities, Exec. Order No. 11905, 41 Fed. Reg. 7703 (1976).

17. Conference with Justice Department officials in November 1976 attended by two FBI representatives.

18. 5 U.S.C. § 552a *et seq*.

19. 8 WEEKLY COMP. OF PRESIDENTIAL DOCUMENTS 1452 (1972). This Presidential Memorandum, dated September 25, 1976, created a 10-member Cabinet Committee to Combat Terrorism and a working group to support the efforts of the Cabinet Committee. The working group now consists of representatives of 23 federal agencies (the District of Columbia Metropolitan Police also participate). The Cabinet Committee is charged with coordinating, among other activities, the worldwide collection of intelligence for the prevention of terrorism. It is in the discharge of this function that an expanded data base on terrorism is an important tool.

20. *Id.*

21. For purposes of the Privacy Act, it appears that at least the Security Office of the State Department is clearly a law enforcement agency. [1974] U.S. CODE CONG. & AD. NEWS 6995: "The term 'law enforcement agency' means an agency whose employees or agents are empowered by State or Federal law to make arrests for violations of State or Federal law." According to 22 U.S.C. § 2667, security officers of the State Department are empowered to make arrests for violations of 18 U.S.C. §§ 111, 112. These sections deal with the protection of certain U.S. and foreign officials. Note that in the instant example we are dealing with activities that fall outside the scope of "physical protection of U.S. personnel and installations abroad, and foreign diplomats and diplomatic installations in the United States," but within the executive mandate to "coordinate activity for the prevention of terrorism," including "the collection of intelligence."

22. 5 U.S.C. § 552a *et seq.*

23. Classification and Declassification of National Security Information and Material, Exec. Order No. 11652, 33 Fed. Reg. 5209 (1972).

24. The Conference Report No. 93-1200 on Pub. L. No. 93-502 (Freedom of Information Act) states that "[t]he conferees intend the term 'criminal law enforcement authority' to be narrowly construed to include the Federal Bureau of Investigation and similar investigative authorities. Likewise, 'national security' is to be strictly construed to refer to military security, national defense, or foreign policy. The term 'intelligence' in subsection (D) of § 552(b)(7) is intended to apply to positive intelligence-gathering activity, counterintelligence activities, and background security investigations by governmental units which have authority to conduct such functions." [1974] U.S. CODE CONG. & AD. NEWS 6291.

25. The exchange of tactical information occurs between working group members on a bilateral basis.

26. *See* note 19 *supra.*

27. Interview with Jean Feixas of the French Ministry of the Interior, Sept. 1976.

12 State Self-Help and Problems of Public International Law

John F. Murphy

Introduction

The basic problem to be addressed in this chapter is the extent to which individual states—either unilaterally or in conjunction with other states—can or should, in accordance with principles of public international law and policy, engage in self-help activities against states that aid or abet, or at a minimum fail to cooperate in preventing and suppressing, individual acts of international terrorism. The specific measures of self-help to be considered include the use of armed force, economic sanctions, international claims, diplomatic protests, and quiet diplomacy. As an organizational matter, these measures will be addressed in descending degree of coerciveness.

State self-help is a subject of vast dimensions and considerable complexity. Time and space limitations preclude any attempt to discuss in detail the content of or the conflicting views on such doctrines as self-defense, humanitarian intervention, reprisals, retorsions, the respective competences of the United Nations Security Council and the General Assembly to apply sanctions or the permissible role, if any, of regional organizations in this area. These subjects, as well as the debates thereon, have been covered extensively elsewhere.[1] At the same time, by necessity, some of these subjects will be briefly considered in the context of discussion of a particular kind of self-help, most particularly, the use of armed force, and the writer will express his opinion on issues that have arisen with respect to them. These opinions, however, will be expressed largely in conclusory form, albeit with some reasons advanced by way of support. The reader who wishes to explore these issues in a more exhaustive fashion may turn to sources cited in the footnotes.

This chapter will focus first on the incident at Entebbe as an extreme example of state self-help arguably justified by the compelling circumstances present at the time. It will then consider a number of circumstances in which at least a colorable case might be made under law and policy for the use of armed force by way of self-help. Next it will examine situations where measures of state self-help not involving the use of armed force—namely, economic sanctions, international claims, diplomatic protests, and quiet diplomacy—might be justified. As to each situation, an attempt will be made to assess the advantages and disadvantages of employing a particular measure of self-help as compared with alternative possibilities.

Throughout, this chapter will attempt to evaluate situations and possible

553

responses thereto in light of the political, economic, and social milieus in which they arise. Such factors are especially relevant in assessing the feasibility of alternative actions available to U.S. decision-makers.

The Unilateral Use of Armed Force:
The Israeli Raid at Entebbe

Brief Factual Background

The salient facts of the Israeli raid at the Entebbe Airport at Uganda may be briefly summarized as follows.[2] On June 27, 1976, four terrorists, members of the Popular Front for the Liberation of Palestine (PLO), took control of an Air France jet shortly after it had taken off from the Athens airport. The hijackers first flew their hostages to Benghazi, Libya, for refueling, and then to Entebbe Airport in Uganda, where they were held for six days in an unused passenger terminal. Israeli discussions with President Idi Amin of Uganda, as well as intelligence reports and other sources of information, indicated quite conclusively that not only was President Amin not making efforts to free the hostages and apprehend the hijackers but was actively involved in support of the hijacking operation.

There was substantial objective evidence that the Uganda government was actively supporting the hijacking operation.[3] To cite only a few examples, when the aircraft landed in Entebbe, six Palestinians, members of one or more divisions of the PLO, joined the hijackers. Ugandan soldiers assisted the hijackers in their surveillance of the hostages. Shortly after landing at Entebbe, the hijackers demanded that 53 prisoners be released (40 incarcerated in Israel, the other 13 elsewhere). President Amin informed the hostages that the hijackers had no grudge against them, but "only against the fascist Israeli government—and if the latter does not agree to the guerrillas' demands, it does not care about the fate of its citizens."[4] The day after the plane arrived in Uganda, all Israelis were segregated in another part of the airport. On June 30, 47 non-Israeli women and children were released and allowed to go to Paris. On July 1, 100 French hostages were released and allowed to leave the country. The 96 Israelis remained at Entebbe under the guard of the hijackers, who were relieved from time to time by Ugandan armed forces.

As all available evidence began to point ineluctably to the futility of attempts to resolve the problem diplomatically, the Israeli government decided to go ahead with a military raid on Entebbe in an effort to rescue the Israeli hostages. Accordingly, on July 3, under cover of darkness, three planeloads of Israeli commandos made a surprise landing at the Entebbe airfield and within less than an hour were airborne with the remaining Israeli hostages. In the course of the raid, 1 Israeli soldier, 3 hostages, 20 Ugandan soldiers, and apparently all of the hijackers were killed. An uncertain number of other persons were wounded. Ten Ugandan aircraft were destroyed, and considerable damage was done to various parts of the airfield. One Israeli woman, who had been taken to a Ugandan hospital earlier in the week, had to be left behind. Never heard from again, she apparently was murdered by Ugandan soldiers in retaliation for the raid. After stopping in Nairobi to refuel and to carry out emergency surgery on the wounded—at least the tacit consent of the Kenya government to do so had been secured in advance—the hostages arrived back in Israel Sunday morning, exactly a week after their takeoff from Lod Airport aboard Air France Flight 139.

The Debates in the U.N. Security Council

Five days after the raid on Entebbe, the Organization of African Unity submitted a complaint to the United Nations Security Council regarding "an act of aggression" by Israel against Uganda.[5] Not surprisingly, their version of the facts regarding the raid at Entebbe differed sharply from those just set forth. The foreign minister of Uganda, Juma Oris Abdalla, and the representative of Mauritania, Moulaye El Hassen, speaking on behalf of the African Group, argued that the Israeli raid constituted aggression under article 2(4) of the U.N. Charter in that it had violated the territorial sovereignty and political independence of a member of the United Nations. According to their version of the facts, not only was the government of Uganda innocent of any collusion with the hijackers, it was making every effort, in cooperation with other governments and the secretary-general, to obtain the freedom of the hostages. Further, they contended that these efforts were leading to a peaceful resolution of the problem when Israel decided "to take the law into its own hands." Accordingly, they argued, the council should adopt a draft resolution, introduced by Benin, Libya, and Tanzania, that would have had the council condemn Israel's flagrant violation of Uganda's sovereignty and territorial integrity and demand that Israel meet the just claims of Uganda for full compensation for the damage and destruction inflicted on Uganda.

In response, the Israeli ambassador to the United Nations, Chaim Herzog, sharply disputed Uganda's version of the facts, repeatedly stressing evidence of Uganda's collaboration with the hijackers and of the imminent danger to the Israeli hostages. On the basis of this version of the events, Herzog turned to a defense of the raid at Entebbe under principles of international law.

Ambassador Herzog first contended that Uganda had violated a basic tenet of customary international law in that it had failed to protect foreign nationals on its territory. He further argued that Uganda's actions constituted a "gross violation" of the 1970 Hague Convention for the Suppression of Unlawful Seizure of Aircraft,[6] which both Israel and Uganda have signed and ratified.

Specifically, Herzog claimed Uganda had violated articles 6, 7 and 9 of the Hague Convention, which read as follows:

Article 6: Upon being satisfied that the circumstances so warrant, any Contracting State in the territory of which the offender or the alleged offender is present, shall take him into custody or take other measures to ensure his presence. The custody and other measures shall be as provided in the law of that State but may only be continued for such time as is necessary to enable any criminal or extradition proceedings to be instituted.

Article 7: The Contracting State in the territory of which the alleged offender is found shall, if it does not extradite him, be obliged, without exception whatsoever and whether or not the offence was committed in its territory, to submit the case to its competent authorities for the purpose of prosecution. Those authorities shall take their decision in the same manner as in the case of any ordinary offence of a serious nature under the law of that State.

Article 9: When any of the acts ... has occurred or is about to occur, Contracting States shall take all appropriate measures to restore control of the aircraft to its lawful commander or to preserve his control of the aircraft. In cases contemplated ..., any Contracting State in which the aircraft or its passengers and crew are present shall facilitate the continuation of the journey of the passengers and crew as soon as practicable, and shall without delay return the aircraft and its cargo to the persons lawfully entitled to possession.

Herzog did not claim that these violations of customary and conventional international law by themselves justified Israel's use of armed force on Ugandan territory. Rather, in this regard he stressed two primary lines of argument. First, citing and quoting O'Connell, he contended that Israel's raid did not violate article 2(4) of the Charter because that provision does not "prohibit a use of force which is limited in intention and effect to the protection of a State's own integrity and its nationals' vital interests, when the machinery envisaged by the United Nations Charter is ineffective in the situation."[7] Second, citing Bowett,[8] he invoked the right of a state under the doctrine of self-defense to take military action to protect its nationals in mortal danger as long as such action is limited to cases where no other means of protection are available and to securing the safe removal of the threatened nationals. In Herzog's view, the situation at Entebbe was in complete accord with the classic formulation set forth in the *Caroline* case, in that there was a "necessity of self-defence, instant, overwhelming, leaving no choice of means and no moment for deliberation."[9]

By way of precedent, Herzog referred, *inter alia*, to France's use of force just a few months before the raid at Entebbe in order to rescue a busload of children held hostage on the Somalia border. The representatives of the terrorists in Somalia had made demands on the French government and had announced that if their demands were not met they would cut the children's throats. In response, French soldiers attacked the terrorists on the Somalia border, killing them and rescuing the children, except for one child who was killed by the terrorists and one child who was taken to Somalia but later returned alive.

During the attack by the French soldiers, fire was directed at them from a Somalia frontier post, seriously wounding a French lieutenant. The French forces returned the fire into Somali territory, causing casualties and damage to the Somalis. Although Somalia complained of the incident in the Security Council, it received little support, and the council took no formal action.

The United States strongly supported the legality of the Israeli raid at Entebbe, but it did so cautiously. In the Security Council debate, U.S. Ambassador William Scranton "reaffirmed" the principle of territorial sovereignty in Africa. He also stated that Israel's breach of the territorial integrity of Uganda, although short in duration and only temporary, would normally be impermissible under the United Nations Charter. However, according to Scranton, the situation at Entebbe involved "unique circumstances," which it was hoped would not arise again in the future. In his words:

[T]here is a well-established right to use limited force for the protection of one's own nationals from an imminent threat of injury or death in a situation where the state in whose territory they are located either is unwilling or unable to protect them. The right, flowing from the right of self-defense, is limited to such use of force as is necessary and appropriate to protect threatened nationals from injury.

The requirements of this right to protect nationals were clearly met in the Entebbe case. Israel had good reason to believe that at the time it acted Israeli nationals were in imminent danger of execution by the hijackers. Moreover, the actions necessary to release the Israeli nationals or to prevent substantial loss of Israeli lives had not been taken by the Government of Uganda, nor was there a reasonable expectation such actions would be taken. In fact, there is substantial evidence that the Government of Uganda cooperated with and aided the hijackers.

A number of the released hostages have publicly related how the Ugandan authorities allowed several additional terrorists to reinforce the original group after the plane landed, permitted them to receive additional arms and additional explosives, participated in guarding the hostages, and according to some accounts, even took over sole custody of some or all of the passengers to allow the hijackers to rest. The ease and success of the Israeli effort to free the hostages further suggests that the Ugandan authorities could have overpowered the hijackers and released the hostages if they had really had the desire to do so.[10]

Ambassador Scranton also emphasized the reasonableness of Israel's conclusion that the hostages were in imminent danger of execution, since the Ugandan government was headed by an individual who had previously rejoiced at the slaying of Israeli athletes at Munich, who had called for the extinction of Israel, and who had praised Hitler's slaughter of six million Jews.

After four days of debate, the Security Council failed to take any formal action. On July 14 the United States and the United Kingdom introduced a resolution that would have had the Security Council condemn hijacking and all other acts that threatened the lives of passengers and crews and the safety of international civil aviation, and call on all states to take every necessary measure to prevent and punish all such terrorist acts. Under the resolution, the council would also have deplored the tragic loss of human life that had resulted from the hijacking of the French aircraft; reaffirmed the need to respect the sovereignty and territorial integrity of all states in accordance with the United Nations Charter and international law; and enjoined the international community to give the highest priority to the consideration of further means of assuring the safety and reliability of international civil aviation. The resolution failed to obtain the necessary majority. The vote was six in favor, none against, with two abstentions.[11]

The draft resolution sponsored by Benin, Libya, and Tanzania was not pressed to a vote.

In a statement made after the vote on the U.S.-U.K. resolution, the U.S. representative, Ambassador W. Tapley Bennett, expressed his delegation's regret that the council had declined to take positive action against the hijacking of the Air France airliner, but he expressed satisfaction that "not a single delegation could bring itself to vote against such a balanced resolution."[12] He again stressed that the "sovereignty and territorial integrity of states must be sustained and protected." Specifically, he emphasized that the United States did not view the raid "as a precedent which would justify any future unauthorized entry into another state's territory that is not similarly justified by exceptional circumstances."[13]

Implications for Future Action

As noted above, the United States—and to a somewhat lesser extent, Israel—adopted an extremely cautious approach in defense of the legality of the raid at Entebbe. U.S. representatives repeatedly stressed the need to protect and sustain the sovereignty and territorial integrity of states; the "exceptional," indeed "unique," circumstances present at Entebbe; and the doctrine of self-defense of one's nationals abroad as the primary, if not the sole, justification for the Israeli use of armed force.

This approach appears eminently sound in law and policy. The incident at Entebbe would seem to be *sui generis* because of the congruence of a number of factors that, the best evidence indicates, were present there:

1. the active involvement of President Amin in, at a minimum, the last stages of the hijacking operation
2. the lack of any indications that steps would be taken by Ugandan authorities to secure the release of the Israeli hostages
3. the Israeli officials' reasonable perception that the hostages were in imminent danger of execution by the hijackers, perhaps with the active participation of Ugandan soldiers

4. Israel's consequent, and reasonable, conclusion that military action was urgently required by the exigencies of the situation
5. the limitation by the Israeli forces of the use of force to the minimum necessary to accomplish the rescue and the swift termination of the use of force upon completion of the mission
6. the absence of any punitive motive on the part of Israel toward Uganda and the limited loss of life and property caused by the raid
7. the acquiescence of the Kenyan government in the refueling of the Israeli planes at the Nairobi airport.

The cautious approach taken by the U.S. government in its defense of the raid at Entebbe is especially noteworthy, because some other extremely prominent authorities on international law have been much less restrained in their defense of the raid. Most particularly, in a letter to the editor of the *New York Times*, McDougal and Reisman defended the raid along the following lines:

There is a bizarre Newspeak quality to the denunciations, in terms of asserted international law, of the Israeli rescue of hijacked passengers from the Entebbe airport in Uganda on July 4.

The initial act of air piracy at Athens was a violation of international law, as was the holding of the hostages for political purposes thereafter. At least one of these acts, piracy, is an international crime subject to universal jurisdiction.

The Israeli action would appear justified as a humanitarian intervention, a doctrine whose roots go back, at least, to Hugo Grotius. Where gross violations of human rights are taking place within a state whose government will not or cannot prevent them, the organs of the international community, or in exigent circumstances a single state, may enter the territory of the defaulting state for the sole purpose of terminating the outrage.

This act is recognized as a lawful humanitarian intervention. For a detailed exploration of the historical application and deep roots in common interest of this doctrine see our "Memorandum on Humanitarian Intervention to Save the Ibos," reprinted in Lillich, "Humanitarian Intervention" (1973).

Another hallowed doctrine of international law, availing Israel in this case and expressing in many forms the common interests of all peoples, is that of "self-help." The forms of this doctrine include self-defense, reprisals, retaliation, impact territoriality, contiguous zones and other equivalents. The core meaning is that if a state is grievously injured but the organized international community is incapable of affording timely redress, the injured party may take necessary and proportionate measures to protect itself and its nationals.

In a context of the most inhumane deprivations and the failure of the Ugandan Government to give protection, it can only be Opposite-speak to describe the rescue operation as an act of aggression against Uganda. The action of the Israelis could not possibly have had the effect of threatening the territorial integrity or political independence of Uganda. This action, on the contrary, was entirely necessary and proportionate to the lawful purposes of the rescue.

The suggestion that, under the circumstances, Israel's action was an invasion of the sovereignty of Uganda involves a complete misunderstanding of sovereignty. Sovereignty even in its most comprehensive conception refers only to that competence of states which international law confers. States are not accorded a competence to exclude themselves from the operative provisions of international law.

It is regrettable that states and international organizations fail to censure the Amin regime. One can only wonder at the Security Council's curious strabismus in focusing righteously on the wrong problem.[14]

With all due respect to the prominence of the writers, it is submitted that this letter constitutes, in effect, an advocates' brief and should not serve as a guide to the use of armed force as a measure of self-help, either for the U.S. government or for other states in the world community. The writers list self-defense as only one of numerous measures of "self-help" involving the use of force, all of which, at least as far as one can tell from the letter, remain fully available to states in spite of the strict limits on the use of force imposed by the United Nations Charter. Especially disturbing, as a possible guide to future state action, is the writers' sentence: "The core meaning [of the doctrine of self-help] is that if a state is grievously injured but the organized international community is incapable of affording timely redress, the injured party may take necessary and proportionate measures to protect itself and its nationals." This sentence is pregnant with ambiguity. "Grievously injured" is patently imprecise phraseology to describe a situation in which a state should be deemed justified under international law to resort to the unilateral use of armed force, even if it is required to be "necessary and proportionate" (terms themselves not free of ambiguity) to the injury inflicted.

The writers' primary rationale for justification for the Israeli raid appears to be the so-called doctrine of humantarian intervention. The historical record indicates that there have been few if any genuine cases of humanitarian intervention.[15] It is also highly debatable whether this doctrine remains viable in light of the United Nations Charter's limitations on the use of force and the OAS charter's strict prohibitions on intervention for any purpose whatsoever.[16] The writer favors the position taken by Franck, which holds that the doctrine of humanitarian intervention is incompatible with principles of modern public international law. At the same time the writer agrees with Franck when he states:

Yet we freely admit that we can imagine situations in which a humanitarian rescue would be highly desirable. With Churchill, we can visualize wanting our country to fight the menace of tyranny for years, and if necessary alone. Undeniably, there are circumstances in which the unilateral use of force to overthrow injustice begins to seem less wrong than to turn aside. Like civil disobedience, however, this sense of superior necessity belongs in the realm not of law but of moral choice, which nations, like individuals, must sometimes make, weighing the costs and benefits to their cause, to the social fabric, and to themselves.[17]

In the raid on Entebbe there was no need to make the difficult choice envisaged by Franck. There, as noted above, the doctrine of self-defense afforded a solid legal as well as moral basis for the action.

Selected Other Situations Arguably Justifying the Use of Force as a Self-Help Measure

Variations on a Theme: Entebbe Revisited

As noted in the preceding section, the primary justification advanced in the Security Council in support of the raid on Entebbe was Israel's right to protect its nationals, a right that, in Ambassador Scranton's words, flowed from the right of self-defense. The question to be addressed here is whether the fact that Israel engaged in the raid to protect *its* nationals was a crucial factor supporting its permissibility. For example, if the hostages at Entebbe had been Kenyan nationals, or the nationals of some other third country, could Israel legitimately have carried out the raid (assuming, of course, which is unlikely, that Israel would have been willing to undertake such a risky operation were its own nationals not involved)?

The conclusion of this writer is that Israel could have done so, at least if it had been requested to do so by Kenya or the other states whose nationals were endangered. The legal rationale for this action would be the doctrine of collective self-defense. Admittedly, the doctrine of collective self-defense is complex and controversial, and its very existence has been challenged by some jurists.[18] Others have claimed that it can be employed only in accordance with the terms of mutual security pacts such as NATO,[19] or in the absence of such pacts, only by states in geographical proximity.[20] Both these proposed limitations seem artificial and non-policy-serving. The entire world community has an interest in protecting innocent individuals from acts of international terrorism. The fact that a particular state does not have the military means to defend its nationals abroad in a situation where another state is actively collaborating with terrorists should not preclude that state from calling on other states with the necessary military capabilities for assistance. As McDougal and Feliciano have suggested, in such a situation each member of the world community "in effect asserts, singly and in combination, defense of the new and more comprehensive 'self.' "[21] Mutual security pacts such as NATO were not designed with individual acts of international terrorism in mind and are therefore entirely inapposite to the problem. Moreover, in an age of global communications and travel—this especially applies, of course, to aircraft hijacking—geographic proximity would seem an irrelevant consideration for purposes of determining the permissible scope of collective self-defense.

An analogy may be drawn, and has been drawn by Bowett, to municipal law principles of self-defense. Writing in 1958, Bowett noted that the common law legal systems recognized self-defense as going beyond the defense of one's own person or property, but that there had to be some close relationship between the person attacked and the person who assists in his lawful defense. That is, the so-called defense of others was limited to those who were members of one's household, or those whom one was under a legal or socially recognized duty to protect.[22] However, more recent cases and commentators recognize the artificiality of such limitations and would seem to support the thesis that "one complete stranger is privileged to defend another whenever it is reasonable for him to do so."[23] For the reasons given above, such an approach should apply *a fortiori* at the international level.

Two other variations of the situation at Entebbe may be briefly mentioned. First, assume that the evidence indicated that the government of Uganda was not actively collaborating with the hijackers but was unable to exercise its responsibility to protect the hostages and that the execution of the hostages by the hijackers was imminent. Egypt attempted to argue that this was at least partially the case after the Larnaca incident. See Evans, pp. 36-37. It is submitted that if all other facts of the raid at Entebbe remained unchanged, the raid could still be justified under the doctrine of self-defense. As Waldock has written:

> The landing of forces without consent, being unmistakably a usurpation of political authority, is *prima facie* intervention. The question is whether it satisfied the principles laid down in the Caroline incident. There must be (1) an imminent threat of injury to nationals, (2) a failure or inability on the part of the territorial sovereign to protect them and (3) measures of protection strictly confined to the object of protecting them against injury. Even under customary law only an absolute necessity could justify an intervention to protect nationals. But, where such necessity existed, intervention seems to have been legally justifiable in the period before the Covenant.[24]

Second, and finally, there would seem to be no question of the legality of the Israeli raid had it been taken with the consent of the Ugandan government. It is a generally recognized principle of international law that a state may intervene in the internal affairs of another state at the request of that country's lawful government.[25] [It may be noted, however, that questions have arisen with respect to past interventions—most particularly the U.S.-Belgian airdrop into the Congo (Stanleyville) in 1964 and the U.S. action in the Dominican Republic in 1965—as to whether the invitation came from the government legitimately in power and whether the use of armed force was solely for the purpose of protecting foreign nationals or was employed to keep the requesting government in power in a situation where a state of belligerency existed requiring neutrality of outside powers.][26] Presumably, no such questions would have arisen in connection with an Israeli intervention authorized by the Ugandan government.

The Use of Armed Force against States Serving as
"Subversive Centers" for International Terrorists

Brian Crozier and other commentators have noted the presence in various parts of the world of what has been described as "subversive centers."[27] Crozier defines these as countries that provide assistance to subversive or terrorist groups who carry out their terrorist activities in other countries. Under this definition, Crozier claims, by far the greatest subversive center in the world is the Soviet Union, actively supported by such East European countries as East Germany, Czechoslovakia, Bulgaria, and Romania. The People's Republic of China, North Vietnam, North Korea, and Cuba are other Communist countries Crozier identified as actively involved in promoting international terrorism.

In addition to the Communist subversive centers, Crozier has claimed that a number of non-Communist but "revolutionary" governments have been supporting, actively or at least occasionally, international terrorism. These include Algeria, Libya, Tanzania, Zambia, the Republic of the Congo (Brazzaville), Zaire, the Popular Democratic Republic of Yemen, Iraq, Syria, and Lebanon (the latter probably involuntarily). In particular, Crozier and others have pinpointed Libya as the most important of the non-Communist subversive centers. According to recent reports, Libya has helped to establish a broad terrorist network, stretching from the Middle East to Africa and Europe.[28] Colonel Muammar el-Qaddafi, Libya's president, has reportedly sent Soviet-made arms to the Irish Republic Army in Northern Ireland, to Moslem guerrillas in the Philippines and Thailand, and to rebels in Chad and Ethiopia. Other reports indicate that the terrorists who murdered members of the Israeli team at the Olympic games in Munich four years ago had been trained in Libya, had their arms smuggled into Munich by Libyan diplomatic couriers, and were later given large rewards by Colonel Qaddafi.

It is a fact that a gang that included the terrorist called "Carlos" took refuge in Libya despite the death of a Libyan minister, in December 1975, after the raid on the Vienna headquarters of the Organization of Petroleum Exporting Countries. Arab and Western diplomats reportedly are convinced that Libya, and possibly Iraq and Algeria, helped plan the raid, whose aim was partly to attract publicity for a newly formed militant group, the Arm of the Arab Revolution.

If Libya has been engaged in such active support of international terrorism, the United Nations Security Council could find, in accordance with article 39 of the Charter, that these activities constitute a threat to international peace and security and call on member states to apply economic sanctions against Libya under article 41 of the Charter or even, although this is more doubtful as a legal proposition, take military action against Libya pursuant to article 42.[29]

The competence of the General Assembly under the "Uniting for Peace" Resolution[30] to call on member states to apply economic sanctions or employ military force against a state like Libya is debatable at best, because as coercive measures or enforcement action they would appear, under the terms of article 11(2) of Charter, as well as the language of the International Court of Justice in the *Certain Expenses* case,[31] to fall within the sole competence of the Security Council. Similarly, the terms of article 53(1) would appear to preclude such "enforcement action" by regional organizations such as the OAS or the OAU in the absence of prior Security Council authorization.[32]

One need not dwell on these complex and debatable issues of the jurisdictional competence of various organs of the international community. The plain fact is that political considerations—most especially the strong influence of the Communist, Arab, and Afro-Asian blocs in the United Nations—rule out such actions as even remote possibilities.

If the United Nations or other international organizations are unable or unwilling to take action against subversive centers such as Libya, to what extent, if at all, may states unilaterally or collectively resort on their own to the use of armed force against such states? It may be noted at the outset that Libya's alleged activities clearly violate established international law principles. To cite but one of several possible examples, the Declaration on Principles of International Law Concerning Friendly Relations Among States in Accordance with the Charter of the United Nations,[33] adopted in 1970 as the authoritative interpretation of the U.N. Charter,[34] provides in pertinent part:

> Every state has the duty to refrain from organizing or encouraging the organization of irregular forces or armed bands, including mercenaries, for incursion into the territory of another state.
>
> Every state has the duty to refrain from organizing, instigating, assisting or participating in acts of civil strife or terrorist acts in another state or acquiescing in organized activities within its territory directed towards the commission of such acts, when the acts referred to in the present paragraph involve a threat or use of force.[35]

However, assuming *arguendo* that the activities of Libya and other states serving as subversive centers violate well-established principles of public international law, it does not necessarily follow that other states may employ armed force in response to these international delicts. The crucial line to be drawn, it would seem, is between the use of force in self-defense and the use of force by way of reprisal. This line is not easily drawn. According to Bowett, the essential difference between self-defense and reprisals lies in the aim or intent of the use of armed force. In contrast to self-defense, reprisals are " 'punitive' in character; their object is 'to compel the offending state to make reparation for the injury or to return to legality, by avoiding further offences.' The right of self-defence does not extend '*en tirer réparation ou . . . infliger punition,*' and the 'essentially preventive and non-retributive character of self-defence' cannot be over-stressed."[36]

Although reprisals utilizing armed force as a matter of self-help were permitted under customary international law, within the strict limitations set forth in the *Naulilaa case,*[37] the law changed dramatically with the adoption of the United Nations Charter. It now appears to be clearly established by the terms of articles 2(3), 2(4), and 51 of the United Nations Charter, by several Security Council resolutions,[38] and by the writings of eminent jurists,[39] that reprisals involving the use or threat of force are illegal. The U.S. Declaration on Principles of International Law concerning Friendly Relations and Co-operation among States provides categorically that "[s]tates have a duty to refrain from acts of reprisal involving the use of force."

According to the facts as they appear at this time, the use of armed force against such subversive centers as Libya would constitute reprisals and thereby contravene public international law. The primary aims of the use of force against Libya would be (1) to punish it for and retaliate against its training of terrorists and its supplying of arms to terrorists around the world; and (2) to compel Libya to make reparations to the injured state and further to prevent such illegal acts by Libya in the future.

Admittedly, a case can and has been made for the legality of reprisals under the Charter, especially when the collective machinery for dealing with such matters established by the United Nations has proved unable to function. Israel especially has strongly supported its reprisal raids against Arab states that harbor terrorist groups directed against Israel.[40] Even Falk—while strongly criticizing Israel's raid on the Beirut Airport of December 26, 1968, in retaliation for an attack two days earlier upon an El Al passenger plane by Palestinian terrorists at the Athens Airport—has suggested a 12-point framework within which to judge state claims to use force in retaliation against prior terroristic acts.[41] It is doubtful, however, whether such a framework would prove workable in practice, especially in the absence of an impartial and effectively functioning third-party decision-maker.

Moreover, there would appear to be overriding policy reasons not to employ armed force against states serving as subversive centers. The dangers of using armed force against the Soviet Union or members of the Communist bloc are obvious. And even such unpopular regimes as those of President Qaddafi in Libya and of President Amin in Uganda have powerful supporters—such as the Soviet Union, the Arab countries, and the Afro-Asian bloc—who would react strongly against an armed attack against Libya or Uganda. In short, the danger to the maintenance of international peace and security of the use of force against subversive centers might be greater than that of international terrorism itself.

State Self-Help Measures Not Involving the Use of Armed Force

Economic Sanctions

Although most authorities support the thesis that reprisals employing the use of armed force are no longer permissible under the United Nations Charter, this injunction does not appear to apply to economic reprisals. It appears generally accepted that a state may resort to economic reprisals as measures of self-help, subject to the accepted, traditional preconditions for armed reprisals, namely (1) there must have been a prior international delinquency against the claimant state; (2) redress by other means must be either exhausted or unavailable; and (3) the economic measures taken must be limited to the necessities of the case and be proportionate to the wrong done.[42]

Again, it may be noted parenthetically that the power of the U.N. Security Council to authorize economic sanctions is expressly recognized by article 41 of the U.N. Charter, and has in fact been exercised against Rhodesia. For the reasons aforementioned, however, such action by the Security Council against subversive centers is simply not feasible. Also as noted earlier, the legal competence of the U.N. General Assembly or of a regional organization to impose economic sanctions is highly questionable. Finally, in any event the political obstacles to the imposition of economic sanctions by a competent organ of the international community appear insurmountable at this time.

The basic question, therefore, may be whether, as a policy matter, the United States, either unilaterally or in conjunction with other like-minded states—primarily, one might suppose, the industrialized countries—should seek to impose economic sanctions against subversive centers like Libya. In the United States, legislation already exists that would enable the United States to impose a variety of economic sanctions against states serving as subversive centers. For example, the Anti-Hijacking Act of 1974 authorizes the president to suspend civil air traffic with any foreign nation that does not abide by the Hague Convention, or that aids and abets terrorist groups, or with any other nation that continues to provide air service to a nation encouraging hijackers.[43] Also, the International Security Assistance and Arms Control Act of 1976-1977 would terminate military and economic assistance to any country granting sanctuary from prosecution to international terrorists unless the president determines that national security considerations justify the continuance of such aid, in which case he must file a report with Congress stating the reasons for his decision.[44]

The unilateral imposition of sanctions by the United States against subversive center states almost surely would be ineffective. In the aircraft hijacking area, many of the offending states do not maintain air transport relations with the United States, and employment of the secondary boycott provisions of the act—*e.g.*, suspending air traffic with France because it continues to maintain air service to Algeria—would create serious diplomatic problems with some of the U.S.'s closest allies. Similarly, as to termination of military and economic assistance under the International Security Assistance and Arms Control Act of 1976-1977, one suspects the economic impact on the target state would be minimal because of limited or even an absence of U.S. military and economic aid to states serving as subversive centers.

For economic sanctions to have any chance of being effective, then, it would appear that a multilateral approach would be required. However, for a variety of reasons, it is recommended that the United States should *not at this time* press for the adoption of a multilateral sanctions convention. The primary reason why such a step would at present be inadvisable is that for the industrialized countries to band together and impose economic sanctions on Third World countries such as Libya or Algeria would surely result in strong, united, and heated response from Communist and Third World countries. The industrialized countries would find themselves isolated, with the great majority of the world community strongly in opposition. In a recent session of the United Nations Human Rights Commission in Geneva, a British proposal to investigate the situation of Uganda in light of widespread reports of atrocities being committed there was shelved because a majority of Communist and Third World countries was opposed to it.[45] In light of this rejection of an eminently reasonable and supportable proposal, one can imagine the strength of the negative reaction to the imposition of economic sanctions on a Third World country by the industrialized states.

This negative reaction, moreover, would most likely have a number of undesirable ramifications. Irreparable damage might be done to the delicate negotiations now taking place between the United States and the Soviet Union in the area of arms control. Equally delicate negotiations in the context of the Conference on International Economic Cooperation and in GATT, between the industrialized countries and the Third World, might also be seriously compromised. In short, measured in terms of a cost/benefit ratio, a multilateral imposition of economic sanctions on states serving as subversive centers would appear likely to result in a situation where the probable costs would far outweigh the possible benefits. Accordingly, less drastic measures of self-help, discussed later, would seem preferable as alternative courses of action.

International Claims

Under the direction of Richard B. Lillich, the Procedural Aspects of International Law Institute has recently completed a substantial working paper for the Department of State on "State Responsibility for Injuries to Aliens Occasioned by Terrorist Activities," which also has been published as a law review article.[46] The study examines in considerable and scholarly detail a variety of sources—such as arbitral decisions, draft codes on state responsibility, League of Nations and United Nations resolutions, and the writings of eminent jurists—in order to adduce principles of state responsibility applicable to incidents of terrorism. On the basis of this review, the study concludes that the law of state responsibility would support, at least in situations where the evidence would indicate "fault" on the part of the respondent state, claims against states for failure to prevent injuries caused by terrorism or for failure to apprehend, punish, or extradite terrorists.

At the same time the study notes that the current law of state responsibility is ambiguous in many areas, especially since the International Law Commission and previous international "law-making" bodies so far have been unsuccessful in agreeing on a codification of the law. Further, at this juncture it is not at all clear as to the extent to which the deliberations of the ILC are specifically focused on possible state responsibility for injuries occasioned to aliens by terrorist activities.

In the conclusion and policy recommendations section of the study, Lillich recommends that "the United States and likeminded governments would be well advised to select a few strong test cases supported by major state responsibility principles considered in this article and press them vigorously and imaginatively in the years ahead."[47] On its face, this recommendation seems eminently sensible and perhaps even incontrovertible. However, it may be worth a moment or two to explore possible difficulties that the implementation of the recommendation might entail.

A primary difficulty has been well noted in the study itself.[48] It is highly unlikely, to understate the matter, that the respondent state would acknowledge international responsibility for its actions or that it would agree to any form of third-party settlement, whether it be international arbitration, the International Court of Justice, or a U.N. organ. Indeed, it is worth noting in passing that in the Entebbe case, the complaint in the Security Council was brought against Israel—although it was Uganda who had aided and abetted the international terrorists—and the U.S.-U.K. resolution that failed to be adopted did not even implicitly accuse Uganda of a breach of state responsibility.

The Lillich study suggests that nonetheless, the mere bringing of international claims might serve a useful function in that they would focus attention on the illegal acts of the respondent state and raise the consciousness of the world community as to the legal principles involved and the respondent state's violation of them.[49] This in itself would be a worthy goal. However, in any individual case, this goal should be balanced against the effect the bringing of such a claim might have on overall relations between the United States and the prospective respondent state, as well as on relations between the United States and third-party states. A formal international claim brought against Third World states like Libya or Uganda might give rise to some of the seriously adverse consequences discussed in the section on economic sanctions. The bringing of such a claim might also have seriously adverse consequences for the integrity of the international judicial process itself. It is at least arguable that bringing highly charged political disputes before international tribunals may undermine state confidence in third-party adjudication. The recent history of the International Court of Justice lends a measure of support to this thesis.

Diplomatic Protests

In his conclusions and recommendations, Lillich, while stating that the obstacles facing the bringing of an international claim against a state supporting international terrorism may be "steep but not insurmountable," suggests that in any event "the avenue of diplomatic protest—short of bringing a formal claim—is always open and frequently worth taking."[50] The writer agrees with this suggestion.

In Lillich's view, the Department of State should protest vigorously against actions by states that hinder or interfere with the prevention or suppression of international terrorism.[51] Moreover, as suggested by Rubin, such protests should be made even if no U.S. nationals are among the terrorists' victims. The United States has a vital interest in inducing other states to refrain from aiding and abetting international terrorism, an interest that transcends the question whether its nationals may be endangered or injured in the course of any particular incident. The U.S.'s expression of "dismay" at the release by France of Abu Daoud would seem a step toward the adoption of such a policy.[52]

There is of course the likelihood that such protests will displease, and even precipitate counter-protests, from many other states in the world community. However, it would appear unlikely that the response would be so severe as to risk the possible adverse consequences discussed in the section on economic sanctions. In other words, the possible benefits of diplomatic protests would appear to outweigh the possible costs.

Quiet Diplomacy

For a variety of reasons, some of which have been considered earlier, in a particular case the State Department may not wish to bring an international claim or lodge a diplomatic protest against a state that is aiding or abetting or at a minimum hindering efforts to combat international terrorism. In such cases the department should express its concern to the state in question and seek, through quiet diplomacy, to induce that state to cooperate more fully with efforts to control international terrorism.

Specifically, the United States should make every effort to induce other states to become parties to and abide by applicable international conventions such as the Tokyo, Hague, and Montreal conventions on civil aviation and the OAS and U.N. conventions on the protection of diplomats, as well as press for the speedy conclusion of a treaty on the taking of hostages, especially now that the U.N. General Assembly has agreed that a 35-nation commission should be established to draft such a treaty.[53] It should also, at the bilateral level, actively attempt to revise its extradition treaties—using the U.S.-Canadian extradition treaty and the U.S.-Cuba Memorandum on hijacking as models—so as to include acts of international terrorism within their terms and to incorporate the principle of *aut dedere, aut judicare.*[54]

Conclusions and Recommendations

In a sense, this section of the chapter is superfluous, because the conclusions and recommendations are set forth in previous sections. It may nonetheless be worthwhile to summarize briefly the most important of these and emphasize the rationale underlying them.

Perhaps the primary conclusion of this chapter is that the United Nations Charter and modern doctrines of public international law have ruled out resort to the use of armed force as a measure of state self-help against other states supporting international terrorism, except in the highly unusual situation where the use of force can be justified as a measure of self-defense. The Israeli raid at Entebbe was such a situation, but as aptly pointed out by U.S. representatives in the Security Council, the circumstances surrounding that incident were "exceptional" if not "unique," and they should not serve as a precedent for future armed incursions by one state into another state's territory.

Another primary conclusion is that economic sanctions, the bringing of international claims, diplomatic protests, and quiet diplomacy are all permissible measures of state self-help under public international law against states supporting international terrorism. However, the use of coercive measures of self-help, such as economic sanctions or even the bringing of formal international claims, may have serious ramifications for relations between the industrialized countries and the rest of the world community. Accordingly, before any decision to take them is made, the costs versus the benefits of the particular action under consideration should be carefully weighed.

In most instances the writer would recommend that with the exception of diplomatic protests, the United States should refrain from the use of the more coercive measures of self-help against states supporting international terrorism. Rather, the creative use of quiet diplomacy is likely to be the most effective measure of self-help that can be employed to induce recalcitrant states to join cooperative efforts to prevent and suppress international terrorism.

Notes

1. *See, e.g.*, 12 M. WHITEMAN, DIGEST OF INTERNATIONAL LAW 1-496 (1971); D. BOWETT, SELF-DEFENSE IN INTERNATIONAL LAW (1958); Schwebel, *Aggression, Intervention and Self-Defense in Modern International Law*, 136 RECUEIL DES COURS 411 (1972, vol. II); Waldock, *The Regulation of the Use of Force by Individual States in International Law*, 81 RECUEIL DES COURS 455 (1952, vol. II).

2. This summary of the facts is based on the account given in W. STEVENSON, 90 MINUTES AT ENTEBBE (1976).

3. Much of this evidence comes from the testimony of the hostages who were released before the Israeli raid at Entebbe. *See, e.g., id.* at 14.

4. *Id.* at 27.

5. The following summary of the debate in the Security Council on the raid at Entebbe is based primarily on the excerpts from 13 U.N. MONTHLY

CHRONICLE 15-21, 67-76 (Aug.-Sept. 1976) and STEVENSON, *supra* note 2, at 148-208.

6. 22 U.S.T. 1641; T.I.A.S. No. 7570; 65 AM. J. INT'L. L. 440 (1972).

7. STEVENSON, *supra* note 2, at 172.

8. *Id.* at 171.

9. *Id.* at 174.

10. *See Statement by Ambassador Scranton*, 74 DEPT. STATE BULL. 181 (Aug. 2, 1976).

11. 13 U.N. MONTHLY CHRONICLE, *supra* note 5, at 15.

12. *Statement by Ambassador Bennett*, 74 DEPT. STATE BULL. 185 (Aug. 2, 1976).

13. *Id.*

14. N.Y. Times, July 16, 1976, at 20.

15. *See generally* Franck & Rodley, *After Bangladesh: The Law of Humanitarian Intervention by Military Force*, 67 AM. J. INT'L L. 275 (1973).

16. *See* 12 M. WHITEMAN, *supra* note 1, at 204-15.

17. Franck & Rodley, *supra* note 15, at 304.

18. *See* 12 M. WHITEMAN, *supra* note 1, at 77-79.

19. *Id.* at 77-84.

20. *Id.*

21. M. McDOUGAL & F. FELICIANO, LAW AND MINIMUM WORLD PUBLIC ORDER 248 (1961).

22. D. BOWETT, *supra* note 1, at 201-02.

23. W. PROSSER, LAW OF TORTS 113 (4th ed. 1971).

24. Waldock, *supra* note 1, at 467.

25. A. ROSS, THE UNITED NATIONS: PEACE AND PROGRESS 209 (1966). A. THOMAS & A. THOMAS, NON-INTERVENTION, THE LAW AND ITS IMPORT IN THE AMERICAS 91 (1956).

26. *See generally* Note, *The Congo Crisis 1964: A Case Study In Humanitarian Intervention*, 12 VA. J. INT'L L. 261 (1972).

27. *See* Brian Crozier, Terrorism: The Problem in Perspective (March 25, 1976) (presented to the Department of State Conference on International Terrorism).

28. N.Y. Times, July 16, 1976, at 1, col. 1.

29. In the absence of the special agreements between member states and the Security Council envisaged by article 43 of the Charter, it is highly doubtful whether article 42 of the Charter would authorize the council to order the use of armed force against a state serving as a subversive center. Rather, it appears that the council's authority would be limited to making recommendations to this effect under article 39. *See* L. GOODRICH, E. HAMBRO, & A. SIMONS, CHARTER OF THE UNITED NATIONS 314, 316 (1969).

30. G.A. Res. 377, 5 U.N. GAOR Supp. (No. 20) 10, U.N. Doc. A/1775 (1950).

31. In the Certain Expenses case, the International Court of Justice, in

analyzing the legal basis for the United Nations peace-keeping forces in the Middle East (UNEF) and in the Congo (ONUC), repeatedly emphasized that these forces were set up with the consent of the nations concerned and did not constitute measures of enforcement. The clear implication of the opinion was that if the consent of the nations concerned had been absent, the forces would have constituted measures of enforcement and their establishment would have been beyond the competence of the General Assembly under the Charter. *Advisory Opinion on Certain Expenses of the United Nations* (art. 17, para. 2 of the Charter), [1962] I.C.J. 151.

32. This issue arose in particularly acute form in the context of the 1965 United States and OAS intervention in the Dominican Republic. For a detailed consideration of that situation, *see* II A. CHAYES, T. EHRLICH, & A. LOWENFELD, INTERNATIONAL LEGAL PROCESS 1150 (1969).

33. G.A. Res. 2625, 25 U.N. GAOR, Supp. (No. 28) 121, U.N. Doc. A/8028 (1970), *reprinted in* 65 AM. J. INT'L L. 243 (1971).

34. *See generally* Rosenstock, *The Declaration of Principles of International Law Concerning Friendly Relations*, 65 AM. J. INT'L L. 713 (1971).

35. See the eighth and ninth paragraphs of the first principle of the declaration.

36. D. BOWETT, *supra* note 1, at 13.

37. 2 REPORTS OF ARBITRAL AWARDS 1012.

38. *See generally* 12 M. WHITEMAN, *supra* note 1, at 161-74.

39. *See id.* at 148-61.

40. For a summary and strong endorsement of these arguments, *see* Blum, *The Beirut Raid and the International Double Standard: A Reply to Professor Richard A. Falk*, 64 AM. J. INT'L L. 73 (1970). *See also* W.M. REISMAN, NULLITY AND REVISION 836ff (1971); Tucker, *Reprisals and Self Defense: The Customary Law*, 66 AM. J. INT'L L. 586 (1972); Lillich, *Forcible Self-Help Under International Law*, 22 NAVAL WAR COLL. REV. 56 (1970); Brownlie, *International Law and the Activities of Armed Bands*, 7 INT'L & COMP. L.Q. 712 (1958).

41. Falk, *The Beirut Raid and the International Law of Retaliation*, 63 AM. J. INT'L L. 415, 440-42 (1969).

42. *See* Bowett, *International Law and Economic Coercion*, 16 VA. J. INT'L L. 245, 252 (1976).

43. Pub. L. No. 93-366; 49 U.S.C.A. § 1514 (Supp. 1976).

44. § 620 A, Pub. L. No. 94-329; 22 U.S.C.A. § 2371 (Supp. 1976). § 115 of P.L. 95-52, the "Export Administration Amendments of 1977," amends § 3 of the Export Administration Act of 1969 by adding at the end thereof the following new paragraph:

(8) It is the policy of the United States to use export controls to encourage other countries to take immediate steps to prevent the use of their territory

or resources to aid, encourage, or give sanctuary to those persons involved in directing, supporting, or participating in acts of international terrorism. To achieve this objective, the President shall make every reasonable effort to secure the removal or reduction of such assistance to international terrorists through international cooperation and agreement before resorting to the imposition of export controls.

45. N.Y. Times, Mar. 12, 1977, at 3, col. 1.

46. Lillich & Paxman, *State Responsibility for Injuries to Aliens Occasioned by Terrorist Activities*, 26 AM. U. L. REV. 217 (1977).

47. *Id.* at 313.

48. *Id.* at 312.

49. *Id.*

50. *Id.* at 313.

51. *Id.* at 312.

52. N.Y. Times, Jan. 12, 1977, at 1, col. 1.

53. U.N. General Assembly, *Provisional Verbatim Record of the Ninety-Ninth Meeting*, 21, A/31/PV.99 (Dec. 15, 1976).

54. For a more thorough discussion of the writer's recommendations regarding actions the United States might take at the bilateral level toward international cooperation in combating international terrorism, *see* Murphy, *Protected Persons and Diplomatic Facilities*, ch. 5 of this report, at 323-326.

13 Private Measures of Sanction

Jordan J. Paust

Introduction

This chapter will explore several claims that are often made to justify the use of private measures of sanction against terrorism. It will also explore legal policies at stake, decision-making trends, and factors conditioning the legal permissibility or impermissibility of using self-help sanction strategies.

General Focus

The claims discussed here, made by private persons to a right to engage in certain types of private sanctions, can be articulated or implicit in events. Authoritative decision-makers and others will respond to these claims leading to a choice or "decision" that the sanction strategy sought by the claimant is or is not legally acceptable. Legally acceptable strategies or conduct will be referred to as "permissible"; legally unacceptable strategies will be labeled "impermissible." "Legal policies at stake" means the goals sought to be served by prescriptions (found in constitutions, treaties, statutes, regulations, "case-law," and other printed rules or in nonprinted legal rules such as customary international law or common law), that is, the policies that lie behind the rules that are relevant to any given problem. The policies are "at stake" if a decision will affect the serving or thwarting of those policies in any given case regardless of some formal procedural or jurisdictional limitation to the contrary. "Conditioning factors" are the predispositional and environmental factors that affected past decisions or impinge on present or future choices. U.S. legal realists and the sociological schools of jurisprudence, as well as many of the political and social science disciplines, recognize these "conditioning factors" as contextual variables that affect human choice concerning rule promotion, creation, invocation, application, and termination.[1]

The main portion of this chapter will survey various claims, decisions, conditioning factors, and some recommendations; the remaining recommendations will be discussed in the concluding section. However, the creation of rigid "rules" or simple "answers" to contextual and normative problems will not be attempted.[2]

This chapter, prepared for this report, was published in substantially similar form in 12 STANFORD J. INT'L LEGAL STUDIES 79 (1977).

This does not mean that there is little or no "law" in this area, but rather that law is not some static, printed set of words on a piece of paper but a dynamic process of human interaction reflecting both what people think and what people do.[3] This balanced emphasis on people's attitudes and behavior is realistic in that it mirrors the shared legal expectations of the community and the actual practices of states, private institutions, value groups, individuals, and other participants in the international legal process. A sanction decision will then be more authoritative and probably more efficacious than one that relies solely on either what people think or do, or on some aspect of these two components of law (such as past court practice, past state practice, or past elite expectation documented in a U.N. General Assembly resolution).

The McDougal-Lasswell value categories (enlightenment, respect, rectitude, wealth, well-being, skill, and power) are used here to facilitate a policy-oriented consideration of the decisions, conditions, and problems of private self-help sanction strategies. Past and possible future self-help responses will be related to the values generally affected by the self-help strategy and to the five decisional tasks identified by McDougal and Lasswell. These five decisional tasks are: (1) the identification and clarification of the legal policies at stake in a given situation; (2) a description of relevant past trends in decision, if any; (3) an analysis of factors that affected those decisions; (4) a projection of future trends; and (5) a recommendation of a continuation or change in policy, institutions, and procedures (policy alternatives).[4] This inquiry will be prefaced by an attempt to identify relevant problems, claims, and policies. Thus the framework proceeds from an introductory overview into more specific problem areas.

An Objective Definition of Terrorism

One final point about the need for a definition: It is not the purpose here to provide an in-depth analysis of the definitional criteria, but a working definition seems necessary to avoid the confusion or ambiguity too often found in the General Assembly or in the literature. An objective definition of international terrorism is required to avoid politically loaded confusion because even though words will not dictate decisions, the impossibility of absolute definitional precision does not necessarily render complete confusion desirable. Furthermore, an objective definition, one that describes terrorism as a process, can be an extremely useful guide for decision-makers confronted with policy, claims, context, and other questions involving legal competence and jurisdiction.[5] The U.N. secretary-general's report on international terrorism reflects the need for an objective definition in its attempt to articulate certain basic definitional components.[6] The 1937 Convention on Terrorism and the efforts of subsequent scholars have identified other components of the process of terrorism.[7]

In this chapter a descriptive definition of terrorism (*i.e.*, one that also describes the terroristic process) will be used. "Terrorism" involves the intentional use of violence or the threat of violence by the precipitator(s) against an instrumental target in order to communicate to a primary target a threat of future violence. The object is to use intense fear or anxiety to coerce the primary target into certain behavior or to mold its attitudes in connection with a demanded power (political) outcome. It should be noted that in a specific context the instrumental and primary targets could well be the same person or group. Also, terror can be caused by an unintended act, but the community does not seem to perceive such activity as terrorism, nor does it seek to regulate terror caused by conduct that does not include intense coercion or acts and threats of violence.

The key to this definition's utility is that it is primarily descriptive. It does not provide an answer to the separate question: whether terrorism used in a given situation is permissible or impermissible. This approach, therefore, is not conclusion-oriented and does not dictate any particular decision about legality or permissibility. Further, this approach does not define away certain types of terrorism as if they do not exist, and it does not advance any particular political preference or seek prior acceptance of an ideological excuse for terror.[8] Thus such a definition can provide a useful basis for politico-legal inquiry into what specific forms of terrorism should be expressly proscribed by new international conventions or domestic criminal legislation.

Private Self-Help Sanctions:
Strategies and Policies

Self-help sanctions exist in nongovernmental domains at the global, regional, state, and substate levels.

As McDougal, Lasswell, and Reisman recognize:

The interaction and interdependence of all individuals of the world have become such common and subtle features of our existence that their magnitude and full import are only rarely appreciated. People cross national boundaries in numbers and with a regularity which have never before been achieved. The ebb and flow of persons has not been restricted to the highly publicized inter-governmental contacts. People from all sectors of national communities travel and intermingle in striving to maximize their wealth, their skill, their understanding and, even, their prestige.[9]

Furthermore, there is an upward surge of transnational interaction with respect to all values;[10] with the increasing interaction and interdependence of peoples, there is an increasing participation of private individuals and groups in the decision-making process. Private choice and conduct increasingly have greater effect on the obtaining, processing, and dissemination of information (intelligence); the promotion of general policies (promotion); the crystallization of policy (prescription); the invocation of relevant prescriptions to circumstance (invocation); and other aspects of decision process.[11] McDougal, Lasswell, and Reisman add:

Most of us are performing some of these decision roles without being fully aware of the scope and consequences of our acts. Because of this, our participation is often considerably less effective than it might be. Every individual cannot, of course, realistically expect or demand to be a decisive factor in every major decision. Yet the converse feeling of pawnlike political impotence, of being locked out of effective decision, is an equally unwarranted orientation. The limits of the individual's role in international as in local processes is as much a function of his passive acquiescence and ignorance of the potentialities of his participation as of the structures of the complex human organizations of the contemporary world.[12]

This recognition is significant in that it relates directly to the existence of "private sanctions" and the possibilities of further involvement by private individuals and groups in a more policy-responsive manner. This helps us to recognize that a realistic approach to law and choice should not focus on questions of whether there should be private involvement in decisions about and sanctions against terrorism, but rather how to make private participation more useful. Additionally, the focus here can move toward the identification of distinctions between permissible and impermissible private sanctions. Such a focus may also promote comprehensive and realistic governmental or governmentally approved responses to impermissible uses of terrorism as a strategy.

McDougal, Lasswell, and Reisman observe that there seems to be developing:

[A]n increasing awareness and concern that mankind has not yet created the legal institutions, or processes of authoritative decision adequate to clarify and secure common interests under conditions of contemporary interdependence. From peoples living in the shadow of possible ultimate catastrophe, yet tantalized by the promise of a potential abundance hitherto unknown in the production and sharing of all values, the demand for a more adequate international, transnational or world law becomes ever more insistent.[13]

Ever more insistent might be the demand by individuals and groups to participate in various sanction strategies designed, on the one hand, to prevent impermissible terrorist acts and, on the other, to punish those who engage in such conduct when governments at the state and international levels seem incapable of applying appropriate and effective sanctions. This trend, already occurring, will be discussed below.

Private Responses: Strategies of Sanctions

In this survey of private response strategies against terrorism, reference will be made to the sanction categorization utilized by McDougal and Feliciano.[14] It is possible, in any given case, that private individuals or groups, just as state actors,[15] will seek to use military, economic, diplomatic, or ideological strategies or some combination of these to promote one or many of the sanction objectives categorized by McDougal and Feliciano as: prevention, deterrence, restoration, rehabilitation, reconstruction, and correction.[16] Thus a focus on merely one sanction objective, by definition or neglect, would be incomplete and ultimately unrealistic. An incomplete focus on the varied aspects and objectives of sanction can also lead to an inaccurate analysis of the utility of various sanction responses and policy-thwarting conclusions about legal permissibility. Possibilities are so numerous that it is incorrect to generalize about, for example, the legality of "military" or "economic" strategies as such. Quite often intensity of coercion is a factor, but each decision must address specific features of context. As disclosed below, the use of these strategies by private groups as sanctions poses significant questions concerning legal permissibility and the utility of such measures in proscribing impermissible terror.

Military Strategies. In the past, military strategy or the use of armed coercion has been utilized by numerous private groups in response to state-initiated or privately initiated terrorism. More recently, all of us have become aware of the spiraling use of terror and countercoercive strategies by private groups in Northern Ireland. Private sanction strategies have been utilized there and elsewhere to *prevent* threats of terrorism; to *deter* more imminent threats of terrorism; to *restore* previous situations by compelling a violator to reduce the frequency, intensity, and scope of coercion unlawfully initiated; to *reconstruct* situations, structures, and processes of interaction; to *modify or eliminate* recurrence of terrorism; and to *correct* individual or group deviation from prevailing norms.

The use of private armies in Northern Ireland or Lebanon or the use of private police in Argentina are examples, in certain situations, of the use of military coercion by private individuals or groups for some or all of these sanction objectives. With the increasing frequency of social violence and the use of terroristic strategy, it is likely that the use of private military coercion will increase as individuals and groups perceive that local law enforcement or military protection is insufficient or even politically or ideologically biased in favor of local or transnational terrorists.

In general, it does not appear that the increased use of private military coercion for prevention or deterrence *per se* will pose significant policy questions. In nearly all societies, the use of private guards at banks, department stores, airports and other transportation centers, business centers, entertainment centers, schools, nuclear and other power facilities, home and resort areas, and other places in order to prevent and deter violence, theft, and other civil or criminal wrongs is not only acceptable in general but widespread. If uncontrolled or misused, however, the widespread use of private guards can pose significant problems for the serving of law and the maintenance of public order. Guards might be used for other purposes, or take anarchistic courses of action to promote their own power and wealth. More important as threats might be the increased use of private military forces for restoration, reconstruction, and correction. This is because the use of military coercion for such objectives will necessarily clash with state claims to a monopoly of the military function for general law enforcement. Moreover, the increased use of military coercion by private individuals and groups can pose threats to state governmental power as well as threats to civic and public order if other groups respond in kind. The complex political struggles in Lebanon and Northern Ireland provide the most notable examples of this dual type of threat.

Economic Strategies. Economic strategies also have been utilized by private groups as sanctions against impermissible terrorism conducted or encouraged by states or other private groups. Attempts have been made to coerce terrorist groups to refrain from engaging in terrorism or to coerce nonsupport of such groups through the use of boycotts, embargoes, labor strikes, and other economically related tactics. Long-term or short-term attempts to prevent and deter terrorism also have been utilized, and nearly all forms of private participation in socioeconomic growth and value redistribution patterns are potential areas for such activity. In global terms, a broader guarantee of socioeconomic human rights for all peoples may help relieve the relative deprivation and social tension that can spawn acts of terrorism and can cut down on the incidence and types of social violence.[17]

Even significant new developments in the promotion of social and economic rights can deter imminent threats of terrorism by meeting certain terrorist base-group demands, thus dissipating the relative acceptability of such strategies in the eyes of base groups and other audiences.

The use of economic strategies to restore previous situations is also possible. On the one hand, private groups have acted to constrain terrorist power and wealth by controlling the economic patterns of support or by destroying the economic resources of terrorist groups. On the other hand, private groups may choose to support groups or institutions targeted by terrorists or considered by terrorists to be opposition groups or institutions. Such control or support can be reflected in trade patterns, banking patterns, cash flows, arms sales or gifts, food distribution patterns, and so forth.

Post-terrorism sanction efforts can also involve economic strategies. Private groups might assist terrorist victims through rehabilitation efforts designed to provide needed economic aid to individuals, groups, or institutions faced with economic loss, starvation, injury, or disease. Private measures of this sort do not appear to pose significant policy questions, but private economic measures aimed at reconstruction or correction will pose threats to state power and law enforcement similar to those posed by the use of private armies or police for the same objectives. There are exceptions, however, as in the case of efforts by private employers or other private groups to reconstruct terrorist group support patterns or to correct the terrorists themselves through economic deprivation and, possibly, by combinations of economic incentives and deprivation within the parameters of state and international law.

Diplomatic Strategies. Diplomatic strategies engaged in by private groups and terrorists are not as likely to be used as other forms of private sanction; but it is possible that two contending private groups could agree to forestall the use of terror or agree to actions that would decrease the probabilities of future terrorism. It is also less likely, but still possible, that private groups will have occasion to employ diplomacy or direct communication techniques to deter terrorists from destroying certain types of property or from executing hostages. Further, religious groups, ideological groups, or others can engage in effective private communications with terrorists to deter imminent harm or destruction and the attendant terror outcome.

Diplomatic strategies employed between private groups can also serve the sanction goals of restoration, rehabilitation, and reconstruction.[18] In certain circumstances, withdrawing the recognition of a terrorist group can effectively counter certain publicity gains that the terrorists may have made. The rehabilitation of resource values destroyed in the course of a terrorist act can also be negotiated in some circumstances.

Ideological Strategies. Ideological strategies designed to influence large groups are possibly the most pervasive form of private responses to terrorism and yet perhaps the least recognized and organized of sanction options. Furthermore, an ideological strategy may have the most significant potential for developing effective private responses to terrorism.

As identified by McDougal and Feliciano, ideological techniques involve:

[T]he selection of symbols to be circulated in the target audience and to the establishment and maintenance of centers and channels of communication through which the symbols chosen are put into circulation. Suitable symbols may be chosen with a view to affecting the expectations, demands, and identifications of people in the audience, to creating attitudes—that is, stresses or tendencies to the commission of acts by which a particular perspective is externalized—and to channeling and directing the existing tension as well as the expected response of the audience.[19]

The media are important in this regard in both a negative and a positive sense. They are capable of enhancing the terror effect and the publicity or communications aspects of terrorist events,[20] but they are also capable of dissipating or channeling such effects in manners contrary to terrorist aims. Educational groups and the media cannot only channel demands, identifications, and expectations away from the coercive, fear-ridden message of terrorist events (and thus counterpose the support of a terrorist challenge as well as the strategy itself), but so can private letters to the editor, speeches, publications, paintings, pictures, and other forms of general communication. Political parties, private business, labor or professional associations, religious groups, ethnic and cultural groups, pressure or special interest groups, entertainment media and other enlightenment groups, and others also can become involved. Such sanction efforts are possible even in states that tend to support or engage in impermissible strategies of terror.

On the other hand, overreaction, with concomitant displays of power symbols and barren slogans, can create counterproductive outcomes and effects in all but totalitarian societies. In the long run, terrorism can be fought by creating an ideological base through (1) deference to authority and strategies oriented toward human rights and the fundamental demands and expectations of all peoples for a wider shaping and sharing of all values, and (2) wider recognition that terrorism, as a strategy, stands in sharp contrast to fundamental goals of self-determination, human rights, and individual dignity.[21]

Legal Policies at Stake

Generally Shared Goals. At stake in varied uses of private sanction strategies are numerous legal policies concerning the promotion of minimum public order, human rights, and fundamental freedoms and the legal policies designed to assure institutional competence of international, regional, state, and substate entities to manage coercive and noncoercive strategies.

Rational decisions as to permissibility require an awareness of the actual legal policies at stake, the context, and projections about the future effects on those legal policies.[22] It is too simplistic, for example, to say that violence is inimical to public order and human dignity; therefore strategies of violent private sanction are illegal. As Reisman reminds us, in a related focus: "[I]nsistence on non-violence and deference to all established institutions in a global system with many injustices can be tantamount to confirmation and reinforcement of those injustices. In certain circumstances, violence may be the last appeal or the first expression of demand of a group or unorganized stratum for some measure of human dignity."[23]

Persuasion versus Coercion. With Reisman's injunction in mind, it is possible to identify and clarify several generally shared goals. One starts with a general preference for strategies of persuasion versus strategies of coercion;[24] then one can identify a general preference that armed coercion "not be used, save in the common interest."[25] Community security and minimum order[26] are also generally preferred, although claims relating to permissible derogation from norms proscribing violence for the purpose of maintaining self-defense or community security in crisis contexts are also relevant.[27] As McDougal and Feliciano disclose: "[N]ot even the most highly centralized and effectively organized municipal public order attempts to prohibit private coercion absolutely; some provision for self-defense in residual, exceptional cases always remains."[28] It is important to keep in mind, however, that permissible military coercion by private participants usually hinges on value-preserving objectives, as opposed to value-extensive strategy;[29] and human rights law identifies the important goal of relative freedom to enjoy rights and a relative prohibition of the intentional "destruction of any of the rights and freedoms" of others.[30]

Value Conservation versus Value Extension. Within U.S. society one can identify a legal distinction between value conservation and value extension. For example, it is unlawful for an individual to kill or injure another (terrorist or otherwise) for the purpose of extending one's power, wealth, or respect in a given group or community.[31] However, the killing of terrorists for at least one value-conserving purpose, self-defense, might be permissible under state law. But this requires a consideration of the actual context, especially the nature and imminence of harm posed to the person claiming a self-defense justification for utilizing a private sanction strategy.

Self-Defense or Defense of Another. There are disparate approaches under state law within the United States concerning another value conservation problem, a problem usually categorized by legal scholars and practitioners as use of force for the "defense of another."[32] Contrary to a contextual and policy-serving approach to law, there are certain state prescriptions and formal rules that categorically limit or prohibit the use of force by a private person for the defense of another.[33] Even in the case of a husband defending his wife and children against a violent attack, such a rule might require the husband to claim that he sought to protect himself from imminent harm, that he feared for his own life.[34] In some states, the killing of a terrorist that is holding family members hostage by a distraught father might itself be prosecutable as murder or manslaughter.[35] The absurdity of such a result, counterbalanced only by formal deference to the monopoly of force claimed by the state to serve public order, seems self-evident, and it is doubtful that widespread adherence to such formal rules occurs through time.[36]

There will be varying contexts in which the claim to engage in permissible self-defense arises. In addition to the example of the distraught father, one can postulate the need for highly trained, relatively "cool" private guards at a nuclear facility to engage in self-defense in case of armed attack on the guards in order to gain access to the installation. Thus should the same rule of self-defense, or defense of another as the case may be, apply to the nuclear guards as to the man on the street since nuclear terrorism could pose greater threats to society than the bomb in the market? Unless the guards are public peace officers, in which case they would not be "private," the approach should be the same. Each claim to engage in self-defense would be tested by a general rule sufficiently open to contextual variations concerning proper application that different types and intensities of responding coercion in any given case could be permissible.

The general rule would require a contextual awareness of the imminence of the type and amount of harm threatened, the type of responding coercion employed, the amount or intensity of responding coercion, the likely effects of the type and amount of responding coercion, and the reasonable necessity for the initiation of the type, amount, and likely effects of the responding coercion.[37] The use of force in any given context must be proportionate to the reasonably apparent necessity presented and must not unduly inflict a risk on others. Excessive or unnecessary force is itself unlawful. Thus in a given case private guards might permissibly engage in much more widespread and intense responding coercion (*e.g.*, with automatic weapons) than the distraught father might utilize if, under the circumstances, such coercion is reasonably necessary and proportionate. Moreover, the nuclear guards may well be defending a broad class of "others" if the attack is part of an effort to cause a nuclear-induced harm to third persons; but no greater type or intensity of coercion than is reasonably necessary and proportionate to the requirements of the circumstance should be permitted. The legal tests are policy-oriented and contextual; no single "answer" for each circumstance is possible.[38] Even an agent of the state, county, or municipal government—a police officer—cannot use responding coercion that is excessive or unnecessary under the circumstances.[39] A police officer, however, may act sooner in his capacity as a law enforcement official, as where the police officer affirmatively investigates threats to law and order. The role of a private police person, however, should be limited to preventive or deterrent functioning when the use of force is contemplated.

Similarly, the law of several states permits tort actions to be brought against an individual who mistakenly seeks to defend another from attack or imminent harm.[40] Such an individual could be sued in tort for assault and battery, although a mistake of fact on the part of the defendant and his lack of criminal *mens rea* allow a defense to a criminal prosecution for murder.[41] Some decision-makers or commentators note that in case of civil suit, the defendant who aids another acts at his peril and "stands in the shoes" of the person the defendant sought to help.[42] If such a person has no defense under the circumstances, the defendant is liable in tort for damages.

Citizen's Arrest. A state can generally authorize other uses of private violence generalized as a right to perform a citizen's arrest. Within the United States, most states allow a citizen to make an arrest, and to use reasonably necessary violence for a felony committed in his presence.[43] In such cases the policy of minimum public order is thought to be advanced by the use of private enforcement measures.[44] Perhaps for the same reason, many states also enact prescriptions that authorize the prosecution of persons who do not cooperate with law enforcement officials or who withhold needed information.[45] This latter type of response to terrorism is more properly considered under state responses than private responses, however, since the response by private individuals is compelled rather than merely authorized.

State Restraints on Private Individuals and Groups. The authorization of private self-defense and private arrest responses under domestic law does not carry over to the international level, where nation-states are obligated to restrain private individuals and groups from exporting their self-defense, arrest, or related responses abroad. States may permit certain measures of private sanction within their own borders, which are tolerable or serving of minimum public order, but there is state responsibility under international law for certain types of failure to regulate private activities threatening minimum public order or other international goals. An example of prescriptions that require states to control the efforts of private groups to engage in transnational acts of counterterror states:

Every state has the duty to refrain from organizing or encouraging the organization of irregular forces or armed bands, including mercenaries, for incursion into the territory of another state.

Every State has the duty to refrain from organizing, instigating, assisting or participating in acts of civil strife or terrorist acts in another State or acquiescing in organized activities within its territory directed towards the commission of such acts. . . .[46]

A similar prescription prohibits related attempts to "organize, assist, foment, finance, incite or tolerate subversive terrorist or armed activities."[47] The U.N. secretariat has stated that a punishable act should include the incitement, encouragement, or toleration of activities designed to spread terror among the population of another state.[48] These prescriptions have historic background. The assassination of King Alexander I of Yugoslavia in 1934, which precipitated the League of Nations effort to create the 1937 Convention on Terrorism, led to a claim by Yugoslavia that Hungary "had been tolerating irredentist activity within its territory directed against the former, and . . . the League [of Nations] Council adopted a resolution declaring it the duty of every state to desist from encouraging or tolerating such activity."[49] Many others support these prescriptions, which are often categorized as prohibitions against aggression or norms of intervention.[50]

As these prescriptions suggest, private activities utilizing violence in other states, whether or not terror outcomes are produced, are the central concern. Thus a state-approved or state-tolerated incursion by private groups into the territory of a neighboring state to engage in sanction activity would entail state responsibility under international law where such acts were not otherwise permissible under state reprisal theory.[51] Similarly, state toleration of private terrorist activity directed against aliens within its own borders will create claims of state responsibility under international law.[52] Additionally, it should not matter that particularly coercive and disruptive private strategies of sanction do not involve the use of armed force but rather are economic or ideological in nature. If private economic or ideological strategy is intense and threatening to relevant world public order and human dignity values, then states should be responsible for the failure to reasonably restrain or control such private strategies, outcomes, and effects.[53]

Permissible Private Responses. Thus far, attention has been directed to general policies at stake when private violence responses to terrorism occur, since it seems easier to generalize about policies at stake concerning violent strategy than about any other form. Furthermore, it seems generally true that most of the economic, ideological, and diplomatic responses to terrorism by private persons or groups are considered permissible.[54]

General Rationale. Instances of private responses to terrorism generally considered to be permissible abound. For example, the withdrawal of support for terrorist groups or their supporters, support of victims, condemnation of terrorists and their tactics, communication with terrorists for the purpose of persuading them to refrain from killing or injuring hostages, and the payment of ransom money for such a purpose all seem generally permissible and even protected under U.S. constitutional law and fundamental human rights law.[55] The only exceptions under U.S. law that come to mind are prescriptions imposing punishment for an intentional misprison of a felony or the intentional aiding and abetting of a felony.[56] Even then, the writer is unaware of any attempt in the U.S. or any foreign state to prosecute a primary victim of terrorism or a third party for communicating with terrorists or participating in the payment of ransom to save the life or limb of an instrumental target held hostage or otherwise threatened. Indeed, to punish the victims of terrorism or sympathetic third persons does not seem to be policy-serving, a realistic deterrent, or even within the long-term interest of governments desirous of maintaining public support. Such punishment would tend to support terrorist claims that the government is no longer capable of protecting the general population, or other targets, or of acting in a rational manner, and that in its death throes, it is striking out at anyone it can reach and punish.

Perhaps in jest, Roger Fisher once suggested that states punish those who pay ransoms without the approval of the attorney general, punish bank employees who knowingly participate in such activity, make such bank employees personally liable to the state for the full amount of any funds (without specifying any theory for state enrichment), and make the payer of ransom liable to anyone who sues the payer up to the amount of the ransom payment (on a theory that payment "injures" others by increasing the risk of future kidnapings).[57] It is rather surprising that Fisher did not recognize the possibilities evident in new laws to make income from kidnapings subject to double taxation; to make attorney general-approved payments in government bonds; to do away with business expense deductions for terrorists using rent-a-cars, dum-dum bullets, special communication devices, and so forth; or to make flights out of the country available only on a charter basis, subject to seasonal scheduling. One might just as well punish rape victims for yielding to, or robbery victims for supporting, the criminal element in our society.[58]

Foreign Legislative Examples. Nearly as threatening and unresponsive to overall policies and a more realistic maximization of long-term governmental authority as Fisher's proposals are examples of foreign legislation that formally prohibit "assisting" antinationalist organizations;[59] corresponding with outlawed organizations;[60] "anything" done that "supports" any claim to bring about secession, or which "disrupts" sovereignty;[61] activity "endangering" the maintenance of law and order;[62] or rendering assistance to terrorists.[63] It should be clear that the punishment of victims or victim sympathizers under these or similar broadly worded prescriptions is not policy-responsive or in the long-term interests of any rational state. Furthermore, the payment of ransom by a victim or victim sympathizer as well as other terrorist-supportive responses should be viewed as a form of self-defense or defense of others by nonviolent means. Section 139 of the Norwegian Penal Code exempts from an obligation to report certain criminal acts those who would expose themselves or their families to danger were they to do so. Common decency requires an extension of such exemptions to all aid-and-assist crimes as well as exemptions for good faith victim sympathizers. Nevertheless, common decency does not always suffice.

Impermissible Private Responses. In any given case, the use of private economic, ideological, or diplomatic responses may be impermissible under international and/or domestic law, and governments could then engage in otherwise lawful and reasonable sanction strategies to prevent or deter the illegal response, to correct the private deviants, and so forth. For example, some antitrust laws would affect certain forms of economic coercion or manipulation of market processes and allow the government to curtail certain practices by criminal sanction. The use of transnational economic coercion also may violate international legal norms and justify the use of certain forms of state or international response.[64] Ideological strategies engaged in by private persons in response to terrorism might run afoul of myriad international, constitutional, and other legal norms and thus permit, if not compel, governmental sanction effort. At stake might be human and constitutional rights of terrorists to due process of law;[65] rights of terrorist sympathizers or others to freedom from racial discrimination or distinctions based on color, sex, language, religion, political or other opinion, national or social origin, property, birth, or other status;[66] rights of terrorist sympathizers and others to be free from coercion that would impair freedoms of thought, conscience, religion, belief, expression, and association;[67] and so forth.

Diplomatic strategies might run afoul of some of the extremely broad foreign state prescriptions noted above that seek to prohibit the destabilization of governmental power or assistance to private terrorist groups.[68] In a given situation, violations of such domestic laws could occur when private victims seek to negotiate with terrorists for the return of a hostage and to pay a demanded ransom. Such governmental restrictions threaten basic freedoms of thought and action, and they should be challenged where possible under international human rights law and local constitutional law. When aliens, such as U.S. businesspeople, negotiate with private terrorists or make ransom payments, some governments view this as illegal private interference in national affairs. Such governments regulate the private persons or institutions within their country through domestic or extraterritorial legislation, or they might charge the foreign state with responsibility for state assistance or toleration of such private responses to terrorism under international law.[69] In these cases the relevant norms of state responsibility and foreign state prescriptions would be at stake. No doubt the payment of some $14 million by a U.S. company to a local terrorist group will have serious implications for the foreign government involved; but greater weight also should be given to fundamental human rights that legally require governments to show the necessity for certain forms of deprivation.

In any one of these "restraints upon private response" situations it is important to keep in mind that fundamental human rights and constitutional policies are always at stake. Accordingly, the state's attempt to restrict such freedoms must be shown, in each case, to be reasonably necessary for the serving of minimum public order and protecting the rights of others and to have been strictly required under the circumstances.[70] From both the legal and pragmatic points of view, efforts must be made to ensure that government restraints are not carried to impermissible excess in violation of international law and its integral component of public expectation.[71] Excesses are counterproductive because of public opinion and because the effects of impermissible excesses can enhance terrorist political rhetoric and promote the overthrow of governments by terrorist elites.[72]

Decisions and Conditioning Factors: Recent Trends

This section will analyze in greater detail recent trends in decision-making concerning private sanction strategies, but the limited data will make the consideration necessarily incomplete. Discernible trends are organized under value headings (enlightenment, respect, wealth, and so forth) that seem most appropriate in terms of the values at stake, the relevant institutional patterns, and the strategy utilized.

Public Opinion: Enlightenment

Education. One implementary response available to the community, yet not specifically mentioned in new instruments on international terrorism, involves the prevention of terrorism through an awareness by members of the legal profession of human dignity goal values, of the fundamental principles of the law of armed conflict, and of human rights. The legal profession should also facilitate a fuller sharing of this awareness. Education is the key to implementing the principles of human rights and the law of war.[73]

The United States, though lacking a far-reaching human rights educational program for civilians, has advocated a more pervasive awareness of international law and has assisted, thereby, in the formation of a "moral" consensus and the broadening of the working foundation of the law (*i.e.*, its meaning and its efficacy in the social process), all of which will discredit and discourage terrorist activities.[74]

Since 1899, states have solemnly declared themselves bound to issue instructions to their armed forces regarding the law of war.[75] The 1949 Geneva Conventions continue this trend and expand the basic obligation of all parties to "respect and to ensure respect" for the conventions "in all circumstances."[76] A common article of the Geneva Conventions provides that contracting parties undertake "to disseminate the text of the present Convention as widely as possible . . . and in particular, to include the study thereof in their programmes of military and, if possible, civilian instruction, so that the principles thereof may become known to the entire population. . . ."[77] Numerous types of civilian education programs on human rights and Geneva law with supplemental media and education usage can be devised,[78] and it is recommended that states do so, both to fulfill Geneva Convention requirements and to broaden "preventive law" measures to combat terrorism.[79] The United States, with its vast educational capacity, has recognized this need and is bound by the Geneva Conventions to implement civilian educational programs, so improvements in implementation by the United States should be made during the next few years. If such programs are not forthcoming from the U.S. government, international lawyers can be more than spectators; they can initiate the process themselves.

Several international entities may be engaged by states or private groups for coordinative, promotional, and advisory services or for limited educational roles. Examples might include U.N. entities such as the United Nations Educational, Scientific and Cultural Organization (UNESCO) and United Nations Institute for Training and Research (UNITAR), or the International Committee of the Red

Cross (ICRC) and its staff and national societies.[80] Indeed, in the light of the U.N. Charter pledge of all members "to take joint and separate action in co-operation with the Organization"[81] and to promote "respect for, and observance of, human rights and fundamental freedoms,"[82] it seems incumbent on all members to initiate civilian education programs, and to seek cooperative educational and other measures that can precipitate an active and viable U.N. entity functioning in this area. While global educational coordination is an important purpose of the United Nations, it is clearly anticipated that signatories will individually ensure respect for all relevant human rights in addition to U.N. efforts.[83] In connection with this expectation, it has been stated by the secretariat that "United Nations human rights instruments as well as the Geneva Conventions appear to belong to the category of treaties setting forth 'absolute obligations' . . . [which are not] dependent upon a corresponding performance by others."[84] Pictet adds that pledges to ensure respect for Geneva law, including educational measures, do not depend on reciprocity or on the existence of signatories' participation in actual conflict. The pledge requires affirmative action on the part of every state to ensure that the principles are "applied universally" and "in all circumstances."[85] Again, education has been recognized by eminent scholars as a key to the implementation of human rights and the laws of war, legal norms that proscribe nearly every form of terroristic strategy. A broader understanding of such can supplement perspectives and foster new expectations that constitute a working foundation of law and the politico-ideological restraint that will have an effect on the use of terroristic strategy and its successes in social process. Education, as a counter to terror conditioning, is of course a critical need in waging an effective ideological war against terrorists.

Media Control and Cooperation. As indicated earlier, the media can play useful roles concerning prevention and reconstruction. Also important are media roles concerning deterrence and restoration objectives through publicity of events and demands on the part of private terrorists and the government. Thus questions concerning the control and cooperation of the private media are very important.

There seems little question as to the permissibility of media participation in the denunciation of terrorist groups and their tactics, the reporting of terrorist incidents, or the publication of other private responses through media channels. Indeed, fundamental constitutional and human rights of freedom of speech, freedom of opinion, freedom of the press, freedom of association, and freedom of participation in government and social process are all at stake.[86] It has been recognized, however, that restrictions on the free exercise of these rights could be permissible in time of crisis when strictly required under the circumstances and within the limits of a democratic society.[87] Moreover, article 18(2) of the 1966 Covenant on Civil and Political Rights would prohibit media "coercion which would impair" the freedom of others to adopt a religion or belief of one's own choice, and article 20 would prohibit any "propaganda for war" and any "advocacy of national, racial or religious hatred that constitutes incitement to discrimination, hostility or violence" if implemented by domestic law. Obviously, the government can request the media's assistance in controlling information provided to the public and to certain terrorists; this approach seems quite successful.[88] The question remains, however, whether the government can demand control of the media through legislation, executive decrees, or other measures.

In some foreign states, broad legislative or executive decrees attempt to control media responses to terrorism. Indeed, some provisions are so broad that media personnel or others using media channels to express their views might be subject to criminal punishment for assisting, supporting, or sympathizing with terrorists or their aims or for disrupting sovereignty and endangering public order.[89]

It is extremely doubtful whether such broad prescriptions can stand the test of necessity within democratic limits.[90] One of the broadest attempts at control specifically directed at the media is the 1973 Uruguayan Decree-Law No. 393/973, which authorized governmental prohibition of "the publication, by means of oral, written or televised media [of] all information, commentaries or impressions which directly or indirectly mentions or refers to those persons who conspire against the nation or against anti-subversive operations, excluding official communication."[91] Other foreign prescriptions would prohibit private media or other responses that incite "hatred" against terrorist groups or their base-groups.[92] Some would prohibit media statements advocating the use of violence against terrorists or their base-groups,[93] and others seek to curb any criticism of government responsive measures.[94] Perhaps the broadest attempt at communication control is contained in the Republic of Korea presidential emergency measure of May 13, 1975, which prohibits fabrication or dissemination of any "falsehood," the making of any false presentation of fact, or any public defamation of the emergency measures.[95]

U.S. adoption of such broad legislative or executive approaches could not pass the international human rights test of necessity within democratic limits or withstand the constitutional challenge likely to occur under the First Amendment. Necessity, in such a case, is ultimately a matter for the courts to decide, and the recent Supreme Court decision concerning the publication of the Pentagon Papers[96] makes it highly unlikely that the Court will allow broad legislative or executive controls of the media, such as those extant in several foreign countries, to stand the test of constitutional challenge. It is most likely that any governmental manipulation of the media for purposes of controlling terrorism will have to be initiated through cooperative and otherwise lawful approaches. However, it appears that such approaches can be creative and highly successful.[97] Furthermore, a greater use of court orders to restrain temporarily certain types of reporting (*e.g.*, location of police, negotiating tactics being utilized, bloody and terror-serving types of reporting) may prove feasible to save lives, preserve due process of law, and prevent added terror and mirror effects.

Outlets for Dissent. Besides consideration of efforts to control or manipulate the flow of private information concerning terrorist events, terrorists, and their objectives, serious thought should be given to providing dissident groups with the means of communicating with other members of society. A communications outlet for groups that, rightly or wrongly, feel "oppressed" could relieve social stress and tension and thereby dissipate the perceived need for other strategies of communication,[98] such as terrorist acts of "propaganda by deed." M. Chérif Bassiouni has made a challenging suggestion that efforts be undertaken to "set up an international radio-television station where liberation movements could have access and broadcast their claims to the world community, avoiding the need to focus attention on them by engaging in particular acts which are dramatic in the eyes of the press."[99] Instead of exercising substantial control over the media, a cooperative and partial control coupled with access or outlet programs should be implemented. More responsible, less sensationalist reporting and commentary should be encouraged since it can have an effect on predispositions toward violence as well as toward simplistic solutions or black-and-white, politicized excuses for human rights deprivation.

Numerous private groups should also be encouraged to investigate, document, disclose, and engage in general preventive strategies regarding instances of institutionalized terrorism so that a greater awareness of these activities and overall enlightenment can lead to more meaningful governmental responses and broader awareness and condemnation of such impermissible acts of terrorism.

Respect, Rectitude, and Moral Suasion

Individuals and groups in high positions of respect and rectitude can participate creatively and effectively in the sanctioning of impermissible acts of terrorism. Professional organizations, religious organizations, civic leaders and their organizations, and all others with relatively high positions of respect can influence predisposition patterns and respond creatively toward general preventive and remedial needs, if not also toward deterrence and restoration in actual cases. The American Bar Association has already responded with a resolution on terrorism,[100] and another law-oriented group, World Peace Through Law, has responded similarly.[101] Church, human rights, other groups, many having transnational bases of support and effect, have undoubtedly also been engaged in private sanction responses. It is important to keep in mind, however, that overreaction to terrorist threats by governments or oppressive measures of control can backfire and lead to loss of support from several types of respect or rectitude groups and institutions.[102] Similarly, approval of, association with, or condoning of terrorists and their strategy can lead to depletion of support for governments, international organizations, or other institutions by respect or rectitude groups and institutions.

Wealth Factors

Questions of the payment of ransom in self-defense or for the defense of another have already been discussed. However, with regard to withdrawal of wealth support to terrorist groups, several interesting questions are worthy of exploration.

Freezing Assets. Can banks or insurance companies freeze assets that are likely to be utilized in support of terrorist causes? Can private individuals breach contracts or suspend the performance of contracts with terrorist groups if performance will only support terrorist activities indirectly? Can private groups confiscate or destroy terrorist weapons or other resources? Can the government regulate any of these interactions? Can the government ban the manufacture or sale of certain terror-saving weapon systems, such as magnum dum-dum bullet systems? Can private groups engage in unrestrained boycott, embargo, or other economic strategy against terrorists and those who tend to support or condone their activities? These are merely some of the problems posed with private sanction activities and wealth processes.

The question whether private wealth institutions can, on their own, freeze assets that are likely to be utilized in support of terrorist activities or causes is intriguing. One runs ultimately into the problem of private breaches of contract. One "solution" to the problem might be the creation of a bank contract clause that allows the bank to freeze assets on its own or at the request of the U.S. attorney general. Contracts, of course, are subject to governmental controls that are reasonably necessary for the promotion of public safety;[103] and governments can regulate this sort of interaction.[104] Government authority aside, the question remains whether private entities can freeze assets or breach private contracts that are otherwise legal when it is reasonably necessary to do so to promote a significant public purpose, or when full performance of the contract would significantly contribute to serious forms of illegality, and the government is unwilling or incapable under the circumstances of meeting the serious threat posed to minimum public order and human dignity.

There is no easy answer. However, if one analogizes to international law, where self-help sanction is more widespread, one can develop a theory justifying such measures as reasonable temporary forms of interference that are generally necessary under the circumstances in order to avert a serious threat to public order and the serving of relevant legal policy.[105] There are several qualifying factors here, however, which must be addressed. The measure must be reasonable under the circumstances and temporary to minimize disruption and facilitate appeals to authoritative decision-makers. The measure must generally be necessary, as with the case of use of violence to defend others when there is threat of a serious felony,[106] and the threat to public order must be serious—a condition that is satisfied by compliance with the necessity standard.

Perhaps these qualifying conditions would severely limit the number of instances in which the freezing of assets by private wealth institutions would be deemed permissible. For example, is it necessary, in order to avert a serious threat of terrorism, to freeze bank assets or to engage in breaches of contracts that are otherwise legal and require performances that are lawful *per se*? Will the courts analogize to criminal law and require imminent threat of death or serious bodily harm? Or will the courts find the freezing of assets to be permissible when reasonable and temporary even where a terrorist threat is not imminent? Must preventive or pre-emptive self-defense await conditions of actual self-defense or defense of others? Given the fact that bank employees and other private sanctioners who find themselves in a situation of predictable but nonimminent terrorism can usually telephone the government's law enforcement entities, it would be a rare situation when the freezing of assets or similar economic measures would actually be necessary. Where reasonable, such actions could avert serious threats of terrorism. The serving of minimum public order and human dignity policies compels a conclusion of permissibility in such a case. This is not to say that any activities that facilitate terrorism can be regulated by private sanctions that would otherwise be impermissible; even the government could not do that. The danger must be generally imminent and the measures generally necessary.[107] Where the danger is predictable but not imminent, the restraint of private measures of this sort is preferable and other governmental and private measures of protection and influence should be utilized.

Transferring Assets. A more serious problem is posed in the United States, however, when the threat is predictable, not imminent but very difficult to avert, as where a bank employee is faced with a request to transfer assets outside the United States for use by terrorists abroad. Can the federal government stop such a transfer of funds? Do the Trading with the Enemy Act and relevant cases provide useful analogies?[108] As U.S. states cannot legislate in areas where there are significant potential disruptions of foreign affairs goals and activities,[109] can private entities engage in conduct with similar potential effects? Can the bank freeze the transfer of funds *until* the federal government can act? Again, no easy answer appears, but the last question may present a viable approach. Even then, however, there should be detailed guidelines governing the private choices made in varying circumstances. If the conduct is deemed permissible to stop the toleration, promotion, and financing of terrorist activities abroad,[110] can private entities be given meaningful guidelines hinged on ambiguous terms of state obligation such as "tolerate," "promote," "assist," or "finance"? Indeed, is the government prepared to make such choices? And if so, what happens to the standard of necessity with regard to private sanction measures or governmental measures? Is the fact of border crossing, or its imminence, sufficiently important to justify an exception?

Possibly the best approach to an overall solution to the transfer of assets problem would involve the creation of new congressional legislation, under the foreign commerce and general welfare powers, that allows the executive branch an opportunity to fulfill its international obligations to refrain from financing, assisting, promoting, or tolerating terrorist activities abroad or acquiescing in organized activities within the United States that are directed toward the commission of such acts. Foreign governments might be sufficiently threatened by local financing and propaganda activities in support of transnational terrorism that they would bring an international claim against the United States. So far, only the British protest of efforts in support of the IRA comes to mind, but other types of activity within the United States could involve the United States in a controversy over claims of assistance, toleration, and acquiescence of foreign terrorist acts. To meet the problem, Congress could delegate to the executive branch the power to regulate the transfer of assets to terrorist organizations. Further, it could delegate to the executive branch related powers to regulate trade with such organizations, governments that utilize terrorism against their own peoples or others, and governments that fail to comply with international norms of state responsibility outlined earlier, the so-called "safe haven" states and others. Apparently such a joint congressional-executive approach would be constitutional under the *Curtis-Wright Export* case.[111]

Transferring Weapons/Breaching Contracts. Other questions, such as whether private entities can stop the transfer of weapons to others or breach contracts when performance is otherwise lawful, seem to present similar policy considerations. The transfer of weapons might be stopped until local police can investigate or the federal government can regulate international transfers. When the terrorist threat is supported only indirectly and thus is not imminent and the sanction approach is not necessary, can there be a lawful breach of contract when performance would merely facilitate terrorism? The answer appears to be no, at least where performance is otherwise lawful.[112] Can private groups confiscate or destroy terrorist weapons or resources? The answer seems to hinge, as in other cases, upon the reasonable necessity to avoid death or serious injury, whether or not there is a contract relationship.[113] Of course, the government could regulate the transfer of weapons to terrorists (magnum force dum-dum bullets, for example, are already illegal)[114] if they only knew who the terrorists were.

Selective Boycotts and Embargoes. The final question addressed in this section is whether private individuals, groups, or institutions can engage in selective boycotts, embargoes, or similar economic strategies against terrorists who necessarily violate international and domestic law. This question seems useful as well for addressing a broader issue—whether a private manipulation of wealth resources is permissible where there are no contractual restraints and no taking or destruction of property occurs. A short answer appears to be yes, the conduct is permissible, provided that there are no violations of international law. Even if violations of international legal norms are threatened, however, it seems arguable that in some cases the violation of international law posed by terrorists justifies otherwise impermissible measures of self-help to sanction violations when the sanctions are necessary and proportionate.[115] The same reasoning should apply to any threats to domestic laws, such as the Sherman Antitrust Act or relevant labor regulations.

A recent claim involving the transnational manipulation of wealth is worth more detailed attention. Recently, certain U.S. Jewish organizations engaged in a tourist boycott activity against Mexico because of dissatisfaction with Mexico's support of, in Jewish eyes, a terrorist organization and its support of General Assembly actions against Zionism.[116] The activity presents the question whether private sanction measures of this sort are permissible. Certainly the freedom to refuse to do business with those engaged in illegal activities is permissible. However, can one use economic coercion against those who merely support terrorists? One may not be compelled to do business with terrorist supporters, but can they be coerced without restraint? It seems that a more policy-responsive answer is that it depends on the nature and intensity of the coercion, the policies at stake, and relevant features of context.[117] In many cases even economic coercion can be permissible; but when such coercion is not necessary or when it is disproportionate, there are other legal policies at stake that can compel a decision of impermissibility. If the response is not necessary, but proportionate and of low intensity, it may still be permissible under certain circumstances. Some forms of coercion are normal in day-to-day social inter-action, but other forms can thwart the serving of fundamental human and constitutional rights to such an extent that legal regulation is possible if not mandatory.[118] In this case the facts are insufficient for a complete answer, but the writer is bothered by the loss of some $9 million by private Mexican groups and entities that may have had nothing to do with any support of terrorists, and one would need to investigate further whether the coercion was intense and there were substantial threats to human rights policies. In general, however, certain levels of economic coercion should be permissible to sanction impermissible support of terrorism.

Well-being Factors

Similar questions concerning breach of contract, prevention of felonies, and use of coercion are presented in a focus on private sanction strategies that relate to well-being processes. Can contracts relating to well-being be breached? Can well-being resources be confiscated, manipulated, or destroyed? Can medical resources be withdrawn? But other questions are also posed: Can private parties bring a cause of action against airlines for terrorist outcomes so as to assure greater preventive effort? Can well-being, as well as other related processes, be utilized to promote socioeconomic conditions less conducive to the spawning of terrorism? Can government regulation of private well-being processes occur when a government objective is to promote socioeconomic conditions that generally thwart the growth of terrorist strategy? In the name of antiterrorism, does the government have greater power to regulate health, wealth, respect, enlightenment, and other value processes?

Intentional Destruction of Well-being Resources. With regard to the first set of questions, relating to breach of contract, defense measures, and prevention of felonies, no significant changes in approaches outlined above seem required by consideration of related private sanction strategy and well-being. The intentional destruction of well-being resources by private individuals, groups, or institutions should be reasonably necessary under the circumstances to avert imminent threat of death or injury. The manipulation of such resources, of course, can be permissible through free choice, but coercive manipulation must be considered with reference to scope, intensity, and effects. There are several human rights policies to keep in mind as well. For example, there are general prohibitions against torture, cruelty, inhumane or degrading treatment or punishment,[119] starvation,[120] deprivation of medical care,[121] summary execution, and numerous things that relate to general well-being. Many of these, in fact, are prohibited *per se*; that is, their use as strategies is never lawful, regardless of claimed necessity.[122]

Deprivation of medical resources serves as an example. There is a basic medical and general human expectation that all persons are entitled to needed medical treatment, supplemented by an expectation applicable in time of armed conflict that all persons placed out of combat by circumstance or choice are entitled to humane treatment, protection, and medical care.[123] An intentional withdrawal of needed medical resources, then, would thwart the serving of such expectations, and there are no pragmatic reasons for thwarting legal policy and medical ethics. On the contrary, the withdrawal of medical resources would be counterproductive in dealing with terrorists and in preventing future forms of social violence. Since cruelty, torture, inhumane punishment, and starvation are also impermissible *per se*, the use of private sanction strategies that seek these outcomes are likewise impermissible. If a distraught father tortures a captured terrorist to learn of the whereabouts of his hostage family, the father's conduct would be impermissible even though a mitigation of penalties imposed would certainly be worth considering.

Private Rights to Sue. The question of suits against airlines poses a sanction approach worthy of special attention. Private individuals should be able to sue any person, group, or institution for negligent or intentional harm, but protection from suits exists in government regulations and court doctrine regarding various public and private entities. The question here goes further: Should recovery of damages against airlines for terrorist outcomes be permitted, regardless of negligence or intent, so as to assure an equitable spread of risk and to promote prevention efforts? A related question might be, should the airlines, as private sanctioners, be free from suit for taking terrorist prevention measures that cause interference with the well-being and respect of certain, or all, passengers? Both these questions are liable to spark reactions among the trial bar and airline lawyers, but special interests should not be the measure for public decisions. A decision to prevent terrorism regardless of the interference with private rights to sue or defend could favor strict liability for airlines when terrorism occurs and a strict defense for airlines sued for reasonable, or even slightly unreasonable, measures of passenger control and routing. A decision to promote normal freedoms might result in a lack of liability *per se* and a lack of defenses for tortious treatment or control of passengers, luggage, and aircraft. Each circumstance, however, should be addressed.

Given the relative infrequency of aircraft incidents in the United States through the use of effective preventive measures, the writer tends to favor leaving tort norms alone. Besides, within certain normative regulations, there is flexibility for responsive policy-serving in given situations.[124]

Civil Liability for Negligence. Related questions concern civil liability of private persons, groups, or institutions for negligence or intentional involvement in connection with terrorism. For example, is a gun shop owner liable for selling illegal dum-dum bullets to persons who use them to commit terrorist acts? The general law of torts, as supplemented by relevant constitutional and international norms, should be sufficient. A gun shop owner who sells illegal bullets to others, for example, should be held strictly liable for the harm caused by the sale of such inherently dangerous and illegal ammunition.[125]

With regard to the more general question of private and governmental responses that seek to prevent terrorism by fostering socioeconomic bases for human dignity, there appears no real problem of permissibility. These measures are permissible, useful, and desirable, if not obligatory upon governments.[126] However, the government has no greater power over private interaction in the name of antiterror than it already possesses in the name of public safety, welfare, and happiness. Of recent interest, for example, is the control of privately owned food supplies exercised by Italian police in June 1976. Local police in Rome barred the shipment of meat collected by butchers for distribution to shops in the city in order "to block the crime of extortion."[127] A terrorist group calling itself the Communist Combat Unit had kidnaped two meat merchants and ordered the sale of 2200 pounds of prime beef in 23 working-class neighborhoods as the primary ransom demand. Local butchers had collected the meat in an effort to comply, but the police stepped in to bar the sale of meat as demanded. The police seizure occurred while one of the merchants was still being held, and posed a precedent for police controls that stands in sharp contrast to the effort by the Hearst family, with government knowledge and apparent approval, to feed the poor of California in response to SLA demands. Although one could justify governmental control of wealth or well-being resources in certain circumstances, when the threat to public order is substantial and the controls are necessary and reasonable under the circumstances, the Italian control of private resources "to block the crime of extortion" would raise serious constitutional questions if copied in this country. What must be addressed in each case, to be policy-serving, are the necessity and reasonableness of the measures adopted and the seriousness of the threat to law and public order posed by the terrorist demand and the countermeasure sought by the police.[128]

Finally, one can note the important efforts made by many private groups, such as the International Committee of the Red Cross, to prevent terrorism and to rehabilitate or reconstruct. These activities are certainly generally permissible and laudable. Present concern does not hinge on the activities of such humanitarian organizations but on the reluctance of far too many governments to allow more creative and effective roles for such organizations and groups to play in combating the inhumanities and injustices that condition violent responses to value deprivation and indignity. For self-interest, if not common interest, greater use of humanitarian organizations should be encouraged.[129]

Skill Factors

It is commonplace now to note that individuals, groups, and institutions with certain skills interact in various ways to terrorist strategies, outcomes, and effects. Of interest here, however, are sanctions recently attempted by various labor or skill unions.

Airline Pilots. Airline pilots are likely to get involved in measures designed to stop the export of terrorism abroad and the practice of some states to provide a safe haven to hijackers and others. One approach suggests that states create a new treaty "which would provide a basis for joint action such as suspension of all air service to countries which fail to follow the basic rules set out in the Hague and Montreal Conventions."[130] In 1973, a diplomatic conference on air security considered this proposal, but it was not acted on. Although there has been some opposition to the strategy, some commentators believe that there is a good possibility that it will be formally adopted in the future, if not on a global basis, at least on a regional basis by means of various bilateral arrangements.[131] The organizational entity most likely to be associated with a global response would be the International Civil Aviation Organization (ICAO), as the United States and Canada have already proposed a draft treaty of this nature to that entity, which proposed a boycott as the primary sanction. If bilateral arrangements are not worked out, and perhaps in some cases even if they are, it is not unlikely that private action will utilize a similar boycott technique supplemented by local ground strikes of airline pilots and air service personnel. Ambassador Bennett has warned the United Nations of the fact that private groups "such as airline pilot associations and labor organizations speak of acting in their own self-defense" regardless of governmental consensus.[132] But Bennett failed to mention that the active pilot group (IFALPA) had already demonstrated the role that private entities could take in sanction objectives by supporting a one-day suspension of air service in several parts of the world.[133] In general, such private measures of sanction are acceptable when they are reasonably necessary self-help efforts to curb terrorism and the fundamental threat posed to international transportation and public order by air hijacking. Measures envisioned are temporary and fairly proportionate responses to state refusal to comply with international norms designed to maximize human rights and minimum public order. The measures envisioned, moreover, involve the "manipulation" of those "contingencies, means, and objectives" that would "be unquestionably lawful assuming that prior sanction had been accorded by an authoritative organ."[134] The fact that private coercion of the intensity envisioned takes place and interferes with state "political independence" does not require a decision of impermissibility where other international norms and a majority of equally significant U.N. Charter goals are served.[135]

It is entirely possible that advance disclosure of these sanction strategies by relevant airline pilot groups, as well as by air companies, will aid this overall preventive effort. If the public knows in advance that airline escapes or hijackings will not be as readily available, that private groups will refuse to participate, there may be fewer attempts to utilize aircraft in carrying out terrorist strategies or escapes. By refusing to fly to safe-haven countries, private groups may aid in preventing greater use of safe havens even when some countries are willing to aid in the promotion of terrorist strategy by what is, in effect, a condonation of terrorism.

Unions and Business Groups. A recent article in the press disclosed that a delegation of labor unions in Portugal had demanded "urgent measures to end a wave of 'fascist terrorism' that has struck northern Portugal" and had threatened "to act themselves if the government does not take steps to curb the violence."[136] Similar claims have arisen in Argentina when business entities demand an end to waves of terrorism or labor unions strike for similar purposes.[137] Indeed, the labor unions in Portugal called "a one-hour work stoppage" in several locations in Portugal to "protest against increasing anti-Communist violence."[138] These trends pose several questions concerning private responses to terrorism by certain skill groups in labor and business sectors. Are labor strikes by local or transnational groups permissible measures of self-help? Are work or business stoppages by local or transnational business groups permissible measures? As with the other questions, there are no easy answers. Permissibility depends on the context and the legal policies at stake.

One can envision breaches of contracts of a local nature and of a transnational nature by such private responses. One can envision minimal and temporary interference with international trade patterns or widespread coercive impact and disruption. And one can also envision minimal and temporary interference with basic social services and fundamental human rights of others or serious disruption and fundamental deprivation. Each of these types of response by private skilled groups, therefore, must be addressed under actual circumstances with reference to types of legal policies at stake. In general, one should favor private measures that pose minimal disruption and deprivation. Certainly many labor and business groups of a transnational nature interact with others each day with levels of persuasion and coercion that are deemed normal and acceptable, but questions arise when the intensity of coercion and deprivation increases.

Power Factors

Numerous private individuals, groups, and institutions play some role in the shaping and allocation of power and the shaping or conditioning of authority.[139] Thus one can envision numerous types of private power-oriented responses to terrorism. Indeed, we have already addressed certain forms of self-defense and defense of others, responses related to the authoritative exercise of power. Furthermore, ideological, legal, or other forms of expectation are also important components of power.[140] The focus here, however, is directed toward private forms of military response to terrorism, rather than the several forms of diplomatic, ideological, and economic strategy under enlightenment and wealth process sections discussed earlier.

Private Armies. One might assume that the problem of private armies is a problem of self-defense or defense of others writ large. To a certain extent this is true, but there are far more significant policy questions posed by the use of private armies to prevent, deter, restore, reconstruct, or correct in response to acts or threats of terrorism than is the case with individual instances of self-defense or defense of others. As stated earlier, it does not generally appear that an increased use of private military coercion for prevention or deterrence as such will pose significant problems for the serving of law and minimum public order. Private armies might take the form of highly trained and well-equipped militia; but if they are privately employed to guard sectors within the inner city or outside the cities in the bedroom communities, to guard large industrial complexes at home or abroad, to guard nuclear facilities for civil nuclear power, to guard important aspects of communication or transportation, and so forth, the employment of military strength for such defensive and deterrent purposes seems permissible. Of course, there are dangers posed by private military units. The power created by private armies can be misused. Private armies could be turned against the state, utilized for border crossings in violation of international law,[141] or used for value extension purposes in violation of local, national, or international legal norms. Some restraint must be imposed, perhaps via state and federal supervision at the national level and some form of international supervision at the international level.

Northern Ireland and Lebanon stand as examples of the dangers of private armies, with or without state approval, to restore *status quo ante*, to reconstruct value losses, or to correct violations of the law and deprivations of certain values such as wealth and well-being. When the use of private armies for such purposes becomes internationalized by outside support or international effects, there are usually serious threats posed to the maintenance of minimum world public order; and if private responses meet private counter-responses, there is serious danger of spiraling social violence[142] and increased destruction of all values. Ideally, the correction of other strategies should be utilized only for reasonably necessary sanction of human right violations when state law enforcement entities are incapable or unwilling to enforce the law or to implement basic human rights of all participants in a given social process. Moreover, private corrective violence must be tested by conditions of necessity and proportionality, the immunity of certain targets and other criteria for policy-serving and contextual-oriented decision, if they are to be allowed at all.[143]

Of particular concern have been the recent spiraling strategies of violence and counterviolence of a terroristic nature in Argentina. A newspaper account states that 40 people were killed in just one week of political assassination and violence. The news story begins:

Nine of the dead were police officers shot down at random from speeding cars by leftist guerrillas, who also wounded four soldiers. A civilian was killed when a bomb exploded in the parking lot of the army's General Command, wounding four colonels.

The 30 other victims were primarily students and labor delegates, kidnapped by groups of armed men in their homes or on the streets at night, and later found shot to death in isolated places.[144]

The patterns of private warfare in Argentina, Lebanon, Northern Ireland, and Spain, to name a few of the recent arenas, are too frequent to be ignored by international legal scholars. Such patterns pose significant domestic, trans-national, and international legal problems—problems intermeshed in typical doctrinal concerns of self-defense, intervention, self-determination, human rights, murder, minimum public order, martial law (or other claims to suspend the efficacy of normal patterns of authority in times of power crisis), kidnaping, preventive detention, subversion, treason, and the like. It is surprising, in view of the growing recognition of the phenomenon and the inadequacy of otherwise ceremonially useful legal labels, that W. Michael Reisman's consideration of the private army problem in 1973 remains the single important attempt to address this issue.[145]

Private Police. Similar problems are posed by the use of private police. However, it is important to note that their widespread use within the United States and by U.S. businesses abroad has led to a general acceptance of their employment for prevention and deterrence purposes by U.S. governmental entities, foreign governmental entities, and others.[146] Although private police can play useful roles, governmental authorities should assure that private police training is appropriate for serving the law, rather than undermining it through the use of illegal equipment or tactics.[147] Furthermore, some controls should be exercised concerning the transnational use of private police with regard to training, equipment, and discipline. It should be made clear to all private police that they should not engage in unlawful activities, value extension strategies, or the more dangerous sanction strategies of correction and reconstruction.[148]

Of recent interest is a news article describing some of the valuable preventive roles played by chauffeurs and police and the creation of a new course in preventive driving for such persons. James Kelly, a former assistant director of the International Association of Chiefs of Police, formed a private company to conduct the training and has already given classes attended by public officials, persons from two domestic companies, and persons from two Latin American companies.[149] One can also envision the creation of other private training courses and the types of domestic and international problems posed by course instruction that might promote violations of international or domestic legal norms in an effort to combat private terrorism. It may be wise to prepare programs of instruction and materials for private use under the auspices of the LEAA so that private training programs and private police efforts do not promote international or domestic illegalities.[150] Special programs may be tailored to special needs and specific groups, such as private guards for civil nuclear facilities, airports, sports facilities, and others. As one can envision the creation of more new training courses, it is recommended that the LEAA fund training programs for various types of private police functioning and that these programs be monitored by the Department of Justice and by an appropriate subcommittee of the House Judiciary Committee. The primary purpose of such monitoring would be to assure that all aspects of the programs are lawful and that no aspect of any governmental or private training program promotes, assists, or tolerates the use of any tactic, weapon, or practice that violates international or domestic legal norms.

Examples of governmental organs violating international legal norms are not difficult to find. In 1975 Malaysia created a highly suspect set of security regulations, the Rukun Tatangga (Community Self-Reliance) regulations. They contain clear illegalities under human rights law, for example, the provision for collective penalties for knowledge of illegal activities by fellow residents or family members. An equally troublesome provision requires village or resident participation in 24-hour patrols of residential areas and stringent controls on movement of persons. Admittedly, there is a precedent for forced enlistment in the service of one's country and for stringent controls of movement in times of crisis.[151] But a maximal approach to a law-serving balance of need and expectations would condition such a governmental dictation by the requirement of the necessity.[152] For such measures to be consistent with human rights law, the deprivations must be strictly required by the necessities posed in times of crisis.[153] It is an educated suspicion that the bombing, however dramatic, of the Malaysian National Monument on August 26, 1975, and the hand-grenading of a Police Field Force barracks in Kuala Lumpur on September 23, 1975, which supposedly compelled adoption of the new security measures, were insufficient reasons for justification under the doctrine of necessity.

Human Rights-Oriented Groups. As disclosed earlier, human rights-oriented groups can play significant roles in overall preventive efforts. Beyond educative and promotion roles connected with enlightenment processes, these groups can utilize their capacities to inspect, investigate, report, advise, protest, publish, and otherwise respond to the use of terrorist strategy and resultant effects.[154] In terms of power process, the creative effort to clarify and disseminate human rights expectations can help to condition the unlawful exercise of power and to shape patterns of authority that will condition power itself.

The power of public protest and the sanction of public opinion should not be ignored by those who seek effective responses to terrorism. Such responses can aid in overall prevention and can even deter imminent terrorist threats where the power of contrary opinion is evident to those who seek to influence by violent deeds of propaganda.[155]

Policy Recommendations

General recommendations, intertwined with the analyses above, are best left in such a context. However, several more specific recommendations that flow from this brief inquiry into legal problems posed by private self-help sanctioning against terrorism should be considered and will be set forth here. There is a need for more detailed study and debate concerning many of the questions raised, and yet there seems little need to inhibit the adoption of several useful measures that seek to assure a more realistic and policy-serving response to terrorism.

Private Assassination and U.S. Policy

There should be no inhibition on the part of the United States to forthrightly condemn terrorism and counterterrorism of all types. This includes private measures of terror and counterterror engaged in either at home or abroad by groups or individuals seeking to "take the law into their own hands" or to engage in claimed "self-defense" measures designed to counter threats or actions from other private groups.

Failure to address the problem and to attempt to condition social expectation away from such activity may have dangerous consequences, as can readily be seen in Lebanon, Northern Ireland, or Argentina, where assassinations of rightists by leftists, and vice versa, have escalated into a sort of private terror war. If the government does not openly condemn such conduct, public attitudes and behavior will be shaped by terrorists and other factors, quite possibly to the detriment of law and authority.

A breakdown of social inhibitions toward the use of violence in general and the use of terroristic strategy in particular might well occur once a spiraling effect begins in this country or if such effects continue abroad and condition the U.S. populace through media awareness of such events. Similarly, related terror-violence by street gangs in New York or Chicago, by mafia participants and others in organized crime, or by actors on our television screens can break down inhibitions that presently thwart various forms of social violence. If terrorism is viewed as a significant threat to law and authority, the federal government should take significantly stronger action (through the use of military, economic, and ideological strategies) against street violence and organized crime. Recent revelations of governmental manipulation of street violence and organized criminal activity and governmental tolerance of illegality cannot help to inculcate in the public perspective an expectation of legality or a social demand for lawful, nonviolent means of social change and control. Such governmental acts can only add to the social revolutionary claims that power, not authority and law, is the guiding force and that power, with its presumed proprieties, can be taken by force.

In short, a government that engages in illegal repressive measures, including campaigns of covert assassination and overt but extralegal forms of detention and censure, may eliminate short-term security threats. Such action, however, can also signify governmental weakness and justify, in the eyes of other terrorists and their supporters, the type of counter-illegalities that are so reprehensible. Politics and ideology are often significantly involved; by ignoring these aspects of decision and response, not only may governmental elites be unprepared to meet long-term security threats, but decisions to engage in unlawful countermeasures, as the Maginot Line hope for stability, could also play into the hands of those who seek finally to destroy the authority-power base of the government and its supporters.

Education as a Key Deterrent

Education is a key to the implementation of human rights and the laws of war, which proscribe nearly every form of terroristic strategy. A broader understanding of these legal norms can supplement perspectives and foster new expectations that constitute a working foundation of legal and politico-ideological restraint upon the successful use of terrorism. Education is critical in waging an effective ideological war against terrorists.

As noted elsewhere,[156] state and federal governmental entities within the United States can play a far more creative, law-serving role in the education of all members of society concerning human, constitutional, and civil guarantees as well as the problems posed to a free society by illegal and inhumane strategies and conditions. Specific approaches are potentially numerous. The federal government could encourage a greater use of high school government and civics classes, senior problems classes, history classes, and other classes for investigation, analysis, and discussion of general human rights norms and their implementation. Related educational programs and concerns can be developed for other levels, including more general but important cooperative and individual-oriented learning in elementary and preschool processes.

These educational efforts can be supplemented by government-sponsored implementation advisory teams working with educational groups and institutions as well as law enforcement agencies, local governmental bodies, media groups, civic organizations, religious groups and institutions, penal institutions, wealth groups and institutions, and others. Government-sponsored fellowships for further study and the development of related efforts in the private sector can be initiated or redirected. Publications of a short, general nature and of more detailed, scholarly format can be stimulated, published, and distributed. Audiovisual forms of communication (*e.g.*, films, slides, television, and radio programs) seminars, conferences, and other enlightenment forums could be encouraged.

Free Media and a Code of Professional Ethics

It is also imperative that the United States maintain a media system that is responsible and free. To impose the media restraints adopted by Uruguay, Argentina, or South Korea, for example, would be not only illegal but unwise as a counter to terrorist threats. It does seem possible, however, to work cooperatively with the media in seeking a responsible and useful reporting of terrorist incidents.

Also of value may be a cooperative airing of the views of media, governmental, and other interested groups concerning the adoption by the media of a code of professional ethics that addresses problems posed by media coverage of terrorist incidents, the hostage-terrorist situation, details of strategy and counterstrategy, and certain effects of terror strategy. Three possible guidelines may be worth future study: that a responsible media (1) will report prosecutions and sanctions imposed; (2) will cooperate with appropriate law enforcement officials to control the release of information of temporary importance to terrorists during a terrorist incident and, if reasonably necessary for law enforcement, soon thereafter; and (3) will not disclose details of law enforcement strategies that might seriously jeopardize the present or future efficacy of law enforcement and endanger the lives of the public, law enforcement officers, or others. There must be a balanced emphasis, however, on relevant human, constitutional, and civil rights.

There seems to be no reason why inquiry could not also proceed at the international or regional level to work out a consensus regarding appropriate media behavior. One might aver that an international or regional effort might dissipate an intra-U.S. consensus, but such criticism ignores at least three aspects. First, it is not known whether an international or regional consensus is possible until effort is expended to create one. Second, if U.S. newspapers, television personnel, and other media entities could agree on a code of professional ethics it may well be that any disparate set of individuals could agree to similar provisions. Third, it may be useful to proceed on two or more levels to develop the best approaches possible at each level. There should be sufficient international concern for such an effort, since the transnational reporting of terrorist incidents can clearly have important transnational effects and could even lead to interstate friction and threats to international peace.

Legislation

Domestic Legislation. Efforts to meet the deficiencies inherent in several legal approaches to the problem of individuals defending others from terroristic threats and attacks might involve the passage of new federal and state legal standards. Here an attempt is made to provide useful examples of such measures. These measures should provide uniformity in approach and fill several gaps in present law.

To stimulate aid to third persons and to thwart certain terror effects, state and federal law might assure civil and criminal immunity for persons acting reasonably in attempting to aid other human beings. Legislation might accomplish this purpose by promulgating the following statutory provisions:

1. No person shall be held civilly liable for using reasonable force while coming to the defense of another when such person reasonably believes that the person aided is in serious danger of losing his life or suffering serious injury. Such civil immunity applies regardless of whether or not a person aided was in fact in danger, provided that the type and amount of force utilized in aid of another was otherwise reasonable and lawful under the circumstances.

2. No person shall be held criminally liable for using a reasonable type and amount of force under the circumstances while coming to the defense of another when such person reasonably believes that the person aided is in serious danger of losing his life or suffering serious injury. Such criminal immunity applies regardless of whether or not a person aided was in fact in danger.[157]

There is an obvious social cost with such legislative measures; some injury or loss may be suffered without civil or criminal liability. It is believed, however, that such injuries and losses will be few or socially *de minimis*, and that the possible benefits from such legislative immunity will be far greater. Moreover, to spread the risk of loss or injury and to compensate victims, it is suggested that federal and state law also provide special "claim and settlement" provisions that are available to the victims of reasonable but mistaken attempts to defend third persons from terrorist threat or attack. Indeed, there seems no reason for a limitation of compensation programs to cases of mistake. All victims of attempts by persons to aid another can be compensated. A special legislative provision might declare that "anyone who suffers injury or loss from the attempt by one person to aid another in preventing a terrorist threat or injury shall be compensated by the state for such loss and/or injury."

An important measure to round out the spread of risks, to compensate losses, and to increase public participation in law enforcement would compensate the person who comes to the aid of another, or to the aid of a law enforcement officer, for any injuries or losses sustained. Further, such a measure would seem to meet any "public purpose concern," all the more so because the individual rendering such aid would be performing a quasi-public service to the community. A provision to compensate in general situations might read:

Any person who lawfully comes to the aid of another thought reasonably to be in danger of suffering loss of life or serious injury shall be entitled to receive from the State compensation for all losses suffered, including reasonable medical and other expenses, as a consequence of rendering such aid or attempting to do so. Included in the calculation of losses suffered shall be reasonable amounts for any injury or pain and suffering thereby sustained.[158]

A related provision that should be useful for supplementing law enforcement in general would compensate an individual for losses sustained while attempting to aid a law enforcement officer. As with the other situations of quasi-public aid, unless there is statutory authority, the individual attempting to render aid will most likely bear the burden of any losses himself. A legislative remedy for this void in compensatory relief might read: "Any person who lawfully comes to the aid of a person(s) reasonably thought to be a law enforcement officer(s) who is reasonably thought to be lawfully enforcing the law shall be compensated by the State for all loss, injury, pain and suffering sustained as a result, including reasonable amounts for medical losses."

International Agreements. Internationally, similar provisions can be incorporated into bilateral and multilateral agreements to assure a more uniform national treatment with regard to state nationals and aliens, and also to assure an immunity of states from liability for acts of their own nationals in foreign territory, under international principles of state responsibility. The drafts recommended above are sufficient to guarantee immunity and compensation for aliens under U.S. law since the drafts apply to "any person," national or otherwise.[159] These drafts could be recommended as uniform rules for foreign state adoption, and the Department of State might also negotiate an inclusion of similar provisions in treaties of friendship, commerce, and navigation to guarantee, on the bilateral level, a uniform approach to state treatment of aliens within their territory. It is theoretically possible, but perhaps unlikely, that states would be interested in a multilateral treaty approach to the treatment of aliens in this manner.

With a bilateral or multilateral treaty, no problem would arise between those who recognize an international minimum treatment rule and those who favor protection of aliens by equal or national treatment approaches. The new treaty would create a standard of immunity and compensation that would apply equally to all persons in the signator state's territory (*i.e.*, to the national and the alien alike). It seems highly useful to work out such agreements as soon as possible. If U.S. citizens are to be encouraged to come to the defense of another person in serious danger here at home, there is ample need to protect such publicly beneficial conduct engaged in by U.S. citizens abroad. There seems no reason to chance an international claim of state responsibility on the part of the United States for the conduct of its citizens abroad or even at home when injury occurs to aliens within the United States. Relevant law in this area is sufficiently vague to compel attempts to devise preventive legislation.

Supplemental Prohibitions of Illegal Weapons. Having worked on the dum-dum bullet controversy here in the United States, the writer finds a significant need to adopt national legislation to supplement legal prohibitions of illegal weapons.[160] Weapon systems proscribed from use *per se* under international law are also clearly illegal under U.S. constitutional law.[161] Supplementary federal statutory law and penalties appear desirable, however, for the following reasons: (1) illegal weapon systems are still available in nearly every gun shop across the country for purchase by terrorists; (2) record use of these weapon systems by those engaged in normal criminal activity is on the increase; and (3) several police officers and other citizens have been killed with these weapon systems in the last few years, but there is insufficient regulation of the manufacture, sale, and use of such illegal weapon systems in the United States at this time.

For this purpose, the following draft amendment to the House draft version of H.R. 3625[162] is offered for executive consideration and possible submission to the House:

Any person who manufactures, produces, or sells weapon systems for use against human beings or uses them to kill or injure a human being when such weapon systems are proscribed for use against human beings under international law, shall be fined not more than $10,000 per incident or imprisoned not more than 10 years, or both; but if death results, such person shall be subject to imprisonment for any term of years or for life. This provision shall have extraterritorial effect to the extent that such is consistent with international law.

With the transnational availability of such illegal weapon systems, the United States might also recommend to foreign states that they adopt similar implementary legislation to supplement or create domestic penal offenses and to establish sanctions for the violation of such international and domestic law. The problems posed are most serious. Without effective sanction, we will witness the spread of the use of illegal weapons against aliens in general, businessmen, tourists, diplomats, and others, with serious threats to the continued existence of law and authority. Furthermore, with the increased interdependence of societies in the global arena, and the increase in alien tourist, business, diplomat, and other ventures into U.S. cities and counties, it seems increasingly likely that the death or injury of an alien by the unregulated use of illegal weapon systems will lead to a claim by a foreign state against the United States of state responsibility for a death or injury by means violative of international law.[163] To leave the country open to such a claim, and the political, ideological, or economic sanctions that can follow, is hardly policy-serving or a rational maximization of self- and common interest. The United States might also benefit greatly from the adoption of a national testing institution that compares effects of weapon systems both outside and within the human body with international and national legal norms to assure compliance with the law.[164]

A Contract Clause

As outlined earlier, banking and other wealth institutions that could obtain a request by a depositor to transfer substantial sums of money to a terrorist group should have a contract clause authorizing them to freeze the transfer of assets for a reasonable time until the federal government can address the situation and take appropriate action. Such a transfer could occur in a matter of minutes by some form of telecommunication and, as far as the writer is aware, present law would most likely prohibit even a temporary interference by the banking institution. Without a banking contract allowing the freezing of assets, the government would be unable to respond in time in certain cases to prevent the transfer of important wealth to the terrorist groups. Furthermore, the banking institution will have to initiate the process, since only it may know of the depositor's intent to transfer assets to a terrorist group.

With the above in mind, the following contract clause is offered:

The _____ bank reserves the right, within a period of 24 hours from receipt of a demand by a depositor to transfer assets to another person or institution, to control assets reasonably suspected of being transferred or utilized to support terrorism or conduct otherwise violative of international law until appropriate governmental authorities can take appropriate action.

As the banking institution that freezes assets will do so until the government can act, it may be appropriate for the government to indemnify the institution in case of any unforeseen losses suffered as a result of its quasi-public role taken in combating international terrorism. If the contract clause is adopted, the writer can foresee no such losses. However, if an effort is made to balance the risks involved by allowing a claim by the depositor for his losses suffered in case of reasonable or other mistake of fact, then the federal government should pay the depositor's claim for at least two reasons: (1) because the overall process of temporary freezes in wealth transfer serves a public purpose, the prevention or deterrence of terrorism in progress (*e.g.*, a ransom demand), or about to occur in the future; and (2) because the banking institution will be encouraged to continue performing a quasi-public function.

It should be noted that some banking institutions may not adopt the proposed contract clause for fear of losing substantial international business. For example, Swiss banks will probably permit no interference with a lucrative pattern of relatively free and anonymous banking and wealth storage. If Swiss banks are unwilling to aid in efforts to stop common theft, governmental corruption, and organized crime through the control of deposited wealth, they are even less likely to feel compelled to change their practices in order to stop terrorism. This seems especially so when trends indicate that terrorism by nongovernmental precipitators poses far less danger to domestic and international social processes than organized crime or governmental corruption. Moreover, a New York bank, predicting a fear of depositor withdrawals and loss of new accounts from Libyan or other customers, may refuse to offer the clause to such foreign depositors, or to any depositor, because of the potential disruption of business with such depositors and others who sympathize with terrorist aims or, perhaps more likely, with an unfettered freedom to engage in international investment and commerce.

In response, one might contend that there is no absolute freedom to engage in unregulated investment and trade, that the temporary disruption envisioned should affect only a few of the bank's depositors, and that the preventive effort could be very useful in thwarting certain terrorist efforts. Nonetheless, the refusal to be bound by such a restriction by several wealthy foreign depositors could lead some banks to conclude that the clause should not be used. Even then, however, some banks might find the clause acceptable to some or all of their depositors and might be willing to participate in this manner in an overall effort to combat terrorism. One cannot really determine the acceptability and utility of such a clause until it is tested.

Conclusion

Individuals, groups, and private institutions can and do respond to terrorism creatively or destructively in terms of serving minimum public order and human dignity. Forms of private response can be as varied as private patterns of social interaction. Choice as to permissibility, then, must be oriented to the context and the relevant legal policies at stake in given cases. Whether private choice, in the long run, will help to prevent and control terrorism and to promote minimum public order and human dignity will depend on popular awareness of and demands for a world of law, justice, and the values of a free society expressed in the human rights instruments of the twentieth century. We can act affirmatively to create such an awareness and demand through the enrichment of the educational process and greater access by all peoples to human intelligence.

We should never forget, as Thomas Paine observed: "He that would make his own liberty secure must guard even his enemy from oppression; for if he violates this duty he establishes a precedent that will reach to himself."[165]

Notes

1. The jurisprudential underpinning for this focus is the interdisciplinary, policy-oriented, and contextual approach to law developed by Myres S. Mc-Dougal and Harold D. Lasswell. *See, e.g.,* Lasswell & McDougal, *Criteria for A Theory About Law,* 44 S. CAL. L. REV. 362 (1971) [hereinafter cited as Lasswell & McDougal]; McDougal, Lasswell, & Reisman, *Theories About International Law: Prologue to a Configurative Jurisprudence,* 8 VA. J. INT'L L. 188 (1968). *See also* H. LASSWELL, A PRE-VIEW OF POLICY SCIENCES (1971); Suzuki, *The New Haven School of International Law: An Invitation to a Policy-Oriented Jurisprudence,* 1 YALE STUDIES IN WORLD PUB. ORDER 1 (1974).

2. As in any area of law, choice is inevitable. *See, e.g.,* note 1 *supra*; H.L.A. HART, THE CONCEPT OF LAW 12 (1961); McDougal, *Fuller v. The American Legal Realists: An Intervention,* 50 YALE L. J. 827 (1941); F. Cohen, *Transcendental Nonsense and the Functional Approach,* 35 COLUM. L. REV. 809 (1935).

3. *See, e.g.,* Lasswell & McDougal, *supra* note 1, at 384, stating: "When decisions are authoritative but not controlling, they are not law but pretense; when decisions are controlling but not authoritative, they are not law but naked power." *See also* note 2 *supra*; Kerstetter, *Practical Problems of Law Enforcement,* ch. 11 of this report, at 535.

4. *See* Lasswell and McDougal, *supra* note 1, at 391-392.

5. *See* M. McDOUGAL & F. FELICIANO, LAW AND MINIMUM WORLD PUBLIC ORDER 56-57, n.136, 62-63, 102, 103, 119, 148-58 (1961) [herein-

after cited as M. McDOUGAL & F. FELICIANO]; *see also* F. Cohen, *supra* note 2.

6. *See* U.N. Report of the Secretary-General, Measures to Prevent International Terrorism Which Endangers or Takes Innocent Human Lives or Jeopardizes Fundamental Freedoms, and Study of the Underlying Causes of Those Forms of Terrorism and Acts of Violence Which Lie in Misery, Frustration, Grievance and Despair and Which Cause Some People to Sacrifice Human Lives, Including Their Own, in an Attempt to Effect Radical Changes, 27 U.N. GAOR, C.6 Annexes (Agenda item 92) U.N. Doc. A/C.6/418, at 6-7 (1972) [hereinafter cited U.N. Doc. A/C.6/418]. These definitional components include: (1) terror outcome, (2) instrumental or "immediate" victims, (3) primary targets ("population" or "broad groups" and others), (4) violence, and (5) political purpose.

7. The Convention for the Prevention and Punishment of Terrorism, Nov. 16, 1937, 19 LEAGUE OF NATIONS Q.J. 23 (1938) [hereinafter cited as 1937 Convention on Terrorism] identified components such as: (1) willful or intentional act; (2) terror purpose ("calculated to create a state of terror in the minds of" the primary target); (3) outcome of death, grievous bodily harm, or loss of liberty to a set of instrumental targets (*e.g.,* heads of state, their families, public servants); (4) outcome of damage to or destruction of public property as an instrumental target; and (5) acts "calculated to endanger the lives of the members of the public." Another factor that seemed to apply to all acts of terrorism was a requirement that acts be "directed against a State" (which most likely was designed to exclude terrorization by governments of their own people and other incidents involving nonstate targets). *See also* U.N. Doc. A/C.6/418, at 6-7, *supra* note 6, at 10-16, 39 n.1. A survey of several definitional components can be found in Hutchinson, *The Concept of Revolutionary Terrorism,* 16 J. CONFLICT RES. 383 (1972) [hereinafter cited as Hutchinson]. Factors identified by Hutchinson include: (1) international conduct, (2) terror purpose, (3) "political" purpose, (4) violent conduct (act or threat), and (5) terror outcome (production of intense fear or anxiety). Other factors identified by Hutchinson that this author finds marginally useful include: (1) "systematic" use or "consistent pattern," (2) atrocious or shocking conduct, (3) arbitrariness, (4) selectivity of targets, (5) indiscriminate affection of targets, (6) irrationality, and (7) immoral or "unjust" activity. In a study on political violence, Eugene Walter describes the process of terrorism as involving three main elements: (1) an act or threat of violence, (2) an emotional outcome, and (3) production of "social effects." He also identifies three types of participants: source, victim, and targets. *See* E. WALTER, TERROR AND RESISTANCE 5, 7-11 (1969). For a slightly less descriptive attempt at definition, *see* Bassiouni, *An International Control Scheme for the Prosecution of International Terrorism: An Introduction,* ch. 8 of this report at 485; Friedlander, *Sowing the Wind: Rebellion and Terror-Violence in Theory and Practice,* 6 DENVER J. INT'L L.

& POL. 83, 84 (1976). The latter approach is insufficiently mindful of the problem of "threats" of violence and the absolute need for terror outcome. *See also* Paust, "NonProtected" Persons or Things, ch. 6 of this report, at 345-349. Nearly every dictionary definition adds these elements. *See, e.g.,* WEBSTER'S THIRD NEW INTERNATIONAL DICTIONARY, "terrorism," at 2361 (1971)("use of terror as a means of coercion . . . threat or violence. . . ."). *See also* Mann, *Personnel and Property of Transnational Business Operations,* ch. 7 of this Report at 399, including "threat or use of violence," but greatly expanding attention to mere "fear" or "alarm" in an overly broad, ultimately unworkable manner); Paust, letter, 68 AM. J. INT'L L. 502 (1974). Again, "terrorism" involves "terror."

8. *See* CANADIAN COUNCIL ON INTERNATIONAL LAW, INTERNATIONAL TERRORISM 55-60, 80 (1974); Paust, *Terrorism and the International Law of War,* 64 MIL. L. REV. 1, 22-27 (1974).

9. McDougal, Lasswell, & Reisman, *supra* note 1, at 188, 189.

10. *See, e.g., id.* at 189-92.

11. *See id.* at 192. For greater exposition of these and other intelligence or decision functions, *see, e.g.,* McDougal, Lasswell, & Reisman, *The Intelligence Function and World Public Order,* 46 TEMPLE L. Q. 365 (1973); Lasswell & McDougal, *supra* note 1, at 387; M. McDOUGAL, H. LASSWELL, & I. VLASIC, LAW AND PUBLIC ORDER IN SPACE 1046-85 (1963).

12. *Id.* at 192-93.

13. *Id.* at 194.

14. *See* M. McDOUGAL & F. FELICIANO, *supra* note 5, at 309-32.

15. Concerning state self-help responses, *compare* Paust, *A Survey of Possible Legal Responses to International Terrorism-Prevention, Punishment and Cooperative Action,* 5 GA. J. INT'L COMP. L. 431, 464-67 (1975), and authorities cited, *with* Murphy, *State Self-Help and Problems of Public International Law,* ch. 12 of this report.

16. *See* M. McDougal & F. Feliciano, *supra* note 5. *Prevention,* as a sanction objective, is an effort to prevent the occurrence of impermissible conduct. *Deterrence,* like prevention, seeks to prevent the occurrence of impermissible conduct, but "is concerned with a threat or challenge . . . that has emerged and been clearly posed and imminently promised." Deterrence "envisages the influencing of the decision that the potential violator will make by affecting his expectations of how the sanctioner will behave and respond." *Restoration* involves "the application of responding coercion for the purpose of compelling the violator to reduce" or stop the unlawfully initiated conduct. *Rehabilitation* involves the "reparation of the destruction of values" suffered because of the unlawfully initiated conduct. *Reconstruction* designates "the long-term purpose of avoiding the recurrence of prohibited coercion by modifying or reorganizing or eliminating particular structures and processes . . . within the violater state [area] . . . ." *Correction* is a sanction strategy directed against particular persons

in order to subject such persons to corrective deprivations, *e.g.*, as with criminal penalty.

17. *But cf.* D. MILBANK, INTERNATIONAL AND TRANSNATIONAL TERRORISM: DIAGNOSIS AND PROGNOSIS 21 (1976) (Research Study, Central Intelligence Agency, PR 76 10030, Apr. 1976), where the author suggests: ". . . a prolonged and general economic upturn can increase local potentials for political violence by causing popular expectations to far outpace governmental capacities to deliver. And in more affluent societies, at least, the attendant emphasis on materialistic values can alienate significant segments of the student and intellectual communities. Indeed, a combination of these last two destabilizing trends contributed, together with the factors cited earlier, to the emergence of a distinctly "revolutionary" political atmosphere in the late 1960s."

18. *See generally* M. McDOUGAL & F. FELICIANO, *supra* note 5, at 311-17.

19. *Id.* at 317.

20. *See generally Patience Key to Method in Handling Terrorists,* Houston Post, Jan. 18, 1976, at 4, col. 5 (UPI interview of Austrian Chancellor Kreisky); M. OPPENHEIMER, THE URBAN GUERRILLA 76 (1969); AMNESTY INT'L, REPORT ON TORTURE 82, 96-97 (1973); J. QUARTIM, DICTATORSHIP AND ARMED STRUGGLE IN BRAZIL 213 (1971); J. MALLIN, TERROR AND URBAN GUERRILLAS 66, 103-04 (1971); *Terrorism: Hearing before the House Comm. on Internal Security,* 93d Cong., 2d. Sess., 3179 (1974) [hereinafter cited as *Terrorism Hearings*] ; *id.* at 3009, 3021; T. GURR, WHY MEN REBEL 4, 13, 212 (1970); R. FOGELSON, VIOLENCE AS PROTEST 143 (1971); A. DALLIN & G. BRESLAUER, POLITICAL TERROR IN COMMUNIST SYSTEMS 24 ff. (1970); R. GAUCHER, THE TERRORISTS 309 (1968).

  See also NATIONAL COMMISSION ON THE CAUSES AND PREVENTION OF VIOLENCE, TO ESTABLISH JUSTICE, TO INSURE DOMESTIC TRANQUILITY, FINAL REPORT I87-207 (1969); SUB-COUNCIL ON ADVERTISING AND PROMOTION OF THE NATIONAL BUSINESS COUNCIL FOR CONSUMER AFFAIRS, VIOLENCE AND THE MEDIA (1972) (mentioning numerous congressional hearings and the surgeon general's study on television).

21. *See, e.g.,* Paust, *A Survey of Possible Legal Responses to International Terrorism: Prevention, Punishment and Cooperative Action,* 5 GA. J. INT'L COMP. L. 431 (1975).

22. *See also,* Lasswell & McDougal, *supra* note 1, at 377-92.

23. Reisman, *Private Armies in a Global War System: Prologue to Decision,* 14 VA. J. INT'L L. 1, 6 (1973). *See also id.* at 32-33. The article is extremely useful for relevant inquiry into violent measures of private self-help. LAW AND CIVIL WAR IN THE MODERN WORLD 252 (J. N. Moore ed. 1974).

24. *See, e.g.,* Reisman, *supra* note 23, at 47-48; McDougal, Lasswell, & Chen, *The Promotion of Respect and Human Rights: Freedom of Choice and World Public Order,* 24 AM. U. L. REV. 919 (1975); M. McDOUGAL & F. FELICIANO, *supra* note 5, at 129-31 *passim.*

25. *See* U.N. CHARTER, preamble; M. McDOUGAL & F. FELICIANO, *supra* note 5, at 93-96 *passim.*

26. *See* M. McDOUGAL & F. FELICIANO, *supra* note 5, at 121 ff.

27. *See id.* at 123-29, 207ff; McDougal, Lasswell, & Chen, *Human Rights and World Public Order: A Framework for Policy-Oriented Inquiry,* 63 AM. J. INT'L L. 237, 256-57, 266-67 (1969); W.M. REISMAN, NULLITY AND REVISION 836-58 (1971).

28. M. McDOUGAL & F. FELICIANO, *supra* note 5, at 128, *citing* JENKS, THE COMMON LAW OF MANKIND 139-43 (1958). *See also* W.M. REISMAN, NULLITY AND REVISION 836ff (1971); H. KELSEN, PRINCIPLES OF INTERNATIONAL LAW 14-17 (1952).

29. For a discussion of value conservation and value extension as they relate to self-defense, *see* M. McDOUGAL & F. FELICIANO, *supra* note 5, at 18-19, 222ff.

30. *See, e.g.,* 1948 Universal Declaration of Human Rights, G.A. Res. 217, art. 30, U.N. Doc. A/810, at 71 (1948) [hereinafter cited as 1948 Universal Declaration of Human Rights]; International Covenant on Civil and Political Rights, Dec. 16, 1966, G.A. Res. 2200, 21 U.N. GAOR, Supp. (No. 16) art. 5(1) at 52, U.N. Doc. A/6316 (1966).

31. For example, killing for vengeance—even if value conservatory and supportable under ancient talion or Jewish law—is unlawful. *See* 40 AM. JUR. 2d, Homicide, § 170, at 457 (1968), *citing* Litchfield v. State, 8 OKLA. CRIM. 164, 126 P.707 (1912).

32. *See, e.g.,* W. LaFAVE & A. SCOTT, CRIMINAL LAW 397-99 (1972).

33. *See, e.g., id.* at 397 n.2; L. WEINREB, CRIMINAL LAW 189 (2d ed. 1975). Many of these, however, allow defense of a third person if the third person is related to the defendant in certain specified ways. *See also* note 35 *infra.*

34. Such prohibition, concerning the defense of related persons, is happily rare. Further, it is contrary to the common law rule. *See* W. LaFAVE & A. SCOTT, *supra* note 32, at 397.

35. Possible exceptions or defenses for the father in such a case, however, might include temporary insanity, necessity, right to prevent a felony, duress, and so forth.

36. *See also* J. VORENBERG, CRIMINAL LAW AND PROCEDURE 370 N.1 (1975) ("practical effect").

37. *See generally* W. LaFAVE & A. SCOTT, *supra* note 32, at 391-97; WEINREB, *supra* note 33, at 177-88; VORENBERG, *supra* note 36, at 361-71; Paust, *Constitutional Prohibition of Cruel, Inhumane or Unnecessary Death,*

Injury or Suffering During Law Enforcement Process, 2 HASTINGS CONST. L.Q. 873 (1975). With regard to international law, *see* M. McDOUGAL & F. FELICIANO, *supra* note 5, at 207ff.

38. *See also* Colorado v. Hutchison, 9 F.2d 275, 276 (8th Cir. 1925).

39. *See* Paust, *supra* note 37, and authorities cited; Mattis v. Schnarr (No. 75-1849) (8th Cir. 1976); Jones v. Marshall, 528 F.2d 132, 139, & 143 (2d Cir. 1975), *citing* Johnson v. Glick, 481 F.2d 1028, 1033 (2d Cir.), *cert. den.,* 414 U.S. 1033 (1973).

40. *See, e.g.,* W. PROSSER, LAW OF TORTS 112-13 (1971).

41. For discussion of the split among states concerning a defense to criminal prosecution in such cases, *see e.g.,* W. LaFAVE & A. SCOTT, *supra* note 32, at 398-99. Concerning civil suit defenses, *see, e.g.,* PROSSER, *supra* note 40, at 113.

42. *See, e.g.,* PROSSER, *supra* note 40, at 113, disclosing his preference for the minority view that an honest mistake made in defense of another should relieve the defendant of civil liability.

43. *See, e.g.,* W. LaFAVE & A. SCOTT, *supra* note 32, at 403 ff.

44. *See id.*

45. *See id.* at 522-27; examples of foreign prescriptions—which approach the problem in a similar vein—include: Norwegian Penal Code, § 139, *see* Summary of Responses to Department of State Circular Airgram Regarding Law and Practice on Terrorism, Norway, 1 (Dec. 1975) [hereinafter cited as Circular, name of country, page, and date of summary] ; *see also id.* § 149; South African Terrorism Act No. 83, § 3 (1967), Circular, South Africa, 1 (Oct. 1975). Foreign prescriptions that adopt a more expansive approach than that of the U.S. legislation include: Uruguayan Military Penal Code, arts. 147-48 (1972), Circular, Uruguay, 2 (Dec. 1975), which would punish the instigation of terrorist activity as well as the public defense of terrorist acts; *see also* Decree-Law 655/972 of Sept. 28, 1972, *id.* at 3 and Decree-Law 393/973 of June 19, 1973, *id.* at 5, which prohibit communications concerning terrorists that are not official communications; Republic of Korea National Security Law No. 549, Circular, Korea, 1 (Sept. 1975), punishing membership in antinational organizations; Republic of Korea Anti-Communist Law No. 643, *id.* punishing those who praise, encourage, or assist antinational organizations; Federal Republic of Germany, Penal Code § 131, Circular, Federal Republic of Germany, 2 (Sept. 1975), punishing the "glorification of violence"; Austria Penal Code, art. 285 *et seq.,* Circular, Austria, 1 (Sept. 1975), punishing membership or contacts with a secret society; Austrian Federal Law for the Protection of the State (1936), *id.* at 2, punishing participation in or with secret armed or military groups; Pakistan Anti-National Activities Act (1974), Circular, Pakistan, 1 (Oct. 6, 1975), suspending constitutional guarantees and punishing antinational activities, associations, support, questioning, and so forth; Pakistan's Defense of Pakistan Ordinance (1971), *id.* at 2-3; Canada's Public Incitement of Hatred Provisions of

Criminal Code, § 281.1, Circular, Canada, 3 (Oct. 1975); South African Terrorism Act (No. 83, 1967), *supra*; South African Unlawful Organizations Act (1960), Circular, South Africa, 2 (Oct. 1975); Spain's Anti-Terrorist Decree Law (Aug. 27, 1975), Circular, Spain, 1-3 (Oct. 1975), punishing nearly any type of encouragement or support of terrorists (direct or indirect); Chile's Decree Law No. 1009 on National Security (May 5, 1975), arts. 2, 5, Circular, Chile, 1-2 (Oct. 1975); Costa Rican Penal Code, arts. 272, 280, Circular, Costa Rica, 2 (Oct. 1975); United Kingdom Prevention of Terrorism Act, Part I (1974), Circular, United Kingdom, 1-2 (Nov. 1975).

46. 1970 Declaration on Principles of International Law concerning Friendly Relations and Co-operation among States in Accordance with the Charter of the United Nations, G.A. Res. 2625, 25 U.N. GAOR, Supp. (no. 28) 123, U.N. Doc. A/8028 (1970) [hereinafter cited as G.A. Res. 2625]. The resolution elaborates the expectations connected with art. 2, para. 4 of the U.N. CHARTER. *See also* United States Draft Convention for the Prevention of Certain Acts of International Terrorism, preamble, art. 10(1), 67 DEP'T STATE BULL. 431 (1972); OAS Convention to Prevent and Punish the Acts of Terrorism Taking the Form of Crimes Against Persons and Related Extortion That Are of International Significance, Feb. 2, 1971, art. 8(a), T.I.A.S. No. 8413, Serie Sobre Tratados [S.S.T.] No. 37, OAS/Off. Doc. OAS/Ser. A/17 [hereinafter cited as 1971 OAS Convention on Terrorism] ; Convention for the Suppression of Unlawful Acts against the Safety of Civil Aviation, signed at Montreal, Sept. 23, 1971, art. 10(1), 24 U.S.T. 564, T.I.A.S. No. 7570 (binding 73 states as of June 30, 1977) [hereinafter cited as 1971 Montreal Convention] ; 1937 Convention on Terrorism, *supra* note 7, at arts. 1(1), 3; G.A. Res. 2131, Declaration on the Inadmissibility of Intervention in the Domestic Affairs of States and the Protection of Their Independence and Sovereignty, 20 U.N. GAOR, Supp. (No. 14) 11-12, U.N. Doc. A/6014 (1965); Draft Code of Offenses Against the Peace and Security of Mankind, 9 U.N. GAOR, Supp. (No. 9), 11-12, U.N. Doc. A/2693 (1954) (*see particularly* art. 2). *See also* LEAGUE OF NATIONS COVENANT, art. 10; L. OPPENHEIM, INTERNATIONAL LAW 292-93 (8th ed., ed. H. Lauterpacht 1955) [hereinafter cited as 1 L. OPPENHEIM] ; 2 L. OPPENHEIM, INTERNATIONAL LAW 698, 704, 751-54 (7th ed., ed. H. Lauterpacht 1952) [hereinafter cited as 2 L. OPPENHEIM] .

47. G.A. Res. 2625, *supra* note 46, at 123. This prescriptive elaboration is listed under a section on art. 2(7) of the U.N. CHARTER.

48. U.N. Doc. A/C.6/418, *supra* note 6, at 26. This would include individual sanctioning of criminal activity. Such individual responsibility can be found in numerous examples of current expectation or traced to customary law as in the 1818 case of Arbuthnot and Ambrister. *See* F. WHARTON, A DIGEST OF THE INTERNATIONAL LAW OF THE UNITED STATES 326 (1886).

49. B. MURTY, PROPAGANDA AND WORLD PUBLIC ORDER: THE LEGAL REGULATION OF THE IDEOLOGICAL INSTRUMENT OF COER-

CION (1968) [hereinafter cited as B. MURTY] 230-31, *citing* Kuhn, *The Complaint of Yugoslavia Against Hungary with Reference to the Assassination of King Alexander,* 29 AM. J. INT'L L. 87 (1936). Kuhn stated that this principle was not well settled in international law by 1935. *Id.* at 89. Murty also notes some of the laws of war that prohibit incitements to assassination.

50. *See, e.g.,* United States v. Arjona, 120 U.S. 479 (1887); 1972 U.N. Doc. A/C.6/418, *supra* note 6, at 30; 2 G. HACKWORTH, DIGEST OF INTERNATIONAL LAW 334-36 (1943); 2 L. OPPENHEIM, *supra* note 46, at 656, 678-80, 698, 704, 751-54, 757-58; Wright, *Subversive Intervention,* 54 AM. J. INT'L L. 521, 533 (1960).

51. Although the 1970 Declaration on Principles of International Law Concerning Friendly Relations, *supra* note 46, prohibits state reprisal action and although there are similar admonishments in Security Council resolutions, recent scholarly attention to state claims and practice suggests retention of state reprisal norms. *See* W.M. REISMAN, NULLITY AND REVISION 836 ff (1971); Lillich, *Forcible Self-Help Under International Law,* 22 NAVAL WAR COLL. REV. 56 (1970); Falk, *The Beirut Raid and the International Law of Retaliation,* 63 AM. J. INT'L L. 415 (1969); Brownlie, *International Law and the Activities of Armed Bands,* 7 INT'L & COMP. L.Q. 712 (1958).

52. See *supra* notes 46 and 47; and claim of Uruguay against France, Circular, Uruguay, 8 (Dec. 1975), *supra* note 45. *See also* L. SOHN & T. BUERGENTHAL, INTERNATIONAL PROTECTION OF HUMAN RIGHTS 23-136 (1973), and authorities cited; 1948 Universal Declaration of Human Rights, *supra* note 30, arts. 1, 2, 3, 5, 7-8, 28.

53. *See generally* Paust & Blaustein, *The Arab Oil Weapon—A Threat to International Peace,* 68 AM. J. INT'L L. 410 (1974); B. MURTY, *supra* note 49; M. McDOUGAL & F. FELICIANO, *supra* note 5, at 29-31, 178-79, 196, 200, 240-41. *Cf.* notes 13, 23, & 51 *supra.*

54. *Cf.,* pp. 589-590 *infra.*

55. *See, e.g.,* U.S. CONST., amendments 1, 5, 9; 1948 Universal Declaration of Human Rights, *supra* note 30, arts. 1, 3, 18-20, 29(2), 30; Paust, *Human Rights and the Ninth Amendment: A New Form of Guarantee,* 60 CORNELL L. REV. 231 (1975).

56. *See, e.g.,* W. LaFAVE & A. SCOTT, *supra* note 32, at 522-27.

57. R. Fisher, N.Y. Times, Mar. 13, 1974, at 40, col. 2.

58. This would, in effect, amount to adoption of the Soviet "objective" theory of crime whereby acts are punishable, regardless of intent, because of their effect on the promotion of "the revolution" and the survival of the state. Presently, the United States does not seek this approach; and although it frowns on the payment of ransom, the decision "can only be made by the family or company of the victim."

59. *See* Republic of Korea, Anti-Communist Law No. 643, Circular, Korea, 1 (Sept. 1975), *supra* note 45; Chile Decree-Law No. 1009, art.2 (1975),

Circular, Chile, 1-2 (Oct. 1975), *supra* note 45; N.Y. Times, May 5, 1975, at 3, col. 5 (trial of 18 religious and political leaders). Concerning notes 56-61, *see also* G. SOREL, REFLECTIONS ON VIOLENCE 124-25 (1950) (terrorist laws and similar government responses).

60. Austria Penal Code, § 285, Circular, Austria, 1 (Sept. 1975), *supra* note 45.

61. Pakistan Anti-National Activities Act (1974), Circular, Pakistan, 1 (Oct. 6, 1975), *supra* note 45. *See also* Defense of Pakistan Ordinance, and Rules (1971), *id.* at 2-3; N.Y. Times, May 9, 1976, at 4, col. 1 (trial of 44 defendants, including several members of Parliament and other political leaders).

62. South African Terrorism Act No. 83 (1967), *supra* note 45. Note the burden of proof in section 2. *See also* N.Y. Times, Apr. 27, 1976, at 2, col. 4 (new Rhodesian national security regulations); Nigerian Armed Forces and Police (Special Powers) Decree No. 24 (1967), Circular, Nigeria, 1 (Mar. 1976), *supra* note 45; Malaysian Emergency Ordinance, arts. 4, 13 (1969), Circular, Malaysia, 1-5 (Mar. 1976), *supra* note 45; Malaysian "Community Self-Reliance" Regulations and "Essential (Security Cases) Regulations" (1975), *id.* at 4-5. *See also* Yim Tak Wai v. R. [1967] Hong Kong Law Reports [H.K.L.R.] (1967), Circular, Hong Kong, 2 (Mar. 1976), *supra* note 45.

63. South African Terrorism Act No. 83 § 3 (1967), *supra* note 45; Chile Decree-Law No. 1009, art. 2 (1975), *supra* note 59.

64. An approach to decision is offered in Paust & Blaustein, *supra* note 53; Paust & Blaustein, *The Arab Oil Weapon: A Reply and Reaffirmation of Illegality,* 15 COLUM. J. TRANS. L. 57 (1976). *See also* p. 586 *supra.*

65. *See, e.g.,* U.S. CONST. art. VI, C1.2 and amends. V & IX; 1948 Universal Declaration of Human Rights, *supra* note 30, arts. 7, 10-11, *cf.* art. 29(2); 1966 Covenant on Civil and Political Rights, *supra* note 30, arts. 14-15. *See also* Paust, *supra* note 55.

66. *See, e.g.,* U.S. CONST., art. VI, C1.2 and amends. V, IX, XIV; 1948 Universal Declaration of Human Rights, *supra* note 30, arts. 1-2; 1966 Covenant on Civil and Political Rights, *supra* note 30, arts. 1-2; International Convention on the Elimination of All Forms of Racial Discrimination, 660 U.N.T.S. 195 (1966).

67. *See, e.g.,* U.S. CONST., art. VI, C1.2 and amends. I. V, IX; 1948 Universal Declaration of Human Rights, *supra* note 30, arts. 18-20; 1966 Covenant on Civil and Political Rights, *supra* note 30, arts. 18-22. *See also* note 53 *supra.*

68. *See* notes 59-63 *supra.*

69. On state responsibility, *see* notes 42-46 *supra.* Recent examples of foreign state interference with private responses include the expulsion of a U.S. company from Venezuela for making payments to a terrorist group and the interference with private efforts to obtain the release of Stanford students held hostage in Africa. This overall problem for aliens in such foreign states is further

complicated by the fact that England and South Africa have prosecuted resident aliens with certain contacts with the forum state for treason when they served in foreign enemy military forces. *See* Joyce v. Director of Public Prosecutions, [1946] A.C. 347 Rex v. Neuman, 3 So. AFRICAN L. R. 1238 (1949) (South African Special Criminal Court of Transvaal, 1946). No cases of prosecution for payment of ransom are known; but another relevant and extremely broad proscription has been adopted by the state of Israel. Israeli Penal Law 5732-1972 (amend. No. 4), Offenses Committed Abroad, in part 2(a) states: "The courts of Israel are competent to try under Israeli law a person who has committed abroad an act which would be an offense if it had been committed in Israel and which harmed the State of Israel, its security, property or economy, or its transport or communication links with other countries." This might cover payment in France of large sums of money as ransom to certain Arab terrorists or the refusal to do business with Israeli companies or persons for racial or religious discriminatory motives, depending on whether such would be an offense if committed in Israel. Presumably this claim to exercise jurisdiction over aliens, beyond the residency and nexus factors in the Joyce and Neuman cases above, would be justified under the protective theory of jurisdiction, but there does not appear to be the usual requirement that the threat be to national security interests and that it be a substantial threat under the circumstances. *Cf.* 1 L. OPPENHEIM, *supra* note 46, at 331-33; C. RHYNE, INTERNATIONAL LAW 117 (1971); McDougal, Lasswell, & Chen, *Nationality and Human Rights: The Protection of the Individual in External Arenas,* 83 YALE L. J. 900 (1974); 22 U.S.C. § 1203 (1906); United States v. Rodriguez, 182 F. Supp. 479 (S.D. Cal. 1960).

70. *See, e.g.,* McDougal, Lasswell, & Chen, *supra* note 27, at 266-67; 1948 Universal Declaration of Human Rights, *supra* note 30, arts. 29(2), 30; 1966 Covenant on Civil and Political Rights, *supra* note 30, arts. 4, 5, 9(1), 10, 19(3), 22(2); European Convention for the Protection of Human Rights and Fundamental Freedoms, Nov. 4, 1950, arts. 10(2), 11(2), 15, 213 U.N.T.S. 221 (1950) [hereinafter cited as 1950 European Convention]; American Convention on Human Rights, Nov. 22, 1969, arts. 13, 15, 22(3)-(4), 27, 29, OAS/Off/Rec./ OEA/Ser.K/XVI/1.1, Doc. 65/Rev.1/Corr.1 (1970), *reprinted in* 65 AM. J. INT'L L. 679 (1971) [hereinafter cited as 1969 American Convention on Human Rights].

71. Excesses that have occurred in Northern Ireland, South Africa, Southern Rhodesia, Bangladesh, Vietnam, Uganda, and elsewhere remain fresh in the memory of international lawyers and are still prominent in newspaper articles. *See, e.g.,* LAW, JUSTICE AND SOCIETY (P. Randall ed. 1972); LEGISLATION AND RACE RELATIONS (M. Horell ed. 1971); Dugard, *South West Africa and the "Terrorist Trial,"* 64 AM. J. INT'L L. 19 (1970); Nanda, *Self-Determination in International Law: The Tragic Tale of Two Cities— Islamabad (West Pakistan) and Dacca (East Pakistan),* 66 AM. J. INT'L L. 321

(1972); N.Y. Times, Apr. 25, 1973, at 2, col. 3. In the case of Vietnam, excesses have occurred on both sides, but the allegations in connection with population control are sometimes overbroad. For indications of other excesses, *see* N.Y. Times, Feb. 4, 1976, at 1, col. 8 (Chile); letter from Theodore A. Coulombis and John A. Micolopoulos, in *id.,* Apr. 21, 1973, at 26, col. 3; letter from Valery Chalidze, Apr. 2, 1973, in *id.,* Apr. 18, 1973, at 46, col. 5; *id.,* Apr. 17, 1973, at 4, col. 4. For a discussion of collective punishments against tribes "suspected" of giving aid to guerrillas, including such measures as new plans for black resettlement, curfews, and the confiscation or destruction of property "useful" to insurgents regardless of military necessity, *see id.,* May 19, 1973, at 9, col. 3. For allegations of torture, assassination, and violent suppression of certain groups, *see id.* at 8, col. 4.

72. *See, e.g.,* M. McDOUGAL & F. FELICIANO, *supra* note 5, at 53, 54 n.129, 86 n.215; M. OPPENHEIMER, THE URBAN GUERRILLA 57, 59-60, 63-64, 66, 69 (1969); T. TAYLOR, NUREMBERG AND VIETNAM: AN AMERICAN TRAGEDY 191-95 (1970); Carroll, *The Search For Justice in Northern Ireland,* 6 N.Y.U.J. INT'L L. & POL. 28, 31-35 (1973); Hutchinson, *supra* note 7, at 392; Paust, *My Lai and Vietnam: Norms, Myths and Leader Responsibility,* 57 MIL. L. REV. 99, 139, 163-65 (1972). The use of terrorism by revolutionaries can also be self-defeating. *See* N.Y. Times, May 20, 1973, at 14, col. 3 (stating that "[l]eftists have lost popularity . . . because of terrorist activities"); *id.,* Mar. 7, 1973, at 1, col. 1 (announcing the ban on PLO operations in the Sudan); Mar. 6, 1973, at 6, col. 1, Mar. 5, 1973, at 7, col. 1; Washington Post, Dec. 2, 1972, at 1, col. 5.

73. *See* J. CAREY, U.N. PROTECTION OF CIVIL AND POLITICAL RIGHTS 17-21 (1970). *See also* Draper, *The Ethical and Juridical Status of Constraints in War,* 55 MIL. L. REV. 169, 183-84 (1972).

74. *See* U.S. DEP'T STATE, PUB. No. 8689, THE ROLE OF INTERNATIONAL LAW IN COMBATING TERRORISM 2 (1973). *See* 4 COMMENTARY, GENEVA CONVENTION RELATIVE TO THE PROTECTION OF CIVILIAN PERSONS IN TIME OF WAR 13, 580-82 (J. Pictet ed. 1958) [hereinafter cited as 4 COMMENTARY] ; M. McDOUGAL & F. FELICIANO, *supra* note 5, at 285, 317-19, 376-78; McDougal, Lasswell, & Chen, *supra* note 27, at 260-62. *See also* Wright, *Toward a Universal Law for Mankind* 63 COLUM. L. REV. 435 (1963).

75. *See* Convention with Respect to the Laws and Customs of War and Land, July 29, 1899, art. 1, 32 Stat. 180 (1902), T.S. No. 403 (effective April 9, 1902).

76. *See* common art. 1 of the 1949 Geneva Conventions, *e.g.,* Convention Relative to the Protection of Civilian Persons in Time of War, dated at Geneva, Aug. 12, 1949, 6 U.S.T. 3516, T.I.A.S. No. 3365, 75 U.N.T.S. 287 (effective Feb. 2, 1956) [hereinafter cited as Geneva Convention No. 4]. *See also* 4 COMMENTARY, *supra* note 74, at 13, 15-16; Paust, *supra* note 72, at 118-28.

77. Geneva Convention No. 4, *supra* note 76, at art. 144; Convention for

the Amelioration of the Condition of the Wounded and Sick in Armed Forces in the Field, dated at Geneva, Aug. 12, 1949, art. 47, 6 U.S.T. 3114, T.I.A.S. No. 3362, 75 U.N.T.S. 31 [hereinafter cited as Geneva Convention No. 1]; Convention for the Amelioration of the Condition of Wounded, Sick and Shipwrecked Members of Armed Forces at Sea, dated at Geneva, Aug. 12, 1949, art. 48, 6 U.S.T. 3217, T.I.A.S. No. 3363, 75 U.N.T.S. 85 [hereinafter cited as Geneva Convention No. 2]; Convention Relative to the Treatment of Prisoners of War, dated at Geneva, Aug. 12, 1949, art. 127, 6 U.S.T. 3316, T.I.A.S. No. 3364, 75 U.N.T.S. 135 [hereinafter cited as Geneva Convention No. 3]. *See also* 4 COMMENTARY, *supra* note 74, at 580-82; International Institute of Humanitarian Law, Guidelines for Military Instruction, Nov. 1972 (San Remo, Italy) [hereinafter cited as Int'l Inst. of Humanitarian Law]; Draper, *supra* note 73, at 184; *G.I.A.D. Draper Addresses JAG School,* 1 ARMY LAW. 1, 2 (1971).

78. *See also* E. CORWIN, UNDERSTANDING THE CONSTITUTION 2-5, 131-32 (4th ed. 1967); SOURCES OF OUR LIBERTIES (R. Perry & J. Cooper eds. 1972).

79. *See* Geneva Convention No. 4, *supra* note 76, art. 33, and the new draft protocols. Concerning human rights and terrorism, *see* 1972 U.N. Doc. A/C.6/ 418, *supra* note 6, at 41; 1971 OAS Convention on Terrorism, *supra* note 46; General Action and Policy of the Organization with Regard to Acts of Terrorism and, Especially, the Kidnapping of Persons and Extortion in Connection with that Crime, June 30, 1970, A.G. Res. 4 (I-E/70) OAS Doc. OAS/Ser. P/I-E.2 (1970), reprinted in INT'L LEGAL MATERIALS 1084 (1970).

80. *See* J. CAREY, *supra* note 73, at 19-21 (noting recent U.N. efforts including lectures, seminars, and fellowships); Veuthey, *The Red Cross and Non-International Conflicts,* 113 INT'L REV. RED CROSS 422 (1970). A private organization has recently suggested several guidelines for action. *See* Int'l Inst. of Humanitarian Law, *supra* note 77. New military efforts could be expanded and copied elsewhere. *See* U.S. DEP'T OF ARMY, SUBJECT SCHEDULE No. 27-1, THE GENEVA CONVENTIONS OF 1949 AND HAGUE CONVENTION No. IV of 1907 (1970); U.S. DEP'T OF ARMY, THE LAW OF LAND WARFARE—A SELF-INSTRUCTION TEXT, PAM. No. 27-200 (1972); U.S. DEP'T OF ARMY, YOUR CONDUCT IN COMBAT: UNDER THE LAW OF WAR, TRAINING CIRCULAR No. 27-12 (1973). For other suggestions as to dissemination and educational implementory techniques, *see* U.N. Report of the Secretary-General, Respect for Human Rights in Armed Conflicts, 24 U.N. GAOR, (Agenda Item 47) 10-11, 116, U.N. Doc. A/8052 (1970) [hereinafter cited as U.N. Doc. A/8052]; U.N. Report of the Secretary-General, Respect for Human Rights in Armed Conflicts, 24 U.N. GAOR, (Agenda Item 61) 41-43, U.N. Doc. A/7720 (1969) [hereinafter cited as U.N. Doc. A/7720]; INTERNATIONAL COMMITTEE OF THE RED CROSS, SOLDIER's MANUAL (1971); UNESCO, Some Suggestions on Teaching About Human Rights, U.N. Doc. Ed. 69/D.37a/A (1968); Paust, *An International Structure for Implementa-*

tion of the 1949 Geneva Conventions: Needs and Function Analysis, 1 YALE STUD. WORLD PUB. ORDER 148 (1974).

81. U.N. CHARTER, art. 56.

82. *Id.,* art. 55(c). Arts. 55(c) and 56 are supplemented by the Geneva Convention No. 4, *supra* note 76, arts. 1, 144-49.

83. *See* U.N. CHARTER, arts. 1(3), 55(c), 56.

84. U.N. Doc. A/7720, *supra* note 80, at 31.

85. *See* 4 COMMENTARY, *supra* note 74, at 15-16, 34, 37 (compulsory minimum). Unless otherwise specified in a particular article, the pledge "prohibited absolutely and permanently, no exception or excuse being tolerated," the following: lack of reciprocity, reprisal, terrorism, political needs, guerrilla needs, or military necessity. *Id.* at 38-40. There the book also notes that the pledge to "ensure" respect requires cooperative international implementary action including cooperative sanction strategy. For a thorough consideration of sanction strategy, *see* M. McDOUGAL & F. FELICIANO, *supra* note 5, at 280-353.

86. *See, e.g.,* U.S. CONST., 1st amend.; 1948 Universal Declaration of Human Rights, *supra* note 30, at arts. 1, 2, 3, 18, 19, 20, 21; 1966 Covenant on Civil and Political Rights, *supra* note 30, arts. 1-2, 9, 18-19, 21-22, 25, *cf.* art. 20; 1950 European Convention, *supra* note 70, arts. 5, 9-11, 14; 1969 American Convention on Human Rights, *supra* note 70, arts. 1, 7, 12-16, 23. *See also* Paust, *supra* note 55; DeBecker v. Belgium, 2 Y.B. CONVENTION ON HUMAN RIGHTS 1959 at 214 (1960); *id.* 1960 at 486 (1961).

87. *See* note 70 *supra.* This issue was not resolved in the *DeBecker case, supra* note 86, since the petitioner withdrew his case after Belgian law was amended. No international forum has attempted to give further guidance.

88. *See, e.g., Patience Key to Method in Handling Terrorists, supra* note 20, adding: "Electricity . . . was cut off, blanking the television screen. The police gave the press only the news that they wanted the gunmen to hear on their transistor radio."

89. *See* notes 59-63 *supra.*

90. *See* note 70 *supra. See also Senate Unit Asks Military Aid Cut for South Korea,* N.Y. Times, Sept. 7, 1974, at 1, col. 4; *South Korea Police Detain and Harass Opposition Leaders, id.,* Jan. 13, 1974, at 1, col. 6; Jan. 9, 1974, at 3, col. 1; J. Cohen, *Lawyers, Politics, and Despotism in Korea,* 61 A.B.A.J. 730 (June 1975). Amnesty International has investigated violations of fundamental human rights in South Korea. *See also* N.Y. Times, Feb. 16, 1976, at 10, col. 1 (India); Feb. 15, 1976, at 12, col. 1 (Chile); at 2, col. 3 (Spain); at 21, col. 1 (South Africa).

91. *See also* Uruguayan Decree-Law 655/972 (Sept. 28, 1972); *supra* note 45; Argentina Decree No. 1454 (1973); Circular, Argentina, 1 (Mar. 1976), *supra* note 45; Argentina Decree No. 2840 (1974), *id.* at 3; H.C. Fragoso, Report on Argentina (1975), *id.* at 5-7 (a report for Int'l Comm. of Jurists).

92. Canadian Penal Code § 281.1, Circular, Canada, 3 (Oct. 1975), *supra* note 45. *See also* Federal Republic of Germany Penal Code § 131, Circular, Federal Republic of Germany, 2 (Sept. 1975), *id.*, Glorification of Violence and Incitement to Racial Hatred; Spain, Anti-terrorist Decree-Law (Aug. 27, 1975); arts. 4, 10, 19 (supposedly patterned after similar British, French and Italian measures), Circular, Spain, 1-2 (Oct. 1975), *id.*; N.Y. Times, Feb. 15, 1976, at 2, col. 3 (Spain). Spanish press controls also occur while governmental investigations are underway. *See id.*, June 18, 1976, at 9, col. 1.

93. *See* note 88 *supra*; Uruguayan Law of State Security and Internal Order, No. 14, 068, arts. 147-48 (July 12, 1972), Circular, Uruguay, 1 (Dec. 1975), *supra* note 45. *See also* Austria Penal Code, art. 99, Circular, Austria, 1 (Sept. 1975), *id.*

94. *See* Chile Decree-Law 1009, arts. 5, 6 (1975), Circular, Chile, 1-2 (Oct. 1975), *supra* note 45; Spain, Anti-Terrorist Decree-Law (August. 27, 1975), arts. 10, 19, Circular, Spain, 2 (Oct. 1975), *id.*; Uruguay Decree-Law 655-972 (Sept. 28, 1972), and Decree-Law 393-973 (June 19, 1973), art. 3, Circular, Uruguay, 3-4, 5 (Dec. 1975); N.Y. Times, May 5, 1976, at 8, col. 5 (S. Korea); *Seoul Jails Defense Lawyer Who Criticized Secret Trial,* Sept. 5, 1974, at 14, col. 1; Jan. 9, 1974, at 3, col. 1; Feb. 2, 1974, at 4, col. 3; Feb. 8, 1974, at 6, col. 4; Mar. 3, 1974, at 9, col. 1; Apr. 4, 1974, at 3, col. 1; note 83 *supra. See also* M. HORRELL, LEGISLATION AND RACE RELATIONS (South African Inst. of Race Relations, 1971).

95. *See* arts. 1, 4. *See also* N.Y. Times, Apr. 27, 1976, at 2, col. 4 (Rhodesian regulations to prohibit the publication of certain information relating to defense, public safety, public order, economic order, or information that might cause alarm and despondency); *id.*, Feb. 15, 1976, at 12, col. 1 (Chilean decree prohibiting false or exaggerated news that causes alarm or disgust); Feb. 16, 1976, at 10, col. 1 (India). *Ex parte* Milligan, United States (4 Wall.) 2 (1866); Brown v. United States, 12 U.S. (8 Cranch) 504 (1814).

96. *See* N.Y. Times v. United States, 403 U.S. 713 (1971); and International Products Corp. v. Koons, 325 F.2d 403 (2d Circ. 1963). *See also* Communist Party of Indiana v. Whitcomb, 414 U.S. 441 (1974); Brandenburg v. Ohio, 395 U.S. 444 (1969) (involving a state terrorism statute); Watts v. United States, 394 U.S. 705 (1969) (threat to the President); New York Times v. Sullivan, 376 U.S. 255 (1974); Garrison v. Louisiana, 379 U.S. 500 (1964); Konigsberg v. Calif., 353 U.S. 252 (1957); *cf.* Cole v. Richardson, 405 U.S. 676 (1972); Near v. Minnesota, 283 U.S. 697, 716 (1934).

97. *See* note 19 *supra. See also* Mann, *Personnel and Property of Transnational Business Operations,* ch. 7 of this report, at 440-443.

98. *See also* T. GURR, WHY MEN REBEL (1970).

99. Bassiouni, discussion, *Symposium: Terrorism in the Middle East,* 7 AKRON L. REV. 395 (1974). *See also* M.C. BASSIOUNI, INTERNATIONAL TERRORISM AND POLITICAL CRIMES xiv-xv, 43-46 (1975). This would

presently be illegal in some countries, *e.g.,* Spain, Chile, Uruguay, South Africa, and South Korea. See notes 91-95 *supra.*

100. *See* ABA International Terrorism Resolution, *reprinted in ABA,* 2 THE INTERNATIONAL LAW NEWS, No. 2, at 4 (1973).

101. *See* World Peace Through Law Resolution, Nos. 11, 12 (Oct. 1975) adopted at the Washington Conference on Law and the World; Proceedings, Abidjan World Peace Through Law Conference, panel on terrorism (Aug. 1973).

102. *See generally* AMNESTY INTERNATIONAL, REPORT ON TORTURE (1973); J. Cohen, *supra* note 90; *Hearings on International Protection of Human Rights Before the Subcommittee on International Organizations and Movements of the House Comm. on Foreign Affairs,* 93d Cong., 1st Sess. (1974); U.N. Panel Asserts Chile Is Continuing Repressive Action, N.Y. Times, Feb. 11, 1976, at 1, col. 8; Mar. 5, 1976, at 6, col. 4; May 28, 1976 (the United States tells South Korea of its concern over human rights). *See also* U.N. Report of the Secretary-General, Torture and Other Cruel Inhumane or Degrading Treatment or Punishment in Relation to Detention and Imprisonment, 30 U.N. GAOR (Agenda Item 74) 1, U.N. Doc. A/10158 and A/10158/Add. 1 (1975).

103. *See generally* El Paso v. Simmons, 379 U.S. 497 (1965); Stone v. Mississippi, 101 U.S. 814 (1879); Restatement, Contracts, § 512; J. CALAMMARI & J. PERILLO, THE LAW OF CONTRACTS 539, 557-60 (1970); J. PAUST & R. UPP, BUSINESS LAW 149 ff (1974). *See also* M. McDOUGAL, H. LASSWELL, & J. MILLER, THE INTERPRETATION OF AGREEMENTS AND WORLD PUBLIC ORDER xx, 30-31, 41-42, 261-62 (1967).

104. *See also* Fuentes v. Shevin, 407 U.S. 67 (1972); Ewing v. Mytinger & Casselberry, Inc., 339 U.S. 594 (1950); Fahey v. Mallonnee, 332 U.S. 245 (1947), national economic crisis due to bank failure; United States v. Pfitsch, 256 U.S. 547 (1921), national emergency in time of war; Stone v. Mississippi, 101 U.S. 814 (1879). Note that Congress also has broad powers to protect civil rights, and, under the 1964 Civil Rights Act, there may be jurisdictional competence to proscribe several types of conspiratorial activity. 18 U.S.C. §§ 241 *et seq.* (1948). Although the president cannot lawfully act alone to regulate these activities, *see generally,* Youngstown Sheet and Tube Co. v. Sawyer, 343 U.S. 579 (1952). *See* Sterling v. Constantin, 289 U.S. 378 (1932); *cf.* Korematsu v. United States, 323 U.S. 214 (1944). *See also* Scheuer v. Rhodes, 416 U.S. 232 (1974); *In re* Yamashita, 327 U.S. 1 (1945); *see* Brown v. United States, 12 U.S. (8 Cranch) 504, 519 (1814); United States v. Toscanino, 500 F.2d 267 (2d. Cir. 1974), *rehearing den.* 504 F.2d 1380 (1974). *See also* United States v. Nixon, 418 U.S. 683 (1974); Marbury v. Madison, 5 U.S. (1 Cranch) 137, 162-63 (1803). The concurrence of corgressional and executive power should be sufficient if the sanction strategy otherwise satisfies the test of reasonable necessity.

105. *See generally* W.M. REISMAN, *supra* note 27; Christol & Davis, *Maritime Quarantine: The Naval Interdiction of Offensive Weapons and Associ-*

ated Material to Cuba, 1962, 57 AM. J. INT'L L. 525, 540-43 (1957); MacChesney, *Some Comments on the "Quarantine" of Cuba, id.* at 592; McDougal, *The Soviet-Cuban Quarantine and Self-Defense, id.* at 597; Mallison, *Limited Naval Blockade or Quarantine-Interdiction: National and Collective Defense Claims Valid under International Law,* 31 GEO. WASH. L. REV. 335 (1962); D.O'CONNELL, 2 INTERNATIONAL LAW 699 ff (1965) (cases of claimed rights to visitation and enquiry); McDougal & Schlei, *The Hydrogen Bomb Tests in Perspective: Lawful Measures for Security,* 64 YALE L. J. 648 (1955); Case of the *Virginius,* 2 MOORE, DIGEST OF INTERNATIONAL LAW 895 (1906); Church v. Hubbart, 6 U.S. (2 Cranch) 187, 234 (1804).

106. *See* notes 32-33, 105 *supra.*

107. *See also* W.M. REISMAN, *supra* note 27; note 51 *supra; cf.* McDougal & Schlei, *supra* note 105.

108. *See* Trading with the Enemy Act, 40 Stat. 415 (1917), as amended, 50 U.S.C. App. § 5 (1964); The Foreign Assets Control Regulations, 31 C.F.R. Part 500 (1967); The Export Control Act of 1949, 63 Stat. 7, *as amended,* 50 U.S.C. App. § 2021 (1964); *cf.* Kent v. Dulles, 357 U.S. 116 (1958); Aptheker v. Secretary of State, 378 U.S. 500 (1964); United States v. Laub, 385 U.S. 475 (1967). Perhaps a better analogy is to the duty of states to not tolerate, finance, promote, and so forth civil strife or acts of terrorism in another state. *See* notes 46-50 *supra.*

109. *See* Zschernig v. Miller, 389 U.S. 429 (1968); *In re* Belemecich's Estate, 375 U.S. 395 (1964); United States v. Pink, 315 U.S. 203 (1942); Hines v. Davidowitz, 312 U.S. 52 (1941).

110. *See* notes 46-50, 108 *supra.*

111. *See* 299 U.S. 304 (1936).

112. *See* note 103 *supra.* The same should apply to employment contracts, lease agreements, purchase agreements, and so forth.

113. *See* notes 32-35 *supra.* A possible exception concerns necessity to prevent *any* felony, but the felony here would at least involve a threat of death or serious injury—at least serious mental anxiety or fear. One might question, however, whether terror outcome alone is "injury." This writer favors a broad, policy-serving approach that would allow private responses to terrorist threats; indeed, the "terrorist" nature of a threat would appear to depend on a perceived threat of death or injury.

114. *See* Paust, *Does Your Police Force Use Illegal Weapons?—An Approach to Decision About Weapons Regulation,* 18 HARVARD INT'L L. J. 19 (1977); Paust, *supra* note 37.

115. *See* W.M. REISMAN, *supra* note 27; Paust & Blaustein, *supra* note 53; note 51 *supra.*

116. *See* Houston Post, Jan. 31, 1976, at 4, col. 1.

117. *See* note 114 *supra.*

118. *See* Paust & Blaustein, *supra* note 53; note 15 *supra.*

119. *See, e.g.,* 1948 Universal Declaration of Human Rights, *supra* note 30, art. 5; Paust, *supra* note 114. *See also* Declaration of Tokyo, Guidelines for Medical Doctors Concerning Torture and Other Cruel, Inhuman or Degrading Treatment or Punishment in Relation to Detention and Imprisonment, adopted by the Twenty-ninth World Medical Assembly in Oct. 1975, *reprinted in* Note by the Secretary General, Human Rights in the Administration of Justice, U.N. Doc. E/AC.57/24 (1976) (Annex contains Declaration of Tokyo).

120. *See, e.g.,* 1948 Universal Declaration of Human Rights, *supra* note 30, art. 25. *See also International Law and the Food Crisis,* 1975 PROCEEDINGS AM. SOC'Y OF INT'L L. 39, 45-52, 57-58, 60 (remarks by Jordan Paust); G. Mudge, *Starvation as a Means of Warfare,* 4 A.B.A. INT'L LAW 228 (1970).

121. *See, e.g.,* 1948 Universal Declaration of Human Rights, *supra* note 30, art. 25. *See also* 1949 Geneva Conventions, *supra* notes 76 & 77.

122. *See, e.g.,* Paust, *Terrorism and the International Law of War,* 64 MIL. L. REV. 1, 11-22 (1974).

123. *See* note 121 *supra.*

124. *See also Dentist, ex-wife fail on hijack damages,* Houston Post, Jan. 24, 1976, at 3, col. 6 (a Houston jury denied $160,000 sought in a damage suit against Eastern Airlines for use of allegedly improper screening procedures—then approved by the FAA). *See also* Evans, *Aircraft and Aviation Facilities,* ch. 1 of this report at note 96. *See also* 1948 Universal Declaration of Human Rights, *supra* note 30, art. 8.

125. *See also* Paust, *supra* note 114; W. PROSSER, LAW OF TORTS 9-11, 492-96, 505-16 (1971); 1948 Universal Declaration of Human Rights, *supra* note 30, art. 8.

126. *See, e.g.,* U.N. CHARTER, arts. 1, 55(c), 56.

127. *See* N.Y. Times, June 17, 1976, at 13, col. 1.

128. *See also* note 70 *supra.*

129. *See also* notes 79-85 *supra.*

130. Stevenson, 67 DEP'T STATE BULL. 645, 647. *See generally* 67 DEP'T STATE BULL. 357-64 (1972); Brower, 67 DEP'T STATE BULL. 444-48 (1972); Evans, *Aircraft Hijacking: What Is To Be Done?* 66 AM. J. INT'L L. 819 (1972) [hereinafter cited as Evans, Aircraft Hijacking]. *See also* Evans, *Aircraft and Aviation Facilities, supra* note 124, at 28-31.

131. *See* Rovine, *The Contemporary International Attack on Terrorism,* 3 ISRAEL Y.B.H.R. 9 (1973). The United States will "support suspension of all air service to countries that fail to abide by the Hague and Montreal Conventions." Letter from Armin Meyer to Jordan J. Paust, June 25, 1973.

132. Bennett, 68 DEP'T STATE BULL. 81, 86 (1973).

133. *See* Evans, *Aircraft Hijacking, supra* note 130, at 819; Stephen, *"Going South"–Air Piracy and Unlawful Interference with Air Commerce,* 4 A.B.A. INT'L LAWYER 433, 442 (1972).

134. *See* W.M. REISMAN, *supra* note 27, at 838.

135. *See* notes 51, 105, 115, 110 *supra*. Also *compare* Evans, panel discussion, INTERNATIONAL TERRORISM 112 (1974), *with* Vlasic, *id.* at 122-23 and Paust, *id.* at 137-38.

136. N.Y. Times, Jan. 31, 1976, at 10, col. 3.

137. *See* N.Y. Times, Apr. 28, 1973, at 7, col. 1.

138. Note 131 *supra.*

139. *See generally* M. McDOUGAL & F. FELICIANO, *supra* note 5; H. LASSWELL, D. LERNER, WORLD REVOLUTIONARY ELITES (1965); H. LASSWELL & A. KAPLAN, POWER AND SOCIETY (1950).

140. *See also* McDougal, book review, *The Three-Mile Limit of Territorial Seas,* 7 A.B.A. INT'L LAWYER 925, 928 (1973), adding: "authority, in the sense of peoples' demands and expectations about how power should be exercised, is itself a most important form of power"; H. LASSWELL, A PREVIEW OF POLICY SCIENCES 27-28 *passim* (1971); W.M. Reisman, *supra* note 23 at 46 (expectations).

141. *See id.* at 3; *cf. id.* at 4-6.

142. *See also id.* at 16; HOUSE COMM. ON INTERNAL SECURITY, STAFF STUDY ON TERRORISM, 93d Cong., 2d Sess., 42 (1974), noting that during most of 1973, "the PFLP and Israeli secret agents engaged in a bloody private war throughout Europe." *See also* N.Y. Times, Mar. 22, 1976, at 6, col. 1 (private "war" in Argentina); Mar. 20, 1976, at 2, col. 3 (private "war" in Spain).

143. *Cf. id.* at 6, 33. Perhaps a useful analogy would be to the self-defense or defense of others set of approaches to choice. Concerning possible claims made by private armies, *see also id.* at 19-22. Concerning uses of private armies in the United States by railroads and other industries in the early twentieth century, *see* references cited in *id.* at 54.

144. N.Y. Times, Mar. 22, 1976, at 6, col. 1. *See also* Houston Post, May 29, 1976, at 15, col. 3 (Lebanon); N.Y. Times, June 7, 1976, at 3, col. 1 (Brazil); June 12, 1976, at 3, col. 5 (Argentina).

145. *See* Reisman, *supra* note 23.

146. For acceptance in the U.S., *see id.* at 2, 27, 54; and J. KAKLIK & S. WILKHORN, PRIVATE POLICE IN THE UNITED STATES (1971). For acceptable use in Argentina, *see* note 137 *supra*. The United States recommends the employment of a private security patrol of home areas if local police patrols are infrequent or nonexistent. *See also* Dalles, *U.S. Firms Combatting Terrorism,* L.A. Times, Oct. 20, 1976, at 1, col. 1; Mann, *supra* note 97.

147. *See also* Report, National Task Force on Private Police, forthcoming.

148. For a discussion of "right-wing death squads" and their illegal tactics in Argentina, including the killing of hundreds of people "in recent months," *see* N.Y. Times, Jan. 14, 1976, at 4, col. 4; Houston Post, Feb. 21, 1976, at 4, col. 3 (A.P.); N.Y. Times, Apr. 4, 1976, at 1, col. 7; June 12, 1976, at 3, col. 5. *See also id.,* June 7, 1976, at 3, col. 1 (Brazil).

These forms of death squad counterterror and terror warfare will probably stimulate claims by others to target police officers as "legitimate" targets, perhaps with the argument that those who violate the law should not be entitled to the protection of the law. Moreover, in addition to violations of domestic law and general norms of international human rights, the use of terror warfare tactics by public or private police would violate the new draft Code of Conduct for Law Enforcement Officials. *See* Note by Secretary-General, Code of Conduct for Law Enforcement Officials, U.N. Doc. E/AC.57/25 (1976); U.N. Report by the Secretary General, Torture and Other Cruel, Inhumane or Degrading Treatment or Punishment in Relation to Detention or Imprisonment, 30 U.N. GAOR (Agenda Item 74) 1, U.N. Doc. A/10260 (1975).

149. N.Y. Times, June 18, 1976, at B1, col. 6.

150. *See also* note 148 *supra*; Paust, *supra* note 37.

151. *See, e.g.*, 1966 Covenant on Civil and Political Rights, *supra* note 30, at art. 4; 1950 European Convention on Human Rights, *supra* note 70, at art. 15; 1969 American Convention on Human Rights, *supra* note 70, at arts. 27, 29. *See also* Paust, *supra* note 72, at 153-56; Kelly, *Legal Aspects of Military Operations in Counterinsurgency,* 21 MIL. L. REV. 95 (1963).

152. *See id; see also* pp. 587-588 *supra*.

153. *See, e.g.,* note 151 *supra*.

154. *See generally* Paust, *supra* note 80; note 102 *supra*.

155. *Cf.* Paust, *supra* note 80, at 209.

156. *See* Paust, *"Nonprotected" Persons or Things,* ch. 6 of this report.

157. *See also* R. PERKINS, CRIMINAL LAW 1018-22 (2d ed. 1969), *citing* the Model Penal Code, § 3.05.

158. More detailed approaches have been adopted by Illinois and Minnesota, and these may be used as models. *See* Illinois Crime Victims Compensation Act, Ill. Stat., ch. 70, § § 74-84 (1973); Minnesota Crime Victims Reparations Act, Minn. Stat., ch. 299.B (1974).

159. *See, e.g.,* Yick Wo v. Hopkins, 118 U.S. 356 (1886).

160. *See* Paust, *supra* note 114.

161. *See id.*

162. H.R. 3625, To amend Title 18, United States Code, to provide a penalty for the use of expanding (dum-dum) bullets in the United States, 94th Cong., 1st Sess., Feb. 25, 1975.

163. *See, e.g.,* United Mexican States (Garcia & Garza) v. United States, U.S.–Mexican Claims Commission, 4. U.N.T.I.A.A. 119 (1926).

164. *See* Paust, *supra* note 114.

165. Paine, *The Rights of Man,* 2 COMPLETE WORKS OF THOMAS PAINE 588 (P. Foner ed. 1945).

**Appendix
Conclusions and
Recommendations**

Introduction

This appendix summarizes the primary conclusions and recommendations of the study as well as their underlying rationales. Before we turn to a consideration of these conclusions and recommendations, a brief word of explanation about the organization of this appendix is in order.

The first section, "General Recommendations of the Study," contains recommendations that transcend or cut across the individual subject matter areas treated in the individual chapters. For example, an international convention that would require states either to impose sanctions on terrorist crimes or to extradite the accused to another jurisdiction for prosecution would apply whether the terrorist act in question was an attack on aircraft and aviation facilities, ocean vessels and offshore structures, or diplomats. In several instances these general recommendations were advanced by more than one member of the working group.

The second section, "Specific Conclusions and Recommendations of the Study," turns to conclusions and recommendations drawn from chapters of the study prepared by individual members of the working group. These chapters in turn fall into two basic categories. The first category includes a consideration of terrorists' threats or attacks on such societal vulnerabilities as nuclear facilities and materials or the personnel and property of transnational corporations. The second category covers procedures and processes relating to the prevention and control of terrorism, such as extradition, expulsion and exclusion, law enforcement measures, and state self-help. These procedures and processes may apply to any or all of the terrorists' threats or attacks included in the first category.

All the general recommendations in the first section of this appendix as well as the conclusions and recommendations of a more specific nature contained in the second section are presented as those of the working group as a whole. However, this is not to say that each conclusion or recommendation obtained the unanimous support of the working group. Quite to the contrary, many of these conclusions and recommendations were sharply challenged and criticized during working group sessions, and no formal votes were taken on them. Nonetheless, they have been included in either the first or the second section of this appendix, as appropriate, unless they clearly enjoyed little or no support from the majority of the working group.

The third section of this appendix includes recommendations that are presented as those of individual working group members. Basically, two tests have been applied in determining whether a particular recommendation should be included in this section. First, in some instances, time constraints precluded the working group from considering the recommendation in any detail. Second, in other instances, discussion in the working group clearly indicated that the recommendation did not enjoy general support and therefore should be attributed only to the individual member who introduced it. The working group agrees, however, that these recommendations, which in many cases are innovative and provocative, are worthy of consideration and deserve inclusion in this chapter.

General Recommendations of the Study

Drafting General Treaty Law

General International Agreements. Despite the erratic nature of recent efforts to draft general treaty law on terrorism, a number of new or renewed multilateral treaty approaches should be considered further. Specifically, the U.S. government should evaluate the feasibility and usefulness of the following kinds of international agreements:

1. *A single convention on legal control of international terrorism, to be drafted in a conference held outside the auspices of the United Nations.* This convention would seek to define the offense, emphasize prosecution, make states that fail to comply liable for damages and make states that condone or cooperate with international terrorists liable for payment of damages to the victims.
2. *International agreements and treaties that would remove territorial sanctuaries for terrorists.* An international convention, for example, would require states either to impose sanctions on terrorist crimes or to extradite the accused to another jurisdiction for prosecution.
3. *An international agreement to aid in the prevention of terrorism against "nonprotected" people.* Such an agreement should emphasize the importance of data collection, warning requirements, cooperative investigatory procedures, extradition or prosecution, an international prosecution tribunal, and specific denial of POW status to terrorists in order to ensure a uniform prosecution effort.

It is recognized, however, that the utility of multilateral treaties is likely to be limited, and that the more like-minded (and thus narrower) the class of states participating in such exercises, the greater will be the likelihood of success either in the drafting effort itself or in the actual operation of the legal regime produced. Governmental policy should take into account that international lawmaking in this as in any other field is not limited to treaties, and that the process of customary international lawmaking may afford some possibilities for overcoming problems created by a lack of pre-existing political consensus on "gut" issues such as sanctuary or the obligation to extradite.

International Tribunal. *The U.S. government should support the establishment of an International Criminal Tribunal as a means of coping with terrorism.* While the idea of an international criminal court presents a number of difficulties, such a tribunal might serve as an alternate jurisdiction for the prosecution of terrorists and might help to mitigate the political difficulties that often surround such prosecutions.

Regional Conventions. *The U.S. government should encourage regional efforts to develop conventions for the control of terrorism, such as the recently adopted Convention of the Council of Europe.*

Promoting Cooperative National Action through International Conference(s)

The United States should consider the usefulness of convening an international conference on the suppression and prevention of terrorism. Such a conference would bring together experts from around the world to discuss means to suppress and prevent terrorist activities and to further international cooperation toward achieving that end. In particular, it would study methods of encouraging states to impose national criminal sanctions for specific acts of terror-violence. Also, a primary goal of such a conference would be to help find ways to deter terror-violence acts such as hijacking, kidnaping diplomats, mailing letter bombs to innocent civilians, and the like.

Educational Programs

There is a role that the federal government can and should play, probably through existing mechanisms and programs, in stimulating more extensive and effective education on terrorism. Specifically, the federal government might encourage greater emphasis in school instruction on issues of human rights as they relate to terrorism.

Government, history, and senior problems classes could be the focus of such instruction, the goal being to make students better aware of the problem of terrorism (as both a direct violation and of a long-range threat to human rights) and thus better able to understand the need to deal with it.

Also, government-sponsored fellowships might encourage further study into the role private sector programs might play in combating terrorism.

In general, the government should stimulate the publication of popular and scholarly material; the production of films, slides, and taped broadcasts; the convening of seminars; and conferences on the subject of terrorism. All these measures would be aimed at further enlightening the public to the danger of terrorism, the threat it poses to democratic government and human rights, and the need and ways to combat it.

At the same time, it is recognized that there are substantial constraints on federal government involvement in this area, for under our system of constitutional government, education is primarily a state rather than a federal responsibility. Accordingly, in most instances the federal government should limit its activities to encouraging and advising on educational programs regarding terrorism, while leaving actual administration to state officials.

Media Guidelines

The working group is concerned about the role of a free and responsible media in sanctioning and reporting terrorism. *Greater attention should be paid by the media and others to the possible relationship between media coverage and terrorist activities with a view to formulating guidelines (nonlegal standards— perhaps a code of ethics) governing the nature and extent of media coverage of terroristic activities.* These standards might address two interrelated problems: (1) the general educational role of the media, which concerns overall effort to assist the public in understanding the threat of terrorism to society, democratic values and human rights (*e.g.,* by making it clear that even legitimate grievances cannot justify the taking of innocent lives), and (2) the role that media coverage of a terrorist event plays in the terrorists' calculations before and during the event, and in the effectiveness of law enforcement officials' efforts to cope with it. Members of the media should seek ways, consistent with the constitutional protection of a free press, to try to ensure that that role does not have the net result of abetting the achievement of terrorist goals. This would require addressing such questions as the need for temporarily withholding the publication news of a kidnaping or extortion threat until the incident has been resolved; avoiding publication of tactical police information; the relationship between tone and emphasis in media coverage and the encouragement of terrorist activity; and the like.

Negotiations: An Inappropriate Subject
for Legislation

Because of the need for government officials to have maximum flexibility in order to adjust their strategies to rapidly changing circumstances, the passage of legislation regarding negotiations with terrorists would be undesirable. Rather, general policy guidelines and *ad hoc* decision-making, plus improved law enforcement techniques, should remain the principal methods for dealing with terrorists.

Specific Conclusions and Recommendations of the Study

Terrorists' Threats and Societal Vulnerabilities

Aircraft and Aviation Facilities   Alona E. Evans

Conclusions

Hijacking, or the diversion of an aircraft from its scheduled destination by force or threat thereof, is a form of terrorist attack against international and domestic civil aviation that achieved spectacular success between 1968 and 1972 and that continues to pose a threat, albeit a declining one. Aircraft hijacking, both international and domestic, has been brought under substantial control through proscriptive international and national legislation, rigorous national security measures, and the enforcement of same. Nevertheless, more can be done at both the national and international levels to further develop controls over aviation terrorism, as the recommendations listed below indicate.

Recommendations

Legislation. *The U.S. government should amend 49 U.S.C. § 1472 so as to implement the Montreal Convention.* Full implementation is necessary if this convention is to have its intended effect in the U.S.

Airport Security. *Airport security programs should be extended to cover General Aviation at the point where general aircraft meet with public air facilities.* As prevention has been the major control over hijacking and the screening program has been very successful, tightening this specific security gap should further inhibit hijacking in the United States.

FAA Security Supervision. *The FAA should increase its supervision of the efficacy of security measures in use in U.S. airports.* The x-ray screening devices can become faulty very quickly, and the FAA's current quarterly inspections are not frequent enough to ensure continuous operating efficiency.

FAA/FBI Areas of Responsibility. *The 1975 Memorandum of Understanding between the Federal Aviation Administration and the Federal Bureau of Investigation should be reviewed.* This review would be for the purpose of clarifying the allocation of responsibility between pilots and ground authorities when an attack has been made on an aircraft.

Sanctions. *A multilateral convention should be concluded that would be designed to enforce, by sanctions, the Tokyo, Hague, and Montreal conventions*

638

and any security convention. This convention would seek to strengthen the need to prosecute or extradite offenders of these conventions and to eliminate "hijack havens."

Nuclear Facilities and Materials   Herbert H. Brown

Conclusions

Nuclear facilities and materials provide targets that could serve terrorist objectives. Although it would be difficult for terrorists to sabotage nuclear facilities or to steal nuclear materials, a trained and skilled group could accomplish these ends. Such a group could be so motivated if it sought to sensationalize its cause, to attack a symbol of modern society, or to extort a major concession from the government. The likelihood of such acts is unclear, but the serious potential harm to public health and safety and to valuable economic resources, and the public fears that would be provoked by nuclear-related terrorism require states to take effective measures to protect against such acts.

Neither the Non-Proliferation Treaty, the IAEA statute, nor any other treaty covers the subject of physical protection of nuclear facilities and materials. States have treated physical protection exclusively within the domain of their national sovereignty to exercise police power and domestic security responsibilities. There are no international agreements mandating the use of uniform physical protection practices among states and none to govern the security of nuclear materials in international transit. There is no systematic exchange among states of technical, administrative, or intelligence information concerning physical protection of nuclear facilities and materials or of information concerning terrorist threat potentials.

No international organization or international coordinative mechanism has been designated or established to plan for or coordinate plans for the contingency of a theft of nuclear materials from one state to another. The efforts of states to commence a dialogue on physical protection matters through the London Suppliers Conference, the *ad hoc* IAEA panels, and bilateral information exchange meetings have been fragmented and piecemeal; they have not been guided by a common integrated purpose or a stipulated objective. These efforts are inadequate for effective contingency planning.

The responsibilities for action and response by states in the event of a theft of nuclear materials across international borders, and indeed the kinds of administrative and logistic actions that would be necessary, are unclear and unarticulated for even the least complex situation, which would be where all states are cooperative. In the more complex situation, where stolen nuclear materials are taken to a state that is unwilling or unable to cooperate in locating and recovering these materials, the potential for confusion among states is great, because no guidelines exist to channel an effective response. In the most extreme case, where the location of stolen nuclear materials is not known, there is no mechanism through which states could plan or effect an efficient and timely coordinated search. The international legal principles of national sovereignty and territorial integrity would complicate and perhaps frustrate emergency actions by one state or several states acting collectively to locate and recover stolen nuclear materials in another state.

Recommendations

Physical Protection Measures. *The United States, in cooperation with other states, should seek to designate an international organization or to establish a formal mechanism to deal with physical protection matters.* Among the possible options, the United States should consider proposing that this mechanism take the form of a standing committee, adjunct to the IAEA but not within the agency's secretariat, with continuing responsibility for the following:

1. To promote free and systematic exchanges of information concerning physical protection measures and terrorist threat analyses among IAEA member states.
2. To sustain a panel composed of technical experts from IAEA member states to monitor regularly, upgrade, and expand, as necessary, the IAEA's recommendations for physical protection.
3. To compile data and report regularly to the IAEA director general and the board of governors on the extent of compliance by member states with the IAEA's recommendations for physical protection.
4. To provide a central information and data base on research and development activities of IAEA member states concerning physical protection systems and vulnerabilities and concerning terrorist threat analyses, and to disseminate regularly this information and data to member states.
5. To provide a forum in which the technical aspects of physical protection and the technical and logistic requirements to locate and recover stolen nuclear materials can be integrated with international legal principles governing the rights and duties of states and the imposition of sanctions where states fail to maintain effective physical protection measures.
6. To stimulate contingency planning among states—outside the forum of this committee and the IAEA—to locate and recover stolen nuclear materials.

An International Convention. *The United States should aggressively seek the agreement of states on the principles and provisions of an international convention that would establish:*

1. the legal basis for national and international physical protection standards that uniformly cover nuclear facilities and nuclear materials at fixed facilities and in transit, including sanctions that may be imposed against states that fail to comply with such standards

2. the rights and duties of states to cooperate with other states in the location and recovery of stolen nuclear materials
3. the institutional mechanisms through which these rights and duties shall be exercised
4. the establishment of a crisis management center or mechanism that would operate in the event of a significant act of nuclear-related terrorism
5. the duty of states to prosecute or extradite individuals responsible for sabotaging nuclear facilities or stealing nuclear materials.

Pending the conclusion of such a convention, the United States should, through the London Suppliers Conference and supplementary bilateral discussions, seek the agreement of states on the foregoing principles. Among the alternatives for implementing these principles, the nuclear supplier states should consider making such principles standard provisions of their bilateral agreements for cooperation on nuclear energy.

Agreements for Cooperation: Stricter Requirements. *The United States should include in its future nuclear energy Agreements for Cooperation—and should negotiate supplementary arrangements to existing U.S. Agreements for Cooperation to include—a provision requiring recipients of U.S.-supplied technology, equipment, and fuel (1) to comply with the IAEA's INFCIRC/225 recommendations for physical protection, and (2) to permit the United States, or the IAEA if the agency is so authorized by the United States, to verify compliance with INFCIRC/225 recommendations.*

Safeguard Agreements: Stricter Requirements. *The United States should include in its future trilateral safeguards agreements with nuclear-recipient states and the IAEA—and should negotiate supplementary arrangements to such existing trilateral safeguards agreements to include—a provision that the IAEA shall be kept informed of the recipient states' application of the IAEA's INFCIRC/225 recommendations for physical protection; and that, further, if so authorized by the United States, the IAEA shall have the right to verify such compliance.* The United States should agree to pay the cost of any such IAEA verification activities.

Ocean Vessels and Offshore Structures   J.D. Nyhart
and J. Christian Kessler

Conclusions

The oceans contain many economic assets that are within the capabilities of terrorists to attack, and which are valuable either economically or symbolically and are therefore potential targets. Under international law, primary jurisdiction over an incident is that of the flag state for vessels under most circumstances, and that of the coastal state for existing continental shelf structures or structures within the territorial sea. The present jurisdictional framework is an inadequate basis for allowing a state to protect assets beyond its territorial sea against terrorism. Resolution of this problem through established international legal forums, especially those dealing with law-of-the-sea matters, will become entangled in broader political issues. However, if a law-of-the-sea treaty emerges that is acceptable to the United States, it is likely to provide an improved basis for national action. In the case of vessels, there exists ample U.S. legislative mandate for preventive and enforcement activity for U.S. enforcement agencies. In the case of structures, additional clarifying legislative amendments would be useful. Furthermore, preventive planning is inadequate.

Recommendations
Coverage and Application of the U.S. Criminal Code

1. *The United States should amend sections 18 U.S.C. 1363 (destruction or injury to property), 18 U.S.C. 6159 (attack to plunder vessel), 18 U.S.C. 2273 (destruction of vessel by nonowner), and 18 U.S.C. 2276 (breaking and entering a vessel), so that they apply to offshore structures.*

2. *The U.S. government should amend 18 U.S.C. § 7 to bring within the special maritime jurisdiction of the criminal code all structures that are owned by U.S. citizens or corporations* and that are not covered by the Outer Continental Shelf Lands Act (OCSLA), the Deepwater Port Act, or the laws of another state governing its continental shelf under the jurisdictional basis provided by the 1958 Convention of the Continental Shelf or a superseding LOS treaty.

3. *If an acceptable law-of-the-sea treaty should result from the current negotiations under U.N. auspices, the United States should ratify that treaty* and enact legislation to extend federal criminal and civil law to all structures within the U.S. economic zone, under the jurisdictional provisions of the treaty.

4. Failing negotiation, ratification, or coming into force of a law-of-the-sea treaty containing economic zone articles, the *U.S. government should consider extending the federal criminal and civil law so as to apply to U.S. structures and objects offshore the U.S. coast that are not covered by the OCSLA or the Deepwater Port Act.*

5. *Upon completion of either the second, third, or fourth recommendation, the Department of State should consider seeking to negotiate bilateral and/or multilateral treaties requiring either extradition or prosecution for those criminal acts committed on or against vessels and/or offshore structures.*

U.S. Agencies; Responsibilities and Planning

1. *The U.S. Coast Guard, the Departments of Defense, State, and Justice, and other interested agencies should negotiate Memorandums of Understanding*

clarifying their respective areas of jurisdiction and responsibility for pre-venting, reacting to, and following up any ocean terrorist incidents. These memorandums should cover future deep-ocean mining activities.

2. Upon such clarification, *the U.S. Coast Guard should complete development of (and make available to private parties as appropriate) a comprehensive set of contingency plans covering prevention of, reaction to, and follow-up after acts of ocean terrorism.* Coast Guard planning would be based on authority provided in 14 U.S.C. § 2 and in the Commandant's Notice 3176 of February 13, 1975. Development of such contingency plans should involve other agencies as indicated by the Memorandums of Understanding referred to above. These contingency plans should be amended to include deep ocean mining activities as soon as development or prototype activities are under way.

Contingency Planning: Industry. *Offshore industries should be required to file their own contingency plans, which would include data regarding pipeline cutoffs and other damage control procedures, responses to fire and pipeline rupture, and the like.* This action would bring these industries more closely into overall government contingency planning and improve security in an area not previously covered by Coast Guard contingency planning. Filing requirements should be consistent with the need to protect proprietary information.

Projecting U.S. Policy. *A low public profile should be maintained with respect to the problem of ocean terrorism.* This would help reduce the possibility that publicity might increase the potential for attacks on ocean facilities.

Design Improvements for Offshore Structures and Vessels. *The National Academy of Engineering Marine Board Panel, the National Advisory Committee on the Oceans and Atmosphere, or a similar body should consider the possible vulnerability of offshore structures, deep-water ports, and vessels to terrorist attack, and the cost-effectiveness of design modifications to minimize it.* A study to determine the cost-effectiveness of various design changes should be made. The U.S.C.G. and U.S.G.S. could require the appropriate construction and design regulations over which they have responsibility to be changed to conform to new standards. Together, these actions would provide additional security in a previously vulnerable area.

*New Weapons: The Threat to Communication Facilities and
New Technological Systems*   Brian M. Jenkins
and Alfred P. Rubin

Conclusions

There are points of vulnerability in our complex technological infrastructure, as well as weapons that in the hands of a very few people can threaten to disrupt our society in ways serious enough that blackmail by fanatic groups or individuals is feasible.

With regard to the weapons that may afford terrorists an increasing capacity for violence and murder, explosives have been and are likely to remain for some time the most reliable and popular instrument of terrorist violence. Terrorists have used bombs to cause property damage, and occasionally to cause limited casualties. With a few recent exceptions in which bombs were planted aboard aircraft, terrorists have not used conventional explosives to kill large numbers of people. Terrorists have rarely used fire as a weapon against people, although they have used incendiary devices, such as bombs, to cause property damage.

Terrorists have also used whatever portable and concealable weapons they have been able to get their hands on. This suggests that as more advanced and exotic weapons become more widely available, terrorists will acquire and use them.

Terrorists have not been associated with any plots involving the use of chemical or biological weapons, with a few exceptions—for example, stolen canisters of mustard gas and "tick letters". Political considerations or moral constraints may be operative here. Plots to poison large numbers of people are more often the product of lunatics than of political extremists.

The historical record provides no evidence that any terrorist group has ever made any attempt to acquire fissionable nuclear material or other radioactive material for use in an explosive or dispersal device. Again, apart from technical difficulties, terrorists may be more subject to political and moral constraints than we normally think.

In sum, in terms of their ability to kill large numbers of people, terrorists have generally operated well below their technological ceiling, perhaps simply because thus far it has been unnecessary for them to escalate the violence beyond what we have seen. They are willing to kill a few to win publicity, to make a point, to create fear; they are rarely willing to kill many to accomplish the same objectives.

Terrorists have exploited the new vulnerabilities of advanced industrial societies in limited and special ways. Ironically, although terrorists are willing to kill "handfuls" of people to gain attention and cause alarm, they apparently are unwilling to anger a large number of people by some act of sabotage that could cause widespread inconvenience. They would rather force the government to take security measures that cause inconvenience. Compelling the British government to surround the Belfast shopping area with a security fence and to search shoppers going in and out is an example. Terrorists have bombed transformers, but they have seldom tried to blow up power stations. They have not interfered with water supplies. They have not forced evacuations by igniting fires in chemical manufacturing plants or by blowing up tanks of hazardous chemicals, although the recent publicity given to accidental chemical spills and fires may provide some inspiration in this direction. They have not attacked liquefied natural gas facilities or tankers carrying LNG; this is, however, a comparatively new technology. Political extremists have on several occasions recently carried out acts of sabotage at nuclear facilities. The intent in these cases appears to have been publicity and disruption, not widespread casualties. In sum, terrorists seem not so willing to kill a lot of people or make a lot of people angry at them and thereby enable the government to crack down on them (with public approval). This constraint will erode in the case of terrorists operating internationally if they can reach sanctuary and if governments are prevented by respect for the sovereignty of other states and by political considerations from responding effectively. If a group does not depend on a local constituency for support and can rely on refuge elsewhere, it may be less concerned about alienating its target population. The vulnerability that modern terrorists have regularly exploited is civil aviation, primarily because airliners have been relatively accessible and convenient containers of hostages or a guaranteed number of victims.

It is impossible within the existing framework of liberty in the United States, and the explicit restrictions on the powers of government contained in the First, Fourth, Fifth, Sixth, Ninth, Tenth, and Fourteenth Amendments to the Constitution, to protect people in the United States fully. Nonetheless, it is possible to reduce the new risks by holding open nonviolent means to effective political action, and by some marginal tightening of legal restrictions on possessing substances with particular potential for politically disruptive effects. It would also seem possible to reduce the likelihood of such blackmail in some cases by making criminal advocating, soliciting, advising about, or teaching methods for achieving the disruption of essential services or amenities or threatening the life or health of people in any section of the country when the effect of such advocacy, solicitation, advice, or teaching would be to increase substantially the likelihood that the acts will in fact be done or when the advocacy, etc., is coupled with the possession of the means to perform such acts, and the items possessed are possessed for use in performing forbidden acts.

Because the limits on governmental action in this area are fixed by the Constitution, no action should be taken without full consultation with the officials of the executive branch of government responsible for assuring compliance with constitutional imperatives, particularly the attorney general. It must be borne in mind that the use of treaty or international agreement cannot, under current approaches taken by the Supreme Court, overcome limitations on the powers of the federal government contained in the Constitution. Even if they could, the political ramifications of attempting to evade constitutional limits on the powers of the Congress by concluding treaty commitments that envisage changes in the criminal laws of the United States are too great to permit recourse to such approaches in this area.

Recommendations

U.S. Criminal Code. *Unauthorized possession of specified destructive substances for which there is no legitimate private use should be forbidden.* Precedent exists for such legislation in the Atomic Energy Act of 1954, as amended. Items that could be specified might include all guided weapons systems—such as heat-

-seeking missiles, and components specifically manufactured for use in them— nerve gases, nonbiodegradable herbicides, and biological substances potentially lethal to humans. Of course, governmental and other socially useful production or use of any of these items could be licensed.

Unauthorized interstate trafficking in specified substances that may have legitimate private uses but that also have significant potential uses as agents to disrupt essential services or amenities or threaten the life or health of people in any section of the country should be forbidden. Precedent exists for such legislation in the Gun Control Act of 1968. Items that could be specified include explosives of any sort, explosive detonators, and incendiary substances. Sales could be licensed on condition that the seller maintains reliable records of purchasers' identities.

Soliciting the unauthorized use of specified substances or weapons in the possession of the solicitor or the person being solicited should be forbidden when that solicitation is likely to produce the unauthorized use of those substances or weapons on targets of high sensitivity. The specified substances and weapons should be those forbidden to interstate traffic but possibly legally possessed. Targets of high sensitivity would include such points of vulnerability as water supply systems, transportation systems, communications systems, energy systems, chemical and biological storage locations, and storage places for radioactive materials. In the absence of an overt act to carry out a conspiracy, even this limited extension of the criminal law might raise constitutional questions. Accordingly, these constitutional questions should be exhaustively explored before this recommendation is implemented.

International Cooperation. *International agreements that restrict the use of specified weapons by states should be vigorously pursued and the widest possible ratification sought.* It would help to diminish the likelihood that irresponsible groups might gain possession of some particularly dangerous substances if national stockpiles were reduced or eliminated. The negotiation and conclusion of agreements such as the Convention on the Prohibition of the Development, Production and Stockpiling of Bacteriological (Biological) and Toxin Weapons and Their Destruction (April 10, 1972) would help toward that end.

International agreements by which countries would undertake to control the possession or use of dangerous substances or weapons by unauthorized individuals or groups within their jurisdiction should be encouraged among those countries whose national legislation would be made more effective by such agreements. While it is not likely that the United States could join in such international agreements without significant questions being raised about the scope of the federal government's constitutional treaty power, other countries might find it easier to implement treaty obligations than to enact municipal legislation in this area without such international commitments.

Foreign countries should be encouraged to enact national legislation to control the possession or use of dangerous substances or weapons by unauthorized individuals or groups within their jurisdiction. The United States could offer technical assistance to help foreign countries identify substances with potential destructive uses and areas in their industrial infrastructure that would be less vulnerable to disruption if subject to special protection by legislation.

Limiting the Sale of Certain Kinds of Weapons. *Measures to limit or control the sale abroad of weapons, destructive devices, and their components should be explored.* National regulations exist in the United States and its allied members of the Coordinating Committee to control the import and export of militarily useful commodities and technical data. It might be possible to gain wider international agreement under which states would find it easier to coordinate measures to limit private exports and imports of interest to terrorists.

International Cooperation in Protective Measures. *Measures to identify certain substances or allow identification of their origin should be explored with other nations.* Even in the absence of agreement on export and import controls, some limit on the dissemination of particularly dangerous or sensitive devices or components might be achieved by tagging them with radioactive nucleides or other substances.

Protected Persons and Diplomatic Facilities
John F. Murphy

Conclusions

The actions the Department of State might take toward the prevention and punishment of attacks on diplomats and diplomatic premises are numerous. Internal policy changes with respect to strategies used when dealing with terrorists, legislative changes that will enhance the government's ability to protect foreign diplomats in the United States and U.S. diplomats abroad, and tighter law enforcement measures implemented with the State Department's encouragement are possible unilateral actions that the United States might take.

Informal arrangements between governments, bilateral agreements, regional arrangements, or multilateral actions are also means the United States might utilize in its efforts to combat terrorism against protected persons.

Recommendations

Federal Legislation. *The U.S. government should give further thought to the feasibility of amending 18 U.S.C. § 122(b)(3) so as to enable the regulation of demonstrations within 500 feet of diplomatic premises located outside of the District of Columbia. Even though the 1976 amendments to 18 U.S.C. appear to* *allow the United States to discharge its international obligations fully under the OAS and U.N. conventions, the above amendment would maximize the protection of foreign diplomats by bringing federal law into accord with the law in the District of Columbia, where a similar measure has worked well.*

Technological Devices for the Protection of Diplomats. *High priority should be given to the research and development of technological devices designed to maximize the protection of diplomats and diplomatic facilities.* Such efforts would appear especially desirable in light of recent attacks on diplomatic personnel and facilities in New York, Washington, and other major cities. Transmitting devices capable of being concealed on a diplomat's person are one example worthy of further study. Such devices should not be employed, however, until they are technologically sophisticated enough to ensure that the diplomat will not become endangered by their use.

Negotiating Strategy and Policy. In the past the United States has on occasion stated that it will not negotiate with international terrorists. Such statements should not be made because they are subject to the misinterpretation that the U.S. government will not even communicate with terrorists during an actual kidnaping or other terrorist incident. It is further recommended that *no policy or strategy for dealing with terrorists should be applied in a rigid, inflexible manner, but should rather be adaptable to individual circumstances.* Some of the variables, among others, that the United States should consider before it determines what action it should take regarding a kidnaping might include the nature of the concessions demanded; the likelihood that the kidnapers will kill their victims if their demands are refused; the possibility of extending the discussions (negotiations) with the kidnapers and thereby enhancing the chances of finding their hideout; and the likely repercussions—both domestic and international—if the kidnaped diplomat is killed. The U.S. government's primary, although not necessarily the exclusive, goal in kidnaping cases should be the safe return of the diplomat.

Bilateral Agreements. *International agreements should be concluded, when feasible, that are modeled after the U.S.-Canada Extradition Treaty of 1971 and the 1973 "Memorandum of Understanding" between the United States and Cuba concerning the hijacking of aircraft, and that are drafted to apply to attacks on diplomats.* The first treaty explicitly calls for extradition in cases that would include attacks on diplomats, and the Memorandum of Understanding incorporates the principle of *aut dedere, aut judicare* but goes beyond the U.N. Convention by requiring that the accused person be submitted to trial for the "offense punishable by the most severe penalty" and by requiring the signatories to prevent the use of their territory as a base for committing the illegal acts covered by the memorandum.

European Convention. *The recent adoption by the Council of Europe of the European Convention on the Suppression of Terrorism is a major regional initiative toward the prevention and suppression of international terrorism. The Department of State should keep itself fully informed of the status of the convention and, when appropriate and feasible, use it as a model for future agreements or sign and ratify it if it is ever opened to non-European states and likely to become an effective "Atlantic" measure.* This convention also employs the *aut dedere, aut judicare* principle, which is seen as one of the most effective legal means of suppressing terrorism.

U.N. Convention: Follow-up. *The United States should undertake a worldwide diplomatic effort to convince as many countries as possible to become parties to the U.N. Convention.* This would be in the interest of maximizing the effectiveness of this convention, which the United States has recently ratified. To this end, the United States should work closely with the U.N. secretary-general.

Data Exchange. *Informal arrangements should be worked out between government officials and appropriate countries to encourage the utilization of the U.N. secretariat to exchange data and ideas concerning security measures for the prevention of attacks on diplomats and to urge other parties to the U.N. Convention to report to the secretary-general on the steps they have taken to carry out their obligations under the convention.* The aim of these actions would be to enhance the prospects that the convention will fully realize its potential as a measure for the protection of diplomats.

Strict State Liability. *The Department of State should study the utility of the concept of strict state liability for injuries to diplomats.* Such a study is encouraged, as both the OAS and U.N. conventions recognize that diplomats require special protection. Even if developing countries faced a special burden in this area, technical assistance programs could be considered to ease that burden.

"Nonprotected" Persons or Things   Jordan J. Paust

Conclusions

Devising strategies to protect "nonprotected" persons or things is one of the most difficult tasks facing the U.S. government in dealing with terrorism. What is perhaps the most effective long-term strategy relates to the need to reemphasize the international duty of nations to respect human rights. Similarly, effort must be made to oppose general excuses for rights violations that are often couched in terms of "innocence," national liberation movement exceptions, aggression, worker struggles, and guerrilla warfare. In several specific instances, educational programs designed to increase public awareness of the problem of terrorism, and ways to deal with it, may seem barely adequate to meet the growing problem, but they can be made more effective. The difficulty is that many terrorists are engaged in an "ideological war" against society when they attack "nonprotected" persons or things, and the best—possibly the only—long-term response that the government and society can adopt, is an "ideological war" against terrorism. But such an effort can utilize numerous substrategies and may ultimately be most effective by assisting the implementation of law by conditioning predispositional patterns for preventive, deterrent, and related sanction efforts. In the recommendations listed below, specific suggestions for international and U.S. government action have been included to undergird more educational and ideological efforts.

Recommendations

Governmental Responses. *Governments should not use the methods of terrorism to combat or sanction terrorism.* Such action would lend credence to terrorist claims concerning the permissibility of using terror as a political weapon and, in the long run, prove counterproductive.

U.S. Government's Public Condemnation of Terrorism. *The U.S. government should continue to publicly condemn serious violations of human rights (including use of torture and terrorism) whether engaged in by governments or by private parties.* This would clarify and supplement a consistent U.S. position on such issues and align concern about terrorism with the Carter administration's newly invigorated concern about human rights. Similarly, the United States should continue to advocate punishment of violators and encourage others to join the international effort to sanction impermissible terrorism.

Government Funding for Special Human Rights/Sanction of Terrorism Programs. *The government should fund and support programs directed at human rights and the promotion of law and justice.* These programs should underscore the link between basic human rights, democratic values, and the impermissibility of terrorism as a strategy to coerce the attitudes and behavior of others. Additional support could come from state boards of education, bar associations, and other government or private groups.

Personnel and Property of Transnational
Enterprises   Clarence J. Mann

Conclusions

The transnational business operation has become a frequent target of terrorist activities over the past few years. Increasingly, attacks have been mounted by relatively large, well-organized, and highly disciplined groups in order to achieve political ends. The transnational enterprise, as a natural ally of political stability, a very effective mode for the organization of capital and technology, and an extension of foreign economic interests, has become a highly symbolic and lucrative target of terrorists whose ultimate objective is to embarrass the host government, erode its authority, and force political change. The costs to the enterprise, both visible and hidden, may far exceed the payments exacted by terrorists. The international investment climate as a whole, as well as international commerce, also suffers. The threat of terrorism is forcing the transnational enterprise to rethink its traditional approach to security and to develop new modes of cooperative action with governmental authorities as well as within the private sector. Because terrorism represents a comprehensive threat to transnational business operations, it requires an equally broad-gauged response.

Recommendations for U.S. Policy

To combat more effectively international terrorism directed against the transnational business operations of U.S. companies, the U.S. government should adopt policies that are designed to allow enterprises maximum flexibility in dealing with terrorism, encourage cooperative measures among enterprises to combat terrorism, and reinforce the general responsibility of states under international law to protect the personnel and property of all aliens against acts of terrorism.

Ransom Policy. *The U.S. government should not foster a prohibition of ransom payments by business enterprises in their dealings with terrorists. Nor should it encourage efforts among states to establish such a prohibition.* Such an approach cannot be justified either from the points of view of the individual victim, the business sector, or society as a whole. It would place business in an impossible personnel position. Further, it would be extremely difficult to enforce and could well work counterproductively in preventing extortion. The United States, however, should respect the decisions of other states to prohibit ransom payments within their jurisdictions.

Hostage Insurance. The U.S. government should take the position that hostage insurance is a private business matter to be regulated by supply and demand within the insurance industry. It should neither encourage the use of hostage insurance, for to do so could well increase the ransom expectations of terrorists; nor should it prohibit hostage insurance, because as recommended above, a prohibition of ransom payments should not be applied to the private sector.

Risk Pooling. *The U.S. government should investigate ways in which changes and clarifications in U.S. tax law could reduce the impact of ransom payments of U.S. enterprises operating in high-risk areas.* Such changes or clarifications, however, should neither subsidize ransom payments nor create special advantages for the enterprise. Rather, they should be limited to enabling legitimate risk-spreading techniques and to ensuring that ransom payments may be fully deducted as ordinary and necessary business expenses to the extent that they are actually paid by the taxpayer for sound business reasons.

Government Subsidies. *The U.S. government should not undertake a program to subsidize the security costs of private enterprise.* In the United States, terrorist activity against business enterprises has not reached a point that would justify such extraordinary measures. Even if it did, serious questions would arise as to whether, to what extent, and what type of private security forces should be encouraged. Moreover, no subsidy should be granted for the security programs of the foreign operations of U.S. enterprises. Such subsidies could be interpreted as interference in the internal affairs of the host country and, in any case, should be granted (if at all) by the host government that has an immediate interest in encouraging such expenditures.

International Protection. *The United States should support and reinforce, where appropriate, the general responsibility of states under international law to protect the person and property of aliens within their jurisdiction against injury, including injury arising from the acts and threats of terrorists.* Nevertheless, the United States should not attempt to establish a higher or special standard of protection with respect to acts and threats of terrorists directed against transnational business operations. There is no clear basis for drawing a distinction between business and any other victim category. Further, any effort to obtain such protection would probably not be well received by foreign governments and could well detract from the general principle of international law applicable to all aliens. By the same token, the United States should not seek to impose a standard of liability under international law with respect to transnational business operations that is more strict than the general standard for aliens based on the fault of a state and its authorized agencies.

Research

The U.S. government should foster research on a wide variety of subjects dealing with the analysis of terrorist activities, their strategies, and the lawful means of prevention in respect to transnational business operations. This research should be undertaken both within the government and within the private sector.

Threat and Risk Analysis. Strategies and methods should be developed to assist management in determining the type and degree of risks involved in locating plants, offices, and other facilities and in securing them, their operations, and their personnel against attack.

Screening Methods. Methods should be developed for use in personnel hiring and in executive and facility protection in order to spot terrorists who attempt to infiltrate a company or an executive's household or who make deliveries or visits to or perform services for company facilities. In many respects, these methods may be similar to those developed by the airline industry for screening passengers and personnel.

Profile Analysis. Methods should be developed for identifying the activities of terrorists in terms of their motivation, their likely targets, the means of terror employed, and the nature of their internal organization. These methods should enable the preparation of individual, group, and country profiles of terrorist activities, as well as their movements and international relationships that are operationally useful to business.

Negotiation Strategy. Alternative strategies must be developed for negotiating with terrorists, depending on the motives involved and the strengths and weaknesses of the parties. These strategies should assist in clarifying the key issues, allow management the greatest degree of flexibility possible, assure a smooth working relationship with the media and with law enforcement and other governmental authorities, and assist in defusing the emotional and ideological pressures at work in the situation.

Hostage Survival. Executives and their families must have a better understanding of the situation that they face as potential hostages and when confronted with the fact of kidnaping. This requires research into psychological stresses to which hostages and their families are subjected prior to, during, and subsequent to kidnaping, and the development of methods and techniques for dealing with those situations.

Crisis Management. Comprehensive methods and techniques must be developed for managing crisis within enterprises faced with terrorist threats, acts, and negotiations. These may require a coordinated, interdisciplinary approach such that a team of executives can deal with all aspects of terrorist threats or attacks, including matters relating to negotiations, financing of ransom payments, legal relationships, medical treatment, family concerns, informants, and technical experts. These methods and techniques also should permit management to arrive rapidly at informed decisions under pressure.

Data Exchange

The U.S. government should establish a data base through which the private sector is kept informed on a current basis, where appropriate, about the activities, movements, and organization of terrorist groups around the world. Such a resource base might be placed within the Department of Commerce, but it should have access as needed to the information of the various governmental intelligence agencies. To preserve the confidentiality of sensitive information and sources, the data should be evaluated and screened before disclosure. In some cases, such as country and terrorist group profiles, the data should be made available on a regular basis to U.S. business enterprises. In other cases, where the data are more sensitive, their disclosure could be limited to the special needs of an enterprise. The flow of data in the United States could be coordinated through the Department of Commerce, while in foreign countries it could be coordinated through security officers and commercial attachés of the U.S. missions to the extent that this does not create embarrassment for or compromise the diplomatic position of these missions. In addition, the utilization of these data could be made more effective if security officers and commercial attachés of the missions are trained in the security needs of the foreign operations of U.S. enterprises.

Private Sector Resource Center

The U.S. government should foster the establishment of a resource center for the private sector, which would be owned and controlled by subscribing businesses. In contrast to the more traditional services offered by private security companies and consultants, the purposes of this center would be to (1) undertake practical research of the type described above under the research recommendation; (2) design and conduct training programs on such matters as hostage survival, negotiation strategy, and crisis management; (3) develop a data system in cooperation with government agencies for keeping businesses currently informed of terrorists' movements and strategies; and (4) offer a crisis management service for businesses in conjunction with law enforcement agencies. While the center would be located in the United States, it could furnish services worldwide to transnational business operations. Government funding might be necessary in the beginning phase. A pilot project might be launched to determine the workability and operating principles for the center. As a privately owned center, it would act as a buffer in data collection and dissemination among the participating enterprises and between the private sector and government agencies. Further, the center would provide the government with valuable insight into the security needs of business as well as the opportunity to analyze and test the practicality and effectiveness of security programs.

Prevention and Control of Terrorism:
International Responses

An International Control Scheme for the Prosecution
of International Terrorism: An
Introduction   M. Chérif Bassiouni

Conclusions

Under the present international legal regime, the process of extradition is cumbersome. It needs to be streamlined and lawful alternatives need to be developed. In addition, the effectiveness of that process faces a serious impediment in the "political-offense exception," and a limitation thereto has to be developed. Judicial assistance and other forms of cooperation in penal matters are varied and might be useful in this regard, but they are seldom employed. Making matters worse, treaties in the field of international criminal law do not contain provisions on judicial assistance and other forms of cooperation in penal matters, and this gap should be filled. More importantly, however, cooperation in penal matters should be increased, as it is a more viable policy alternative than is the attempt to elaborate substantive treaties on terrorism.

Recommendations

Multilateral Treaty Defining the Exception to the Political Offense Exception. *A multilateral treaty defining the "exception to the political-offense exception" in extradition should be considered.* Such a treaty would list those internationally recognized crimes that are to be excluded from the "political-offense exception" in existing and future treaties, laws, and state practice.

International Conference on Judicial Assistance. *An international conference of governmental legal experts on the topic of judicial assistance and other forms of cooperation in penal matters should be convened.* Such a conference should prepare a Draft Treaty on Judicial Assistance and Other Forms of Cooperation in Penal Matters.

Expanded Use of Extradition

1. The U.S. should rely on multilateral treaties as an alternative to bilateral treaties as a basis for extradition.
2. Continued reliance on reciprocity or comity as a basis for extradition should be encouraged.
3. The United States should enter into special agreements with states that deny extradition of U.S. nationals or deny extradition for offenses for which the death penalty could be imposed in an effort to overcome these obstacles to extradition. These agreements should provide:
   a. that the relator shall be returned to the requested state after trial, whether acquitted or convicted, and, if convicted, that the sentence be carried out in the requested state
   b. that the relator shall not be subject to the death penalty

Data Collection and Dissemination of Information. *A central data collection office should be established in the United States.* Other states should be invited to assist this office in collecting and disseminating through periodic publication the following information: (1) reported acts of terrorism; (2) prosecution; (3) trial; (4) sentence; (5) extradition or other forms of surrender; and (6) execution of the sentence and release.

Use of the International Court of Justice. *The United States should resort to and encourage other states to resort to the International Court of Justice for resolving disputes* regarding provisions in treaties and conventions that require states to "prosecute or extradite" individuals who commit terrorist acts.

State Responsibility

1. The U.S. government should encourage by international convention the establishment and enforcement of sanctions against states that fail to carry out their responsibilities with respect to international terrorism.
2. The Department of State should clearly enunciate as the policy of the United States that it considers breaches of international obligations relating to international terrorism as giving rise to state responsibility.
3. The Department of State should espouse the claims of U.S. nationals against foreign states for injurious and wrongful acts arising out of terrorist activities when such states fail to carry out reasonable safety and security measures, or fail to carry out their duty to prosecute or extradite.

National Task Force on the Prevention and Suppression of Terrorism. *With a view to making U.S. governmental responses to terrorism more effective, a special national task force should be assembled under the chairmanship of a sub-cabinet-level presidential appointee.* The national task force would consist of representatives from the Departments of Defense, Justice, State, Transportation, Energy, and Commerce; the CIA, the FBI, the Federal Aviation Administration, the National Security Council, and it should be the body to coordinate all government activities in the area of terrorism. The national task force should have a permanent office and staff and should override all agencies with respect to the control of terrorism and the development of policy where there is federal jurisdiction.

Apprehension and Prosecution of Offenders: Some Current Problems   Alona E. Evans

Conclusions

The antiterrorist treaties enjoin member states to extradite offenders or to submit them to prosecution. State practice indicates that deportation is the more common method of rendition of offenders than extradition. Present policies and practices of states with regard to extradition, exclusion, and expulsion should be reviewed for the purpose of establishing a common standard of international rendition. Historical, philosophical, and jurisprudential considerations may prevent states from arriving at an affirmative definition of the political offense, but the defense of the political offense as an obstacle to legal control of international terrorism can be curtailed by selective elimination of offenses from this category in absolute terms, *i.e.,* without exception. Submission of an international terrorist to prosecution is the duty of the state to which he has been surrendered or of the state that, denying rendition, has retained custody of the offender. Where a state has failed to prosecute or has apparently prosecuted *pro forma*, a realistic appraisal of the situation with a view to a policy determination directed against the delinquent state, *e.g.*, the institution of an economic boycott, can be made only on the basis of knowledge of the meaning of "submit to prosecution" in the criminal justice system of the delinquent state. Consequently, there is a need for the concerted development of a fund of information about policy and practice regarding the criminal justice systems of civilized states. The grant of political asylum to an offender is a distinctly separate matter from the obligation to submit an offender to prosecution; it must be considered subsequently to prosecution and on different terms. A greater knowledge of the practical operations of the criminal justice systems of various states, coupled with widespread development of judicial assistance procedures in criminal matters, would allay much of the reluctance of states to surrender international terrorists for prosecution or to undertake prosecution themselves. International cooperation looking to the establishment of an international minimum standard of criminal justice is needed before "extradite or submit to prosecution" becomes a widely meaningful formula for the legal control of international terrorism.

Recommendations

Extradition, Exclusion, and Expulsion: State Policy. *A study of contemporary policy and practice of states with respect to the use of extradition, exclusion, and expulsion of international terrorists should be undertaken under private or governmental auspices.* The study should determine the extent of use of each method as a means of international rendition of such offenders to states where they are wanted for prosecution, and reasons why extradition appears to be used less frequently than exclusion and expulsion as a means of international rendition. A clearinghouse of information about instances of extradition, exclusion, and expulsion of international terrorists should be established. A suggested location would be the Criminal Justice Division of the Department of Justice.

Common Standards of Exclusion and Expulsion: Multilateral Convention. *A multilateral convention should establish a common standard regarding the use of exclusion and expulsion for purposes of international rendition with procedural safeguards for the interests of the offender as well as those of the states involved.* Once such a common standard has been established, substitute "lawful return" for "extradition" in the treaty injunction "extradite or submit to prosecution."

Emphasizing Obligation to Prosecute Offenders. *States party to the antiterrorist conventions are under an international obligation to prosecute the offender, whether prosecution follows lawful return or takes place in the state in which* *the offender was found.* A clearinghouse of information regarding instances of prosecution of international terrorists should be established with a view to determining the extent to which such prosecution takes place, and reasons for discrepancies in bringing offenders to trial and in sentencing. A suggested location would be the Criminal Division of the Department of Justice.

Defense of the Political Offense. *It should be recognized that the defense of the political offense is historically, philosophically, and jurisprudentially accepted by many states.* The need to circumscribe "political offense" by selected elimination of offenses from this category in absolute terms—*i.e.,* without exception—should be emphasized.

Political Asylum. *The formula "extradite or submit to prosecution" should be amended to recognize that prosecution is a separate act from the grant of political asylum to an offender after he has been prosecuted.*

Judicial Assistance. *There should be emphasis on the need for widespread development of various methods of judicial assistance in criminal matters through bilateral and, where feasible, multilateral agreements as an inducement to lawful rendition and prosecution of international terrorists by states concerned about the quality of the criminal justice systems in other states.*

Criminological Policy   M. Chérif Bassiouni

Conclusions

It is commonly accepted that a terrorist is an ideologically motivated offender, *i.e.,* a person who engages in acts of terror-violence not for personal gain but to accomplish a power outcome. Such a person rejects in whole or part the social, political, or economic system of the society of which he or she is a member. Random violence is the usual strategy used to accomplish such a power outcome. Unfortunately, terrorism cannot be easily separated from other forms of violence. As a result, the general tolerance of terrorism may breed acceptance of violence. When a specific target is chosen, the means employed will depend on the anticipated psychological effects of the violent action. In this regard, the role of the media and their use by terrorists should be better understood generally. Efforts to curtail their negative use should be recognized as being indispensable to the effective prevention and suppression of terrorism. Prosecution, followed by imprisonment, can be used to counter terrorism, but the most effective deterrent is preventive law enforcement.

Numerous U.S. agencies are interested in the enforcement of international criminal law; however, their interests and activities are overlapping and uncoordinated. Moreover, the United States is insufficiently involved, at the governmental level, in international criminal law activities of other countries and of private or public international organizations.

Recommendations

Molding Public Opinion. *The U.S. government should deemphasize the significance of the dangers and threats of terrorism.* This policy would help prevent the creation of a climate of fear and apprehension among the general population. Emphasis on such dangers and the helplessness of society makes the psychological impact of terror-violence activities more effective and can induce terrorists to commit such acts. Information about the successful prevention and suppression of terrorist activities should be regularly publicized.

Educational Programs. *At the national level, the Law Enforcement Assistance Administration and the Department of Health, Education, and Welfare should provide funds for the development of programs of education in law* with respect to criminal justice, violence, human rights, peaceful resolution of international conflicts, and world public order. Law-focused educational programs exist in some twenty-five states in the United States with funding by LEAA, state commissions, and bar associations, and new programs are being planned by state boards of education. HEW has a program for global education, which includes an international law component.

At the international level, the United States should participate in and encourage educational programs concerned with the prevention of violence and the protection of human rights, sponsored by the United Nations, UNESCO, and private international organizations.

Training Programs. *The U.S. government should develop new training materials and help prepare qualified instructors to assist U.S. local law enforcement agencies* in their efforts to implement new techniques for preventing and controlling terrorists activities. The United States should also encourage and participate in similar programs that may be instituted by other countries or by international organizations, such as Interpol.

Death Penalty. *The U.S. government should for policy reasons oppose resorting to the death penalty for terrorists,* for by attracting would-be martyrs, it may be counterproductive.

Preventive Detention. *The U.S. government should study the constitutional aspects of restricting or denying bail to accused terrorists pending trial,* on the grounds of dangerousness and their potential flight from prosecution.

Harmonization of Criminal Laws and Penalties. *The United States should encourage interested countries to harmonize their criminal laws and penalties for* *terrorist acts* as a means of improving the effectiveness of apprehension and prosecution of such offenders. To that end, a U.S. study of comparative criminal law should be undertaken by a public agency or by private groups or institutions with public funding. The results of such a study should be widely publicized.

U.S. International Efforts. *The federal government should encourage U.S. experts and scholars to participate in public and private international gatherings, conferences, and seminars* and should facilitate such participation through a special funding program, so that U.S. policy and efforts in combating all forms of violence can be better known to the world community.

Defense of the Last-Resort Necessity. *The defense of "last-resort necessity" should be recognized as a mitigating factor for acts falling within the definition of "international terrorism"* if the person was acting to secure his personal freedom or safety.

Practical Problems of Law Enforcement   Wayne
A. Kerstetter

Conclusions

Law enforcement officials in the United States and in Western Europe are concerned about certain ambiguities in the scope of their authority to deal with international terrorism. Positive, incremental improvements in the law enforcement capacity to respond to terrorism are needed, although in the view of law enforcement officials, the ultimate solution to the problem lies in political and not in law enforcement action. More importantly, specific, limited steps should be taken to close certain loopholes in the law enforcement response to terrorism. Imaginative initiatives in these areas might support a new balance between international order and national freedom, which would aid in making this a safer world.

Recommendations

Narrow Scope of Political Crimes Exception in Extradition Treaties. *The United States should give special emphasis to narrowing the scope of the political crimes exception in extradition treaties with countries that share its commitment to the prevention of terrorism.* While ideological controversies allow territorial sanctuaries for terrorists, consideration of narrow political interests often frustrate effective law enforcement coordination between countries committed to the prevention of terrorism. Limiting the scope of the political crimes exception in extradition treaties with countries who share the U.S. commitment to prevent terrorism would reduce the impact of these narrow political interests.

Executive Branch Clarification of Law Enforcement Authority. *Recent statutes and executive orders should be reviewed to ensure that they: (1) provide law enforcement and security officials with appropriate authority to discharge their responsibilities to combat terrorist activities; (2) do not impose unnecessary and undue restrictions on antiterrorist law enforcement activities; and (3) provide adequate guidelines for officials discharging their responsibilities to combat terrorism.*

A review of Executive Order 11905 discloses a serious lack of definition of key terms. Both the Privacy Act of 1975 and the Freedom of Information Act contain ambiguities of concern to law enforcement officials. The Presidential Memorandum establishing the Cabinet Committee to Combat Terrorism charges the committee with the responsibility to "coordinate, among the governmental agencies, ongoing activity for the prevention of terrorism. This will include such activities as the collection of intelligence worldwide. . . ." It is unclear precisely what this memorandum was intended to authorize. In the sensitive area of intelligence, such ambiguity is unwise.

Centralized Data Base on Terrorism. *The executive branch of the U.S. government should consider development of a data base on terrorism by centralizing the collation and analyses of information about terrorists and terrorist activities currently collected by various U.S. agencies. Realistic guidelines should be adopted defining what information is to be collected, analyzed, and disseminated in order to ensure that this activity is kept within appropriate limits.*

Accurate and timely intelligence is crucial to an effective law enforcement response to terrorism and is essential to the prevention of terrorist activities because it provides the only substantial possibility of preventing terrorist incidents. Once hostages have been taken or a bomb planted, law enforcement officials can attempt only to limit the amount of damage suffered and to capture the terrorists. And these efforts at damage control must be carried out in the surroundings and circumstances chosen by the terrorists, no matter how difficult this renders those tasks.

Hence prevention and interception are particularly desirable enforcement efforts. Prevention by means of additional security for possible targets is extremely expensive both in terms of dollars and in terms of interference with the normal movement of people in society. Possible targets are almost limitless. The consequence of "securing" all of them is a fortress society.

The interception of terrorist activities has a great appeal both in terms of effectiveness and of economic and social costs. But an interception strategy is impossible without effective means to collect, collate, analyze, and disseminate information about terrorist activities. To be sure, there are real limits to the effectiveness of an interception strategy and social costs in its use.

An interception strategy will not be totally effective (and should not exclude preventive security measures), but it should reduce the numbers of incidents. It will entail social costs, but these can be minimized and controlled by proper safeguards.

Currently, information relevant to the prevention of terrorism is gathered by many different agencies. This information must be brought together for analysis because the development of intelligence involves piecing together numerous items of information from many sources into an indicative whole. Unless a structure or procedure exists to collate this information, several agencies are likely to sit with unintelligible pieces of information, unaware of their relevance to a larger whole.

Establishing Legal Authority for Data Collection and Utilization. *If the collation and analysis of terrorism information is centralized, as suggested above, care should be taken to ensure that the appropriate legal authority has been established for this action and that effective guidelines for the activity are promulgated.*

Whether or not Article II of the Constitution vests authority in the president to authorize this activity on his own, political wisdom suggests that consultation with Congress in the matter is advisable.

Care should be taken to obtain guidance and support from the highest levels of the executive branch in the development of a realistic and appropriate set of guidelines for the collection, storage, and dissemination of this information. These guidelines should provide a precise standard regarding what information is to be collected and stored, to whom and under what circumstances it will be disseminated, and how long it will be maintained before being purged.

Consideration also might be given to establishing judicial or quasi-judicial review for certain threshold decisions, for example, when to start and when to purge a file on an individual. The key element in such review would be the articulation of realistic standards that allow for the uncertainty inherent in intelligence gathering and at the same time impose meaningful restrictions on the process. Such standards can be developed only in close cooperation with officials involved in field operations.

State Self-Help and Problems of Public International
Law   John F. Murphy

Conclusions
Measures of state self-help with respect to states that harbor, or at least do nothing to prevent and suppress the actions of, international terrorists should be employed cautiously and only as a last resort. The incident at Entebbe Airport in Uganda may be *sui generis*, or at least highly unusual, because of the congruence of a number of factors that, the best evidence indicates, were present

there: (1) the active involvement of President Idi Amin of Uganda in the last stages of the hijacking operation; (2) the lack of any indications that steps would be taken to secure the release of the Israeli hostages; (3) the reasonable perception of Israeli officials that the hostages were in imminent danger of execution by the hijackers; (4) the consequent and reasonable conclusion by Israel that military action was urgently required by the exigencies of the situation; (5) the limitation by the Israeli forces of the use of force to the minimum necessary to accomplish the rescue, and the swift termination of the use of force upon completion of the mission; (6) the absence of any punitive motive on the part of Israel toward Uganda and the limited loss of life and property caused by the raid; and (7) the acquiescence of the Kenyan government in the refueling of the Israeli planes at the Nairobi airport.

Economic sanctions, whether applied unilaterally, bilaterally or regionally, or globally, against states aiding international terrorists appear supportable under principles of public international law. However, economic sanctions have not worked well in practice (*witness* Cuba, Rhodesia), and they should be employed in any event only in extreme cases after other, less coercive forms of self-help have been tried. These might include international claims, public diplomatic protests, and quiet diplomatic expressions of concern.

The following recommendations explore, in descending order of intensity of coercion, the primary types of self-help that states might employ against other states that aid and abet international terrorism.

Recommendations

The Use of Armed Force. *As it has previously, the Department of State should stress the* sui generis *nature of the incident at Entebbe and support generally the limitations that international law places on the use of force by states against other states in the name of combating international terrorism.* To this end, the State Department should stress the primary emphasis assigned by the United Nations Charter to avoiding the use of armed force and to settling disputes peacefully.

Economic Sanctions. *The State Department should not at this time press for the adoption of multilateral or regional conventions enabling states' parties to impose economic sanctions against a state that harbors international terrorists, even if that state is not a party to the convention.* Rather, the United States should make every effort to induce other states to become parties to and abide by applicable international conventions such as the Tokyo, Hague, and Montreal conventions on international civil aviation and the OAS and U.N. conventions on the protection of diplomats. In addition, it should press for the speedy conclusion of a convention on the taking of hostages along the lines of the West German initiative. It should also, at the bilateral level, actively attempt to revise its extradition treaties, using the U.S.-Canadian extradition treaty and the

U.S.-Cuba Memorandum on hijacking as models, so as to include acts of international terrorism within their terms and to incorporate the principle of *aut dedere, aut judicare.* Only if all further efforts at international cooperation with recalcitrant states fail should the State Department renew and pursue proposals for the application of economic sanctions.

The U.S. government (Congress and the executive) should evaluate carefully the utility of legislation compelling the president to impose economic sanctions against countries that grant safe haven to terrorists. Past experience indicates that amendments and legislation of this type (*e.g.,* the early version of the so-called Hickenlooper Amendment) tend to exacerbate already delicate U.S. foreign relations with the target state and fail to induce it to take action favorable to U.S. interests.

International Claims. *A first step the State Department should take in the area of international claims is to seek to ensure the inclusion of provisions applicable to states that aid international terrorists in the Document on State Responsibility that is ultimately to be adopted by the International Law Commission. These provisions should specify in precise terms the rights and responsibilities of states in this area.* Further, the department should strongly encourage the ILC to complete its work on state responsibility on a high-priority basis.

As suggested by Professor Lillich, the United States may wish, in selected cases, to bring international claims against states that aid international terrorists. However, the decision to bring such a claim should be taken only after the most careful consideration of its effect on overall relations between the United States and the prospective respondent state, as well as on relations between the United States and third party states. Moreover, the agreement of the respondent state to submit the claim to international adjudication should be sought. Absent such agreement, the claim would probably serve only to lend weight to a diplomatic protest, because the international tribunal with which it was filed would most likely decline jurisdiction.

Diplomatic Protest. The Department of State should protest vigorously against actions by states that hinder or interfere with the prevention or suppression of international terrorism. Moreover, as suggested by Professor Rubin, where standing exists, such protests should be made even if no U.S. nationals are among the terrorists' victims.

Quiet Expressions of Concern. *For a variety of reasons, the State Department may not wish to bring an international claim or lodge a diplomatic protest against a state that is hindering efforts to combat international terrorism. In such cases the department should express its concern to the state concerned and seek, through quiet diplomacy, to induce that state to cooperate more fully with efforts to control international terrorism.*

Private Measures of Sanction   Jordan J. Paust

Conclusions

Individuals, groups, and private institutions can and do respond to terrorism creatively or destructively in terms of serving minimum public order and human dignity. Forms of permissible private response—whether ideologic, diplomatic, economic, or military—can be as varied as private patterns of social interaction, and permissible responses should be encouraged in order to thwart terrorism and its impact. Choice as to permissibility of private response must be oriented to context and relevant legal policies at stake in given cases. Whether private choice, in the long run, will help to prevent and control terrorism and to promote minimum public order and human dignity will ultimately depend on popular awareness of and demands for a world of law, justice, and the values of a free society expressed in the human rights instruments of the twentieth century. We can act affirmatively to create such an awareness and demand through the enrichment of the educational process, greater access by all peoples to human intelligence, and broader use of ideological strategy. Of more specific import is the problem posed by the role of a free but responsible media concerning use of several sanction categories (*e.g.*, prevention, deterrence) and the reporting of terrorist incidents.

Recommendations

Public Condemnation of Terrorism. *The U.S. government should forthrightly condemn private and public measures of terror, whether engaged in at home or abroad by individuals or groups.* This policy would help condition social expectation away from such terrorist activity. Failure to do so might allow public attitudes to be shaped by terrorists.

Federal Training of Private Police. *The U.S. government should encourage the development of private police to assure that their tactics, equipment, and training are within relevant international and domestic legal standards.* The LEAA should begin by funding investigative and cooperative efforts (*e.g.*, pamphlets, training programs).

Federal and State Legislation. *The Department of State should encourage the National Commission on Uniform Law to consider, in the context of their present and future work, the amendment of federal and state law to assure civil and criminal immunity for persons acting reasonably to aid terrorism victims, to compensate a victim if the victim is further injured by the person giving aid, and to compensate the individual for losses sustained while attempting to aid a law enforcement officer.* These laws would stimulate aid to third persons and victims of terrorist attacks, and would thwart certain terror effects.

Additional Recommendations of Individual Working Group Members

New Weapons: The Threat to Communication Facilities
and New Technological Systems   Brian M.
Jenkins and Alfred P. Rubin

Chain of Responsibility for Those Supplying Weapons or Other Help to Terrorists. *Nations that fail to meet international standards of security for aliens in their territory, or fail to meet their obligations under general international law to prevent their territory from being used as a base for armed bands attacking the territory of other states, bear international responsibility for their defaults to the extent that those defaults contribute to injury done to other states. The United States should state a position at every appropriate opportunity asserting such responsibility against haven states.* The general international law in this area is evidenced by consistent state practice, including the assertions of the Ugandan representative in the U.N. Security Council immediately after the Entebbe incident, and is partially codified in UNGA Res. 2625 (xxv) adopted by consensus on October 24, 1970 and UNGA Res. 3314 (xxix) adopted by consensus on December 14, 1974.

"Nonprotected" Persons or Things   Jordan J. Paust

Children, Medical Personnel, and Food Supplies: Special Protection. *The U.S. government should seek agreements for the special protection of children, medical personnel, and food supplies that might be administered by special agencies of the United Nations.* Such protection should be based on a general consensus among governments, such as that underlying the Declaration of the Rights of the Child, and on international human rights law. This approach should lessen overall attacks on certain types of targets and may provide the best first effort at multilateral proscription of terrorist attacks on "nonprotected" persons.

Implementation Advisory Teams. *Government-sponsored implementation advisory teams should be established to advise and assist local government and community groups in their own efforts to counter terrorism.* These teams would increase coordination between federal and local efforts to counter terrorism and general anti-human rights attitudes and activities. They would also be able to provide assistance that may be beyond the capacity of the local government or group to obtain.

666

Bilateral and International Agreements: A U.N. Resolution. *The 1949 Geneva Convention provisions on training and general education concerning human rights in time of armed conflict should serve as a model for new bilateral and international agreements on a general human rights education and implementation program.* These efforts could begin with a U.N. resolution calling for cooperative educational and advisory approaches to implement general human rights in an effort to sanction international terrorism.

State Sanctions. *Legislation authorizing executive action to cut off communications and transportation to states that provide "safe havens" for terrorists should be introduced and supported to supplement present executive powers.* In addition to these, "self-help" military and economic sanctions should also be considered where necessary and proportionate (*e.g.,* military evacuation missions). In each case, executive flexibility seems desirable as international law already compels a showing of *necessity* for intensely coercive "self-help" military or economic sanction.

Amendment to the United States Code. *Title 18 of the United States Code should be amended to provide a penalty for the commission of acts of international terrorism at home or abroad.* This would eliminate existing gaps in U.S. law and assure the nation's ability to implement several international treaties relating to terrorism and the general customary international norms that are also violated by acts of international terrorism.

Practical Problems of Law Enforcement   Wayne
A. Kerstetter

International Detention Center. *The Department of State should explore the possibility of supporting the establishment of an international detention center for convicted terrorists.* Such a center might reduce the problem that countries currently face when they hold a terrorist and then become targets for further terrorist activities aimed at securing the release of the detained terrorist.

Private Measures of Sanction   Jordan J. Paust

Avoiding Punishment of Victims. *The U.S. government should avoid punishing victims of terrorism or striking out at innocent persons or groups. To do otherwise could play into the hands of terrorists.*

Federal and State Legislation. *The U.S. government should enact new federal laws to create a federal tort remedy and civil damage relief by victims against perpetrators for acts of international terrorism committed against U.S. nationals* *abroad.* Such legislation would fill a present gap in the law and contribute to the overall effort to sanction impermissible terrorism.

Treaties. *The United States should sponsor as a protocol to the 1949 Geneva Conventions and other relevant treaties a guarantee of a private cause of action in domestic courts against terrorists for effective compensatory relief.* Such measures would assure adequate implementation of the human right to an effective remedy and greater private sanction effort against terrorists and terrorism generally.

The U.S. government should negotiate for inclusion in Treaties of Friendship, Commerce, and Navigation provisions to protect those persons who come to the aid of victims of terrorist attacks. These provisions would supplement internationally a similar effort being made domestically. A multilateral treaty might be possible between states that recognize an international minimum treatment rule.

Illegal Weapon Systems: Legislation. *The executive should support the proposed amendment to H.R. 3625 (amending title 18 of the United States Code with respect to the use of dum-dum bullets) to supplement legal prohibitions against the use of any weapon system that violates international law.* Such legislation is necessary because certain illegal weapon systems are readily available and are being used increasingly against police and other citizens. Legislation would also help the U.S. government fulfill its state responsibility to protect aliens within the United States from death or injury by weapons that are illegal under international law.

New Contract Clause: Right to Freeze Assets. *The U.S. government should encourage banking and other wealth institutions to have a contract clause authorizing them to freeze for 24 hours, assets that the institution suspects are being transferred to support terrorism.* Such a clause would give governmental authorities time to take appropriate action to prevent the transfer of these funds to terrorist groups, and allow banking institutions to take preventive action without incurring civil contract liability.

American Society of International Law: Working Group on Legal Aspects of International Terrorism

Professor M. Chérif Bassiouni
De Paul University College of Law
25 East Jackson Boulevard
Chicago, Ill. 60604

Herbert H. Brown, Esq.
Hill, Christopher & Phillips
1900 M Street, N.W.
Washington, D.C. 20036

Professor Alona E. Evans
Wellesley College
Wellesley, Mass. 02181

Professor C. Clyde Ferguson, Jr.
FOB 400
Harvard Law School
Cambridge, Mass. 02138

Dr. Robert L. Friedheim
Institute for Marine & Coastal
    Studies
University of Southern California
Los Angeles, Calif. 90007

John Lawrence Hargrove, Esq.
Director of Studies
American Society of International Law
Washington, D.C. 20008

Brian M. Jenkins
Rand Corporation
1700 Main Street
Santa Monica, Calif. 90406

Wayne A. Kerstetter, Esq.
Center for Studies in Criminal Justice
University of Chicago
Chicago, Ill. 60637

J. Christian Kessler
Lulejian & Associates, Inc.
5205 Leesburg Pike
Falls Church, Va. 22041

Clarence J. Mann, Esq.
Assistant General Counsel
Sears, Roebuck & Co.
Sears Tower
Chicago, Ill. 60684

Professor John F. Murphy
University of Kansas Law School
Lawrence, Kan. 66045

Professor J.D. Nyhart
Massachusetts Institute of Technology
Cambridge, Mass. 02139

Professor Jordan J. Paust
University of Houston College of Law
3801 Cullen Boulevard
Houston, Tex. 77004

Professor Alfred P. Rubin
The Fletcher School of Law and Diplomacy
Tufts University
Medford, Mass. 02155

Index

About the Contributors

M. Chérif Bassiouni is professor of law at DePaul University College of Law, Chicago, Illinois.

Herbert H. Brown, Esq. practices law in Washington, D.C., with the firm of Hill, Christopher and Phillips.

Brian M. Jenkins is with the Rand Corporation, Santa Monica, California.

J. Christian Kessler is a systems analyst with the firm of Lulejian and Associates, Falls Church, Virginia, specializing in energy systems safeguards and regulatory policy.

Wayne A. Kerstetter, Esq. is associate director of the Center for Studies in Criminal Justice at the University of Chicago, Chicago, Illinois.

Clarence J. Mann, Esq. is assistant general counsel with Sears, Roebuck & Co., Chicago, Illinois.

J.D. Nyhart is associate professor of management, Department of Ocean Engineering, Massachusetts Institute of Technology, Cambridge, Massachusetts.

Jordan J. Paust is associate professor of law at the University of Houston College of Law.

Alfred P. Rubin is professor of international law at the Fletcher School of Law and Diplomacy, Tufts University, Medford, Massachusetts.

About the Authors

Alona E. Evans is Elizabeth Kimball Kendall Professor of Political Science at Wellesley College. She is vice-president of the American Society of International Law, a member of the Board of Editors of the *American Journal of International Law* (to which she is a frequent contributor), and chairman of the Committee on International Terrorism of the International Law Association.

John F. Murphy is professor of law at the University of Kansas School of Law, where he served as associate dean from January 1975 to July 1977. He has been in the private practice of law and has also been an attorney with the Office of the Legal Adviser of the U.S. Department of State. He has published a wide variety of articles on international law and policy, including several on the control of international terrorism.

About the Society

The American Society of International Law was organized in 1906 and incorporated by special Act of Congress in 1950. Its objects are "to foster the study of international law and to promote the establishment and maintenance of international relations on the basis of law and justice."

Concerned with problems of international order and the legal framework for international relations for more than 70 years, the Society serves as a meeting place, forum and collegial research center for scholars, officials, practicing lawyers, students, and others. The Society is hospitable to all viewpoints in its meetings and in its publications. Those publications include the leading periodicals, *The American Journal of International Law* and *International Legal Materials.* In addition, the Society publishes books, reports, and the occasional papers series, *Studies in Transnational Legal Policy,* produced by an extensive Research and Study Program under the supervision of its Board of Review and Development.

The Society's membership, which exceeds 5000, is drawn from some 100 countries. Membership is open to all, whatever their nationality or profession.